GREAT LIVES FROM HISTORY

AMERICAN HEROES

Great Lives from History

American Heroes

Second Edition

Volume 3

Presidents and First Ladies
Religion
Social Reform
STEM
Appendixes

Editor
D. Alan Dean

SALEM PRESS
A Division of EBSCO Information Services, Inc.
Ipswich, Massachusetts

GREY HOUSE PUBLISHING

Cover photo: Chris Hurtt via iStock

Copyright © 2019 by EBSCO Information Services, Inc., and Grey House Publishing, Inc.

Great Lives from History: American Heroes, published by Grey House Publishing, Inc., Amenia, NY, under exclusive license from EBSCO Information Services, Inc.

All rights reserved. No part of this work may be used or reproduced in any manner whatsoever or transmitted in any form or by any means, electronic or mechanical, including photocopy, recording, or any information storage and retrieval system, without written permission from the copyright owner. For information, contact Grey House Publishing/Salem Press, 4919 Route 22, PO Box 56, Amenia, NY 12501.

∞ The paper used in these volumes conforms to the American National Standard for Permanence of Paper for Printed Library Materials, Z39.48 1992 (R2009).

Publisher's Cataloging-In-Publication Data
(Prepared by The Donohue Group, Inc.)

Names: Dean, Dewayne A., editor.
Title: American heroes / [editor, Dewayne A. Dean].
Other Titles: Great lives from history.
Description: [Second edition]. | Ipswich, Massachusetts : Salem Press, a division of EBSCO Information Services, Inc. ; Amenia, NY : Grey House Publishing, [2019] | Includes bibliographical references and index.
Identifiers: ISBN 9781642650587 (set) | ISBN 9781642653595 (v. 1) | ISBN 9781642653601 (v. 2) | ISBN 9781642653618 (v. 3)
Subjects: LCSH: Celebrities--United States--Biography. | Heroes--United States--Biography. | United States--Biography. | LCGFT: Biographies.
Classification: LCC CT214 .A47 2019 | DDC 920.073B--dc23

FIRST PRINTING
PRINTED IN THE UNITED STATES OF AMERICA

Contents

Complete List of Contents vii

Presidents and First Ladies
Abigail Adams 661
John Adams 664
Dwight D. Eisenhower 668
Betty Ford 672
Andrew Jackson 675
Thomas Jefferson 678
John F. Kennedy 682
Abraham Lincoln 686
Dolley Madison 689
James Madison 692
Barack Obama 695
Eleanor Roosevelt 699
Franklin D. Roosevelt 702
Theodore Roosevelt 707
George Washington 710

Religion
Sister Thea Bowman 717
Mary Baker Eddy 718
Barbara Harris 724
M. Hasna Maznavi 726
Thomas Merton 728
John R. Mott 731
Sally J. Priesand 735
Zaid Shakir 737
Avi Weiss 738

Social Reform
Ralph David Abernathy 743
Jane Addams 746
Susan B. Anthony 750
Gloria Anzaldúa 753
Ella Baker 756
John Brown 758
Olympia Brown 762
Luisa Capetillo 765
Mary Ann Shadd Cary 767
Lourdes Casal 769
César Chávez 771
Helen Fabela Chávez 774
Kimberlé Williams Crenshaw 775

Dorothy Day 777
Eugene V. Debs 780
Dorothea Dix 784
Frederick Douglass 787
W. E. B. Du Bois 790
Marian Wright Edelman 793
Sue Kunitomi Embrey 797
Betty Friedan 799
Marcus Garvey 803
Emma Goldman 806
Emma González 809
Fannie Lou Hamer 811
Harry Hay 814
Aileen Clarke Hernandez 817
Samuel Gridley Howe 820
Dolores Huerta 824
Larry Itliong 829
Jesse Jackson 831
Marsha P. Johnson 834
Mother Jones 837
Frank Kameny 840
Helen Keller 843
Martin Luther King, Jr. 847
John L. Lewis 850
Malcolm X 854
Cherríe Moraga 857
Bree Newsome 859
Queen Noor 861
Rosa Parks 863
Alice Paul 866
Elizabeth Peratrovich 869
Ai-jen Poo 871
A. Philip Randolph 873
Sylvia Rivera 877
Bayard Rustin 879
Edward Snowden 881
Elizabeth Cady Stanton 883
Mary Tape 888
Reies López Tijerina 890
Sojourner Truth 892
Harriet Tubman 895
Nat Turner 898
Ida B. Wells-Barnett 899
Elie Wiesel 901

STEM
Benjamin Banneker 907
Steven Chu 909
Albert Einstein 911
Grace Murray Hopper 914
Edwin Powell Hubble 918
Mae C. Jemison 921
Katherine G. Johnson 923
Mary Golda Ross 925
Steve Wozniak 926
Chien-Shiung Wu 929

Appendixes
Chronological List of Entries 935
Alphabetical List of Entries 941
Subject Index 947

COMPLETE LIST OF CONTENTS

Volume 1
Publisher's Note vii
Introduction ix
Complete List of Contents xiii

Aeronautics and Spaceflight
Neil Armstrong 3
Bessie Coleman 8
Jimmy Doolittle 10
Amelia Earhart 13
John Glenn 16
Hazel Ying Lee 20
Shannon W. Lucid 22
Christa McAuliffe 25
Ellen Ochoa 27
Sally Ride 30
Alan Shepard 33
Sunita Williams 37
Orville and Wilbur Wright 39
Chuck Yeager 43

Art
Ruth Asawa 49
Judith F. Baca 51
Jean-Michel Basquiat 53
Barbara Carrasco 55
Keith Haring 56
Edmonia Lewis 58
Maya Ying Lin 60
Georgia O'Keeffe 63
Maria Tallchief 67
Martin Wong 70

Athletics
Muhammad Ali 75
Jack Dempsey 78
Lou Gehrig 82
Althea Gibson 85
Michael Jordan 88
Michelle Kwan 91
Martina Navratilova 94
Jack Nicklaus 97
Jesse Owens 100
Jackie Robinson 103
Bill Russell 106

Babe Ruth 108
Serena Williams 112
Babe Didrikson Zaharias 115

Business
Andrew Carnegie 121
Bill Gates 125
Andrea Jung 128
Indra Nooyi 130
John D. Rockefeller 132
Sheryl Sandberg 136
George Soros 138
Dave Thomas 140
Madam C. J. Walker 142

Education
Elizabeth Cabot Agassiz 149
Mary McLeod Bethune 151
Fabiola Cabeza
    de Baca Gilbert 155
Huping Ling 157
Juliette Gordon Low 159
Anne Sullivan 162
Booker T. Washington 165

Entertainment
Joan Baez 171
Lynda Carter 174
Ellen DeGeneres 176
Duke Ellington 177
Aretha Franklin 180
Katharine Hepburn 184
Billie Holiday 187
Nancy Kwan 190
Bruce Lee 192
Stan Lee 195
Dolly Parton 198
Prince 202
Fred Rogers 205
Selena 208
Nina Simone 209
James Stewart 211
Oprah Winfrey 215
Anna May Wong 218

Environment
Rachel Carson 223
Van Jones 226
Winona LaDuke 232
John Muir 234
Margaret Murie 237
Henry David Thoreau 239

Exploration
Robert D. Ballard 245
Daniel Boone 248
Richard Byrd 252
Meriwether Lewis and William
    Clark 255

Invention
Patricia Bath 263
Alexander Graham Bell 265
George Washington Carver 268
Lee De Forest 271
John Deere 276
Charles Richard Drew 279
George Eastman 282
Thomas Alva Edison 286
Thomas L. Jennings 290
Hedy Lamarr 293
Garrett Augustus Morgan 296

Journalism
Walter Cronkite 303
Ann Curry 306
Margaret Fuller 308
William Lloyd Garrison 311
Katharine Graham 316
Maria Hinojosa 319
Edward R. Murrow 321
Ida Tarbell 325

Volume 2
Complete List of Contents vii

Literature
Mercedes de Acosta 331
Maya Angelou 333
James Baldwin 336

Complete List of Contents

Pura Belpré 339
Judy Blume 342
Giannina Braschi............................344
Sandra Cisneros 347
Ta-Nehisi Coates...........................349
Martha P. Cotera...........................351
Emily Dickinson 353
Henry Louis Gates, Jr....................358
bell hooks 361
Zora Neale Hurston.......................363
Jhumpa Lahiri 365
Toni Morrison 368
Lola Rodríguez de Tió 370
Susan Sontag.................................372
Harriet Beecher Stowe 374
Walt Whitman 377
August Wilson................................381

Medicine
Clara Barton 387
Martha Bernal 390
Elizabeth Blackwell 392
Deepak Chopra..............................396
Margaret Chung 398
Jane L. Delgado 399
Gertrude Belle Elion 402
Sanjay Gupta.................................405
David Ho.......................................408
Joseph LeDoux..............................410
Antonia Novello 415
Susan La Flesche Picotte 417
Jonas Salk.....................................420
Margaret Sanger...........................423
Nora D. Volkow 427

Military
Omar Nelson Bradley 435
Stephen Decatur 438
Mary A. Hallaren 442
Oveta Culp Hobby 444
Stonewall Jackson 447
Robert E. Lee 451
Chester W. Nimitz.........................455
John J. Pershing 458
Loreta Janeta Velázquez...............462
Cathay Williams............................464

Native American Leaders
Crazy Horse 469
Geronimo 474
Chief Joseph.................................477
Kamehameha I 480
Lili'uokalani..................................484
Wilma Mankiller 487
Nanyehi...490
Red Cloud 493
John Ross 496
Sacagawea....................................499
Sitting Bull 503
Sarah Winnemucca.......................506

Politics/Law
Madeleine Albright 511
Louis D. Brandeis 515
William J. Brennan 518
Ralph Bunche................................521
Norma V. Cantú............................524
Elaine L. Chao 525
Shirley Chisholm 527
Judy M. Chu.................................529
Clarence Darrow 531
Helen Gahagan Douglas 534
William O. Douglas 538
Tammy Duckworth 540
Geraldine Ferraro 542
Heather Fong................................547
Benjamin Franklin 549
Ruth Bader Ginsburg 553
Al Gore..555
Nikki Haley 558
Alexander Hamilton......................559
Learned Hand...............................564
Patrick Henry 567
Mazie Hirono 570
Charles Evans Hughes 572
Daniel Ken Inouye 577
Marí-Luci Jaramillo 580
Barbara Jordan 582
Robert F. Kennedy 586
Robert M. La Follette...................590
Belva A. Lockwood 594
Huey Long 597
John Marshall...............................601
Thurgood Marshall 605

Vilma Socorro Martínez................608
Harvey Milk 610
Patsy Mink 613
Ralph Nader 615
Sandra Day O'Connor...................617
Thomas Paine...............................622
Rachel Paulose 625
Colin Powell..................................626
Jeannette Rankin 630
Condoleezza Rice.........................633
Felisa Rincón de Gautier..............636
Margaret Chase Smith..................638
Sonia Sotomayor 642
Adlai E. Stevenson II 645
Norman Thomas............................649
Earl Warren 654

Volume 3
Complete List of Contents vii

Presidents and First Ladies
Abigail Adams 661
John Adams..................................664
Dwight D. Eisenhower..................668
Betty Ford 672
Andrew Jackson 675
Thomas Jefferson 678
John F. Kennedy...........................682
Abraham Lincoln 686
Dolley Madison.............................689
James Madison.............................692
Barack Obama..............................695
Eleanor Roosevelt 699
Franklin D. Roosevelt 702
Theodore Roosevelt 707
George Washington......................710

Religion
Sister Thea Bowman 717
Mary Baker Eddy 718
Barbara Harris 724
M. Hasna Maznavi 726
Thomas Merton.............................728
John R. Mott.................................731
Sally J. Priesand 735
Zaid Shakir...................................737
Avi Weiss 738

Social Reform

Ralph David Abernathy 743
Jane Addams 746
Susan B. Anthony 750
Gloria Anzaldúa 753
Ella Baker 756
John Brown 758
Olympia Brown 762
Luisa Capetillo 765
Mary Ann Shadd Cary 767
Lourdes Casal 769
César Chávez 771
Helen Fabela Chávez 774
Kimberlé Williams Crenshaw .. 775
Dorothy Day 777
Eugene V. Debs 780
Dorothea Dix 784
Frederick Douglass 787
W. E. B. Du Bois 790
Marian Wright Edelman 793
Sue Kunitomi Embrey 797
Betty Friedan 799
Marcus Garvey 803
Emma Goldman 806
Emma González 809
Fannie Lou Hamer 811
Harry Hay 814
Aileen Clarke Hernandez 817
Samuel Gridley Howe 820
Dolores Huerta 824
Larry Itliong 829
Jesse Jackson 831
Marsha P. Johnson 834
Mother Jones 837
Frank Kameny 840
Helen Keller 843
Martin Luther King, Jr. 847
John L. Lewis 850
Malcolm X 854
Cherríe Moraga 857
Bree Newsome 859
Queen Noor 861
Rosa Parks 863
Alice Paul 866
Elizabeth Peratrovich 869
Ai-jen Poo 871
A. Philip Randolph 873
Sylvia Rivera 877
Bayard Rustin 879
Edward Snowden 881
Elizabeth Cady Stanton 883
Mary Tape 888
Reies López Tijerina 890
Sojourner Truth 892
Harriet Tubman 895
Nat Turner 898
Ida B. Wells-Barnett 899
Elie Wiesel 901

STEM

Benjamin Banneker 907
Steven Chu 909
Albert Einstein 911
Grace Murray Hopper 914
Edwin Powell Hubble 918
Mae C. Jemison 921
Katherine G. Johnson 923
Mary Golda Ross 925
Steve Wozniak 926
Chien-Shiung Wu 929

Appendixes

Chronological List of Entries ... 935
Alphabetical List of Entries 941
Subject Index 947

Presidents and First Ladies

The most important president for a historical discussion of heroes and role models in America's civic life is George Washington. After his death and into late in the nineteenth century, some Americans sought to deify Washington in terms reminiscent of classical mythological figures, Roman caesars, or religious figures. Washington had shown extraordinary military leadership during the Revolutionary War, he was a great statesman, and he was America's founding president. For those captivated with the spirit of civic religion, it was natural that Washington should be celebrated in quasi-religious terms. The most important monument that survives expressing this attitude is the painting inside the dome of the United States capitol building called the *Apotheosis of George Washington*. Apotheosis means achievement of divine status. Painted in 1865 by Constantino Brumidi, it depicts George Washington rising to the heavens in glory, flanked by female figures representing Liberty and Victory.

This hyperbolic style of discourse is related to another, more homely one, exemplified by the story of George Washington and the cherry tree. It originated in the fifth edition of Mason Locke Weems's *The Life of George Washington*, published in 1806. Weems's book was enormously popular. After giving a thorough biographical account, it goes on "to show that his unparalleled rise and elevation were due to his Great Virtues." Weems's story of the cherry tree, in which young George confesses to his father that he cannot tell a lie, was picked up by William Holmes McGuffey who included in his textbooks for children known as *McGuffey's Readers*. First published in 1836 and in print for almost a century, generations of Americans grew up reading the edifying story.

The apotheosis discourse, embodied in the painting at the United States capitol, focused on Washington's public accomplishments. It fused mythological ideas about heroes, Roman notions of statehood, and Christian religious symbolism in order to celebrate a hero of democracy. For the most part, this style of discourse has faded from view. The story of Washington's childhood honesty, however, with its focus on private virtue and rooted in a moral and didactic discourse, rather than a political one, has survived for much longer. Today, the fictitious but humble exemplary tale remains familiar to most Americans, while the apotheosis discourse has receded into history.

An 1846 daguerrotype of the White House by John Plumbe. (Library of Congress)

ABIGAIL ADAMS

First Lady of the United States (1797-1801), educator, writer, and feminist

Born: November 22, 1744; Weymouth, Colony of Massachusetts
Died: October 28, 1818; Quincy, Massachusetts
Area of Achievement: Women's rights, education, literature, government and politics, business

An early proponent of humane treatment and equal education for women, Abigail Adams wrote eloquent, insightful letters that provide a detailed social history of her era and her life with John Adams.

Abigail Adams (National Gallery of Art)

EARLY LIFE

Abigail Adams, born Abigail Smith, was one of four children of William Smith, minister of North Parish Congregational Church of Weymouth, and Elizabeth (Quincy) Smith from nearby Braintree, Massachusetts. Massachusetts Both parents were members of prominent New England families of merchants, statesmen, and ministers. From her parents, Abigail learned a conservative, rational Puritanism. She retained throughout her life a solid Christian faith and shared with her Puritan forebears a belief in the fundamental depravity of humankind. These religious convictions influenced her political opinions.

Observing her mother's example, Abigail learned her future roles as wife and mother, duties instilled in girls from an early age during this time in American history. As a minister's wife, Elizabeth Smith provided relief for the town's poor, nursed the town's sick, and presented herself as a model wife. She was nurturing and kind to her children.

In eighteenth century Massachusetts, education was prized. In government-supported schools, boys studied Latin, Greek, French, mathematics, and literary arts in preparation for higher education either at Harvard College or abroad. Girls, however, were educated almost exclusively at home, receiving only rudimentary training in reading and writing; some remained illiterate. They learned domestic skills such as sewing, fine needlework, and cooking, which were considered vital preparation for marriage. Abigail received only informal home instruction yet shared with her sisters the advantage of a keen intellect and unlimited access to her father's extensive library.

In her early adolescence, Abigail was encouraged in her studies by a young watchmaker and scholar, Richard Cranch. Although self-educated, Cranch conveyed his passion for scholarship to Abigail and to her sisters Mary and Elizabeth. It was through Cranch, who wedded Mary, that Abigail met her future husband.

Abigail proved a shrewd judge of character when at the age of nineteen she married Harvard-educated lawyer John Adams. Although they were not social equals—he was from a markedly less prominent family and practiced a profession that was poorly regarded—the match proved exceedingly profitable and satisfying for both parties. In John, Abigail found a man who appreciated and even encouraged her forthrightness and her intellectual ability, while John in turn received emotional, financial, and intellectual support from Abigail.

> "*If we mean to have heroes, statesmen and philosophers, we should have learned women.*"

LIFE'S WORK

Abigail Adams is best known for her remarkably detailed, eloquent letters. Although many creative outlets were considered unsuitable for women to pursue, letter writing was a socially sanctioned literary art for women in the eighteenth century. Abigail, who felt compelled to write, naturally selected that medium.

During her first ten years of marriage, however, Abigail's letter writing was not prolific as she was kept extraordinarily busy with domestic affairs. Enduring five pregnancies in seven years, she also suffered the death of an infant daughter. In addition, she was plagued by several physical afflictions including frequent colds, rheumatism that caused acute swelling of her joints, and insomnia.

During these early years, she moved her household several times to remain with John in his work. The turmoil of their lives as they uprooted their family paralleled the contemporary political events in which John played a leading role. This was a pattern they would repeat throughout his working life and would include residences in Boston, Philadelphia, New York, Paris, and London. Abigail demonstrated repeatedly that she was extraordinarily adaptable and found pleasure in observing foreign customs. She always, however, longed for the idealized pastoral life in Braintree that she had shared with John during their first few years of marriage.

In 1775, John embarked for Congress on the first of frequent extended absences from Abigail. With her husband away, Abigail weathered several personal tragedies, including a difficult pregnancy in 1777, during which she apparently suffered from toxemia and finally eclampsia, a condition that is usually fatal to the infant and often to the mother. A remarkable series of letters were written between John and Abigail during this period; in them, Abigail expressed loneliness and fear for her unborn child. The child, a girl, was indeed stillborn. John and Abigail's letters provide invaluable information on the social history of parent-and-child relationships.

The pattern of intimate and frequent letters continued over the next twenty-five years as John, an extraordinarily ambitious man, accepted political positions that removed him from home for periods often extending to years. While Abigail considered their separation as a patriotic sacrifice, she nevertheless frequently expressed her loneliness to John, imploring him to return home.

Because she was a married woman, Abigail was legally prevented from owning property in her own name. Notwithstanding, she repeatedly demonstrated her ingenuity and self-sufficiency. During their first ten years together, John's legal fees and the income from their farm supported the family. As events took him farther from home, his legal practice was largely abandoned and Abigail assumed most financial duties. She never welcomed the addition to her already burdensome domestic responsibilities, yet she consistently proved herself a competent manager. Abigail deplored debt and worked to ensure that her family avoided it. She successfully ran the farm for four years during which she was responsible for the odious chore of collecting rents from several tenants as well as supervising agricultural production. Scarcity of labor and acute inflation made the task a difficult one. After four years, she lessened her burden by renting the farm.

In 1778, Abigail began requesting luxury goods from John, who was then serving as a diplomat in France. She then profitably sold these items, which, because of war shortages and inflation, were scarce in Massachusetts. At the same time, Abigail also purchased land and

---

Remembering the Ladies

Abigail Adams wrote a letter to Congress in 1776, demanding that women not only have a voice in the new nation but also have freedom from cruelty and abuse at the hands of men. She warned that without representation and legal protection, women would be positioned to rebel and to follow no laws.

Remember the ladies, and be more generous and favorable to them than your ancestors. Do not put such unlimited power into the hands of the Husbands. Remember all Men would be tyrants if they could. If particular care and attention is not paid to the Ladies we are determined to foment a Rebellion, and will not hold ourselves bound by any laws in which we have no voice, or Representation.

That your Sex are Naturally Tyrannical is a Truth so thoroughly established as to admit of no dispute, but such of you as wish to be happy willingly give up the harsh title of Master for the more tender and endearing one of Friend. Why, then, not put it out of the power of the vicious and the Lawless to use us with cruelty and indignity without impunity. Men of Sense in all Ages abhor those customs which treat us only as the vassals of your Sex.

Source: Abigail Adams, "Remember the Ladies," in *Living History America*, edited by Erik Bruun and Jay Crosby (New York: Tess Press, 1999), pp. 150-151.

speculated in currency. Through these endeavors, she kept her family solvent.

During the ten years in which she saw her husband only sporadically, Abigail expanded her literary interests, exploring, partly through John's guidance, political theory, biography, and history. She also wrote voluminously, to John, to other family members, and to friends. It was during this period that Abigail wrote to John of her political views regarding women's roles in the new nation. Her famous letter of March 31, 1776, in which she requested John to "Remember the Ladies," established Abigail's reputation as an early proponent of women's rights. In context, however, it is clear that Abigail wrote not of political rights per se but of women's legal rights, specifically those that guaranteed them protection from physical abuse. At the time, divorce, although allowed in a few extreme instances, was generally unavailable. In addition, women abrogated all rights to property ownership upon marriage, which in turn made them ineligible to vote because property ownership was a key qualification for voting.

Abigail also advocated equal education for women. She argued for equal education within the context of her perception of women's traditional domestic roles. The concept of "Republican motherhood" held that because women taught the sons who were destined to become leaders, women had an important role in maintaining the existence of an informed citizenry capable of supporting a republican government. To teach their sons successfully, these women required an education equal to that of boys and men, which Abigail hoped would be supported by law.

Although she is now considered an early advocate of women's rights, Abigail saw her own life as highly traditional. An adept manager of her family's resources, she nevertheless viewed her role as currency speculator, land purchaser, and farmer as aberrant and a patriotic sacrifice. She was comfortable only, it seems, in her domestic role, and in that, as in all else, she excelled. Abigail lived to see her son John Quincy establish a successful diplomatic and political career. Several personal tragedies marred her happiness, including the death of her son Charles from alcoholism when he was thirty years old and her daughter Nabby's brutally painful mastectomy and subsequent death from breast cancer.

Until 1800, when John retired from government office, Abigail functioned at times as host during his several years as a diplomat, first in England, then in France. She also served two terms as the vice president's wife during the George Washington administration and finally as First Lady during her husband's presidency from 1797 to 1801.

During the last eighteen years of her life she retired with her husband to Quincy (formerly Braintree) and lived in relative domestic peace surrounded by children, grandchildren, sisters, nieces, and nephews. At the family's Quincy farm, Abigail pursued her lifelong hobby of gardening. Dying of typhoid fever in 1818, she was mourned by John, who, lamenting the loss of his "dearest friend," survived his wife by eight years.

SIGNIFICANCE

Abigail Adams always functioned within the prescribed social roles for women of her time. She was an affectionate, protective mother who cared for her children physically and emotionally her entire life. She provided intellectual and emotional companionship as well as financial support for her brilliant but irascible husband John Adams. Although Abigail for a time functioned as merchant, farmer, and speculator, she viewed these roles as a patriotic sacrifice to support the political career of her husband.

While her own marriage provided her intellectual and emotional satisfaction, she condemned the tyranny of men over women and longed for legal protection for women. Women's education she hoped would one day rival that of men. She also yearned for the day when women would be able to limit the number of children they had. Nevertheless, her life must be viewed within the context of her eighteenth century world, where she functioned primarily within the domestic sphere. She was not a public advocate for women's rights; the term "women's rights" was not even used in her time. Yet, she did not view her role within her marriage as less valuable than that of her husband. To Abigail and to John, marriage was a true partnership.

She was a supremely shrewd, able woman who took every advantage available to her to expand her intellectual horizons, and she enjoyed a wide correspondence through her letters. In addition to providing an idea of this remarkable woman's psyche, Abigail Adams's copious letters give a detailed social history of her era and details into the character of her husband and of several other political leaders, including her close friend Thomas Jefferson.

Mary E. Virginia

FURTHER READING

Adams, Abigail. *The Book of Abigail and John: Selected Letters of the Adams Family, 1762-1784.* Edited by L. H. Butterfield, Marc Friedlaender, and Mary-Jo Kline. Boston: Northeastern University Press, 2002. This revised text includes a foreword by David McCullogh, author of a best-selling biography of John Adams. Abigail's letters are her literary achievement—eloquent, informative, and illuminating.

Akers, Charles W. *Abigail Adams: An American Woman.* Boston: Little, Brown, 1980. Written specifically for the college undergraduate and high school student, Akers's work is admirably detailed and readable. Abigail's life is well grounded in historical context.

Gelles, Edith B. *Portia: The World of Abigail Adams.* Bloomington: Indiana University Press, 1992. An insightful biography of Adams, viewing her not only as John's wife and John Quincy's mother but also within the context of her domestic and predominantly female world. This work requires a knowledge of fundamental historical events, so it should be read in conjunction with a broader history, such as that of Akers. Includes an instructive introductory chapter, footnotes, a bibliography, and a chronology.

Levin, Phyllis Lee. *Abigail Adams: A Biography.* New York: St. Martin's Press, 1987. By far the most detailed biography of Adams, making extensive use of research sources. Unlike other biographers, Levin provides ample discussion of Abigail's life during the years after John Adams's retirement, although Levin does so against the backdrop of John Quincy's career. Similarly, Abigail's earlier life is viewed against John's career. Just shy of five hundred pages, the work contains footnotes, a bibliography, and a family tree.

Nagel, Paul C. *The Adams Women: Abigail and Louisa Adams, Their Sisters, and Daughters.* New York: Oxford University Press, 1987. While not exclusively about Abigail, Nagel's work is useful for placing Abigail's life within the context of her close female relations, including her sisters Mary and Elizabeth. Despite his admiration of her intellect, Nagel provides a portrait of Adams that is largely unsympathetic, making her appear domineering.

Withey, Lynne. *Dearest Friend: A Life of Abigail Adams.* New York: Simon & Schuster, 2001. Withey judges Adams by twentieth century standards rather than understanding her within her historical context. The author focuses extensively on Abigail's political views while paying scant attention to her more notable successes in her domestic roles, viewing Abigail as a "prisoner" in her world.

JOHN ADAMS

2nd President of the United States (1797-1801)

As a member of the Continental Congress, Adams helped bring the American colonies to the point of independence in 1776. As one of the new nation's first diplomats, he helped negotiate the treaty that ended the American War of Independence. As the second president of the United States, he kept the young nation out of war.

Born: October 30, 1735; Braintree, Colony of Massachusetts
Died: July 4, 1826; Quincy, Massachusetts
Area of Achievement: Law, politics, diplomacy, writing

EARLY LIFE

John Adams was born in Braintree, Massachusetts, where his family had lived for nearly a century. His father was a farmer and a town constable who expected his eldest son, John, to become a Congregational minister. The young Adams attended the Free Latin School in Braintree and then enrolled at Harvard College in 1751. On graduation in 1755, he taught school for a while at Worcester before deciding to abandon the ministry to take up law instead. In 1758, the intelligent, studious Adams returned to Braintree to practice law in what was still a country town only 10 miles from Boston.

Six years later, he married Abigail Smith, a woman who matched him in intelligence and ambition and perhaps exceeded him in practicality. Together, the couple had five surviving children, of whom their son John Quincy would become the sixth president of the United States. Short and already stocky (colleagues later called him rotund), Adams seemed to be settling into the life of a successful country courthouse lawyer who might, in time, aspire to a seat in the legislature when, in 1765, the English parliament altered American colonial politics forever by passing the Stamp Act. The ensuing Stamp Act crisis offered to the ambitious Adams a quick route to popularity, influence, and public office. He did not miss his chance.

John Adams (National Gallery of Art)

LIFE'S WORK

In 1765, John Adams denounced the stamp tax in resolutions written for the Braintree town meeting. When they were reprinted around the colony, his reputation as an opponent of English arrogance began to grow. Those in Boston who led the opposition to English taxes (including John Adams's distant relative, Samuel Adams) began to bring him more actively into their campaigns. He moved to Boston and won a seat in the Massachusetts General Court. He became, in effect, the local antigovernment party's lawyer, writing some of its more important public papers for the Boston town meeting and defending its members in court against charges brought by the Crown.

When Parliament answered the 1773 Boston Tea Party with the Coercive (or Intolerable) Acts in 1774, the general court chose Adams as a delegate to the intercolonial congress scheduled to meet in Philadelphia that fall, to discuss what the colonies should do. He wrote a "Declaration of Rights," which the First Continental Congress adopted, which based colonial rights to self-government not only on their charters and on the inherent rights of Englishmen but also on "the immutable laws of nature." Those were the grounds on which many colonists would soon challenge not merely England's right to tax them but also England's right to govern them at all. In good part, those were the grounds that underlay the Declaration of Independence.

Before the Congress met again, war began at Lexington in April 1775. When Adams arrived at the Second Continental Congress in the spring of 1775, he already believed that the only true constitutional connection between the colonies and England was through the king—a position he set out in newspaper essays signed "Novanglus." He had not yet, however, openly called for a severing of all ties to the mother country. He had seen the colonists' rage run out of bounds in the Stamp Act riots of 1765. He had been disturbed and angered by the joy with which some colonists greeted the closing of civil and criminal courts in Massachusetts when English authority collapsed in the colony. He was worried that a revolution might get out of hand and establish not liberty, but mob rule. Although such worries stayed very much in his mind, by the time the Second Continental Congress met, Adams realized that there were no practical alternatives left but armed resistance or submission to Parliament. At the Congress, therefore, he worked both openly and by guile to bring reluctant and sometimes timid delegates to accept the inevitability of independence. When the Congress finally agreed to act, after more than one year of war, it was Adams who wrestled Thomas Jefferson's declaration through to adoption on July 4, 1776.

Adams had applauded Thomas Paine's *Common Sense* when it appeared in January 1776, but he disliked the very democratic plan of government advocated by Paine. The kind of government Adams favored can be seen most clearly in the plan he drew up for Massachusetts' revolutionary constitution. Adams thought the purpose of the American Revolution was to preserve old liberties, not to establish new ones, and that the new Constitution ought to conserve as much of England's admirable constitutional heritage as possible. The constitution he drafted included relatively high property qualifications for voting and holding office (to ensure stability); it left the structure of Massachusetts' government much as it had been before independence, except for replacing English officials with elected American ones.

> "*Human nature with all its infirmities and depravation is still capable of great things. It is capable of attaining to degrees of wisdom and goodness, which we have reason to believe, appear as respectable in the estimation of superior intelligences.*"

For more than a year after independence, Adams served on a variety of committees in Congress and in Massachusetts, doing work that was as exhausting as it was important. In October 1777, he withdrew from Congress and returned to Massachusetts, but in November, Congress named him one of its emissaries to France, charged with raising loans for the republic across Europe and with negotiating treaties of friendship, trade, and alliance, especially with the French nation.

That alliance was concluded before Adams arrived in Paris, but he stayed on and was immediately caught up in the roiling jealousies that were endemic at the American mission there. Adams especially disliked and distrusted Benjamin Franklin, whose demeanor, integrity, honesty, and morals he judged inferior to his own. Adams returned to Massachusetts in August,1779, but by December, he was back in France to help negotiate a peace treaty with England. He feuded with Franklin almost constantly over which of them was responsible for what in conducting the republic's diplomacy, but ultimately, all three peace commissioners (Adams, Franklin, and John Jay) agreed to negotiate a separate treaty between the United States and England, a treaty that did not directly involve France.

Though Franklin was responsible for the broad outlines of the agreement, Adams worked out some crucial compromises, without which the treaty may well have failed. Adams persuaded the English, for example, to concede to American fishing rights off the Newfoundland and Nova Scotia coasts in return for the new nation agreeing to open its courts to Loyalists. Adams stayed on for a year in France after the war ended in 1783 and then moved to London as the United States' first minister to the Court of St. James in 1785. He spent three years there, trying with little success to iron out problems between the United States and England (mostly involving noncompliance with the peace treaty).

While in London, he wrote the three-volume *A Defense of the Constitutions of the United States of America* (1787–1788), in which he explained his conservative and primarily English approach to the proper constitution of civil governments. The work was frank in its praise of the basic principles of the English constitution and earnest in its cautions about the risks of letting government rely too heavily on popular majorities to determine policy and law. Indeed, some Americans began to consider Adams soft on aristocracy and even monarchy. The first volume of *A Defense of the Constitutions of the United States of America* appeared in time to influence the thinking of delegates at the Constitutional Convention.

Adams returned home in 1788, and he was chosen as George Washington's vice president under the new Constitution of 1787. He did not like the job. "My country," he wrote to his wife, "has in its wisdom contrived for me the most insignificant office that ever the invention of man contrived or his imagination conceived." For the next eight years, nevertheless, he served Washington loyally, presiding over the Senate and breaking tie votes in favor of Federalist policies. His reward came in 1797, when, as Washington's chosen successor, Adams defeated Jefferson and became the second president of the United States.

Adams's presidency was at best only a partial success. He had hoped, as Washington had in 1789, to become president of a united people. By the time he took office, however, the people had already divided themselves into two rival political parties: the Federalists (ostensibly led by Adams) and the National (or Jeffersonian) Republicans, led by Adams's vice president and old friend, Thomas Jefferson. Under the election rules of the time, Jefferson, as the runner-up candidate, became the vice president, which, due to ever-widening partisanship, created internal interference with which Adams had to contend.

Furthermore, world affairs all but guaranteed that his presidency would be troubled. As Adams took office, for example, the United States was already dangerously close to war with France. The French, who had already fought their own revolution and created a republic of sorts, were at war with England and were angry that the United States had refused to aid France, a conflict called the XYZ Affair. By 1797, the French were beginning to seize American ships on the high seas. When American peace commissioners, whom Adams had sent to France to try to work things out short of war, reported that the French had demanded bribes to begin serious negotiations, Americans reacted angrily. Adams asked Congress to prepare for a war that seemed inevitable, but, at the same time, he refused to abandon his efforts to avoid it if possible. For the remainder of his presidency, Adams stuck to the same policy—prepare for war, but work for peace—until (just as he left office) it yielded a new treaty of amity between the United States and France.

In the meanwhile, the Federalist Party, influenced by Alexander Hamilton more than by Adams, forced through Congress very high (and very unpopular) taxes to pay for the war they confidently expected to begin at any moment. These taxes sparked an uprising in rural Pennsylvania, where farmers attacked tax collectors under the misapprehension that the money was to fund a standing military; leaders of the Fries's Rebellion, as it came to be known, were convicted of treason and faced capital punishment, but were pardoned by Adams.

Thomas Jefferson (right), Benjamin Franklin (left), and John Adams (center) meet at Jefferson's lodgings, on the corner of Seventh and High (Market) streets in Philadelphia, to review a draft of the Declaration of Independence. (Library of Congress)

Moreover, Federalist congressmen passed, and Adams signed, the unpopular Alien and Sedition Acts in 1798. The first act raised to fourteen the number of years an immigrant had to live in the country before becoming a citizen and was evidently designed to prevent recent Irish immigrants from voting against Federalists, whom they rightly believed to be pro-English. The second, the Sedition Act, made the publication of virtually all criticism of federal officials a crime. Both laws lost whatever legitimacy they may have had in the eyes of the public when the supposedly imminent war, which might have justified them as national defense measures, failed to come.

Federalist judges and prosecutors enforced the laws anyway, jailing, for example, several prominent Republican newspaper editors for violating the Sedition Act by criticizing Adams (though no Federalist editor ever went to jail for vilifying Jefferson). The partisan application of the law left Adams and the Federalists saddled with a reputation as opponents of free speech as the election of 1800 approached. Adams was further crippled by growing divisions in his own party (Hamilton actually campaigned against him) and by the slow pace at which his diplomacy worked. Most voters did not know, for example, until after they had voted, that Adams's policy had succeeded and that a lasting peace with France had been arranged.

In the election of 1800, Adams lost to Jefferson by eight electoral votes. Exhausted, bitterly disappointed, and tired as well of the constant bickering and criticism, public and private, of the previous four years, Adams retired from public life on the day Jefferson was inaugurated. He returned to his home in Quincy to spend his time farming, reading, corresponding with Jefferson, and writing an occasional essay on law or history. He died on July 4, 1826, a few hours after his great antagonist and greater friend, Jefferson, died in Virginia.

SIGNIFICANCE

Throughout his life, John Adams never got the praise he thought was his due. He was an important writer in the years preceding independence, but none of his writings had the broad impact of John Dickinson's *Letters from a Farmer in Pennsylvania, to the Inhabitants of the British Colonies* (1767–1768) or the great popular appeal of Thomas Paine's *Common Sense*. In the long run, however, through his writings on government and constitutions, Adams contributed as much or more to the development of republican constitutional thought than all but two or three of the founders.

His work in Europe negotiating the Treaty of Paris (1783) was at times brilliant, but it was the colorful and cunningly rustic Benjamin Franklin who caught the public's eye. Adams was president of the United States, but he immediately followed Washington in that office and inevitably Americans compared the two and found Adams the weaker president. Adams claimed that he did not seek the people's praises, but all of his life he watched men who were no more intelligent than he, no more dedicated to the republic, and no more successful in serving it win the kind of warm public applause that seemed beyond his grasp. He was respected but not revered, and he knew it.

Broadly speaking, Adams made three major contributions to the revolution and the new republic. First, he worked in Massachusetts and in Congress to keep the revolution from running amok and destroying what was good in the English political tradition. He demonstrated to skeptical Tories and doubtful rebels, by both his words and his work, that independence need not be an invitation to anarchy, despotism, or mob rule, and so he helped make independence an acceptable alternative to submission. Second, with Jay and Franklin, he protected

American interests in the double-dealing diplomatic atmosphere of Paris and London during the war, and he won for the republic a treaty that secured its independence as well as the vast undeveloped territories and other economic resources it needed to survive and develop. Third, as president, he kept the new republic out of what would have been a bitter, divisive war fought under a new, untested Constitution; thanks to Adams's skillful foreign policy, the republic did not have to face its first war under the Constitution for another twelve years.

Yet Adams never completely accepted the more democratic implications of the revolution, and so, by the end of his career, he was both one of the most important of the republic's founders and one of the least appreciated.

Robert A. Becker

FURTHER READING

Adams, Abigail. *The Book of Abigail and John: Selected Letters of the Adams Family, 1762-1784*. Ed. L. H. Butterfield, Marc Friedlaender, and Mary-Jo Kline. Boston: Northeastern UP, 2002. Print.

Adams, John. *The Portable John Adams*. Ed. John Patrick Diggins. New York: Penguin, 2004. Print.

Allen, Brooke. "John Adams: Innocent Sage." *Hudson Rev.* 64.2 (2011): 259–69. Print.

Cappon, Lester J., ed. *The Adams-Jefferson Letters: The Complete Correspondence between Thomas Jefferson and Abigail and John Adams*. 2 vols. Chapel Hill: U of North Carolina P, 1959. Print.

Clancy, Thomas K. "The Framers' Intent: John Adams, His Era, and the Fourth Amendment." *Indiana Law Jour.* 86.3 (2011): 979–1061. Print.

Cornish, Paul Joseph. "John Adams, Cicero and the Traditions of Republicanism." *Michigan Academician* 41.1 (2012): 22–37. Print.

Ferling, John E. *Adams vs. Jefferson: The Tumultuous Election of 1800*. New York: Oxford UP, 2004. Print.

Freidel, Frank, and Hugh Sidey. "John Adams." *The Presidents of the United States of America*. Washington: White House Historical Assn., 2006. *WhiteHouse.gov*. Web. 3 Sept. 2015.

Grant, James. *John Adams: Party of One*. New York: Farrar, 2005. Print.

Jensen, Merrill. *The Founding of a Nation: A History of the American Revolution, 1763-1776*. New York: Oxford UP, 1968. Print.

McCullogh, David. *John Adams*. New York: Simon, 2001. Print.

Morris, Richard B. *The Peacemakers: The Great Powers and American Independence*. New York: Harper, 1965. Print.

Shaw, Peter. *The Character of John Adams*. Chapel Hill: U of North Carolina P, 1976. Print.

Smith, Page. *John Adams*. 2 vols. Garden City: Doubleday, 1962. Print.

Taylor, C. James, ed. "John Adams: Domestic Affairs." *American Presidents*. Miller Center of Public Affairs, U of Virginia, 2015. Web. 3 Sept. 2015.

Dwight D. Eisenhower

34th President of the United States (1953-1961)

Born: October 14, 1890; Denison, Texas
Died: March 28, 1969; Washington, D.C.
Area of Achievement: Military, politics

During World War II, Eisenhower served with distinction as Allied commander for the invasions of North Africa, Italy, and France. He won the presidential elections of 1952 and 1956 and guided the United States through eight years of relative peace and prosperity.

Early Life

Although born in Texas, where his parents lived briefly, Dwight D. Eisenhower grew up in the small town of Abilene, Kansas. The Eisenhowers were a close-knit family and belonged to the Brethren Church, part of the heritage of ancestors who had immigrated to Pennsylvania from Germany during the eighteenth century. The third of seven sons (one of whom died as an infant), Dwight enjoyed a secure childhood, completed high school, and worked in a creamery for two years before entering West Point on the basis of a competitive examination. West Point appealed to him because it offered a free college education.

As a cadet, Eisenhower excelled at football until a knee injury ended that career. He proved a conscientious but not exceptional student and was graduated sixty-first in a class of 164. At graduation in 1915, he stood five feet eleven inches tall and weighed 170 pounds. His classmates remembered and respected "Ike," as did his boyhood friends, as likable, honest, and confident, a person with a quick temper but a quicker infectious grin. He had

Dwight D. Eisenhower (Wikimedia Commons)

an expressive face, blue eyes, and light brown hair that thinned and receded when he was a young man.

Eisenhower's early military years were uneventful except for his marriage in 1916 to Mamie Geneva Doud of Denver, Colorado. The two had met in Texas during his first assignment at Fort Sam Houston. They became parents of two sons, the first of whom died as a child.

LIFE'S WORK

During the 1920s and 1930s, Eisenhower demonstrated exceptional organizational skill and an ability to work with others. In 1926, Eisenhower, who had been merely an average student at West Point, finished first among 275 in his class at the Army's elite Command and General Staff School. When General Douglas MacArthur served as the Army's chief of staff, Eisenhower assisted him, and then served as his senior assistant in the Philippines. MacArthur once evaluated Eisenhower as the most capable officer in the Army.

Eisenhower's personality and his performance during maneuvers in the summer of 1941 impressed the Army's chief of staff, General George C. Marshall. Both in 1941 and in 1942, Eisenhower won two promotions, jumping from lieutenant colonel to lieutenant general. In June 1942, Marshall appointed Eisenhower European Theater Commander. The next year, as general, Eisenhower became Supreme Allied Commander and won fame as the leader of the multinational invasion of Europe in June 1944.

After accepting Germany's surrender, Eisenhower served as the Army's chief of staff. He retired from the Army in 1948 and became president of Columbia University. His book *Crusade in Europe*, published the same year, sold millions of copies and gave him financial security. Two years later, President Harry S. Truman recalled Eisenhower to active duty as Supreme Commander of the North Atlantic Treaty Organization (NATO) forces.

In May 1952, Eisenhower again retired from the Army to seek the Republican Party's nomination for president, an office that leaders in both parties had urged on him for years. With his decisive victory in the November election, Eisenhower embarked on a second career, one even more important than the first.

> "*War is mankind's most tragic and stupid folly; to seek or advise its deliberate provocation is a black crime against all men. Though you follow the trade of the warrior, you do so in the spirit of Washington — not of Genghis Khan. For Americans, only threat to our way of life justifies resort to conflict.*"

As president, Eisenhower set his primary foreign policy objective as maintaining the international role the United States had assumed during the previous decade. More specifically, he intended to end the fighting in Korea, reduce military spending, and lessen the intensity of the Cold War while still adhering to the policy of containment. Militarily, Eisenhower pursued a policy of strategic sufficiency rather than superiority. This policy, as well as a reduction of the capacity to fight limited wars, made possible cuts in the defense budget.

In 1953, Eisenhower approved an armistice in Korea and the next year rejected the advice of his secretary of state and the chairman of the Joint Chiefs of Staff, among others, and refused to intervene in the French war in Indochina. The United States took the lead, however, in establishing the Southeast Asia Treaty Organization as an attempt to accomplish in a region of Asia what NATO had accomplished in Europe. During this same period, Eisenhower also approved Central Intelligence Agency covert activity that helped overthrow the governments of Iran and Guatemala and thereby contributed to the growing acceptance of undemocratic action in the name of freedom.

Eisenhower addresses American paratroopers prior to D-Day. The General was talking about fly fishing with his men as he always did before a stressful operation. (Wikimedia Commons)

In 1955, he helped terminate the post-World War II occupation of Austria and then, at Geneva, Switzerland, became the first president in a decade to meet with Soviet leaders. That same year and again in 1956, Eisenhower reacted to crises in the coastal waters of the People's Republic of China, in Hungary, and in Suez in a manner that helped prevent these crises from escalating into greater violence.

On the domestic side, Eisenhower followed a moderate path. He accepted the New Deal programs and even expanded those covering labor, Social Security, and agriculture. Although he cut the budget of the Tennessee Valley Authority and reduced federal activity and regulations regarding natural resources, Eisenhower championed the nation's largest road-building project (the Federal Aid Highway Act of 1956) and federal development of the Saint Lawrence Seaway. He also approved spending increases in health care. Fiscally, Eisenhower cut taxes and controls, and each year balanced or nearly balanced the budget. The nation's gross national product, personal income, and house purchases all climbed. Inflation proved negligible, averaging 1.5 percent per year. Fundamental to Eisenhower's public philosophy was his belief that only a sound economy could sustain a credible, effective foreign policy.

In the presidential election of 1956, Americans gave Eisenhower a second, even greater, landslide victory over his Democratic opponent Adlai E. Stevenson, despite Eisenhower's major heart attack in 1955 and his operation for ileitis in 1956. Voters approved his moderate policies and, like the friends of his youth and the military personnel with whom he worked, responded positively to his famous grin. His dislike of politics and his lifelong refusal to discuss personalities in public also struck responsive chords. Even his hobbies of golf, fishing and hunting, bridge and poker, and cookouts embodied widespread American values.

Eisenhower's second term continued the basic policies and themes of the first. He steadfastly resisted demands from Democrats and from conservative Republicans to increase defense spending, although he expanded the ballistic missile program after the Soviets launched the world's first human-made earth-orbiting satellite (*Sputnik*) in 1957. In 1958 (in Quemoy) and in 1958–1959 (in Berlin), Eisenhower again handled crises with deliberation. After he hosted the visit of Soviet leader Nikita S. Khrushchev, Eisenhower looked forward to a Paris summit meeting in May 1960, and to a visit to the Soviet Union as his final contribution to promoting peace. On the eve of the conference, the Soviets shot down an American spy plane over Soviet territory. The U-2 incident, named for the plane, ruined the conference, canceled Eisenhower's planned visit to the Soviet Union, and dashed his hopes to improve relations between the two superpowers.

Domestic highlights of Eisenhower's second term included his ordering troops to Little Rock, Arkansas, to maintain order while the city's high school racially integrated its classes. In the same year, 1957, Eisenhower signed the first civil rights act in eighty-two years. Important symbolically, the act produced little change in the lives of black Americans. The same proved true of another civil rights act in 1960. In response to *Sputnik*, Eisenhower established the National Aeronautics and Space Administration (NASA) and approved the National Defense Education Act, providing the first substantial federal aid to higher education in almost a century.

Criticism of Eisenhower dealt mostly with three subjects. First, he refused to exercise any public leadership in response to Senator Joseph McCarthy's excessive and unsubstantiated accusations of disloyalty directed against numerous Americans, including General Marshall. Second, after the U.S. Supreme Court ruled in 1954 that separate-but-equal facilities were unconstitutional, Eisenhower refrained from lending his moral or political support for implementation of the ruling or for promotion of civil rights in general. The third area of criticism concerned his sparse defense budget and the limited range of responses it permitted in time of crisis. Eisenhower's confidence and public support, however, kept him from altering his positions because of such criticism.

In his presidential farewell address, Eisenhower warned the nation of the threat to democracy from the influence of the military-industrial complex, which benefited from massive military budgets. He retired to his Gettysburg, Pennsylvania, farm and wrote his memoirs. Most contemporary observers agreed that, had the Constitution permitted and had he been willing to run, Eisenhower easily would have won a third term.

Significance

Eisenhower, the career military officer, curtailed defense spending, pursued a foreign policy that emphasized conciliation rather than conflict, and presided over eight years of peace. An advocate of gradual domestic change, Eisenhower watched his most prominent appointee, Chief Justice of the United States Earl Warren, use his position and influence to bring sweeping changes to society. As a Republican president, Eisenhower, who disliked politics and favored limitations on the terms of senators and representatives, proved the most able politician of his generation. He adhered to definite policies, faced a Democratic Congress for six of his eight years in the White House, and suffered domestic and foreign setbacks, yet he gave the country eight years of economic growth and prosperity and left office with undiminished popularity.

Eisenhower obviously was a capable, complex man, but the key to his success seems to have been his ability to radiate straightforward honesty and uncomplicated common sense. The events of the decades following his presidency the international arms race, war, riots, Watergate, inflation, declining standard of living, and uncontrollable budget deficits have greatly enhanced respect for Eisenhower's accomplishments. Indeed, according to many, he joined the ranks of the nation's ten greatest presidents.

Keith W. Olson

Further Reading

Ambrose, Stephen E. *Eisenhower*. 2 vols. New York: Simon, 1983–1984. Print.

Boyle, Peter G. *Eisenhower*. New York: Pearson, 2005. Print.

Burk, Robert F. *The Eisenhower Administration and Black Civil Rights*. Knoxville: U of Tennessee P, 1984. Print.

Divine, Robert A. *Eisenhower and the Cold War*. New York: Oxford UP, 1981. Print.

Eisenhower, David. *Eisenhower: At War, 1943–1945*. New York: Random, 1986. Print.

Eisenhower, David. *Going Home to Glory: A Memoir of Life with Dwight D. Eisenhower, 1961–1969*. New York: Simon, 2010. Print.

Eisenhower, Dwight D. *The Eisenhower Diaries*. Ed. Robert H. Farrell. New York: Norton, 1981. Print.

Filipink, Richard M. *Dwight Eisenhower and American Foreign Policy during the 1960s: An American Lion in Winter*. Lanham: Lexington, 2015. eBook Collection (EBSCOhost). Web. 9 Sept. 2015.

Gilbert, Robert E. "Dwight D. Eisenhower: The Call of Duty and the Love of Applause." *Jour. of Psychohistory* 38.1 (2010): 49–70. Print.

Griffith, Robert. "Dwight D. Eisenhower and the Corporate Commonwealth." *American Historical Rev.* 87 (1982): 87–122. Print.

Madsen, Grant. "The International Origins of Dwight D. Eisenhower's Political Economy." *Jour. of Policy Hist.* 24.4 (2012): 675–708. Print.

Mayer, Michael S. "With Much Deliberation and Some Speed: Eisenhower and the Brown Decision." *Jour. of Southern History* 52 (February, 1986): 43–76. Print.

Polsky, Andrew J. "Shifting Currents: Dwight Eisenhower and the Dynamic of Presidential Opportunity Structure." *Presidential Studies Quarterly* 45.1 (2015): 91+. Print.

Walch, Timothy. *Herbert Hoover and Dwight D. Eisenhower: A Documentary History*. New York: Palgrave, 2013. eBook Collection (EBSCOhost). Web. 9 Sept. 2015.

Wukovits, John. *Eisenhower*. New York: Palgrave, 2006. Print.

Betty Ford

First Lady of the United States (1974-1977)

Born: April 8, 1918; Chicago, Illinois
Died: July 8, 2011; Rancho Mirage, California
Area of Achievement: Public health, government and politics, women's rights

Ford was a popular, outspoken first lady of the United States. In the White House, she was an advocate for a number of women's issues. She was diagnosed with breast cancer soon after becoming first lady, which led her to join the emerging women's health movement. After leaving the White House, she founded and chaired the Betty Ford Center, an internationally known institution for the treatment of substance abuse.

Early Life

Betty Ford was born Elizabeth Ann Bloomer in Chicago on April 8, 1918, the third child and only daughter of William and Hortense (Neahr) Bloomer. When Ford was two years old, the family moved to Grand Rapids, Michigan, where she had a comfortable upbringing. Ford's early years were full of friends, family, and social activities. Tragedy, however, touched her family at age sixteen when her father died. At his funeral, she learned that her father had been an alcoholic.

A lifelong love of dance began when Ford started taking lessons at the age of eight. For two years during high school, she attended the well-respected Bennington School of Dance in Vermont, where she became acquainted with modern dance innovator Martha Graham. Ford aspired to dance in Graham's regular company and, at the age of twenty, she moved to New York to pursue that goal. Though talented, she was not invited to join Graham's main group. Her mother, who was uncomfortable with the idea of her daughter living alone in New York, encouraged Ford to return to Grand Rapids, and she did.

Life's Work

Ford worked at a local department store as a fashion coordinator and also taught dance. In 1942, she was married to William Warren, a man she had known for years. Like her father, Warren struggled with alcoholism. The marriage ended in divorce five years later.

In 1947, Betty met Gerald Ford, a lawyer who also was from Grand Rapids. Their romance progressed and they

Betty Ford (Library of Congress)

were married on October 15, 1948. Ford was elected to the US House of Representatives less than one month later. The couple set up house near the capitol and Ford became active in political and social causes. She was active in the Congressional Club, gave tours to visiting constituents, and campaigned when her husband was running for reelection.

The Ford family grew quickly: Between 1950 and 1957, the couple had four children. Her husband was away from home for as many as 258 days a year doing congressional business or supporting fellow Republicans. The burden of raising the family fell almost exclusively on Ford, and it took a toll. Recurring physical problems from a pinched nerve in her neck as well as low self-esteem led her to consult a psychiatrist, whom she saw for a number of years.

In 1973, the Fords had decided that they would retire to Grand Rapids after one more term in the House. Then, President Richard M. Nixon named Gerald Ford to succeed the disgraced Spiro Agnew as vice president of the United States in October 1973. Less than one year later, on August 9, 1974, Gerald Ford became president after Nixon left office following his impeachment. Betty Ford became first lady of the United States.

After five years of First Lady Pat Nixon's formality, Ford was a breath of fresh air. She wanted to be an active first lady, and it was apparent that she intended to speak her mind frequently, to the displeasure of her husband's West Wing staff.

Ford's abbreviated tenure in the White House kept her from developing an ongoing White House program or project. Building on a lifetime as a homemaker and political partner, she became an advocate for women's issues. At least part of her activity was unintentional. Shortly after becoming first lady she was diagnosed with breast cancer. At the time, Americans were reluctant to discuss breast cancer and other women's health issues. Ford made the conscious decision to tell the public about her cancer and subsequent radical mastectomy. She said, "My feeling was if I had it, others had it, and if I said nothing, their lives would be gone." The announcement came at a time when breast cancer was rarely discussed in public. After leaving the hospital and completing chemotherapy, Ford continued to be an advocate for regular mammography exams and for health education. Her advocacy was a part of the emerging women's health movement in the 1970s.

On a Campaign trip in Texas Ford, aka "First Momma," greets the crowd gathered at San Jacinto Battlefield Park for a Bicentennial Celebration. (Wikimedia Commons)

"*Being a lady does not require silence.*"

The first lady became a vocal supporter of the Equal Rights Amendment (ERA) as well. The ERA had already been passed by thirty-four state legislatures, but four others were needed for passage at the federal level as an amendment to the US Constitution. Ford made telephone calls and wrote notes to members of the state legislatures where votes were pending. She aroused the ire of anti-ERA forces that were annoyed with her lobbying efforts. She asserted that she was only expressing her opinion, but she finally backed away from active support when it seemed that her efforts might affect her husband politically.

Ford encouraged her husband to appoint more women to government positions. Taking her views into consideration, President Ford named Carla Hills to serve as secretary of Housing and Urban Development. Anne Armstrong was appointed US ambassador to the Court of St. James. Ford was also hopeful that her husband would nominate the first woman to the US Supreme Court, but when he had the opportunity, he named John Paul Stevens instead.

A defining moment for Ford occurred in August 1975, when she appeared on the CBS television program 60 Minutes. The program coincided with the anniversary of the Ford administration's first year in office. The first lady startled interviewer Morley Safer with her enthusiastic support for Roe v. Wade (1973). She also told Safer that she would not be surprised if her children tried marijuana, and she would not be shocked if her daughter had an affair. The public reaction was immediate, and much of it was negative. Over time, however, public opinion reversed and Ford saw her popularity rise for her candor.

Ford's popularity rose so much that a campaign button from the 1976 presidential election read "I'm Voting for Betty's Husband." However, her husband was defeated by Jimmy Carter in the 1976 elections.

After leaving the White House, the family grew increasingly concerned with Ford's drinking and dependence on prescription drugs. They conducted an intervention to help her face her problems. She entered a rehabilitation program in California and was so grateful for the help she received there that she founded the Betty Ford Center in Rancho Mirage, also in California, for the treatment of substance abuse. Over the years, the center became one of the most well-known treatment centers in the world. Ford stepped down as the chair of the board of trustees in 2005 and was succeeded by her daughter, Susan Ford. Ford also remained a vocal advocate of women's rights, speaking at numerous engagements and fund-raising events. In 1991, she was presented the Presidential Medal of Freedom by George H. W. Bush, and she received a Congressional Gold Medal in 1999.

Gerald and Betty Ford became the first US president and first lady to live into their nineties. Gerald Ford died at age ninety-three in 2006, and Betty Ford traveled cross-country to take part in memorial services for her husband in California, Michigan, and Washington, DC. She underwent operations in 2006 and 2007 for blood clots in her legs, after which she curtailed her public appearances. Ford died at age ninety-three on July 8, 2011, at the Eisenhower Medical Center near her home and the Betty Ford Clinic in Rancho Mirage.

Significance

As one scholar observed, Ford's legacy was more in her example than in the success or failure of the causes she supported. Well liked by Americans who admired her candid and unpretentious style, she was an active first lady who was, in many ways, ahead of her time. Her public policy forays achieved mixed but well-publicized results.

Perhaps Ford's greatest achievement in the White House was that she brought breast cancer out of the closet, so to speak. Her frank openness about breast cancer most likely saved lives and is credited with contributing to what was a burgeoning women's health movement in the 1970s. After leaving the White House, she confronted her own demons and faced the realities of her substance abuse. Her status as a public figure helped the nation talk openly about two previously taboo subjects, breast cancer and substance abuse, bringing awareness and encouraging countless Americans to seek treatment.

One of the most popular and well-respected first ladies, Ford's candor and resilience in the face of personal tragedies and challenges have enlightened and improved the lives of Americans. One scholar referred to her as "an American hero," a well-deserved title. Ford died of natural causes in 2011, at Eisenhower Medical Center in Rancho Mirage. Her memorial service had over 800 attendees including First Lady Michelle Obama and former President Bill Clinton.

Myra G. Gutin, updated by Micah L. Issitt

Further Reading

Ford, Betty, and Chris Chase. *The Times of My Life.* New York: Harper, 1978. Print. Ford's autobiography follows her from childhood through the tumultuous events of 1974 to 1977, when she served as first lady, and through her successful treatment for alcohol and drug dependency.

Greene, John Robert. *Betty Ford: Candor and Courage in the White House.* Lawrence: UP of Kansas, 2004. Print. The most comprehensive and thoughtful discussion of Ford, this book incorporates primary and secondary materials as it assesses her effectiveness in the White House and in the years after.

Gutin, Myra G. "Betty Ford." *The President's Partner: The First Lady in the Twentieth Century.* Westport: Greenwood, 1989. Print. Classifying Ford as a political surrogate and independent activist, this study looks at Ford's speeches, media relations, and social activities while serving as first lady.

_____, and Leesa E. Tobin. "'You've Come a Long Way Mr. President': Betty Ford as First Lady." *Gerald R. Ford and the Politics of Post- Watergate America.* Ed. Bernard J. Firestone and Alexej Ugrinksy. Vol. 2. Westport: Greenwood, 1993. Print. This chapter discusses Ford as a political spouse and White House activist. Focuses special attention on her speeches, media relations, and her appearance on 60 Minutes.

Joslyn, Heather. "Betty Ford, Outspoken Health Advocate." *Chronicle of Philanthropy* 23.16 (2011): 18. Print.

Nemy, Enid. "Betty Ford, Former First Lady, Dies at 93." *New York Times.* New York Times, 8 July 2011. Web. 6 Dec. 2013.

Radcliffe, Donnie. "Betty Ford Dies at 93: Former First Lady Founded Iconic Clinic." *Washington Post.* Washington Post, 8 July 2011. Web. 6 Dec. 2013.

Tobin, Leesa E. "Betty Ford as First Lady: A Woman for Women." *Presidential Studies Quarterly* 20 (1990): 761–767. Print. Written by the Ford Library archivist responsible for processing the papers of the first lady and her staff, this article describes their significance in understanding women's issues in the 1970s.

Weidenfeld, Sheila. *First Lady's Lady: With the Fords at the White House.* New York: Putnam's, 1979. Print. Weidenfeld, who served as Betty Ford's press secretary, discusses her years with the First Lady in chronologically arranged entries.

ANDREW JACKSON

7th President of the United States (1829-1837)

Born: March 15, 1767; Waxhaw Settlement, Colony of Carolinas
Died: June 8, 1845; Nashville, Tennessee
Area of Achievement: Politics, military

Possessing the characteristics of the roughly hewn Western frontiersman—in contrast to the aristocratic propensities of the eastern and Virginia "establishment"—Jackson came to symbolize the common person in the United States and the rise of democracy.

EARLY LIFE

Andrew Jackson was born into a family that had come from County Antrim, Ireland. His father, also named Andrew, arrived in America in 1765 and died shortly before his son, the future president, was born. The younger Jackson's teenage years were "rough and tumble." Acquiring little formal education, Jackson made his way through early life by hand-to-mouth jobs, helping his two older brothers support their widowed mother.

During the Revolutionary War, the British invaded Waxhaw, an event that shaped much of Jackson's subsequent life and career. His two brothers were killed, and his mother died of cholera while caring for prisoners of war. Jackson, taken prisoner by the British, was orphaned at the age of fourteen, a situation that taught him independence, both in action and in thought.

In 1784, Jackson went to Salisbury, North Carolina, apprenticed to the law firm of Spruce McKay. Within three years, he was admitted to the bar, and in 1788, Jackson made the decision to go west, to Nashville, Tennessee, to seek his fortune.

While Jackson pursued a legal career as a practicing attorney, superior court solicitor, and judge, he also ventured into other activities. He became an avid horse breeder and racer, as well as a plantation owner. Jackson had no formal military training, but he quickly earned a reputation as an Indian fighter, and it was undoubtedly his experience in this area that led to his election in 1802 as major general of the western Tennessee militia. In 1791,

Andrew Jackson (Wikimedia Commons)

Jackson married Rachel Donelson Robards, who had, she thought, been recently divorced from Lewis Robards. The divorce decree had not been issued in Virginia at the time Andrew and Rachel were wed in Natchez, Mississippi. Three years later, when Jackson learned of the error, he and Rachel remarried, but this action did not stop enemies from slandering his wife in subsequent political campaigns.

Jackson was one of few serious duelists in American history (Aaron Burr was another), and his most famous confrontation was with Charles Dickinson, essentially over a problem that started with race horses. On the occasion, Jackson wore a borrowed coat that was too large for him. When Dickinson fired, he aimed for the heart, located, he thought, at the top of Jackson's coat pocket. Because the coat was too big, the top of the pocket was below Jackson's heart. Dickinson hit the target, but Jackson still stood. Dickinson exclaimed, "Great God, have I missed?" Jackson then fired at Dickinson, mortally wounding him. Dickinson lived for a time after being shot, and it was characteristic of Jackson not to allow anyone to tell Dickinson that he really had hit his opponent; he died thinking that he had missed. Jackson was seriously wounded in the duel, and he convalesced for several weeks.

Jackson was a tall, thin man, six feet one inch in height, usually weighing 150 pounds. His nose was straight and prominent, and his blue eyes blazed fiercely whenever he lost his temper, which was often. During the early years, his hair was reddish-brown; in old age, it was white. He had a firmly set chin and a high forehead. Paintings and daguerreotypes suggest a man accustomed to giving orders and having them obeyed.

> "*As long as our government is administered for the good of the people, and is regulated by their will; as long as it secures to us the rights of persons and of property, liberty of conscience, and of the press, it will be worth defending.*"

LIFE'S WORK

Jackson became a nationally known figure during the War of 1812. Though he had been elected to his rank rather than earning it by training and experience, he soon proved to be a capable leader. He endeavored to neutralize the Creek Indians in Alabama, who periodically attacked white settlers. He accomplished this objective at the Battle of Horseshoe Bend. So tough and unremitting was he at this engagement that his soldiers began to call him Old Hickory. His greatest battle was against the British at New Orleans. Amazingly, there were some two thousand British casualties, and less than a dozen for the army of Westerners, black people, and pirates that Jackson had put together. Although the war was essentially over before the battle took place—news traveled slowly before the advent of modern communications—Jackson became a national military hero, and there was talk in some quarters of running him for president of the United States.

After the war, in 1818, President James Monroe ordered Jackson and his army to Florida, to deal with Indian problems. While there, Jackson torched Pensacola and hanged two Englishmen whom he thought were in collusion with the Indians as they attacked settlers across the border in Alabama. Jackson's deeds in Florida caused diplomatic rifts with Spain and England, and he clearly had exceeded his orders, but his actions appealed to a pragmatic American public, and the general's popularity soared.

When Jackson became a presidential candidate in 1824, some believed that it was the office to which all of his previous activities pointed. If ever there was a "natural" for the presidency, his supporters argued, it was Andrew Jackson. His opponents feared that if Jackson were elected, there would be too much popular government; Jackson, they argued, might turn the republic into a "Mobocracy." Worse yet, he had little experience with foreign policy, and his confrontational style might create one diplomatic crisis after another.

Jackson missed the presidency in 1824, although he received more electoral votes than anyone else. It was necessary to get a majority of electoral votes—more than all the other candidates combined. Because there was no majority in 1824, the election was decided by the House of Representatives, which selected John Quincy Adams; Jackson protested that Adams's victory was engineered by a "corrupt bargain" with Henry Clay, whom Adams appointed as secretary of state after Clay's supporters in the House ensured Adams's election. In 1828, however, there was no doubt that Jackson would defeat Adams. A political "revolution" had occurred in the four-year term. In 1824, four candidates amassed altogether less than a half million popular votes. In 1828, however, two candidates, Jackson and Adams, collected about 1,200,000, meaning that in four years 800,000 voters had been added to the polls—in large part the result of liberalized voting qualifications—and most of them voted for Jackson.

Jackson's great objective while in office was "executive supremacy." He reasoned: Who was the only government official universally elected to office? The answer was the president. Was it not reasonable, then, that the president was the chief symbol of the American people? Further, if he were the chief symbol, should not the executive branch be as powerful, or more so, than the Congress or the Supreme Court? This concept of executive supremacy displeased numerous congressional leaders. Congress had dominated the federal government since the Revolution, out of a general distrust of administrative centralization. After all, Britain's king George III was a "typical" administrator.

Jackson pursued executive supremacy in a number of ways. One was the patronage system, by which he appointed friends to office. His enemies referred to this policy as the "spoils system"; Jackson called it "rotation in office." The number of those displaced, however (about 10 percent of the government workforce), was no greater than previous or future executive terms. Another procedure that strengthened Jackson's presidency, perhaps the most important, was the "county agent" system that Martin Van Buren created for the Democratic Party. The forerunners of what became known as "county chairmen," these agents enabled the Democrats to practice politics on a grassroots level, going door to door, as it were, to collect votes and support for the president.

An important part of Jackson's drive for executive supremacy was the presidential veto. He used this constitutional device twelve times, more than all of his predecessors put together. Moreover, he made good use of the "pocket veto." (If a bill comes to the president less than ten days before Congress adjourns, he can "put it in his pocket" and not have to tell Congress why he disapproves of it. A "pocket veto" enhances presidential power by preventing Congress from reconsidering the bill, an action that caused presidential critics to call Jackson "King Andrew I.") Though he was not the first president to use the pocket veto—James Madison was first—Jackson made more extensive use of it than any of his predecessors.

Perhaps the most significant presidential veto in American history was Jackson's rejection, in 1832, of the re-charter bill, a bill that would have re-chartered the Bank of the United States. Among other things, Jackson argued that the executive had the power to judge the constitutionality of a bill brought before him. According to Jacksonian scholar Robert Remini, Jackson's veto on this bill caused an ascendancy of presidential power that did not abate until Richard M. Nixon's resignation in 1974.

In foreign affairs, Jackson conducted a lively policy that gained new respect for the United States from major European powers. He nurtured good relations with England by a conciliatory attitude on the Maine-Canada boundary question and promising to exempt many English goods from the harsh tariff of 1828 (the Tariff of Abominations). He even held out the prospect of lowering the tariff against the British through a treaty. His positive stance on boundary lines and the tariff helped re-open full West Indies trade with the British. Although Jackson may have been an Anglophobe most of his life, it is nevertheless true that he gained concessions from the English that had been denied to his predecessor, the so-called Anglophile, Adams.

The United States almost went to war with its oldest and most loyal ally while Jackson was president. The United States presented France with a "spoliation" bill, going back to the depredations of American shipping during the Napoleonic Wars. When, for various reasons, the French government refused payments, Jackson's tone became strident. In a message to Congress, he said that a "collision" was possible between the two governments if the French remained obstinate. Ultimately, Britain intervened and urged the French to settle the "American matter," because of mutual problems developing with Russia.

Though Jackson personally believed that Texas would one day be a part of the American Union, he did not push its annexation while in office, for he feared that the slavery question that Texas would engender would embarrass his chosen presidential successor, Van Buren. After Van Buren was safely elected, Jackson publicly supported the annexation of Texas, which took place in 1845, the year Jackson died.

While Jackson was president, reforms occurred on state levels. Numerous state constitutions were revised or rewritten, all with liberal trends. Women found it easier to prosecute abusive husbands and, increasingly, they could purchase property and dispose of it as they chose, without getting permission from their nearest male kin. Prison reforms began in some states, and mentally ill people were treated for their illnesses rather than being thought to be possessed by the devil. Public education systems started in several states, notably Massachusetts and New York. In all these reforms, suffrage ever widened, exemplifying the belief that political participation should be based on white manhood rather than property qualifications. Noted scholar Clinton Rossiter has shown that the Jacksonian presidency changed the base of American government from aristocracy to democracy without fundamentally altering its republican character.

After serving as president from 1829 to 1837, Jackson happily returned to the Hermitage. There, he continued as the father figure of his country, receiving dignitaries from around the world, and giving advice to those who followed him in the presidential office. He was especially pleased to see his protégé, James K. Polk, win the office in 1844 and become widely known as "Young Hickory." Jackson died at the Hermitage on June 8, 1845.

Significance

It is fair to say that Andrew Jackson was first and foremost a beneficiary of rising democratic spirits in the United States. When he attained power, he put his stamp upon events and promulgated additional steps toward democracy. He suggested some reforms, many of which were ultimately enacted. He wanted senators to be popularly elected, as were members of the House of Representatives. He wanted additional judges to take the heavy burden off the judicial system. He believed that the United States Post Office should be reshaped into a semiprivate organization. He suggested some reforms that were not enacted but were widely discussed. He believed that a president should serve for six years and then be ineligible for further election. He thought that the electoral college should either be abandoned or drastically reformed, because, in his opinion, it did not always reflect the will of the electorate.

It is widely held that Jacksonian America heralded the "positive state," where government dominates the private sector. Jackson's presidency is frequently cited as starting the trend toward federal centralization. Jackson's legacy is most visible in his personification of the common American man, even though he, himself, was hardly a "common" man. His was an age of entrepreneurship in which it was believed that government should not grant privileges to one group that it withholds from another. This thought has motivated many reform philosophies in the twentieth century, not the least of which was the civil rights movement. In this and other significant ways, Andrew Jackson has spoken to Americans of subsequent generations.

Carlton Jackson

FURTHER READING

Brogdon, Matthew S. "Defending the Union: Andrew Jackson's Nullification Proclamation and American Federalism." Rev. Of Politics 73.2 (2011): 245–273. Print.

Burstein, Andrew. The Passions of Andrew Jackson. New York: Knopf, 2003. Print.

Ellis, Richard E. Andrew Jackson. Washington, DC: CQ P, 2003. Print.

Gatell, Frank Otto, and John M. McFaul, eds. Jacksonian America, 1815-1840: New Society, Changing Politics. Englewood Cliffs: Prentice, 1970. Print.

Inskeep, Steve. Jacksonland: President Andrew Jackson, Cherokee Chief John Ross, and a Great American Land Grab. New York: Penguin, 2015. Print.

Langguth, A. J. Driven West: Andrew Jackson and the Trail of Tears to the Civil War. New York: Simon, 2010. Print.

Moser, Harold D, et al. The Papers of Andrew Jackson: 1830. Knoxville: U of Tennessee P, 2013. Print.

Pessen, Edward. Jacksonian America: Society, Personality, and Politics. Rev. ed. Urbana: U of Illinois P, 1985. Print.

Remini, Robert V. Andrew Jackson. 3 vols. Baltimore: Johns Hopkins UP, 1998. Print.

Remini, Robert V. Andrew Jackson and the Bank War: A Study in the Growth of Presidential Power. New York: Norton, 1967. Print.

Remini, Robert V. The Election of Andrew Jackson. Philadelphia: Lippincott, 1963. Print.

Remini, Rovert V. Martin Van Buren and the Making of the Democratic Party. New York: Columbia UP, 1959. Print.

Rossiter, Clinton L. The American Presidency. New York: Harcourt, 1956. Print.

THOMAS JEFFERSON

3rd President of the United States (1801-1809)

Born: April 13, 1743; Shadwell, Colony of Virginia
Died: July 4, 1826; Charlottesville, Virginia
Area of Achievement: Politics, law, diplomacy, architecture

A genuine revolutionary, Thomas Jefferson was one of the early and effective leaders of the movement to overthrow British rule in North America. After laboring to create a free, prosperous, enlightened, and agrarian republic, Jefferson served as the third president of the United States.

Thomas Jefferson (Wikimedia Commons)

Early Life

The man generally considered the first thoroughgoing democrat in US history began life as a Virginia aristocrat. His father, Peter Jefferson, had indeed come from yeoman stock but commended himself to the upper class as an expert surveyor, reliable county officer, and energetic planter. The elder Jefferson then joined that upper class by marrying Jane Randolph. From his parents, Thomas Jefferson inherited wealth, status, and a tradition of public service.

Educated at first in private schools kept by Anglican clergymen William Douglas and James Maury, Jefferson descended to Williamsburg in 1760, to study at the College of William and Mary. A proficient student, he completed the requirements for his degree within two years but stayed on to read law with George Wythe, an uncommonly learned and humane jurist. In his student years, Jefferson, along with his favorite professor, William Small, and Wythe, was frequently a guest in the governor's palace. Admitted to the bar in 1767, the young bachelor attorney became acquainted with all of Virginia by the strenuous but interesting practice of attending the quarter sessions of county courts. Jefferson soon stood among the leaders of his profession.

Entering the House of Burgesses in 1769, Jefferson already owned more than 2,500 acres inherited from his father, who had died in 1757. His marriage to the young widow Martha Wayles Skelton doubled his property in 1772, and the death of Martha's father in 1774 doubled it again, while increasing his slaves to more than two hundred. The Wayles inheritance also brought a large indebtedness, but in 1774, Jefferson might count himself the most fortunate of men, with a lovely wife and a robust baby daughter, a personal fortune, and a position near the top of Virginia's society and politics. He was imposing in appearance, standing more than six feet tall, with plentiful red hair, strong features, and an attitude of vitality and interest. Yet he was also shy and avoided public appearances whenever he could; he was at his very best in the cordial intimacy of the drawing room or the dining table.

Life's Work

In 1774, Virginia chose to support Massachusetts against the assaults of the Coercive (or Intolerable) Acts. To that support, Jefferson contributed the first of his major political writings, *A Summary View of the Rights of British America* (1774). In 1775, he was a delegate of Virginia in the Continental Congress in Philadelphia, supporting George Washington's newly formed Continental army in the defense of Massachusetts. Here, for a few months, Jefferson's sentiments were too radical for the majority, but when independence seemed all but inevitable in June 1776, Congress placed him (with Benjamin Franklin and John Adams) on the special committee to draft a Declaration of Independence. Though slightly amended in committee and again on the floor of Congress, the Declaration of Independence is largely Jefferson's work.

For the next several years, Jefferson avoided continental service, preferring the considerable scene of action near his growing family and estate. With Wythe and Edmund Pendleton he drew up a new legal code for the state. He also prepared a plan for the gradual ending of slavery but declined to bring it before the House of Delegates. He also postponed his plans for a general scheme of education and for the separation of church and state. Elected governor in 1779, he found that office an ordeal. To the minor confusion of moving government from Williamsburg to Richmond was added the major trauma of a full-scale British military invasion of his state. Just before Jefferson's second term ended in June 1781, he had to flee into the Blue Ridge Mountains to escape a raiding party sent to Monticello expressly to capture him.

> "*We hold these truths to be self-evident, that all men are created equal, that they are endowed by their Creator with certain unalienable Rights, that among these are Life, Liberty, and the pursuit of Happiness.—That to secure these rights, Governments are instituted among Men, deriving their just powers from the consent of the governed, That whenever any Form of Government becomes destructive of these ends, it is the Right of the People to alter or to abolish it, and to institute new Government, laying its foundation on such principles and organizing its powers in such form, as to them shall seem most likely to effect their Safety and Happiness.*"

Already discouraged by his last months as governor, Jefferson was cast into the deepest depression of his life by his wife's death in 1782. He never remarried, but he did accept reappointment to Congress, where, in 1783 and 1784, he worked on the monetary system of the United States, basing it on the plentiful Spanish dollar and applying the rational decimal system to fractional coins. He also drafted a comprehensive scheme for organizing the western territories of the United States. He introduced the idea of rectangular surveys and proposed local self-government from the start. His division of the terrain into eighteen jurisdictions, while convenient for the participatory democracy he had in view, would have long delayed statehood for any of them. A provision barring the introduction of slavery after 1800 failed to win the support of the nine states required under the Articles of Confederation, but Congress did adopt Jefferson's plan, replacing it instead with the Land Ordinance of 1785 and the Northwest Ordinance of 1787. Meanwhile, Jefferson had accepted a diplomatic mission to France; in 1785, he replaced the aged Benjamin Franklin as minister.

The five years in Europe were busy and happy. A tour of France and northern Italy confirmed Jefferson's architectural taste and enlarged his knowledge of agriculture. He flirted with an artistic Englishwoman, Maria Cosway, and enjoyed visiting John Adams in England, though he did not care for English society in general. By mail he kept up with the movement to disestablish religion in Virginia, where his own bill was finally passed under the expert guidance of James Madison. He also encouraged Madison and other correspondents in their drive toward a new federal constitution. In France, he sought help against the Barbary pirates and urged France to remove prohibitions or costly restrictions on such American commodities as tobacco and whale oil. His closest friends were liberal aristocrats such as the Marquis de Lafayette, whose leading role in the early stages of the French Revolution Jefferson followed with interest and encouragement.

Intending a brief visit only, Jefferson returned to the United States at the end of 1789, but he promptly accepted the post of secretary of state from President Washington. After settling his two daughters in Virginia, he took up his duties in the temporary capital, New York City. There he helped bring about the trade of votes that made possible Alexander Hamilton's federal assumption of state Revolutionary War debts and the permanent location of the Federal District on the Potomac River. The government then moved, temporarily, to Philadelphia.

In 1791, Jefferson and Madison began to organize the first opposition party under the new Constitution. Their avowed object was to overturn not Washington but his secretary of the treasury, Hamilton. Washington almost always sided with Hamilton against his rivals, however, so it was really a case of going against a popular president by forcing him to fire a considerably less popular minister and change his policies. Vigorously protesting Hamilton's Bank of the United States and his avowed intention to reach a friendly understanding with Great Britain, Jefferson and his growing party accused Hamilton of secret designs to reestablish aristocracy and monarchy, and even return the United States to the British Empire.

In the spring of 1793, Jefferson opposed Washington's Neutrality Proclamation and initially supported the representative of the new French republic, Edmond Charles Genet. Genet, however, far overreached Jefferson's idea of propriety by licensing privateers to prey on British shipping, setting up prize courts in American seaports and raising an army based in Kentucky to attack Spanish Louisiana. Jefferson had the unpleasant task of opposing all this, while trying to contain the zeal of the many new Democratic societies that were supporting Genet. This crisis passed when Genet's group fell from power in France, and after a harrowing yellow fever epidemic paralyzed the American government in the late summer, Jefferson returned to present Congress with his report on the foreign commerce of the United States. He then resigned and spent three years improving his estate and carrying on a lively exchange of letters with his political friends.

The odd workings of the original electoral system made Jefferson vice president in 1797, after he had finished a close second behind his now-estranged rival, John Adams, in the contest for president. Discreet in public, he acted behind the scenes to stiffen resistance to Adams and his Federalist majorities in Congress during the undeclared naval war with France. Jefferson wrote the Kentucky Resolutions against the partisan Alien and Sedition Acts of 1798; his friend John Breckinridge steered them through the Kentucky legislature. The resolutions contained the extreme doctrine that a state might nullify an act of Congress; the effect, however, was to let off steam until the Federalists and their acts passed from the scene.

Fearful that Adams might sneak in for a second term, every Jeffersonian elector cast one ballot for Jefferson and another for Aaron Burr of New York in the election of 1800. This produced a tie, unintended by the mass of voters, and threw the election into the lame-duck Congress that had been elected in 1798. Enough Federalist congressmen preferred Burr to Jefferson to produce a stalemate for several weeks, but Jefferson finally prevailed; Burr, as vice president, found Jefferson depriving him of federal patronage and Governor George Clinton depriving him of influence in New York. Burr thus began on the course that led to his seeking Federalist support for

The Jefferson Memorial in Washington, DC. (Wikimedia Commons)

his political comeback, which in turn produced the famous duel, fatal to Alexander Hamilton, and finally the adventures in the West that led Jefferson to arrest Burr and try him for treason.

Jefferson's first term in office was one of the most popular and successful in the history of the presidency. After many a bad turn, Washington and Adams had secured peace with all the major foreign powers and all the American Indian tribes capable of threatening America's frontiers. By cordially maintaining these arrangements—even with Britain—Jefferson presided over four years of peaceful and prosperous expansion. Yet he proved to be different from his predecessors. With the expert help of Albert Gallatin, secretary of the treasury, and James Madison, secretary of state, he greatly reduced the army, the navy, and the foreign diplomatic corps. His congressional majorities reduced the federal judiciary and repealed the unpopular excises, including the tax on distillations that had set off the Whiskey Rebellion in 1794. The Twelfth Amendment to the Constitution ended forever the confusion of presidential and vice presidential votes.

Jefferson did incur the expense of sending several ships to the Mediterranean, where various North African states were holding American sailors for ransom and demanding tribute that Federalist presidents, and various European governments, had customarily paid. Even in this, Jefferson hoped to save money in the long run, by putting a stop to criminal behavior that, he believed, civilized nations should never have tolerated in the first place.

Among the accomplishments for which Jefferson is most remembered was his acquisition of the Louisiana Territory from Napoleon Bonaparte, emperor of France, in 1803. Although initially seeking only access to West Florida and the Mississippi River via New Orleans, Jefferson agreed to purchase 828,000 square miles, a move that doubled the country's land area. The Lewis and Clark expedition was organized in order to explore and survey the new territory.

During Jefferson's second term, the supposedly neutral United States relied on its role supplying both France and Britain in the Napoleonic Wars (1803–15), a strategy that failed when both belligerents decided to prohibit US trade with their enemy. Britain inflamed American passions by impressing American merchant sailors in its effort to reclaim British defectors. Seeking to pressure the combatants, Jefferson called for a wholesale ban on US exports to Europe, the Embargo Act of 1807, which backfired and had severe economic repercussions. It was replaced with the Non-Intercourse Act of 1809, which sanctioned only the belligerents.

In private life several years later, but hardly in retirement, Jefferson maintained an extensive political and philosophical correspondence, especially with John Adams, the two now fully reconciled. He also labored long and finally successfully to establish the University of Virginia in nearby Charlottesville. Jefferson and Adams both died on July 4, 1826, while their fellow citizens were celebrating the fiftieth anniversary of the Declaration of Independence.

Significance

Thomas Jefferson was brilliant, versatile, energetic, and creative, but he was neither original nor systematic. He contributed no great books to the American tradition, but rather a number of ringing phrases about natural rights, the impositions of tyrants, the virtue of the people, and the beneficence of free inquiry. With Abraham Lincoln, he is the most quotable American public figure, and every conceivable political view has been bolstered by his maxims. Jefferson further helped this trend by being inconsistent in such important areas as the power of the national government, the proper treatment of dissenters, and the crucial question of slavery.

Yet he was perfectly consistent on many points. A true son of the Enlightenment, he believed that scientific study and education would cure the ills of humankind, and he rejected as superstitious all those parts of religion that dwelt on mysterious or miraculous interventions in human affairs. He detested the very idea of inherited power or status and believed that differences among races and national groups were the result of environment. He always believed that government should be kept to a minimum, that standing armies were not republican, and that the true strength of a people resided in the widest possible distribution of virtue, learning, and property; not in armies, national treasuries, or government agencies.

Early in life, he had supposed that the United States might not extend beyond the Appalachians, for he still shared the classical view that republics must be small. By the time he had retired from the presidency, however, he had conceived that all North America might be "an Empire for Liberty

Robert McColley

Further Reading

Boorstin, Daniel J. *The Lost World of Thomas Jefferson.* New York: Holt, 1948. Print.

Ellis, Joseph J. *American Sphinx: The Character of Thomas Jefferson.* New York: Knopf, 1996. Print..

Ferling, John E. *Adams vs. Jefferson: The Tumultuous Election of 1800.* New York: Oxford UP, 2004. Print.

Gish, Dustin A., and Daniel P. Klinghard. "Republican Constitutionalism in Thomas Jefferson's Notes on the State of Virginia." *Jour. of Politics* 74.1 (2012): 35–51. Print.

Gutzman, Kevin R. C. "Thomas Jefferson's Federalism, 1774Â1825." *Modern Age* 53.3 (2012): 74–80. Print.

Jefferson, Thomas. *The Papers of Thomas Jefferson.* Ed. Julian P. Boyd. 31 vols. Princeton: Princeton UP, 1950–2004. Print.

Levy, Leonard. *Jefferson and Civil Liberties: The Darker Side.* Cambridge: Belknap, 1963. Print.

McCoy, Drew R. *The Elusive Republic.* Chapel Hill: U of North Carolina P, 1980. Print.

Malone, Dumas. *Jefferson and His Time.* 6 vols. Boston: Little, 1948–81. Print.

Miller, John Chester. *The Wolf by the Ears.* New York: Oxford UP, 1977. Print.

"Napoleonic Wars and the United States, 1803–1815." *Milestones.* Office of the Historian, Bureau of Public Affairs, United States Dept. of State, n.d. Web. 9 Sept. 2015.

Onuf, Peter, ed. "Thomas Jefferson: Foreign Affairs." *American Presidents.* Miller Center of Public Affairs, U of Virginia, 2015. Web. 9 Sept. 2015.

Schwabach, Aaron. "Thomas Jefferson, Slavery, and Slaves." *Thomas Jefferson Law Rev.* 33.1 (2010): 1–60. Print.

Sheldon, Garrett Ward. *The Political Philosophy of Thomas Jefferson.* Baltimore: Johns Hopkins UP, 1991. Print.

Wills, Garry. *Inventing America: Jefferson's Declaration of Independence.* Boston: Houghton, 2002. Print.

John F. Kennedy

35th President of the United States (1961–1963)

Born: May 29, 1917; Brookline, Massachusetts
Died: November 22, 1963; Dallas, Texas
Area of Achievement: Politics, military

Combining intelligence with personal charm, Kennedy became a model to millions around the globe, inspiring them to seek new goals and to work toward those goals with self-confidence. His assassination is still studied and debated.

Early Life

John F. Kennedy was born in Brookline, Massachusetts, an inner suburb of Boston. He was the second son of Joseph P. Kennedy, a businessman rapidly growing wealthy, and Rose Fitzgerald Kennedy, daughter of former Boston mayor John Francis "Honey Fitz" Fitzgerald. He was educated at Choate School in Connecticut and graduated from Harvard in 1940. While his earlier years were plagued by illness and his grades were often mediocre, he revealed himself to be an original thinker. His senior thesis was published as *Why England Slept* (1940), largely by the efforts of Joseph Kennedy's friends. John Kennedy was able to travel widely in Europe in 1937 and 1938 and to spend the spring of 1939 in Britain, where his father was United States ambassador. Still there when World

John F. Kennedy (National Archives and Records Administration)

War II began in September, he assisted in caring for American survivors of the first torpedoed passenger ship, gaining a sense of realism about war.

As US entrance into the war became likely, he entered the US Navy as an ensign, September, 1941, six feet tall but extremely thin and looking younger than his years. A thatch of often rumpled, sandy hair added to his boyish appearance. He was sent to the South Pacific where he commanded PT 109, a patrol torpedo boat. The boat was sunk in action on August 2, 1943, and Kennedy not only rescued survivors but also swam for help though badly injured. Awarded the Navy and US Marine Corps medal, he briefly commanded another boat but soon went on sick leave and was discharged for disability as a full lieutenant in December, 1944. Because of his injury, coming in the wake of earlier illnesses, he was often sick.

Life's Work

Kennedy had thought of writing as a career and covered the United Nations Conference at San Francisco, April–July, 1945, and the 1945 British elections for the New York *Journal-American*. His older brother, Joseph Jr., slated to be the family's political success, had been killed in the war in Europe, and John took up that task. In 1946, he ran for the House of Representatives from the Eleventh District of Massachusetts, narrowly gaining the Democratic nomination but winning the November election with 72.6 percent of the vote. The district sent him to Washington for three terms, during which time his record was mixed. In favor of public housing and an opponent of the then reactionary leadership of the American Legion, he was friendly with Senator Joseph McCarthy of Wisconsin, whose "red-baiting" began in 1950. Plagued by a painful back, he was diagnosed in 1947 as having Addison's disease also, then usually fatal, and was often absent from the House. He showed more interest in national issues than local ones and became deeply interested in foreign policy. He rejected his father's isolationism, supported the Truman Doctrine and the Marshall Plan, but joined right-wing critics of the so-called loss of China to Mao Zedong. In 1951, he toured Europe and Asia for several weeks and returned better balanced regarding a Soviet threat to Western Europe and the significance of Asian anti-colonialism.

Unwilling to spend many years gaining seniority in the House, in 1952 Kennedy ran against Henry Cabot Lodge for the United States Senate. Despite illness, explained to the public as wartime injuries or malaria, he campaigned effectively, helped by family money and friends, building his own political organization. He won 51.5 percent of the vote and would be easily reelected in 1958.

He married Jacqueline Lee Bouvier on September 12, 1953, and they had two children, Caroline, born November 27, 1957, and John Jr., born November 26, 1960. A third child, Patrick Bouvier Kennedy, born in August, 1963, lived only a few hours. Jacqueline Kennedy's beauty, charm, and linguistic skills helped the future president on countless occasions.

As a senator, Kennedy gained national publicity by working to cure the economic ills of all of New England. He continued to speak out on foreign policy, often against French colonialism in Indochina or Algeria. He finally turned away from McCarthy as the Senate censured the latter. During one long illness, he put together another book, *Profiles in Courage* (1956), based heavily on others' research, winning a Pulitzer Prize and good publicity. One result of Kennedy's growing national reputation was his almost becoming Adlai E. Stevenson's running mate in the 1956 presidential election. While older politicians often regarded him as a rich young man with no serious intentions, his popularity was growing among voters.

Kennedy began, in 1956, to work for the 1960 Democratic presidential nomination. His brother Robert observed the Stevenson campaign, and afterward, the brothers began building a national organization. Finding his health improving, thanks to the use of cortisone, Kennedy made speeches throughout the country and created a "brain trust" of academic and other specialists who could advise him on policy. To win the nomination and then the 1960 election, Kennedy had to overcome anti-Catholicism and his own image as too young and inexperienced. Campaigning hard both times, he convinced millions of voters that he was intelligent and prepared for the office as well as a believer in the separation of church and state. He named as his running mate Lyndon B. Johnson of Texas, Democratic majority leader in the Senate, who was strong where Kennedy was weak, especially in the South. In televised debates with his opponent, Vice President Richard Nixon, Kennedy appeared competent and vigorous; Nixon, exhausted from campaigning, did poorly. Kennedy won the election by 303 electoral votes to 219, with a popular vote margin of only 119,450 out of 68,836,385, so narrow a victory that it limited his political strength. He named a cabinet representing all factions of the Democratic Party and including two Republicans. Despite the administration's New Frontier label, it was balanced between liberals and conservatives.

As president, Kennedy sought a constant flow of ideas of all shades of opinion. He held few Cabinet meetings, preferring the informality of task forces on various problems. To reach the public, he used "live" televised press conferences. A handsome face, no longer gaunt and pained, the thatch of hair, plus Kennedy's spontaneity and wit, captivated millions. His inaugural address had promised boldness, especially in the Cold War, and he acted on that in agreeing to a Central Intelligence Agency plan for an invasion of Cuba to overthrow Fidel Castro. When the CIA fumbled and the Cuban exile invaders were killed or captured at the Bay of Pigs, Kennedy publicly took the blame and found his popularity rising. He went to Europe to meet French president Charles de Gaulle, who warned against American involvement in Vietnam, and also Nikita S. Khrushchev of the Soviet Union, finding the Communist leader tough, belligerent, and unwilling to help solve any problems.

In domestic matters, Kennedy accomplished little during his thousand days in office. He sought and obtained minor increases in the minimum wage and Social Security coverage, plus money for public housing, and forced a temporary rollback in steel prices. Jacqueline Kennedy supervised a notable redecoration of the White House in Early American style. Only late in his brief term did Kennedy take up the issue of civil rights, because of increasing violence in some southern states. He took executive action where he could and proposed an anti-poll-tax amendment to the Constitution, which passed the Congress while he was still president. He also called for increased federal power to enforce voting rights and a major civil rights act to include the opening of public accommodations and an end to job discrimination.

Kennedy was more active in foreign affairs. Concerned about Soviet moves in the developing world, he founded the Peace Corps and the Alliance for Progress. After the Bay of Pigs and his encounter with Khrushchev, he became "hard line," appointing such militant anticommunists as John McCone as CIA director and General Curtis LeMay as commander of the Air Force. He also vowed that the Western powers would remain in West Berlin.

The major event of Kennedy's foreign policy was the crisis that arose when Khrushchev tried to establish nuclear missiles in Cuba in 1962. Using all of the

Kennedy's address to the people of Berlin, June 26, 1963. (Wikimedia Commons)

information and ideas he could get from another task force and forcing his advisers to debate their ideas in his presence, he chose to blockade Cuba and threaten Khrushchev, keeping in reserve an air attack on the missile sites. Khrushchev withdrew the missiles and countless millions around the world were relieved that no nuclear war took place.

> "*Let every nation know, whether it wishes us well or ill, that we shall pay any price, bear any burden, meet any hardship, support any friend, oppose any foe to assure the survival and the success of liberty.*"

Kennedy learned from the Cuban missile crisis. Afterward he was interested in "peace as a process," as he put it in the spring of 1963; the United States and the Soviet Union had to find ways to end the nuclear threat. Kennedy established a "hotline" for communication between the White House and the Kremlin and negotiated a treaty that stopped American and Russian outdoor nuclear tests, reducing radioactivity in the atmosphere. It is this, Kennedy's admirers say, that indicates how he would have acted in a second term. Yet Kennedy also listened to advisers who insisted that the United States send troops to Vietnam to go into combat and show the South Vietnamese army how to fight. Skeptical, Kennedy agreed, saying that if this did not work he could change his mind and withdraw the American forces.

Tragically, Kennedy did not live to follow that plan. In Dallas on a trip to heal a split among the Texas Democrats, he was assassinated on November 22, 1963.

Significance

Kennedy represented a new generation in American politics, for whom World War II and the Cold War were the major events, rather than the 1920s and the Depression of the 1930s. He brought with him a style different from that of Presidents Harry S. Truman and Dwight D. Eisenhower, a contemporary style without formality and with wry, self-deprecatory humor. While his actual accomplishments were limited largely to proposing domestic legislation and to steps toward détente in foreign policy, he inspired millions in the United States and abroad to reach toward new goals in a spirit of confidence that they could make a difference. As did another assassinated president, Abraham Lincoln, Kennedy left a legacy of legend, in this case of Camelot or a new King Arthur's court engaged in serving good ends.

Kennedy has remained one of the most admired and highly rated American presidents of the late twentieth and early twenty-first centuries. The year 2013 marked the fiftieth anniversary of the Kennedy assassination, a pivotal event in the minds of those who remember where they were when it happened as well as those who were born long after it took place. A poll conducted by Peter Hart and Geoffrey Garin around the time of the fiftieth anniversary revealed that 75 percent of respondents surveyed questioned the Warren Commission's finding that the assassination was the work of a single gunman, Lee Harvey Oswald.

Robert W. Sellen

Further Reading

Dallek, Robert. *An Unfinished Life: John F. Kennedy, 1917–1963*. Boston: Little, 2003. Print.

Dallek, Robert, and Terry Golway. *Let Every Nation Know: John F. Kennedy in His Own Words*. Naperville: Sourcebooks MediaFusion, 2006. Print.

Douglass, James W. *JFK and the Unspeakable: Why He Died and Why It Matters*. New York: Simon, 2010. Print.

Frankel, Max. *High Noon in the Cold War: Kennedy, Khrushchev, and the Cuban Missile Crisis*. New York: Ballantine, 2004. Print.

Hodgson, Godfrey. *JFK and LBJ: The Last Two Great Presidents*. New Haven: Yale UP, 2015. *eBook Collection (EBSCOhost)*. Web. 9 Sept. 2015.

Kennedy, John F., and Martin W. Sandler. *The Letters of John F. Kennedy*. New York: Bloomsbury, 2013. Print.

Logsdon, John M. *John F. Kennedy and the Race to the Moon*. New York: Palgrave, 2010. Print.

Manchester, William. *One Brief Shining Moment*. Boston: Little, 1983. Print.

Matthews, Christopher. *Kennedy and Nixon: The Rivalry That Shaped Postwar America*. New York: Simon, 1996. Print.

Parmet, Herbert S. *Jack: The Struggles of John F. Kennedy*. New York: Dial, 1980. Print.

Parmet, Herbert S. *JFK: The Presidency of John F. Kennedy*. New York: Dial, 1983. Print.

Picker, Lenny. "A Pivotal Moment: Fifty Years Later." *Publishers Weekly* 5 Aug. 2013: 33–40. *Literary Reference Center Plus*. Web. 9 Sept. 2015.

Rorabough, W. J. *Kennedy and the Promise of the Sixties*. New York: Cambridge UP, 2002. Print.

Sabato, Larry. *The Kennedy Half-Century: The Presidency, Assassination, and Lasting Legacy of John F. Kennedy*. New York: Bloomsbury, 2013. Print.

Schlesinger, Arthur M., Jr. *A Thousand Days*. Boston: Houghton, 1965. Print.

Talbot, David. *Brothers: The Hidden History of the Kennedy Years*. New York: Free, 2007. Print.

Widmer, Ted, and Caroline Kennedy. *Listening In: The Secret White House Recordings of John F. Kennedy*. New York: Hyperion, 2012. Print.

ABRAHAM LINCOLN

16th President of the United States (1861-1865)

Born: February 12, 1809; Sinking Spring Farm, Kentucky
Died: April 15, 1865; Washington, D.C.
Area of Achievement: Politics, law

A towering figure in American history, Lincoln played a leading role in the abolition of slavery and is generally credited with primary responsibility for preserving the Union through the unprecedented challenges of the Civil War.

Abraham Lincoln (Wikimedia Commons)

EARLY LIFE

Abraham Lincoln was born on the same date that the great British naturalist Charles Darwin was born. The place of his birth, Sinking Spring Place, was a farm three miles south of Hodgenville, Kentucky. Lincoln's mother was the former Nancy Hanks, and his father was Thomas Lincoln, both natives of Virginia whose parents had taken them into the Kentucky wilderness at an early age. Thomas Lincoln was a farmer and a carpenter. In the spring of 1811, they moved to the nearby Knob Creek Farm.

The future president had a brother, Thomas, who died in infancy. His sister, Sarah (called Sally), was two years older than he. Much has been made in literature of his log-cabin birth and the poverty and degradation of Lincoln's childhood, but his father—a skilled carpenter—was never abjectly poor. The boy, however, did not aspire to become either a farmer or a carpenter. A highly intelligent and inquisitive youth, he considered many vocations before he decided upon the practice of law.

In Kentucky during his first seven years, and in Indiana until he became an adult, Lincoln received only the rudiments of a formal education, about a year in total. Nevertheless, he was able to read, write, and speak effectively, largely through self-education and regular practice. He grew to be approximately six feet, four inches tall and 185 pounds in weight. He was angular and dark-complected, with features that became familiar to later generations.

Moving with his family to Spencer County, Indiana, in December, 1816, Lincoln learned to use the American long ax efficiently on the Pigeon Creek Farm, where his father constructed another simple log cabin. He grew strong physically, and, largely through books he was able to borrow from neighbors, he grew strong mentally as well. The death of his mother from "the milk sick" in the summer of 1818 left both the boy and his sister emotionally depressed until the arrival of their stepmother, Sarah Bush Johnston Lincoln, from Elizabethtown, Kentucky. This strong and resourceful widow brought love and direction back to Lincoln's life and introduced him to her lively children, Elizabeth, Matilda, and John D. Johnston, then aged twelve, eight, and five, respectively.

While in Indiana, Lincoln was employed in 1827 as a ferryman on Anderson Creek and on the Ohio River into which it flowed. Then, in cooperation with Allen Gentry and at the behest of Gentry's father, he took a flatboat full of goods down the Mississippi River to New Orleans in 1828. Another childhood companion of this time was Lincoln's cousin, Dennis Hanks, who, in his later years, would relate many colorful stories about the future president's boyhood.

In March, 1830, the family moved to central Illinois, where Thomas Lincoln had heard that the farming was superior. They situated their cabin on a stretch of prairie in Macon County, some ten miles west of Decatur. There Lincoln split many rails for fences, although not as many as would later be accredited to the Rail-Splitter. Another nickname he earned in Illinois that would serve him well in his later political career was Honest Abe. His honesty in business dealings became legendary.

> "*My poor friends, you are free, free as air. You can cast off the name of slave and trample upon it; it will come to you no more. Liberty is your birthright. God gave it to you as He gave it to others, and it is a sin that you have been deprived of it for so many years. But you must try to deserve this priceless boon. Let the world see that you merit it, and are able to maintain it by your good works. Don't let your joy carry you into excesses."*

Again, in the spring of 1831, Lincoln took a flatboat laden with supplies down the Mississippi River to New Orleans, this time commissioned by Denton Offutt and in the company of John Hanks and John D. Johnston. Hanks would later claim that the sight of a slave auction on this visit to the busy southern city stirred in Lincoln his famous opposition to slavery, but historians now discredit this legend. Upon his return, Lincoln, having reached maturity, struck out on his own for the village of New Salem, Illinois.

LIFE'S WORK

Lincoln had been promised a store clerk's position in New Salem by Offutt and worked at this task for almost a year before the store "winked out." Then, in the spring of 1832, he served as a captain of volunteers in the Black Hawk War for thirty days. This service was followed by twenty days under Captain Elijah Iles and thirty days under Captain Jacob M. Early as a mounted private seeking to discover the whereabouts of the Indian leader for whom the war was named. While he saw no action, the war soon ended, and Lincoln returned home something less than a war hero.

Immediately upon returning to New Salem, Lincoln threw himself into an election for the lower house of the Illinois state legislature but, having no reputation, failed to win the seat. He was a loyal supporter of Henry Clay for president and therefore a Whig, but Clay failed also. In desperation, Lincoln became a partner in a store with William Berry, but its failure left him with an eleven-hundred-dollar "national debt." In 1834, however, and in 1836, 1838, and 1840 as well, Lincoln won consecutive terms in the state house of representatives. He also served as postmaster of his village from 1833 to 1836 and as deputy county surveyor from 1833 to 1835. Effective in these roles and being groomed for a leadership position in the legislature by Whigs such as John Todd Stuart, Lincoln studied law and passed the state bar examination in 1836.

New Salem was too small a village to sustain a lawyer, and Lincoln moved to the new capital city of Springfield in April, 1837, to join the law firm of Stuart and Lincoln. This firm was successful, and Lincoln won more cases than he lost, but Stuart wanted to devote more time to his political career. In 1841, the partnership was dissolved, and Lincoln joined, again as junior partner, with the master lawyer Stephen T. Logan. Finally, in 1844, he formed his last partnership, taking on young William H. Herndon as his junior partner.

In 1839, Lincoln met his future wife, Mary Todd, at the home of her sister, the wife of Ninian Edwards. Lincoln and Edwards were already Whig leaders and members of the influential Long Nine. Lincoln and Todd intended to marry in 1841, but on January of that year, he suffered a nervous breakdown, broke the engagement, and then cemented it again. Their marriage took place at the Edwards home on November 4, 1842. From this union would be born four children: Robert Todd (1843), Edward Baker (1846), William Wallace (1850), and Thomas, called Tad (1853). Their home, purchased in 1844, was located at Eighth and Jackson streets.

When Clay again ran for president in 1844, Lincoln campaigned energetically on his behalf, but Clay was defeated once again. Two years later, Lincoln canvassed the district on his own behalf and won his sole term in the U.S. House of Representatives over the Democrat Peter Cartwright. During this term, which ran from 1847 to 1849, the Mexican War was still in progress, and Lincoln followed the Whig leadership in opposing it. For this decision, he suffered among the voters at home and had to content himself with the single term. Before leaving Washington, however, he patented a device for lifting riverboats over the shoals.

During the early 1850s, Lincoln concentrated upon his legal practice, but perhaps his most famous legal case came much later, in 1858, when he defended Duff Armstrong successfully against a charge of murder. Lincoln was a friend of Duff's parents, Jack and Hannah, and took the case without charging a fee. His use of an almanac in this case to indicate the brightness of the moon on the night of the purported murder is celebrated in the annals of courtroom strategy.

The passage of the Kansas-Nebraska Act in 1854 and the Supreme Court decision in the *Dred Scott* case in 1856 aroused Lincoln's antislavery fervor and brought him back into active politics. In 1855, he campaigned as an Anti-Nebraska (later Republican) candidate for the US Senate but was compelled to stand aside in favor of his friend Lyman Trumbull, the eventual victor. A year later, Lincoln campaigned on behalf of presidential candidate John C. Frémont. Then, in 1858, he contended with his archrival, Stephen A. Douglas, for another Senate seat.

Before engaging in the famous debates with Douglas, Lincoln gave his most famous speech to date at Springfield, in which he proclaimed, "A house divided against itself cannot stand"; this government cannot endure permanently half slave and half free." This House Divided Speech set the tone for his antislavery attacks in the debates that followed. Lincoln was a Free-Soiler and was truly outraged by Douglas's stance on slavery. Many observers thought that Lincoln had won the debates, but largely because of a pro-Democratic apportionment, Douglas won reelection. Nevertheless, the fame Lincoln achieved through these debates assured his consideration for a presidential nomination in 1860.

The Republican Convention of that year was held in Chicago, where Lincoln was especially popular. Then, too, the original leading candidates, William Seward and Salmon Chase, detested each other; accordingly, their delegates turned to Lincoln as a "dark horse" when their favorites destroyed each other's chances. The Democrats then split their support with the dual nominations of Stephen A. Douglas and John C. Breckinridge. What was left of the old Whig Party split the South further by nominating as the Constitutional Union nominee John Bell of Tennessee.

Lincoln grew the dark beard associated with him during his campaign. He did not campaign actively but was elected over his divided opposition with 173 electoral

Allan Pinkerton, President Lincoln, and Major General John A. McClernand. In his role as head of Union Intelligence Services during the war, Pinkerton foiled an assassination attempt against Lincoln. His wartime work was critical in raising Pinkerton's profile and helping to bolster the reputation of his Pinkerton National Detective Agency, which pioneered the American private detective industry. (Library of Congress)

votes, while Breckinridge amassed 72, Bell 39, and Douglas merely 12. Lincoln had the necessary majority of the electoral college but did not have a majority of the popular votes—no one did. The division in the country at large was made even more coldly clear when seven southern states seceded over his election.

Inaugurated March 4, 1861, Lincoln took a strong stand against secession; when newly armed Confederate troops fired upon and captured Fort Sumter on April 12-13, 1861, he announced the start of the Civil War by calling for seventy-five thousand volunteers and a naval blockade of the southern coast. Four more states then seceded, and the War Between the States began in earnest, lasting four years.

During the war, President Lincoln often visited the fighting front, intercepted telegraphic messages at the War Department, and advised his generals as to strategy. He was a remarkably able wartime leader, but he was deeply dissatisfied with his highest-ranking generals in the field until he "found his general" in Ulysses S. Grant.

In the midst of the struggle, Lincoln drafted his Emancipation Proclamation, calling for the freedom of the slaves. A few months later, in 1863, he wrote and delivered his most famous speech, the Gettysburg Address. This speech summed up the principles for which the federal government still fought to preserve the Union. Upon being reelected in 1864, over Democratic nominee General George B. McClellan, the president gave another stirring speech in his Second Inaugural Address. Final victory was achieved only after the defeat of Confederate general Robert E. Lee's Army of Northern Virginia at Appomattox Courthouse on April 9, 1865. Less than a week later, on April 14, Lincoln was assassinated by the southern partisan actor John Wilkes Booth at Ford's Theatre in Washington, expiring the following morning. Secretary of War Edwin Stanton then was heard to say: "Now he belongs to the ages."

SIGNIFICANCE

More books have been written about Lincoln and more legends have been told about him than about any other individual in American history. This sixteenth president often is regarded as the greatest leader the United States has yet produced or is likely to produce, yet he came from humble stock, and little was given him that he had not earned.

Lincoln was the first Republican president, was twice elected, and had to fight a cruel war yet remained sensitive, humble, and magnanimous to the end. It was his intention, had he lived, to "bind up the nation's wounds" with a speedy and liberal method of reconstruction. His death assured the opposite, or Radical Reconstruction.

Lincoln's greatest achievements were the preservation of the federal Union and the liberation of the slaves. The former was achieved with the cessation of fighting in the South, which came only days after his death. The latter was brought about at last by the Thirteenth Amendment to the Constitution a few months later.

Joseph E. Suppiger

FURTHER READING

Donald, David Herbert. *Lincoln*. New York: Simon, 1995. Print.
Fornieri, Joseph R. *Abraham Lincoln, Philosopher Statesman*. Carbondale: Southern Illinois UP, 2014. Print.
Gienapp, William E. *Abraham Lincoln and Civil War America: A Biography*. New York: Oxford UP, 2002. Print.
Goodwin, Doris Kearns. *Team of Rivals: The Political Genius of Abraham Lincoln*. New York: Simon, 2005. Print.
Guelzo, Allen C. *Lincoln's Emancipation Proclamation: The End of Slavery in America*. New York: Simon, 2004. Print.
Herndon, William H. *Herndon's Lincoln: The True Story of a Great Life*. 3 vols. Chicago: Belford, 1889. Print.
Kunhardt, Philip B., Jr. *New Birth of Freedom: Lincoln at Gettysburg*. Boston: Little, 1983. Print.
Lamon, Ward Hill. *The Life of Abraham Lincoln*. Boston: Osgood, 1872. Print.
McPherson, James M. *Abraham Lincoln*. New York: Oxford UP, 2009. Print.
Nicolay, John G., and John Hay. *Abraham Lincoln: A History*. 10 vols. New York: Century, 1890. Print.
Oates, Stephen B. *With Malice Toward None*. New York: Harper, 1977. Print.
Sandburg, Carl. *Abraham Lincoln: The Prairie Years*. 2 vols. New York: Harcourt, 1926. Print.
Sandburg, Carl. *Abraham Lincoln: The War Years*. 4 vols. New York: Harcourt, 1939. Print.
Thomas, Benjamin. *Abraham Lincoln*. New York: Knopf, 1952. Print.
Vidal, Gore. *Lincoln*. New York: Random, 1984. Print.
Von Drehle, David. *Rise to Greatness: Abraham Lincoln and America's Most Perilous Year*. New York: Holt, 2012. Print.

DOLLEY MADISON

First Lady of the United States (1809-1817)

Born: May 20, 1768; Guilford County, Colony of North Carolina
Died: July 12, 1849; Washington, D.C.
Area of Achievement: Culture and society

First Lady Dolley Madison's popularity and social acumen made her a political asset to President James Madison. The leading social figure in the capital city for years, she was arguably the most beloved and important American woman of her times, and she served as a role model for future First Ladies.

Dolley Madison (Wikimedia Commons)

EARLY LIFE

Dolley Madison was the daughter of John and Mary Coles Payne, who moved to Piedmont, North Carolina, from Virginia. It was there that Dolley was born in 1768. The following year, the Payne family moved back to their native Virginia. In 1783, after freeing his slaves, John again moved his family, this time to Philadelphia, Pennsylvania, where the Paynes raised their eight children in the strict disciplinary tradition of the Quaker Society of Friends. Dolley was also raised modestly, as her father had failed in business.

In 1790 Dolley married John Todd, Jr., a successful lawyer and Quaker. Dolley and John had two sons: John Payne in 1790 and William Temple in 1792. Tragedy struck when the yellow fever epidemic hit Philadelphia in 1793 and claimed the lives of Dolley's husband, both of his parents, and Dolley's son William, leaving her a young widow with an infant child. The strong-willed Dolley was determined to persevere and make something of herself. Among her many courters at this time was the "Father of the Constitution" and author of the Bill of Rights, Representative James Madison of Virginia. They seemed to make an unlikely couple, as the longtime bachelor James was seventeen years Dolley's senior. He was also unlike most of the dashing gentlemen of his time, because he had not been a soldier, did not dance, and did not ride horses. However, Dolley eventually fell for the intelligent but dour James. They were married on September 15, 1794, and enjoyed a happy but childless marriage. After abandoning her Quaker roots for James's Episcopalianism, she was disowned by the Quakers.

LIFE'S WORK

Dolley appears to have completely shed her conservative Quaker upbringing after her second marriage and developed a love of music, gardens, and socializing. She also acquired a taste for fashion that could not have been further from the social standards of the day that included bright colors, scandalously low-cut dresses, and a bold hairstyle of large curls. Incredibly, for much of the early nineteenth century she was at the center of social life in Washington, D.C. During this time, Dolley was quite possibly the most widely known and beloved woman in the country. A highly capable woman, Dolley managed the Madison family plantation when James was away in Washington, D.C. Admired for her outgoing, pleasant personality, her legacy belongs to her famous social events. Even among present-day First Ladies, Dolley is widely considered to have been the most talented social hostess in the history of the White House. In this endeavor she was aided by what appears to have been a deep, selfless, and genuine love of people and a knack for remembering everyone's name.

In 1801, newly elected President Thomas Jefferson appointed James as his secretary of state. As a widower, Jefferson asked James's wife Dolley to help serve as the White House's social hostess. For eight years she presided over the social affairs of the Jefferson White House. This was followed by another eight years during which her husband was president of the United States from 1809 to 1817. It was Dolley who presided over the nation's first inaugural ball in 1809.

Among the Washington social crowd and much of the nation, Dolley was hailed as "Queen Dolley," "Lady Presidentress," or the "Queen of Washington City." Her socials were the events of the social season, and all of Washington awaited an invitation. Breaking with tradition, she served American dishes for dinner (even contacting people all over the country for recipes), re-arranged rooms to better accommodate her guests, and defied convention by sitting at the head of the table at dinners.

Dolley set a precedent for future First Ladies when she renovated and redecorated the White House. Strategically, she invited members of Congress to the White

House so they could see the poor condition of the building; after securing congressional funding for the renovation project, she even worked with the supervising architect. She successfully blended European flair with American homespun simplicity in her entertaining and invited a wide array of guests to the White House. Although the historical record is far from complete, she seems to have made a positive impression on almost every visitor to the White House. She also emerged as a fashion trendsetter as the nation took a keen interest in her taste for European attire, jewels, bird plumes, and even what became known as "the Dolley Madison turban." Details of her social events and attire were reported in newspapers.

> *"It is one of my sources of happiness never to desire a knowledge of other people's business."*

Along with her successful social role, she was the perfect political partner for James. In comparison with his subdued seriousness, she was funny, talkative, and engaging. As was the norm for women of the eighteenth and nineteenth centuries, Dolley had little formal education and was not as well read or intellectual as her predecessor, Abigail Adams. She had been tutored at her childhood plantation home in Virginia and had received some education at a Quaker school in Pennsylvania. Yet, in an era during which women rarely spoke publicly and took no interest in politics, Dolley functioned as an adviser to her husband on both social and political matters. She traveled with him, campaigned with him, and appeared in public with him. James was proud of his wife's accomplishments. He appears to have recognized her social abilities and his limited interpersonal skills. He often sought and took her advice, appreciating her political astuteness, warm personal touch, and legendary tact.

Even though James had been the secretary of state, it was Dolley who was the diplomat. She took no formal or public role in politics and claimed to not be interested in political affairs. However, her actions revealed her many political contributions to James's presidency. Many historical accounts exist of Dolley disarming her husband's political opponents, charming his potential supporters, and captivating statesmen, dignitaries, and other White House guests. Dolley made sure she invited every member of Congress to dinner at least once during legislative sessions. In doing so, she was a century ahead of her time as the first presidential spouse to blend White House social events with political agendas. She also held socials in honor of U.S. accomplishments, including the capture of British ships during the War of 1812.

When the British sacked the capital city and set the White House ablaze during the War of 1812, Dolley was among the last Americans to leave. The president and cabinet had already evacuated the city. Refusing pleas to abandon the capital city, Dolley watched the approach of the British through a spyglass. Unconcerned about her own safety, she thought to load as many White House archives as possible (including official papers, china, and silver, as well as such artifacts as the famous Gilbert Stuart portrait of George Washington) onto a wagon while the British army literally marched into the city. With a wagon full of priceless items, she fled to Virginia at the last possible moment. Her courageous act inspired a nation stung by the defeat and the August 24, 1814, burning of the White House. After the war an unfazed but heroic Dolley continued entertaining in her temporary quarters in a private home on Penn Avenue in Washington, D.C. She proclaimed to a cheering city, "We shall rebuild Washington!"

Madison attends a ball at the Tomlinson's Hotel in Washington to celebrate the American victory at the battle of Craney Island, 8th December 1812. (Wikimedia Commons)

Significance

After James's second term as president ended in 1817, he and Dolley returned to Montpelier, their plantation home in Virginia, where they enjoyed a comfortable retirement highlighted by the many visitors and guests who attended Dolley's parties. Dolley continued to support her husband's political work by taking dictation for him through his failing health during the last years of his life. James Madison died in 1836 and, in the autumn of 1837, Dolley returned to the capital city to live. She moved into a small home that James had built some years earlier. Back in Washington, Dolley returned to the social and political life, enjoying an honorary seat on the Senate floor, attending social events, and receiving lifetime franking privileges from Congress. She wisely sold James's official papers to the government for $30,000 to both assure their preservation and provide for herself financially. She remained a central figure until her death in 1849.

Dolley Madison loved living in the White House and was perhaps the first presidential spouse as well as one of the few women prior to the twentieth century to develop an identity of her own beyond that of her husband. She fashioned the social side of the office of First Lady and consequently became a role model for many future First Ladies. On her death, President Zachary Taylor aptly described her as "Our First Lady for a half-century."

Robert P. Watson

Further Reading

Anthony, Carl Sferrazza. *First Ladies: The Saga of the Presidents' Wives and Their Power, 1789-1961.* New York: William Morrow, 1990. Contains a chapter on each First Lady, including Dolley. Anthony provides both personal and political details of Dolley's life.

Arnett, Ethel Stephens. *Mrs. James Madison: The Incomparable Dolley.* Greensboro, N.C.: Piedmont Press, 1972. A source for Dolley's life before meeting James Madison and later in the White House. Examines her personality and character.

Cote, Richard N. *Strength and Honor: The Life of Dolley Madison.* Mount Pleasant, S.C.: Corinthian Books, 2004. A well-researched, comprehensive biography of the woman Cote describes as the "best loved first lady of the nineteenth century."

Gould, Lewis L., ed. *American First Ladies: Their Lives and Their Legacy.* New York: Garland, 1996. Contains a chapter on each First Lady that includes an examination of their contributions to the presidency. Includes a helpful bibliography.

Hunt-Jones, Conover. *Dolley and the "Great Little Madison."* Washington, D.C.: American Institute of Architects Foundation, 1977. Hunt-Jones explores the Madisons' marriage, their long life together, and Dolley's influence on her "Great Little Madison."

Ketcham, Ralph. *James Madison: A Biography.* Charlottesville: University Press of Virginia, 1990. Insights on the life and presidency of the fourth president. Dolley is discussed periodically, but it also benefits one studying Dolley to know James Madison, his times, and life in the Madison White House.

Madison, Dolley. *The Selected Letters of Dolley Payne Madison.* Edited by David B. Mattern and Holly C. Shulman. Charlottesville: University Press of Virginia, 2003. Contains a carefully edited selection of letters to and from Madison. Also features short, factual essays placing Madison's letters within the context of her life and times, and biographies of the people mentioned in the letters.

Truman, Margaret. *First Ladies: An Intimate Group Portrait of White House Wives.* New York: Random House, 1995. Contains numerous discussions of Dolley's sense of style, famous social events, renovation of the White House, and heroism during the War of 1812. The book is written in a conversational, non-academic style and is very readable.

James Madison

4th President of the United States (1809-1817)

Born: March 16, 1751; Port Conway, Colony of Virginia
Died: June 28, 1836; Orange, Virginia
Area of Achievement: Politics, law, diplomacy, philosophy

Madison was the primary architect of the U.S. Constitution and the fourth U.S. president. His lasting reputation is based less on his conduct as president or as secretary of state than on his contribution to the writing of the Constitution and securing its ratification. He also is remembered for helping to establish the new government and political parties, and for being a superior legislator and nation-builder.

James Madison (Wikimedia Commons)

EARLY LIFE

James Madison was the son of James Madison Sr. and Nelly Conway Madison. James Jr. was the eldest of twelve children. The family was not wealthy but lived in comfortable circumstances. Young Madison was enrolled at the age of eleven in the boarding school of Donald Robertson, and he studied under him for five years. He studied two additional years at home under the tutelage of Thomas Martin, an Anglican minister. In 1769, Madison entered Princeton. Because of his previous training, he was able to complete the four-year course in two years, graduating in September 1771. This effort took a toll on his health. He appears to have suffered from depression and nonepileptic seizures. </p>

In May 1776, Madison began his political career as a member of the convention that drew up the Virginia constitution. He was then elected to the Virginia Assembly. There, Madison joined with Thomas Jefferson in an effort to disestablish the Church of England. They eventually became lifelong friends and close political associates. Madison was not reelected, but he was chosen by the legislature in 1778 to the governor's council. Despite his unimposing five-foot, six-inch stature and a slender frame and boyish features, Madison obviously made an impression upon the legislature with his intelligence and diligence. He was never a great orator, but he was an agreeable, persuasive speaker. He possessed great political skill and generally was a dominating figure in legislative bodies throughout his career.

In December 1779, Madison was chosen a delegate to the Continental Congress. He took his seat in March 1780 and quickly established himself as one of the most effective and valuable members of that body. For most of the next forty years, he would play an important, and at times major, role in the critical years of the early republic.

LIFE'S WORK

In the Continental Congress, James Madison took a nationalist position. He often collaborated with Alexander Hamilton. He labored hard to strengthen the government and amend the Articles of Confederation to give it the power to levy duties. Madison wrote an earnest address to the states, pleading for national unity, but it was to no avail, and the amendment failed.

In 1784, Madison was elected to the Virginia legislature, where he worked to defend religious freedom. His famous "Memorial and Remonstrance against Religious Assessments" helped defeat a scheme by Patrick Henry to impose a general assessment for the support of religion. Madison then pushed Jefferson's "Bill for Religious Liberty" to passage, completing the disestablishment of the Anglican Church begun in 1779. Madison's "Memorial and Remonstrance" foreshadowed the clause on religious liberty in the First Amendment to the U.S. Constitution.

Madison was a delegate to the Annapolis Convention of 1786, and he was named to the Virginia delegation to attend the federal convention at Philadelphia in 1787. When the Constitutional Convention opened in May, Madison had prepared an extensive proposal to revise the Articles of Confederation. The Virginia Plan, presented by Edmund Randolph but based on Madison's ideas, became the basis of discussion throughout the summer months. Madison led the movement to grant the federal government greater authority over national affairs. While he did not always carry his point of view, he clearly was the dominating figure in the convention, so that he is often called the "Father of the Constitution." The journal that he kept on the convention is the most complete record of the proceedings available.

Madison also played a prominent role in securing the ratification of the Constitution in Virginia. His influence was crucial in overcoming the opposition of Patrick Henry and George Mason. In retrospect, perhaps his most important work was in cooperating with Alexander Hamilton and John Jay in writing a series of essays for New

York newspapers that were later collected and published in 1788 as *The Federalist*, also known as the Federalist papers. Madison wrote nearly thirty of the eighty-five essays, which are justly celebrated today as still the most authoritative commentary on the US Constitution and a major contribution to political science. His most notable contributions were his reflections on the plural society in numbers ten and fifty-one; the dual nature of the new government, federal in extent of powers and national in operation, in number thirty-nine; and the interrelationship of checks and balances in number forty-eight.

Madison was elected to the House of Representatives, and within a week of entering the House in April 1789, he began the work of establishing a strong and effective central government. He led the movement to establish revenues for the new government by imposing import duties; he presented a motion to create the Departments of State, Treasury, and War and gave the executive broad powers over these offices; and he proposed a set of constitutional amendments that eventually became the Bill of Rights.

Madison served in the first five Congresses. His inherent conservatism manifested itself in his growing opposition to Hamilton's fiscal policies and the government's pro-British tendency. After 1790, Madison organized the congressional alliances that became the basis for the first national political parties. More than Jefferson, Madison deserves to be called the founder of the modern-day Democratic Party.

> "*The people are the only legitimate fountain of power, and it is from them that the constitutional charter, under which the several branches of government hold their power, is derived.*"

On September 15, 1794, at the age of forty-three, Madison married a young widow, Dolley Payne Todd. It proved to be a long and happy marriage, and the young wife, Dolley Madison, gained a reputation as a famous hostess during her husband's presidential years.

Madison retired from Congress in 1797. Federalists, taking advantage of the hysteria generated by the XYZ Affair and the quasi-war with France, passed the Alien and Sedition Acts to curb foreign- and native-born critics of the administration. Madison and Jefferson drafted resolutions adopted by the Kentucky and Virginia legislatures in 1798. These resolutions not only criticized the Alien and Sedition Acts but also struck down the doctrine of nullification for states' rights. In later years, Madison argued that these statements were protests intended primarily to secure the cooperation of the states, but they also expressed positions dangerous to the unity of the new republic. Nevertheless, these resolutions contributed to the overthrow of the Federalists and secured the election of Jefferson in 1800. Jefferson brought his longtime friend into the government as his secretary of state.

Later, in 1807, Madison became president, primarily a result of support from Jefferson, but his presidency was beset by many problems in the early years of the nineteenth century. Foreign relations with Britain, which had been deteriorating for many years, came to a breaking point in 1812. The final straw for Madison was the Royal Navy "impressing," or seizing and putting to work, American sailors. In what has often been termed the Second War for American Independence, the United States saw the burning of its newly built capital, Washington, and a failed invasion of Canada, among other humiliations. Despite this, the young country managed victory in 1814 and in so doing gained pride, territory, and a measure of security against the British-aligned Potowatomis, Shawnees, and other Plains Indian nations.

In the closing years of his presidency, Madison signed bills establishing a standing army and enlarging the naval establishment, reauthorizing the Bank of the United States, and passing a protective tariff. He did, however, veto an internal improvement bill as unconstitutional. He left office on March 4, 1817, and except for participation in the Virginia Constitutional Convention in 1829, his political career was over. He lived his remaining years quietly at Montpelier. Occasionally, he offered advice to his successor, James Monroe, and he wrote defending his actions over his long career. He also devoted time to arranging his notes on the Constitutional Convention for publication. They were not published until 1840, four years after his death on June 28, 1836.

Significance

James Madison was truly a nation-builder. Perhaps the outstanding political theorist and political writer in a generation that produced many first-rate thinkers, Madison often carried his position by sheer brilliance and cool, dispassionate reasoning. He lacked the dramatic style often useful in public life. He advanced because of his abilities and not because of his personality. He was a first-rate legislator, one of the most effective this country has produced. He was, on the other hand, only an average administrator. He failed to provide dynamic leadership during his presidency, especially during the War of 1812.

There are certain consistent themes throughout his career. First, there were his efforts to secure freedom of conscience and other personal rights and liberties. Second, he consistently supported and advanced the republican form of government based broadly on the popular will. Finally, throughout his life his devotion to the union was paramount. One of the last actions of his life was to write a document entitled "Advice to My Country." It concluded with the advice that the union "be cherished and perpetuated."

C. Edward Skeen

Further Reading

Brant, Irving. *The Fourth President: A Life of James Madison.* Indianapolis: Bobbs, 1970. Print.

Broadwater, Jeff. *James Madison: A Son of Virginia & a Founder of the Nation.* Chapel Hill: U of North Carolina P, 2012. Print.

Brookhiser, Richard. "James Madison." *American History* 46.5 (2011):64–69. Print.

Cooke, Jacob E., ed. *The Federalist.* Middletown: Wesleyan UP, 1961. Print.

Gutzman, Kevin R. C. *James Madison and the Making of America.* New York: St. Martin's, 2012. Print.

Ketcham, Ralph. *James Madison: A Biography.* New York: Macmillan, 1971. Print.

Koch, Adrienne. *Jefferson and Madison: The Great Collaboration.* New York: Knopf, 1950. Print.

Matthews, Richard K. *If Men Were Angels: James Madison and the Heartless Empire of Reason.* Lawrence: UP of Kansas, 1995. Print.

Meyers, Marvin, ed. *The Mind of the Founder: Sources of the Political Thought of James Madison.* Indianapolis: Bobbs, 1973. Print.

Moore, Virginia. *The Madisons: A Biography.* New York: McGraw, 1979. Print.

Rutland, Robert Allen. *James Madison: The Founding Father.* Columbia: U of Missouri P, 1997. Print.

Stagg, J. C. A. *Mr. Madison's War: Politics, Diplomacy, and Warfare in the Early American Republic, 1783-1830.* Princeton: Princeton UP, 1983. Print.

Stagg, J. C. A., ed. "James Madison: Foreign Affairs." *American Presidents.* Miller Center of Public Affairs, U of Virginia, 2015. Web. 4 Sept. 2015.

Wills, Garry. *James Madison.* New York: Times, 2002. Print.

Barack Obama

44th President of the United States (2009-2017)

Born: August 4, 1961; Honolulu, Hawaii
Area of Achievement: Law, politics

The first African American elected president of the United States, Obama previously worked as a US Senator from Illinois, a lawyer, community organizer, author, and law school professor. He was awarded the Nobel Peace Prize in 2009.

Early Life

Barack Hussein Obama (bah-RAHK hoo-SAYN oh-BAH-mah) was born in Honolulu, Hawaii, on August 4, 1961. His mother was Stanley Ann Dunham, an American born and raised in Kansas, and his father was Barack Obama Sr., a Kenyan of the Luo-speaking people. Obama's parents were married on February 2, 1961, while students at the University of Hawaii, but they divorced in 1964. His mother subsequently married Lolo Soetero, an Indonesian, and went with him and her son to

Barack Obama (Wikimedia Commons)

live in Jakarta, Indonesia, in 1967. After completing a graduate degree at Harvard University, the elder Obama returned to Kenya and saw his son only one more time, in 1971. He died in a road accident in 1982. From the remarriages of his parents, Obama has several half brothers and half sisters.

> "A good compromise, a good piece of legislation, is like a good sentence; or a good piece of music. Everybody can recognize it. They say, 'Huh. It works. It makes sense.'"

From 1967 to 1971, Obama studied at public and parochial grade schools in Jakarta. He returned to Honolulu for the rest of his primary education and graduated from high school in 1979. His favorite sport became basketball. He lived with his maternal grandparents, who had moved to Hawaii from their home in Kansas. His mother lived with him from 1972 to 1977, then she returned to Indonesia to pursue her anthropological research. She died of cancer in 1995 in Hawaii.

The individuals most influential in forming Obama's character were his mother and grandmother, both of whom were born and raised in small-town Kansas and valued family, work, and plain speaking. As a youth, he experimented with drugs, a decision for which he later expressed regret.

Obama began his college career at Occidental College in Los Angeles in 1979 before transferring two years later to Columbia University in New York. At Columbia, he earned a degree in political science and international relations in 1983. He remained in New York until 1985, when he moved to Chicago to work as a community organizer on the city's South Side. After a two-month tour of Europe and Africa in mid-1988, he entered Harvard Law School and became the first African American to serve as president of the Harvard Law Review.

After graduating from Harvard, Obama returned to Chicago to practice civil rights law and teach constitutional law at the University of Chicago Law School. He emerged as not only a community organizer but also a community leader. In 1992, he married fellow Harvard Law graduate Michelle Robinson. They had two daughters, Malia in 1998 and Natasha (better known as Sasha) in 2001. Obama's introspective memoir, *Dreams from My Father: A Story of Race and Inheritance* (1995), became a best seller. He began to contemplate a political career.

LIFE'S WORK

Although Obama considered running for mayor of Chicago, his strongest community roots were in the area of south Chicago that formed the Thirteenth District of the Illinois Senate. In March of 1996, he won the Democratic Party nomination for the district unopposed. He carried the November 5 election with more than 80 percent of the vote. Obama won reelection in 1998, this time for a four-year term, obtaining just under 90 percent of the vote. In 2002 he won another four-year term, running unopposed. Obama was defeated in a 2000 bid for the Illinois First Congressional District seat, losing the Democratic primary by a wide margin to the incumbent congressman, Bobby Rush.

In the Illinois senate, Obama introduced or supported legislation that reformed the state's welfare system, provided tax relief for low-income families, and supported labor interests. Democrats won control of the senate in 2003, and Obama was named chairman of the Health and Human Services Committee. With more power to shape and pass legislation, he moved to improve health care for children, standardize access to health care statewide, and monitor hospital quality. He also responded to labor demands related to equal pay, overtime, and protection of whistleblowers. He addressed police issues related to domestic violence, racial profiling, and evidence-gathering in potential capital punishment cases. He was noted for his bipartisan approach to writing and supporting legislation.

In 2002, Obama began considering a future run for a US Senate seat and engaged Chicago political strategist David Axelrod for his campaign. Sweeping through the 2004 spring primary, he won a solid majority for the nomination. He further enhanced his rising political profile by giving a charismatic address that summer to the Democratic National Convention. In the November election, Obama trounced his conservative Republican opponent, Alan Keyes, a last-minute substitute for a previous Republican candidate who had resigned amid a marriage scandal.

Obama's position in the US Senate provided him a national and international stage on which to act. With Republican senator Richard Lugar, he sponsored the Lugar-Obama Nuclear Proliferation Act of 2007 to reduce conventional weapons of warfare. He also teamed with Republican senator Tom Coburn to produce the Federal Funding Accountability and Transparency Act of 2006 that created a website, USAspending.gov, to enhance transparency in government finance. Obama also supported legislation for campaign finance reform, energy

Obama hugs Donna Vanzant, the owner of North Point Marina, as he tours damage from Hurricane Sandy in Brigantine, New Jersey on 31 October 2012. (Wikimedia Commons)

efficiency, and children's health insurance. A member of the Committee on Foreign Relations, he traveled to Europe, the Middle East, and Africa.

Obama next set his sights on the Democratic presidential nomination, announcing his candidacy at the beginning of 2007. His opposition to the Iraq War and support of health care reform, as well as his charismatic skills as an orator, quickly placed him among the frontrunners. His main opponent became then Senator Hillary Clinton of New York, who emphasized Obama's lack of experience and expressed doubts that his rhetoric could be turned into tangible action. By June, after a protracted primary campaign, Obama had edged past Clinton to achieve the necessary majority of delegates for the nomination. At the Democratic National Convention in August, Obama selected Senator Joseph Biden of Delaware as his running mate.

Obama's Democratic ticket ran against a Republican duo of Senator John McCain of Arizona and Alaska governor Sarah Palin. McCain and Palin presented themselves as "mavericks," while Obama and Biden championed "change you can believe in." Obama continued his highly successful fund-raising campaign, rejecting both official public funding and lobbyist support. Opting for private funding, much of which came in small amounts from individual donors, he accumulated well over half a billion dollars, an unprecedented amount to raise privately. His campaigns also made innovative use of the Internet. He took part in three televised debates with McCain and was generally judged to have won them all. Further weakening the McCain campaign was its association with the presidency of George W. Bush, whose popularity sank under the weight of a major economic crisis and unpopular wars in Iraq and Afghanistan. In the final weeks of the 2008 campaign, opinion polls showed the Obama-Biden ticket leading McCain-Palin by a significant margin.

For the general election on November 4, voter turnout was estimated at over 60 percent, relatively high by modern American standards. More than 130 million votes were cast, with nearly 70 million (53 percent) going to Obama. Electoral college results were 365 to 173 in favor of the Democratic ticket, which ran strongest in the populous states of the East Coast, West Coast, and upper Midwest. The Republican ticket claimed nearly 60 million votes (47 percent), prevailing in the South, Southwest, and lower Midwest. The Democratic Party also won overwhelming majorities in both houses of Congress. At a victory rally on the night of his election, Obama addressed a massive crowd in downtown Chicago's Grant Park, where forty years earlier police and protesters had clashed in one of the most turbulent Democratic conventions in history. Until his inauguration on January 20, 2009, Obama and his transition team worked with the outgoing Bush administration to deal with the mounting global financial and economic collapse.

Obama took office as the United States' first African American president amid a vast array of economic, social, and international challenges. He was awarded the Nobel Peace Prize that year in recognition of his "efforts to strengthen international diplomacy and cooperation between peoples." The award stirred controversy, since America remained heavily involved in two wars, and the Nobel committee was criticized by some for acting prematurely to honor a president mere months into his term. The committee, however, argued that Obama had "captured the world's attention and given its people hope for a better future." Obama's first term as president saw him sign the Patient Protection and Affordable Care Act (also known as Obamacare) into law on March 23, 2010, as well.

Obama ran for a second term as president against former Massachusetts governor Mitt Romney. The

November 6, 2012, election went to Obama, who won his second term with 332 electoral votes against Romney's 206. Obama began his second term on January 20, 2013.

Obama's second term focused primarily on US domestic issues. Obama sought to pass gun control legislation following the December 2012 Sandy Hook Elementary School shooting in which twenty children and six school employees were fatally shot by one gunman. Obama also advocated for the US Supreme Court to overturn as unconstitutional the 1996 Defense of Marriage Act and California's 2008 Proposition 8, both of which opposed same-sex marriage, and he championed equal rights for the lesbian, gay, bisexual, and transgendered (LGBT) communities.

In September 2014, Obama announced in a speech before the United Nations General Assembly that the United States would be taking the lead in responding to such global crises and conflicts as the Ebola virus outbreak in West Africa and Russian aggression in the Ukraine. He also stated his administration's intent to dismantle the so-called Islamic State (a militant extremist group also known as ISIL or ISIS) and called on the rest of the world to join America in training and equipping soldiers to fight the terrorist organization. He issued an executive order on pledging American troops to help fight ISIS in the Middle East. He also issued one expanding pardons for illegal immigrants, which proved controversial.

Obama saw a major victory in June 2015, when the Supreme Court declared Obamacare constitutional. Though he pledged to close Guantanamo Bay and was not successful, he did open up relations with Cuba. He visited the country in late March 2016, the first US president to do so in eighty-eight years. He met with Cuban leaders to discuss normalization. The embargo against Cuba, in place since the 1950s, remained held up by Congress.

Obama's final year in office was somewhat overshadowed by the race to elect his successor. Obama endorsed the Democratic nominee, Hillary Clinton, for the presidency, but Republican nominee Donald Trump won the election. On January 20, 2017, Donald Trump was inaugurated and Obama officially left the White House.

Significance

Although the Obama presidency faced unprecedented, paralyzing dilemmas, its mere existence was a major milestone in American history. In his November 4, 2008, victory speech in Chicago's Grant Park, Obama proclaimed that his ascension to the presidency had proved that "America is a place where all things are possible." His campaign emphasized "change" and "hope" as its main themes, and his election symbolized for many Americans the changing of long-held racial attitudes and hope for a more unified future. The fight against ISIS and Obamacare will figure in Obama's legacy, though the nature of that legacy has yet to be determined.

Edward A. Riedinger

Further Reading

Baker, Peter. "Paths to War, Then and Now, Haunt Obama." New York Times. New York Times, 13 Sept. 2014. Web. 25 Sept. 2014

Dionne, E. J., Jr. "The Case for Barack Obama." Time 12 Nov. 2012: 42–47. Print.

Freddoso, David. The Case Against Barack Obama: The Unlikely Rise and Unexamined Agenda of the Media's Favorite Candidate. Washington, DC: Regnery, 2008. Print.

Jacobs, Lawrence. "Yes, He Did: Why Obama is the Most Consequential Second-Term President since FDR." Huffington Post. TheHuffingtonPost.com, 11 Jan. 2016. Web. 15 Apr. 2016.

Jones, Erik, and Salvatore Vassallo, eds. The 2008 Presidential Elections: A Story in Four Acts. New York: Palgrave, 2009. Print.

Kesler, Charles R. I Am the Change: Barack Obama and the Crisis of Liberalism. New York: Harper, 2012. Print.

Maraniss, David. Barack Obama: The Story. New York: Simon, 2013. Print.

Obama, Barack H. The Audacity of Hope: Thoughts on Reclaiming the American Dream. New York: Crown, 2006. Print.

---. Dreams from My Father: A Story of Race and Inheritance. New York: Three Rivers, 1995. Print.

"Obama's Second Term: A Timeline." The Hill. News Communications, 3 July 2015. Web. 15 Apr. 2016.

Olive, David. An American Story: The Speeches of Barack Obama. Toronto: ECW, 2008. Print.

Pierre, Robert E., and Jon Jeter. A Day Late and a Dollar Short: High Hopes and Deferred Dreams in Obama's "Postracial" America. Hoboken: Wiley, 2010. Print.

"President Obama's Moment." Editorial. New York Times. New York Times, 9 May 2012. Web. 25 Sept. 2014.

Price, Joann F. Barack Obama: A Biography. Westport: Greenwood, 2008. Print.

"Remarks by President Obama in Address to the United National General Assembly." whitehouse.gov. US Government, 24 Sept. 2014. Web. 25 Sept. 2014.

Todd, Chuck, and Sheldon Gawiser. How Barack Obama Won: A State-by-State Guide to the Historic 2008 Presidential Election. New York: Vintage, 2009. Print.

ELEANOR ROOSEVELT

First Lady of the United States (1933-1945)

Born: October 11, 1884; New York City, New York
Died: November 7, 1962; New York City, New York
Area of Achievement: Politics, diplomacy, activism

As First Lady and as a private citizen, Roosevelt worked for civil rights, women's rights, and domestic and international peace and justice.

EARLY LIFE

Anna Eleanor Roosevelt (ROH-zeh-vehlt) was the first child of Elliott Roosevelt and Anna Livingston Ludlow Hall Roosevelt. Her beautiful and aristocratic mother, who was only twenty years old when Eleanor was born, was more involved in the social life of her contemporaries than in the needs of her daughter. Elliott Roosevelt, although handsome and charming, was troubled by problems associated with alcoholism. As a result of her parents' self-absorption, Eleanor's early childhood was lonely and somber despite her family's wealth and social position.

Anna Roosevelt died of diphtheria in 1892, depressed and discouraged by her husband's drinking and irresponsibility. Eleanor idolized her father and imagined that she would live with him and that they would travel to exciting places together. In reality, however, Elliott's attitude toward Eleanor, although expressed in loving words, was characterized by thoughtlessness. Elliott died on August 14, 1894, of complications related to his drinking.

After her father's death, Eleanor lived with her maternal grandmother Mary Livingston Ludlow Hall. A strict disciplinarian, Hall insisted on a regimented life for her grandchildren. Despite her grandmother's insistence that she wear unfashionable clothes and a back brace to improve her posture, and despite the dreary atmosphere of Hall's New York townhouse, Eleanor's childhood was not as miserable as some writers have suggested. She had, for the first time in her life, a stable and orderly home. Her grandmother and aunts were sympathetic and supportive of her academic and athletic activities, and the family's

Eleanor Roosevelt (National Archives and Records Administration)

country estate at Tivoli was a pleasant place with spacious grounds for a child to roam.

Eleanor remained in this environment until the age of fifteen, when she was sent to Allenswood, a girls' boarding school in England. Presided over by Mademoiselle Marie Souvestre, Allenswood provided a rigorous academic environment that encouraged young women to think and act independently. Eleanor came into her own at boarding school. She was an outstanding student, was active in sports, was held in the highest esteem by her fellow students, and was a protégée of Mademoiselle Souvestre. She took from Allenswood an intellectual self-possession, an increased sense of tolerance, and a commitment to public activity.

LIFE'S WORK

At eighteen, Eleanor Roosevelt returned to New York, at her grandmother's insistence that she make her debut. Although in her own memoirs Roosevelt describes herself as shy and awkward at this period of her life, her contemporaries remembered her as attractive and sought-after by the more thoughtful young men. One young man who was particularly interested was her fifth cousin once removed, Franklin D. Roosevelt. (FDR), at the time a Harvard student. The two became secretly engaged in November, 1903, and were married in March, 1905, after a courtship during which his rather possessive mother tried to raise obstacles.

> "You gain strength, courage and confidence by every experience in which you really stop to look fear in the face. You are able to say to yourself, 'I have lived through this horror. I can take the next thing that comes along.' ... You must do the thing you think you cannot do."

During the years before her marriage, Roosevelt had become involved in volunteer work in New York City. There she had found a sense of usefulness and satisfaction that social life had never held for her. She worked with the Junior League to teach settlement house children, and she joined the Consumers' League, helping to investigate women's working conditions in factories and department stores. She had firsthand exposure to urban poverty, and her commitment to improving the lives of the less fortunate dates from this period of her life.

After their wedding, Eleanor and Franklin settled in New York City in a townhouse adjoining his mother's home. During the next eleven years, Roosevelt had six children: Anna (1906); James (1907); Franklin (1909), who lived only seven months; Elliott (1910); Franklin, Jr. (1914); and John (1916). Her life was filled with domestic responsibilities and with her mother-in-law's interference in the younger Roosevelts' household. Those were years of little personal satisfaction for Roosevelt. She had little involvement with friends or work outside her family.

In 1910, Franklin began his political career by winning a seat in the New York state legislature. Roosevelt also began her public life. She enjoyed the role of political wife, especially because it brought her into contact with the issues and figures of the day. Contrary to some reports, she was not opposed to woman suffrage during this period. She had not given the issue much thought until FDR came out in support of votes for women in 1911. Then she realized that "if my husband were a suffragist I probably must be too."

In 1913, the Roosevelts moved to Washington, D.C., where Franklin served as assistant secretary of the Navy under President Woodrow Wilson. There, during World War I, Eleanor organized the Red Cross canteen and the Navy Red Cross. She knitted, entertained troops, and served food to servicemen. She visited soldiers in the hospital and raised money for a recreational center for wounded men. Her work often lasted from 9:00 a.m. until long past midnight.

The war years also brought her heartache and disillusionment when she learned of her husband's affair with her social secretary, Lucy Mercer. Roosevelt offered to divorce Franklin at this time, but he refused. Certainly, the Roosevelts' decision to continue their marriage was made partly because divorce was a serious liability in politics in the early twentieth century, but also because Franklin realized that his wife's special skills would be invaluable in his career. For Eleanor, the Lucy Mercer episode encouraged her to seek her own fulfillment in the world outside her marriage.

After an unsuccessful run for the vice presidency in 1920, Franklin developed polio in 1921. Spurred by these events, Eleanor became involved in politics both in women's issues and in the Democratic Party. During the 1920s, she became active in the League of Women Voters and the Women's Trade Union League, which supported protective legislation for women. She became acquainted with such activist women as Esther Lape and Elizabeth Read, who introduced Roosevelt into a community of independent women. With her friends Marion Dickerman and Nancy Cook, she built a cottage called Val-Kill on the grounds of the Roosevelt family estate at Hyde Park. There they created a partnership that managed a furniture crafts factory and also published the Women's Democratic News. With her friends, she also purchased Todhunter, a private girls' school in New York City. She taught there three days a week until she became First Lady in 1933. Teaching fulfilled a dream from her days at Allenswood, gave her immense satisfaction, and brought her into contact with the young people she always loved.

With the phenomenal energy that characterized her whole life, Roosevelt also entered Democratic politics, first as a representative of her husband during his convalescence and then in her own right as a spokesperson for women and social reform. She organized Democratic women in New York, traveled and spoke for Democratic Party candidates, and advocated the election of women to public office.

When Franklin was elected governor of New York in 1928 and president of the United States in 1932, Eleanor worked with the Women's Division of the Democratic National Committee to involve women in the election process and to ensure that women were appointed to positions in the administration. Among those whom she brought to her husband's attention was Frances Perkins,

Roosevelt in the mess hall at an Army airfield in the Galapagos Islands (Wikimedia Commons)

the secretary of labor, the first woman ever appointed to a presidential cabinet.

Roosevelt had feared that the position of First Lady would mean curtailing her own political and reform activities, but she discovered new opportunities to promote her primary concerns, such as equal rights and the concerns of the poor and dispossessed. She held regular press conferences that were open only to women reporters, gave radio interviews and lectures, and wrote a syndicated newspaper column called "My Day." In addition, she supervised the responses to the thousands of letters she received, sometimes sending a personal note or a check. She also traveled throughout the country as the president's "eyes and ears," seeing for herself the conditions on farms, in mines and factories, and in the homes of the poor during the Depression. She brought representatives of excluded groups to the White House, frequently seating them next to the president so that he could hear their stories.

A primary commitment of Roosevelt's adult life was to civil rights for African Americans. She had grown up in an isolated and prejudiced environment, but living in Washington, D.C., had made her aware of the evils of racism. Her advocacy took the form both of symbolic gestures, as when she insisted on placing her chair in the center of the aisle between black and white sections at a segregated meeting of the Southern Conference on Human Welfare in 1939, and of quiet lobbying, as in her role of messenger between her husband and the National Association for the Advancement of Colored People (NAACP). She supported federal legislation to outlaw lynching and, during World War II, worked to eliminate discrimination in the armed forces.

During the war, Eleanor endeavored to ensure women's participation in all aspects of the mobilization, visited troops in hospitals and in the field, and sought to continue the many New Deal social reforms jeopardized by the country's focus on the international crisis.

Franklin died in April of 1945, during his fourth term as president. Roosevelt continued her public life, perhaps feeling freer because she was no longer perceived as a politician's wife. She turned many of her efforts to international matters, an extension of her longstanding interest in building a lasting peace. She had earlier been an advocate of the League of Nations and the World Court, and now President Harry S. Truman appointed her as a delegate to the newly formed United Nations, where she served until 1953. She chaired the committee that produced the 1948 Declaration on Human Rights and was nominated four times for the Nobel Peace Prize.

The "First Lady of the World" showed concern for the victims of war and oppression parallel to her continuing domestic interests in civil rights and women's issues. Roosevelt's last public role was as the chairperson of President John F. Kennedy's Commission on the Status of Women, in which capacity she supported full access by women to economic and political opportunities. She died in New York City on November 7, 1962, of a rare type of tuberculosis.

SIGNIFICANCE

Eleanor Roosevelt's life bore out the advice she had written to women in 1930, "to be ready to go out and try new adventures, create new work for others as well as herself, and strike deep roots in some community where her presence will make a difference in the lives of others."

Roosevelt defined a new role for women in American public life. Although during much of her life she filled a position as the wife of a prominent politician, her contributions stand on their own. With compassion and a commitment to humanitarian interests, she helped to place the issues of racial and gender justice on the national agenda. She was an advocate for all excluded groups, using her public visibility as a means to bring their concerns to national attention and using her influence to promote changes in attitudes and in legislation. On the international scene, she reached out to the victims of injustice and poverty, legitimizing and promoting their well-being.

To women of future generations, Roosevelt became a model of energy, humanity, and courage. Always an example of impeccable courtesy, she could also confront leaders of the Soviet Union or the proponents of segregation and state her case. She demonstrated the need to redefine power as not only the authority to move armies or to control economic might but also the ability to inspire, to question the status quo, and to work for equality without the expectation of personal gain.

Mary Welek Atwell

FURTHER READING

Cook, Blanche Wiesen. *Eleanor Roosevelt*. Vol. 1. New York: Viking, 1992. The first volume of a projected two-volume study, Cook's sensitive biography places Eleanor Roosevelt in the context of a rich emotional life and emphasizes her lifelong strengths.

Glendon, Mary Ann. *A World Made New: Eleanor Roosevelt and the Universal Declaration of Human Rights*. New York: Random House, 2001. Recounts how Roosevelt and others in 1947 began drafting the Universal Declaration of Human Rights, which was adopted by the United Nations the following year. Includes a legal analysis of the declaration and its applicability to the twenty-first century.

Hoff-Wilson, Joan, and Marjorie Lightman, eds. *Without Precedent: The Life and Career of Eleanor Roosevelt*. Bloomington: Indiana University Press, 1984. An excellent collection of articles on Roosevelt's character and contributions. The essays introduce fine scholarship dealing with the major themes in her life.

Lash, Joseph P. *Eleanor and Franklin*. New York: W. W. Norton, 1971. The first part of a two-volume biography of Roosevelt. Lash had full access to Roosevelt's papers.

---. *Eleanor: The Years Alone*. New York: W. W. Norton, 1972. The second volume of the biography looks at Roosevelt's life after her husband's death. Lash's personal friendship with Roosevelt enabled him to provide a warm and comprehensive picture of her life.

Roosevelt, Eleanor. *The Autobiography of Eleanor Roosevelt*. New York: Harper & Brothers, 1961. Three volumes consolidated into one, this autobiography is indispensable to the student but provides a picture that is too self-effacing.

---. *My Day: The Best of Eleanor Roosevelt's Acclaimed Newspaper Columns, 1936-1962*. Edited by David Emblidge and Marcy Ross. New York: Da Capo Press, 2001. A selection of Roosevelt's syndicated newspaper columns in which she expresses her views on the New Deal, World War II, human rights, and other issues.

Youngs, J. William T. *Eleanor Roosevelt: Personal and Public Life*. 3d ed. New York: Pearson/Longman, 2006. A biography that touches on Roosevelt's life at home and in the public eye.

FRANKLIN D. ROOSEVELT

32nd President of the United States (1933-1945)

Born: January 30, 1882; Hyde Park, New York
Died: April 12, 1945; Warm Springs, Georgia
Area of Achievement: Politics

Displaying extraordinary personal courage and perhaps the most astute political leadership America has ever witnessed, Roosevelt dominated American government for a longer period than has any other president of the United States.

EARLY LIFE

Franklin D. Roosevelt was a member of an American aristocratic family of great wealth. James and Sara Roosevelt, of Dutch and English ancestry, educated their only child with private tutors and European tours. At Groton School in Massachusetts, Roosevelt came under the influence of Rector Endicott Peabody, who prided himself on grooming future politicians and instilling in his charges a lifelong commitment to public service.

By 1900, when Franklin enrolled at Harvard University, he was an impressive young man six feet two inches tall, handsome, with a patrician nose and majestically deep-set eyes. In his junior year, he fell in love with his fifth cousin, Eleanor Roosevelt. Eleanor was the daughter of President Theodore Roosevelt's younger brother, Elliott, who died from alcoholism when she was ten. In 1905, Franklin married Eleanor, over the objections of his mother, who tried to postpone the wedding.

Following Harvard, Roosevelt dabbled briefly with the practice of law before turning to the real love of his life:

Franklin D. Roosevelt (National Archives and Records Administration)

politics. In 1910, he entered the political arena for the first time, running for the New York State senate. Fellow Democrats skeptically observed his entrance into the race for several reasons: his aristocratic bearing, his tendency to look down his nose at people, his unfamiliarity with working-class voters in the Hyde Park–Poughkeepsie area, and the fact that he was a former Republican. The political climate, however, demanded a reformer, and Roosevelt, following in the footsteps of his cousin Theodore, could fill the bill by pointing to the ugly specter of corruption within the opposition party. During the campaign, FDR (as he came to be known) showed he was different from the average "cheap-talking" politician, displaying a pragmatic unorthodoxy that later endeared him to the nation. He even campaigned for office in an automobile, an unusual political act for a time when most people eyed the horseless carriage with suspicion. Victory was his, however, and Roosevelt became only the second Democrat elected from his district to the New York State senate since the Civil War. He was on his way.

It was not an easy path to success. Experiences in the New York senate taught him the limits of progressive, reformistic power. When he challenged Charles F. Murphy's Tammany Hall political machine of New York City over the Democratic nomination for the United States Senate, he met defeat. He gradually learned, however, to moderate his reform tendencies. This later proved to be his first major lesson in the school of politics. Following his reelection in 1912, Roosevelt jumped at the opportunity to join Woodrow Wilson's administration in the capacity of assistant secretary of the Navy under Josephus Daniels. In doing so, young FDR may have imagined himself following the example of Theodore Roosevelt, who had achieved the governorship of New York, the vice presidency, and the presidency after serving in the same position. The Navy Department afforded FDR a chance to hone his administrative skills and strengthen his political ties throughout the Democratic Party to the point that, by 1920, delegates to the national convention were willing to exploit his famous name by nominating him for the vice presidency as James M. Cox's running mate. Cox and Roosevelt suffered defeat in the Republican landslide that swept Warren G. Harding and Calvin Coolidge into office. FDR remained basically unchanged throughout these events, still a somewhat immature young man who maintained very few strong convictions.

All this changed in August, 1921, when Roosevelt contracted polio while vacationing at Campobello Island, his family's resort off the Maine seacoast. His health was shattered, but a new Roosevelt slowly began to emerge. Paralyzed from the waist down, and wealthy enough to retire at the age of thirty-nine, he fought to regain his vigor. First, he had to overcome the frustration that resulted from the wearing of heavy steel braces that prohibited him from walking unaided. Second, he had to ignore the pleas of his mother (whom he worshiped but who urged him to withdraw from politics) and listen to his wife and his personal secretary, Louis McHenry Howe, who plotted to restore him to some semblance of health. During this period of recovery, Eleanor became his "legs," going where he could not go, doing what he could not do physically, and generally learning the art of politics.

> "*Let us not be afraid to help each other — let us never forget that government is ourselves and not an alien power over us. The ultimate rulers of our democracy are not a President and Senators and Congressmen and Government officials but the voters of this country.*"

Life's Work

In 1924, FDR showed that Roosevelt the fighter had superseded Roosevelt the dedicated aristocrat when he appeared at the Democratic National Convention to give his

Roosevelt broadcasting from his Hyde Park, New York, home on November 4th, 1938. (Wikimedia Commons)

"Happy Warrior Speech" nominating Alfred E. Smith for president. Smith lost the nomination, but Roosevelt did not lose his political career to polio. Instead, it seemed to give him a strength of character he had rarely shown before the Campobello incident. In 1928, while Smith was losing his home state of New York by 100,000 votes to Herbert Hoover, Roosevelt was winning the governorship by 25,000, thus becoming the front-runner for the 1932 Democratic presidential nomination. Reelected by an unprecedented 725,000 votes in 1930, Roosevelt, aided by his national campaign manager, James A. Farley, began his first run for the presidency. Capturing the nomination on the third ballot, Roosevelt pledged himself to create, if elected, a "new deal" for the American people.

The 1932 presidential campaign pitted Roosevelt against the Republican incumbent, Herbert Hoover. With the country three years into the Great Depression, Roosevelt wisely ran a pragmatic campaign fluctuating between alternative ideological positions, allowing Hoover's record to speak for itself, and leaving the decision to the American electorate. On November 8, 1932, the people spoke giving him a 472–59 electoral victory over Hoover. When Roosevelt took office on March 4, 1933, the nation was mired in the worst depression in American history. There were approximately thirteen million unemployed people 25.2 percent of the workforce. As a mood of apprehension gripped the country, Roosevelt tried to calm the panic-stricken populace when he said,

During the crucial one hundred days that followed his inaugural speech, Roosevelt began the New Deal. He quickly satisfied the public's overwhelming desire for leadership and action by issuing executive orders and introducing legislation that a frightened Congress quickly rubber-stamped. Roosevelt acted in four critical areas: finance, industry, agriculture, and relief (welfare). In combating the Depression, he gave the nation no panacea but offered the means through which it might be able to survive the crisis. He did not end the Depression but many of his programs and the laws he signed got the country through the Depression and remained an effective part of the federal government long after his death. In finance, the Emergency Banking Act (1933) and the Banking Act of 1933, also known as the Glass-Steagall Act, saved the banking structure and helped prevent a future crisis by creating the Federal Deposit Insurance Corporation. The Truth-in-Securities Act (1933) and the Securities Exchange Act (1934) brought Wall Street under tighter public regulation. In industry, the National Industrial Recovery Act (1933) offered both business and labor opportunities for greater self-government. Later, through the National Labor Relations Act (1935), he concentrated more on allowing labor unions the right to organize. In agriculture, Roosevelt tried to restore farmers' prosperity through the Agriculture Adjustment Act (1933) by subsidizing certain farm products they could not afford to sell at market prices. In relief, FDR straddled the line between welfare and public works. At first, the New Deal doled out money to unemployed people through the Federal Emergency Relief Administration (1933) and sent young men to work camps through the Civilian Conservation Corps (1933).

After the one hundred days had passed, FDR turned away from welfare and made government jobs a primary goal of his administration. Listening to his advisers, Harry Hopkins and Harold L. Ickes, Roosevelt made the federal government the employer of the last resort through the Civil Works Administration (1933), the Public Works Administration (1933), and the Works Progress Administration (1935). In particular, the WPA, which averaged 2,112,000 on its monthly payrolls from 1935 to 1941, was the largest, most visionary, and probably most effective federal relief program ever created. Perhaps the most long-lasting reform achieved by Roosevelt was the Social Security Administration (1935), granting unemployment compensation and old-age pensions.

Roosevelt's New Deal programs generated billions of new dollars throughout the American economy, increasing incomes and causing tax revenues to "trickle up" to the federal and state governments. The jobs also raised the hopes of millions of voters who came to believe that

Roosevelt signing the declaration of war against Germany, marking US entry into World War II in Europe. Senator Tom Connally stands by holding a watch to fix the exact time of the declaration. (Library of Congress)

Roosevelt had saved them from financial disaster. He was the man who put food on their tables, shoes on their feet, and a roof over their heads. In brief, the New Deal was political dynamite, and Roosevelt was the New Deal. The president's charismatic leadership, his inspirational speeches and informal "fireside chats," made him an unbeatable campaigner, as his 1936 Republican opponent learned. Roosevelt crushed Kansas Governor Alfred M. Landon by the largest electoral margin in recent American history, 523 to 8.

In less than three years, Roosevelt created an imperial presidency and vastly enlarged the federal bureaucracy, thus prompting criticisms from conservatives and the Supreme Court. When the Court began invalidating some New Deal programs such as the National Industrial Recovery Act (*Schechter Poultry Corp. v. United States*, 1935) and the Agriculture Adjustment Act (*Butler v. United States*, 1936), he struck back. In 1937, Roosevelt tried to pack the Court with New Dealers by introducing the Federal Judiciary Reorganization Bill. Although the bill failed to pass Congress, Roosevelt prevailed in this struggle, since the Court's later decisions proved more favorable to New Deal legislation. Still, the court-packing scheme suggested dictatorial ambitions and damaged Roosevelt's reputation in some circles. His popularity further declined as the nation slid deeper into the Depression in 1938, and the president, determined to keep his working majority in Congress, attempted to purge conservative Democrats from his party. This tactic also failed. By 1939, the New Deal, for all practical purposes, was dead.

As the New Deal passed into history, new dangers loomed on the horizon. Totalitarian regimes in Germany, Japan, and Italy threatened the position of the United States in the world. Roosevelt himself recognized that the leaders of these regimes, Adolf Hitler, Hideki Tōjō, and Benito Mussolini, would necessitate some changes in American foreign policy when he said that "Dr. Win the War" would have to replace "Dr. New Deal." In this way, he reluctantly began to shift American diplomacy in the direction of confronting these aggressors. After Germany invaded Poland on September 1, 1939, precipitating a declaration of war by Great Britain and France, Americans debated whether their country should maintain its isolation or aid its British and French allies. While Roosevelt was preaching neutrality, he won an unprecedented third term, a 449–82 electoral victory over his 1940 Republican opponent, Wendell Lewis Willkie.

When the war came to the United States, it struck with a fury. Possibly no aspect of Roosevelt's foreign policy has evoked more controversy than the role he played in leading the United States into World War II. On December 7, 1941, a little more than a year after he promised that "this country is not going to war," Japanese planes swept down on the American naval base at Pearl Harbor, Hawaii, nearly destroying the United States Pacific Fleet. The declaration of war that followed prompted his critics to complain that he had tricked his nation into war. While the Roosevelt administration made numerous errors in judgment, Roosevelt did not intentionally expose the military installation to attack to drag a reluctant and isolationistic American people into the war.

Shortly after the "day of infamy," Roosevelt met with British prime minister Winston Churchill in the first of several Washington conferences forming a "grand alliance" between the two world leaders and their nations. At the first meeting, Roosevelt agreed to the idea that the Allies should place top priority on defeating Germany and Italy, while fighting a holding action against Japan in the Pacific theater. In fact, throughout the war, Roosevelt actively planned and executed top military and diplomatic decisions that affected its outcome and the postwar world. Together with Churchill and Soviet premier Joseph Stalin, he agreed to the formulation of the United Nations. At the Yalta Conference (February, 1945), Roosevelt made another of his extremely controversial decisions that would affect public opinion long after he was gone. In return for Stalin's promise to enter the war against Japan and to allow free elections in the Soviet bloc nations, Roosevelt acquiesced to Russia's hegemony in eastern Poland and other territories occupied by Soviet troops. Because these decisions were kept secret by the chief signatories, Roosevelt never felt the full fury of his critics before his death on April 12, 1945.

Significance

In electing Roosevelt to an unprecedented four terms of office, the American people lent credence to the belief that Roosevelt was the greatest leader ever to hold the presidency. This view was further substantiated by the 1982 survey conducted by Professor Robert K. Murray of Pennsylvania State University among a thousand historians with doctoral degrees; only Abraham Lincoln ranked ahead of Roosevelt as the best president in American history. Those who admire FDR have praised his leadership, confidence, and flexibility in the face of economic crisis and war. The Social Security Act has changed since its initial implementation, but continues to provide financial support to disabled and elderly Americans. Nevertheless, some historians have criticized Roosevelt's ambitions as dictatorial for circumventing the Constitution and in his effort to seat New Deal–friendly justices on the Supreme Court. Conservatives have decried Roosevelt for allowing the national debt to grow during his presidency, while others point to the recession that occurred when FDR reined in deficit spending and implemented economic austerity measures. Since Roosevelt's presidency both liberal and conservative presidents have resorted to deficit spending, and political debate over its use and misuse continues into the twenty-first century.

Roosevelt created the imperial presidency, in the process setting a precedent for leadership by which all his successors have been evaluated. He took the executive branch, which had lost much of its power and glory, and expanded it beyond the limits achieved by any twentieth century American chief executive. Circumstances such as depression and war, and the force of his indomitable personal character, allowed him to restructure the office into its present form. Proponents have praised the FDR's restructuring of the executive office for expanding both its responsibilities and capabilities, while critics say such changes encroach on the normal powers and functions of Congress and the Supreme Court. In 1939 he issued Executive Order 8248, creating the Executive Office of the President and shifting the powerful Bureau of the Budget from the Treasury Department to the White House.

Although Roosevelt's primary claim to greatness lay in domestic achievements, he made major contributions in foreign policy as well. He was the president who led America to victory over the Axis powers and then achieved the first détente with the new superpower: the Soviet Union. It was in the arena of American politics and government, however, that Roosevelt made his greatest imprint. Even his critics must concede that his impact on the nation was extraordinary.

Christopher Schnell

Further Reading

Beschloss, Michael. *The Conquerors: Roosevelt, Truman, and the Destruction of Hitler's Germany, 1941–1945.* New York: Simon, 2002. Print.

Brands, H. W. *Traitor to His Class: The Privileged Life and Radical Presidency of Franklin Delano Roosevelt.* 5th printing. New York: Anchor, 2013. Print.

Burt, Sally. "The Ambassador, the General, and the President: FDR's Mismanagement of Interdepartmental Relations in Wartime China." *Jour. of Amer.-East Asian Relations* 19.3/4 (2012): 288–310. Print.

Daniels, Roger. *Franklin D. Roosevelt.* Urbana: U of Illinois P, 2015–2016. Print.

Davis, Kenneth Sydney. *FDR, Into the Storm, 1937–1940: A History.* New York: Random, 1993. Print.

Freidel, Frank. *Launching the New Deal.* Boston: Little, 1973. Print.

Freidel, Frank. *Franklin D. Roosevelt: A Rendezvous with Destiny.* Newtown: American Political Biog. P, 2006. Print.

McElvaine, Robert S. *Franklin Delano Roosevelt.* Washington, D.C.: CQ P, 2002. Print.

Neal, Steve. *Happy Days Are Here Again: The 1932 Democratic Convention, the Emergence of FDR and How America Was Changed Forever.* New York: Morrow, 2004. Print.

Pious, Richard M. "The Historical Presidency: Franklin D. Roosevelt and the Destroyer Deal: Normalizing Prerogative Power." *Presidential Studies Quarterly* 42.1 (2012): 190–204. Print.

Rofe, J. Simon, and John M. Thompson. "Internationalists in Isolationist Times—Theodore and Franklin Roosevelt and a Rooseveltian Maxim." *Jour. of Transatlantic Studies (Routledge)* 9.1 (2011): 46–62. Print.

Schlesinger, Arthur M., Jr. *The Age of Roosevelt*. 3 vols. Boston: Houghton, 1957–1960. Print.

Shaw, Stephen K., Franklin Williams, and William D. Pederson. *Franklin D. Roosevelt and the Transformation of the Supreme Court*. London: Routledge, 2015. *eBook Collection (EBSCOhost)*. Web. 8 Sept. 2015.

THEODORE ROOSEVELT

26th President of the United States (1901-1909)

Born: October 27, 1858; New York City, New York
Died: January 6, 1919; Oyster Bay, New York
Area of Achievement: Politics, military, conservation

As twenty-sixth president of the United States, Roosevelt energetically led America into the twentieth century. Popular and effective, he promoted major domestic reforms and a larger role for the United States in world affairs. In so doing, he added power to the presidential office.

Theodore Roosevelt (Library of Congress)

EARLY LIFE

Theodore Roosevelt (ROH-zeh-vehlt) was born into a moderately wealthy New York City mercantile family in New York City. His father, Theodore, Sr., was of mostly Dutch ancestry; his mother, Martha Bulloch of Georgia, came from a slaveholding family of Scots and Huguenot French. (During his political career, Roosevelt would claim an ethnic relationship with practically every white voter he met; among his nicknames besides TR and Teddy was Old Fifty-Seven Varieties.) He was educated at home by tutors and traveled with his parents to the Middle East and Europe.

As a child, Roosevelt was puny, asthmatic, and was literally unable to see much of the world until he was fitted with thick eyeglasses at the age of thirteen. He grew determined to "make" a powerful body, and by strenuous exercise and force of will, Roosevelt gradually overcame most of his physical shortcomings. Shyness and fear were other weaknesses he conquered. "There were all kinds of things of which I was afraid at first," he later admitted in his *Theodore Roosevelt: An Autobiography* (1913). "But by acting as if I was not afraid I gradually ceased to be afraid." Insecurity, however, was one demon that he never exorcised.

While becoming athletic and assertive, Roosevelt retained his wide-ranging intellectual curiosity. At Harvard University, from which he was graduated in 1880, his absorption with both sports and books made him something of an oddity. Yet career plans remained uncertain. Dull science classes dimmed his earlier interest in becoming a naturalist. A year at Columbia University Law School from 1880–81 did not stimulate an interest in a legal career. While attending Columbia, he married Boston socialite Alice Hathaway Lee in 1880; completed his first book *The Naval War of 1812*, which was published in 1882; and entered politics in the autumn of 1881 by election to the New York legislature as a Republican representative from Manhattan. For the remainder of his life, except for brief military glory in the Spanish-American War, writing and politics would absorb most of his overflowing energy.

LIFE'S WORK

At the age of twenty-three, Roosevelt, the youngest member of New York's legislature, attracted attention because of his anticorruption stance and his flair for the dramatic. He instinctively knew how to make his doings interesting to the press and the public. Personality flaws were obvious from the beginning of his political career (egotism, impulsiveness, a narrow-minded outlook, and occasional ruthlessness), yet Roosevelt's virtues were equally apparent and won for him far more admirers than enemies: extraordinary vitality and intelligence, courage, sincerity, conviviality, and, usually, a willingness to make reasonable compromises.

> *"It is not the critic who counts, not the man who points out how the strong man stumbled, or where the doer of deeds could have done better. The credit belongs to the man who is actually in the arena; whose face is marred by the dust and sweat and blood; who strives valiantly; who errs and comes short again and again, because there is no effort without error or shortcoming; who knows the great enthusiasms, the great devotions and spends himself in a worthy cause; who at the best, knows in the end the triumph of high achievement, and who, at worst, if he fails, at least fails while daring greatly; so that his place shall never be with those cold and timid souls who know neither victory or defeat."*

In February 1884, Alice gave birth to a baby girl, who the couple named Alice Lee Roosevelt. Within two days, however, Alice died from what is believed to have been undiagnosed kidney failure or postpartum preeclampsia. Distraught over his young wife's death, Roosevelt sent the newborn to live with her aunt, Roosevelt's older sister, Anna "Bamie" Roosevelt and regained custody of her when she was three years old.

Following the death of Alice, Roosevelt temporarily retired from politics and for the next two years operated cattle ranches that he owned in the Badlands of the Dakota Territory, where he found time to write *Hunting Trips of a Ranchman* (1885), the first of a trilogy of books on his Western activities and observations. Ranching proved financially unprofitable, but outdoor life made Roosevelt physically more robust and helped ease the pain of Alice's death. In 1886, he returned to New York and married Edith Kermit Carow, who raised young Alice alongside the couple's four sons and a daughter.

Also in 1884, Roosevelt was the unsuccessful Republican nominee for mayor of New York City and he began work on a six-volume history of America's Western expansion, *The Winning of the West* (1889–96).

Roosevelt did not seek another elected office until he won the governorship of New York in 1898, but in the meantime, he served in three appointed positions: member of the United States Civil Service Commission (1889–95), president of New York City's Board of Police Commissioners (1895–97), and assistant secretary of the Navy (1897–98). He resigned the latter post when war with Spain broke out in 1898. Eager for combat, he organized a volunteer cavalry regiment known as the Rough Riders. Most of the land fighting between the United States and Spain occurred in Cuba, and the image of Colonel Roosevelt leading a charge up San Juan Hill (in actuality, Kettle Hill) became a public symbol of this brief, victorious war with "Teddy" as a national hero. In November of 1898, he was elected governor of New York and quickly published a new book, *The Rough Riders* (1899), which a humorous critic said should have been titled "Alone in Cuba."

As governor of New York (1899–1900), Roosevelt pursued a vigorous program of political reform. The Republican state machine who wanted him out of New York promoted his nomination for vice president on the national ticket in 1900. With reluctance, thinking that office might be a dead end, Roosevelt was finally persuaded to accept the nomination, thus becoming President William McKinley's running mate in 1900.

Within a year, McKinley died by an assassin's bullet, and Theodore Roosevelt, at age forty-two, was sworn in as the youngest chief executive in the nation's history. Physically, the new president had an aura of strength despite his average height, spectacles, small hands and feet, and high-pitched voice. His wide, square face; prominent, firm teeth; and massive chest overrode any hint of weakness.

The presidency, Roosevelt once observed, was a "bully pulpit," and he wasted no time in exhorting America toward new horizons in both domestic and foreign policy. Yet Roosevelt was painfully aware that he had become president by mishap. Not until his overwhelming election to a full term in 1904 did he believe that the office was truly his.

Within the nation, President Roosevelt called for a Square Deal for both capital and labor. He saw himself as chief arbiter of conflicts between economic groups; government, he believed, should represent everyone equitably. Believing in capitalism yet convinced that big corporations were too powerful and arrogant, he began a policy of "trust busting." Roosevelt's administration was the first to use successfully the Sherman Antitrust Act (passed in 1890) to break up business monopolies. Actually, Roosevelt believed more in regulation than in "busting," but he hoped to frighten big business into accepting regulation. Privately, he was convinced that, for

Colonel Roosevelt and his Rough Riders at the top of the hill which they captured, Battle of San Juan (Library of Congress)

modern America, industrial and financial combinations were inevitable; he desired to subordinate both big business and labor unions to a stronger central government, which he viewed as the proper instrument for protecting the general interest.

The Hepburn Act, which for the first time gave the Interstate Commerce Commission regulatory power over railroads, was a significant accomplishment of Roosevelt's presidency as were the Pure Food and Drug Act and the Meat Inspection Act, all passed in 1906. Conservation of natural resources was another Roosevelt goal. Over both Democratic and Republican opposition, he cajoled Congress into limiting private exploitation of the nation's wilderness, mineral, and water resources and withdrew the Grand Canyon from mining claims. His administration doubled the number of national parks and tripled the acreage of national forests. Fifty-one wildlife refuges were established. Conservation was probably Roosevelt's most passionate cause and one of his most enduring legacies. In 1947 over 110 square miles were preserved and named the Theodore Roosevelt National Park.

In foreign policy, Roosevelt is remembered by the proverb he once used: "Speak softly and carry a big stick." In practice, however, he bifurcated that approach; he spoke softly toward nations whose power he respected, while saving the big stick for small or weak countries. High-handedly, he "took Panama" to use his own words away from the nation of Colombia in 1903 so as to build an isthmian canal; the next year, he proclaimed a protectorate over all of Latin America the Roosevelt Corollary to the Monroe Doctrine. As for the Far East, Roosevelt worried over but respected the rising power of Japan. He wanted the Japanese to thwart Russian expansionism but not to dominate Asia. He assumed that Great Britain and the United States would draw closer in worldwide interests; he viewed Germany, Japan, and Russia as probable enemies of a future Anglo-American alliance.

Roosevelt did not run for reelection. He had pledged after his 1904 triumph that he would not seek or accept another nomination. It was a promise he later regretted. The Republican Party in 1908 chose Roosevelt's close personal friend William Howard Taft who, with Roosevelt's blessing, easily won the presidency. Yet Taft's troubled term (1909–13) split the Republicans into Progressive and Old Guard wings, and by 1910, Roosevelt angrily decided that Taft had capitulated to the Old Guard. Consequently, Roosevelt attempted to regain the White House in 1912. After losing a bitter contest to Taft for the Republican nomination, Roosevelt burst into the general election as a third party (Progressive, or Bull Moose Party) candidate, thus virtually guaranteeing victory for Democratic nominee Woodrow Wilson. Roosevelt's personal popularity allowed him to finish second in the 1912 presidential election, but without a viable national organization, he lost heavily to Wilson in the electoral count. Taft ran third.

Roosevelt spent most of the remainder of his life writing books, exploring Brazil's backcountry, and criticizing President Wilson, whom he hated. He wanted to fight in World War I but was refused a commission. With his health weakened by infections contracted in Brazil, Theodore Roosevelt died in his sleep on January 6, 1919, at the age of sixty.

SIGNIFICANCE

"The Republican Roosevelt," as one historian termed him, is usually ranked among the best American presidents. An inspirational leader and superb administrator, he revitalized the presidency. His career seemed to defy the adage that power corrupts. In mental prowess, he had few equals in American political history; indeed, Roosevelt ranks among the rarest of human types: an intellectual who was also a man of action.

Ideologically, Roosevelt defies simple definition. Whether he was an "enlightened" conservative or a "Progressive" liberal remains in dispute. Roosevelt himself refused to accept labels. He viewed himself as a moral leader who combined practicality and idealism for the purpose of unifying the nation's opposing economic and social interests into a mutually beneficial synthesis.

Coming to the presidency at the dawn of the twentieth century, Roosevelt understood that America was fast becoming a complex urban and industrialized nation and that a new balance was needed between individualism and the collective good. In foreign policy, Roosevelt acted on his conviction that the old isolationism was no longer possible and that the United States, because of its growing strength, was destined to be a world power.

William I. Hair

FURTHER READING

Beale, Howard K. *Theodore Roosevelt and the Rise of America to World Power*. Baltimore: Johns Hopkins UP, 1956. Print.

Cordery, Stacy A. *Theodore Roosevelt: In the Vanguard of the Modern*. Belmont: Thomson, 2003. Print.

Goodwin, Doris Kearns. *The Bully Pulpit: Theodore Roosevelt, William Howard Taft, and the Golden Age of Journalism*. New York: Simon, 2014. Print.

Gould, Lewis L. *The Presidency of Theodore Roosevelt*. Lawrence: UP of Kansas, 1991. Print.

Harbaugh, William Henry. *Power and Responsibility: The Life and Times of Theodore Roosevelt*. New York: Oxford UP, 1975. Print.

Morris, Edmund. *The Rise of Theodore Roosevelt*. New York: Coward, 1979. Print.

Morris, Edmund. *Theodore Rex*. New York: Random, 2001. Print.

O'Toole, Patricia. *When Trumpets Call: Theodore Roosevelt After the White House*. New York: Simon, 2005. Print.

Pringle, Henry F. *Theodore Roosevelt: A Biography*. New York: Harcourt, 1931. Print.

Ricard, Serge. "An Atlantic Triangle in the 1900s: Theodore Roosevelt's 'Special Relationships' with France and Britain." *Jour. of Transatlantic Studies (Routledge)* 8.3 (2010): 202–12. Print

Rofe, J. Simon and John M. Thompson. "Internationalists in Isolationist Times-Theodore and Franklin Roosevelt and the Rooseveltian Maxim." *Jour. of Transatlantic Studies (Routledge)* 9.1 (2011): 46–62. Print.

Roosevelt, Theodore. *Selected Speeches and Writing of Theodore Roosevelt*. Ed. Gordon Hutner. New York: Vintage, 2014. Print.

Roosevelt, Theodore. *The Writings of Theodore Roosevelt*. Ed. William H. Harbaugh. Indianapolis: Bobbs, 1967. Print.

Thompson, J. Lee. *Never Call Retreat: Theodore Roosevelt and the Great War*. New York: Palgrave Macmillan, 2013. Print.

West, Mark. "Theodore Roosevelt and the Golden Age of Children's Literature." *Jour. of Amer. Culture* 33.2 (2010): 121–25. Print.

GEORGE WASHINGTON

1st President of the United States (1789-1797)

Born: February 22, 1732; Bridges Creek, Colony of Virginia
Died: December 14, 1799; Mount Vernon, Virginia
Area of Achievement: Politics, military

As commander in chief of the Continental army during the American Revolution, president of the Constitutional Convention of 1787, and first president of the United States, Washington was the principal architect of the nation's independence and its federal political system.

EARLY LIFE

Born into a family of middling standing among Virginia's planter elite, George Washington was the eldest son of his father's second marriage. A favorite of his half brother Lawrence Washington of Mount Vernon, young George capitalized on this brother's marriage into the prominent Fairfax family and the inheritance of Lawrence Washington's estate. Thus, despite his losing his father at age eleven and his being a low-priority heir to his father's lands, he was by his mid-twenties able to achieve greater

George Washington (Wikimedia Commons)

prominence both in estate and position than his ancestors.

His connections allowed him to succeed Lawrence Washington as a major and adjutant of militia in 1752, and the following year he carried a message from Virginia's governor to the French forces encroaching on Virginia-claimed lands in the upper Ohio valley. In 1754, Lieutenant Colonel Washington surrendered a small Virginia detachment under his command to French forces in southwestern Pennsylvania. Thus began the French and Indian War (1754-63), known in Europe as the Seven Years' War (1756-63).

Washington's war record was solid but undistinguished, except for his well-recognized bravery during General Edward Braddock's defeat on the Monongahela River in 1756. Failing to receive the royal military commission he sought, he returned to Mount Vernon, engaged in modern farming techniques, expanded his land holdings, and, in 1759, married a wealthy widow, Martha Dandridge Custis. Their marriage was childless, but Washington adopted her two children.

Life's Work

Elected to the Virginia House of Burgesses, George Washington never achieved a reputation of outspokenness comparable to that of, say, Patrick Henry. A delegate to the First and Second Continental Congresses, Washington impressed his colleagues with his mastery of military affairs and was selected by them to serve as commander in chief of the newly formed Continental army in 1775. He took command of the mostly New England force shortly after its defeat at Breed's (Bunker) Hill and immediately sought to reform it into an effective fighting force. Containing the British forces inside Boston during the winter of 1775-76, he forced them to evacuate the city the following spring. Action then moved to New York City, where he suffered defeats on Long Island and Manhattan Island and was eventually driven across the Hudson River into and across New Jersey. His counterattacks at Trenton and Princeton during the winter of 1776-77 revived American hopes and allowed his forces to winter in northern New Jersey.

The following year, he countered the two-pronged British invasion from Canada down the Lake Champlain-Hudson Valley route and from New York via sea against Philadelphia by sending General Horatio Gates with some of his regulars to join local units in combating the northern invasion and by leading the Pennsylvania campaign himself. In the latter area, Washington was soundly defeated by General William Howe's forces but escaped to rebuild his army during the bitter winter at Valley Forge. General Gates won a remarkable victory at Saratoga that encouraged the French government to recognize the United States. The subsequent alliance with France allowed the Americans to continue their efforts and forced the British to concentrate their naval and military forces against an ever-widening war that eventually saw combat from the Indian Ocean to the Caribbean Sea.

The new international conflict caused the British to withdraw from Philadelphia to New York in 1778. When Washington sought to destroy their forces at Monmouth, New Jersey, the result was an indecisive battle that could have turned into a rout had not the American commander personally rallied his troops. For the next three years, Washington headquartered his forces near West Point, New York, while combating some British raids and pinning the British forces in the New York City-Long Island vicinity. When the British developed a southern strategy to return Georgia and the Carolinas to their empire, Washington countered by sending Generals Benjamin Lincoln and Horatio Gates to the region. The result was defeat for both officers at Charleston and Camden. In early 1781, Washington sent Nathanael Greene southward, and Greene was able to conduct an effective area defense that thwarted General Charles Cornwallis's attempts to conquer the Carolinas. Exasperated, Cornwallis sought to cut off Greene's supply line and to draw him northward by invading Virginia. At this point, Washington coordinated with the French general, the comte de Rochambeau, commander of a French expeditionary force in Rhode Island, and through him Admiral Count François de Grasse, commander of the French West Indian fleet, to unite their forces against Cornwallis in Virginia. The resultant surrender of Cornwallis at Yorktown in October, 1781, effectively ended British attempts to reintegrate the United States into the British Empire even though the treaty of peace would not be signed until 1783.

After Washington resigned his commission in 1783 (a remarkable event in itself, since most observers expected him to become another Oliver Cromwell), he maintained a high public profile during the next several years but did not seek major positions until 1787, when he became a delegate to the Constitutional Convention and presiding officer of that body. Although his position precluded his taking an active part in the deliberations, he played a significant behind-the-scenes role in the convention and, by lending his name to the final document, helped to ensure its eventual ratification.

Washington and other military officers riding on horseback in a victory parade in New York City. (Library of Congress)

> "*America is open to receive not only the Opulent and respectable Stranger, but the oppressed and persecuted of all Nations And Religions; whom we shall wellcome to a participation of all our rights and previleges.*"

During the convention and the ratification process, it was assumed that Washington would become the first chief executive of the new government. Elected president in 1789, he established precedents for the new office that are still followed. Unlike modern presidents, who receive the privileges and prestige of the office, Washington lent his public reputation to the presidency and thereby enhanced its repute.

His government faced difficult tasks in the fields of administrative organization, foreign relations, and economic policy. Influencing each of these areas would be both the clash of personalities and the clash of political interests. Washington sought to resolve the issues without involving himself in the controversy. For the most part, except in the area of foreign policy, he was successful.

One of the most critical areas was the creation of an independent executive system, which was not fully developed in the Constitution. Here Washington prevailed over those desiring to use the Senate as sort of a privy council under the "advise and consent" clause, and those, such as Alexander Hamilton, desiring a parliamentary cabinet system with the major executive officers responsible to the Congress. Among Washington's other achievements were the creation of federal administrative agencies separate from those of the states; the introduction of orderly and stable relationships between officials based on law, instructions, and precedents; the maintenance of high standards of integrity, honesty, and competence; the recognition of claims of locality upon political appointments (often called "senatorial courtesy"); and the dominance of federal authority over individuals, demonstrated decisively in the suppression of the Whiskey Rebellion of 1794. Some of Washington's administrative policies, such as the use of the veto only in relation to constitutional questions, did not long survive his presidency. In the same vein, his use of the cabinet as a consultative body had a short life.

Other developments during his tenure can be attributed less to Washington's personal efforts than to the circumstances of the time or to the role of others. The creation of the judicial system was largely the responsibility of Roger Sherman, the Bill of Rights that of James Madison. The latter also formulated the first national revenue system. Hamilton created a financial system that funded government debts, instituted a national central bank, and established a national mint and stable currency. Washington either actively endorsed or did not oppose (in itself an act of endorsement) these efforts.

In military affairs, Washington often used his secretary of war as a cipher and conduit in a field where he had considerable expertise. His greatest disappointment in this field was Congress's rejection of his proposals for a national military system; instead, it passed the Militia Act of 1792, which left the nation without any effective defense posture.

In foreign affairs he closely worked with Thomas Jefferson in his first administration and followed the often misguided instincts of Hamilton in the second. Jay's Treaty of 1794 was the most divisive event of his tenure and did far more to encourage partisan politics than did any other policy matter. Despite the political consequences of Washington's diplomacy, he is generally given appreciative accolades for his maintenance of neutrality in the Anglo-French struggle that drew most of the Western world into its vortex.

Washington undoubtedly believed that the greatest weakness of his administration was the development of partisan politics. Both the president's supporters and his opponents favored a consensual political environment that saw partisan activities as divisive of national solidarity and indicative of corruption and personal ambition. The main intent of Washington's farewell address was to warn against political parties.

His final legacy to the presidency was the decision not to run for reelection in 1796 and the consequent two-term tradition that continued until 1940. He established a precedent of turning the office over to a duly elected successor instead of waiting for either death or revolt to remove him from office. Washington did not believe that his presence in the office was indispensable, and he instinctively knew that the peaceful transfer of power to a duly elected successor constituted an important building block in erecting a stable nation.

His retirement from the presidency in 1797 did not remove him entirely from public service. When the Quasi War with France broke out in 1798 (and ended in 1800), President John Adams called Washington back to command the army with the rank of lieutenant general. In this capacity he normally remained at Mount Vernon and delegated much of the running of the army to Major General Hamilton. Washington died after a short illness in late 1799.

Significance

No American figure has for so long dominated the national scene as has George Washington. For nearly twenty-five years, Washington remained the symbol of American nationhood, commanding its armies in a war for national independence, presiding over the convention that drafted its fundamental political charter, and transforming that charter's vague articles into political reality as the first chief magistrate of the republic.

As both general and president, he shaped the American military tradition with its subordination to civilian authority. As president, he established the contours of the American federal system and, even though he opposed its development, the party system. A far better statesman than general, still, he is probably better remembered for his military than for his political contributions to American history.

David Curtis Skaggs

Further Reading

Alden, John R. *George Washington: A Biography*. Baton Rouge: Louisiana State UP, 1984. Print.

Allen, William B. "The Moral Foundations of Political Choices: George Washington, Foreign Policy, and National Character." *Rev. of Faith & Intl. Affairs* 9.4 (2011): 3–12. Print.

Burns, James MacGregor, and Susan Dunn. *George Washington*. New York: Times, 2004. Print.

Countryman, Edward. "Getting to Know George Washington." *Southwest Rev.* 94.2 (2009): 132–46. Print.

DeConde, Alexander. *Entangling Alliance: Politics and Diplomacy Under George Washington*. Durham: Duke UP, 1958. Print.

Ellis, Joseph J. *His Excellency: George Washington*. New York: Knopf, 2004. Print.

Flexner, James Thomas. *George Washington*. 4 vols. Boston: Little, 1965–72. Print.

Freeman, Douglas Southall. *George Washington*. 7 vols. New York: Scribner's, 1948–57. Print.

Hofstadter, Richard. *The Idea of a Party System: The Rise of Legitimate Opposition in the United States*. Berkeley: U of California P, 1969. Print.

Kammen, Michael. *A Season of Youth: The American Revolution in Historical Imagination*. New York: Oxford UP, 1978. Print.

Langston, Thomas S., and Michael G. Sherman. *George Washington*. Washington, DC: CQ P, 2003. Print.

Larson, Edward J. *The Return of George Washington: 1783–1789*. New York: Morrow, 2014. Print.

McCullough, David. *1776*. New York: Simon, 2005. Print.

Washington, Austin. The Education of George Washington: How a Forgotten Book Shaped the Character of a Hero. Washington, DC: Regnery, 2014. Print.

Washington, George. *This Glorious Struggle: George Washington's Revolutionary War Letters*. Ed. Edward G. Lengel. Charlottesville: U of Virginia P, 2010. Print.

Weems, Mason Locke. *The Life of Washington*. Ed. Marcus Cunliffe. Cambridge: Harvard UP, 1962. Print.

Weigley, Russell F. *The American Way of War*. New York: Macmillan, 1973. Print.

Wills, Garry. *Cincinnatus: George Washington and the Enlightenment*. Garden City: Doubleday, 1984. Print.

Religion

The Pew Research Center's Religious Landscape Study (2014–2015) was one of the most thorough demographic studies of religion ever conducted in America. It was based on a survey of more than 35,000 Americans in all fifty states. According to the survey, an overview of religious affiliation in America looks like this:

Christian	70.6%
Jewish	1.9%
Muslim	0.9%
Buddhist	0.7%
Hindu	0.7%
Unaffiliated	22.8%

More than seventy percent of Americans identified as Christian in the survey. The breakdown by Christian denomination was as follows: 25% of Americans identified as Evangelical Protestant, 15% as Mainline Protestant, and 20% as Catholic. Historically Black Protestants accounted for about 7%. Mormons were 1.6%. Eastern Orthodox Christians, Jehovah's Witnesses, and other groups each made up less than one percent of all those surveyed.

Reports for several years now have indicated that the religiously unaffiliated, a group sometimes called the "nones," is the fastest growing religious group in America. The majority of those called unaffiliated identified as "nothing in particular" (16%) or as agnostic (4%). But the rise of the "nones" doesn't appear to represent a disavowal of religion per se. Only three percent of Americans identified at atheists, according to Pew, and that number has remained relatively stable for decades.

It's clear that religion remains important to the vast majority of Americans. This is no surprise in a nation that began, according to an influential historical narrative, with the Pilgrims at Plymouth Plantation, a colony founded as an experiment in religious freedom in 1620. And the core principle of religious liberty is enshrined in the First Amendment: "Congress shall make no law respecting an establishment of religion, or prohibiting the free exercise thereof." With these sixteen words, the framers of the Constitution gave affirmation to the principle that has made today's religious pluralism possible.

Interfaith Chapel at the University of Rochester in Western New York. (Wikimedia Commons)

Sister Thea Bowman

Religious leader, educator, and singer

Born: December 29, 1937; Yazoo City, Mississippi
Died: March 30, 1990; Canton, Mississippi
Area of Achievement: Music: spirituals, religion and theology, social issues

A teacher, scholar, and evangelist, Bowman became known for her spoken and sung presentations to Catholic audiences. Her spirituality advocated intercultural understanding, inclusiveness, and black empowerment. Even while facing incurable cancer, she taught by example to live as fully as possible.

Early Life

Eagerly awaited after many childless years of marriage, Bertha Elizabeth Bowman, the great-granddaughter of slaves, was born to Mary Esther Coleman, a teacher, and Theon Bowman, a physician. Raised in segregated Canton, Mississippi, Bowman experienced a vibrant black community and culture alongside discrimination. Vivacious and inquisitive, at the age of nine Bowman decided to convert to Catholicism. Having sampled Christian denominations, she found inspiration in the good works of Catholic sisters, brothers, and priests at Holy Child Jesus Mission.

Five years at a Jim Crow public school failed to help Bowman reach grade-level reading standards. Her parents decided to transfer her to Holy Child Jesus School, where the instruction of the Franciscan Sisters of Perpetual Adoration (FSPA) helped her to excel in academics. The sisters' pedagogy encouraged advanced students to help the less advanced, a lesson in community building that shaped her educational philosophy and spirituality. At age fifteen, Bowman convinced her reluctant parents that she wished to become a Franciscan sister, thus necessitating her move to Saint Rose High School in La Crosse, Wisconsin, where the order's motherhouse was located. The sole African American aspirant, she experienced both acceptance and racism in the Midwest. Tuberculosis slowed Bowman, but she flourished as a Franciscan and received the name Thea. Returning to Canton to teach, during summers she completed her education, first at Viterbo College and then at the Catholic University of America, where in 1972 she completed a Ph.D. in English literature in preparation for college teaching.

Life's Work

Bowman mastered the European and American literary canons and immersed herself in African American studies. By the early 1970's, she had built a reputation as a popular speaker and singer of spirituals and gospel hymns who encouraged audiences to embrace black spirituality and liturgy. The influence of Franciscan spirituality on her life's work became clear. Like Francis of Assisi, she preached with song; she modeled peace in a racially charged society; and she shared her appreciation of God's diverse creation with all people.

> "*I think the difference between me and some people is that I'm content to do my little bit. Sometimes people think they have to do big things in order to make change. But if each one would light a candle we'd have a tremendous light.*"

Upon her return to Viterbo in 1972, where she taught literature and headed the English Department, Bowman inspired students with her spirited and rigorous approach to learning. An accomplished soloist, she founded and directed the Hallelujah Singers, an integrated group of student performers.

In 1978, Bowman returned to Canton to assist her elderly parents and to embark on a new project for the diocese of Jackson, the development of a Catholic interracial and intercultural awareness ministry. Indefatigable, she traveled throughout the country proclaiming the value of African American spiritual traditions for all Catholics. To African Americans she spoke of the need to cherish their history and culture. To white Catholics she explained how African American religious practices could enhance their experience of God. In 1980, Bowman was one of the founders of the Institute of Black Catholic Studies at New Orleans's Xavier University, and she taught on its faculty. She also regularly presented papers at the annual William Faulkner conference at the University of Mississippi.

After receiving a diagnosis of advanced cancer in 1984, Bowman continued teaching, speaking, and singing. In 1987, television's *60 Minutes* introduced her to her largest and most diverse audience. Accolades including the Harriet Tubman Award of the National Black Sisters' Conference and the Laetare Medal of the University of Notre Dame were accompanied by honorary degrees from Georgetown University and others. A highlight of her influence came when she addressed the

American Catholic bishops at their annual conference in 1989. From her wheelchair, she sang and spoke of the gifts and the needs of African American Catholics. A few months later, in March of 1990, Bowman died in Canton, Mississippi.

Significance

During a time of social and religious upheaval, Bowman challenged the African American Catholic laity and clergy to embrace their culture, their strengths, and their Catholicism to transform themselves and their society. She used her talents as a teacher, speaker, and performer to advocate for an inclusive Catholic community, open to and strengthened by differences of race and gender. Her joy and faithfulness to her life's work, even while suffering, were a source of inspiration to countless people.

The Sister Thea Bowman Black Catholic Educational Foundation was established to raise scholarship money for African Americans. Bowman had conceived of the foundation as early as 1984. By 2015, the foundation had put more than 150 African American students through college.

Bowman was considered for canonized sainthood, and has been designated a Servant of God. At the United States Conference of Catholic Bishops' 2018 Fall General Assembly, the Committee on Canonical Affairs and Church Governance indicated unanimous support for the advancement of Bowman's canonization cause on the diocesan level.

Anne Klejment

Further Reading

Cepress, Celestine, ed. *Sister Thea Bowman, Shooting Star: Selected Writings and Speeches*. Winona, Minn.: St. Mary's Press, 1993. Autobiographical notes with Bowman's thoughts on African American religious culture, diversity, and reflections on life while facing death.

Koontz, Christian, ed. *Thea Bowman: Handing on Her Legacy*. Kansas City, Mo.: Sheed & Ward, 1991. Two works of Bowman's accompany appreciations of her life.

Nutt, Maurice J., comp. and ed. *Thea Bowman: In My Own Words*. Ligouri, Mo.: Ligouri Publications, 2009. Meditations from Bowman's talks and writings.

Smith, Charlene, and John Feister. *Thea's Song: The Life of Thea Bowman* Maryknoll, N.Y.: Orbis Books, 2009. A revealing authorized biography based on archival, oral, and other sources documenting Bowman's activities.

Mary Baker Eddy

Religious leader

Born: July 16, 1821; Bow, New Hampshire
Died: December 3, 1910; Newton, Massachusetts
Area of achievement: Religion and theology

A deeply religious thinker, Mary Baker Eddy established the Church of Christ, Scientist—the first church movement to be founded in the United States by a woman.

Early Life

The youngest of six children, Mary Morse Baker was born on her parents' New Hampshire farm. Her father, Mark Baker, was a respected farmer whose deep interest in theology prompted him to engage in serious religious debates with his neighbors. Mary's mother, Abigail Ambrose Baker, had grown up as the daughter of a prominent deacon of the Congregational church in nearby Pembroke and was known for her tender solicitude toward her family and neighbors. Both parents were devout members of the Congregational church; Mary was nurtured in their Calvinist faith and joined the church herself at the age of twelve.

As a young girl, Mary began her formal education in 1826. An intelligent, highly sensitive child, Mary suffered from ill health that frequently kept her at home. She became a diligent reader and an avid writer of poetry. Mary received individual instruction from her second brother, Albert, who served as a schoolmaster at Mary's school when he was twenty. Her brother's instruction provided Mary with an education well in advance of that commonly available to young women of the period, and she was introduced to the rudiments of Greek, Latin, and Hebrew as well as contemporary works of literature and philosophy.

In December of 1843, Mary Baker was married to Major George Washington Glover, a successful builder with business interests in the Carolinas. The newlyweds eventually settled in Wilmington, North Carolina. By June of 1844, George Glover's investments in building supplies for a project in Haiti were lost, and he was stricken with yellow fever. He died on June 27, forcing his pregnant and impoverished widow to return to her parents' home. Despite her dangerously poor health, Mary gave birth in September to a healthy son, whom she named George in honor of his late father.

Mary Baker Eddy (Wikimedia Commons)

When Abigail Baker died in 1849, her daughter's grief and precarious health made further care for the boisterous young George Glover even more difficult. Mark Baker's second marriage less than one year later forced Mary and her son to leave the Baker house. Mary went to stay with her sister Abigail Tilton, but George Glover was placed in the care of Mary's former nurse. Mary was devastated by her separation from her son, but her family insisted that reuniting the two would further strain Mary's tenuous health.

In 1853, Mary was married to Daniel Patterson, a dentist who promised to provide a home for her and her son. That promise was never fulfilled, however, and Patterson's failings as a husband became increasingly evident. Mary's son moved with his foster parents to the West; they later told him that his mother had died. Mary's new husband was often absent in the course of his itinerant practice, and the couple found lodgings in various communities in New Hampshire. In the spring of 1862, while on commission to deliver state funds to Union sympathizers in the South, Patterson was taken prisoner by Confederate forces.

Barely able to care for herself, Mary sought relief from her persistent ill health at an institute in New Hampshire that promoted hydropathy, or the water cure. Finding little improvement during her visit, she traveled to Portland, Maine, to visit Phineas P. Quimby, a clockmaker who had developed a reputation as a magnetic healer and hypnotist. After her first treatment at his office, Mary experienced a marked improvement in her health. In her enthusiasm to learn more about the methods Quimby used, she sought to reconcile Quimby's ideas with the spiritually based biblical healings with which she was so familiar.

Reunited with her husband in December of 1862 after his escape from prison, Mary returned to New Hampshire, where she experienced relapses of ill health. She sought relief by visiting Quimby at various times but could not discover a permanent cure for her illnesses. After Quimby's death in early January of 1866, Mary was seriously injured when she fell on icy pavement in Lynn, Massachusetts, on February 1.

After being taken to a nearby house, Mary eventually regained consciousness sufficiently to persuade her doctor and friends to move her to her lodgings in nearby Swampscott, where she was given little hope of recovery from the injuries to her head and spine. Visited by a clergyman on the Sunday after her accident, she asked to be left alone with her Bible. Turning to the ninth chapter of Matthew, she read the account of Jesus' healing of the man sick of the palsy (paralysis). Upon reading the story, she felt a profound change come over her and found that she was fully recovered from her injuries. Rising from her bed to dress and then greet the friends who waited outside her door, Mary astonished them with the rapidity and completeness of her healing, one that she credited to the power of God alone.

> "*True prayer is not asking God for love; it is learning to love, and to include all mankind in one affection. Prayer is the utilization of the love wherewith He loves us.*"

LIFE'S WORK

During the decade from 1866 to 1876, Mary Patterson's outward life seemed little improved, yet her conviction that she could discover the source of her healing experience inspired her to continue her study of the Bible. Her husband deserted her soon after her healing; they were divorced in 1873, and she resumed using the surname Glover.

Although her financial situation was precarious and she was still separated from her son, Mary realized that, at the age of forty-five, she was healthier than she had ever been in her entire life. For three years after her recovery, she dedicated herself solely to searching the Bible for answers to her questions regarding spiritual healing, withdrawing from social pursuits and her temperance movement activities in order to record the revelations she was gaining through her studies. She lived frugally in a series of boardinghouses, began sharing her notes and interpretations of Bible passages with individuals who seemed receptive to her new ideas, and occasionally offered instruction in her healing methods in exchange for the cost of her room and board. A group of committed students eventually began to gather around her. In October of 1875, she managed to publish the first edition of her work, entitled *Science and Health*, with the financial assistance of some of her students.

It was in March of 1876 that Asa Gilbert Eddy, a native of Vermont who was ten years her junior and worked in Massachusetts as a salesperson for the Singer Sewing Machine Company, became one of Mary's students. Asa Eddy, better known as Gilbert, became a successful healer. At a time when many of her most talented students were challenging her authority and attempting to undermine her teachings, Mary came to rely on Gilbert Eddy's sound judgment and his steady support of her leadership. The two were married on January 1, 1877.

Around this time, Mary Baker Eddy began revising *Science and Health*, adding five new chapters. This two-volume second edition was so rife with typographical errors that only the second volume was circulated. During this time, Eddy began to lecture weekly at the Baptist Tabernacle in Boston. The success of her public sermons led her to make a motion at a meeting of her students in 1879 that they organize a church; it was called the Church of Christ, Scientist. In Eddy's own words, the purpose of this church was "to commemorate the word and works of our Master, which should reinstate primitive Christianity and its lost element of healing."

The new church was incorporated under a state charter, and Eddy was designated its president and appointed its first pastor. By the winter of 1879, Eddy and her husband

First Church of Christ, Scientist in Boston, Massachusetts. (Wikimedia Commons)

had moved to rooms in Boston to be nearer to the growing church. She continued to teach new adult students about Christian Science, and the church established a Sunday school for the instruction of children in 1880. That same year, Eddy published the first of her many pamphlets: a sermon entitled Christian Healing. In an effort to give a more solid legal foundation to her classes, Eddy applied for a state charter in order to incorporate the Massachusetts Metaphysical College, a school dedicated to furthering the spread of her healing method by ensuring that students received unadulterated instruction directly from her.

Earlier, Mary Baker Eddy had begun revising and expanding *Science and Health* once again. The third edition of *Science and Health,* which appeared in 1881, was the first accurate edition of her writings to incorporate part of the treatise she used to instruct students in her classes. This publishing enterprise brought Eddy into contact with one of the leading printers of her day: John Wilson of the University Press in Cambridge, Massachusetts. Prospects for selling all one thousand copies of the third edition were not promising, but Wilson was convinced that Eddy would be able to finance the printing of her book through its sales. By 1882, the book had gone back to print for two additional editions of one thousand copies each.

Other publishing activities began. In April of 1883, Eddy published the first issue of *The Journal of Christian Science*. Originally a bimonthly periodical with articles designed to explore issues of interest to both newcomers and longtime students of Eddy's religion, the *Journal* was expanded to become a monthly publication and was one of the first authorized organs of the Christian Science church. A sixth edition of *Science and Health* appeared in 1883; it was the first to contain Eddy's "Key to the Scriptures," a section initially consisting of a glossary with her metaphysical interpretations of biblical terms and concepts. By 1885, nine additional printings were made, bringing the total number of copies in circulation during the book's first ten years to 15,000.

The years following the publication of the sixth edition of *Science and Health* were prosperous ones, with many new students working to spread Christian Science and its healing practice throughout the United States. Nevertheless, several events occurred in the period from 1889 to 1892 that radically altered the structure and direction of the Christian Science church. Schisms among her students and the burdens resulting from those who increasingly relied on her personal leadership in all matters led Eddy to close her college at the height of its popularity and resign her post as pastor of the Boston church. Services continued to be conducted in Christian Science churches, but students voted to adjourn the activities of the National Christian Scientist Association for three years beginning in 1890. Withdrawing to a new home in Concord, New Hampshire, Eddy commenced work on a major revision of *Science and Health* to be published as the fiftieth edition in 1891.

September 23, 1892, marked the establishment of Eddy's newly reorganized church: the First Church of Christ, Scientist, in Boston, Massachusetts, also known as The Mother Church. She consulted with attorneys familiar with Massachusetts statutes in order to find a legal means to incorporate her church that would place its corporate government on a solid basis without encouraging undue attachment to her personal authority. The new charter provided a powerful centralized structure in the form of a five-member board of directors responsible for management of the church's affairs; it also fostered the practice of democratic self-government already established in the branch churches outside of Boston that were affiliated with the growing church movement. All members of these branches were invited to apply for concurrent membership in The Mother Church. Eddy was henceforth designated as the Discoverer and Founder of Christian Science. To her mind, this title expressed the scientific aspect of her work—emphasizing her role in formulating and articulating its religious teachings in much the same way that scientific laws and principles are formulated and articulated, but not created, by those who discover them.

In October of 1893, the building of the new church edifice was begun in Boston's Back Bay area, with the cornerstone of the church laid in May of 1894 and the first service held on December 30, 1894. Eddy took the unusual step of ordaining the Bible and *Science and Health*, rather than human ministers, as pastors of the church. When she published the *Manual of The Mother Church* in 1895, setting forth the rules by which the church was to be governed, she made provisions in its bylaws for the election of lay readers who would read texts from the Bible and from *Science and Health* relating to twenty-six topics she set forth.

The texts were selected by a special committee; the resulting lesson sermons were studied daily by individual members and were read Sundays at Christian Science church services throughout the world. These changes were instituted by Eddy in order to avoid the adulteration of her teachings through personal preaching. In this way, she believed that the healing message contained in the Bible and in her book would speak directly to all who attended her church without the injection of personal opinion or conflicting interpretations. In 1898, Eddy established a board of education to provide for the formal instruction of students in Christian Science by those who were approved to serve as teachers. She also established a Board of Lectureship to which practitioners (ordained healers within the church) and teachers of Christian Science were appointed. These lecturers were responsible for preparing and delivering public lectures on Christian Science in order to introduce and clarify its teachings to those unfamiliar with the religion. The Christian Science Publishing Society was created through a deed of trust and was charged with the responsibility for publishing and distributing *Science and Health* and Eddy's other books as well as *The Christian Science Journal* and the newly founded periodical, *The Christian Science Week*ly (renamed *The Christian Science Sentinel* in 1899). In 1902, Eddy completed work on her final major revision of *Science and Health*; it was the 226th edition of the book known as the Christian Science textbook.

Although she enjoyed the relative peace and seclusion of her New Hampshire estate, known as Pleasant View, Eddy faced bitter personal attacks in the popular press during the early twentieth century that threatened to undermine her church. These articles reflected the sensational "yellow journalism" of the period. Few pieces were more damaging than those published by Joseph Pulitzer, whose *New York World* newspaper claimed that Eddy was near death from cancer and that her alleged fortune of $15 million was being wrested from her control. Refusing to meet with Pulitzer's reporters, Eddy granted audience to representatives of several other leading newspapers and press associations. After answering three brief questions concerning her health, Eddy gave evidence of her well-being by departing to take her daily carriage ride.

Despite Eddy's efforts to disprove the rumors concerning her health, her son George was approached by the publishers of the *New York World* and was encouraged, on the basis of the paper's erroneous accounts of his mother's welfare, to begin legal proceedings to determine Eddy's mental competence and ability to conduct business affairs connected with her church. Although funded by Pulitzer's newspaper fortune, this lawsuit ultimately collapsed after a panel appointed to determine Eddy's competence held a one-hour interview and established that she was in full possession of her mental faculties.

Refusing to back down in the face of these personal attacks, Eddy was prompted to establish a trust for her

---

Eddy's Advice To Her Followers

This extract is from Mary Baker Eddy's introduction to her frequently reprinted pamphlet No and Yes, in which she offers advice and encouragement to her followers on how to practice Christian Science beliefs properly. This passage is broadly representative of Eddy's writing style.

To kindle in all minds a common sentiment of regard for the spiritual idea emanating from the infinite, is a most needful work; but this must be done gradually, for Truth is as "the still, small voice," which comes to our recognition only as our natures are changed by its silent influence.

Small streams are noisy and rush precipitately; and babbling brooks fill the rivers till they rise in floods, demolishing bridges and overwhelming cities. So men, when thrilled by a new idea, are sometimes impatient; and, when public sentiment is aroused, are liable to be borne on by the current of feeling. They should then turn temporarily from the tumult, for the silent cultivation of the true idea and the quiet practice of its virtues. When the noise and stir of contending sentiments cease, and the flames die away on the mount of revelation, we can read more clearly the tablets of Truth.

The theology and medicine of Jesus were one,—in the divine oneness of the trinity, Life, Truth, and Love, which healed the sick and cleansed the sinful. This trinity in unity, correcting the individual thought, is the only Mindhealing I vindicate; and on its standard have emblazoned that crystallized expression, CHRISTIAN SCIENCE.

A spurious and hydra-headed mind-healing is naturally glared at by the pulpit, ostracized by the medical faculty, and scorned by people of common sense. To aver that disease is normal, a God-bestowed and stubborn reality, but that you can heal it, leaves you to work against that which is natural and a law of being. It is scientific to rob disease of all reality; and to accomplish this, you cannot begin by admitting its reality. Our Master taught his students to deny self, sense, and take up the cross. Mental healers who admit that disease is real should be made to test the feasibility of what they say by healing one case audibly, through such an admission,—if this is possible. I have healed more disease by the spoken than the unspoken word.

The honest student of Christian Science is modest in his claims and conscientious in duty, waiting and working to mature what he has been taught. Institutes furnished with such teachers are becoming beacon-lights along the shores of erudition; and many who are not teachers have large practices and some marked success in healing the most defiant forms of disease.

Dishonesty destroys one's ability to heal mentally. Conceit cannot avert the effects of deceit. Taking advantage of the present ignorance in relation to Christian Science Mind-healing, many are flooding our land with conflicting theories and practice. We should not spread abroad patchwork ideas that in some vital points lack Science....

Source: Mary Baker Eddy, *No and Yes* (Boston, 1919).

property in order to preserve its orderly transfer to the church after her death. More important, Eddy was impelled to launch an enormous new undertaking: She directed the Trustees of the Publishing Society to establish a daily newspaper to be known as *The Christian Science Monitor*, which began publication in 1908. By bringing national and international events into clearer focus for its readers, *The Christian Science Monitor* would fulfill Eddy's vision of its purpose: to combat the apathy, indifference, and despair that were common responses to world affairs through its spiritually enlightened, problem-solving journalism. After witnessing the fruition of her long-cherished hopes, Eddy died quietly in her sleep near the end of 1910.

SIGNIFICANCE

Regardless of one's perspective on the validity of her religious beliefs, Mary Baker Eddy clearly led a remarkable life—one full of extraordinary success despite the prejudices that confronted her as a woman attempting to establish a spiritually minded religious movement during an age of rampant materialism. Novelist and humorist Mark Twain, who was one of Eddy's most outspoken critics, once remarked that she was "probably the most daring and masterful woman who has appeared on earth for centuries."

A pragmatic and capable administrator who inspired her followers by her example of single-minded dedication, Eddy was equally comfortable in her role as a religious thinker—one who refused to compromise her conscience "to suit the general drift of thought" and was convinced of the importance of maintaining the intellectual and spiritual purity of her writings. Her church remains an active presence in the United States and throughout the world, and her book *Science and Health* was recognized by the Women's National Book Association in 1992 as one of seventy-five important works by "women whose words have changed the world."

Wendy Sacket

FURTHER READING

Eddy, Mary Baker. *Mary Baker Eddy: Speaking for Herself.* Boston: Writings of Mary Baker Eddy, 2002. Includes two of Eddy's books: her memoir, Retrospection and Introspection, first published in 1891, and Footprints Fadeless, a defense of one of her critics, written in 1901-1902, and published here for the first time. Jana K. Reiss, religion editor for Publishers Weekly, provides an introduction, analyzing Eddy's writings and placing Eddy's life and work in the context of late nineteenth century American religion and society.

Gill, Gillian. *Mary Baker Eddy*. Reading, Mass.: Perseus Books, 1998. Feminist biography. Gill portrays Eddy as a powerful woman who broke free from conventional gender roles to introduce radical new ideas. While acknowledging Eddy's faults, Gill is generally sympathetic, emphasizing her subject's gifts as a religious leader, administrator, and promoter of Christian Science.

Gottschalk, Stephen. *The Emergence of Christian Science in American Religious Life.* Berkeley: University of California Press, 1973. Although its examination of Christian Science from the perspective of intellectual history may make it less easily accessible to general readers, this work sets forth the distinctive contributions Christian Science has made to American theology and culture.

Orcutt, William Dana. *Mary Baker Eddy and Her Books.* Boston: Christian Science Publishing Society, 1950. Written by a distinguished bookmaker who worked closely with Eddy from 1897 to 1910 and helped design the oversize subscription edition of Science and Health that was released in 1941, this memoir provides an intriguing window on Eddy's career as an author.

Peel, Robert. *Mary Baker Eddy: The Years of Discovery.* New York: Holt, Rinehart and Winston, 1966.

---. *Mary Baker Eddy: The Years of Trial.* New York: Holt, Rinehart and Winston, 1971.

---. *Mary Baker Eddy: The Years of Authority.* New York: Holt, Rinehart and Winston, 1977. Written by a Harvard-educated scholar who had unprecedented access to church archival materials, this monumental three-volume biography remains the definitive work on Eddy's life. Although Peel was himself a Christian Scientist, his work gives evidence of his conscientious effort to provide "a straightforward, factual account free from either apologetics or polemics."

Satter, Beryl. *Each Mind a Kingdom: American Women, Sexual Purity, and the New Thought Movement, 1875-1920.* Berkeley: University of California Press, 1999. Focusing on the New Thought Movement in general, and Eddy's Christian Science in particular, Satter describes American women's intellectual and psychological relationships to progressive social movements and self-improvement cults during the late nineteenth and early twentieth centuries. She concludes that participation in these movements gave disenfranchised middle-class white women a way to escape their homes and refashion society and gender roles.

Thomas, Robert David. *"With Bleeding Footsteps": Mary Baker Eddy's Path to Religious Leadership.* New York: Alfred A. Knopf, 1994. Trained in the theories of psychoanalysis, Thomas brings this psychological perspective to bear on his study of Eddy's character and behavior. Despite his serious, scholarly approach, Thomas fails to provide a complete assessment of Eddy's significance as a religious leader and seems to fall short of bringing his subject fully alive. Nevertheless, this biography is useful as one of the few fair-minded studies of Eddy to have appeared since Peel's three-volume work, cited above.

Barbara Harris

Religious leader

Born: June 12, 1930; Philadelphia, Pennsylvania
Area of Achievement: Religion

A lifelong advocate for the full inclusion of women and people of color in church life and in society, Harris broke through nearly two millennia of religious tradition when she was consecrated a bishop of the Episcopal Church.

Early Life

Barbara Harris was born in 1930 to Walter Harris and Beatrice Price Harris, lifelong members of the Episcopal Church, in the Philadelphia suburb of Germantown. She was the middle of three children in the family. As a child of the Great Depression, she grew up in a home that emphasized the importance of both work and sharing. Her father supported the family through odd jobs and repair work. He also carefully tended the fruit trees growing in the family's yard. During World War II he worked in a steel mill. Harris's great-grandmother, who lived with the family when Harris was small, had been a slave, and she told many stories about the hardships of life under slavery. The children's grandmother cleaned the local school, and sometimes she took young Harris along to help her.

Harris's mother, Beatrice, was an active lay member of St. Barnabas Church, where the family worshiped. St. Barnabas was an all-black Episcopal parish. Located in the same city where Absalom Jones, the first African American to be ordained a priest, had founded his church, St. Barnabas carried on a proud tradition. The church was strongly oriented toward social justice and service, although it also preached values of the Christian gospel in living one's daily life.

As a child and teenager Harris stayed active in church life. She organized a young adults group, which grew to more than fifty members, and regularly played the piano for church-school programs. She enjoyed her music lessons, practiced on an old Steinway piano, so much that she thought briefly of making a career of music.

However, Harris's other interests were stronger. While a student at Philadelphia High School for Girls, she got an reporting assignment with the *Pittsburgh Courier*, writing a weekly column about school life. After she graduated in 1948, she enrolled at the Charles Morris Price School of Journalism, aiming for a career with the press.

Life's Work

With the return of millions of former service members to colleges and their jobs after World War II and with the swing back to "normality" in American society, it was not the optimum time for a talented young black woman to start a journalistic career. Harris needed a job, and when she heard of an opening for a nurse's aide at a local hospital, she applied and was accepted. Despite her resolve to work hard and do well at anything she tried, she hated the job. When she learned of an opening for a receptionist at a children's hospital, she applied for the job and was hired.

Harris's work at the children's hospital led to a fortunate chance at a bigger job, when the father of one of her friends from high school offered her a job in his firm, Joseph V. Baker Associates. This was a black-owned public relations firm that promoted white-owned products and companies within black communities. The plan was for Harris to learn every aspect of the company's work, from the ground up. She did this so well that within ten years she became the company's president. In all, she was employed at Baker Associates for nineteen years, from 1949 to 1968. During this time she was married briefly, a marriage that ended in divorce. In 1968 she went to work for the Sun Oil Company, where she served as head of the community relations department.

Throughout this time period she continued to be active as an Episcopal laywoman. One of her major projects was the St. Dismas Society, which involved visiting prisons, leading services there, and befriending prisoners. In 1968 she transferred her membership from her home church of St. Barnabas to the Church of the Advocate in North Philadelphia. The latter church and its rector, Paul Washington, were in the vanguard of support for the burgeoning Civil Rights movement, the campaign to empower the poor, and, soon, the push for equality for women within the Episcopal Church.

The cause for women's equality within the Episcopal Church was to soon have its first victory within the church structure, and it was at Harris's Church of the Advocate that this first victory took place. Three retired bishops ordained eleven women to the priesthood there in 1974. The ordination was technically valid at the time but irregular, because the church's general convention had voted against allowing women to be priests in both 1970 and 1973. Nevertheless, a strong current was gathering in favor of women's ordination. The ceremony at Philadelphia was carefully planned, with wide press coverage. Harris, who fully supported women's ordination by this time, volunteered to carry the cross in the opening procession.

When the 1976 general convention authorized women's ordination, Harris began to wonder if the priesthood might be her calling, too. With the diocese of Philadelphia's approval, she entered an alternate course of study leading to the diaconate and then to the priesthood, taking courses at Villanova University and Hobart and William Smith Colleges.

> "We have to remain vigilant and keep revisiting situations to make sure that we are still paying attention to what needs to be done."

After ordination as a deacon in 1979 and as a priest in 1980, Harris served in parish ministries on an interim basis. She was priest-in-charge at Norristown's St. Augustine of Hippo Church from 1980 to 1984. However, her background in administration and social advocacy soon won her an appointment as executive director of the Episcopal Church Publishing Company and editor of *The Witness*, a progressive periodical focused on the need to confront social issues. Her hard-hitting articles and editorials there drew wide attention within the Episcopal Church, some of it admiring and some quite the opposite.

There were so many admirers of Harris by this time that when the diocese of Massachusetts needed a new suffragan (assistant) bishop, her name was placed in nomination. In the American Episcopal Church, bishops are chosen first by vote of clergy and lay representatives from the diocese and are then confirmed by approval at the triennial general convention. Usually the election process takes several ballots, as it did in Harris's case; she was elected on the sixth ballot. Although her election was normal in that sense, the issues it raised were not.

The Anglican Communion, like the Roman Catholic and Orthodox branches of Christianity, regards bishops as possessing special authority. They are believed to constitute an unbroken line to Jesus Christ, who charged Simon, Peter, and his other disciples with leadership of his church. Before the selection of Harris, all such bishops had been men. Coming only thirteen years after the church's acceptance of women priests, Harris's selection shocked the more conservative elements of the Episcopal Church once again. The greatest outrage was that she was a woman. There were also objections to her irregular preparation (not a seminary graduate), her race, and her marital status (divorced), but all these traits had several or many precedents within the Episcopal Church's recent history. Women priests and bishops have also been considered roadblocks to ecumenical outreach with the Catholic Church, although some Catholics see the existence of women priests as a hopeful sign that their church also can change.

Many Episcopalians expected that in her new role, Harris would serve as the leader of a movement for more radical social change. Although she continued to speak out, however, most of her work as a suffragan bishop was pastoral. She oversaw churches, sorted out parish disputes and problems, and performed standard duties such as confirming new members and ordaining clergy.

Almost fourteen years after her consecration as a bishop in 1989, she retired at the mandatory age of seventy-two. A slight, energetic woman with relatively good health and many friends, she worked for several years after retirement as an assisting bishop in the Washington, DC, diocese.

In 2010, Harris suffered a stroke in her home in Massachusetts. She appears to have made a full recovery and preached at an ecumenical worship service in the historic Tabernacle in Oak Bluffs, Massachusetts, on September 5, 2010. Her sermon was entitled "It Isn't Easy Being Green".

SIGNIFICANCE

Harris played a pivotal role in the changes that have turned the once-staid Episcopal Church into a body shaken by radical changes. Her removal of the gender barrier to the church's highest rank paved the way for other women bishops. In 2006 another barrier fell when

Katharine Jefferts Schori became the twenty-sixth presiding bishop of the Episcopal Church.

Harris's career has been both symbolic of and a spur to further change in the Episcopal Church; to a lesser extent her career has influenced other mainstream Christian churches as well. These changes mirror, and attempt to cope with, events in the larger, secular society and world. The changes are aimed at a more inclusive church, one where social justice goals are viewed as a natural outcome of the work that Jesus himself did. As Harris's story shows, these goals are controversial within the church, but the trend has been toward their realization.

Emily Alward

FURTHER READING

Bozzuti-Jones, Mark Francisco. *The Miter Fits Just Fine! A Story about the Right Reverend Barbara Clementine Harris*. Cambridge: Cowley, 2003. Print..

Evans, Sara M. *Tidal Wave: How Women Changed America at Century's End*. New York: Free, 2010. Print.

Harris, Barbara Clementine. *Parting Words: A Farewell Discourse*. Cambridge: Cowley, 2003. Print.

Nicholson, Aleathia Dolores. "Barbara Harris." In *Epic Lives: One Hundred Black Women Who Made a Difference*. Ed. Jessie Carney Smith. Detroit: Visible Ink, 1993. Print.

House of Deputies Special Study. *Shared Governance: The Polity of the Episcopal Church*. New York: Church, 2012. Print.

Palmer, Michael D., and Stanley M. Burgess. *The Wiley-Blackwell Companion to Religion and Social Justice*. Malden: Wiley, 2012. Print.

Turner, Renee D. "The First Woman Episcopal Bishop: Elevation of Christian Social Activist Barbara C. Harris Causes Religious Stir." *Ebony* May 1989: 40. Print.

M. HASNA MAZNAVI

American Muslim leader

Born: c. 1986; California
Area of Achievement: Religion; Social Reform

When M. Hasna Maznavi founded the Women's Mosque of America, building on the precedent of women's mosques in Islamic history, she forged a vision of Islamic religious renewal that united Islamic tradition with American values of equality and women's empowerment.

EARLY LIFE

While some details of M. Hasna Maznavi's early life are not available in the public record, we know that she was born around 1986 and that she was raised in southern California. There, with her family, she attended the Garden Grove mosque. Her sister was the president of the mosque's Muslim youth group, and Maznavi has said in interviews that in that mosque at that time, men and women prayed together in the same space. Later, as the Muslim community grew, influences from other Muslim countries and traditions led to the construction of a new mosque with architecture that separated male worshipers from female ones.

For Maznavi, segregation by gender in mosques is not by itself a problem; a problem arises when the spaces for women—and the women themselves—are made marginal in the mosque. In the new mosque that was built in Garden Grove, for example, there was a beautiful dome, and the main area for prayers was under the dome. But the area for women during prayers was up some stairs and in a balcony. During off-hours, Maznavi came to the mosque to sit and pray in the main space under the dome, but she was not allowed. Maznavi has also said that when she was a child she loved mosques—the spaces, the architecture, and the experiences that she had there—and that she entertained a dream of one day building a mosque.

As a teenager, Maznavi was active in the Muslim community in Los Angeles. In the period after the 9/11 attacks when many ordinary Muslims in America were threatened with death or subject to other forms of harassment and hate crimes, she volunteered in the civil rights department at the Council of American-Islamic Relations in Los Angeles (CAIR-LA). It was while working for CAIR that she decided to pursue a career in media. She attended the University of California at Berkeley, graduating with a bachelor's degree in communications. Then she went to the University of Southern California for a master's degree in film and television production.

LIFE'S WORK

After school, Maznavi found work in Los Angeles as a comedy writer. She also continued to practice her faith and to deepen her understanding of Islam. In the years prior to founding the Women's Mosque, Maznavi led an interfaith group, attended conferences and workshops, and attended *Jummah*, or Friday prayer, at a variety of mosques in the region. Friday is the traditional day of assembly for Muslims. But Maznavi felt that it was difficult to find a mosque where she felt entirely at home.

Muslims make up 1.1% of the United States population, and the largest group of American Muslims (about thirty-five percent of all Muslims in America) are African Americans. There are over 2,000 mosques in the United States. Because there are so many different Muslim traditions from different Muslim nations, and because Islam has had a long and complex history, it can be difficult to make generalizations about Islam. But scholars have pointed to the prevalence of women as both scholars and leaders in the early days of Islam and contrasted this with their diminished role in many mosques today. This is often attributed to the influence of Wahhabism, a strict reformist version of Islam that arose in the eighteenth century and that has spread its influence across much of the Muslim world.

Many Muslims today—like Maznavi—believe that it would be beneficial to the Muslim community at large to stimulate a revival of the role of women in the *Ummah*, or the community of Muslims. This was, in fact, the topic of a conference held at the University of California in Santa Barbara that Maznavi attended in 2012 called "The Reconstituting of Female Authority in Islam." She attributed the conference with changing her life. Inspired by the conference, Maznavi enrolled in Al-Rawiya College and studied Islamic history, including the history of the development of *Shari'a*, or Islamic law.

Reflecting on her disappointing experiences at local mosques, and inspired by what she had learned about the history of women in Islam, Maznavi decided to found a women's only mosque, similar in concept to a women's only college. Together with Sana Muttalib, she found space in an interfaith community center that was originally a synagogue. On January 30, 2015, the Women's Mosque held its first women's only Friday service, a historic first in the United States. Typically, Friday services are the same as the ritual prayers that are performed by Muslims at other times during the week, only with the presence of an imam who leads the prayer and delivers a sermon, called the *khutbah*. There are no "career" clergy people in Islam, and the imams are usually community members who are esteemed and asked to speak. The first sermon at the Women's Mosque was given by Edina Lekovic from the Muslim Public Affairs Council.

> "*This is a place where Muslim women can come and experience inspiration and then return with that to their communities.*"

It is important to understand that women's mosques, although not very common in most Muslim communities, are relatively common in some, and they were historically much more common than they are today. In China, among the millions of Hui Muslims who reside there, female imams and women's mosques have flourished for many centuries, far from the influence of Wahhabism. Mosques for women also exist, although to a lesser extent, in Syria, Egypt, India, Palestine, Yemen, and other countries. For this reason, Maznavi corrected the first media accounts—and there was a lot of media attention when the Women's Mosque opened—that presented the Women's Mosque as a modernizing intervention or as a subversive act. This understanding was not only provincial, she wrote in a Huffington Post article, it reinforced a sensationalized and fundamentally ignorant view of Muslim women (and Muslim men, too): "As tempting as it may be to believe that we Muslim women are a monolithically oppressed group of Jasmines waiting to be saved from big bad bearded Muslim men, this couldn't be further from the truth." She also emphasized that the wider Muslim community supported her effort, including numerous (male) leaders in Islam.

SIGNIFICANCE

The Women's Mosque sees itself as part of a revival of the historic role that women played in earlier eras in Islam. But this renewal of religious energy and ideas from within Islam has been inspired, too, by modern or Western ideals, such as democratic values and the women's movement. In the same vein, one of the questions on the mosque's FAQ asks whether the mosque is a conservative idea or a progressive one. The answer is carefully framed: it refuses the terms of the question and asserts inclusivity, and it affirms both "orthodoxy" and openness to "flexibility."

In this way, Hasna Maznavi and the Women's Mosque have charted a course that seeks to empower women and do it from within Islam, based on Islamic principles and precedent. Perhaps the greatest significance of the Women's Mosque, beyond the opportunities it affords women to study Islam and take on leadership roles in the community, has been to affirm the compatibility of these diverse trends, spanning the modern and the traditional, in order to tie together communities and emphasize connectedness.

D. Alan Dean

FURTHER READING

Street, Nick. "First All-Female Mosque Opens in Los Angeles." *Aljazeera*, Feb. 3, 2015. http://america.aljazeera.com/articles/2015/2/3/first-all-female-mosque-opens-in-los-angeles.html.

Elkhaoudi, Salma. "Women's Mosque of America: In the Founder's Own Words." *Muslimgirl.com*. http://muslimgirl.com/10157/womens-mosque-america-interview-m-hasna-maznavi/.

"FAQ." *The Women's Mosque of America* (website). http://womensmosque.com/faq/.

Maznavi, M. Hasna. "9 Things You Should Know about the Women's Mosque of America—and Muslim Women in General." *Huffington Post*, May 20, 2015. https://www.huffingtonpost.com/m-hasna-maznavi/9-things-you-should-know-about-the-womens_b_7339582.html.

Mohamed, Besheer. "New estimates show U.S. Muslim population continues to grow." *Pew Research Center*, Jan. 3, 2018. http://www.pewresearch.org/fact-tank/2018/01/03/new-estimates-show-u-s-muslim-population-continues-to-grow/.

Paludi, Michele A. and J. Harold Ellens. *Feminism and Religion: How Faiths View Women and Their Rights.* Santa Barbara: Praeger, 2016.

Sobh, Mariam. Muslim Women in Los Angeles Start a Mosque of Their Own." *Religion News Service*, Feb. 2, 2015. https://religionnews.com/2015/02/02/muslim-wom

Tatlow, Didi Kirsten. "A Model of Inclusion for Muslim Women." *New York Times*, Oct. 9, 2012. https://www.nytimes.com/2012/10/10/world/asia/10iht-letter10.html.

THOMAS MERTON

Trappist monk and writer

Born: January 31, 1915; Prades, France
Died: December 10, 1968; Samutprakarn, Thailand
Areas of Achievement: Religion and theology, literature, social reform

Merton is best known for his spiritual autobiography The Seven Storey Mountain, *in which he explores how one might become a spiritual person in a nonspiritual age. His later works continued the search for spirituality through his experiences as a monk, and though for a time he seemed to be renouncing the world, he became a sort of prophet seeking to reform it.*

EARLY LIFE

Thomas Merton (MURT-ehn) spent the early years of his life being shuttled between France, England, and the United States. His parents, artists Owen Merton and Ruth Jenkins Merton, were from New Zealand and the United States respectively, but had met and married in Europe and had settled in the small town of Prades in the French Pyrenees, where Thomas (actually registered at birth as Tom) was born.

The family did not stay long in Prades, however, leaving in 1916 to escape from World War I. They lived on Long Island, New York, with Ruth's parents. Five years later, when Thomas was only six, his mother died of cancer. After that, he lived variously with his father, his mother's parents, other relatives, and family friends. In 1925 his father took him to the south of France to live, where he spent two unhappy years at a French school. Young Merton was happier in England, where he and his father moved in 1928. He attended Oakham School, wrote for the school paper, and eventually became its editor.

In 1931 his father died of a brain tumor. After graduating from Oakham in 1933, Merton had a disastrous year at Clare College, Cambridge, where he spent most of his time partying; he also might have fathered an illegitimate child. In 1934 he withdrew from Cambridge, returned to New York, and enrolled at Columbia University.

Merton did well at Columbia, completing bachelor's and master's degrees and writing a thesis on the mystical poetry of William Blake. He continued to live a bohemian life but also began to become interested in religion,

Thomas Merton (Wikipedia)

especially Roman Catholicism, although he had been raised in the Anglican Church. He converted to Catholicism in 1938 and expressed an interest in becoming a priest or a monk. He also was interested in a writing career. He produced several novels that no one would publish but succeeded in publishing some poems and book reviews. He also took a position teaching English at St. Bonaventure College (now University) in New York.

Still seeking to become a monk, Merton applied to the Franciscans, but was turned down by them. He then went on a retreat at the Abbey of Our Lady of Gethsemani in rural Kentucky and knew immediately it was the place for him. He entered the monastery permanently on December 10, 1941.

Life's Work

Except for a few trips to conferences in his later years, Merton spent the rest of his life at the monastery or in Louisville, Kentucky, on brief outings. The monastery Merton chose was a strict one that belonged to the Cistercian Order of the Strict Observance, also known as the Trappists. He took vows of poverty, chastity, and obedience and found himself in an institution in which he and his fellow monks were expected to spend most of their time in communal prayers and manual labor while eating a meager diet and wearing simple robes. They also were to be silent most of the time and use sign language instead of speaking.

> "To say that I am made in the image of God is to say that Love is the reason for my existence, for God is love. Love is my true identity. Selflessness is my true self. Love is my true character. Love is my name."

Merton discusses his decision to subject himself to this strict discipline in his best-selling autobiography *The Seven Storey Mountain* (1948). His idea was to free himself from the dissipated, undisciplined life he had led before entering the monastery. His original view was that he had to reject the world entirely, but he slowly gave up this idea. In the last ten years of his life especially, he saw his mission as one of reaching out to humanity while still maintaining his distance from the world.

For a while Merton even thought that, in order to purify himself and devote himself to God, he would have to give up his writing, but writing was too strong a drive in

---

Kentucky's Silent Abbey

The embrace of it, the silence! I had entered into a solitude that was an impregnable fortress. And the silence that enfolded me, spoke to me, and spoke louder and more eloquently than any voice, and in the middle of that quiet, clean-smelling room, with the moon pouring its peacefulness in through the open window, with the warm night air, I realized truly whose house that was, O glorious Mother of God!

How did I ever get back out of there, into the world, after tasting the sweetness and the kindness of the love with which you welcome those that come to stay in your house, even only for a few days, O Holy Queen of Heaven, and Mother of my Christ!

It is very true that the Cistercian Order is your special territory.

Merton's gravesite at the Abbey of Gethsemani. (Wikimedia Commons)

him. To his surprise, he found that his superiors in the monastery encouraged him to write, though they did also censor what he produced. Merton thus found himself in the paradoxical situation of having joined a monastery dedicated to the rule of silence and yet being able to speak, through his writings, to the world outside the monastery. Furthermore, he was quite candid about this paradox and about his struggles over his writings. He also struggled over his desire for greater solitude.

The Trappists were a communal order, and the monks at Gethsemani spent most of their time together. Merton soon decided that a hermit's life would be ideal, like that practiced at some other, more contemplative monasteries. However, his superiors told him it was God's will that he remain a Trappist, and he did, though he eventually won concessions, including a little hut that he used as a private hermitage on the monastery's grounds.

Merton wrote about his struggles with his monastic life in several journals he published, notably *The Sign of Jonas* (1953) and *Conjectures of a Guilty Bystander* (1966). He also wrote books on contemplation, such as *New Seeds of Contemplation* (1961), in which he connected contemplation and prayer with community, wrote that contemplation was not just for monks, and argued that it must be accompanied by compassion for others.

Acting on his conviction that the truly spiritual person, even a solitary monk like himself, must connect to the world, Merton in his last years began writing about political issues. He opposed the Vietnam War, called for racial harmony, denounced nuclear weapons, and supported nonviolence. Also in these years he began to explore other spiritual traditions, such as Zen Buddhism, Daoism, and Sufi mysticism.

Exploring these traditions led him to Asia in late 1968, where he met the Dalai Lama and attended a religious conference in Bangkok, Thailand. He died there on December 10, 1968, after he was accidentally electrocuted.

Significance

Merton became instantly famous with the publication of *The Seven Storey Mountain*, a spiritual autobiography depicting his search for meaning in an apparently meaningless world. The book struck a chord in the postwar world of 1948, as did some of his later works in which he tried to explain prayer and contemplation through his personal experiences. Paradoxically, even though *The Seven Storey Mountain* ended by renouncing the world, it nevertheless appealed to that world as it spoke to all who were eager to follow him in his search for spirituality in a secular era.

Merton became a prophet for his era, trying to lead people away from mindless conformity and faith in technology. He tried to show them a path of contemplation through which they might connect with the deepest, most interior part of their being, and by doing so connect with God.

Sheldon Goldfarb

Further Reading

Cunningham, Lawrence. *Thomas Merton and the Monastic Vision*. Grand Rapids, Mich.: William B. Eerdmans, 1999. Clear and informative account of Merton's life after he joined the monastery and of the works he composed there. Discusses Merton's views on prayer. Includes a useful annotated Further Reading.

Elie, Paul. *The Life You Save May Be Your Own: An American Pilgrimage*. New York: Farrar, Straus and Giroux, 2003. An examination of Merton alongside Catholics Dorothy Day, Flannery O'Connor, and Walker Percy. These writers, taken together, paint a vivid portrait of the "Catholic moment" of the mid-twentieth century.

Furlong, Monica. *Merton: A Biography*. San Francisco, Calif.: Harper & Row, 1980. Overview of Merton's life, with useful discussion of his work as a teacher of novice monks. At times seems unsympathetic, presenting him as suffering from neuroses.

Kramer, Victor A. *Thomas Merton*. Boston: Twayne, 1984. Includes a biographical sketch and a discussion of Merton's major works. Also includes a useful chronology, a Further Reading, and an index.

Labrie, Ross. *The Art of Thomas Merton*. Fort Worth: Texas Christian University Press, 1979. Literary analysis of Merton's writings. Discusses his struggle over whether he could be both a monk and a writer. Index, Further Reading.

Mott, Michael. *The Seven Mountains of Thomas Merton*. Boston: Houghton Mifflin, 1984. The authorized biography. Focuses on the details of Merton's everyday life rather than on the nature of his achievements. Illustrations, Further Reading, index.

Padovano, Anthony. *The Human Journey: Thomas Merton, Symbol of a Century*. Garden City, N.Y.: Doubleday, 1982. Focuses on Merton's significance as a symbol of his age. Places him in the American context.

Shannon, William H. *Thomas Merton: An Introduction*. Cincinnati, Ohio: St. Anthony Messenger Press, 2005. Revised edition of *Something of a Rebel*. Includes a clear and informative biographical sketch, an insightful examination of Merton's continuing significance, a discussion of his most important writings, and an explanation of his notion of contemplation. Index.

Shannon, William H., Christine M. Bochen, and Patrick F. O'Connell. *The Thomas Merton Encyclopedia*. Maryknoll, N.Y.: Orbis Books, 2002. A good resource that outlines Merton's life and writings in an easy-to-read encyclopedic format. Includes name and subject indexes and a Further Reading.

John R. Mott

Religious leader

Born: May 25, 1865; Livingston Manor, New York
Died: January 31, 1955; Orlando, Florida
Area of Achievement: Religion and theology; activism

The central figure in at least four worldwide Christian movements, Mott combined missionary zeal and personal piety with administrative efficiency. Cowinner of the Nobel Peace Prize in 1946, he is widely regarded as the founder of the ecumenical movement, the most significant religious movement of the twentieth century.

Early Life

John R. Mott (mawt) was the third of four children and the only son of John Stitt Mott and Elmira Dodge Mott. When he was only four months old, his father, a farmer, moved the family to Postville, Iowa, where he entered the lumber business and soon became the leading lumber and hardware dealer in town. While working in his father's lumberyard, Mott learned to keep meticulously accurate and detailed records, which he continued to do throughout his life. John Mott expressed his individuality early when, at age eleven, on his own initiative he added the initial "R" (for "Raleigh") to his name.

Mott acquired from his mother much of his personal piety, together with an almost insatiable desire for knowledge. Elmira was an earnest Methodist and subscribed regularly to such magazines as *Harper's Weekly*, *The Youth's Companion*, *The Christian Advocate*, and *The Guide to Holiness*, all of which were eagerly devoured by young Mott. The family also had a relatively large library, and his mother told him much about European history and

John R. Mott (Wikimedia Commons)

public affairs, both absorbing interests of his in later years. At the age of thirteen, Mott came under the influence of an Iowa Quaker evangelist, J. W. Dean. Shortly thereafter, a young circuit-riding Methodist pastor, the Reverend Horace E. Warner, not only instilled in him the desire and purpose to obtain a college education but also convinced his parents to make it possible for him to do so.

In the fall of 1881, Mott, at age sixteen, enrolled in Upper Iowa University, a small Methodist preparatory college at nearby Fayette. His primary interests in his years there were English literature, history, and philosophy, with special emphasis on politics, constitutional law, and logic. He joined the Philomathean Society, a debating club, and won prizes in historical and political oration and debate. Mott's debates and orations, in preparation for a political career, were to prove highly useful to him in later years, as did his nearly complete mastery of *Robert's Rules of Order* (1876).

During his years at Upper Iowa, Mott was not particularly religious, although he did become a charter member of the local Young Men's Christian Association (YMCA). His decision to transfer to Cornell University in Ithaca, New York, seems to have been motivated primarily by a need for wider horizons in his preparation for a career in politics and law, but also by a desire to attend a large secular institution in hopes of escaping religious influences. Such was not to be. On Friday evening, January 15, 1886, Mott attended a lecture by J. E. K. Studd, a famous English cricketer from Cambridge (later to be knighted and become lord mayor of London), and heard Studd utter three sentences that changed his life. As Mott took his seat, having arrived late, Studd announced his text: "Seekest thou great things for thyself? Seek them not. Seek ye first the kingdom of God." Mott later wrote, "These words went straight to the springs of my motive life. I have forgotten all else that the speaker said, but on these few words hinged my life-investment decision. I went back to my room not to study but to fight." Following an interview with Studd the next day, Mott wrote his parents of his decision "to devote my whole life and talents to the service of Jesus."

Mott immediately began a period of intensive Bible study and prayer, along with holding religious services in the local jail. He was elected vice president of the Cornell YMCA, whose membership rapidly grew from 40 to 150. In the summer of 1886, he was selected to represent Cornell at the first international and ecumenical Christian Student Conference, a gathering of 251 young men from eighty-nine colleges and universities in the United States and Canada, at Mount Hermon, Massachusetts, under the leadership of the evangelist Dwight L. Moody. Mott returned to Cornell from Mount Hermon determined to complete his education and to devote his life to missionary work. He was elected president of the Cornell YMCA, and its membership rapidly grew to 290. He also was instrumental in raising the money for a building for the Cornell YMCA. In 1888, he was graduated with degrees in philosophy, history, and political science, along with membership in Phi Beta Kappa.

LIFE'S WORK

Rejecting several opportunities for further study and travel, Mott agreed to a trial period of one year as student secretary of the International Committee of the YMCA. This involved extensive traveling to college campuses and coordination of campus Christian activities. Mott was to remain in this position not one year but for the next twenty-seven years until 1915, at which time he became the committee's general-secretary until 1931. Only four months into his new job, however, Mott also accepted the additional responsibility of chair of the newly organized Student Volunteer Movement for Foreign Missions, the missionary branch of the YMCA, the YWCA, the American Inter-Seminary Missionary Alliance, and the Canadian Intercollegiate Missionary Alliance. This post Mott would hold until 1920, and he continued to solicit funds for it most of his life. Its slogan, The Evangelization of the World in This Generation, was the title of one of his most important books (1900). Mott had an almost uncanny ability to seek out other capable leaders and to inspire them by his own contagious enthusiasm and zeal. In addition to Mott's extensive travels, he sent out others to work with student Christian groups on various campuses. By 1925, his efforts had resulted in the recruitment of more than ten thousand American and Canadian student volunteers for various mission boards.

In November of 1891, Mott married Leila Ada White, an English teacher and graduate of Wooster College, at her family home in Wooster, Ohio. White accompanied him in much of his travel and was a devoted wife and partner for nearly sixty-one years, until her death in 1952. The Motts had four children: John Livingstone, Irene, Frederick Dodge, and Eleanor, all of whom grew up in Montclair, New Jersey, while their father commuted to offices in New York City when not traveling elsewhere. Mott is described by his biographers as six feet tall, with handsome features and an impressive bearing. His reddish-brown hair, gray in later years, topped a large, finely molded head. Photographs indicate his most impressive facial feature to have been his thick, shaggy eyebrows.

His entire physique suggested strength: square shoulders and square head, firm mouth, and dark brown, piercing eyes. Small wonder that at least one student is said to have emerged from a conference with Mott and commented, "It was like being in to see God!"

Mott defined his life's work as one of weaving together Christian movements particularly among students all over the world. In 1893, he organized the Foreign Missions Conference of North America in an effort to unite missionary work on that continent. He was repeatedly elected to its executive committee and was made an honorary life member in 1942. Mott also was one of the leaders in founding the World's Student Christian Federation (WSCF) in Badstena, Sweden, in 1895, and he became its first general-secretary. In this role, he organized student movements in China, Japan, India, New Zealand, and Australia, as well as in Europe and the Near East. International meetings were held in such unlikely places as Tokyo, Constantinople, Jerusalem, Beijing, and Madras. By 1925, the WSCF claimed the membership of more than 300,000 young men and women in more than three thousand colleges and universities in twenty-seven different nations. Mott served as chair of its executive committee from its inception until 1920, then as general chair until 1928.

A high point in Mott's career came in June of 1910, when he was elected chair of the World Missionary Conference, attended by more than twelve hundred delegates, in Edinburgh, Scotland, which Mott himself called "the most notable gathering in the interest of the worldwide expansion of Christianity ever held, not only in missionary annals, but in all Christian annals." Mott was also made chair of a "continuation committee" to carry on the work of the Edinburgh conference until the next one. He toured the Far East in this role and organized regional missionary councils in various nations, including India, Japan, Korea, and China. Mott spent his days organizing these councils and his evenings addressing huge throngs of students. Although he spoke through interpreters, his impassioned words were interrupted time and again by applause. Mott deserves much of the credit for the leading role assumed by the "younger churches" in later missionary conferences throughout the world. Against strong opposition, he recruited Roman Catholic and Eastern Orthodox Christians into ecumenical groups. The "continuation committee" was succeeded by the International Missionary Council in 1921, with Mott as its chair. In 1942, when he retired from that position, he was named its "honorary chairman."

Mott's travels on behalf of various Christian causes were prodigious. Following extensive trips throughout the United States and Canada, he made his first visit to Europe in 1891. For the next sixty years, he crossed the Atlantic both ways almost annually, occasionally twice or three times, and the Pacific at least fourteen times, in all logging well over two million miles and visiting eighty-three countries. One indication that these travels were far from pleasure junkets is that Mott was often afflicted by motion sickness not only on sea travels, but on trains as well. When he accepted the Nobel Peace Prize in 1946 (after his first intercontinental flight), this "world citizen" received congratulatory messages from seven chiefs of state and numerous other world leaders. He died January 31, 1955, a few months before his ninetieth birthday, and was buried in the Washington Cathedral. Among his last recorded words were these: "While life lasts I am an evangelist."

Significance

For many years, Mott was the central figure in at least four major world Christian movements: president of the World's Alliance of YMCAs, general-secretary and later chair of the World's Student Christian Federation, chair of the International Missionary Council, and the first

Mott receives the Distinguished Service Medal for his relief work during World War I. (Library of Congress)

honorary president of the World Council of Churches. As an American Methodist layman, he was awarded an honorary doctor of divinity degree by the (Russian) Orthodox Theological Institute of St. Sergius, in 1940. He declined many prestigious opportunities during his career, including President Woodrow Wilson's offer to become United States ambassador to China and offers of the presidencies of Princeton University, Oberlin College, and Yale Divinity School. At President Wilson's request, he served on the Mexican Commission in 1916 and the Special Diplomatic Mission to Russia (the "Root Mission") in 1917, utilizing the latter as an opportunity to bring the Russian Orthodox Church into the ecumenical network. Mott was awarded the Distinguished Service Medal for his fund-raising work and other service during World War I, at the conclusion of which he also made significant contributions to the peace conferences at Versailles. In addition to the Nobel Peace Prize, which he shared with the pacifist Emily Greene Balch in 1946, he was the recipient of eight honorary degrees: the Imperial Order of Meija from Japan, the Order of the Saviour from Greece, the Order of the Holy Sepulchre from Jerusalem, the Prince Carl Medal from Sweden, the Order of the White Rose from Finland, the Second Order of the Crown from Siam, the Order of Polonia Restituta from Poland, and the Order of the Italian Crown and he was made a chevalier, and later an officer, of the French Legion of Honor. He raised more than $300 million for his various Christian causes, most of it for World War I relief work.

> "*It is possible for the most obscure person in a church, with a heart right toward God, to exercise as much power for the evangelization of the world, as it is for those who stand in the most prominent positions.*"

Although a brilliant organizer and fund-raiser, Mott also had deep spiritual strength. "Organize as though there were no such thing as prayer," he said, "and pray as though there were no such thing as organization." President Wilson once called him "the world's most useful man."

Mott was typical of much of early twentieth century American religious thought. An evangelical liberal, he eagerly embraced the "social gospel" and applied it to missions and other burning issues of his day. Mott was probably influenced as well by the "social Darwinism" of the period; there was unbounded optimism in the popular slogan The Evangelization of the World in This Generation. This slogan did not originate with Mott, although he made it his own. Yet it is also clear that he knew the difference between the "evangelization" of the world and its "conversion." He simply wanted the Christian Gospel to be preached to the entire world and sincerely believed it could be done in a single generation. Perhaps in part because of his lack of a seminary education, Mott was not deterred by theological niceties in urging ecumenical cooperation. He made the words of Jesus, "that they all may be one," into an ecumenical rallying cry.

In his speech responding to the 1946 Nobel Peace Prize, Mott characterized his career: "My life might be summed up as an earnest and undiscourageable effort to weave together all nations, all races, and all religious communions in friendliness, in fellowship, and in cooperation." In its 1965 tribute to him, on the one hundredth anniversary of his birthday, the General Board of the National Council of Churches called Mott "the greatest missionary statesman since the Apostle Paul." If anyone ever deserved the title of founder of one of the most important religious movements of the twentieth century, the ecumenical movement, it was John R. Mott.

C. Fitzhugh Spragins

FURTHER READING

Fisher, Galen M. *John R. Mott: Architect of Cooperation and Unity.* New York: Association Press, 1952. Written shortly before his death, this volume is very positive throughout in its analysis of Mott's many contributions. The book contains many quotations from distinguished churchmen in praise of Mott's work. The concluding chapter compares Mott's service with that of Saint Paul.

Hopkins, Charles Howard. *John R. Mott, 1865-1955: A Biography.* Grand Rapids, Mich.: William B. Eerdmans, 1979. The definitive biography of Mott, by an emeritus professor of history at Rider College, Philadelphia, this is a detailed, straightforward, and well-documented account of Mott's career and influence. The result of fifteen years of research, this volume tends to emphasize Mott's social concern and the details of his travels, perhaps to the neglect of his evangelicalism and churchmanship.

Howe, W. Tracy, and Nancy Reece, eds. *Strengthening the Organizational Heart: Fifteen Timeless Lessons from Legendary YMCA Leader, John R. Mott.* Franklin, Tenn.: Providence House, 2006. Mott summarized what he had learned in fifteen basic principles. YMCA leaders examine his precepts to describe how they can be applied to contemporary issues.

Mackie, Robert C. *Layman Extraordinary: John R. Mott, 1865-1955.* New York: Association Press, 1965. A brief monograph of nearly unbridled praise and enthusiasm on behalf of Mott and his accomplishments.

Mathews, Basil. *John R. Mott: World Citizen.* New York: Harper and Brothers, 1934. This book was authorized by Mott to describe the principles and experiences of his life as examples for young people. An excellent portrayal of his personality and character written some twenty years before his death, this volume portrays Mott as one who applied the principles of business to the work of Christian missions.

Mott, John R. *Addresses and Papers.* 6 vols. New York: Association Press, 1946-1947. Mott wrote at least sixteen books himself, as well as many shorter works, which are included in these volumes. His personal papers and his comprehensive archives of the World's Student Christian Federation are in the Mott Collection of the Yale Divinity School Library, New Haven, Connecticut.

Rouse, Ruth. *John R. Mott: An Appreciation.* Geneva: World's Student Christian Federation Press, 1930. A well-balanced portrayal of Mott in midcareer by an admirer and historian of the ecumenical movement.

---. *The World's Student Christian Federation: A History of the First Thirty Years.* London: S.C.M. Press, 1948. Mott wrote the foreword to this volume, which traces the WSCF from its origins prior to Vadstena, Sweden, in 1895, to High Leigh, England, in 1924, with appropriate attention to Mott's contributions.

Woolverton, John F. *Robert Gardiner and the Reunification of Worldwide Christianity in the Progressive Era.* Columbia: University of Missouri Press, 2005. This biography of Gardiner, a leader in the Christian ecumenical movement, includes a discussion of Mott.

SALLY J. PRIESAND

Rabbi

Born: June 27, 1946; Cleveland, Ohio
Area(s) of significance: Religion and theology, women's rights

As the first woman to achieve ordination to the rabbinate through a theological seminary, Priesand broke a barrier to women's full participation in Jewish religious life and modeled a new role for temple leadership, in which rabbi and congregation work together in affirming Judaic tradition and values.

EARLY LIFE

Sally J. Priesand (PREE-sand) was born to Irving Theodore Priesand and Rose Elizabeth Welch in 1946, a part of the post-World War II baby boom. During Sally J. Priesand's childhood, the family lived on Cleveland's east side, where they were active in the Jewish community. As a child, Priesand attended classes at the Conservative Community Temple, although she later reflected that she did not enjoy them or feel religious. When she was in junior high school, the family moved to the city's west side, where she and her brothers were the only Jews in their schools. Perhaps in compensation, Priesand enthusiastically took part in youth activities offered by the Reform temple, Beth Israel, her parents joined. The Temple Sisterhood gave her a scholarship to a summer camp institute at Zionsville, Indiana. She loved the camp, which allowed her to give sermons and to take other roles in services. Priesand traces her ambition to become a rabbi back to these experiences.

In high school, she contacted Hebrew Union College (HUC) in Cincinnati, asking about its undergraduate program and its seminary. The reply on the latter was equivocal and not totally negative. She entered the undergraduate college's program in Judaic studies, offered in cooperation with the University of Cincinnati. During college, she was part of a small circle of women students who, if not as single-minded as Priesand, were likewise serious about Jewish worship and tradition. These friends offered much-needed moral support as Priesand's ambitions became known and controversial on campus.

At this time, the HUC seminary was headed by a remarkable president, Nelson Glueck. A distinguished archaeologist as well as a rabbi, Glueck had announced that he was eager to ordain a qualified woman. Priesand was admitted to rabbinical studies with the implicit understanding that if she completed her course work satisfactorily, she would be ordained. Priesand continued to do well with her academics. She also spoke to outside groups and took High Holiday student assignments (although not all congregations were happy to have her). For her rabbinical thesis she chose an ambitious topic, "The Historic and Changing Role of the Jewish Woman." On June 3, 1972, she was ordained as a rabbi by Alfred Gottschalk, Glueck's successor.

Life's Work

Priesand's first position was assistant rabbi at Stephen Wise Free Synagogue in New York City. She served seven years there, and she was promoted to associate rabbi. When the lead rabbi approached retirement, it became clear that she had little or no chance of succeeding him. Beginning the search for a post that matched her qualifications and hopes, she bumped into the glass ceiling. Few congregations searching for a rabbi would consider a female candidate. For the next two years she served in a part-time post at Temple Beth El in Elizabeth, New Jersey, and worked as a chaplain at Lenox Hills Hospital in Manhattan.

> "I do think the feminist movement is important because it is time for us to overcome psychological and emotional objections. We must fulfill our potential as creative individuals."

In 1981, she became rabbi at Monmouth Reform Temple in Tinton Falls, New Jersey. It was a middlesized congregation, whose 365 families were willing to accept a female rabbi and work with her in cooperative worship and service. Priesand had believed originally that a larger congregation was a measure of success for a rabbi, but her attitude changed during the years at Monmouth. Leading prayer and worship, studying and teaching the Torah, and conducting the services that mark lifecycle events are important duties, no matter what the setting. At this temple she was able to develop a unique partnership with the congregation so that members were empowered in their faith. She stayed at the Monmouth Reform Temple for twenty-five years, until her retirement in 2006. Priesand participated in a conference called "First Lights" with other female rabbis, which conducted interviews with women rabbis in order to archive their stories for future generations. In 2012, on the 40th anniversary of her ordination, Priesand and the other 3 first women rabbis gathered at the Annual Convention of the Central Conference on American Rabbis in commemoration of their efforts for gender equality in the Jewish faith.

The Rabbi Sally J. Priesand WRJ Award was created to honor the 45th anniversary of Priesand's ordination. The award is given out once every year to a graduating Hebrew Union College-Jewish Institute of Religion Cincinnati campus woman, chosen because she "exemplif[ies] the mission and values of WRJ and embod[ies] the qualities that Rabbi Priesand has exhibited throughout her career, including her clarity of vision, her commitment to excellence, her professionalism, her dedication to the continuity of Reform Judaism, her passion, and her perseverance."

Although in this work Priesand fulfilled her own career ambitions, she was cast in another role, that of pioneer. Once in the rabbinate, she was in demand as an exemplar of newly empowered women within Judaism. She carried this out within her own congregation by ensuring that girls and women participated equally in worship and in committee assignments. In the wider world, she worked with many organizations in the Reform movement to encourage fuller representation of women. She has also been an active member of community groups, working for such causes as housing for the homeless, Planned Parenthood, and Holocaust studies. In 1975, her book, *Judaism and the New Woman*, based on her extensive research for her rabbinic thesis, was published. HUC awarded her an honorary doctorate in 1998, and its Sally J. Priesand Visiting Professorship has been funded to support Jewish women's studies.

Significance

Priesand's achievements represented a rare intersection of her own ambitions and talents with the spirit of her times. Since 1922 Reform Judaism had held that nothing in Jewish law forbade women rabbis, yet in the following half-century none had been recognized in American life. The cultural transformations of the 1960s and early 1970s put the egalitarian ideals of American society to a reality test. Even before the women's movement gathered force, the drive for civil rights challenged long-established racial injustices. Many young Jews had put their lives on the line by joining African-American freedom riders in the South, finding racial discrimination an obvious case of the world needing repair. Thus, when Priesand argued for women's ordination based on each person's right to pursue her own dreams and reach her potential, she struck the right note for a receptive audience.

Two years after Priesand became a rabbi, Sandy Eisenberg Sasso was the first woman ordained in Reconstructionist Judaism. Amy Eilberg, ordained in 1985, was the first female rabbi in the Conservative movement. By the opening of the twenty-first century, female rabbis numbered in the hundreds. At the same time, movements for ordaining female clergy were consolidating in many Christian denominations. As one of Priesand's friends told her, she carried the dreams of many others.

Emily Alward, updated by Micah L. Issit

Further Reading

Kimmel, Elizabeth Cody. "Sally Priesand." In *Ladies First: Forty Daring American Women Who Were Second to None.* Washington, D.C.: National Geographic Society, 2006. Short but illuminating essay highlighting early experiences that helped shape Priesand's rabbinical career.

Nadell, Pamela S. *Women Who Would Be Rabbis.* Boston: Beacon Press, 1998. A survey of the women who aspired to be rabbis during a century of change in Judaism. Contains a long chapter on Priesand's quest.

Priesand, Sally Jane. "New Jersey Q and A: Rabbi Sally J. Priesand, Reflections of a Woman Who Dared." Interview by Sally Friedman. *The New York Times,* September 19, 1993. Interview in which Priesand reflects on her experiences as a reluctant pioneer, how her personal beliefs had changed, and the "tests" of illness and loss in her life.

Zaid Shakir

Muslim American scholar

Born: May 24, 1956; Berkeley, California
Also known as: Ricky Daryl Mitchell (birth name)
Area of achievement: Religion; Education

One of the most respected and influential Muslim leaders in the United States today, Zaid Shakir was born in Berkeley, California, in 1952 and converted to Islam in 1977. He is a co-founder of Zaytuna College, the first Muslim liberal arts college in the United States.

Early Life

Zaid Shakir was born in Berkeley, California, on May 24, 1956. His parents were of African, Irish, and Native American descent. Shakir's birth name was Ricky Daryl Mitchell; he adopted the name Zaid Shakir when he converted to Islam at age twenty-one. When he was a young boy, his parents moved to Atlanta, Georgia, and then to New Britain, Connecticut. In both places, Shakir grew up in mostly poor, black neighborhoods. After graduating from high school, Shakir joined the United States Air Force. At that time in his life, Shakir investigated a number of religious traditions and practices, studying transcendental meditation and several forms of Christianity in addition to Islam. In 1977, he converted to Islam.

Leaving the Air Force, Shakir obtained a bachelor's degree in international relations from American University in Washington DC, graduating summa cum laude. Later he earned a master's in political science from Rutgers University in New Jersey. Shakir's interest in social justice and activism began to find expression at this time. While he was a student at Rutgers, he led a university campaign for divestment from South Africa. He also co-founded a religious organization, the New Brunswick Islamic Center.

> "*Hatred is the refuge of wretched souls. Try to find some love in your life and... spread it around.*"

Life's Work

Shakir then traveled to Cairo, Egypt, to study Arabic for one year. He returned to the United States, settling in New Haven, Connecticut, where he became an Islamic community activist and organizer. He also taught political science and Arabic at Southern Connecticut State University and served as a chaplain at Yale University.

In 1994, he moved to Syria to study Arabic, Islamic law, and Quranic studies. He stayed there for seven years, meeting many of Islam's top scholars and graduating from the Abu Noor University in Syria with a degree in Islamic studies. He was the first American male to earn a degree from that prestigious school. Returning to the United States, Shakir began an affiliation with the Zaytuna Institute in Hayward, California. The institute was founded in 1996 by Shaykh Hamza Yusuf, an influential Islamic scholar. Shakir taught Arabic, law, and Islamic spirituality at the institute. He also developed a seminary program to train students in Islamic studies reading both classical and contemporary Islamic thinkers.

In 2010, Shakir co-founded Zaytuna College, together with Shaykh Hamza Yusuf and Hatem Bazian, colleagues from the institute. Located in Berkeley, California, Zaytuna College is a small, four-year Muslim liberal arts college and the first institution of its kind in the United States. Zaytuna teaches traditional Islam, with a focus on the Ashari and Maturidi schools of theology. The college combines the Western concept of a liberal arts college with the traditional Islamic practice of Quranic studies. It has a diverse student body and accepts both men and women as students. Following traditional Muslim gender codes, classrooms are divided down the middle with male

Zaid Shakir (Wikimedia Commons)

and female students sitting on opposite sides. Zaytuna is small, with about 54 students and seventeen professors, but in 2015 it received accreditation from the Western Association of Schools and Colleges (WASC), an academic organization that oversees public and private colleges and universities in the United States.

The college has developed a curriculum that integrates traditional Islamic scholarship with topics from the western philosophical tradition. Zaytuna does not receive government funding. All financial support for students is obtained through other channels, and support is frequently provided by the college.

Shakir has published a number of books, beginning with *Scattered Pictures: Reflections of an American Muslim*, published in 2005 by Zaytuna Institute. He, like many other influential Muslim leaders in the United States, has denounced the rise of militant Islam.

Significance

Those who have met Zaid Shakir often remark on his approachable and down to earth personality. An inspiration to millions of American Muslims, Shakir was acquainted as a young man with racism and poverty before joining the armed forces. He converted to Islam while in the Air Force. From that moment, with his religious faith as a base, Shakir has virtually moved mountains. He obtained advanced degrees in international relations and Islamic studies, taught, became an activist, and eventually co-founded the first Muslim liberal arts college in the United States. He is widely recognized today as an important Muslim scholar and faith leader. He has promoted interfaith dialogue and spoken often of Islam's peaceful vision for society.

Dewayne Dean

Further Reading

"Bill Moyers talks with Imam Zaid Shakir." *Bill Moyers Journal.* June 22, 2007. https://www.pbs.org/moyers/journal/06222007/transcript2.html

"New Islamic Directions – Imam Zaid Shakir." *New Islamic Directions.* https://www.newislamicdirections.com/about/

Shakir, Zaid. S*cattered Pictures: Reflections of an American Muslim.* Hayward, CA: Zaytuna Institute, 2005.

Smith, Jane I. *Islam in America (second edition).* New York: Columbia University Press, 2009.

Winston, Kimberly. "Zaytuna College Recognized as First Accredited Muslim College in the U.S." Washington Post, March 18, 2015. https://www.washingtonpost.com/national/religion/zaytuna-college-recognized-as-first-accredited-muslim-college-in-the-us/2015/03/18/4b4e58e2-cd9a-11e4-8730-4f473416e759_story.html

Avi Weiss

Rabbi

Born: June 24, 1944; New York City, New York
Also known as: Avraham Haim Yosef haCohen Weiss
Area of achievement: Religion; Social Reform; Education

Weiss is known for his worldwide activism on behalf of Jewish causes and as the key figure in the Open Orthodox movement within Judaism.

Early Life

Avraham Haim Yosef haCohen Weiss was born on June 24, 1944, in New York City. He was raised in the city's Orthodox Jewish community and, after high school, attended Yeshiva University in the Washington Heights area of New York City. In 1968, he was ordained as a rabbi at the Rabbi Isaac Elchanan Theological Seminary at Yeshiva University. Influenced by the progressive, anti-war, and social justice activism of the 1960s, Avi Weiss incorporated protest and activism into a modern vision for Orthodox Jewish religious life as early as his college years.

Life's Work

In 1970, Weiss joined the Student Struggle for Soviet Jewry (SSSJ), an organization founded in 1964 by Yaakov Birnbaum. SSSJ agitated on behalf of Jews living in the Soviet Union, and in the 1960s had become a force in uniting many other Jewish organizations and communities around that cause, above all in New York City. SSSJ held frequent marches and demonstrations with messaging that drew upon Biblical symbolism, such as the blowing of the shofar or the story of the Exodus, to characterize the struggle to free Soviet Jewry. Religious symbolism was combined with a distinctly modern protest style. One of the SSSJ slogans from the period ("1-2-3-4, open up the Iron Door; 5-6-7-8, let our people emigrate") would be used as the title of a book by Weiss many years later (*Open Up the Iron Door*, 2015). By the time that Weiss joined, SSSJ was drawing crowds of around 20,000 people and holding events in Madison Square Garden. In 1982 Weiss was named the national chair of SSSJ, a position he held for the next seventeen years.

In 1973, Weiss became the rabbi of the Hebrew Institute of Riverdale in the Bronx, a synagogue. Weiss led the congregation there until his retirement in 2015. In the 1980s, Weiss was a passionate activist. For several years, he traveled around the world following Kurt Waldheim to protest his public appearances. Waldheim was an Austrian politician who had served as the fourth Secretary-General of the United Nations. He was accused by the World Jewish Congress of having lied about the extent of his involvement in Nazi crimes during World War II. In 1985, Weiss traveled to Bergen-Belsen to protest President Ronald Reagan's visit with the German Chancellor Helmut Kohl to an historic German military cemetery that held, among others, the graves of Nazi soldiers. In 1989, Weiss led a demonstration at a Carmelite convent that had opened just outside the site of the Auschwitz concentration camp. For Weiss and others, the presence of the nuns was an attempt to "Christianize" Holocaust memory.

Weiss is also a vocal supporter of the State of Israel and an opponent of the Oslo Accords, which established mutual recognition between the State of Israel and the Palestinian Liberation Organization (PLO) that was headed by Yasir Arafat. The Oslo Accords also established a framework for a two-state solution. Weiss was opposed to Israel's recognition of the PLO, and he was unhappy with the Oslo framework for a two-state solution. Weiss supports the expansion of Israeli settlements, and has said, "I believe it's very fair for there to be natural growth [of the settlements]. Imagine someone turning to an American family saying you can't have more children, or if you have more children you can't add a home." Weiss became the personal rabbi of American Jonathan Pollard when the latter was arrested and sentenced to life in prison for having spied for the state of Israel. He also lobbied unsuccessfully for Pollard's release. In 2001, Weiss publicly criticized President George W. Bush when the latter spoke of "Israeli-Palestinian violence," asserting that Israel acted in self-defense, while Palestinians were terrorists.

Weiss has been arrested several times for protesting the cause of Palestinian statehood, and he organized a boycott against several major United States newspapers that he thought were anti-Israel. In 2015, Weiss wrote an op-ed on the occasion of the United States Supreme Court decision to legalize same-sex marriage. He asserted his support for the legislation while affirming that he would never participate in same-sex wedding ceremonies; he

Avi Weiss (Wikimedia Commons)

went on to praise the "exemplary lives" of many homosexual Jews. Weiss has authored several books about religious activism, including *Principles of Spiritual Activism* (2001), *Spiritual Activism: A Jewish Guide to Leadership and Repairing the World* (2008), *Open Up the Iron Door: Memoirs of a Soviet Jewry Activist* (2015), and *Journey to Open Orthodoxy* (2018).

Weiss used his position as rabbi at the Hebrew Institute of Riverdale to develop a style of Modern Orthodox Judaism that he eventually came to call Open Orthodoxy. In general, Modern Orthodox Judaism attempts to relate to the modern world while remaining observant of Jewish law and adhering to Jewish values. Open Orthodoxy, as a particular form within this movement, was once described by Weiss as "expressing vibrancy, inclusivity and non-judgmentalism." In practice, this has meant incorporating into Orthodox Judaism some features of modern democratic social tolerance, especially regarding the roles in society that woman are allowed to occupy. Weiss himself has stated that the "key issue today is inclusivity." In 1999, Weiss established Yeshivat Chovevei Torah (YCT) in Riverdale, a rabbinic seminary that affirms the values of Open Orthodoxy.

In 2009, Weiss ordained a woman, Sara Hurwitz, as an Orthodox religious leader, bestowing on her the title *maharat*. The word is an acronym formed from the Hebrew words for "lawful" (halakhic), "spiritual," and "Torah leader"; it was invented by Weiss. A maharat (plural *maharatot*) is theoretically able to assume many roles of authority in Orthodox Judaism while still respecting the myriad rules regarding gender divisions that are an important part of Jewish law. He later agreed to call her by the title "Rabba," the female form of "Rabbi," a move that set off a storm of controversy within Orthodoxy. Also in 2009, he founded Yeshivat Maharat, a school to train more women as maharatot.

In 2017, as the dispute between Weiss's apparently more "liberal" Orthodoxy and the rest of the Orthodox community became more heated, the Yeshivat Chovevej Torah, Weiss's rabbinic seminary, attempted to distance itself from the phrase "Open Orthodoxy," issuing a statement that declared that the term had become too controversial. In 2018, it was revealed that the rabbinical court system in Israel had categorically stopped recognizing the rabbinic authority of more than 120 rabbis who had all been ordained at Yeshivat Chovevej Torah.

Significance

As the rabbi of an important synagogue in the Riverdale neighborhood in the Bronx, Avi Weiss is a prominent figure in New York's Jewish community. Weiss pioneered a form of modern Orthodoxy called Open Orthodoxy, and he made headlines when he arranged for a new position of limited religious leadership in Orthodoxy that is available to women. For this, he has drawn strong criticisms from other sectors of Orthodox Judaism. He is also well-known as an activist for Jewish and pro-Israel causes and as a writer.

Dewayne Dean

Further Reading

Chabin, Michele. "Rabbinical court in Israel rejects 'liberal' American rabbis." *Religion News Service*. May 30, 2018. https://religionnews.com/2018/05/30/rabbinical-court-in-israel-rejects-liberal-american-rabbis/

Ginsberg, Johanna. "Closing A Chapter On 'Open Orthodoxy.'" *The New York Jewish Week*. August 16, 2017. https://jewishweek.timesofisrael.com/closing-a-chapter-on-open-orthodoxy/

Mindell, Cindy. "Conversation with...Rabbi Avi Weiss." *Jewish Ledger*. March 2013. http://www.jewishledger.com/2013/03/conversation-with-rabbi-avi-weiss/

Pogrebin, Abigail. "The Rabbi and the Rabba." *New York Magazine*. July 11, 2010. https://nymag.com/news/features/67145/

Weiss, Avi. *Open Up the Iron Door: Memoirs of a Soviet Jewry Activist*. Jerusalem: Toby Press, 2015.

———. *Journey to Open Orthodoxy*. Jerusalem: Urim Publications, 2018.

Social Reform

The history of social reform in America can be traced to its founding as a political experiment. The American Revolution, the Declaration of Independence, and the United States Constitution gave reality to revolutionary ideas and ideals that many around the world found inspiring. In particular, the guarantee of religious liberty and the disestablishment of religion that is contained in the founding documents expressed the values of the English Dissenters. The Dissenters were Protestants who disagreed with the established church in England. Many radical ideas—religious, political, and moral ones—were associated with the tradition of Dissent. What was marginal in England thus became the norm in America. In the eighteenth and early nineteenth centuries, marginal and progressive ideas about society, morals, and manners had a strong presence in America. Influenced by these Christian spiritual values, an amazing variety of reform movements flourished, especially in the North in the nineteenth century: women's rights, pacifism, the temperance movement, prison reform including the abolition of debtor's prison, movements to improve the conditions of the working class or to abolition of the death penalty, and others. There were also many experimental communities founded that did away with private property.

The most significant reform movement was the one to abolish slavery. As the decades wore on in that struggle, social reformers who had relied for years upon the power of moral persuasion began to realize that political strategies were needed. The effort to abolish slavery ultimately led to the Civil War—a great and costly political intervention. The United States government before the war was largely decentralized; after the war, it became increasingly centralized. Thus in the era of Reconstruction and after, reform movements became increasingly political in nature. The earlier movements, rooted in religious tradition, were primarily focused on appeals to conscience and sought to change lives and behavior. Beginning in the late nineteenth century with the expansion of federal powers, changing laws would become at least as important and changing minds.

Suffrage parade in New York city, 1912. (National Archives and Records Administration)

Ralph David Abernathy

Activist, religious leader, and educator

Born: March 11, 1926; Marengo County, Alabama
Died: April 17, 1990; Atlanta, Georgia
Areas of achievement: Civil rights; Radio and television; Religion and theology; Social issues

A major figure in the Civil Rights movement, Abernathy was a minister, political activist, author, and college administrator. His leadership led to the passage of laws granting equal rights to all U.S. citizens.

Ralph David Abernathy (Library of Congress)

EARLY LIFE

Ralph David Abernathy, Sr. (A-ber-NA-thee) was born on March 11, 1926, on his father's five-hundred-acre farm near Linden, Alabama. Abernathy was the tenth of twelve children born to William L. Abernathy and Louivery Valentine Bell Abernathy. When his grandmother, midwife Ellen Bell, delivered him, she told Louivery that Abernathy was a strange child who would be "known throughout the world." While his siblings worked in the fields on the family farm, young Abernathy assisted his mother in the kitchen.

Commanding respect was of utmost importance to Abernathy. At an early age, he observed that ministers were accorded respect at all times, so he decided to become a minister. Farming also was a well-respected profession. His father's farming success made the Abernathys more prosperous than the town's white residents, who held the family in great esteem. One day, when Abernathy was on an errand to the country store to sell eggs from the farm, a white man confronted him. As the man prepared to hit Abernathy, the store owner admonished him not to put his hands on W. L. Abernathy's son, which brought about an immediate change in the man's behavior.

During his senior year of high school, Abernathy was drafted to serve in World War II. While he was serving in the U.S. Army, his father died from a stroke. W. L.'s advice—"If you ever see a good fight, get in it and win it"—shaped Abernathy's life's work.

LIFE'S WORK

Abernathy received an honorable discharge from the Army in 1945 after a serious bout of rheumatic fever. He returned to his Alabama home and received a G.E.D. With the aid of the G.I. Bill, Abernathy enrolled in Alabama State College (now Alabama State University), where he majored in mathematics and served as president of the Student Council. He put his father's words of wisdom into action when it was revealed that faculty members were being served better food than students in the dining hall on campus. Abernathy organized his first demonstration, encouraging students to boycott the dining hall until their food improved. The protest was an immediate success: The students were served fried chicken the next night. Abernathy later led a protest that resulted in improved housing for male students on campus.

> *"Bring on your tear gas, bring on your grenades, your new supplies of Mace, your state troopers and even your national guards. But let the record show we ain't going to be turned around."*

Shortly after his mother's death in 1947, Abernathy heard the call to preach. He graduated from Alabama State in 1950 and during the summer became the first black radio disc jockey in Montgomery, Alabama. While pursuing graduate studies in sociology at Atlanta University (now Clark Atlanta University), he met a young minister named Martin Luther King, Jr.

Abernathy was encouraged by his pastor to begin theological studies after completing graduate school. The pastor's logic was that if Abernathy did not go to seminary immediately, he would get busy with work and start a family and never attend. Abernathy returned to Montgomery and became the dean of men at Alabama State while also serving as a supply pastor at Eastern Star Baptist Church in neighboring Demopolis.

In 1952, Abernathy became the pastor of the historic First Baptist Church in Montgomery and married schoolteacher Juanita Odessa Jones. Their first child, Ralph, Jr., died only two days after his birth in August, 1953. They soon became parents to three children—Juandalynn, Donzaleigh, and Ralph III—who frequently participated in the nonviolent marches and demonstrations of the Civil Rights movement. Their son Kwame was born in 1971. The Abernathy children were raised with a responsibility to help humanity and serve others.

Abernathy and King were reunited in 1954 when King became the pastor of Dexter Avenue Baptist Church in Montgomery. The families became inseparable and met for dinner daily to make plans to achieve social justice and racial equity through nonviolent methods in the coming years. The opportunity to use the strategies they discussed presented itself much sooner than they anticipated.

The Women's Political Council (WPC), an activist group headed by Alabama State professor Jo Ann Gibson Robinson, invited Abernathy and other local pastors to join them in addressing the cruel treatment of black passengers on Montgomery buses. African Americans were forced to pay their fare at the front of the bus, then exit and reenter through the back door. Sometimes the bus pulled off before the black passenger could get to the back door. On one occasion, a woman was dragged to the next stop when the driver closed the door on her arm. Two women had also been arrested for noncompliance with Jim Crow laws. The WPC presented its concerns to local leaders but was ignored.

After Rosa Parks's arrest on December 1, 1955, for refusing to give up her seat on the bus, a boycott of Montgomery buses was proposed for the day of her hearing. National Association for the Advancement of Colored People (NAACP) president E. D. Nixon asked Abernathy to lead the boycott. Abernathy organized a meeting of clergy and distributed leaflets in the community, which resulted in a front-page story in the Sunday *Montgomery Advertiser* and a 381-day boycott. The successful protest was an early milestone in the Civil Rights movement.

For the next thirteen years, Abernathy and King led African Americans toward equality through nonviolent protest. The activists often were confronted with billy clubs, fire hoses, and worse: Two bombs were set at Abernathy's home and church when he and King were in Atlanta meeting to organize the Southern Christian Leadership Conference (SCLC) in 1957. In spite of the danger, death threats, arrests, and deaths of many staunch supporters of the movement, Abernathy continued to champion equality for all. The Civil Rights Act of 1964 and the Voting Rights Act of 1965 are two pieces of legislation made possible through the efforts of Abernathy and other supporters.

In 1961, Abernathy became pastor of West Hunter Baptist Church in Atlanta at the urging of King. King had returned to Atlanta on the advice of his father, who thought Alabama had become too explosive. Abernathy served as senior pastor at the church until his death in 1990.

In early April of 1968, Abernathy, King, and others went to Memphis to support striking sanitation workers. On the evening of April 4, the men were preparing to go

---

Abernathy's Autobiographical Writings

Ralph David Abernathy's 1989 autobiography, *And the Walls Came Tumbling Down*, provides detailed information about his efforts to combat oppression of people of color. The 638-page book, divided into sixteen chapters, opens with his birth and his grandmother's proclamation that he would be famous. Abernathy describes the rich family history that instilled in him a desire to serve humanity.

The chronicle Abernathy provides of his involvement in the Civil Rights movement is not a simple list of names, places, and dates, but an abundant account of the lives of the individuals involved in the protests. *And the Walls Came Tumbling Down* not only explores what he and other civil rights leaders did, but also examines their decision-making process and the emotional impact of those decisions on the leaders and their families. The book gives the reader a different view of Abernathy and Martin Luther King, Jr., that shows them both as leaders and also as everyday men with families, making them both heroic and human.

Abernathy can be seen in the left background, wearing a fur cap. His three children march on the front line, holding hands. From left to right the children are: Donzaleigh, Ralph David III, and Juandalynn Abernathy. (Wikipedia)

to the Reverend Billy Kyle's home for dinner when King was shot while standing on the balcony of the Lorraine Motel. Abernathy found King lying on the balcony, gravely wounded. King was taken to the hospital, where he died in Abernathy's arms.

Abernathy became the president of the SCLC after King's death. He and King's widow, Coretta Scott King, led a march to support the Memphis sanitation workers on April 8, 1968. He continued to agitate for freedom and equality through his work with the Poor People's Campaign in May, 1968; the United Farm Workers' grape pickers strike; and an American Indian demonstration at Wounded Knee in 1973. Abernathy also met with President Richard M. Nixon and legislators to discuss poverty.

In 1970, Abernathy introduced the idea of honoring King's January 15 birthday with an annual holiday. He lobbied Congress in 1982 for the extension of the Voting Rights Act of 1965, which was passed. In 1989, he published his autobiography, *And the Walls Came Tumbling Down*.

In March of 1990, Abernathy was hospitalized. He died on April 17 while on his way to an operating room to have blood clots removed.

Abernathy received more than three hundred awards and seven honorary doctorates in his lifetime. The Ralph David Abernathy Memorial honors his career as a minister, his work as a political activist, and his life as a family man. It is located in Atlanta on Ralph David Abernathy Boulevard between Formwalt and Cooper Streets.

In 2009, his alma mater, Alabama State University, opened Ralph David Abernathy Hall, the new home to its College of Education.

Significance

Abernathy provided an ideal balance with King in leading the Civil Rights movement. While King outlined the overall strategy, Abernathy formulated the tactics to achieve that strategy. His autobiography offers a firsthand, eyewitness account of the movement. After King's death, Abernathy assumed leadership of the SCLC and trained future generations of civil rights activists.

Trevy A. McDonald

Further Reading

Abernathy, Donzaleigh. *Partners to History: Martin Luther King, Jr., Ralph David Abernathy, and the Civil Rights Movement*. New York: Crown, 2003. This coffee table book chronicles the Civil Rights movement through photographs, first-person accounts, and excerpts from Abernathy's and King's sermons and speeches.

Abernathy, Ralph David. *And the Walls Came Tumbling Down: An Autobiography*. New York: Harper & Row, 1989. This autobiography explores Abernathy's early childhood experiences and his calls to the ministry and political activism. His involvement in the Civil Rights movement is detailed.

Axelrod, Alan. *Minority Rights in America*. Washington, D.C.: CQ Press, 2002. This collection examines issues, events, organizations, and individuals related to minority rights in the United States.

Garrow, David J. *The Walking City: The Montgomery Bus Boycott, 1955-1956*. Brooklyn, N.Y.: Carlson Publishing, 1989. Abernathy's master's thesis, *The Natural History of a Social Movement: The Montgomery Improvement Association*, is published as a chapter in this book.

Hare, Kenneth M. *They Walked to Freedom, 1955-1956: The Story of the Montgomery Bus Boycott*. Champaign, Ill.: Spotlight Press, 2005. This book documents the bus boycott through rich stories and photographs from the archives of the *Montgomery Advertiser*.

Jane Addams

Social reformer and educator

Born: September 6, 1860; Cedarville, Illinois
Died: May 21, 1935; Chicago, Illinois
Area of Achievement: Social reform, education, women's rights

Addams, a writer of hundreds of books and articles and a cofounder and director of the Hull House settlement in Chicago, promoted a variety of social reforms designed to facilitate the adjustment to urban, industrial America from 1890 to 1935.

Early Life

Jane Addams (AD-amz) was born in the village of Cedarville in northern Illinois. Her father, John Huy Addams, owned a local mill and had investments in land and other enterprises in several states; his belief in civic responsibility led him to represent his district in the Illinois senate from 1854 to 1870. Her mother, Sarah, died when Jane was barely two years old, and an older sister supervised the Addams household until John Addams remarried in 1868. Anna Haldeman Addams, the widow of a Freeport merchant, was a self-educated woman with a high regard for social position, travel, dress in general, the cultural aspects of life. Jane received tutelage from her stepmother in these areas, which supplemented the information she gleaned from books in the local subscription library, conveniently located in John Addams's house. Her formal education began in the village school in Cedarville; in 1877, she entered nearby Rockford Female Seminary (of which her father was a trustee), an institution dedicated to instilling in young women religious piety, cultural awareness, and domesticity. That Jane became president of her class, valedictorian, and editor of the class magazine attests her popularity and intellectual qualities.

Shortly after Jane's graduation from the seminary, in 1881, John Addams died. This shock combined with Jane's indecision about a career to produce several years of irresolution and depression. She began medical study at the Woman's Medical College in Philadelphia, but poor health forced her to leave after a few months. She was then bedridden for six months following an operation on her spine to correct the slight curvature caused by childhood spinal tuberculosis. At the urging of her stepmother, she toured Europe for twenty-seven months from 1883 to 1885, absorbing Old World culture with Anna and a few

Jane Addams (Library of Congress)

college classmates. Her purposelessness persisted after her return. She accompanied her stepmother to Baltimore for two winters and engaged in some charity work there, but her nervous depression continued. It was not until her second trip to Europe, in 1887-1888, in the company of her former teacher, Sarah Anderson, and college friend, Ellen Gates Starr, that she perceived a means to reconcile her intellectual and cultural interests with a useful career. In London she visited Toynbee Hall, a social settlement in the city's East End, and discussed the institution's social and cultural activities with its founder, Canon Samuel A. Barnett. She also toured the People's Palace, an institute for the working class. These experiences acquainted her with the attempts of other educated men and women to deal with the problems of modern society by living and working in a poor neighborhood. Before leaving Europe she discussed her plan for founding a Chicago settlement with Starr; a few months after arriving home, the two women opened Hull House, on September 18, 1889.

Life's Work

While the model of Toynbee Hall initially influenced Addams's establishment of Hull House, the ethnically mixed population around the Halsted Street settlement had a greater impact on its development in the 1890's. When the two women residents moved into the old Hull

> ### Ethics
>
> Addams' experiences at Hull House provided her with a vantage point that few other reformers enjoyed. Observations of the ordinary led her to formulate social theories. For example, her reflections on the activities of neighborhood children led to a remarkable book, *The Spirit of Youth and the City Streets* (1909), in which she discussed the importance of the natural instinct toward play among children and the "urban democracy" exhibited on the playground.
>
> The neighborhood was also a place where social experimentation could occur, where ideas could be translated to practice, for Addams was a rare combination of social theorist and pragmatic reformer. As such, she attracted other educated and talented people to join the settlement, many of whom were young women who faced the same career quandary with which she had dealt in the 1880's. She was willing to draw on the observations and ideas of this group in formulating her own programs. This open-minded deference to ideas, including those of William James and John Dewey, may have been her greatest strength in attempting to apply democratic idealism to an urban industrial setting in new ways that represented a profound break from the genteel tradition in which she was reared and educated.
>
> Her attitude toward war rested on the same ideal of Progressive democracy as her social theories. Like other Progressives, she believed that war destroyed social progress and moral civilization. Unlike most other Progressives, however, she could not support U.S. involvement in the war, citing as her reasons the sanctity of human life and the irrationality of war as an instrument of change. As a practical idealist, she supported such postwar initiatives as the League of Nations, the World Court, and the Kellogg-Briand Pact, hoping that they would serve as instruments to direct world public opinion against war. In international affairs, as well as in industrial relations, Addams was always willing to pursue numerous programs, never losing her faith in achieving human progress through social change. once autobiography, publicity for Hull House, and a consideration of reform ideas in the twenty years preceding its publication.

mansion, they had no formal program of activities and sought to establish contact with their neighbors by sharing their literary enthusiasms in a series of "reading parties." Soon, however, the needs of area residents dictated programs. A wide variety of activities evolved in the first decade, including classes, clubs, social and cultural events, and a day nursery. Many of these activities drew on the cultural backgrounds of immigrants; Greeks staged classical Greek dramas at the Hull House Theater, and Italian and German immigrants discussed Dante and Johann Wolfgang von Goethe. As the functions of the settlement multiplied and Hull House added new buildings, Addams stood as the central figure still a young woman, her brown hair drawn back into a bun, her pleasant face distinguished by pensive dark eyes radiating goodwill and competence.

Her changed awareness of the nature of urban problems began to emerge in the 1890's. While her original impulse in establishing Hull House had reflected the religious and humanitarian principles of her early years, a combination of circumstances now led her to consider the causes of poverty and maladjustment to industrial society. Florence Kelley, who came to Hull House as a resident in the early 1890's, contributed her infectious interest in scientific investigations of the neighborhood as a basis for reform proposals. Her work culminated in the 1895 publication of Hull-House Maps and Papers: A Presentation of Nationalities and Wages in a Congested District of Chicago, Together with Comments and Essays on Problems Growing Out of the Social Conditions, a series of essays by Hull House residents, including "The Settlement as a Factor in the Labor Movement," by Addams.

> "*What after all, has maintained the human race on this old globe despite all the calamities of nature and all the tragic failings of mankind, if not faith in new possibilities, and courage to advocate them.*"

Addams was critical of current labor practices, an outgrowth of her involvement in the unsuccessful mediation of the Pullman strike in 1894. She also criticized the response to the depression of 1893-1894 by existing charitable organizations, which too often stressed laziness and other individual vices as the determinants of poverty. Her developing view was to consider the underlying causes of labor problems and social ills: the dislocation caused by modern industrial organization. Her promotion of scientific inquiry was abetted by members of the new Department of Sociology at the University of Chicago, particularly Albion Small who encouraged her to publish in the *American Journal of Sociology*, which he began editing in 1896.

Addams's far-flung activities of the early 1900's aimed at achieving harmony between industrialism, on the one hand, and traditional ideas of morality and culture, on the other. She was particularly interested in children and their development through educational and social activities. She promoted public parks and playgrounds in Chicago, established a kindergarten at Hull House, and set up a Hull House camp for neighborhood children outside the city. She promoted reform in education, believing that traditional educational methods and subjects insufficiently prepared children for modern life. She served on the Chicago Board of Education from 1905 to 1908 and was a founder of the National Society for the Promotion of Industrial Education. (Founded in 1906, the Society's efforts culminated in the 1917 Smith-Hughes Act, which provided federal support for vocational education in high schools.) She was also a founding member of the National Child Labor Committee, which supported compulsory education laws as well as restrictive legislation for child labor in factories.

By the time she published her autobiographical masterpiece, *Twenty Years at Hull House* (1910), Addams was widely recognized as an expert in social problems and a spokesperson for major programs for progressive reform. A leading suffragist (and officer of the National American Woman Suffrage Association from 1911 to 1914), she was attracted by the woman's suffrage and industrial justice planks of the Progressive Party in 1912. She delivered a stirring speech seconding Theodore Roosevelt's nomination at the party's convention in Chicago and subsequently traveled more than seven thousand miles campaigning for the party. When Woodrow Wilson won the election, she opined that he would pursue a program of Progressive democracy. The war in Europe in 1914 impaired Progressive aspirations for reform, however, and directed Addams's attention to the cause she would pursue for the rest of her life: world peace.

Peace delegates to the International Congress of Women which was held at the Hague, the Netherlands in 1915. The delegates include: British feminist and peace activist Emmeline Pethick-Lawrence (1867-1954), social activist and writer Jane Addams (1860-1935), and Annie E. Malloy, president of the Boston Telephone Operators Union. (Library of Congress)

During the period of American neutrality, until April, 1917, Addams worked for international arbitration, believing that neutral nations could resolve the war's causes and mediate with the belligerents. With Carrie Chapman Catt, she issued a call to women to attend a conference in Washington in January, 1915, resulting in the formation of the Woman's Peace Party, with Addams as its chair. Later in the year, she was elected president of the International Conference of Women at the Hague. (When the group reorganized after the war as the Women's International League for Peace and Freedom, she was elected president and retained the post until 1929.) When mediation did not materialize and the United States entered the war, she did not support the war effort, although in 1918 she worked for Herbert Hoover's Department of Food Administration, which she viewed as a humanitarian response to the upheaval of war. Her patriotism came under attack, and the Daughters of the American Revolution withdrew her lifetime honorary membership. In the years following the war, she continued to search for ways to ensure lasting peace; her efforts were recognized by the award of the Nobel Peace Prize in 1931, which she shared with Nicholas Murray Butler.

Her final years were marked by tributes and honors from organizations throughout the world. Her activities were hampered, however, by failing health. She underwent major surgical operations and suffered a heart attack in the early 1930's; she died on May 21, 1935. Following

Ethics

Addams' experiences at Hull House provided her with a vantage point that few other reformers enjoyed. Observations of the ordinary led her to formulate social theories. For example, her reflections on the activities of neighborhood children led to a remarkable book, *The Spirit of Youth and the City Streets* (1909), in which she discussed the importance of the natural instinct toward play among children and the "urban democracy" exhibited on the playground.

The neighborhood was also a place where social experimentation could occur, where ideas could be translated to practice, for Addams was a rare combination of social theorist and pragmatic reformer. As such, she attracted other educated and talented people to join the settlement, many of whom were young women who faced the same career quandary with which she had dealt in the 1880's. She was willing to draw on the observations and ideas of this group in formulating her own programs. This open-minded deference to ideas, including those of William James and John Dewey, may have been her greatest strength in attempting to apply democratic idealism to an urban industrial setting in new ways that represented a profound break from the genteel tradition in which she was reared and educated.

Her attitude toward war rested on the same ideal of Progressive democracy as her social theories. Like other Progressives, she believed that war destroyed social progress and moral civilization. Unlike most other Progressives, however, she could not support U.S. involvement in the war, citing as her reasons the sanctity of human life and the irrationality of war as an instrument of change. As a practical idealist, she supported such postwar initiatives as the League of Nations, the World Court, and the Kellogg-Briand Pact, hoping that they would serve as instruments to direct world public opinion against war. In international affairs, as well as in industrial relations, Addams was always willing to pursue numerous programs, never losing her faith in achieving human progress through social change. once autobiography, publicity for Hull House, and a consideration of reform ideas in the twenty years preceding its publication.

---

mansion, they had no formal program of activities and sought to establish contact with their neighbors by sharing their literary enthusiasms in a series of "reading parties." Soon, however, the needs of area residents dictated programs. A wide variety of activities evolved in the first decade, including classes, clubs, social and cultural events, and a day nursery. Many of these activities drew on the cultural backgrounds of immigrants; Greeks staged classical Greek dramas at the Hull House Theater, and Italian and German immigrants discussed Dante and Johann Wolfgang von Goethe. As the functions of the settlement multiplied and Hull House added new buildings, Addams stood as the central figure still a young woman, her brown hair drawn back into a bun, her pleasant face distinguished by pensive dark eyes radiating goodwill and competence.

Her changed awareness of the nature of urban problems began to emerge in the 1890's. While her original impulse in establishing Hull House had reflected the religious and humanitarian principles of her early years, a combination of circumstances now led her to consider the causes of poverty and maladjustment to industrial society. Florence Kelley, who came to Hull House as a resident in the early 1890's, contributed her infectious interest in scientific investigations of the neighborhood as a basis for reform proposals. Her work culminated in the 1895 publication of Hull-House Maps and Papers: A Presentation of Nationalities and Wages in a Congested District of Chicago, Together with Comments and Essays on Problems Growing Out of the Social Conditions, a series of essays by Hull House residents, including "The Settlement as a Factor in the Labor Movement," by Addams.

> "*What after all, has maintained the human race on this old globe despite all the calamities of nature and all the tragic failings of mankind, if not faith in new possibilities, and courage to advocate them.*"

Addams was critical of current labor practices, an outgrowth of her involvement in the unsuccessful mediation of the Pullman strike in 1894. She also criticized the response to the depression of 1893-1894 by existing charitable organizations, which too often stressed laziness and other individual vices as the determinants of poverty. Her developing view was to consider the underlying causes of labor problems and social ills: the dislocation caused by modern industrial organization. Her promotion of scientific inquiry was abetted by members of the new Department of Sociology at the University of Chicago, particularly Albion Small who encouraged her to publish in the *American Journal of Sociology*, which he began editing in 1896.

Addams's far-flung activities of the early 1900's aimed at achieving harmony between industrialism, on the one hand, and traditional ideas of morality and culture, on the other. She was particularly interested in children and their development through educational and social activities. She promoted public parks and playgrounds in Chicago, established a kindergarten at Hull House, and set up a Hull House camp for neighborhood children outside the city. She promoted reform in education, believing that traditional educational methods and subjects insufficiently prepared children for modern life. She served on the Chicago Board of Education from 1905 to 1908 and was a founder of the National Society for the Promotion of Industrial Education. (Founded in 1906, the Society's efforts culminated in the 1917 Smith-Hughes Act, which provided federal support for vocational education in high schools.) She was also a founding member of the National Child Labor Committee, which supported compulsory education laws as well as restrictive legislation for child labor in factories.

By the time she published her autobiographical masterpiece, *Twenty Years at Hull House* (1910), Addams was widely recognized as an expert in social problems and a spokesperson for major programs for progressive reform. A leading suffragist (and officer of the National American Woman Suffrage Association from 1911 to 1914), she was attracted by the woman's suffrage and industrial justice planks of the Progressive Party in 1912. She delivered a stirring speech seconding Theodore Roosevelt's nomination at the party's convention in Chicago and subsequently traveled more than seven thousand miles campaigning for the party. When Woodrow Wilson won the election, she opined that he would pursue a program of Progressive democracy. The war in Europe in 1914 impaired Progressive aspirations for reform, however, and directed Addams's attention to the cause she would pursue for the rest of her life: world peace.

Peace delegates to the International Congress of Women which was held at the Hague, the Netherlands in 1915. The delegates include: British feminist and peace activist Emmeline Pethick-Lawrence (1867-1954), social activist and writer Jane Addams (1860-1935), and Annie E. Malloy, president of the Boston Telephone Operators Union. (Library of Congress)

During the period of American neutrality, until April, 1917, Addams worked for international arbitration, believing that neutral nations could resolve the war's causes and mediate with the belligerents. With Carrie Chapman Catt, she issued a call to women to attend a conference in Washington in January, 1915, resulting in the formation of the Woman's Peace Party, with Addams as its chair. Later in the year, she was elected president of the International Conference of Women at the Hague. (When the group reorganized after the war as the Women's International League for Peace and Freedom, she was elected president and retained the post until 1929.) When mediation did not materialize and the United States entered the war, she did not support the war effort, although in 1918 she worked for Herbert Hoover's Department of Food Administration, which she viewed as a humanitarian response to the upheaval of war. Her patriotism came under attack, and the Daughters of the American Revolution withdrew her lifetime honorary membership. In the years following the war, she continued to search for ways to ensure lasting peace; her efforts were recognized by the award of the Nobel Peace Prize in 1931, which she shared with Nicholas Murray Butler.

Her final years were marked by tributes and honors from organizations throughout the world. Her activities were hampered, however, by failing health. She underwent major surgical operations and suffered a heart attack in the early 1930's; she died on May 21, 1935. Following services at Hull House, she was buried in the cemetery at Cedarville.

SIGNIFICANCE

Jane Addams was in the vanguard of Progressive reformers. Rather than exhibiting a populist-type aversion to modern industrial conditions, she shared with other urban reformers a belief that social, political, and economic relationships could be modified in a democratic fashion to deal with changed conditions. The belief in evolutionary change toward a new "social morality" was the theme of her first book, *Democracy and Social Ethics* (1902), a collection of essays on such diverse topics as charity organizations, family relationships, women in domestic employment, labor-management relations in industry, education, and the roles of bosses and reformers in politics.

In 1973 Jane Addams was inducted into the National Women's Hall of Fame. On December 10, 2007, Illinois celebrated the first annual Jane Addams Day. In 2008 Jane Addams was inducted into the Chicago Gay and Lesbian Hall of Fame. Addams was inducted into the Chicago Literary Hall of Fame in 2012. Also, in 2012 she was inducted into the Legacy Walk, an outdoor public display which celebrates LGBT history and people. In 2014, Jane Addams was one of the first 20 honorees awarded a 3-foot x 3-foot bronze plaque on San Francisco's Rainbow Honor Walk paying tribute to LGBT heroes and heroines. In 2015, Addams was named by Equality Forum as one of their 31 Icons of the 2015 LGBT History Month.

Richard G. Frederick

FURTHER READING

Addams, Jane. *Democracy and Social Ethics*. Edited by Anne Firor Scott. New York: Macmillan, 1902. Reprint. Cambridge, Mass.: Belknap Press, 1964. Originally published in 1902, this book was a compilation of earlier magazine articles (revised for the book), which addressed the problem of applying ethics to an evolving democratic system. This edition includes an excellent introduction to the life and thought of Addams by the editor.

---. *The Social Thought of Jane Addams*. Edited by Christopher Lasch. Indianapolis, Ind.: Bobbs-Merrill, 1965. An excellent introduction to Addams through her published and unpublished writings. Following a biographical introduction by Lasch, the material is organized under five subject headings, which reflect Addams's diverse interests.

---. *Twenty Years at Hull House with Autobiographical Notes*. New York: Macmillan, 1910. A good source for understanding Addams and the Progressive reform movement, as the book is at once autobiography, publicity for Hull House, and a consideration of reform ideas in the twenty years preceding its publication.

Davis, Allen F. *American Heroine: The Life and Legend of Jane Addams*. New York: Oxford University Press, 1973. A balanced biography that establishes Addams's writing and other activities in a broader cultural context. The most realistic appraisal of her accomplishments.

Farrell, John C. *Beloved Lady: A History of Jane Addams' Ideas on Reform and Peace*. Baltimore: Johns Hopkins University Press, 1967. The first study to analyze the thought of Addams, rather than concentrate on her humanitarian sentiments or involvement in settlement activity. Particularly good in demonstrating that her ideas often conflicted with later historical accounts of the "average" Progressive reformer.

Joslin, Katherine. *Jane Addams: A Writer's Life*. Urbana: University of Illinois Press, 2004. Joslin argues that Addams's emergence as a public figure stemmed from her books and essays. She describes how Addams rejected scholarly writing in favor of a combination of fictional and analytical prose that appealed to a wide readership.

Knight, Louise W. *Citizen: Jane Addams and the Struggle for Democracy*. Chicago: University of Chicago Press, 2005. An insightful account of the early years of Addams's life, from 1860 through 1899, which depicts her personality flaws as well as her compassion.

Lasch, Christopher. *The New Radicalism in America, 1889-1963: The Intellectual as a Social Type*. New York: Alfred A. Knopf, 1965. In a perceptive essay on Addams, Lasch examines her early life and motivation for reform; he finds that her gradual emergence as an adherent to the "new radicalism" (marked by interest in educational, cultural, and sexual reform) was based on the conflict between the genteel values of her parents' generation and her own perceptions of life and society.

Levine, Daniel. *Jane Addams and the Liberal Tradition*. Madison: State Historical Society of Wisconsin, 1971. An intellectual biography of Addams, which asserts that she was a radical in urging rapid change. The book deals with three facets of her life: Hull House, her publicizing of social problems, and activism in national affairs.

Linn, James Weber. *Jane Addams: A Biography.* New York: D. Appleton-Century, 1935. An admiring but thorough biography by Addams's nephew. Not interpretive, but valuable for detail, as the author had access to all of Addams's manuscripts and files prior to her death, and discussed with her the proposed biography.

SUSAN B. ANTHONY

Feminist and social reformer

Born: February 15, 1820; Adams, Massachusetts
Died: March 13, 1906; Rochester, New York
Area of Achievement: Women's rights, social reform

A gifted and tireless worker for feminist causes, Anthony was for five decades the preeminent voice and inspiration of the woman suffrage movement.

EARLY LIFE

Susan Brownell Anthony was the second child of Daniel and Lucy Read Anthony. Her mother, a sullen, withdrawn woman, grudgingly accepted her domestic role as housewife and mother of six. Susan loved but pitied her mother and learned from her more what to avoid than what to emulate. Her father, in contrast, always loomed large in his daughter's eyes. A radical Quaker, Daniel Anthony was liberal in creed and illiberal toward those who tolerated the social evils that he so adamantly despised. Strong-willed and independent of mind, Daniel Anthony taught his children to be firm in their convictions and to demonstrate their love for God by working for human betterment.

As an owner of a small cotton mill, Daniel Anthony had the means to provide for his daughter's education. A precocious child, Anthony took full advantage of her opportunities, first attending the village school and later receiving private instruction from a tutor hired by her father. At the age of seventeen, Anthony left with her older sister Guelma for a Quaker boarding school in Philadelphia. Anthony's seminary training, however, was cut short by the Panic of 1837. With mounting business debts, Daniel Anthony was forced to auction his cotton mill, homestead, furniture, and even personal belongings, and to relocate as a dirt farmer on a small tract of land outside Rochester, New York.

In response to the family crisis, Susan Anthony left boarding school, secured a teaching position, and began sending half of her two-dollar weekly salary home to the family. For the next decade, Anthony remained in the classroom, instructing her pupils in the three R's, even as she augmented her own education with extensive reading and study. Intelligent yet unpretentious, Anthony matured into an athletic, tall, and slender woman with thick brown hair and warm blue eyes. Hardly the ugly, unsexed "battle-ax" her future enemies portrayed her to be, Anthony was courted by several suitors and remained single largely because none of her admirers, in her opinion, equaled her father in character or conviction.

> "*Woman must not depend upon the protection of man, but must be taught to protect herself.*"

Like her father, Anthony was a reformer who yearned for a society free from the evils of slavery and alcoholism. An idealist but not a dreamer, Anthony worked actively in these reform efforts, serving during her twenties as president of the Canajoharie Daughters of Temperance. In 1849, at her father's request, Anthony resigned from teaching to take over management of the family farm near

Susan B. Anthony (Library of Congress)

Rochester. This relocation enabled Daniel Anthony to devote his full attention to a new business venture (an insurance agency that eventually made him prosperous again). The move also allowed Anthony to commit herself more fully to reform activity.

LIFE'S WORK

While still a teacher in Canajoharie, Anthony read a newspaper account of a meeting in nearby Seneca Falls-Woman's Rights Convention (1848), where a group of sixty-eight women and thirty-two men issued a Declaration of Women's Rights. This declaration demanded free education, equality of economic opportunity, free speech, the right to participate in public affairs, and the right to vote. As a schoolteacher making only one-third the salary of her male colleagues, Anthony sympathized with many of these demands for equal rights. Her Quaker upbringing, however, had convinced her that no person should participate in a government that waged war or condoned slavery, and she was thus not yet ready to take up the cause of woman suffrage.

In 1851, while attending an antislavery lecture in Seneca Falls, Anthony met the renowned Elizabeth Cady Stanton. The two women developed an instant friendship that led to a strong partnership in reform work. Together they organized the Woman's State Temperance Society of New York and petitioned the state legislature for a prohibition law. On numerous occasions during the 1850's, Anthony left Rochester for Seneca Falls to care for Stanton's children while their mother was away on speaking tours.

Although agreeing with Stanton on most issues, Anthony for several years refrained from embracing Stanton's call for woman suffrage. Gradually, however, the arrogance and disregard of many male reformers for the rights of women altered Anthony's view. Finally, in 1853, after the male delegates of the New York Woman's Temperance Society monopolized the annual convention and rudely ousted Stanton as president, Anthony declared her full allegiance to the women's crusade for equal rights and political equality.

Anthony's political conversion brought new life to the fledgling woman movement. An experienced worker willing to assume the time-consuming chores that no one else wanted, Anthony labored around the clock for feminist causes, organizing women into local associations, scheduling conventions and arranging speakers, seeking contributions, and paying administrative expenses. During the winter of 1854-1855, Anthony personally visited fifty-four of the sixty New York counties, collecting signatures in support of legal rights for married women.

When the legislature failed to act, Anthony promised to return with petitions every year until the inequities were rectified. For five years the tireless Anthony kept her promise, and in 1860, following a stirring address by coworker Stanton, the New York legislature granted property and guardian rights to married women. Much to Anthony's and Stanton's dismay, however, two years later the same body repealed portions of the marriage reform bill. This setback confirmed what Anthony had been saying for a decade: Benevolent legislation alone was insufficient; women would be fully protected only when they enjoyed full political powers.

For Anthony and her associates, the decade of the 1860's was eventful but largely disappointing. Before the Civil War, Anthony campaigned hard for the American Anti-Slavery Society, and during the war she helped establish the Women's Loyalty League to lobby for a constitutional amendment that would abolish opposition to and guarantee civil and political rights for all Americans. Nevertheless, despite her lifelong commitment to black rights, after the war Anthony opposed both the wording of the Fourteenth Amendment, because it inserted the word "male" in reference to citizen's rights, and the Fifteenth Amendment, for its failure to include the word "sex" in protecting voting rights for all citizens.

Berated by her former allies, who insisted that women must not endanger the long-awaited liberation of slaves with additional demands for women's rights, Anthony countered the accusations by asserting that if reformers linked these two great causes, then the moment in history called by some "the Negro's hour" could be the woman's hour as well. This controversy ultimately split the women's movement. Following an explosive Equal Rights Association convention in 1869, Anthony and Stanton organized the National Woman Suffrage Association (NWSA), a "for women only" organization committed to the passage of a national woman suffrage amendment. The more conservative reformers established the American Woman Suffrage Association (AWSA), a rival body that focused its efforts at the state rather than the national level.

At this time, Anthony's commitment to feminist goals did not deter her from other reform activities. In 1868, Anthony organized the Working Woman's Association in a futile attempt to unionize woman workers and build female solidarity across class lines. In the same year,

Anthony and Stanton allied themselves with the eccentric millionaire George Francis Train and began publishing a radical newspaper entitled *The Revolution*. On its masthead was the motto: Principle, not policy; justice, not favors. Men, their rights, and nothing more: Women, their rights and nothing less. This paper, which opened its columns to editorials on greenback currency, divorce laws, prostitution, and a variety of other controversial issues, survived only two years and left Anthony with a debt of ten thousand dollars. It took six years, but Anthony ultimately repaid the entire debt from income she earned delivering suffrage lectures on the Lyceum circuit. Following this experience, Anthony determined to disassociate herself from other controversial reforms and focus all of her energy on the crusade for woman suffrage.

In 1872, Anthony gained national media attention when she registered and voted in the presidential election. Several weeks later, a federal marshal issued her an arrest warrant for illegal voting. While awaiting trial, Anthony went on a whirlwind tour delivering the lecture "Is It a Crime for a U.S. Citizen to Vote?" Her defense was that the Fourteenth Amendment made her a citizen, and citizenship carried with it the right to vote. During her trial, the judge refused to allow her to testify on her own behalf, demanded that the jury render a guilty verdict, and fined her one hundred dollars. Outraged by this travesty of justice, thousands sent contributions to the NWSA treasury. Although she lost the trial, Anthony (who never paid the fine) won added respect for herself and her cause.

Anthony spent the last three decades of her life recruiting and training a new generation of suffragist leaders, including, among many others, Anna Howard Shaw and Carrie Chapman Catt. In 1889, at the age of sixty-nine, Anthony worked to secure a merger of the rival NWSA and AWSA. Three years later, she accepted the presidency of the unified National American Woman Suffrage Association and she served in this capacity until 1900, when she passed her mantle of leadership onto her handpicked successors. As honorary president emeritus,

Susan B. Anthony, the "Dowager Empress" of the early woman's rights movement, is seated at the center. Around her are Laura Clay, Anna Howard Shaw (front row, second from left), Alice Stone Blackwell (front row, far right), Annie Kennedy Bidwell, Carrie Chapman Catt, Ida A. Husted Harper (back row, far right), and Rachel Foster Avery (front row, second from right). Also believed to be pictured are Winfred Harper and Mary Hayes (Wikimedia Commons)

Anthony remained the dominant figure in the movement until the time of her death in March, 1906.

SIGNIFICANCE

When Anthony joined the women's rights movement, women had little social, professional, or educational standing. They were denied the right to vote, to hold office, or to be tried by their peers. As wives, they lost their legal individuality, having no rights to inherit property, keep earnings, sign contracts, or claim more than one-third of their husbands' estates. As mothers, they lacked legal custody or control over their own children. By the time of Anthony's death, however, 80 percent of American colleges, universities, and professional schools admitted women. In many states women had legal control over their own earnings and property and, in case of divorce, generally were awarded custody of their children. Although much discrimination remained, reform legislation along with advances in the medical treatment of women had increased the life expectancy of women from forty to fifty-one years. In four states, women enjoyed full suffrage rights, and in the majority of the remaining states, women voted in school or municipal elections.

Many of these changes were in part a consequence of the Industrial Revolution, which freed many women from a portion of their domestic chores, created new opportunities for employment, and provided increasing numbers with the wealth and leisure to sponsor reform work. The improved status of American women, however, was also a result of the heroic efforts of individuals who endured decades of hardship and ridicule in their quest for equal rights. For more than half a century, Anthony campaigned tirelessly for feminist goals. A radical visionary, the "Napoleon of Feminism" was also a shrewd, practical politician who did more than any other reformer to change the minds of men toward women, and of women toward themselves. Although vilified throughout much of her career, by the time of her death Anthony was the heroine of a second generation of suffragists, who in 1920 would win the victory she had fought so hard to achieve.

Terry D. Bilhartz

FURTHER READING

Barry, Kathleen. *Susan B. Anthony: A Biography of a Singular Feminist.* New York: New York University Press, 1988. Scholarly but readable biography, explaining how Anthony's family background, education, and Quaker upbringing, and the early temperance movement, produced a woman with a striving for social justice. Outlines Anthony's involvement in the abolition and suffrage movements.

Buhle, Mary Jo, and Paul Bulhe. *A Concise History of Woman Suffrage: Selections from the Classic Works of Stanton, Anthony, Gage, and Harper.* Urbana: University of Illinois Press, 1978. An abridged volume of the basic sources of the woman suffrage movement. Provides useful selections from the writings of Anthony and other eminent suffrage leaders.

DuBois, Ellen Carol, ed. *The Elizabeth Cady Stanton-Susan B. Anthony Reader: Correspondence, Writings, Speeches.* Boston: Northeastern University Press, 1992. Collection of letters, speeches, and other written works tracing the relationship and political development of the two women. DuBois provides critical commentary to illuminate the women's writings and experiences.

Edwards, G. Thomas. *Sowing Good Seeds: The Northwest Suffrage Campaigns of Susan B. Anthony.* Portland: Oregon Historical Society, 1990. Anthony traveled to Oregon in 1871, 1896, and 1905 to campaign for woman suffrage. Edwards uses newspaper accounts of her trips to describe how Anthony organized her campaign and obtained publicity and support for women's right to vote.

Flexner, Eleanor. *Century of Struggle: The Woman's Rights Movement in the United States.* Cambridge, Mass.: Harvard University Press, 1959. An overview of the women's rights movement that offers insights into the intellectual origins of American feminism. It remains the standard history of the suffrage crusade.

Harper, Ida H. *The Life and Work of Susan B. Anthony.* 3 vols. Indianapolis: Bowen-Merrill, 1898-1908. The authoritative biography, written with Anthony's assistance. The only source for numerous Anthony papers that were destroyed after its publication.

Lutz, Alma. *Susan B. Anthony: Rebel, Crusader, Humanitarian.* Boston: Beacon Press, 1959. A well-documented, straightforward biography. Informative, but like the other dated biographies, it makes no attempt to penetrate beyond the surface record of events.

Sherr, Lynn. *Failure Is Impossible: Susan B. Anthony in Her Own Words.* New York: Times Books, 1995. Excerpts from Anthony's speeches and letters. Sherr provides commentary about Anthony's life and career.

Truman, Margaret. *Women of Courage.* New York: William Morrow, 1976. A popular collection of biographical sketches of noted American women. The Anthony essay concentrates on her arrest, trial, and conviction for illegal voting in the 1872 presidential election.

GLORIA ANZALDÚA

Writer and scholar

Born: September 26, 1942; Harlingen, Texas
Died: May 15, 2004; Santa Cruz, California
Area of Achievement: Scholarship, literature, social issues, gay and lesbian issues

Anzaldúa is best known as the founder of border theory, which explores the geographical, bodily, and emotional conflicts inherent in Chicano identity. Her works connect notions of indigenous mythology, the implications of language use among Spanish speakers in an English-dominant society, Chicana lesbian sexuality, and spiritual activism.

EARLY LIFE

Gloria Anzaldúa (Wikimedia Commons)

Gloria Evangelina Anzaldúa (AHN-zahl-DOOuh) was born in the Rio Grande Valley of south Texas to Urbano and Amalia Anzaldúa. The eldest of four children, Anzaldúa and her family spent time working on various ranches and farms as migrant workers throughout her adolescence. When Anzaldúa was eleven years old, her parents made the decision to relocate the family to Hargill, Texas, so the children would have the opportunity to attend school. In *Borderlands/La Frontera: The New Mestiza* (1987), Anzaldúa described the punishment inflicted by white teachers upon her and other Chicano students for speaking Spanish. The pain of those experiences resonated throughout her life.

In 1962, Anzaldúa graduated from Edinburgh High School and began taking courses at Texas Women's University. Tuition proved to be too expensive, and she was forced to withdraw from school. Anzaldúa later earned her bachelor's degree from the University of Texas-Pan American in 1969 and began teaching in primary and secondary schools. She had been a writer throughout high school and resumed her dedication to writing during this period. She earned a master's degree in English and education from the University of Texas at Austin in 1972.

Anzaldúa later returned to the University of Texas in 1974 to work toward a doctoral degree in literature. She was involved as an activist in several groups while in Austin, but she ultimately felt unsupported by her doctoral department and made the decision to relocate to the San Francisco area to pursue her writing.

Life's Work

Anzaldúa's firsthand experiences with racism, sexism, classism, and heterosexism in south Texas influenced her autobiographical writings, poetry, and essays. While attending a writing retreat with other women and experiencing the elitism and racism of other individuals present, Anzaldúa had the idea for the collection *This Bridge Called My Back: Writings by Radical Women of Color* (1981), which she co-edited with Cherríe Moraga. This foundational feminist text offered a space for women of color to share their experiences and frustrations in the forms of poetry, essays, and theories.

After the publication of *This Bridge Called My Back*, Anzaldúa continued to write and eventually published her essays and poetry in *Borderlands/La Frontera*. This text is considered the basis for border theory. Within the text, Anzaldúa rejects a stable notion of identity for Chicanas because borders of space, mind, language, and body are constantly in flux. Chicanas, according to Anzaldúa, must constantly negotiate these shifting borders and address what it means to be mestiza, or individuals of mixed identity. This mestiza consciousness requires Chicanas to embrace all aspects of their identity, including the indigenous. *Borderlands/La Frontera* both critiques and examines Chicano culture on the grounds of sexism, heterosexism, and elitism related to language. Anzaldúa reclaims and re-imagines the histories of various female figures relevant to Chicana mestiza identity because they have previously been subject to the accounts of patriarchal historians and storytellers.

> "Why am I compelled to write? Because the writing saves me from this complacency I fear. Because I have no choice. Because I must keep the spirit of my revolt and myself alive. Because the world I create in the writing compensates for what the real world does not give me. By writing I put order in the world, give it a handle so I can grasp it. I write because life does not appease my appetites and hunger."

Indigenous Nahua female figures are important in Anzaldúa's theory, so the forced mistress and translator to

This Bridge Called My Back

Coedited by Gloria Anzaldúa and Cherríe Moraga, *This Bridge Called My Back: Writings by Radical Women of Color* (1981) is a text that defies simple categorization because it not only contains autobiographies, poems, essays, stories, manifestos, and theories, but also voices the oppressions and experiences of women of color based on race, gender, sexuality, and class. The text was revolutionary on numerous levels considering its publication history, content, and authorship. The anthology initially was published by Persephone Press, primarily a publisher of work by white women. The second publication came in 1983 after Persephone shut down; this edition was released by Kitchen Table: Women of Color Press, which counted Moraga among its founders and had the express purpose of publishing the works produced by women of color. When Kitchen Table ceased operations, Third Woman Press, founded by Norma Alarcón, published the third edition of *This Bridge Called My Back*.

The content of the text was groundbreaking for its attention to issues relating specifically to women of color because the essays, poems, and stories come directly from these women. The Combahee River Collective's "A Black Feminist Statement" is a manifesto describing the goals and beliefs of a group of African American women, many of whom were lesbians, in response to movements that ignore their identities. In "Chicana's Feminist literature: A Re-Vision Through Malintzín/or Malintzín: Putting Flesh Back on the Object," Alarcón explores the uses and abuses of the figure of Malintzín Tenepal in Chicano culture and the ways Chicana authors respond to and write about this historical figure. Also present are poems such as Donna Kate Rushin's "The Bridge Poem," mary hope lee's "on not bein," and Chrystos's "I Walk in the History of My People." The women within *This Bridge* were, through the writing and publication of their works, bringing their marginalized status in U.S. society to the center and interrogating it, therefore defying the notion of the center and redefining the margin.

Hernán Cortés, Malintzín Tenepal, is no longer a traitor to the indigenous people; rather, she is the forgotten and abandoned mother of all mestizas. Mythological deities such as Coatlicue and Coyolxauhqui also are redeemed in Anzaldúa's work. She reimagines the histories of La Llorona and La Virgen de Guadalupe. In Anzaldua's text, these women are no longer subject to virgin/whore dichotomies or the monstrous historical interpretations previously offered by religious and historical patriarchs. *Borderlands/La Frontera* defies categorization because it contains elements of history, mythology, prose, poetry, and linguistics.

Anzaldúa began the Ph.D. program in literature at the University of California at Santa Cruz and in 1990 published the anthology *Making Face, Making Soul/Haciendo Caras: Creative and Critical Perspectives by Feminists of Color*. She also published two children's books, *Friends from the Other Side: Amigos del otro lado* (1993) and *Prietita and the Ghost Woman/Prietita y la llorona* (1995). Along with AnaLouise Keating, Anzaldúa published *Interviews/Entrevistas* (2000), a collection of interviews with Anzaldúa conducted over the course of nearly twenty years. In a subsequent collaboration, Anzaldúa and Keating edited and published *This Bridge We Call Home: Radical Visions for Transformation* (2002). This anthology, released more than twenty years after the publication of *This Bridge Called My Back*, expands the earlier conversation to include the voices of men and women, as well as people of color and whites. The text expressed Anzaldúa's growing concept of feminism that included transformation and activism grounded in work on public and individual levels.

While working on numerous projects, Anzaldúa continued to teach and work toward her doctoral degree; however, she did not live to receive it. She died on May 15, 2004, of complications from diabetes. The University of California at Santa Cruz posthumously awarded Anzaldúa her doctorate.

SIGNIFICANCE

In *Borderlands/La Frontera*, Anzaldúa urges Chicanas to reject a singular approach to identity and instead work to interrogate and understand the various aspects inherent in a new mestiza consciousness: race, gender, sexuality, class, location, language, and history. Her work is the foundation for Border Theory and has fundamentally impacted queer, Chicana/o, and feminist studies. Her commitment to writing, collaborating, teaching, and public speaking, as well as her emphasis on spiritual activism, identity, and creativity are Anzaldúa's legacy.

The National Women's Studies Association honors Anzaldúa, a valued and long-active member of the organization, with the annual Gloria E. Anzaldúa Book Prize, which is designated for groundbreaking monographs in women's studies that makes significant multicultural feminist contributions to women of color/transnational scholarship.

Erin Ranft

Further Reading

Anzaldúa, Gloria. *The Gloria Anzaldúa Reader*, edited by AnaLouise Keating. Durham, N.C.: Duke University Press, 2009. Released posthumously, AnaLouise Keating compiled and edited several works by Anzaldúa that were previously unpublished.

---. "Now Let Us Shift." *In This Bridge We Call Home: Radical Visions of Transformation*, edited by AnaLouise Keating and Gloria Anzaldúa. New York: Routeldge, 2002. One of the last works published by Anzaldúa before her death, this essay details her theory on the path to conocimiento, or deep knowledge. Individual work, according to Anzaldúa, will lead to transformation and spiritual activism.

_____, and AnaLouise Keating. *Interviews/Entrevistas*. New York: Routledge, 2000. A collection of interviews with Anzaldúa, each containing an introductory retrospective interview with Keating.

Pérez, Emma. "Gloria Anzaldúa: La Gran Nueva Mestiza Theorist, Writer, Activist, Scholar." *NWSA Journal* 17, no. 2 (Summer, 2005): 1-10. Pérez analyzes the theories within Anzaldúa's work.

Yarbro-Bejarano, Yvonne. "Gloria Anzaldúa's Borderlands/La Frontera: Cultural Studies, 'Difference,' and the Non-Unitary Subject." *Cultural Critique* 28 (1994): 5-28. In this article, Yarbro-Bejarano examines Anzaldúa's theory of mestiza consciousness, as well as the positive and negative responses to this work.

Ella Baker

Civil rights organizer and activist

Born: December 13, 1903; Norfolk, Virginia
Died: December 13, 1986
Area of Achievement: Education, social issues

Working behind the scenes of the Civil Rights movement, Baker was a grassroots community organizer whose primary aim was to teach uneducated working class African Americans the skills necessary to achieve social and economic empowerment. Baker worked especially hard to train African American youths as social activists.

Early Life

Ella Josephine Baker was born in Norfolk, Virginia, to Georgianna (Anna) Ross Baker and Blake Baker. Her father worked for the railroad, and her mother was active in community service through the Baptist church. In 1910, Baker's father moved the family to Littleton, North Carolina, to escape growing racial violence in Norfolk, but he continued to work there and rarely saw his children. Consequently, Baker's mother was her greatest influence during her childhood. Family and community were important to Baker's mother, who believed that it was an obligation to help those less fortunate. This lesson made a deep and lasting impression on Baker.

In 1918, Baker enrolled in Shaw University, a Baptist preparatory school and university for African American students. After graduating from high school, Baker remained at Shaw and earned her bachelor's degree. There

Ella Baker (Afro American Newspapers/Getty Images)

she developed her social activist skills as a member of the debate team and school newspaper editor. Baker often found herself challenging established school policies. In 1927, she graduated from Shaw as class valedictorian.

After graduation, Baker moved to New York City's Harlem neighborhood, where she met many socialist radicals who shaped her political thought. Throughout the 1930's, Baker honed her skills as a community organizer and youth programs developer for a host of grassroots and government organizations in New York City. In the late 1930's, Baker married T. J. Roberts. Indicative of her fierce independence, however, she did not take her husband's surname. The couple divorced in 1958.

LIFE'S WORK

In 1940, Baker was hired by the National Association for the Advancement of Colored People (NAACP) as an assistant field secretary to organize and conduct fundraising and membership drives. She resigned from the NAACP for personal reasons in 1946 but continued to work with the organization unofficially. Into the early 1950's, Baker worked with several smaller, local civil rights groups. In 1952, she became the first woman president of New York City's NAACP branch and concentrated on eliminating racism and segregation in the city's schools by organizing and leading several protests.

Baker shifted her attention to civil rights struggles in her native South after the Montgomery bus boycott began in 1955. In 1956, Baker organized direct action campaigns in the South through the civil rights group In Friendship. One year later, she helped organize the Southern Christian Leadership Conference (SCLC). Baker moved to Atlanta in 1958 to become the SCLC's first full-time staff member and organized the Crusade for Citizenship. She left the SCLC the next year to once again focus on grassroots movements in smaller communities that were overlooked by the SCLC and the NAACP.

> "Oppressed people, whatever their level of formal education, have the ability to understand and interpret the world around them, to see the world for what it is, and move to transform it."

In 1960, Baker helped form the Student Nonviolent Coordinating Committee (SNCC). Comprising mostly African American college students, this organization concentrated on involving poor and undereducated African Americans in the Civil Rights movement. During 1963 and 1964, Baker, through SNCC, organized the Freedom Vote, Freedom Summer, and Freedom School campaigns in Mississippi. She also orchestrated the Mississippi Freedom Democratic Party's participation in the 1964 Democratic National Convention.

In the late 1960's, SNCC became increasingly militant and violent in its attitude and actions. Although SNCC moved away from Baker's original vision for the group, her support never wavered in spite of her reservations about the group's philosophy and tactics. Despite her continued support, Baker's role in SNCC diminished with time.

By the early 1970's, failing health had limited Baker's physical participation as an organizer, but she remained a respected activist who spoke out against a variety of social ills, including war and political persecution. She also supported the women's rights and Puerto Rican political independence movements, and she spoke out against apartheid in South Africa. Baker died in her Harlem apartment on her birthday in 1986, after a long battle with Alzheimer's disease.

SIGNIFICANCE

Although Baker worked with the NAACP, SCLC, SNCC, and many other civil rights organizations, she remained loyal only to her core beliefs and values, which respected the young, the impoverished, and the undereducated. When an organization began to exhibit qualities that were contrary to her ideals, Baker moved on to groups more closely aligned with her values. Beyond fighting racism, she sought to eliminate the sexist attitudes that permeated African American culture at the time. Refusing to join any particular political party or subscribe to a specific political ideology, Baker was an intensely independent community organizer and activist who cherished social justice over political affiliations.

Mark T. Vail

FURTHER READING

Bohanon, Lisa Frederikson. *Freedom Cannot Rest: Ella Baker and the Civil Rights Movement*. Greensboro, N.C.: Morgan Reynolds, 2005. Provides a general overview of Baker's work during the 1950's and 1960's.

DeLaure, Marilyn Bordwell. "Planting Seeds of Change:

Ella Baker's Radical Rhetoric." *Women's Studies in Communication* 31, no. 1 (Spring, 2008): 1-28. Scholarly analysis of some of Baker's most famous and influential speeches as an organizer and activist.

Grant, Joanne. *Ella Baker: Freedom Bound.* New York: John Wiley & Sons, 1998. This biography focuses on Baker's work within the Civil Rights movement from the 1940's through the 1960's.

Ransby, Barbara. *Ella Baker and the Black Freedom Movement: A Radical Democratic Vision.* Chapel Hill: University of North Carolina Press, 2003. A comprehensive biography of Baker's life from early childhood on. Focuses on both her personal life and professional work.

JOHN BROWN

Abolitionist

Born: May 9, 1800; Torrington, Connecticut
Died: December 2, 1859; Charles Town, Virginia
Area of achievement: Social reform

Thanks to the notoriety that Brown received from a single dramatic act of rebellion, his name has come to symbolize the struggle over the abolition of slavery in the United States. His action was the catalyst for change from polite debate and parliamentary maneuvering aimed at modification of the institution to physical violence and a direct onslaught on southern territory and the supporters of slavery.

EARLY LIFE

A native of Connecticut, John Brown was born in a state that, like many others in New England in 1800, was agriculturally exhausted and in religious turmoil. His parents, Owen and Ruth (Mills) Brown, were affected by both problems at his birth. Economically, the Brown family was barely at the subsistence level. John's father moved from job to job: farmer, carpenter, handyman. Though the family descended from the early Mayflower settlers, they were never able to capitalize on their ancestry. Religiously, Owen Brown was a harsh practitioner of the piety of his Puritan forebears, and he instilled in his son a lifelong fear and adoration of a militant and volatile God.

The elder Brown had been married twice and fathered sixteen children. His first wife, John's mother, suffered from mental disease as did others in her family. According

John Brown (Wikimedia Commons)

to some accounts, John did not take well to his stepmother, but there is little evidence to support this conjecture. The peripatetic life of the family was probably more disturbing to him. When John was five, his father moved to Hudson, Ohio, following the line of the moving frontier. Again, the family was without the necessary capital to take advantage of the opportunities available in the rich Ohio Valley. His father became a herdsman and then a tanner, a vocation that the son quickly mastered. His father had some plans for his son which included sending him to Plainsfield, Massachusetts, to study for the ministry. John did not stay long, however, either because of poor preparation or because of his poor eyesight.

John Brown returned to Hudson to help his father with the cattle and the tanning shop. At the age of twenty, he married Dianthe Lusk, who bore him seven children in twelve years of married life. She, like his mother, had mental problems. Dianthe Brown died in 1831, and within a year of her passing, Brown married Mary Anne Day, then sixteen, who bore him thirteen more children in twenty-one years. Brown, possessing a modicum of education in a frontier region, became a surveyor as well as a tanner like his father. Also like his father, Brown was a mover. In 1825, he moved to Pennsylvania, cleared land,

and set up what was to become a successful farm and tannery. He also became a postmaster, but still he was unsatisfied. Quick fortunes were being made in land and business speculation, and Brown sold off his holdings and moved back to Ohio. There he hoped to take advantage of land speculation and canal building contracts. He lost heavily and began pyramiding debt while turning to cattle and sheep selling. His creditors moved in on him and he was compelled to declare bankruptcy.

LIFE'S WORK

Brown's work in the woolen business brought him a partnership with another man, Simon Perkins, to establish a wool brokerage in Springfield, Massachusetts. Fluctuating prices and market instability, however, confounded his efforts to make a success of the business. He was also accused of "weighting" the packs of hides, which were sold by weight to English markets. The collapse of this last business venture was followed by numerous lawsuits, one involving sixty thousand dollars for breach of contract. Brown settled his affairs as best he could. He was fifty years old and virtually penniless, with a large family to support.

Even as a young man, Brown had learned from his father the biblical precept that it was sinful to earn one's living from the sweat of others and that slavery was wrong. In Ohio both he and his father had lent their resources to aiding the underground movement of runaway slaves. John Brown's barn at his farm in Pennsylvania was a station in that movement, and he formed a League of Gileadites among black people in Springfield to encourage them to defend both themselves and fugitive slaves.

Brown's activity in New England brought him in touch with men whose lives would never be the same after meeting him. Gerrit Smith, a New York benefactor of abolitionism who owned much of the Adirondack Mountains, was attracted to Brown. He had given land for use by runaway slaves in a small community known as North Elba. He gave Brown a farm from which he could train and educate the former slaves. Given the severe climate, short growing season, and lack of arable land in the region, not to mention Brown's spotty record as a farmer, problems developed. Brown himself declared that he felt "omnipotent" in his new role as guide and exemplar to the black people in his charge.

Within two years, however, he was in Akron, Ohio. His mind was turned to developing a grand plan for an attack on slavery. As early as 1847, he had talked about gathering a band of men from the free states to make forays into slave territory to rescue black slaves from bondage. He talked of setting up a mountain stronghold as a base of terrorist activity, but the ideas did not take coherent form until the Fugitive Slave Act, part of the Compromise of 1850, was passed. The Kansas-Nebraska Act, four years later, further agitated him and his sons, five of whom moved to the territory to help make Kansas a free state. In May, 1855, John Brown, Jr., wrote a mournful letter to his father explaining the conditions and imploring him to send arms to battle proslavery forces. Brown dispatched his family to North Elba again and set out for Kansas with a wagonload of guns and ammunition.

Brown found his sons impoverished and ill when he arrived at Osawatomie. Though he was to join the colony as a surveyor, he quickly assumed leadership of the local militia and made Free Soil a vengeance-wreaking crusade. His group fought in the ineffectual Wakarusa War and then, after the sacking of Lawrence by proslavery forces, he and his party, which included four sons and two others, ritually slaughtered five settlers at Pottawatomie. He had reached a personal turning point, viewing himself as an instrument in the hands of an angry God.

> "*Whereas slavery, throughout its entire existence in the United States, is none other than the most barbarous, unprovoked and unjustifiable war of one portion of its citizens against another portion, the only conditions of which are perpetual imprisonment and hopeless servitude, or absolute extermination, in utter disregard and violation of those eternal and self-evident truths set forth in our Declaration of Independence.*"

Brown's own colony was overrun and burned and one of his boys killed in retaliation. Brown now was gray in hair and features, with a bent back and glittering gray-blue eyes; he had grown a full beard that was streaked with gray, which made him appear older than his fifty-six years. His fervent attitude toward slavery fired his listeners, many of whom, such as Franklin Sanborn, Thomas W. Higginson, Theodore Parker, Gerrit Smith, G. L. Stearns, and Samuel Gridley Howe, were ripe for the leadership that Brown promised. He met with these members of the Massachusetts State Kansas Committee, and they responded with some arms and ammunition and money to take with him to Kansas again.

Kansas had no stomach for bloodshed in 1857 as it

Larger than lifesize, bronze sculpture of Brown and an African-American youth, by Joseph P. Pollia. Installed at John Brown's Farm, near Lake Placid, New York, 1935. (Wikimedia Commons)

moved closer to voting the issue of free or slave, and Brown now thought of a daring plan to liberate slaves in the South itself. In the spring of 1858, he visited the colony of runaway slaves in Catham, Canada, to gain volunteers. His money gone, he turned again to Smith and the Massachusetts group. They argued for a delay, gave him some money and supplies, and Brown again headed for Kansas, this time under the name of Shubel Morgan. There he led a raid on some plantations in Missouri in which one planter was killed and some slaves liberated. Brown was now a wanted man with a bounty on his head. He headed for Canada with the slaves in tow and then proceeded east, making speeches in Cleveland and Rochester to solicit funds. Again the old group came through with thirty-eight hundred dollars, knowing full well that Brown was bent on violence.

It was Harpers Ferry that became fixed in Brown's mind; to the commander in chief of a provisional army for liberation it was an ideal objective. The federal arsenal in the town was noted for the quality of arms and its technology since its creation in 1798. The complex of forges, shops, tool and die works, and assembly areas turned out rifles and handguns in an assembly line process that foretold mass production. John Hall of Maine had gained a contract in 1819 to turn out breech-loading rifles using his idea of interchangeable parts, and his contract was renewed yearly until 1844, when a totally new rifle plant was built to produce the Standard United States Model military rifle. The skilled workers were mostly transplanted northerners who were regarded as "foreigners" by local southerners. A canal and a railroad as well as a macadam road led to the town of three thousand, which included 1,250 free blacks and some eighty-eight slaves.

The Brown contingent of fourteen white and five black people established themselves in a farm five miles from the Ferry to lay plans for their attack. On Sunday, October 16, 1859, they marched by night down the dirt road leading to the town. By mid-morning, the men had taken both the town and its leading citizens.

Brown did not know what to do with his victory. He had control of the engine house, the federal armory, the railroad, and the town of Harpers Ferry, and the very magnitude of his success overwhelmed and confused him. He let a train continue, certainly with the knowledge that the passengers would alarm state and federal officials. He did nothing about searching out possible followers from the town population or the countryside. He had guns, powder and shells, and a well-situated natural fortress, as well as a small though very devout band of followers. Brown lost his revolutionary compass at this critical moment. His willingness to fight was not in question. Shots were fired and lives were taken until Lee's troops stormed the engine house and cut Brown down. Though he was not severely wounded, there was little recourse for his men but to surrender.

The military quickly restored order and moved Brown to prison while dispatching squads to investigate the farm that had been the band's headquarters. There they found letters and documentation that implicated Brown's northern associates in the Harpers Ferry venture. Why Brown had kept, let alone brought with him, these damning materials is uncertain. He certainly treasured his association with successful and influential men, and given his life on the margin of society, this connection was important enough to be sustained with physical evidence. Furthermore, Brown was concerned about the shifting commitment of antislavery reformers and therefore by keeping documentation he could hold them to the course. The discovery of these materials, however, proved the conspiracy case against Brown and his men and threw fear into those who had aided them.

Of the twenty-one men who had followed Brown to Harpers Ferry on October 16, only eleven remained alive. Brown had seen two of his sons killed in the melee that followed the arrival of the militia from Charlestown (modern Charles Town, West Virginia) and Lee's marines. On October 18, he was jailed in Charlestown to await indictment, which came a week later.

Brown, Aaron Stevens, Edwin Coppoc, Shields Green (the black man who had chosen to go with Brown despite the admonition and concerns of Frederick Douglass), and John Copeland were all indicted on October 25 for treason against Virginia, for conspiring with slaves to rebel, and for murder. All of them pleaded not guilty and requested separate trials. The court agreed and determined that Brown would be tried first.

The prosecution was headed by Charles Harding, state attorney for Jefferson County, and Andrew Hunter, a seasoned Charlestown attorney. The court was presided over by Judge Richard Parker, who had just begun the semiannual term of his circuit court and already had a grand jury seated. Turner had just gaveled the court to order when Brown's defense attorney read a telegram from one A. H. Lewis of Akron, Ohio, declaring that Brown's family was suffering from hereditary insanity. It proceeded to list the people on his mother's side who were known to have severe mental problems. The inference was that Brown himself was insane and therefore not fit for trial. His attorney had shown Brown the telegram and Brown admitted to his mother's death by insanity and the fact that his first wife and two of his sons were afflicted. Brown, however, rejected the plea of insanity on his behalf, though he apparently gave his attorney permission to use the document. The judge ruled out the plea on the basis that the evidence was in unreliable form. He also rejected a delay to enable Brown to get a new attorney.

Brown's trial began on October 27, 1859, and lasted less than four days. He was carried to the court each day in a litter, and with each day, he became more irritated with his court-appointed attorneys. They had been joined by a twenty-one-year-old Boston attorney, George Hoyt, who had been retained by some Brown supporters who hoped to learn more about the case on behalf of the group of backers who were facing possible indictment as coconspirators. Botts and Green gratefully withdrew from the defense team, leaving the inexperienced Hoyt alone. Legal help soon came in the form of Samuel Chilton of Washington and Hiram Griswold of Cleveland, who were persuaded to take up what Brown himself realized was a lost cause.

The prosecution's case was devastating. Brown's request that he be tried as commander in chief of a provisional army, according to the laws governing warfare, was rejected. Brown's vision of himself as a messianic leader of a noble crusade against slavery was ignored. On October 31, at 1:45 p.m., the case went to the jury, which, after only forty-five minutes, declared Brown guilty on all counts. The verdict cast a pall on the audience, which days before had been vociferous in its rage against Brown. Brown himself said nothing as he lay quietly on his cot. The sentence of death by hanging was passed on November 2, with the date for execution set for December 2.

The coconspirators captured with Brown were tried as well and all sentenced to the same fate. Brown had visited with them in jail, calling on them to be firm and resolute and to implicate no one. Friends of Brown had sought to bring his wife from North Elba, but Brown insisted that she remain at home. Only on the afternoon before his execution did she visit with him and then stand by to claim his body.

Governor Henry Wise was besieged with demands for clemency, threats, and warnings of plots to free Brown. Martial law was proclaimed in Charlestown, and fifteen hundred soldiers, including a company of cadets from Virginia Military Institute commanded by Stonewall Jackson, ringed the gallows on December 2.

John Brown's death on a rope in Charlestown was but the end of a beginning. The larger crisis that Brown had foreshadowed soon came with a character of violence and death that would have perhaps given even Osawatomie pause. The South, by insisting on dealing with Brown's case, had arrogated to itself police authority over what was a crime against federal property. It thereby threw down a gauntlet of defiant sectionalism and states' rights.

None of this was lost on Brown's supporters in the North, who, after suffering gag rules in Congress blocking their petitions against slavery, after almost thirty years of relentless electioneering, pamphleteering, lecturing, haranguing, debating, and propagandizing against slavery, and after suffering dismaying defeats at the hands of every branch of government and in virtually every attempt to work within the system, were ready to exploit John Brown's fateful end.

Antislavery reformers took charge of the body, and by wagon, train, and steamer they took it to the hills where Brown had felt "omnipotent." It was a cortege that would be duplicated six years later on the death of Abraham Lincoln—a slow, somber taking of martyred remains home. Through Lake Placid and on to the little village of North Elba they took Brown, and near his little home they buried him. Gerrit Smith, the man who had given him the land, was not with him at the burial. Smith had become mentally deranged after Brown's capture and was institutionalized. Others who were closely involved with Brown, such as Frederick Douglass, found it convenient to flee to Canada or travel abroad. Brown, the guerrilla fighter and terrorist who had taken the struggle against slavery beyond rhetoric, had made clear that the approaching confrontation would be violent.

Significance

John Brown was a tragic figure central to the great tragedy of Civil War America. Whether he was a hero in that era is, at best, controversial. There seems little doubt that had his earlier ventures been successful, he would have melded with other entrepreneurs of the moving frontier and probably been lost as another subject representing an enterprising nation. A failure as a businessperson, he turned all of his energies to what became for him a holy mission: rooting out the evil of slavery. Social, economic, and political displacement encouraged many in his region to seek redress. Brown, however, personalized these conflicts to an extreme degree and placed himself at a point from which there was no turning back.

Jack J. Cardoso

Further Reading

Boyer, Richard O. *The Legend of John Brown: A Biography and a History*. New York: Alfred A. Knopf, 1972. This is a fine piece of biography that takes the story of Brown up to his arrival in Kansas in 1855. Boyer died before he could complete the second volume.

Malin, James C. *John Brown and the Legend of Fifty-six*. Philadelphia: American Philosophical Society, 1942. Malin's work is highly critical of Brown's activities in Kansas and of Brown personally. It is useful, however, for its detail of that period of Brown's life.

National Park Service. *John Brown's Raid*. Washington, D.C.: Superintendent of Documents, 1974. Here is an outstanding piece of work based on reports by William C. Everhart and Arthur L. Sullivan that gives sweep and substance to Brown and his men at Harpers Ferry in the space of sixty-eight pages.

Oates, Stephen B. *To Purge This Land with Blood: A Biography of John Brown*. New York: Harper & Row, 1970. Oates's book is a full biography of Brown and establishes the point of view that Brown's puritanical heritage was at the base of his thought and action. He also has something to say in a bibliographical essay. See also his article "John Brown and His Judges: A Critique of the Historical Literature" in *Civil War History* vol. 17, 1971, pp. 5-24.

Reynolds, David S. *John Brown, Abolitionist: The Man Who Killed Slavery, Sparked the Civil War, and Seeded Civil Rights*. New York: Alfred A. Knopf, 2005. Reynolds's biography is generally sympathetic toward Brown. He portrays Brown as a Puritan in the tradition of Oliver Cromwell and Jonathan Edwards—a man who saw the world as a battle of good versus evil, and who sought to avenge the evil of slavery.

Sanborn, Franklin B., ed. *The Life and Letters of John Brown*. New York: Negro Universities Press, 1891. This is a book to be used carefully as it is biased toward Brown. However, the gathering of Brown's letters makes this a valuable resource.

Stauffer, John. *The Black Hearts of Men: Radical Abolitionists and the Transformation of Race*. Cambridge, Mass.: Harvard University Press, 2002. During the 1850's, Brown, Gerrit Smith, and two African Americans, Frederick Douglass and doctor/scholar James McCune Smith, formed an interracial alliance to abolish slavery. Stauffer describes how the men worked to promote abolition and other social issues, and how their revolutionary zeal waned after Brown's 1859 raid on Harpers Ferry.

Villard, Oswald Garrison. *John Brown, 1800-1859: A Biography Fifty Years After*. Gloucester, Mass.: Peter Smith, 1910. Villard's biography is still a standard work on Brown and his time. It cannot be ignored in any study.

Olympia Brown

Protestant cleric and social reformer

Born: January 5, 1835; Prairie Ronde Township, Michigan
Died: October 23, 1926; Baltimore, Maryland
Area of Achievement: Religion and theology, women's

Olympia Brown (Library of Congress)

rights

Among the first Americans to demand that higher education be opened to women, Brown managed to graduate from college and become one of the first women ordained a minister. She was also prominent in the woman suffrage movement.

EARLY LIFE

Olympia Brown was the first of four children born to Asa and Lephia Brown. Her parents were pioneers who made the eight-hundred-mile trip from their native Vermont to live on the frontier in Michigan Territory during the year before she was born. In contrast to many of their neighbors, the Brown family was one in which education played a vital role. When the children were young, they were taught by their mother, a woman passionate about education, who pasted together articles from newspapers and journals to make books for her children.

Lephia and Asa Brown were also strong in their religious faith, Universalism. They taught their children the main tenets of this religion—a detail that would greatly influence Olympia's later life. In 1837, when Michigan attained statehood and began a state-wide public school system, the Browns built a one-room schoolhouse on their property and took the necessary steps to secure pupils and teachers. After attending Cedar Park Seminary in nearby Schoolcraft, Michigan, the fifteen-year-old Olympia taught at the family schoolhouse. At this time in her life, she experienced sexual discrimination for the first time: She wanted to continue her education, but few colleges admitted women.

After many debates with her father, Olympia and her younger sister left home in 1854 to attend Mount Holyoke Female Seminary in South Hadley, Massachusetts. Although the courses she took deepened her hunger for learning, she left Mount Holyoke after only one year because of its rigid Calvinistic atmosphere and the sexual discrimination she perceived behind the façade of female education. Once again, she struggled to find an institution that would admit women, and she suffered many rejections. Finally, when she was twenty years old, she was accepted at Antioch College in Yellow Springs, Ohio. Antioch was an institution that imposed no religious conversion on its students.

> "*The grandest thing has been the lifting up of the gates and the opening of the doors to the women of America, giving liberty to twenty-seven million women, thus opening to them a new and larger life and a higher ideal.*"

LIFE'S WORK

As had been the case in Brown's education up to that moment, Antioch's educational system was discriminatory, as male and female students were given different assignments. Brown's religious background told her that all humans were created equal, so she refused to accept the system and became the only female student to complete the men's assignments, orations on various topics, a discipline taboo at that time for American women. Brown also was responsible for bringing to the school other women speakers. It was, in fact, while listening to one of the few women ministers in America that Brown sensed her own destiny.

After graduating from Antioch in 1860, Brown struggled for entrance into a theological college. Once admitted, she again endured sexual harassment. She also struggled to perfect her speaking voice and had to fight for ordination. She finally was ordained at the Universalist Divinity School of St. Lawrence University in 1863. Within a year, she received the call to her first full-time parish in Weymouth Landing, Massachusetts. This assignment began a series of assignments to parishes struggling so hard that male ministers turned them down or gave up on them.

Although Brown's first official work for the women's movement began while she was attending Antioch College, it was not until her tenure at Weymouth Landing that she began winning national prominence for her role in the movement's 1867 Kansas campaign, which sought to secure the vote for women in that newly settled territory. Although she had been given many promises concerning arrangements and accommodations that would be in place during the campaign, Brown faced disorganization, a collapsing support base in the Republican Party, and sweltering heat. She also worked almost entirely on her own, as the promised arrangements for a traveling companion also fell through. In Kansas, she was alone, an unmarried woman, hundreds of miles from home and within fifty miles of deadly wars between settlers and Native Americans. She was completely dependent on pioneer farmers for her conveyance, housing, support, and, at times, the means of escape in the face of sometimes hostile crowds. Although the Kansas campaign ultimately failed to achieve its objective, Elizabeth Cady Stanton was so impressed with the fear that the ninety-pound Olympia Brown aroused among opposition speakers that she began trying to persuade Brown to work full-time in the suffrage movement.

Brown chose to remain in her field for the time being, accepting her next religious call to the Universalist Church in Bridgeport, Connecticut, in 1870. Three years later, she married John Henry Willis. Although those around her had feared that marriage would distract her from both the ministry and the women's cause, Brown discovered in her husband one who supported her on every front. He changed his own job to meet the demands of hers and relocated when her work made it necessary. He also supported her then radical decision to keep her maiden name, Brown.

In 1874, Brown gave birth to her first child, John Parker Willis, and then discovered that while she had been on maternity leave some members of her congregation had begun lobbying for a male minister. Although the majority of the congregation supported Brown, she resigned. By 1876, Brown had given birth to a second child, Gwendolen Brown Willis. In 1878, she was appointed to a struggling church in Racine, Wisconsin. In her hands, the Racine parish not only survived, it flourished as an educational and cultural center. The Racine church would prove, however, to be Brown's last full-time ministerial position.

Although Brown never completely quit the ministry, she dedicated her final decades to full-time work within the fight for women's equality. She was active in many organizations, including the Wisconsin Suffrage Association, the Wisconsin Federation of Women's Clubs, the Federal Suffrage Association, the National Woman Suffrage Association, and the Woman's Party.

During the winter of 1917, when she was more than seventy years old, Brown participated in a march on Washington, D.C., in support of woman suffrage. She was among the people who witnessed several men attacking the marchers and then saw President Woodrow Wilson have the women arrested, instead of their attackers. The following year, she again marched in Washington, this time personally burning some of the president's speeches before the crowds. Finally, in 1920, when she was eighty-five years old, she was able to vote in her first election. She then dedicated her remaining six years to worldwide equality by active participation in the Women's League for Peace and Freedom, the League of Nations, the League of Women Voters, and the American Civil Liberties Union.

Significance

Although Olympia Brown had relatives who ran an Underground Railroad station in their home, she herself never knew the plight of American slaves at first hand. She also had no firsthand knowledge of the abuses of factory workers or of the hardships of immigrants. Nevertheless, hers is an important story in American history. She lived on the American frontier; she shocked college administrators by wearing the costume named after Amelia Bloomer and refusing chaperones; she was ordained into the ministry at a time when the mere idea of such a thing was heresy to many; she knew and was respected by some of the most important leaders in the woman suffrage movement; and she was one of the few prominent figures of the movement still alive in 1920 when the Nineteenth Amendment was passed.

Olympia Brown experienced sexual discrimination

both within the educational system and within churches. During her lifetime, she argued against prevailing notions of womanhood, accused novelists of portraying women as insipid, and railed against the notion that young girls should be taught to be "little ladies." At a time in American history when women of her class were expected to be "quiet angels" in their homes, she was politically astute and vocal, taking on the weaknesses in the political positions of prominent figures such as Ralph Waldo Emerson and Frederick Douglass, in their presence. Through it all, she refused to let go of her personal doctrine that all people are created equal and that women are people, too.

Anna Dunlap Higgins

FURTHER READING

Baker, Jean H., ed. *Votes for Women: The Struggle for Suffrage Revisited.* Oxford, England: Oxford University Press, 2002. A solidly researched work that places Brown in the national struggle for woman suffrage.

Brown, Olympia. *Suffrage and Religious Principle: Speeches and Writings of Olympia Brown.* Edited by Dana Greene. Metuchen, N.J.: Scarecrow Press, 1983. Collection of some of Brown's major writings and speeches.

Buhle, Mari Jo, and Paul Buhle, eds. *The Concise History of Woman Suffrage: Selections from the Classic Work of Stanton, Gage, and Harper.* Urbana: University of Illinois Press, 1978. Like Baker's book, this is an important work that helps place Brown in the larger picture of woman suffrage. Many readers should find this updated version more reader-friendly than the original source, which was published in 1868.

Coté, Charlotte. *Olympia Brown: The Battle for Equality.* Racine, Wis.: Mother Courage Press, 1988. A full-length biography, this book also includes two of Brown's best-remembered addresses and lists the whereabouts of most of the other documents by and about Brown, most of which are located at Radcliffe College in Cambridge, Massachusetts.

Emerson, Dorothy May, ed. *Standing Before Us: Unitarian Universalist Women and Social Reform, 1776-1936.* Boston: Skinner House Books, 2000. This work contains a biographical sketch of Brown and Brown's own "The Higher Education of Women." The book also confirms Brown's status as the first woman ordained to the Universalist ministry.

LUISA CAPETILLO

Puerto Rican activist and writer

Born: October 28, 1879; Arecibo, Puerto Rico
Died: April 10, 1922; San Juan, Puerto Rico
Area of Achievement: Activism, women's rights, social issues, literature

Best known as a labor leader and champion of the working class, Capetillo also was a pioneer feminist in Puerto Rico. As a writer, Capetillo denounced religion, capitalism, the exploitation of workers by political parties, and the patriarchal system that kept women from full economic and social independence.

EARLY LIFE

Luisa Capetillo Perone (kah-peh-TEE-yoh) was born to Luisa Margarita Perone, a domestic worker, and Luis Capetillo Echevarria, an unskilled laborer, on October 28, 1879, in Arecibo, Puerto Rico. Although they were

Capetillo wearing men's clothing. (Wikimedia Commons)

members of the working class, Capetillo's parents ensured that she had an education and exposed her to many forms of literature. In addition to her education, Capetillo assisted her mother in domestic service to wealthy families in Arecibo. Capetillo's mother's passion for literature and experience as a domestic worker no doubt influenced Capetillo's later work.

In 1898, having fallen in love with and been courted by Manuel Ledesma, Capetillo gave birth to her first child, Manuela. Ledesma was the son of a wealthy dignitary, and his family never approved of the relationship. Shortly after the birth of their second child, Gregorio, Ledesma and Capetillo separated.

While working as a reader in a cigar factory, Capetillo became deeply involved with the Free Federation of Workers (Federacion Libre de Trabajadores, or FLT). Her position as a reader exposed Capetillo to important political and philosophical works as well as news from around the world. At this time, her activism flourished as she traveled throughout Puerto Rico to participate in strikes and speak at rallies. Her knowledge and eloquence allowed Capetillo to emerge as a leader in the male-dominated labor movement.

In 1904, Capetillo began writing for newspapers and magazines, which eventually led to the publication of her first book, *Ensayos libertarios* (*Libertarian Essays*, 1907), which employs socialist and anarchist rhetoric to advocate for an equal society free from exploitation of laborers and women.

> *"Do not buy finery or jewels, because books are worth more than they are. Adorn your understanding with their precious ideas, because there is no luxury that dazzles like the luxury of science."*

LIFE'S WORK

By the early 1900's, Capetillo's articulate perspectives and skilled organizing had made her the best-known woman labor leader in Puerto Rico. As an active member of the FLT, Capetillo used her prominence to reach female workers by publishing a magazine called *La mujer*. In an effort to raise money to sustain the magazine, Capetillo published her second book, *La humanidad del futuro* (*Humanity's Future*, 1910). *La humanidad del futuro* depicts Capetillo's vision of a utopian society and advocates for a reform of social services including health and education, as well as free love, vegetarianism, and communal responsibility.

In 1911, Capetillo gave birth to Luis, her third child, who was the result of a brief relationship with a married pharmacist. The same year, she published her most renowned book, *Mi opinión sobre las libertades derechos y deberes de la mujer* (*My Opinion About the Freedom, Rights, and Duties of Women*), which is considered the first feminist treatise in Puerto Rico and possibly Latin America. In a collection of essays, the book provides a comprehensive feminist analysis of issues such as sexual exploitation, domestic and other women's work, education, politics, motherhood, and religion. Capetillo's work concludes that education is the key to women's emancipation.

In 1912, Capetillo began working as an international labor organizer. Her work brought her to New York, where she wrote for a Hispanic labor newspaper and other labor publications. Her labor work eventually took her to Ybor City, a section of Tampa, Florida. While in Florida, Capetillo collaborated with a variety of cigar workers to organize for better working conditions, higher wages, and the right to unionize.

Three years later, Capetillo moved to Havana, Cuba, to participate in labor rallies and strikes. In 1915, she was arrested in Havana for wearing pants in public. This incident and her anarchist activities led to her deportation to Puerto Rico in 1916.

While in Puerto Rico, Capetillo published her final book *Influencias de las ideas modernas* (*Influences of Modern Ideas*, 1916). The work reiterates many of the same subjects in *Mi opinión sobre las libertades, derechos, y deberes de la mujer* in a compilation of letters, a three-part play, and a number of personal reflections. After the publication of *Influencias de las ideas modernas*, Capetillo continued to write for labor publications and promote her books. From 1919 to 1920, Capetillo lived in New York City, where she worked as a reader in a cigar factory, ran a hostel, and wrote.

In 1920, Capetillo returned to Puerto Rico to start an education project called Escuela Granja Agricola (Agricultural Farm School). The project would teach children agricultural and leadership skills in addition to a traditional education. However, before that dream could come to fruition, Capetillo died on April 10, 1922, from tuberculosis.

SIGNIFICANCE

Capetillo's work as a labor organizer and feminist activist

not only brought together the working class of Puerto Rico but also revealed gender disparities within progressive movements and political revolutions. As the first feminist treatise in Puerto Rico, her *Mi opinión sobre las libertades, derechos, y deberes de la mujer* captured the social history and experiences of Puerto Rican women in the early twentieth century. Furthermore, her prominence as an international labor leader revealed a commonality among working women throughout North America. Capetillo's legacy has given generations of labor and feminist activists a historical context in which to base their work.

Erin E. Parrish

FURTHER READING

Capetillo, Luisa. *A Nation of Women: An Early Feminist Speaks Out—Mi opinión sobre las libertades, derechos, y deberes de la mujer.* Edited with an introduction by Félix V. Matos Rodríguez. Houston, Tex.: Arte Público Press, 2004. Matos Rodríguez provides a short biography of Capetillo and a historiography of her works. This text also includes a translation of Capetillo's landmark feminist treatise.

Hewitt, Nancy A. "Luisa Capetillo: Feminist of the Working Class." In *Latina Legacies: Identity, Biography, and Community*, edited by Vicki L. Ruia and Virginia Sanchez Korral. New York: Oxford University Press, 2005. Includes a brief biography, historical context, and an analysis of Capetillo's significance.

Valle Ferrer, Norma. *Luisa Capetillo, Pioneer Puerto Rican Feminist.* New York: Peter Lang, 2006. Valle Ferrer provides an in-depth biography and study of Capetillo's life. Appendix includes selections from Capetillo's final book, Influencias de las ideas modernas

MARY ANN SHADD CARY

Abolitionist and journalist

Born: October 9, 1823; Wilmington, Delaware
Died: June 5, 1893; Washington, D.C.
Area of Achievement: Journalism, women's rights, law

A pioneering educator and lifelong advocate of equality for African Americans, Cary wrote and lectured widely in support of abolition and black emigration to Canada, and after emancipation was achieved, she participated in the woman suffrage and temperance movements. She was also first African American woman newspaper publisher and the first black woman to enter Howard University Law School.

EARLY LIFE

Mary Ann Shadd Cary was born Mary Ann Shadd, the first of thirteen children of Harriet Parnell, a mulatto woman born in North Carolina, and Abraham Shadd, a shoemaker descended from a German soldier named Hans Schad and a free black Pennsylvania woman named Elizabeth Jackson, who married in 1756. Like her father and paternal grandfather, Mary Ann was born free. The fact that her grandfather and great-grandfather had been butchers by trade secured the status of the Shadd family within the black middle class of Wilmington, Delaware, where she grew up. However, their comparative material prosperity did not spare free blacks, such as the Shadds, from the black codes that Delaware enacted during the 1830's to restrict the freedoms of former slaves.

At an early age, Mary Ann was exposed to the

Mary Ann Shadd Cary (Wikimedia Commons)

movements to abolish slavery and achieve political and social equality for free African Americans. Her father was active in local and national social protests throughout his life. He offered his homes in Wilmington and later in West Chester, Pennsylvania, as stations on the Underground Railroad, which was used by people escaping from southern slavery. He also solicited subscriptions for abolitionist newspapers such as William Lloyd Garrison's *Liberator*. In 1831, Abraham Shadd was one of three authors and signatories of a statement condemning the American Colonization Society, which worked to ship freed slaves to Africa. He was also among the first five African Americans on the board of managers of the American Anti-Slavery Society when that organization began in 1833.

During 1833, the Shadd family escaped from the increasing harshness of Delaware's black codes by moving to nearby West Chester, Pennsylvania. There, Mary Ann received six years of private instruction provided by local Quakers, under whom she studied Latin, French, literature, and mathematics. In 1840, when she was seventeen and her schooling was completed, she returned to Wilmington and opened a school for African American children. Throughout the 1840's, she taught not only in Wilmington but also in West Chester and Norristown, Pennsylvania, and in Trenton, New Jersey, where she failed in an effort to establish another school for African Americans in 1844.

LIFE'S WORK

In 1849, Mary Ann Shadd entered the public debate on obtaining black equality. During that year, she published a letter in Frederick Douglass's newspaper, *The North Star*, and also published a pamphlet, *Hints to the Colored People of the North*, in which she stressed education, morality, and economic self-help as the means through which African Americans could integrate themselves into American society. Passage of the Fugitive Slave Act by the U.S. Congress in 1850 permitted federal marshals to reclaim runaway slaves even after they reached free states. That law added new urgency to Mary Ann's emerging activism.

After attending an antislavery convention in Toronto, Canada, in September, 1851, Mary Ann decided to join the thousands of free and slave-born African Americans who were emigrating to Great Britain's Canadian colonies. After giving up her teaching job in New York City, she settled in the town of Windsor (now in Ontario). There she opened a school with the support of the American Missionary Association and became that organization's only black missionary in Canada West. In 1852, Mary Ann published *Notes of Canada West*, an essay extolling the benefits of life in Canada to potential African American migrants. By the end of the decade, Mary Ann's parents as well as several siblings had also moved to Canada.

Mary Ann's advocacy of Canadian immigration and racial uplift challenged the established leadership of Henry Bibb, another immigrant, who had established the newspaper *Voice of the Fugitive* in 1851. The friction between Mary Ann and Bibb came to a head in 1853, when the American Missionary Association responded to Bibb's criticisms of Mary Ann by withdrawing its support of her school. On March 24, 1853, the day after her Windsor school closed, Mary Ann began publishing and editing her own newspaper, the *Provincial Freeman*, in Toronto. She was the first African American woman to do so, even though the conventions of the time required her to list a man as the newspaper's editor on its masthead.

The *Provincial Freeman* provided Mary Ann with a public voice with which to articulate her support of black immigration to Canada and racial integration and to critique other abolitionists. The newspaper also published letters and articles debating woman suffrage and women's participation in the public sphere. Mary Ann spread her message further and solicited subscriptions for her newspaper by lecturing in the United States. She was one of only a few black women who spoke publicly during that period. In 1855, she moved her newspaper from Toronto to Chatham.

> *"It is better to wear out than to rust out."*

On January 3, 1856, Mary Ann married Thomas Cary, a free-born African American and barber who relocated to Toronto during the early 1850's and had three children from an earlier marriage. Mary Ann's marriage to Cary was unusual, in that she and her husband traveled back and forth between the separate homes they maintained in Chatham and Toronto. They had two children together: Sara Elizabeth, born in 1857, and Linton, born in 1860.

Mary Ann continued editing the *Provincial Freeman* until it folded in 1860 because of insufficient funds. After her husband's death later that same year, Mary Ann taught briefly in Michigan, opened another school in Chatham with her sister, and continued to publish articles in the abolitionist press. At the urging of the black nationalist leader Martin Delaney, Mary Ann traveled throughout the

United States in 1863 to encourage African American men to join the Union army during the Civil War. After the war ended, the promise of Reconstruction and diminishing employment opportunities for African Americans in Canada prompted Mary Ann's permanent return to the United States in 1867. She worked as a teacher in Detroit before moving to Washington, D.C., in 1869.

As Mary Ann settled into life as a teacher, and later as a school principal, in Washington, D.C., she began to pay more attention to women's issues in her social activism. She attended the yearly meetings of the National Women's Suffrage Association during the early part of the decade and wrote frequently for Frederick Douglass's newspaper *New National Era* in support of woman suffrage, a position that diverged from the African American community's primary goal of obtaining the vote for black men. After ratification of the Fifteenth Amendment gave black men the vote in 1870, Mary Ann herself attempted to register to vote several times. In 1880, she established the short-lived Colored Women's Progressive Franchise Association. She also advocated temperance as a means of promoting black self-sufficiency.

Meanwhile, Mary Ann became the first black woman to enter Howard University Law School. She began her legal studies there in 1869 and combined being a law student with being a teacher and school principal until she received her degree in 1883. Throughout the 1880's, she practiced law in Washington and continued to lecture and write on strategies of racial uplift. She died of stomach cancer in Washington, D.C., on June 5, 1893, during her seventieth year.

Significance

Mary Ann Shadd Cary is remarkable, not only for her notable firsts in the fields of journalism and law, but also for the space that she carved out for herself as a woman activist during the long African American struggle to obtain racial equality. She defied the mainstream social convention that a woman's rightful place was in the home by inserting herself into public debate, first on the issue of abolition of slavery and extension of civil rights to free blacks, and later in her advocacy of woman suffrage. She also defied the assumptions of other African American activists who asserted that gender equality should be subordinate to racial uplift. Her career as an educator, lecturer, and newspaperwoman—which did not cease with marriage and motherhood—was its own protest against the twin sets of limitations that she faced as an African American and as a woman.

Mary Ann's former residence in the U Street Corridor was declared a National Historic Landmark in 1976. In 1987 she was designated a Women's History Month Honoree by the National Women's History Project. In 1998, Mary Ann was inducted into the National Women's Hall of Fame. She was also honored by Canada, being designated a Person of National Historic Significance. In 2018 the New York Times published a belated obituary for her.

Francesca Gamber

Further Reading

Cimbala, Paul A. "Mary Ann Shadd Cary and Black Abolitionism." In *Against the Tide: Women Reformers and American Society*, edited by Paul A. Cimbala and Randall M. Miller. Westport, Conn.: Praeger, 1997. This essay places Mary Ann Shadd Cary within the broader community of African American abolitionists and in relation to the particular concerns of black women activists.

Ferris, Jeri. *Demanding Justice: A Story About Mary Ann Shadd Cary*. Minneapolis: Carolrhoda Books, 2003. Illustrated children's book about Shadd Cary.

Rhodes, Jane. *Mary Ann Shadd Cary: The Black Press and Protest in the Nineteenth Century*. Bloomington: Indiana University Press, 1998. A thorough recent treatment of Shadd Cary's life, this book pays special attention to her years as a newspaper editor and publisher and the role she played in the antebellum black press.

Silverman, Jason H. *Unwelcome Guests: Canada West's Response to American Fugitive Slaves, 1800-1865*. Millwood, N.Y.: Associated Faculty Press, 1985. Contests the view that Canada provided a safe haven for African Americans by describing the obstacles and racism that immigrants such as the Shadds faced there.

LOURDES CASAL

Cuban-born writer, scholar, and activist

Born: April 5, 1938; Havana, Cuba
Died: February 1, 1981; Havana, Cuba
Area of Achievement: Scholarship, literature, poetry, activism

As a public intellectual, Casal contributed scholarly research and literary production in the form of poetry, essays, and fiction. Widely anthologized, Casal's work grappled with continuously evolving views on the tensions among gender, race, class, and nationality, expressing for many readers their own struggles.

Early Life

Lourdes Emilia Irene de la Caridad Casal y Valdés (LOHR-dehs kah-SAHL) was born into a middle-class family to a physician-dentist father and an elementary schoolteacher mother. As a china mulata of African, Chinese, and Spanish descent, Casal experienced firsthand the class and race tensions in Cuba under Fulgencio Batista.

An ardent and accomplished student at the Universidad Católica de Santo Tomás de Villanueva, her wide-ranging interests led her from the school of engineering to psychology and on to literature and political science. While a student at university, Casal supported Fidel Castro and the anti-Batista group, but after Castro took power, she became disillusioned with the revolutionary movement. Casal belonged to the El Puente literary group and publishing house, and when it was closed for publishing "bourgeois" literature, she was among those arrested. Although she initially was in favor of the Cuban Revolution, by 1962 she had changed her mind and was opposed to Fidel Castro's government.

Casal traveled to Africa and ultimately moved to New York City, where she completed her clinical training, began teaching and writing, and became a naturalized citizen. She wrote Chinese Cuban history and anti-Castro essays and became politically active, arguing for open dialogue between the United States and Cuba. She wrote poems, stories, essays, and academic studies. She received a Ph.D. in psychology from New School for Social Research in 1975.

Life's Work

In 1972, Casal published *El caso Padilla*, a critical review of Cuba's imprisonment and censorship of dissident poet Heberto Padilla, in 1971. Many scholars assert that El caso Padilla signaled a change in Casal's political trajectory from opponent back to sympathizer with revolutionary Cuba. She reached out to the Cuban exile community, establishing an unprecedented rapport.

At the invitation of the Cuban government in May, 1973, Casal became the first exile to return to Cuba. Upon her return to the United States five months later, she was doubtful about the viability of democracy in Latin America, given Augusto Pinochet's coup in Chile and the problems inherent in the Cuban national process. In November and December, 1978, Casal gathered with other Cuban exiles to form the Group of Seventy-five in Havana. Castro and other Cuban officials met with the group for discussions in *El Diálogo* (*The Dialogue*), a discourse that led to the emancipation of thirty-six hundred political prisoners from Cuban jails.

Casal taught at Rutgers and the City University of New York, among other institutions. In 1972, she founded the Institute for Cuban Studies at Rutgers to promote free and open exchange between Cuba and the United States and serve as a clearinghouse for credible information on Cuba through publications, exchange programs, and art projects. Currently, the Center for Cuban Studies in New York documents Cuba's intellectual, social, historical, cultural, and political changes since the revolution. It includes the Lourdes Casal Library, which houses research materials on the visual arts, including books, periodicals, and ephemera.

Casal was in Cuba during the Mariel boatlift in the summer of 1980, at an Institute for Cuban Studies conference. While in Cuba, her health rapidly deteriorated, and she died on February 1, 1981.

Significance

Cubans on the island and those in the diaspora face an artificial but no less divisive separation, a political and cultural border, but Casal determined there should be dialogue between the two groups, worked to build bridges between them. She searched energetically for alternate ideas about Cuba's situation, believing that resuscitating communication among all Cubans, regardless of their location or politics, was paramount. To honor the memory of Casal, once a professor at Rutgers, the Department of Psychology faculty there each year select a graduating senior to receive the Lourdes Casal Memorial Award in recognition of both intellectual excellence and social commitment. It is a fitting tribute to a scholar, artist, and leader.

Jan Voogd

Further Reading

Casal, Lourdes. *Revolution and Race: Blacks in Contemporary Cuba. Latin American Program Working Paper Series No. 39*. Washington, D.C.: Woodrow Wilson International Center for Scholars, 1979. This working paper represents the distillation of Casal's scholarly reflection on the issues she also considered in her essays, poetry, and fiction.

"Lourdes Casal." In *Daughters of the Diaspora: Afra-Hispanic Writers*, edited by Miriam DeCosta-Willis. Miami, Fla.: Ian Randle, 2003. The section on Casal includes several examples of her work along with critical analysis and a brief biography.

"Lourdes Casal." In *The Norton Anthology of Latino Literature*, edited by Ilan Stavans and Edna Acosta-Belen. New York: W. W. Norton, 2011. Examines examples of Casal's poetry in the broader context of Latino literature.

Negron-Muntaner, Frances, and Yolanda Martinez-San Miguel. "In Search of Lourdes Casal's 'Ana Veldford.'" *Social Text* 25, no. 3 (2007): 57-84. Durham, N.C.: Duke University Press. This article reprints and explicates Casal's most often anthologized and enduring poem, "For Ana Veldford."

César Chávez

Union leader and civil rights activist

Born: March 31, 1927; Yuma, Arizona
Died: April 23, 1993; San Luis, Arizona
Area of Achievement: Activism; social issues

Chávez was the most prominent Latino civil rights leader of the period, and as founder of the United Farm Workers (UFW), he helped to promote the conditions of migrant field workers, most of whom were of Mexican ancestry. Using aggressive but nonviolent tactics, he persuaded employers to recognize the UFW as the bargaining agent for some fifty thousand workers in Florida and California.

Early Life

César Estrada Chávez (SAY-zahr CHAH-vehz) was raised in a hardworking, close-knit family that was deeply committed to the Catholic Church. His father, Librado Chávez, owned a small grocery store, pool room, and auto repair shop. After the Great Depression began in 1929, Librado lost his business, in part because he trusted a dishonest neighbor in purchasing property, and the family was forced to move into an old adobe house on the small farm owned by Librado's widowed mother, Mama Tella. Chávez later described his life on the farm as happy and

César Chávez (Library of Congress)

secure, and despite the poverty, he said that the family always had enough to eat.

The young Chávez did not do well in school, probably because his family spoke only Spanish at home. His teachers used corporal punishment whenever he spoke his native language, but he later said that the embarrassment of making mistakes in English was worse than the spankings. When white families from the South moved into the region in 1936, there were frequent fights between white and Chicano children. Chávez resented that the principal always seemed to blame the Chicanos. Because no Catholic Church was close to the family farm, Mama Tella gave Chávez most of his formal religious training. Never a skeptic, he would later write that her lessons in Christianity provided a foundation for the moral direction of his life.

In 1937, Chávez's father suffered a severe sunstroke, Mama Tella died, and the state took over the family farm because of unpaid taxes. Like thousands of others, the Chávezes moved to California, where they traveled from place to place in search of work picking fruits and vegetables. Wages were low, and housing conditions were miserable. Chávez attended some sixty-five different

Chávez visits César Chávez school in 1974, a year after the school opened. (Wikimedia Commons)

elementary schools, sometimes for only a few days. In 1942, the year that he graduated from the eighth grade, an accident left his father unable to work, forcing Chávez to leave school and work in the fields.

In 1944, Chávez joined the U.S. Navy so he would not be drafted into the Army. He disliked the regimentation and strongly resented the military's discrimination against minorities. He later described his two years of service as the worst in his life. Although he once sailed on a crew transport to the Mariana Islands, he never participated in combat. He observed that Latinos and other minorities rarely were in positions of leadership, and while on leave he was briefly arrested for refusing to sit in a segregated area in a theater. After completing his military service, Chávez returned to California to resume working in the fields. In 1948, he married Helen Fabela. The couple settled in Delano and would eventually have eight children.

Life's Work

In 1952, Chávez was introduced to the idea of collective organization by his parish priest, Father Donald McDonnell, who was strongly committed to the Catholic Church's doctrines on workers' rights. McDonnell provided Chávez with relevant papal encyclicals and books on labor history and social movements. Chávez was particularly impressed by Mahatma Gandhi's philosophy of using nonviolent protests in pursuit of social justice. Shortly thereafter, Chávez met Fred Ross, a militant leader in Saul Alinsky's Community Service Organization (CSO). Ross was urging Mexican Americans organize politically, emphasizing issues of voter registration, housing discrimination, police abuse, and public education. Chávez began working for the CSO, first as a volunteer and then as a full-time employee. By the late 1950's, he was a regional leader of the organization.

In 1962, Chávez resigned from the CSO because of its refusal to organize a union devoted to improving the conditions of farm laborers. He joined with Dolores Huerta to establish the National Farm Workers Association, which became the United Farm Workers (UFW) three years later. For the organization's logo, Chávez chose the colors red and black, and his brother Richard designed an Aztec eagle without wings, which was easy to draw on homemade flags. One of the major challenges of the union, which was primarily composed of poor Chicano workers, was to collect enough dues to pay for its activities.

Chávez and the UFW captured national attention for the first time during a five-year grape strike in the region of Delano, California. Shortly after the strike began in 1965, Chávez led a twenty-one-day, 250-mile protest march from Delano to Sacramento. In December, Chávez called for a national boycott of grapes produced by the two largest grape-growing corporations in Delano. In 1968, when many strikers became impatient with Chávez's nonviolent tactics, he went on a twenty-five-day hunger strike in order to persuade his followers not to resort to violence. The widely publicized fast, which lasted from February 15 to March 11, was quite successful in gaining sympathy for the UFW. On the day that Chávez broke the fast, a rally of six thousand supporters, including Senator Robert F. Kennedy, assembled in Delano. The strike ended in 1970, when the UFW finally reached a collective bargaining agreement with the grape-growing corporations, covering more than ten thousand workers.

"History will judge societies and governments — and their institutions — not by how big they are or how well they serve the rich and the powerful, but by how effectively they respond to the needs of the poor and the helpless."

> **Chávez, Huerta, and the United Farm Workers**
>
> Dolores Huerta's efforts at organizing poor people predated those of César Chávez. In 1955, she cofounded the Stockton chapter of the Community Service Organization. A former schoolteacher who delivered impassioned speeches, Huerta became known as "La Pasionaria" (the Passionate One). Recognizing her dedication and communication skills, Chávez selected her to be the cofounder of the National Farm Workers Association in 1962. For more than three tumultuous decades, the two leaders had a symbiotic relationship. While Chávez was the face of the union, Huerta played a crucial role in formulating its goals and strategies. In 1965, she directed the union's national grape boycott, and the next year, she negotiated a landmark contract between the union and the Schenley Wine Company. Although she also was known for her radical socialist ideas, she served as an effective lobbyist in Washington and Sacramento. She was arrested at least twenty-two times for participating in demonstrations and other forms of nonviolent civil disobedience.

By the 1970's, the UFW was generally recognized as the nation's vanguard union of farmworkers, and it continued to organize strikes and boycotts. In 1972, Chávez undertook a twenty-four-day fast to protest an Arizona law that outlawed secondary boycotts. Although the fast failed to achieve its objectives, it succeeded in prompting the registration of thousands of Latino voters. The UFW's activities helped convince California's legislature to pass the Agricultural Labor Relations Act of 1975, which provided the right of collective bargaining to farmworkers in the state. Because growers often hired undocumented workers from Mexico as strikebreakers, the UFW supported stricter enforcement of the nation's immigration laws.

During the 1980's, Chávez changed his position on immigration and became an outspoken proponent of immigrants' rights. He also began to concentrate much of his attention on the health hazards posed by pesticides. To publicize the issue, he held a thirty-six-day fast, which was accompanied by nightly masses with thousands of sympathizers. Before he finally ended the fast, doctors warned that he had begun to burn muscle tissue and could experience kidney failure.

Chávez faced growing frustrations and challenges during the early 1990's. The UFW experienced internal dissent and was beset with serious financial difficulties, especially after two lawsuits that required it to pay more than $7 million. Chávez was forced to increase the number of fund-raising rallies. At the same time, he stepped up efforts to increase membership. On April 23, 1993, while in Arizona on UFW business, he began another fast but was convinced to call it off because of his deteriorating health. That night, he died in his sleep.

Significance

Although most farmworkers continued to receive low wages and live in poverty, Chávez's activities within the UFW promoted greater sympathy for their plight and achieved at least some amelioration for union members. After his death, he became a symbol of heroic personal sacrifice in pursuit of greater social justice. His birthday has been declared a state holiday in California and Texas and an optional holiday in Arizona and Colorado.

Thomas Tandy Lewis

Further Reading

Collins, David. *César Chávez*. Minneapolis, Minn.: Lerner, 2005. A good summary that is written primarily for young readers, presenting Chávez as an inspiration and positive role model.

Etulain, Richard W., ed. *César Chávez: A Brief Biography with Documents*. New York: Bedford/St. Martin's, 2002. Primarily a supplementary text for college courses, this useful book includes a chronology, bibliographical essay, and collection of original documents.

Giswold del Castillo, Richard, and Richard A. Garcia. *César Chávez: A Triumph of Spirit*. Norman: University of Oklahoma Press, 1995. A relatively short biography that is well-written, balanced, and based on abundant research.

Jensen Richard, and John Hammerback. *The Words of César Chávez*. College Station: Texas A&M University Press, 2002. A collection of Chávez's speeches and correspondence organized into major periods, with chapter introductions emphasizing rhetorical analysis.

Levy, Jacques E. *César Chávez: Autobiography of La Causa*. New York: W. W. Norton, 1974. The author has taken selections from Chávez's taped interviews, producing an unsurpassed primary source of personal insights into the man and his life until the early 1970's.

Pawel, Miriam. *The Union of Their Dreams: Power, Hope, and Struggle in César Chávez's Farm Worker Movement.* New York: Bloomsbury, 2009. Written by a Pulitzer Prize-winning journalist, this book presents a poignant account of the movement and the people who made it, including both accomplishments and failures.

Stavans, Ilan, ed. *César Chávez.* Santa Barbara, Calif.: Greenwood, 2010. A collection of essays that captures the multiple aspects of a complex person and his career.

Helen Fabela Chávez

Labor activist

Born: January 21, 1928; Brawley, California
Died: June 6, 2016; Bakersfield, California
Area of Achievement: Activism; social issues

As the wife of the United Farm Workers (UFW) organizer and founder César Chávez, Helen Chávez was heavily involved and influential in the union. She balanced her domestic responsibilities with working in the fields and helping other migrant farmworkers.

Early Life

Helen Fabela Chávez (fah-BEHL-ah CHAH-vehz) was born Helen Fabela in Brawley, California, on January 21, 1928. Her parents were Mexican immigrants Vidal Fabela and Eloisa Rodriguez, who met in Los Angeles, California, and married in 1923. The Fabela family were migrant farmworkers in the California valleys. Like many Mexican Americans, they worked long hours for low wages in unhealthy conditions. These factors, as well as inadequate housing, took a toll on Chávez's health. She became malnourished and anemic.

Chávez's values of the traditional Mexican familial structure were formed by her mother's dedication to her role as mother and wife. Eloisa would work only temporarily in the fields, focusing most of her attention on the needs of her family, while Vidal was active in the Comisión Mexicana, a group dedicated to maintaining the Mexican community. When Chávez was twelve years old, her father died, leaving the family in a difficult financial situation. To help support her mother and siblings, Chávez and her older sister made the difficult decision to stop attending school and work full time at the DiGiorgio Corporation, a major fruit grower. Chávez also worked for local ranches packing grapes, and when the season ended, she worked in nearby stores as a clerk.

In 1943, the same year she began working full time, Chávez met César Chávez at a malt shop named La Baratita. Although César served in the U.S. Navy from 1944 to 1946 and continued to work seasonally as a migrant field worker with his family, the two dated whenever they could. In October, 1948, the young couple married. César and Helen Chávez had eight children over the next ten years, and Chávez's roles as a mother and wife became central in her life.

Life's Work

Chávez began her activism while living in the "Sal Si Puede" ("Get Out If You Can") barrio of San Jose, California. Her husband became involved in the Community Service Organization (CSO), and Chávez often helped with the bookkeeping and office work, such as writing out daily reports. She often is credited with convincing César to speak with CSO organizer Fred Ross, whom her husband had avoided until Chávez's intervention. Chávez was very supportive of her husband's responsibilities with the CSO. She later began attending local division meetings and conventions, and by the late 1950's, she was participating in civic protests. One protest in particular, devoted to the unemployed local workers, convinced César to form an organization completely dedicated to the struggles of farmworkers.

In 1962, César and Dolores Huerta founded the National Farm Workers Association (NFWA). César worked as an unpaid volunteer when the organization was launched, so Helen had to return to the fields in order to support her family. She worked long hours and was paid very little. Chávez worked out of necessity, and because of her working-class background and upbringing, she understood that the fight to change the lives of the farmworkers was imperative to the Hispanic community. Over the next few years, Chávez, her children, and her extended family assisted in promoting the ideology and goals of the National Farm Workers Association.

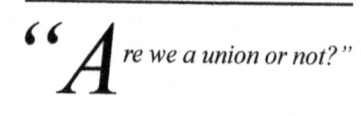

> "*Are we a union or not?*"

By 1965, Chávez had joined the picket lines while still supporting her family. In October of the same year, she was detained by police for shouting "Huelga" ("Strike") at a protest at the W. B. Camp and Sons farm. César's activism in the farmworkers' struggle had evolved into the formation of the United Farm Workers Organizing Committee through the National Farm Workers Association's mergers with other organizations that had similar goals. The United Farm Workers (UFW) was established in 1966, and Chávez continued to protest the unfair treatment of agricultural laborers with UFW members and her family. Her most public arrest came in 1978 with César at the G & S Produce Company in Yuma, Arizona. Both later were released and given suspended sentences.

César Chávez died in his sleep on April 23, 1993, and more than fifty thousand people attended his funeral in Delano, California. Later that year, César's friends and family founded the César E. Chávez Foundation, an organization that aims to educate people about his life and career and to inspire individuals and communities to carry on his work for civil rights.

In August 8, 1994, Helen Chávez attended a White House ceremony with President Bill Clinton, in which she accepted the posthumous award of the Medal of Freedom to her husband. In 2008 Helen Chávez was awarded Latina of the Year by the National Latino Peace Officers Association of Los Angeles Chapter. On May 18, 2011, she and other members of her family joined Secretary of the Navy Ray Mabus to announce that a new naval ship would be named the USNS *César Chávez*. During the announcement, Helen Chávez noted that her husband did not believe he should be singled out for praise because "he knew there were many César Chávezes, so many men and women in the movement who made great sacrifices and achieved great things." For that reason, Helen, her family, and the farmworker movement explained that the USNS *César Chávez* was named in honor of all Latinos who "helped build America and served their country."

On June 6, 2016, Chávez died at a Bakersfield hospital at the age of 88.

Significance

Helen Chávez's role in the fight for migrant farmworkers' rights is defined by her dedication to her family. Her values played an influential part in the onset of her family's involvement in "La Causa." She is often revered for upholding traditional Mexican values and supporting the conventional familial gender roles. While Chávez did value these roles, it is important to remember that at times she was the primary breadwinner while César worked unpaid to form the NFWA. She also protested in the fields and endured multiple arrests and police harassments. Her support, financially and emotionally, helped to change the poor working conditions farm laborers previously had to tolerate.

Monica E. Montelongo

Further Reading

Etulain, Richard W., ed. *César Chávez: A Brief Biography with Documents*. New York: Palgrave, 2002. Chávez's role as a supporter of "La Causa" is shown through her participation and influence in the activism of her husband.

Levy, Jacques E., and César Chávez. *César Chávez: Autobiography of La Causa*, 2d ed. Minneapolis: University of Minn. Press, 2007. A historical account of "La Causa" from César Chávez, including Helen's role and perspective on supporting her husband.

Rose, Margaret Eleanor. "Mujer Valiente: Helen Chávez, the Interdependence of Family Life, Work, and Union Activism." In *Women in the United Farm Workers: A Study of Chicana and Mexicana Participation in a Labor Union, 1950 to 1980*. Los Angeles: University of California, Los Angeles, 1988. Includes a formative and substantial biographical chapter on the life of Helen Chávez, including her early childhood and introduction to social activism.

KIMBERLÉ WILLIAMS CRENSHAW

Educator, lawyer, and scholar

Born: 1959; Canton, Ohio
Area(s) of significance: Law; civil rights; social issues; activism and dissidence

Crenshaw is a founding theorist of an academic movement called critical race theory. She has done substantial research into issues related to race, class, and gender. Because of her expertise in law, Crenshaw also is considered a leading authority in the realm of civil rights.

Early Life

Kimberlé Williams Crenshaw was born in Canton, Ohio, in 1959. She began her career as an academic at Columbia University, where she began to grapple with the marginalizing effects of race and gender. As she completed courses in Africana studies, she began to notice that areas of

Kimberlé Williams Crenshaw (Wikimedia Commons)

inquiry concerning women of color were severely under investigated.

She earned her undergraduate degree from Columbia in 1981 and went on to earn her juris doctorate from Harvard Law School in 1984 and her master of laws degree from the University of Wisconsin-Madison in 1985. At Wisconsin, she also earned the William H. Hastie Fellowship. Crenshaw was a law clerk for Shirley Abrahamson of the Wisconsin Supreme Court in 1985-1986.

Life's Work

Crenshaw's work has focused on illuminating the varying ways in which racism, sexism, and classism marginalize groups and individuals. She has established herself as an authority on constitutional and civil rights law and has done work related to immigration, international law, education, and criminal law. Crenshaw assisted the legal team that represented Anita Hill in the confirmation hearings for then-Supreme Court nominee Clarence Thomas in 1991, and in 2001, she wrote a paper for the United Nations Conference on Racism. In 1996, Crenshaw cofounded the African American Policy Forum, a think tank whose goal was to deconstruct and challenge public discourse on discrimination and injustice.

> "The way we imagine discrimination or disempowerment often is more complicated for people who are subjected to multiple forms of exclusion. The good news is that intersectionality provides us a way to see it."

In 1992 and 1995, Crenshaw was the Samuel Rubin Visiting Professor at Columbia University. In 1986, she began teaching at the University of California at Los Angeles (UCLA) School of Law. Her position at UCLA allowed her the flexibility to lecture nationally and internationally and continue to pursue scholarship on issues related to race, politics, civil rights, and legal theory. Crenshaw was selected as UCLA's professor of the year in 1991 and 1994. In 2007, she was nominated to the Fulbright Chair for Latin America in Brazil, and in 2008, she was named an Alphonse Fletcher Fellow. The same year, she was granted an in-residence fellowship at the Center for Advanced Study in the Behavioral Sciences at Stanford University.

Crenshaw has written, edited, or contributed to books such as *Critical Race Theory: Key Writings That Formed the Movement* (1995) and *Words That Wound: Critical Race Theory, Assaultive Speech, and the First Amendment* (1993). She also has published several journal articles. Crenshaw published the scholarly book *On Intersectionality: Essential Writings of Kimberle Crenshaw* in 2012, and the following year, published two books exploring the modern approach to race in America; *The Race Track: Understanding and Challenging Structural Racism and Reaffirming Racism: The Faulty Logic of Colorblindness, Remedy and Diversity*. Crenshaw also served as executive director of the African American Policy Forum and was one of the architects of the organization's "My Brothers Keeper" initiative that seeks to create employment and educational opportunities for young men of color. Crenshaw is credited with spearheading critical race theory as an academic discipline and theoretical movement. Her sociological construct of intersectionality, a term she coined in 1989, became a conceptual tool useful in analyzing patterns of inequality and oppression that affect people in "postracial" American society and the international community.

Significance

Crenshaw's scholarship examines and exposes racism, classism, and sexism. Giving voice to the black female perspective, her work has provided critical insight into American society's treatment of underrepresented groups.

Kidogo A. Kennedy, updated by Micah L. Issitt

Further Reading

Crenshaw, Kimberlé. "A Black Feminist Critique of Antidiscrimination Law." In *Philosophical Problems in the Law*, edited by David M. Adams. 4th ed. Florence, Ky.: Wadsworth, 2005. Crenshaw outlines her theory that the combination of race and sex creates a form of discrimination against black women that was not previously recognized or examined, legally or academically.

---. "A Preference for Deception: A Legal Scholar Shows How the Language of Civil Rights Is Stolen by Those Trying to Halt Affirmative Action." *Ms.* 18, no. 1 (Winter, 2008): 34. Crenshaw examines the rhetoric used by affirmative action opponent Ward Connerly—emphasizing terms such as "discrimination" and "racial preference"—in his efforts to get voters to outlaw the social program in several states.

_____, et al., eds. *Critical Race Theory: Key Writings That Formed the Movement*. New York: New Press, 1995. A compilation of essays by leading critical race theorists that challenge dominant assumptions related to issues of race, class, and gender.

Matsuda, Mari J., et al. *Words That Wound: Critical Race Theory, Assaultive Speech and the First Amendment*. Boulder, Colo.: Westview Press, 1993. Four influential critical race theorists comment on ways in which speech can injure various populations and provide an interpretation of the First Amendment as it relates to these injuries.

Dorothy Day

Social reformer and journalist

Born: November 8, 1897; Brooklyn, New York City
Died: November 29, 1980; Manhattan, New York City
Area of Achievement: Social reform, journalism, religion and theology, publishing, peace advocacy

Co-founder of a radical Roman Catholic social movement, the Catholic Worker, and editor and publisher of its paper, Day linked traditional piety to immediate relief for the needy and to nonviolent direct action to end injustice and warfare.

Early Life

The third of the five children of John I. Day and Grace Satterlee, Dorothy Day was born in Brooklyn, New York, into a comfortable home. At the time of Dorothy's birth, John Day, the ambitious son of an impoverished Confederate surgeon, was a clerk, but advanced to sports editor, columnist, and partner in the Hialeah Racetrack venture later in life. During prosperous periods, the family employed a domestic servant. Reared in Protestant churches, the Days were not regular churchgoers when their children were growing up. On her own initiative, Dorothy was baptized into the Episcopal church as a teenager.

Shortly after Dorothy started school, the family moved across the continent to the San Francisco Bay Area, where John accepted a position as sports editor at one of the city's major papers. The 1906 earthquake devastated the family's home and ruined John's employer. Resettled in Chicago, the Days experienced unaccustomed poverty. The family rented a grim tenement apartment above a saloon, and Grace assumed the duties once performed by the maid.

Parental protectiveness failed to shield the children from social reality and radicalism. Their seedy neighborhood provided an observant child such as Day with an education about injustice. A precocious reader, she devoured the writings of muckrakers and socialists, whose lurid realism inspired progressive reform during the early twentieth century. She enjoyed writing and performed well enough in high school to win a coveted Hearst scholarship to the University of Illinois. As an undergraduate, Day nurtured her talent in the Scribblers' Club and

Dorothy Day (Wikimedia Commons)

reinforced her radical leanings by joining a socialist group, experiencing student poverty, and reading whatever interested her. In 1916, after two years of mediocre academic performance, she quit the university and joined her family in New York, where her father had assumed a promising position after the failure of still another of his employers.

LIFE'S WORK

At age eighteen, armed with a thin portfolio of writings from small-town newspapers, Day became a reporter, despite her father's edict that women belonged at home. Hired as a lowly features writer by a New York-based socialist daily, the *Call*, Day wrote vividly about women workers, a series much admired by the reform-minded Russell Sage Foundation. Soon the *Call* sent Day to cover strikes, riots, birth control activists, and the peace movement. Perhaps the rookie reporter's greatest coup was an interview of Russian revolutionist Leon Trotsky weeks before the czar was overthrown.

Day's career was boosted when Floyd Dell hired her to assist him with the editing of *The Masses*, Greenwich Village's chic radical monthly. Within a few months, wartime censorship shut down the magazine, leaving Day without regular work. At the urging of a friend, she traveled to Washington and picketed for woman suffrage in front of the White House. The pair was arrested a few times and jailed, along with members of the militant National Woman's Party. At the notorious Occoquan Workhouse Day, the women engaged in a hunger strike, and Day scuffled with guards over inmate conditions. Ironically, Day never voted in a national election on principle. Throughout her life, she preferred direct action, especially picketing, to the debates and deals of politicians. She joined in this demonstration out of boredom and a desire to address the treatment of political prisoners in American penal institutions.

> "The greatest challenge of the day is: how to bring about a revolution of the heart, a revolution which has to start with each one of us?"

Between 1918 and 1924, a period of drift, Day fell in and out of love, was married and divorced, and traveled throughout Europe and the United States. She published a novel of disillusionment, *The Eleventh Virgin* (1924),

---

Dorothy Day's Early Years

In *The Long Loneliness* (1952) Dorothy Day details her life, including her earliest years of coming to terms with the ideas of God and "right and wrong."

> We did not search for God when we were children. We took Him for granted. We were at some time taught to say our evening prayers. "Now I lay me," and "Bless my father and mother." This done, we prayed no more unless a thunderstorm made us hide our heads under the covers and propitiate the Deity by promising to be good.

> Very early we had a sense of right and wrong, good and evil. My conscience was very active. There were ethical concepts and religious concepts. To steal cucumbers from Miss Lynch's garden on Cropsey Avenue was wrong. And it was also wrong to take money from my mother, without her knowledge, for a soda. What a sense of property rights we had as children! Mine and yours! It begins in us as infants. "This is mine." When we are very young just taking makes it mine. Possession is nine points of the law. As infants squabbling in the nursery we were strong in this possessive stance. In the nursery might made right.

---

patterned on her life, and entered into a common-law marriage with Forster Batterham, a biologist with whom she had a daughter, Tamar. Her search for self-purpose led her into the Roman Catholic Church in 1927, which precipitated a break with Batterham, whose commitments to anarchism and atheism made him hostile to organized religion. Day tried to maintain her friendships with radicals and for a few years sought work within the radical movement. Before 1931, she wrote a few articles for the *New Masses,* a communist literary magazine, and was a propagandist for a communist front group.

Accepting a contract to write dialogue in Hollywood, Day moved with Tamar to California. Uncomfortable in this bourgeois setting, she left for Mexico. On their return to the United States, Day wrote for Catholic magazines but felt unfulfilled. A radical at heart and a Catholic convert with a social conscience, Day wanted to help change the social order that created injustice. Writing about it was not enough, especially when she saw the human suffering caused by the Depression.

In 1932, she met the person who helped her to resolve her vocational crisis. Peter Maurin, twenty years Day's senior and a French immigrant, was a devout Catholic, well read in Catholic and social issues, and committed to nonviolent revolution. Encouraged by her platonic friend, Day founded *The Catholic Worker*, a tabloid edited, published, and at first largely written by her. Within five years, the paper reached nearly 200,000 readers each month. Lively writing about work and social injustice and a sense of urgency attracted readers, many of whom wanted to put radical Catholic social ideals into practice. The bold works of art that graced its pages, as well as its trademark penny cover price, added to the paper's appeal.

The Catholic Worker movement started with the paper, the feeding of the hungry, and later the establishment of houses of hospitality, where homeless people could find shelter without the annoying difficulties of welfare bureaucracies and the condescension of do-gooders. A clothing room outfitted the tattered. All were to be treated with dignity, each person an ambassador of Christ. Peaceful protests aroused social consciences. Catholic Workers picketed with striking workers, taught black children in Harlem how to draw, and spoke at the U.S. Capitol against the military draft. The movement spread to other American cities, including Boston, St. Louis, Washington, and Seattle. By 1941, twenty-seven cities had Catholic Worker houses.

Like her contemporaries in the radical movement, Day predicted that the Depression of the 1930's was evidence that American capitalism was dying from its own structural weaknesses. To replace it, she envisioned Christian community: voluntary, cooperative, nonviolent, egalitarian, and distributist, based on production for need and not for profit. A just society would help to prevent evil. In the meantime, Day and the Catholic Worker movement supported stopgap measures, the right of workers to unionize, earn fair wages, and improve industrial safety. Maurin's "green revolution," an alternative to industrialism and urbanization, was translated into Catholic Worker farming communes, the first of which was founded within a few years. On the communes, Catholic Worker families, volunteers, and guests theoretically would live in rural simplicity and produce food for their own use. The contrasts between theory and reality posed some of the more problematic aspects of the Catholic Worker movement. Intellectuals, unemployed industrial workers, and the frail were rarely equipped to run a farm.

A socialist opponent of World War I, Day was predisposed to Christian pacifism. Clinging to the belief that the possession of arms leads to war, the Catholic convert believed that human life was sacred and must be protected. Since she understood violence to be an ever-escalating condition, each conflict breeding greater violence to counter it, Day found no moral justification for war. To critics who scoffed at nonviolence, she replied that spiritual weapons, prayer, penance, and fasting, were the best defense against evil. During World War II, however, the novelty of Catholic pacifism divided the Catholic Worker movement. Dissenting volunteers claimed that war was a lesser evil than fascism.

Day put pacifism into practice in several ways. She opposed the military draft and supported the right of conscientious objection. Urging noncooperation with the war effort, Day suggested that workers should not take jobs in defense plants, and she refused to pay war taxes. When Japanese Americans were sent to armed detention camps for the duration of the war, she was one of a handful who criticized the federal government order. The use of the atomic bomb on civilian targets likewise sparked her outrage. In the Cold War era, Day promoted peace through nonviolence and was arrested for challenging compulsory Civil Defense air raid drills. The nuclear arms race and its potential for global holocaust emboldened Day to educate the bishops of the Catholic Church about pacifism when they gathered in Rome for the Second Vatican Council (1962-1965). During the Vietnam War, she supported new Catholic peace groups and was widely credited for building the foundation of modern Catholic pacifism.

Weakened by heart trouble for more than a decade and barely able to write her monthly column, Day died in 1980 at the age of eighty-three.

Significance

Day revitalized American Catholicism. She found ways for volunteers to work for a nonviolent revolution within the church and to care for the immediate needs of the poor and oppressed. Her inclusive understanding of Christian community led to the establishment of the first true Catholic pacifist movement in the United States. Her steady leadership for nearly fifty years made the Catholic Worker one of the most durable of American alternative movements. Her deep faith and good judgment preserved Catholic Worker religious orthodoxy and prevented church officials from silencing her or dismantling the controversial movement.

Day's powerful writing attracted volunteers and introduced pacifism and nonviolent direct action to Catholics. During the Second Vatican Council, Day was among those who moved the Catholic Church toward pacifism. She was justly celebrated for her contributions to nonviolent change by the American bishops in a 1983 pastoral statement on peace.

Since 1933, the Catholic Worker movement has challenged many injustices: poverty, war, and racism. In death, Day lives through her writings, the work of her followers, and in the memories of all who have been touched by her deep faith in Christian radicalism. The Catholic Worker, still sold for a penny, and Catholic Workers throughout the United States, England, Canada, Australia, and Mexico bring Day's message of nonviolent revolution to a new generation.

Anne Klejment

FURTHER READING

Coles, Robert. *Dorothy Day: A Radical Devotion.* Reading, Mass.: Addison-Wesley, 1987. Psychiatrist Coles's brief study features excerpts from taped interviews with Day, but offers surprisingly little psychological analysis.

Day, Dorothy. *Dorothy Day, Selected Writings: By Little and by Little.* Edited by Robert Ellsberg. Maryknoll, N.Y.: Orbis Books, 1992. A wide-ranging anthology of Day's writings on social and spiritual issues drawn from published works. Ellsberg's well-crafted biographical introduction is based on a personal relationship with Day and careful scholarship.

---. *The Long Loneliness.* New York: Harper & Row, 1952. An autobiography written primarily to explain her conversion and the work of the Catholic Worker movement especially relating to the poor, the labor movement, gospel pacifism, and nonviolent social revolution. Weak on the period from 1918 through 1924.

Klejment, Anne, and Alice Klejment. *Dorothy Day and "The Catholic Worker": A Bibliography and Index.* New York: Garland, 1986. Helpful for researchers. Lists all known publications by Day, indexes The Catholic Worker from 1933 through 1983, and comments on selected titles.

McNeal, Patricia. *Harder than War: Catholic Peacemaking in Twentieth-Century America.* New Brunswick, N.J.: Rutgers University Press, 1992. Examines leading American Catholic peace organizations and peace advocates with emphasis on the formative role played by Day and her movement in the emergence of Catholic pacifism.

Miller, William D. *A Harsh and Dreadful Love: Dorothy Day and the Catholic Worker Movement.* New York: Liveright, 1973. Dated, but an interesting history of the Catholic Worker movement with portraits of many key figures and quotations from volunteers.

O'Connor, June. *The Moral Vision of Dorothy Day: A Feminist Perspective.* New York: Crossroad, 1991. Views Day as a writer, convert, radical, and moralist and presents her as an occasionally anti-feminist feminist.

Piehl, Mel. *Breaking Bread: The Catholic Worker and the Origin of Catholic Radicalism in America.* Philadelphia: Temple University Press, 1982. A demanding but rewarding work that explains the religious context of the movement. Roughly covers events to 1965.

Roberts, Nancy L. *Dorothy Day and the Catholic Worker.* Albany, N.Y.: State University of New York Press, 1984. One of the most readable accounts of Day's life at the Catholic Worker, with a focus on Day the advocacy journalist.

Zwick, Mark, and Louise Zwick. *The Catholic Worker Movement: Intellectual and Spiritual Origins.* New York: Paulist Press, 2005. Examines the intellectual and spiritual influences that led Day and Peter Maurin to organize the Catholic Worker movement.

EUGENE V. DEBS

Labor leader and social reformer

Born: November 5, 1855; Terre Haute, Indiana
Died: October 20, 1926; Elmhurst, Illinois
Area of Achievement: Labor law; union organization

Debs's work in the organization of labor and the adoption of social welfare legislation had a significant impact on the American economy and government. He campaigned several times for the presidency of the United States as a representative of the Socialist Party.

EARLY LIFE

Eugene V. Debs was the third child of six who survived to

Eugene V. Debs (Library of Congress)

adulthood and the first son of Jean Daniel Debs and Marguerite Marie Bettrich Debs. His parents had emigrated in 1849 from France, lived briefly in were chosen and Cincinnati, and settled in Terre Haute, opening a grocery store that provided the family with a modest but sustaining income.

After reading *Les Misérables*, Debs' father decided to name his son after Victor Hugo and Hugo's compatriot and fellow novelist, Eugène Sue. Debs early became aware of the wretchedness of poverty and the dream of its eradication. His formal education was perhaps less influential; in 1871, against his parents' wishes, he left high school, worked for the Terre Haute and Indianapolis Railroad, and in December, 1871, was promoted to the position of fireman.

Debs was employed as a railroad man for two years. In 1873, as a result of the financial panic and the subsequent economic depression, he lost his job, moved to East St. Louis, and at first hand witnessed the realities of urban beggary and desperation. After his return to Terre Haute the next year, he secured employment in a wholesale grocery company and participated in the cultural and civic institutions of the small mid-western city. He established, along with others, the Occidental Literary Club, served as its president, and provided a platform for such national figures as the atheist propagandist and orator Robert Ingersoll, the former abolitionist Wendell Phillips, who had embraced the cause of labor, and the poet James Whitcomb Riley. The visit to Terre Haute of Susan B. Anthony, and the refusal of the literary club to sponsor her speech, brought him into contact with the cause of women's rights and the hostility that the intrepid suffragist constantly encountered.

LIFE'S WORK

In February, 1875, although no longer involved in the industry, Debs became a member of the newly established Vigo Lodge of the Brotherhood of Locomotive Firemen, rose rapidly to prominence in union circles, and with labor support was elected first as Terre Haute city clerk and then, in 1884, as a representative to the lower house of the Indiana General Assembly. His legislative record reveals a dedication to labor issues, the sponsoring of railroad workers' safety and employers' liability bills, and the abortive support of a law extending the ballot to Indiana women.

The year 1885 was a momentous one in Debs's life and career. A photograph taken sometime later shows him clean-shaven, with a receding hairline, and smart clothes. On June 9, 1885, he married Katherine Metzel, the stepdaughter of a Terre Haute druggist. He was grand secretary of the Brotherhood of Locomotive Firemen and editor of its magazine; before the year's end, he left his positions in the grocery warehouse and as state legislator and devoted himself fully to the cause of labor organization.

> "Your Honor, years ago I recognized my kinship with all living beings, and I made up my mind then that I was not one bit better than the meanest on earth. I said then, and I say now, that while there is a lower class, I am in it; and while there is a criminal element, I am of it; and while there is a soul in prison, I am not free."

In the pages of the union's official publication, Debs frequently commented on labor strategies and the structure of unionization. He was opposed to strikes except as a last resort. He believed that the use of boycott was a terrible example of economic coercion. He dissociated himself from any project that would effect an "amalgamation" of labor organizations and the dissolution of the independent craft unions.

The 1888 strike against the Chicago, Burlington and Quincy Railroad, which concluded in defeat for the union, had an important impact on Debs and modified his attitude toward labor organization. If not yet advocating the establishment of an industrial union, he urged that the railway unions develop a federation similar to the American Federation of Labor, and, by numbers and a united front, win concessions on wages and other terms and conditions of employment. His efforts and those of other railroad labor leaders reached a brief fruition in 1889, in the establishment of a Supreme Council of the United Orders of Railroad Employees, combining in a federation firemen, brakemen, and switchmen. The organization was too weak, however, to resolve disputes among its members, caused bitterness and estrangement among the railroad unions, and at its 1892 annual convention, Debs reluctantly sponsored a successful resolution dissolving this experiment in labor federation.

Disillusioned by the impotency of the Supreme Council of the United Orders of Railroad Employees, believing that a federation of craft unions would not prove effective in ameliorating labor conditions, Debs turned to the creation of an industrial railroad union. The American Railway Union (ARU), founded in Chicago in June, 1893, with Debs serving as president, represented a threat not only to railroad corporations but also to the railroad unions of craftsmen and to the American Federation of Labor. It proposed to organize all railroad workers, coal miners, and longshoremen employed in the industry, irrespective of their skills. Reflecting the racism of the 1890's, it barred black Americans from membership. (Debs, however, opposed such exclusionary language in its constitution.)

The year 1893 was an unpropitious time to form a new labor organization. There was another financial panic and another depression; the ranks of the unemployed swelled, and the breadlines in the cities grew longer. On the other hand, the depression caused railroad men to desert the unions; before a year was over, the ARU had become the largest single labor union in the United States, with a membership of more than 150,000. In April, 1894, it won a brilliant victory and a wage increase after an eighteen-day strike against the Great Northern Railroad. Yet its triumph was transitory: A month later began the strike and lockout at the Pullman Palace Car Company outside Chicago. The employee-inhabitants of Pullman town had long been resentful of the unwillingness of the company to sell them the houses in which they lived, to accord them political rights in the selection of town officials, and to lower rents as wages were reduced in September, 1893. Against the advice of Debs and other ARU officers, in May, 1894, they struck, and, the next month, sent their delegates to the first annual convention of the industrial union that by coincidence was meeting in Chicago. Their accounts of exploitation and deprivation swayed the convention to support a boycott of all railroad companies with Chicago terminals unless they refused to link Pullman cars to their passenger trains.

The Pullman Strike of 1894 pitted the ARU against the General Managers Association, a trade organization of twenty-four railroad companies with terminals in Chicago. Allied with management were the judges of the federal courts, the Democratic administration of Grover Cleveland, and particularly Attorney General Richard Olney. Olney was determined to crush the railroad workers and to destroy their union. He attained both objectives. Borrowed from the Chicago, Milwaukee, and St. Paul Railroad, appointed as special district attorney, Edwin Walker successfully petitioned the federal court in Chicago to grant an injunction that prohibited the ARU, its president, and other officials from any further supervision of the strike. They could not speak, write instructions, or use telegraph or telephone lines to support ARU members who had paralyzed railroad traffic, not only in and out of Chicago but also in twenty-seven Western states and territories. Unemployed railroad workers were transported from the East to replace striking employees, and on July 4, 1894, federal troops appeared in Chicago by Cleveland's order. Labor had suffered one of the most devastating defeats in its history. The ARU was wrecked, its members blacklisted, and the Pullman workers were forced to return to their jobs under the old conditions. Debs was sentenced to six months' imprisonment in Woodstock Jail for violating the federal court's injunction.

The failure of the ARU and the subsequent incarceration converted Debs to socialism as a preferable economic system. Within two years after his release, he joined the Social Democratic Party (in 1901, it became the Socialist Party of America), served on its executive board, and, in 1900, ran for president of the United States. It was the first of five campaigns. Debs used his candidacies as forums for education, attracting large crowds, arguing that socialism and democracy were compatible, standing on party platforms that advocated, among other things, woman suffrage, industrial safety legislation, shorter workdays, and the abolition of child labor. He received 96,978 votes in 1900, 402,406 in 1904, and eight years later, a climactic vote of 897,011, representing 6 percent of the electorate.

World War I and the entry of the United States in April, 1917, marked the end of the socialist electoral momentum. In June, 1917, Congress passed the Espionage Act (amended the next year to include nine new federal criminal offenses) to enforce the Selective Service Act and to suppress verbal opposition to the war. Debs was angered by the imprisonment of many of his socialist colleagues under the congressional legislation. On June 15,

Debs with a group of young Socialists in Chicago. (Wikimedia Commons)

1918, in Canton, Ohio, he addressed the Ohio Socialist Party Convention. In a long and sometimes eloquent speech, he expressed sympathy for his incarcerated socialist comrades, excoriated the United States Supreme Court, and criticized conscription and the United States' participation in the European conflagration. He did not directly counsel draft resistance or illegal action in the military forces or say anything to promote the success of the German army. Nevertheless, he was arrested, indicted, and, in September, 1918, tried in a Cleveland courtroom, convicted, and sentenced to ten years' imprisonment. His appeal to the United States Supreme Court his attorneys arguing that the Espionage Act violated the First Amendment guarantee of freedom of speech was concluded in March, 1919, with a Justice Oliver Wendell Holmes, Jr., opinion affirming the conviction.

Debs, sixty-three years old, confronted a decade of imprisonment. Depressed at times by his confinement in Atlanta Penitentiary, elated at others by the steady flow of sympathetic letters and visitors, in 1920 he ran once more for president, the only candidate ever to have done so while in prison.

Ironically it was Republican president Warren G. Harding who ordered Debs's release on Christmas Day, 1921. The socialist leader was not able to unite his party, which had been torn by dissension over the war and by the emergence of two communist political organizations. His personal popularity, however, had not waned. He spoke out against violent revolution, criticized the Soviet government, and worked to revise Socialist Party fortunes. Hampered by failing health, he continued his speaking tours throughout the country, edited the *American Appeal*, and, in a last pamphlet, pleaded the case of Nicola Sacco and Bartolomeo Vanzetti. He died on October 20, 1926, in Lindlahr Sanatorium in a Chicago suburb and was buried in his hometown of Terre Haute.

Significance

Although the ARU failed and the Socialist Party declined in influence during his lifetime, Debs left behind him important legacies in the currents of twentieth century American history. The ARU served as a model of the industrial organization of labor, emulated by the establishment of the more enduring Congress of Industrial Organizations. The Socialist Party of America, under his leadership, impelled the major political parties of Democrats and Republicans to co-opt reformist elements in their rival's platform. The abolition of child labor, maximum hour and minimum wage legislation, the protection of employees in the workplace, woman suffrage, and the graduated income tax became part of state and federal legal codes or amendments to the U.S. Constitution.

Debs's conviction and incarceration under the Espionage Act educated the American public and the Supreme Court about the dangers of suppressing dissent and the crucial relationship between the free speech guarantee and the preservation of democratic institutions. Perhaps most important, his dedication to the alleviation of poverty, to social justice, and to peace has inspired other Americans in later generations and has contributed to the richness of American political life.

David L. Sterling

Further Reading

Chace, James. *1912: Wilson, Roosevelt, Taft, and Debs: The Election That Changed the Country*. New York: Simon & Schuster, 2004. Relates the events of the 1912 presidential election, including Debs's campaign on the Socialist Party ticket.

Debs, Eugene Victor. *Writings and Speeches of Eugene V. Debs*. New York: Hermitage Press, 1948. A collection of Debs's works, with an introduction by Arthur M. Schlesinger, Jr., including an abridged version of the Canton speech for which the socialist leader was convicted and imprisoned for violation of the Espionage Act. The book further exhibits the quality of Debs's rhetorical skills.

Ginger, Ray. *The Bending Cross: A Biography of Eugene Victor Debs*. New Brunswick, N.J.: Rutgers University Press, 1949. The most colorful and readable study of Debs's life, narrative in form, but perpetuating a mythic portrait of the socialist leader.

Lindsey, Almont. *The Pullman Strike.* Chicago: University of Chicago Press, 1942. The only systematic account of the conflict between the Pullman workers and the ARU on one side and the railroad corporations and the Cleveland administration on the other. The author emphasizes employee grievances relative to conditions in Pullman, Illinois, and, along with a careful analysis of the course of the strike, presents the reactions and recommendations of the United States Strike Commission in its aftermath.

Morgan, H. Wayne. *Eugene V. Debs: Socialist for President.* Syracuse, N.Y.: Syracuse University Press, 1952. Focuses on the five presidential campaigns as well as on the history of the party between 1900 and 1925.

Peterson, J. C., and Gilbert C. Fite. *Opponents of War: 1917-1918.* Madison: University of Wisconsin Press, 1957. One of many such studies, a wide panorama of the suppression of dissent during World War I, the closing of German-language and socialist newspapers, the prosecutions under the Espionage Act, and the antilibertarian record of the Woodrow Wilson administration.

Salvatore, Nick. *Eugene V. Debs: Citizen and Socialist.* 2d ed. Urbana: University of Illinois Press, 2007. The best and most analytic biography to date. The author argues that Debs's career can be viewed in an American tradition of radical reformism rather than as an attempt to implant into American politics an alien European ideology.

Shannon, David A. *The Socialist Party of America: A History.* New York: Macmillan, 1955. An overview of the fortunes of the Socialist Party from its origins in 1901 to the early 1950's, placing Debs in a context of intraparty factionalism.

Dorothea Dix

Educator and social reformer

Born: April 4, 1802; Hampden, Maine
Died: July 17, 1887; Trenton, New Jersey
Area of achievement: Social reform

A crusader for the rights of the mentally ill, Dix devoted her life to establishing psychiatric hospitals to provide proper care for those with mental and emotional problems and set the stage for worldwide reforms in the care and treatment of people with mental disabilities.

Early Life

Dorothea Lynde Dix had a difficult childhood. By his family's standards, her father married below his station. Because married students were not accepted at Harvard, where he was studying at the time, he was sent to manage family holdings in Maine—nothing less than the frontier during the early nineteenth century. Never a financial success, he did win some notice as a traveling Methodist preacher and a writer of tracts. Thus, Dorothea was often without her father, and unfortunately, her mother was often too ill to give her the attention that young children require.

Dorothea's happiest memories of her solitary childhood revolved around visits to her paternal grandparents in Boston. Her grandfather, a successful if curmudgeonly physician, and grandmother provided a warm welcome. Dorothea's first exposure to public service came from watching her grandfather practice medicine. She had few playmates her own age and was four years older than her nearest sibling. At least one biographer believes that isolation from children and involvement with adults led to a high degree of self-interest and blocked the development of personal emotional commitment. In any case, she

Dorothea Dix (Wikimedia Commons)

never married, and most, though not all, of her friendships were with people involved in her charitable endeavors.

When Dix was around the age of twelve and unhappy at home, she began to live permanently with her then-widowed grandmother. To her dismay, her grandmother insisted on both academic and social discipline, and Dorothea's sense of rejection was actually worsened. After two years, she was sent off to live with a great-aunt, where she finally found a congenial home. Although still a teenager, she was allowed to open a school for small children, which she ran successfully for three years before returning to Boston. Two years later, in 1821, she opened a school for girls. Education for women was unusual—public schools accepted girls only for the few months when many boys were out for agricultural labor—and even more unusual was Dix's insistence on including natural science in the curriculum. Dorothea Dix proved to be a gifted teacher, and she seemed to have found her life's work. In a gesture that was a harbinger of her future, she added a program for poor girls who otherwise had no opportunity for schooling.

Ill health—apparently tuberculosis—and the collapse of a romance with her cousin resulted in a new direction for Dix. While recovering her strength during the mid-1820's, she became interested in Unitarianism and the ideas of William Ellery Channing. This Christian sect's emphasis on the goodness of humanity and the obligation to serve it would inspire her for the rest of her life. A new attempt to run a school, however, led to her complete collapse in 1836 and her doctor's orders never to teach again.

LIFE'S WORK

While recuperating, Dorothea Dix visited England. During her two-year stay with the William Rathbone family, she met a variety of intellectuals and reformers. When she returned to the United States, she found that the deaths of her mother and grandmother had left her financially independent. She spent several years seeking some focus for her life. Then, in 1841, she was asked to teach Sunday school for women at the East Cambridge Jail. She found the innocent and guilty, young and old, sane and insane crowded into the same miserable, unheated facility. Those regarded as insane were often chained or otherwise restrained. Her discussions with humanitarians such as George Emerson, who would become a longtime friend, led her to understand that conditions in East Cambridge Jail were, if anything, better than those in most jails. There was virtually no distinction made between mental illness and impairment, and in the entire country there were only about 2,500 beds specifically for those with emotional problems. Dix quickly had a sense that she had come upon something important that needed doing.

Dix's first move was to demand and get heat for the insane in the East Cambridge Jail. Then, after talking with other reformers, including Samuel Gridley Howe and Charles Sumner (later a radical Republican leader during Reconstruction), she began a survey of facilities for the insane in Massachusetts. Although the McLean Psychiatric Hospital was relatively progressive, most of the mentally ill were kept in local poorhouses, workhouses, and jails. She visited every one. Conditions were horrendous. Patients were often locked in dirty stalls, sometimes for years, and many were chained to the floor. Many were virtually naked, and physical restraint was virtually universal. She also found time to discuss treatment with the best doctors, finding that much more humane treatment was being successfully used in leading hospitals in Europe and a few in the United States. More common in the United States were strong sedatives to induce quiescence and the application of shocks, such as surprise dousings with ice water, to bring individuals back to reality.

After eighteen months, Dix prepared a petition to the Massachusetts legislature. The petition stated psychiatric facilities should provide for physical health and comfort (she would later expand this to prisons) and seek, with kindness and support, to cure diseased minds. When it was published, this document at first produced embarrassment and denial and then attacks upon the author. Her friends—Howe, Sumner, and others—rushed to defend her. She had her first victory when a bill providing for more and better accommodations for the mentally ill was passed. Her career was beginning to take shape.

Dix's initial investigations had occasionally taken her outside Massachusetts, where she found conditions to be generally worse than in her home state. From the mid-1840's to the mid-1850's, she traveled many thousands of miles around the United States and Canada, finding and exposing the suffering of the indigent insane. Although she did not travel to the far West (she did work in Texas), Dix visited almost every one of the thirty-one states of that era.

Dix developed an investigative technique in which, by means of simple persistence and will, she forced her way into every facility where the insane were kept. There followed dramatic revelations of suffering and abuse that shamed all but the most hardened and/or fiscally conservative. Finally, she launched a petition to the legislature for the necessary funds and regulations to ensure improved care. She found the inevitable compromises necessary in any political campaign frustrating, but she settled for whatever state legislatures would fund and began again.

Results varied. New Jersey and Pennsylvania established state psychiatric hospitals as a result of Dix's efforts. New York, however, rejected her call for six hospitals and only expanded the beds available in an existing facility. In 1845, with the help of Horace Mann and George Emerson, Dix expanded her efforts to prison reform and published a manual on that subject. Proper care for the mentally ill, however, remained her main focus.

> "*I have had so much at heart. Defeated, not conquered; disappointed, not discouraged. I have but to be more energetic and more faithful in the difficult and painful vocation to which my life is devoted.*"

From 1845 to 1846, Dix worked in Kentucky, Tennessee, Louisiana, Alabama, Georgia, and Arkansas, and she was working her way up the Mississippi when, in September, she collapsed in Columbus, Ohio. By December, she was sufficiently recovered to resume traveling, and in January, 1847, she presented a petition to the Illinois legislature, which resulted in the passage of a bill creating a psychiatric hospital. Later that year and in the following year, she had similar successes in Tennessee and North Carolina. Her fame was growing enormously, as were the respect and love with which Americans regarded her. One of the greatest marks of the latter came in 1863, when Confederate troops invading Pennsylvania stopped a train on which Dix was riding. A North Carolina officer recognized her, and the train was released to continue on its way. Not even the passions of Civil War could change people's feelings about Dorothea Dix.

Despite local successes—between 1844 and 1854 Dix persuaded eleven states to open hospitals—Dix recognized by the late 1840's that only a national effort would resolve the problems of the insane. No more than one-fourth of those needing care got it. She began to push for a federal effort, suggesting that five million acres of public land be committed to set up a fund to provide care for insane, epileptic, and mentally impaired Americans. A bill to this effect was introduced in Congress in 1848. Dix was provided with a small office in Washington from which to lobby. Questions about cost and constitutionality blocked the various versions of the bill until 1854, when, to her joy, it passed both houses. Her exultation was brief, however, for President Franklin Pierce vetoed the bill on the grounds that Congress had no authority to make such grants outside the District of Columbia. It was the final blow—the effort was abandoned.

Exhausted and ill, Dix planned to renew efforts in individual states, but friends and doctors persuaded her to rest. She visited friends in England, and within two weeks she was involved in efforts to reform psychiatric care there. She went so far as to go personally to the home secretary, Sir George Grey, to argue for improvements in Scotland. Before she left, a Royal Commission to investigate the problem was in the works. She also helped to sustain a reform effort in the Channel Islands before touring the Continent, where she visited hospitals, asylums, and jails, exposing problems and demanding change. The force of her personality seems to have made her irresistible; even Pope Pius IX was forced to initiate improvements in the Vatican's handling of the mentally ill.

Dix's return to the United States in 1856 brought a large number of requests for aid. She was soon traveling again, seeking various reforms and funding. In the winter of 1859 alone, she asked state legislatures for a third of a million dollars, and in 1860, she got large appropriations for hospitals in South Carolina and Tennessee. The outbreak of the Civil War brought reform work to a halt, and Dix promptly volunteered her services.

After being appointed superintendent of U.S. Army nurses, Dix spent four years of very hard work developing the Medical Bureau from a service set up for an army of ten thousand to one that could handle more than that many casualties from one battle. Unfortunately, she was too straitlaced at the age of sixty to cope with the rough-and-tumble style of the military. Her New England Puritanism showed in her tendency to think that an army doctor who had had a few drinks should be dishonorably discharged. Although her work in ensuring the provision of nurses and medical supplies at the beginning of the war was of great importance, in 1863 her authority was quietly reduced, to her bitter disappointment. After the war, Dix spent another fifteen years traveling as the advocate of the insane. Worn out in 1881, she retired to the hospital (the first created by her efforts) in Trenton, New Jersey, where she lived until her death in 1887.

SIGNIFICANCE

Dorothea Dix's importance can be seen from simple statistics. In 1843, the United States had thirteen institutions for the mentally ill; in 1880, it had 123. Of the latter, 75 were state-owned, and Dix had been a key factor in the founding of 32 of them. She had also been able to get a number of training schools for the mentally impaired established, and specialized training for psychiatric nurses had begun.

More important, the lives of many unfortunate people had been made easier thanks to Dix's efforts. The idea that the insane, even if poor, deserved humane care and treatment intended to help them recover had been established in the United States. Dix's efforts began a process that has continued since her death and has left the United States a world leader in the treatment of mental illness.

Fred R. van Hartesveldt

Further Reading

Brown, Thomas J. *Dorothea Dix: New England Reformer.* Cambridge, Mass.: Harvard University Press, 1998. This study of Dix provides new insight into her passions and methods.

Dain, Norman. *Concepts of Insanity in the United States, 1789-1865.* New Brunswick, N.J.: Rutgers University Press, 1964. A useful description of attitudes and problems that Dix had to confront during her career.

Dix, Dorothea. *Asylum, Prison, and Poorhouse: The Writings and Reform Work of Dorothea Dix in Illinois.* Edited by David L. Lightner. Carbondale: Southern Illinois University Press, 1999. Dix traveled to Illinois in 1846 and 1847 to publicize the need for more humane treatment of prisoners, the insane, and the poor. This book is a collection of her writings during that trip, including a series of newspaper articles about conditions in jails and poorhouses. There also are two memorials she presented to the state legislature: one describes the treatment of inmates at a state penitentiary, and the other urges the establishment of a state insane asylum. Lightner has provided detailed notes and introductions to these documents, and in a concluding essay he assesses the immediate and continuing impact of Dix's work.

---. *On Behalf of the Insane Poor: Selected Reports.* New York: Arno Press, 1971. A valuable source of Dix's ideas and opinions expressed in her own words. Her eloquence and passion shine through.

Gollaher, David. *A Voice for the Mad: A Life of Dorothea Dix.* New York: Free Press, 1995. A balanced biography highlighting Dix's strengths and weaknesses, her efforts in the area of legislative reform, and her second career as head of the Civil War nurses.

Marshall, Helen. *Dorothea Dix: Forgotten Samaritan.* Chapel Hill: University of North Carolina Press, 1937. Although it is sometimes overly sympathetic to its subject, this is a solid and well-written biography.

Snyder, Charles M., ed. *The Lady and the President: The Letters of Dorothea Dix and Millard Fillmore.* Lexington: University Press of Kentucky, 1975. Provides interesting insights into one period in Dix's life.

Tuke, Daniel. *The Insane in the United States and Canada.* London: M. K. Lewis, 1885. This contemporary description of the problems Dix tried to solve gives a valuable perspective of the situation. It is very useful for modern students trying to achieve an understanding of her work.

Frederick Douglass

Escaped slave, writer, publisher, and civil rights activist

Born: February, 1817?; Tuckahoe, Maryland
Died: February 20, 1895; Washington, D.C.
Also known as: Frederick Augustus Washington Bailey

Frederick Douglass (Wikimedia Commons)

(birth name)

Areas of Achievement: Abolitionism; Civil rights; Diplomacy; Government and politics; Journalism and publishing; Literature

Douglass was one of the best-known African Americans involved in the emancipation movement before the Civil War. He published the abolitionist newspaper The North Star and gained international attention when, in 1845, he published his autobiography, Narrative of the Life of Frederick Douglass, an American Slave.

EARLY LIFE

Frederick Douglass was born a slave in Maryland, possibly in February, 1817. He had little contact with his mother, Harriet Bailey, and never knew the identity of his father. At the age of twenty-one, he fled north to New Bedford, Massachusetts, where he was protected by white abolitionists. To the surprise of his protectors, Douglass showed extraordinary skill with words. He had learned to read during his youth, which might have exposed him to the cause of abolitionism. Drawing themes from the abolitionist newspaper *The Liberator*, Douglass gave speeches under the auspices of the Massachusetts Anti-Slavery Society. There, he met abolitionist leader William Lloyd Garrison, founder of *The Liberator* and a major figure in the abolitionist movement. Douglass was one of a significant number of fugitive slaves who joined Garrison's abolitionist cause.

During this period, Douglass published the autobiography that soon achieved widespread recognition: *Narrative of the Life of Frederick Douglass, an American Slave* (1845). Shortly after its publication, he left the United States for England, possibly out of fear that bounty hunters might seek him out and return him to slavery. While he was in England, Douglass received contributions from abolitionist supporters on both sides of the Atlantic, enabling him to purchase his freedom and return to America in 1847.

LIFE'S WORK

Douglass's Autobiographies

Frederick Douglass's *Narrative of the Life of Frederick Douglass, an American Slave* (1845), his first autobiography, was supplemented by two later works, *My Bondage and My Freedom* (1855) and *Life and Times of Frederick Douglass, Written by Himself* (1881). These three works shed light on the evolution of Douglass's self-image and public persona.

Douglass's first autobiography was intended to provide proof of his slave origins and his escape from bondage by fleeing to the North. Years later, in *Life and Times of Frederick Douglass*, he wrote that he had lived "several lives," including as a slave, a fugitive, and a (somewhat) free man. It is possible that Douglass sought in both *My Bondage and My Freedom* and *Life and Times of Frederick Douglass* to clarify or correct certain impressions he had conveyed in the 1845 book, including the contention that his father had been white. Perhaps because some skeptics claimed that Douglass's literary abilities could only be explained by his having white ancestry, Douglass backtracked from the statement. In *My Bondage and My Freedom*, he referred to his father as "a white man or nearly white." By the time *Life and Times of Frederick Douglass* was published, he claimed to have no idea of his father's identity.

Another issue that changed with the passage of time was the degree to which Douglass claimed to have resisted the power of masters over slaves. Each of the three autobiographical works treats this issue differently, particularly with regard to Douglass's relations with his master Edward Covey, whom Douglass challenged openly and even physically.

Some commentators note similar subjective "image making" with respect to Douglass's depiction of his mother and grandmother and female slaves in general. Feminist scholars such as Angela Davis note that Douglass had a tendency to equate the African American struggle for freedom with his and other black men's struggle for manhood. Selected quotations most often emphasize female slaves' helplessness as slave owners abused them physically and sexually. This emphasis presents female slaves' goal as escaping suffering, while male slaves seek to establish and assert independence and agency.

In 1847, Douglass and Garrison parted company after disagreements over the use of violence to end slavery and modes of raising funds. Douglass moved to Rochester, New York, and founded his own abolitionist paper, *The North Star* (later published under his own name as *Frederick Douglass' Newsletter* and *Douglass' Monthly*)— a move that widened the breach with Garrison. At the same time, Douglass's "alternative" articles on the subject of slavery and emancipation continued to attract supporters, raising his profile well beyond the Northeastern states. It might have been this growing fame that prompted the government to consider recruiting Douglass as a semiofficial propagandist in the antislavery debate that would grow more intense with the election of Abraham Lincoln in 1860.

During the Civil War, Douglass publicly supported Lincoln's antislavery position. In addition, he became involved in the challenge of applying a bill signed by Lincoln on July 17, 1862. The bill called for the recruitment of African Americans to serve in segregated regiments in the Union Army. In 1863, Douglass launched a recruitment campaign in *Douglass' Monthly*, listing eight factors that should motivate African Americans to enlist. He argued that enlistment was an obligation of the citizenship that African Americans had acquired through the Emancipation Proclamation of 1863. He also maintained that military service was a visible means of gaining self-respect and the respect of others. His own two sons, Charles and Lewis, both joined the first black regiment in the Union Army. Although Douglass apparently hoped that his service as a recruiter, which merited a government salary, would lead to an official military commission, this hope was not realized. For the duration of the war, he traveled throughout the North delivering speeches in support of the war effort.

> "*They cannot degrade Frederick Douglass. The soul that is within me no man can degrade. I am not the one that is being degraded on account of this treatment, but those who are inflicting it upon me...*"

Along with wartime activities came a longer-term goal in Douglass's public life: gaining for emancipated black men the same voting rights as white men. This aim was not achieved until many years later. As Douglass began to call for African American voting rights, he sought (not always successfully) to ally his cause with that of the Equal Rights Association (until 1866 the Women's Rights Convention) headed by Susan B. Anthony and Elizabeth Cady Stanton.

In the years after the Civil War, Douglass began dedicating his efforts to political causes, particularly support of the Republican Party. He was relieved when Ulysses S. Grant won the presidential election of 1868 and Andrew Johnson, the candidate against whom Douglass had campaigned, was defeated in the Democratic primary. The prominence Douglass gained as a supporter of the Union government allowed him to play official roles in government affairs. A first task assigned to him by Grant came in 1870, when the United States was considering challenging Spanish rule in the colony of Santo Domingo. Douglass served as one of several secretaries to an 1871 exploratory commission sent to the island.

More indicative of Republican Party support for Douglass as a spokesman for African American political participation was his role in 1872 as one the electors at large (serving without any association with a particular electoral district) of New York's electoral college. Another chance to play a political role came in the mid- 1870's when President Rutherford B. Hayes appointed Douglass federal marshal of the District of Columbia. Although this post involved mainly ceremonial duties (as did his next appointment, as recorder of deeds for the District of Columbia in 1880), Douglass continued to try to publicize his views on key issues. One was his support for pressuring Spain to end the lingering slave system in Cuba; another was his involvement in the growing debate over migration to northern states by black agriculturalists unable to earn a living in the South.

The capstone of Douglass's government service came after he backed Benjamin Harrison's presidential candidacy in 1888. Harrison appointed him minister-resident and consul general to Haiti. Apparently, however, political and commercial pressure to seek compromises with the Haitian government caused Douglass to lose faith in his diplomatic mission. He resigned this post in 1891. Four years later, Douglass died in Washington, D.C.

SIGNIFICANCE

Douglass was one of the best-known figures of pre-Civil War abolitionist activism. He raised the awareness of many Americans through his widely read autobiography. Perhaps equally important, he gained broad recognition during his many years as a public servant, filling several midlevel posts within the federal government.

Byron Cannon

Further Reading

Douglass, Frederick, and Angela Y. Davis. *Narrative of the Life of Frederick Douglass, an American Slave: A New Critical Edition.* San Francisco, Calif.: City Lights Books, 2010. This edition of Douglass's autobiography includes Davis's lectures from her days as a militant activist in the late 1960's. It attempts to reinterpret positions reflected in earlier editions of Douglass's autobiography, adding a feminist approach to issues raised by Douglass.

Lampe, Gregory P. *Frederick Douglass: Freedom's Voice, 1818-1845.* East Lansing: Michigan State University Press, 1998. This carefully documented biography of Douglass covers many aspects of his career that were either unknown, overlooked, or given minor attention in Benjamin Quarles's 1948 biography.

Mieder, Wolfgang. *"No Struggle, No Progress": Frederick Douglass and His Proverbial Rhetoric for Civil Rights.* New York: Peter Lang, 2001. Analyzes intended meaning implied by Douglass's choice of particular phrases, some very famous (such as Lincoln's "Government of the people, by the people, and for the people"), as the basis for moral and rhetorical lessons on race and equality.

Quarles, Benjamin. *Frederick Douglass.* 2d ed. New York: Da Capo Press, 1997. An update of Quarles's 1948 biography of Douglass, this source concentrates on Douglass's personal experiences and contacts, most of which are closely documented by a variety of contemporary primary sources, including letters and newspaper accounts.

W. E. B. Du Bois

Writer, scholar, educator, and civil rights activist

Born: February 23, 1868; Great Barrington, Massachusetts
Died: August 27, 1963; Accra, Ghana
Also known as: William Edward Burghardt Du Bois
Areas of Achievement: Civil rights; Education; Journalism and publishing; Literature; Scholarship; Social issues; Social sciences

Best known for his contribution to African American civil rights and scholarship, Du Bois founded the Niagara Movement, which was the precursor to the National Association for the Advancement of Colored People (NAACP). He also produced a body of academic writing that included journals and books on African Americans and their place in American society.

Early Life

William Edward Burghardt Du Bois (BURG-hahrt doo-BOYS) was born in Great Barrington, Massachusetts, a town of approximately five thousand residents. Du Bois knew little about his father, Alfred Du Bois, but had a close relationship with his mother, Mary Burghardt. His mother was a key figure in his life and insisted on a proper education for her son. Du Bois suffered little discrimination himself during his early years and enjoyed a simple, but comfortable, childhood in New England.

Du Bois was an intellectual standout early on, and after graduating from high school, he received a scholarship to Fisk University, a black school in Nashville,

W. E. B. Du Bois (National Portrait Gallery)

Tennessee. While attending Fisk, he traveled to rural areas, meeting African Americans and teaching in rural schools for little or no pay. At the age of nineteen, Du Bois taught in log cabins that were built before the Civil War and mingled with black people who lived in poverty, as well as farmers and former slaves. He began to think about helping African Americans in their struggle to succeed in the post-Civil War South. After growing up in a predominantly white New England neighborhood, Du Bois's time at Fisk allowed him to develop relationships with other African Americans for the first time.

Du Bois excelled in academics, and after graduating from Fisk, he entered Harvard University. He entered as a junior, because Harvard did not recognize his degree from Fisk. Du Bois was intellectually stimulated by the university but remained apart from the main culture. While studying at Harvard, he developed a desire to study in Germany. He applied for a scholarship that had been established by President Rutherford B. Hayes but was denied. After writing a scathing letter to Hayes, Du Bois was granted funds to study in Berlin.

Du Bois studied in Germany for two years, from 1892 to 1894, and met some of the most important European intellectuals of the time. This was a period of enlightenment for Du Bois, and when he returned from Germany, he had a clear vision for his life and career. He returned to Harvard and, in 1896, completed his doctoral dissertation, *The Suppression of the African Slave Trade to the United States of America, 1638-1870*. Du Bois became the first African American to receive his doctorate from Harvard.

LIFE'S WORK

After graduating from Harvard, Du Bois accepted a teaching position at Wilber force College, a black school in Ohio. He taught Latin and Greek. While he was there, he met and fell in love with Nina Gomer. The two were married in 1896.

> "The theory of democratic government is not that the will of the people is always right, but rather that normal human beings of average intelligence will, if given a chance, learn the right and best course by bitter experience."

In the fall of 1896, Du Bois accepted a temporary instructor's position at the University of Pennsylvania, where he was asked to study the social conditions of African Americans in Philadelphia's Seventh Ward. He had no students, no office, and very little interaction with the rest of the faculty. He was paid a meager salary of nine hundred dollars but proceeded to conduct a comprehensive study, interviewing more than five thousand residents of the Seventh Ward. Du Bois classified the area by social conditions, mapped the district, and compiled more than two centuries of history of the African American population in Philadelphia. He finished the work in the spring of 1898, and his investigation was published as *The Philadelphia Negro: A Social Study*. The landmark study became the launch pad for his life's work.

In 1896, Du Bois began teaching sociology at Atlanta University in Georgia. He published prolifically during his years there, including his most famous work, *The Souls of Black Folk: Essays and Sketches* (1903). Du Bois's work at the university became well known, and he founded the Atlanta University Studies, a series of studies on the social conditions of African Americans. Du Bois worked to become a source of information rather than a social reformer during these years. Using scientific methods to examine the social conditions of African Americans, he published comprehensive studies, including *Health and Physique of the Negro American* (1906), *Economic Cooperation Among Negro Americans* (1907), *The Negro American Family* (1908), *Efforts for*

The Souls Of Black Folk

In his classic work, *The Souls of Black Folk: Essays and Sketches* (1903), W. E. B. Du Bois captured the essence of African American life after the Emancipation Proclamation. He used a series of essays, poems, and personal stories and drew upon African American literary works that were popular during his lifetime, such as slave narratives, to depict African Americans' living conditions. Scholars view this book as one of his most important works. Du Bois examined race relations from historical, sociological, and philosophical perspectives and directly addressed the rise of black leadership in America. Du Bois expressed his opposition to the ideas of Booker T. Washington, whose approach to seeking equality Du Bois deemed "accommodationist." Du Bois encouraged African Americans to pursue higher education as a path to success and status.

Social Betterment Among Negro Americans (1909), *The College Bred Negro American* (1910), *The Common School and the Negro American* (1911), *The Negro American Artisan* (1912), and *The Morals and Manners Among Negro Americans* (1914).

While at Atlanta University, Du Bois published a total of 2,172 pages, which formed an encyclopedia of problems African Americans faced. It was his goal to provide as much information as possible in a form that would be available to scholars around the world. During this time, Du Bois lectured throughout the United States and corresponded with leading intellectuals from around the world, including Max Weber, a major figure in the fields of sociology and economics.

When funding became a problem, the Atlanta University Studies came to an end. In 1910, Du Bois was invited to join the Tuskegee Institute, one of the leading African American institutions of the time, run by Booker T. Washington. However, Du Bois had a fundamental disagreement with the underlying philosophy put forth by Washington. Washington believed that African Americans should seek technical training so that they could work, accumulate wealth, and thus obtain status in American society. Du Bois believed that higher education was the key to success for African Americans, and he opposed Washington's accommodationist policies. Du Bois referred to the institute as the "Tuskegee Machine" and declined the invitation to join its faculty. Instead, he organized the Niagara Movement, which later became the National Association for the Advancement of Colored People (NAACP).

Du Bois became the editor and publisher of *The Crisis*, a magazine that became the voice of the NAACP as well as a venue for important African American writers and intellectuals. In 1920, *The Crisis*'s circulation was more than 100,000. It was the main literary source that called attention to the African American problem in the United States. Several early Harlem Renaissance writers, such as Langston Hughes, had their work published in the magazine.

During the 1920's, Du Bois published tirelessly. He produced such works as *Dark Water* (1920), *The Gift of Black Fall* (1924), and numerous scholarly essays. He wrote twenty-one books in all, including two novels, *The*

Niagara Movement leaders Du Bois (seated), and (left to right) J.R. Clifford, L.M. Hershaw, and F.H.M. Murray at Harpers Ferry. (Wikimedia Commons)

Quest of the Silver Fleece (1911) and *Dark Princess: A Romance* (1928). He also organized a series of Pan-African Congresses and was active in investigating the problems of Africans in countries dealing with colonialism. He traveled widely throughout Europe and Asia, lecturing on numerous topics and meeting dignitaries and scholars from around the globe, including the Soviet Union and China.

After resigning from the NAACP, Du Bois returned to teaching at Atlanta University in 1933, and became the head of the Sociology Department. From 1935 to 1940, he published three more volumes of work: *Black Reconstruction: An Essay Toward a History of the Part Which Black Folk Played in the Attempt to Reconstruct Democracy in America, 1860-1880* (1935), *Black Folk Then and Now: An Essay in the History and Sociology of the Negro Race* (1939), and *Dusk of Dawn: An Essay Toward an Autobiography of a Race Concept* (1940). In 1940, he founded *Phylon*, a social science quarterly. In 1947, he published *The World and Africa: An Inquiry into the Part Which Africa Has Played in World History*. Du Bois eventually became the vice chairman of the Council of African Affairs.

In the 1950's, during the Korean War, Du Bois got involved in world peace initiatives and founded the Peace Information Center. This project led to the formation of the Stockholm Initiative, which called for an end to war, aggression, and the use of atomic weapons. As Du Bois became more idealistic, he began to lean toward socialism, embracing Marxism as a philosophical and ideological movement. As Du Bois's beliefs became more widely known, the U.S. government began to scrutinize his work at the Peace Information Center. When the Justice Department demanded that the organization register as a foreign agent under the Foreign Agents Registration Act of 1938, Du Bois refused, explaining that the center was founded and operated by Americans. The Justice Department claimed that the organization was a Soviet communist agency, and Du Bois was tried for failing to register. Although he was eventually acquitted, he remained bitter about his treatment by the government and the media.

After the indictment and trial, his influence in the United States waned, and his popularity began to fade. African American leaders increasingly distanced themselves from him. In 1961, the president of Ghana, Kwame Nkrumah, invited Du Bois to move to Ghana. Du Bois did so, and two years later, he became a Ghanaian citizen. He died in Ghana on August 27, 1963, at the age of ninety-five, and was given a state funeral. Du Bois's final resting place is his former home in Accra, which was converted into a research center, memorial, and museum.

SIGNIFICANCE

Du Bois spent a lifetime gathering knowledge necessary to improve the lives of African Americans. He became one of America's first sociologists and established one of the earliest sociology departments in the country. His tireless work, writing abilities, and intellectual skills were a testament to his belief that higher education would help African Americans succeed in life. The establishment of the NAACP also had far-reaching effects on the Civil Rights movement of the 1960's. Through his efforts, Du Bois also was able to effect change around the world, especially in Africa. He was a pioneer in using scientific methods to study inequality, and his books remain relevant to the discussion of race in America. Scholars are constantly rediscovering his intellectual prowess and his contributions to the Civil Rights movement in the United States.

Jerry W. Hollingsworth

FURTHER READING

Du Bois, W. E. B. *The Autobiography of W. E. B. Du Bois: A Soliloquy on Viewing My Life from the Last Decade of Its First Century.* New York: International, 1968. A comprehensive account of Du Bois's life and work, including discussions of his views, philosophies, and travels.

---. *The Philadelphia Negro: A Social Study.* Philadelphia: University of Pennsylvania Press, 1899. The landmark study of Philadelphia's Seventh Ward that launched Du Bois's career.

---. *The Souls of Black Folk: Essays and Sketches.* 1903. Reprint. New York: Pocket Books, 2005. Written at the beginning of Du Bois's intellectual career, this book examines the race problem through a series of folktales, poems, and personal stories.

Lewis, David Levering. *W. E. B. Du Bois: The Fight for Equality and the American Century, 1919-1963.* New York: Henry Holt, 2000. Pulitzer Prize-winning biography that concentrates on the second half of Du Bois's life and career.

Morris, Aldon. "Sociology of Race and W. E. B. Du Bois: The Path Not Taken." In *Sociology in America: A History*, edited by Craig Calhoun. Chicago: University of Chicago Press, 2007. Frames Du Bois as one of the pioneers of sociology in America.

MARIAN WRIGHT EDELMAN

Social reformer

Born: June 6, 1939; Bennettsville, South Carolina
Area of Achievement: Civil rights, education, social reform

Edelman created the Children's Defense Fund, an advocacy and public education association dedicated to improving conditions for children in the United States.

EARLY LIFE

Marian Wright Edelman (EH-dehl-muhn) was born in Bennettsville, South Carolina, to Arthur Jerome Wright and Maggie Leola Bowen Wright. Her father, a Baptist minister, said that "service is the rent we pay for living." Hence, helping others was the basic duty of all people and an essential part of her early family life. Her parents taught by example. They built a home for the elderly in which Marian cleaned and cooked. Her parents reared five of their own children and cared for twelve foster children over the years.

Marian's education emphasized international understanding. After she completed high school at Marlboro Training High School, she attended Spelman College in Atlanta, Georgia. During her junior year, she received a

Marian Wright Edelman (Wikimedia Commons)

Merrill Scholarship to study at the University of Paris and at the University of Geneva during the academic year 1958-1959. In the summer of 1959, she participated in a student exchange study tour of East Germany, Poland, Czechoslovakia, and the Soviet Union. These experiences broadened her perspective on humanity. She returned to the United States unable to accept the indignities of segregation, under which she had grown up and lived.

In 1960, Marian received her bachelor's degree from Spelman College as the valedictorian of her class. During that same year, black college students were conducting sit-in demonstrations at college campuses throughout the South. Her own participation in a sit-in at Atlanta's city hall led her to be arrested along with fourteen other students. Marian's civil rights activism, coupled with her international experiences and her family's commitment to service, shaped her life. Instead of choosing to pursue graduate work in Russian studies and traveling abroad, she decided to become a lawyer and use the law to effect social change.

While she pursued higher education, she continued learning from other cultures through educational service. Her achievements led to her becoming a John Hay Whitney Fellow from 1960 to 1961 at Yale University.

During the summer of 1962, she worked in Crossroads Africa, a work project in the Ivory Coast, West Africa. Wright eventually received an LL.B. degree from Yale University in 1963. With her law degree in hand, Wright was poised to launch her career as a civil rights attorney.

LIFE'S WORK

From 1963 to 1964, Marian Wright worked in New York City at the headquarters of the National Association for the Advancement of Colored People (NAACP), where she served as a staff attorney for the NAACP Legal Defense and Educational Fund. Because the NAACP was working in cooperation with other civil rights groups on the Voter Education Project in Mississippi, Wright moved to Mississippi, where she became the first black woman to be admitted to the bar. Because she had to work with federal law, she also became a member of the bar in Washington, D.C., and in Massachusetts. From 1964 to 1968, she served as the director for the NAACP Legal Defense and Educational Fund in Jackson, Mississippi, where she successfully defended the Head Start Program from political attacks, helped to get student demonstrators out of jail, became involved in school desegregation issues, and risked injury and arrest in the process.

> "Service is the rent we pay for being. It is the very purpose of life, and not something you do in your spare time."

As part of her Head Start activities, Wright served on the board of the Child Development Group of Mississippi, a representative for one of the largest Head Start projects in the United States. Her advocacy for the poor of Mississippi led her to give testimony before the Senate and to work as a liaison between the Poor People's Campaign and Congress. In the course of this work, Wright came in contact with Peter Edelman, a Jewish lawyer who served as an assistant to Senator Robert F. Kennedy. Wright married Peter D. Edelman on July 14, 1968. Theirs was one of the first interracial marriages to take place in Virginia after the state's anti-miscegenation laws had been declared unconstitutional. The couple eventually reared three sons: Joshua, Jonah, and Ezra.

In 1968, Marian Wright Edelman toured Eastern Europe, India, Israel, East Africa, and Southeast Asia. From 1968 to 1973, she served as coeditor with Ruby G. Martin of the Washington Research Project of the Southern

> ### "Exactly What My Parents Did"
>
> In her memoir *Lanterns* (1999), Marian Wright Edelman remembers the people who positively influenced her life, including her parents, who raised her and her siblings in racially segregated Bennettsville, South Carolina. Edelman's parents sought to improve life for African American children in their community, and their example influenced Edelman's career.
>
> My belief that I and others could do more than complain, wring hands, or give in to despair at the wrongs rife in the world stems from my parents' examples.... Because the public playgrounds and many public services were closed to Black children, Mama and Daddy made our church a hub for children...
>
> My outrage about children who die needlessly from preventable diseases and curable sickness today is a result of my parents' sadness over the senseless death of little Johnny Harrington, who lived three doors down from our church parsonage and did not get a tetanus shot after stepping on a nail. His good and hard-working grandmother didn't have the money or the knowledge to take him to the emergency room and nobody acted until it was too late.
>
> My concern for safe places for children to play and swim comes from the lack of public playgrounds for Black children when I was growing up and our exclusion from the swimming pool near my home where I could see and hear White children splashing happily.... I almost drowned in a segregated public lake in Cheraw, South Carolina, that lacked adequate lifeguard surveillance. Daddy and Mama built a playground behind our church with a skating rink and swings and sliding boards and lights so children could play at night and Mama opened a canteen with sodas and snacks so young people could have someplace safe and fun to go...
>
> My concern for children without homes and parents unable to care for them comes from the foster children my mother took into our home after Daddy died...
>
> An elderly White man asked me what I did for a living when I was home for my mother's funeral in 1984. I realized and told him I do, perhaps on a larger scale, exactly what my parents did: serve and advocate for children and the poor.

Center for Public Policy, headquartered in Washington, D.C. The project used litigation to promote equal employment opportunity, monitored various federal programs in such areas as child care and school desegregation, and worked with community groups. This organization became the parent organization of the Children's Defense Fund, which became incorporated in 1973. In 1971, Edelman and her husband moved to Boston, from where she continued to travel regularly to Washington, D.C., as a partner of the Washington Research Project. She became a trustee of Yale University, the second woman to serve in this capacity in the university's 270-year history. She also served from 1971 to 1973 as director of the Harvard University Center for Law and Education, part of the Office of Economic Opportunity's legal services program. The organization emphasized reform in education through research and action related to the legal implications of educational policies.

In 1973, Edelman became a founder and the president of the Children's Defense Fund (CDF), an advocacy and public education association for children's issues that has become one of the best-known and best-connected of all lobbies, with an annual budget of $10 million and staff of more than 120. Soon, as the director of the nation's most effective organization for children's issues such as teen pregnancy, prenatal care, early childhood education, health services, child care, adoption, child labor, and child welfare, Edelman became known as "the children's crusader." Through CDF, Edelman seeks to make it "un-American" for any child to grow up poor, lacking adequate health care, food, shelter, child care, or education.

To allow Edelman to spend more time at her organization's headquarters, she and her family returned to Washington, D.C., in 1979. As the spokesperson for CDF, Edelman has avoided the politics of confrontation, choosing instead to forge alliances with other groups that seek to lessen the effects of poverty, injustice, inadequate health care, insufficient education, and family violence.

During the course of her tenure as director of CDF, Edelman has testified about the human and public costs the United States would face if it continued to fail to provide adequate funds and resources to meet the needs of American children and families. Such problems became greater in the 1980's as increasing numbers of children and families faced poverty as a result of economic recession, structural change in the economy, stagnating wages, tax and budget policies that favored the well-to-do, lack of state enforcement of child support payments, and greater dependency on welfare by the growing number of female-headed households. Edelman uses statistics and personal testimony to demonstrate that children have become the poorest Americans and will become a permanent "underclass" if public policy fails to address the needs outlined by CDF. Her passion is also mixed with optimism, since she not only stresses the problems but also provides remedies to build the broadest constituency to protect the children and alleviate poverty through education, legislation, and welfare reform.

Edelman has been a member of numerous committees addressing social, educational, and public policy, such as the advisory council of Martin Luther King, Jr., Memorial Library, the advisory board of Hampshire College, the Presidential Committee on Missing in Action (1977), the Presidential Committee on International Year of the Child (1979), and the United Nations International Children's Emergency Fund (UNICEF). She has also served on many boards of directors, such as those of the Eleanor Roosevelt Institute, the Carnegie Council on Children (1972-1977), and the Martin Luther King, Jr., Memorial Center. She has served as trustee for the March of Dimes, the Joint Center for Political Science, the Yale University Corporation (1971-1977), and the Aetna Center. In 1980, she became the chair of the Spelman College Board of Trustees, becoming the first African American and the second woman to serve in that role. Through the years, Edelman has worked closely with First Lady Hillary Rodham Clinton, a friend since 1969 and former staff attorney for the Children's Defense Fund. After the election of Bill Clinton as president, Edelman consulted with the First Lady on national health care issues and legislation but indicated that she did not want any administrative appointment.

Her outstanding contributions have been recognized with many awards. Edelman has been the recipient of sixty-eight honorary degrees from such institutions as Smith College, Columbia University, Swarthmore College, Rutgers University, Georgetown University, and Yale University. Named one of the Outstanding Young Women of America in 1966, Edelman continued to be recognized for her outstanding achievements. She received the Mademoiselle magazine award (1965), the Louise Waterman Wise Award (1970), the National Leadership award from the National Women's Political Caucus (1980), the Black Women's Forum award (1980), and the Eliot Award of the American Public Health Association (1987). She was named a MacArthur Foundation Fellow in 1985. Edelman also was honored with the Albert Schweitzer Humanitarian prize from Johns Hopkins University (1987), the Hubert Humphrey Civil Rights award, and the AFL-CIO award (1989). In 1991, the Jackie Robinson Foundation recognized her decency and dedication to working on the behalf of children.

SIGNIFICANCE

Edelman's leadership in shaping programs and legislation to improve life for American children made her one of the nation's most effective lobbyists for the young. She argued that conditions must be changed to provide a better environment for the development of the nation's future leaders. In the course of her work, she also contributed significantly to the efforts to obtain equal rights for all citizens, particularly African Americans and women.

Dorothy C. Salem

FURTHER READING

Atkins, Norman. "Marian Wright Edelman." *Rolling Stone*, December 10, 1992. This interview examines the personality behind Edelman's public career.

Bouton, Katherine. "Marian Wright Edelman." *Ms.*, July/August, 1987. The author describes Edelman's attempts to juggle career and family while leading the Children's Defense Fund.

Edelman, Marian Wright. *Families in Peril: An Agenda for Social Change.* Cambridge, Mass.: Harvard University Press, 1987. This book compares the status of black and white children and families in America. It discusses problems resulting from inadequate attention and a lack of public policies and programs to deal with these issues.

---. *Lanterns: A Memoir of Mentors.* Boston: Beacon Press, 1999. A tribute to the people who helped shaped Edelman's life, including her parents, teachers, and civil rights activists Martin Luther King, Jr., and Fannie Lou Hamer.

---. *The Measure of Our Success: A Letter to My Children and Yours.* Boston: Beacon Press, 1992. Edelman presents a blend of personal advice, homilies, and analysis of experiences in this work, which was on best-seller lists for several weeks.

---. *The Sea Is So Wide and My Boat Is So Small: Charting*

a Course for the Next Generation. New York: Hyperion, 2008. Edelman examines the progress of the children's rights movements and lays out goals for the future in a series of open letters to various people, including her grandchildren, national leaders, and Martin Luther King, Jr.

Jones, Arthur. "A Voice for the Poor in D.C." *National Catholic Reporter,* March 24, 2000. A profile of Edelman that focuses on her efforts to help poor people in the United States.

Kaus, Mickey. "The Godmother." *New Republic,* February 15, 1993. This article provides a critical look at some of the basic arguments put forth by Edelman during her leadership of the Children's Defense Fund.

SUE KUNITOMI EMBREY

Activist and educator

Born: January 6, 1923; Los Angeles, California
Died: May 15, 2006; Los Angeles, California
Birth name: Sueko Kunitomi
Area of Achievement: Activism, education

Driven by a powerful sense of justice, Sue Kunitomi Embrey raised awareness about the World War II incarceration of Japanese Americans through her work with the Manzanar Committee. Her advocacy culminated in congressional acknowledgment and presidential apology for internment as well as the transformation of the former Manzanar confinement camp into the Manzanar National Historic Site.

EARLY LIFE

Sue Kunitomi Embrey grew up with six siblings during the Great Depression in the Little Tokyo district of Los Angeles, California. Her issei (first-generation Japanese American) parents, Gonhichi and Komika Kunitomi, immigrated to the United States and brought with them traditional Japanese values that required adjustment in their American life. However, two aspects of tradition remained unchanged: male dominance and shared responsibilities within the family. Her father's dominance was potent when he told her that she could not attend college because she was female and Japanese. Her responsibilities increased dramatically with the sudden death of her father in December 1937, and she was needed to work in her mother's store seven days a week.

The December 7, 1941, attack on Pearl Harbor would be one of the defining experiences of Sue Kunitomi Embrey's life—it resulted in the incarceration of her family at the Manzanar War Relocation Authority (WRA) Camp in Lone Pine, California. On February 19, 1942, President Franklin D. Roosevelt had issued executive Order 9066, which authorized the forced containment of 120,000 Japanese Americans. The Kunitomi family was sent to the camp when Kunitomi was nineteen years old.

The ten WRA camps, including Manzanar, were enclosed in barbed wire and had watchtowers manned by armed military police. The euphemistically named "apartments" at the site had no insulation and were heated by oil burners and lit by a single lightbulb in the ceiling. There was little privacy in the apartments or the shared latrines, and meals served in mess halls resulted in the dismantling of family unity.

While living at the Manzanar camp, Kunitomi began work as reporter and editor of the Manzanar Free Press internee newspaper. After nearly eighteen months at Manzanar, Kunitomi obtained leave clearance in October 1943. She moved to Madison, Wisconsin, and when her

Sue Kunitomi Embrey (Wikimedia Commons)

> **Internment Camp Newspapers**
>
> The Japanese press suffered severely in the aftermath of the Japanese attack on Pearl Harbor on December 7, 1941. US military officials desired total suppression of Japanese-language publishing, whereas civilian authorities merely urged its control. Nevertheless, all Japanese American papers on the West Coast were shut down by mid-May, 1942. In contrast, the inland press, including the *Rocky Nippon*, *Colorado Times*, Utah *Nippo*, and the relocated *Pacific Citizen*, continued and to some degree thrived during the war. Newspapers also quickly developed within internment camps.
>
> Although officially sanctioned, internment camp newspapers enjoyed some autonomy. *The Manzanar Free Press*, for example, was headquartered in the Office of Official Reports and was subject to censorship by the camp director. In practice, however, the paper's editors received little interference. The director even authorized a Japanese-language edition during the paper's second year. While barred from directly criticizing federal policies that had led to the mass Japanese American incarceration, Free Press editors were allowed to print factual stories on legal challenges to those policies. The Free Press was circulated by mail to all internment camps. The Japanese American press was restored to vitality by the end of the war, with the new *Nichi Bei Times* established in 1946 to reconnect individuals separated by incarceration. Similarly to the *Nichi Bei Shinbun*, the *Nichi Bei Times* became the leading Japanese American newspaper.

application for admission to the University of Wisconsin was denied because of her Japanese heritage, she moved to Chicago and worked for the Newberry Library, where her political awareness was nurtured by her diverse colleagues.

Life's Work

After the war, Kunitomi's mother returned to Los Angeles, and Kunitomi joined her there in 1948. Despite blatant housing and employment discrimination, she secured a house for her family and a job with the Los Angeles County Department of Education. In 1947, she joined a nisei (second-generation Japanese American) group supporting the liberal presidential candidate Henry Wallace. When Wallace was defeated, the group became the Nisei Progressives. Kunitomi met the activist Garland Embrey at a Nisei Progressive party in 1948 and married him in November 1950, despite opposition to interracial marriage and a consequent estrangement with her mother that ended only with the birth of her sons, Gary and Bruce.

Sue Kunitomi Embrey was also able to fulfill her dream of higher education; defying her father's edict, she earned a BA in English from California State College in 1969 and a teaching credential and MA from the University of Southern California (USC) in 1972. She worked for the Los Angeles Unified School District for ten years and taught kindergarten, first grade, and special education in addition to teaching at colleges including USC and the University of California at Santa Barbara and Los Angeles. At this time, she was also active with the United Teachers Los Angeles union. Embrey was also involved in advocacy for the United Farm Workers, the anti–Vietnam War movement, affirmative action, and equality in housing and jobs.

> "*Democracy is a fragile concept, only as good and as strong as the people who practice it. Let us tell the world that we are a people, strong and resolute, acknowledging the errors of the past in order not to repeat them in the future.*"

In 1969, Embrey was invited to join activists on the first Manzanar Pilgrimage to raise awareness about Japanese internment. In a nationally televised interview during this event, Embrey described the terrible conditions of the camp and recounted the injustices her family suffered while there. The Manzanar Committee was formed in 1970 by Embrey and other former internees. Embrey endured hostility for over three decades in her role as chair of the committee and as the result of her campaign to raise awareness about the camps and anti-Japanese discrimination. Her fortitude ultimately resulted in Manzanar being designated a California State Landmark in 1972, a National Historic Landmark in 1985, and a National Historic Site in 1992. Embrey also helped form the organization E.O. 9066 Inc. and campaigned for the government to offer redress and reparations for internment. She remained involved in the Manzanar site through the

1990s. Embrey died at a Los Angeles hospital on May 15, 2006, at the age of eighty-three.

Significance

Embrey is best remembered for her seminal work in preserving the Manzanar site, advocating for redress and reparations, and educating Americans about Japanese internment. The Manzanar Pilgrimage is an annual event that continues after her death, and the Manzanar Committee carries on her work advocating for Japanese Americans, offering the yearly Sue Kunitomi Embrey Legacy Award for activism. Through her work in education and community activism, Embrey spoke out against discrimination and in support of social justice. Her publications include *The Lost Years: 1942–1946* (1976), an overview of internment. Embrey's determination transformed a dark chapter of American history into a positive lesson that a democratic society can acknowledge discrimination, apologize, and make amends. Despite hostility from her community, Embrey drew strength from her Japanese heritage and was able to refocus a community and reshape history.

Diana Meyers Bahr

Further Reading

Commission on Wartime Relocation and Internment of Civilians. *Personal Justice Denied: The Report of the Commission on Wartime Relocation and Internment of Civilians.* Seattle: U of Washington P, 1997. Print. A report from the commission, established in 1980 by an act of Congress, that investigated the incarceration of Japanese Americans and made redress and reparations possible.

Howard, John. *Concentration Camps on the Home Front: Japanese Americans in the House of Jim Crow.* Chicago: U of Chicago P, 2008. Print. Provides new perspectives on the Japanese American incarceration in a study of two detention camps established in Arkansas in the segregated South.

Muller, Eric L. *Free to Die for Their Country: The Story of the Japanese American Draft Resisters in World War II.* Print. Chicago: U of Chicago P, 2001. Print. Tells the story of the United States government drafting Japanese Americans out of detention camps for military duty and imprisoning those who resisted.

Betty Friedan

Writer and feminist

Born: February 4, 1921; Peoria, Illinois
Died: February 4, 2006; Washington, D.C.
Area of Achievement: Women's rights, journalism, social reform

Friedan's book The Feminine Mystique (1963) energized an untold number of women and helped spark the second wave of the feminist movement. Although Friedan became a leader in the continuing struggle for women's rights, she also was a controversial figure. She later advocated against radical feminism and sexual politics and argued instead for unity with men in common struggle for gender equality.

Early Life

Betty Friedan (free-DAN) was born Betty Naomi Goldstein in Peoria, Illinois, to jeweler Harry Goldstein and former journalist Miriam Horowitz Goldstein. Friedan recalled that her mother gave up a career in journalism to be a homemaker and mother. This, Friedan believed, explained her mother's enthusiastic encouragement of her

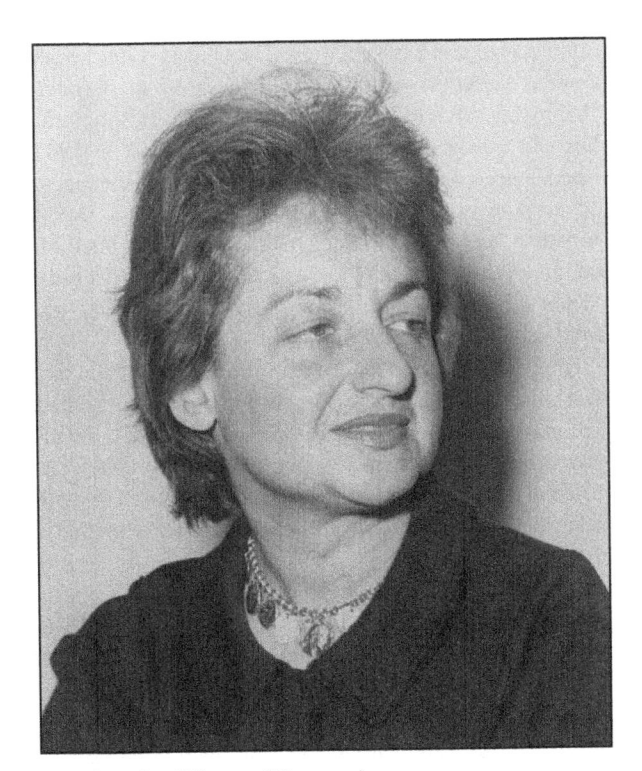

Betty Friedan (Library of Congress)

daughter's journalistic endeavors in high school, college, and beyond.

Friedan graduated from Smith College in 1942, summa cum laude, and later did graduate work at the University of California, Berkeley, studying with the famous child psychologist Erik Erikson. She received a fellowship for her studies and was about to accept a second, which would have allowed her to complete a doctorate, when she quit school. She decided that becoming an academic was too "tame"; she preferred the more active world of reporting. Accordingly, she returned to New York City, where she worked as a reporter for *The Federated Press*, a labor news service. It was wartime, and women were encouraged to fill jobs while men were overseas as soldiers. In 1946 she became a reporter for *U.E. News*, a weekly union paper.

Once the war ended, however, women were expected to give up their jobs so that returning veterans could find work. Friedan lost her reporting position and had to take a position as a researcher. This was a "woman's job," which involved doing the research and often much of the writing for articles that were then published under the male authors' bylines.

In the postwar era, women also were expected to return to their traditional domestic roles to get married, settle down, and have children. Thus began a time when women were presented with idyllic visions of being "happy housewives" at home in the suburbs raising families and caring for their homes and husbands. In 1947, Friedan accepted this vision and married Carl Friedan, an advertising executive; they had three children: David, Jonathan, and Emily. Friedan had, however, kept her job, taking a year's maternity leave after her first child's birth. When she requested her second leave, however, she was fired.

Friedan now tried to live up to the ideals of the day, working hard to find the so-called feminine fulfillment her mother had never found in domestic life. Eventually moving to a house in Rockland County, New York, Friedan reared her family, but she also continued to write, contributing articles to several magazines for women.

Life's Work

A popular topic in the media of the postwar period was the idea that women's education was not preparing them adequately for their roles as women. That is, women went to colleges where they received educations they would never be able to apply in careers, since their proper role as women was to be housewives. Too much education was making them discontent with this role in life. The focus was on the inappropriateness of women's education, but Friedan began to see that what was wrong was not education but the role expectations that limited the choices of educated women.

Based on a 1957 survey of her classmates from Smith College, Friedan wrote an article for *McCall's* magazine on the issue of women and education, but her work was rejected by the male editor as too unbelievable. She was then asked to write the same story for *Ladies' Home Journal*, but the article that was published revealed the opposite of what Friedan had originally written. *Redbook* also considered and refused to do the story. Friedan realized that she would have to write a book to get her ideas into print, because her ideas threatened the very identity and existence of magazines geared to women.

In her first book, *The Feminine Mystique* (1963), Friedan coined the now-famous phrase "feminine mystique" to describe the prescribed female role of the postwar years. Although reviewers were largely hostile or cautious, the book caused shock waves throughout the country among readers, because thousands of American women identified with the "nameless, aching dissatisfaction" that she described. Friedan's readers were to become part of the energy that would instigate the second wave of the feminist movement, beginning in the late 1960's.

> "*Men weren't really the enemy — they were fellow victims suffering from an outmoded masculine mystique that made them feel unnecessarily inadequate when there were no bears to kill.*"

By 1966, Friedan, sensing that words were not enough to make change, began putting her energies into organizing for women's rights. In that year, she attended a conference in Washington, D.C., of all the state Commissions on the Status of Women. The delegates, who shared their frustrations at having state and local governments dismiss their concerns, soon organized what was to become the National Organization for Women (NOW). Friedan wrote NOW's statement of purpose. The organizing conference of the new group was held in October of 1966, with about three hundred members, and Friedan was elected the first president, a post she held until 1970 (one year after her divorce in May, 1969). In 1969 she

> ### "The Problem That Has No Name"
>
> Betty Friedan's book *The Feminine Mystique* (1963) countered the conventional wisdom of midcentury America by legitimizing women's dissatisfaction with their roles as wives and mothers. In the first chapter of the book, Friedan described women's unhappiness as "the problem that has no name."
>
> "The problem lay buried, unspoken, for many years in the minds of American women. It was a strange stirring, a sense of dissatisfaction, a yearning that women suffered in the middle of the twentieth century in the United States. Each suburban wife struggled with it alone. As she made the beds, shopped for groceries, matched slipcover material, ate peanut butter sandwiches with her children, chauffeured Cub Scouts and Brownies, lay beside her husband at night she was afraid to ask even of herself the silent question—'Is this all?'
>
> "For over fifteen years there was no word of this yearning in the millions of words written about women, for women, in all the columns, books and articles by experts telling women their role was to seek fulfillment as wives and mothers.. . . For over fifteen years women in America found it harder to talk about the problem than about sex. Even the psychoanalysts had no name for it.. . .
>
> "If I am right, the problem that has no name stirring in the minds of so many American women today is not a matter of loss of femininity or too much education, or the demands of domesticity. It is far more important than anyone recognizes. It is the key to these other new and old problems which have been torturing women and their husbands and children, and puzzling their doctors and educators for years. It may well be the key to our future as a nation and a culture. We can no longer ignore that voice within women that says: 'I want something more than my husband and my children and my home.'"

also cofounded the National Association for the Repeal of Abortion Laws (now known as NARAL Pro-Choice America) with Bernard Nathanson.

Continuing her activism, Friedan became a major organizer of the Women's Strike for Equality, which took place on August 26, 1970, the fiftieth anniversary of the date women won the right to vote. During this time, Friedan joined the debates over sexual politics. She was opposed to a feminist politics that condemned males as oppressors of women and girls, that embraced notions of female separatism, and that supported lesbian sexuality as a political issue. She argued that sexual politics was divisive and that it diverted attention from what she considered the real political and economic issues of most women.

In 1971, Friedan helped organize and was the coconvener of the National Women's Political Caucus (with Gloria Steinem and Bella Abzug). The caucus was formed to encourage and support women and prowomen candidates for public office. By 1972, however, Friedan was beginning to back out of political activism, focusing her energies on writing, speaking, and teaching. In that year, she was invited to teach as a visiting professor at Temple University. This was followed by invitations to teach at Yale in 1974 and at Queens College of the City University of New York in 1975. It was around this time as well that Friedan was exploring what she called the "second stage," defined by her as the sex-role revolution that must include men. This new focus was reflected in her course titles at Temple, Yale, and Queens: "The Sex-Role Revolution, Stage II."

In 1975, Friedan was named Humanist of the Year by the American Humanist Association, and she received an honorary doctorate of humane letters from Smith College. The following year saw the publication of her second book, *It Changed My Life: Writings on the Women's Movement* (1976). In this book Friedan described her work over the previous years and included a journal of her experiences. Her third book, *The Second Stage* (1981), further explored her growing concern with the need to overcome the polarization between women and men and to achieve the human wholeness that she saw as the ultimate promise of feminism. In addition, she was concerned about a damaging myth she saw growing in American culture that of the superwoman who could have it all: career, marriage, and family. Her book argued that the time for reacting against male dominance and focusing on work outside the home was passing as women's goals were being won. Women now needed to begin to unite with men in building a new society of male-female equality.

Although a logical extension of Friedan's previous work, *The Second Stage* unleashed a great controversy. Many feminists turned on Friedan, saying that she had betrayed the women's movement by buying into popular ideas about the importance of the traditional family and the need to gain the approval of men. Moreover, she was faulted for focusing on the problems of middle-class white women and neglecting women of color and the poor. By the early 1990's, however, she insisted that while she still considered herself a feminist, she was not concerned with women as a separate special interest group.

Friedan's next book was *The Fountain of Age* (1993), which she wrote to face her own denial and dread of aging. However, in the process of her research she found a major contradiction between the typical view that aging is a time of loss and debility and the realities of the lives of the aging people she interviewed. She notes that for women the aging process is changing because of differences in the way women are defining themselves (a change she helped bring about with her leadership in the feminist movement). She developed the phrase "fountain of age" (a play on "fountain of youth") to describe the new generativity experienced by both women and men as they grow older. Friedan held a variety of academic appointments. She became Distinguished Visiting Professor and director of the New Paradigm Project at Cornell University and also taught at New York University, the University of Southern California, and Mount Vernon College as the George Mason Professor of Social Evolution. She also lectured worldwide. Beyond academia she organized and directed the First Women's Bank and Trust.

In her 2000 autobiography *Life So Far*, Friedan described her married life as stormy to the point of physical battles. Her husband Carl once said much the same when, following the couple's divorce, he admitted, in describing Friedan, "It took a driven, superaggressive, egocentric almost lunatic dynamo to rock the world the way she did. Unfortunately, she was the same person at home, where that kind of conduct doesn't work. She simply never understood this." Friedan was well-known among colleagues for her abrasiveness, fits of temper, and tendency to monopolize the spotlight. According to Germaine Greer, a writer and feminist who did not share Friedan's philosophy, Friedan also was very feminine and dressed in stylish clothes.

Billington; Friedan; NOW co-chair and Washington, D.C., lobbyist Barbara Ireton (1932-1998); and feminist attorney Marguerite Rawalt (1895-1989). (Wikimedia Commons)

Friedan divided her time at homes in Washington, D.C., and Sag Harbor, New York. She died at her Washington home on February 4, 2006, from congestive heart failure. It was her eighty-fifth birthday.

SIGNIFICANCE

Friedan's effect on the American women's movement, and on American culture, is immeasurable. Indeed, her name, along with that of Gloria Steinem, has become synonymous with feminism in the United States. Friedan first gave voice to the dissatisfaction of housewives caught in the postwar ideology of the feminine mystique, then cofounded and led feminist organizations such as NOW. In her later years she focused first on the second stage and then on aging. She always was willing to be controversial, to follow her own star, and always spoke for many who identified with her insights. On a practical level, Friedan worked successfully with others for economic parity with men, and for genderneutral language, maternity leave, abortion rights, and childcare centers for working women.

Biographer David Horowitz suggested that it was less

Friedan's experience as a housewife than it was her youthful communist sympathies, evidenced by her journalistic work for labor unions, that led her to reject the midcentury stereotype of American womanhood. Whatever her inspiration, historians regard The Feminine Mystique as among the most influential nonfiction books of the twentieth century. More than 3 million copies of the book have been sold, and it has been translated into numerous languages. Although a flamboyant, divisive figure, Friedan continued to personify women's struggle for equity, even after her death.

Eleanor B. Amico

Further Reading

Behm, Barbara. *Betty Friedan: Speaking Out for Women's Rights.* Milwaukee, Wis.: Gareth Stevens, 1992. This book discusses Friedan's views of women's rights and her impact on the women's movement.

Friedan, Betty. *It Changed My Life: Writings on the Women's Movement.* New York: Random House, 1976. Perhaps the most autobiographical of Friedan's books, this work documents her activism in the women's movement and provides various entries from her journal.

Hennessee, Judith. *Betty Friedan: Her Life.* New York: Random House, 1999. Hennessee portrays Friedan as a "woman of paradoxes," a feminist who did not like women. The biography covers her youth and early ambitions, including her desire to be an actor, but focuses on the women's movement and her ongoing conflicts with leading feminists such as Gloria Steinem and Bella Abzug.

Horowitz, Daniel. *Betty Friedan and the Making of the Feminine Mystique.* Amherst: University of Massachusetts Press, 1998. Horowitz contends that many of Friedan's ideas came from her study of humanistic psychology and from her participation in the labor movement of the 1940's.

Sherman, Janann, ed. *Interviews with Betty Friedan.* Jackson: University Press of Mississippi, 2002. A collection of published interviews with Friedan conducted over the course of her career. Part of the Conversations with Public Intellectuals series.

Marcus Garvey

Civil rights activist

Born: August 17, 1887; Saint Ann's Bay, Jamaica
Died: June 10, 1940; London, England
Also known as: Marcus Mosiah Garvey, Jr.; the Black Moses
Areas of Achievement: Business; Civil rights; Social issues

As founder of the Universal Negro Improvement Association (UNIA), Garvey made a major contribution to the course of African American history. The UNIA tried to create for people of African descent in the United States and abroad various means for enhancing their sense of self-respect and capacity for social and material improvement. Although the slogan "Back to Africa" is frequently associated with his movement, "black nationalism" might be a more appropriate term.

Early Life

Marcus Mosiah Garvey, Jr., was one of eleven children born to Marcus Mosiah Garvey and Sarah Jane Richards; only one other child survived. Garvey's father was a mason, and his mother worked part-time in the fields, part-time as a domestic servant. At the age of fourteen, Garvey went to Jamaica's capital city, Kingston, where he started work in a printing firm and rose to the rank of master printer. Involvement in union politics led to conflicts with his employers and his decision to leave

Marcus Garvey (Wikimedia Commons)

Jamaica. In 1914, while Garvey was temporarily back in Jamaica, he founded the Universal Negro Improvement Association and African Communities League, which would later be better known as the Universal Negro Improvement Association (UNIA). His cofounder was Amy Ashwood, who later became his first wife.

The UNIA's goals included fostering fellowship among African Americans, "civilizing" African tribes, and establishing agencies to support the rights of people of African descent worldwide. Its motto was "One God, one aim, one destiny."

In 1916, Garvey came to the United States after spending several years in Central America and England. In England, he had collaborated with the Sudanese-Egyptian editor of *The African Times and Orient Review*. Although he contributed a 1913 article on African Americans in the West Indies, he began to look beyond Jamaica to embrace black people on all continents, a cause that later was associated with the "Back to Africa" movement.

Life's Work

Garvey's biographers often attribute his dedication to the UNIA to his admiration for Booker T. Washington, whose autobiography, *Up from Slavery* (1901), and whose work as the first head of the Tuskegee Institute in Alabama influenced him greatly. He was in touch with Washington by 1915, a year before his arrival in the United States. Garvey's first U.S. lecture tour brought him into contact with several prominent African American leaders of the time, including W. E. B. Du Bois. His ties with Du Bois, however, were short-lived. By the mid-1920's, the two black nationalist leaders had parted ways and even developed a mutual enmity. Garvey's view of how the goals of the UNIA could be achieved shifted in this period. While his early emphasis had been on improving educational opportunities, he began to discuss the need to found all-black business and industrial enterprises.

In 1918, Garvey began publication of a weekly newspaper titled *The Negro World*, which became the mouthpiece of the UNIA. In 1919, as he was beginning to rise to prominence, Garvey launched an ambitious but ill-fated plan to foster closer economic ties between Africa and the West. He conceived of the Black Star Line (BSL), an oceanic steamship line owned and operated by African American investors. Its goal was to obtain a substantial portion of what its founders predicted would be a growing market in Africa for goods from the Western Hemisphere, as well as the market in the Americas for African exports. Shortly after it began operations, however, the BSL ran into legal trouble connected with the marketing of its shares. Although some supporters claimed that the prosecution was racially and politically motivated, Garvey was convicted of fraud in 1923 and sentenced to five years in prison. After serving part of his term, Garvey had his sentence commuted by President Calvin Coolidge in 1927.

After his release, Garvey returned to Jamaica, where he continued to devote himself to the UNIA. Soon, he was able to set up branch offices of the UNIA in various Jamaican towns. In 1928, he returned to Europe, where he met representatives of a number of African movements, including the West African Students Union.

Garvey founded another newspaper, *The Blackman*, in 1929, the same year he organized the Sixth International UNIA Convention. The event drew more than ten thousand supporters, including activists from around the world. The pomp and circumstance of this convention lent a new aura to Garvey's style of leadership. Garvey appeared clad in flowing robes wearing a plumed hat, while officials of the UNIA wore military-style uniforms and carried swords.

In 1931, Garvey launched the Edelweiss Amusement

Garvey giving the Declaration of Rights of the Negro Peoples of the World. (Library of Congress)

> ### Garvey and the Universal Negro Improvement Association
>
> By 1920, only six years after the founding of the Universal Negro Improvement Association (UNIA), the organization had reached several milestones. In the Western Hemisphere, membership grew rapidly, reportedly surpassing four million in 1920. This was the year of the first UNIA international convention held in New York's Madison Square Garden. At the convention, founder Marcus Garvey announced that two concrete steps had been taken to achieve the group's goal of self-sufficiency for Africans and African Americans. One step, the founding of the Black Star Line of steamships, later caused serious legal troubles for the association and Garvey himself. The second step, an investment program, was inaugurated with the goal of providing black-produced consumer goods and services for the black market.
>
> The UNIA combined steps such as these (creating institutions, each with its own UNIA-appointed board of directors) with efforts to support an emerging international pan-African movement. The organization was concerned with preparing Africa—then still almost entirely colonial—for a successful independent future. These efforts made it clear that Garvey's UNIA sought to grow in political and economic potential (and possibly become an actual political party) in the Americas, Europe, and ultimately on the African continent itself.

Company (named after Edelweiss Park, his headquarters location in Jamaica), a philanthropic foundation to provide support for African American artists in marketing their artwork internationally.

Garvey is most commonly associated with the Back to Africa movement. While this movement is typically thought to involve African American migration to the African "homeland," Garvey's efforts were more closely related to a broader pan-African movement championed by a number of Africans after the near-collapse of Europe's African colonies in World War I. Speeches by UNIA vice president William Sherrill suggested that the UNIA was drawing attention to Africa in order to help native Africans improve their lives and gain opportunities. Although UNIA rhetoric included references to possible support for uprisings against whites in Africa, Garvey indicated that he felt that economic and technical assistance was the real key to "modernism" in Africa. For example, he was involved in efforts to attract African Americans to investment schemes that could help Africans establish businesses and export goods to America.

Most of Garvey's projects focused on Liberia, which, after severing ties with the original American Colonization Society, was struggling to establish a political and socioeconomic system based on the United States. The UNIA tried to raise a five-million dollar private loan to help Liberia free itself from white capitalist ventures (eventually dominated by the rubber industry and the Firestone Company). Garvey even proclaimed that the UNIA was prepared to set up its headquarters in the Liberian capital of Monrovia. The ambitious ventures—including a plan for a Liberian black business school launched by Cyril Critchlow, one of the directors of the troubled Black Star Line—proved to be beyond the UNIA's practical capacities.

> *"God and Nature first made us what we are, and then out of our own created genius we make ourselves what we want to be. Follow always that great law. Let the sky and God be our limit and Eternity our measurement."*

Between the time he left the United States in 1927 and 1935, Garvey resided in his native Jamaica, where he directed UNIA operations from headquarters in Kingston. During this period, he actively participated in Jamaican politics. He founded the People's Political Party in 1929 and ran several successful campaigns under a banner supporting the cause of the working class, women, and the poor.

Garvey spent his final years in England, where he had established ties with leaders of other black nationalist groups. He died there in 1940.

SIGNIFICANCE

Garvey was an icon of black nationalism throughout his career and even after his death. The UNIA remained active into the 1950's, and Garvey's name was frequently invoked in rallies in the United States and abroad. His reputation was greatest among Caribbean islanders and their diaspora communities in other countries.

Byron Cannon

FURTHER READING

Cronon, E. David. *Black Moses: The Story of Marcus Garvey and the Universal Negro Improvement Association.* 2d ed. Madison: University of Wisconsin Press, 1987. First published in 1960, this scholarly study was long regarded as the most influential work on Garvey.

Grant, Colin. *Negro With a Hat: The Rise and Fall of Marcus Garvey.* New York: Oxford University Press, 2008. Detailed, readable biography exploring the interior life of the black nationalist leader.

Hill, Robert A., ed. *The Marcus Garvey and Universal Negro Association Papers.* 10 vols. Berkeley: University of California Press, 1990. Definitive collection of primary documents about Garvey and his movement. Contains most of Garvey's own letters, newspaper editorials, and speeches.

Martin, Tony. *Marcus Garvey, Hero: A First Biography.* Dover, Mass.: Majority Press, 1983. Less detailed than Judith Stein's closely documented study, this biography is a very readable, more personal, account of Garvey's life.

Stein, Judith. *The World of Marcus Garvey: Race and Class in Modern Society.* Baton Rouge: Louisiana State University Press, 1991. Comprehensive scholarly biography of Garvey covering the main stages of his career, including his ties with the international pan-African movement.

EMMA GOLDMAN

Lithuanian-born activist and feminist

Born: June 27, 1869; Kovno, Lithuania
Died: May 14, 1940; Toronto, Canada
Area of Achievement: Activism, social issues, women's rights

Goldman expounded anarchist principles in speeches across the United States, attacking repressive government, religion, militarism, and sexism.

EARLY LIFE

Emma Goldman (GOHLD-muhn) showed her rebellious spirit early, fighting with her autocratic father and despotic teachers. She passed the entrance examinations for admission to a German-language secondary school, but she could not attend when her religious teacher refused to provide a certificate of character because she did not show proper respect for authority.

When her family moved to St. Petersburg, Goldman was exposed to socialist and anarchist critiques of capitalism and of government. She accepted the idea that violence was justified to bring about change. However, her true inspiration was anarchist Peter Kropotkin, who believed in a normal evolution to a better society with social revolutions serving only to clear the way for progress. Private property sanctified by state and religion was the basis of oppression; once those obstacles were transcended, a stateless society based on freedom and voluntarism would evolve.

In December, 1885, Goldman accompanied her older sister in emigrating to America. They settled in Rochester, New York, and Goldman went to work in the city's clothing factories. Her marriage to a fellow clothing

Emma Goldman (Library of Congress)

worker ended in divorce within a year; however, under existing naturalization law marrying a citizen automatically made Goldman a citizen of the United States.

The execution of four anarchists for alleged participation in the Chicago Haymarket bombings (1886) made Goldman disillusioned with American freedom. Working for low wages under harsh and arbitrary conditions in the clothing factory owned by the chairman of the United Jewish Charities of Rochester convinced her that German Jewish factory owners deliberately exploited needy Russian Jews.

Her experience with Jewish capitalism in Rochester and her difficulties with religious teachers in Russia led Goldman to repudiate both religious and secular Judaism. The first issue of Goldman's monthly magazine, *Mother Earth*, had a lengthy article condemning nationalism, with special emphasis on Zionism.

LIFE'S WORK

On August 15, 1889, Goldman moved to New York City, determined to launch a career propagandizing radical ideas. She was quickly accepted by the anarchist community and often asked to lecture. On her first day in New York Goldman met Alexander Berkman, who became her lover and constant companion (when they were not in prison) until his death in 1936. Goldman was very open about her love affairs, which always began passionately and often ended in lifelong friendships.

Berkman and Goldman were repulsed by the July, 1892, gun battle at the Homestead steel plant near Pittsburgh between strikers and Pinkerton detectives hired by Henry Clay Frick, chairman of Carnegie Steel, in which ten workers died. Berkman decided Frick should be punished. With Goldman's help he bought a pistol, entered Frick's office July 23, and wounded but did not kill him. Berkman was imprisoned for fourteen years after a trial during which he hid Goldman's complicity.

Goldman kept speaking up. In 1893 she was sentenced to a year in prison, accused of inciting a riot by a speech to striking workers. While in prison she decided to move beyond Yiddish- and Russian-speaking audiences and become an apostle of anarchism to the American public. As she ranged across the country, hostile press coverage and attempts by police to suppress her made "Red Emma" the best known and most frightening example of dangerous radicalism.

After Leon Czolgosz claimed to have been inspired by Goldman to assassinate President William McKinley, pressure to silence her intensified, although extensive

Defense of Free Speech

Emma Goldman used attempts to prevent her from being heard as occasions to energize defenders of freedom of speech. In Chicago in 1908 a police captain literally dragged her off the platform. News reports aroused prominent citizens to form a free speech league, and when Goldman returned in 1910 she spoke without molestation. After being forced out of San Diego in 1912 and 1913 by vigilantes protected by the police—on one of these occasions, one of her companions was tarred and feathered—she was triumphantly invited back in 1915 by a committee of civic leaders.

Her 1910 tour was one of her most successful, both in raising money and in starting five successful free speech fights. In that year, however, the University of Wisconsin disgraced itself when the regents and president of the university bowed to a public outcry and disciplined a faculty member for announcing Goldman's speech to his classes. Protests by the class of 1910 finally led to placement of a plaque on campus in 1915 dedicating the university to freedom of speech.

The most lasting of Goldman's contributions to free speech was enlisting Roger Baldwin in 1911. He went on to organize the National Civil Liberties Bureau, which fought to protect civil rights during the 1919-1920 Red Scare and ultimately led to the founding of the American Civil Liberties Union. Through that organization the influence of Goldman's fight for free speech extends to the present.

government efforts revealed no connection. In 1908, the federal government legally denaturalized her ex-husband, automatically revoking Goldman's citizenship, planning to bar her reentry as an undesirable alien if she ever left the country.

In her lecture tours Goldman basically restated Kropotkin's sweeping criticism of capitalism, religion, and nationalism. Applying his insights to the American scene, she described the repressive forces denying true freedom to Americans, whether workers prevented from unionizing or intellectuals inhibited from speaking out critically. Goldman also lectured on new European plays and

Goldman addressing a rally at Union Square, New York, 1916. (Wikimedia Commons)

novels, stressing their radical social content. She attacked the institution of marriage, arguing that it treated women as objects, making the survival of true love improbable. After activist Margaret Sanger was arrested in 1915 on obscenity charges for advocating birth control, Goldman added birth control information to her lectures. Goldman was contemptuous of the idea that women's suffrage would fundamentally change government.

Early in 1917 Goldman began concentrating on antiwar speeches. In July, she and Berkman were sentenced to two years in prison for opposing conscription. They were deported to the Soviet Union in December, 1919. At first the two enthusiastically supported the new regime. Able to speak Russian, they were not dependent on government handouts for information, and Goldman soon became appalled by the savage repressive actions of the government. They left Russia in December, 1921.

> "There are...some potentates I would kill by any and all means at my disposal. They are Ignorance, Superstition, and Bigotry — the most sinister and tyrannical rulers on earth."

Left-leaning liberals refused to believe her accounts of what she had seen; liberal weeklies refused to accept her articles. Her 1923 *My Disillusionment in Russia* received little attention. No one Goldman approached was willing to join her in publicly protesting Soviet persecution of dissidents. She continued to lecture and in 1931 published a widely ignored autobiography.

Upon the outbreak of the Spanish Civil War in 1936, Goldman rallied to support the anarchist armies in Catalonia. In 1940, she was in Canada raising funds for Spanish refugees when she suffered a fatal stroke. Once dead, Goldman was permitted to reenter the United States for burial in Chicago.

Significance

Goldman was at least partially successful in becoming an apostle of anarchism to America. Her notoriety as a dangerous subversive made her a celebrity. Papers announced her arrival in town. Although most coverage was negative, attacks on her aroused curiosity and swelled her audiences beyond the already converted. She became adept at witty responses to those who came to jeer and, more importantly, educated open-minded individuals, who came out of curiosity, about progressive social causes.

As continuous revelations of Soviet brutality erupted, beginning with the Great Purge of the 1930's, Goldman's critique of communism became more acceptable to liberals. The major revival of her fame came with the rise of the New Left in the 1960's. Her ideas on feminism and her attacks on state power and on conformity strongly influenced a new generation. Goldman's major books came back into print and remain so in the twenty-first century.

Milton Berman

Further Reading

Drinnon, Richard. *Rebel in Paradise: A Biography of Emma Goldman.* Chicago: University of Chicago Press, 1961. Detailed life by a sympathetic New Left scholar.

Falk, Candace. *Love, Anarchy, and Emma Goldman.* New York: Holt, Rinehart and Winston, 1984. Stresses Goldman's private life.

_____, et al. *Made for America, 1890-1901.* Vol. 1 in Emma Goldman: A Documentary History of the American Years. Berkeley: University of California Press, 2003.

---. *Making Speech Free, 1902-1909.* Vol. 2 in Emma Goldman: A Documentary History of the American Years. Berkeley: University of California Press, 2004. These two volumes contain letters, articles and speeches, and government documents dealing with efforts to suppress and deport Goldman.

Goldman, Emma. *Living My Life.* 2 vols. New York: Alfred A. Knopf, 1931. A 993-page narrative of her struggles against authorities. Very open account of her sex life.

Rudahl, Sharon. *A Dangerous Woman: A Graphic Biography of Emma Goldman.* New York: New Press, 2007. A celebration of Goldman's life using comic-book techniques.

Solomon, Martha. *Emma Goldman.* Boston: Twayne, 1987. Focuses on Goldman as a writer, discussing her rhetorical devices and platform performance.

Weiss, Penny, and Loretta Kensinger, eds. *Feminist Interpretations of Emma Goldman.* University Park: Pennsylvania State University Press, 2007. Fifteen essays analyze what is still valuable in Goldman's insights for modern feminism.

EMMA GONZÁLEZ

Gun control activist

Born: November 11, 1999; Florida
Areas of Achievement: Social Reform; Politics/Law

In the aftermath of the 2018 school shooting in Parkland, Florida, in which seventeen students and staff were killed, a handful of high school students—survivors of the shooting—were at the forefront of a national wave of youth activism against gun violence. Among them was seventeen-year-old Emma González, a Cuban-American whose passionate speech at a gun control rally three days after the shooting was viewed millions of times on social media and helped to galvanize the movement.

EARLY LIFE

Emma González was born November 11, 1999, in Florida. Her father, Jose González, emigrated from Cuba in 1968, initially settling in New York. Emma was raised in Parkland, Florida, a town near Fort Lauderdale with a population of around 35,000 people. Emma has two older siblings. She attended the Marjorie Stoneman Douglas High School in Parkland, where she was the president of the school's gay-straight alliance. Her favorite high school subjects were creative writing and astronomy.

The Stoneman Douglas High School was the scene of a mass shooting that occurred in February 2018 during Emma's senior year. On Valentine's Day, a troubled teen and a former student at the high school entered the building with a weapon and opened fire. Seventeen students and staff were killed and another seventeen were wounded. González was in class when the fire alarm went off; the students filed out the doors where they found SWAT teams already in place. The authorities indicated to the students that the incident was a "Code Red," meaning the highest level of imminent danger. Following the direction of the authorities, the students re-entered the school building and took cover in the auditorium. González crouched with other students on the floor between rows of folding seats until the incident was over.

According to a 2018 CNN analysis, it was nearly the 300th school shooting in the United States since 2009. For comparison, Canada and France each had two school

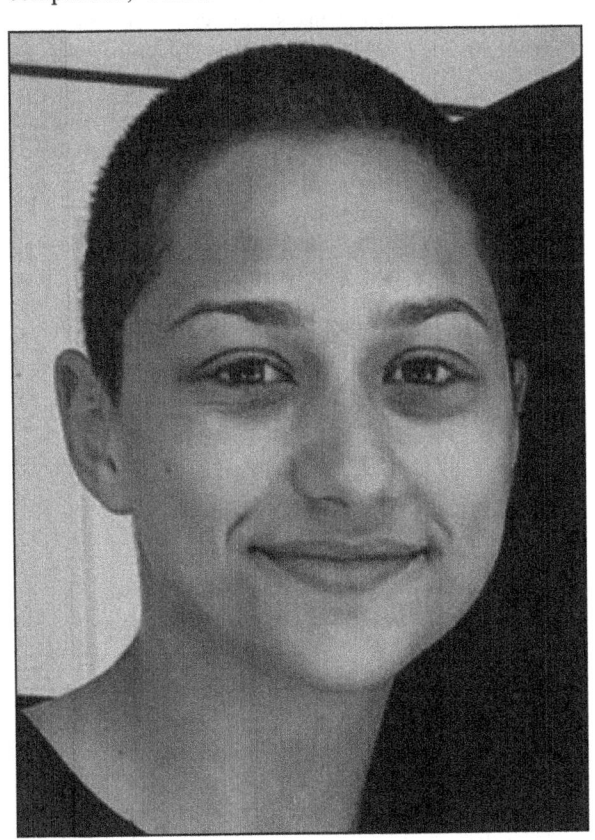

Emma González (Wikimedia Commons)

shootings in the period 2009–2018, and Germany had one. The United Kingdom, Italy, and Japan—like most nations in the world—had zero. The country in second place for the most school shootings was Mexico, with only eight. One reason, it is generally thought, for the high incidence of gun violence in the United States is the prevalence of guns in the population. The United States is home to only 4.4% of the global population, yet it has nearly 42% of the world's guns.

Life's Work

The day after the shooting, González received a text from a fellow student, David Hogg, telling her that CNN was looking for another student to appear alongside him in an interview on cable television with Anderson Cooper that evening. Hogg, who had an internship his senior year with the *South Florida Sun-Sentinel*, was an unusually articulate and media-savvy high school student. Hogg can perhaps be credited with sparking the new post-Parkland youth activism and their commitment to gun control. When he was being interviewed by Laura Ingraham in the first national interview with a Parkland student to air following the shooting, he interrupted her to say, "Can I say one more thing to the audience? *I don't want this just to be another mass shooting. I don't want this to be something that people forget.*"

Gonzalez made such an impact in the wake of the Stoneman Douglas High School shooting that marchers used her image to show support for the anti-gun violence movement. (Wikimedia Commons)

> "When we've had our say with the government — and maybe the adults have gotten used to saying 'it is what it is,' but if us students have learned anything, it's that if you don't study, you will fail. And in this case if you actively do nothing, people continually end up dead, so it's time to start doing something."

Media appearances and activist opportunities picked up pace in days following the shooting. A rally for gun control was quickly organized in Fort Lauderdale. Several Parkland high school students were invited to speak at the rally, and González was among them. Although it was only a day or two after after the shooting when González agreed to speak and began working on a speech, she poured her heart into the effort. She settled on a speech that castigated the failure of politicians to institute gun control laws. The speech was built around the repeated phrase, "We call B.S." González's speech was broadcast nationally, and video of the speech was watched millions of times in the next few days on social media and other platforms.

Thanks as much to her demeanor as to the speech itself, González became an instant celebrity. A Cuban-American bisexual female with a shaved head, González is telegenic. Writer Rebecca Mead in the *New Yorker* magazine was quick to highlight her "uncanny" resemblance to Maria Falconetti, the actress in Carl Theodor Dreyer's silent film masterpiece, *The Passion of Joan of Arc* (1928). Mead also pointed to a deeper resemblance: Joan in Dreyer's film is a powerful and authoritative figure because she is "innocent" and even naive, not because she is "wise" and sophisticated. Over the following weeks and months, González was invited to write op-eds for the *New York Times* and was profiled by *Glamour* and other magazines.

González spent most of 2018 as an activist before beginning college in the fall at New College of Florida in Sarasota. On March 14, 2018, exactly one month after the shooting, nearly one million young people across the country walked out of class to mark National School Walkout, a protest against the school shooting epidemic. On March 21, 2018, the March for Our Lives took place in Washington, DC. The event was first announced by fellow student Cameron Kasky. It was organized by Never Again MSD, begun by a group of students in the days after the shooting, including Kasky, Alex Wind, Sofie Whitney, González and Hogg. With over 200,000 participants and organized entirely by students, the event was among the largest student-led demonstrations in Washington DC since the Vietnam War era.

SIGNIFICANCE
In the years before Parkland, official and public responses to school shootings had developed into a familiar pattern: statements of grief and condolences, expressions of frustration with the status quo, followed by pledges on the part of politicians to find solutions to the problem of gun violence in America. After the Parkland shooting, something else happened. The school students themselves organized, began to speak out, and became a potent political force. Within months, the students of Marjorie Stoneman Douglas High School had organized one of the largest youth demonstrations ever held in Washington DC since the 1960s. Several students became leaders in the new activism, including David Hogg, Alfonso Calderon, Sarah Chadwick, Emma González, and Cameron Kasky. González's "No B.S." speech, delivered at a rally three days after the shooting, was a critical event in galvanizing the movement and giving it a national spokesperson.

The activists wanted 2018 to be a watershed year for passing meaningful gun control laws across the nation. They worked hard, too, to increase voter turnout among young people in the 2018 mid-term elections, and several of the students spoke of their long-term commitment to opposing the National Rifle Association, the nation's largest pro-gun lobbying group. Three weeks after the shooting, Florida's governor Rick Scott signed a law that banned bump stocks and raised the gun buying age to 21 years. The law also imposed a three-day waiting period for the purchase of firearms. Many other states, too, made changes to their gun ownership laws in the months following Parkland, inspired by the activism of the survivors. The new laws primarily banned bump stocks, expanded background checks, restricted ownership, or increased wait periods.

D. Alan Dean

FURTHER READING
Alter, Charlotte. "The School Shooting Generation Has Had Enough." *TIME* magazine, March 22, 2018.
Cook, Philip, and Kristin Goss. *The Gun Debate: What Everyone Needs to Know*. New York: Oxford University Press, 2014.
Fisher, M., & Keller, J. "What Explains U.S. Mass Shootings? International Comparisons Suggest an Answer." *New York Times*, Nov. 11, 2017. https://www.nytimes.com/2017/11/07/world/americas/mass-shootings-us-international.html. Accessed Dec. 15, 2018.
Grabow, Chip, and Lisa Rose. "The US has had 57 times as many school shootings as the other major industrialized nations combined." *CNN.com*. https://www.cnn.com/2018/05/21/us/school-shooting-us-versus-world-trnd/index.html. Accessed Dec. 15, 2018.
Mead, Rebecca. "Joan of Arc and the Passion of Emma Gonzalez." *The New Yorker*, March 26, 2018.
Vasilogambros, Matt. "After Parkland, States Pass 50 New Gun-Control Laws." Pewtrusts.org. https://www.pewtrusts.org/en/research-and-analysis/blogs/stateline/2018/08/02/after-parkland-states-pass-50-new-gun-control-laws.
Waldman, Michael. *The Second Amendment: A Biography*. New York: Simon & Schuster, 2015.

FANNIE LOU HAMER

Civil rights activist

Born: October 6, 1917; Montgomery County, Mississippi
Died: March 14, 1977; Mound Bayou, Mississippi
Area of Achievement: Civil rights, social reform, government and politics, women's rights

Born a child of sharecroppers and a descendant of slaves, Hamer rose to prominence as a fearless and eloquent advocate for African American voting rights and as a leader in the larger Civil Rights movement. Her name became symbolic of the movement.

EARLY LIFE
Fannie Lou Hamer (HAY-mur) was born Fannie Lou Townsend in Montgomery County, Mississippi. She was the granddaughter of slaves and the last of twenty children born to James Lee Townsend and Lou Ella Bramlett. Her father was a Baptist preacher and bootlegger, her mother a domestic servant, and both were sharecroppers. The family was very poor; meals often consisted of greens and gravy or bread and onions. They lived in a small

Fannie Lou Hamer (Library of Congress)

wooden house without running water or electricity. When Hamer was six years old, she was offered a reward of canned fish and Cracker Jacks candy from the sharecropper boss if she proved how well she could pick cotton. Excited, she passed the test and ended up joining her siblings and working in the fields twelve to fourteen hours a day.

Hamer attended school for several years, but for blacks the school was open for four winter months only, when field-workers could be spared. Still, she learned to read and write, won spelling bees, and sharpened her quick mind. Tragically, she contracted polio as a child and limped with a disabled leg for the rest of her life.

When Hamer was eleven, her family rented their own land, the first step toward independence, and bought three mules, two cows, a plow, and even a car. Two years later, however, someone, most likely a white neighbor who did not want the family to succeed, poisoned the mules, and the family was forced back to sharecropping. In 1939, Hamer's father died, and soon after her mother was injured in an accident that deprived her of sight in one eye.

Life's Work

Hamer married Perry "Pap" Hamer in 1945, and the couple resettled in nearby Sunflower City. They had their own home, with cold running water. They were able to have children of their own, but they took in and later adopted two girls, whom they raised as daughters. Hamer worked three jobs: picking cotton, supervising other field workers, and cleaning the home of the Marlowes, the plantation owners. The third job showed her how the white population lived, with standard amenities in homes of the day.

Life changed for Hamer in 1962. At a meeting conducted by civil rights workers from the North, she learned that African Americans had the right to vote. When the organizers called for people to register, Hamer raised her hand. This was no small decision. Though the law gave people the right to vote regardless of race, across the South there was much intimidation. African Americans were beaten, fired from their jobs, or killed if they dared to assert their constitutional rights; often, their property was vandalized and their homes burned.

Pap chose not to register, but Hamer, knowing that registering to vote could affect her family and its livelihood, followed through on her pledge. On August 31, 1962, she was one of seventeen African Americans who met activists in the nearby town of Indianola and boarded a bus to take them to register. Voting officials asked the group to copy out a section of the Mississippi state constitution and explain its meaning. Hamer and the others, predictably, failed the test. On the return trip, the bus was stopped by police, ostensibly for being "too yellow," and the driver was arrested and fined thirty dollars.

News of Hamer's attempt to register spread quickly, and Pap's boss threatened to evict the family from the land they worked. The Hamers moved out of their home and stayed with friends in Ruleville. Targeted intimidation ensued, including gunshots in their direction, and the Hamers left the county. Voting rights workers learned of Hamer's courage as well, and they asked her to speak at a meeting of the Student Nonviolent Coordinating Committee (SNCC) in Nashville, Tennessee. Prior to this invitation, Hamer had never left her area of northern Mississippi. In Nashville, she addressed groups and spoke with reporters. When she returned to Ruleville, Pap was fired from his job, and the Hamers lost their home. Hamer took a job with the SNCC, making speeches, recruiting volunteers, and helping to build the organization.

In January of 1963, at the age of forty-five, Hamer finally passed the test and became a registered voter. Her struggle was far from over, however. Six months later, on

June 9, she and a group of fellow activists were at a bus station in Winona, Tennessee, traveling home from a meeting. The entire group was arrested and beaten brutally with leather straps in jail. The event left Hamer scarred for life, but it galvanized her resolve. The group sued the officers who had beaten them, but an all-white jury acquitted the defendants on all charges.

As the 1964 presidential elections approached, civil rights workers felt that the Mississippi Democratic Party did not represent their views, so they formed the Mississippi Freedom Democratic Party (MFDP). As a member, Hamer went to the Democratic National Convention in Atlantic City, New Jersey, that summer. The MFDP sought to replace the Mississippi Democratic Party's all-white delegation. Hamer spoke eloquently, arguing that the state deserved a representatively diverse delegation. The national party rejected the MFDP's request. Hamer, nevertheless, tried to enter the convention, singing what would become her trademark song, "This Little Light of Mine." Though ejected, her attempt was covered on the evening news across the nation. Later that year, Hamer ran for Congress, earning thirty thousand votes, not enough to win the race. In 1968, the MFDP was chosen to represent Mississippi Democrats at the national convention, and Hamer was a delegate.

In 1969, Hamer started the Freedom Farm Cooperative and was invited to the White House for a conference on health and nutrition. She also started a child care center for children of single and working mothers, bringing the Head Start program to rural Mississippi. She helped build homes for poor families through Young World Developers. She was awarded honorary degrees from Shaw University in Raleigh, N.C., Howard University in Washington, D.C., Morehouse College in Atlanta, and Columbia College in Chicago.

> "*I feel sorry for anybody that could let hate wrap them up. Ain't no such thing as I can hate anybody and hope to see God's face.*"

Plagued by her earlier fight with polio and by the injuries she suffered in 1963, Hamer's poor health, which included diabetes, affected her throughout the late 1960's and the 1970's. She was diagnosed with breast cancer in 1976, the same year that her hometown of Ruleville celebrated Fannie Lou Hamer Day. She died in Mound Bayou, Mississippi, on March 14, 1977, at the age of fifty-nine. United Nations ambassador Andrew Young spoke at her funeral, and she was buried in Ruleville. Her gravestone reads, "I'm sick and tired of being sick and tired."

SIGNIFICANCE

Hamer's life provides a stark example of personal accomplishments made through sheer will. Rising from the depths of poverty and living with pain through her life, she became a leader of the movement to bring African Americans to the polls. In so doing, she helped to empower a long-oppressed people, and to make them a significant and powerful force in the democratic process and in the shaping of twentieth century American history.

Barry Stewart Mann

FURTHER READING

Donovan, Sandy. *Fannie Lou Hamer*. Chicago: Raintree, 2004. Part of the African American Biographies series for young readers, with short chapters, accessible text, and ample sidebars. Includes generous photographs, a glossary, a simple time line, a short bibliography, and an index.

Haskins, Jim. *One More River to Cross: The Stories of Twelve Black Americans*. New York: Scholastic, 1992. Targeted for adolescents and young adults, this volume includes a sixteen-page chapter on Hamer that is both readable and informative. It sets her among civil rights leaders such as Ralph Bunche, Shirley Chisholm, and Malcolm X. The book includes a bibliography and an index.

Lee, Chana Kai. *For Freedom's Sake: The Life of Fannie Lou Hamer*. Urbana: University of Illinois Press, 1999. A scholarly, comprehensive, and unsentimental rendering of Hamer's life and achievements. Includes several photographs, exhaustive notes, a bibliography, and an index.

Mills, Kay. *This Little Light of Mine: The Life of Fannie Lou Hamer*. New York: Plume, 1994. At 390 pages, a comprehensive and heartfelt account, complete with chronology, a list of individuals important in Hamer's life and work, extensive notes, and an index.

Olson, Lynne. *Freedom's Daughters: The Unsung Heroines of the Civil Rights Movement from 1830-1970*. New York: Scribner, 2001. A fascinating account that includes Hamer in a parade of women, black and white, who kept the Civil Rights movement moving forward. Olson profiles more than sixty women, going beyond prominent figures like Ida B. Wells-Barnett and Rosa Parks to place in context more obscure figures such as Mary Burks, Daisy Bates, and Penny Patch. The book provides plenty of photographs, endnotes, a bibliography, and an index.

Rubel, David. *Fannie Lou Hamer: From Sharecropping to Politics.* Englewood Cliffs, N.J.: Silver Burdett Press, 1990. A juvenile biography written with lively prose and plenty of background information about life in the South in the mid-twentieth century. The book has photographs, illustrations, and maps. Includes a timetable of events, an index, suggested readings, and an introduction by former U.N. ambassador Andrew Young.

Harry Hay

Gay rights activist

Born: April 7, 1912; Worthing, England
Died: October 24, 2002; San Francisco, California
Also known as: Henry Hay, Jr.
Area of Achievement: LGBTQ rights

An important early gay rights activist, Communist, and labor organizer, Hay founded the Mattachine Society in 1950, the most significant gay rights group in the United States before the Stonewall era. He also founded the Radical Faeries, a gay spiritual movement.

Early Life

Harry Hay Jr. was born in England in 1912. His father was a businessman and an engineer who managed mines for Cecil Rhodes in South Africa. When Harry Jr. was two years old, his father moved the family to Chile, where he took a job managing a copper mine that was owned by the Guggenheims. In 1916, when Harry Jr. was four years old, Harry Sr. resigned from his job after losing a leg in an accident at the mine. He moved his family to California in the United States. By the time of the move, Harry Sr. and his wife Margaret had three young children: Harry Jr., Elizabeth (born in 1914), and a newborn, John. In California, Harry Sr. purchased a citrus farm that turned a profit, and he bought a home in Los Angeles for his family. Los Angeles in 1916 was a bustling, sunny city of about 500,000 inhabitants and already home to a rapidly expanding movie industry. Harry Jr. would spend the rest of his childhood and much of his adult life there.

Hay was always frank about his early sexual experiences and his developing awareness of his sexuality. Hay would come to believe that gay men were not just males who happened to prefer males; he believed that homosexuals comprised a kind of third sex—even a "separate people" apart from heterosexual society, with unique spiritual gifts and capacities and unique cultural forms.

Life's Work

The word "homosexual" was still relatively novel when Hay first encountered it in Edward Carpenter's *The Intermediate Sex* (1908), a book Hay discovered in the public library in Los Angeles. Carpenter was a visionary thinker, writer, and radical who had been friends with Walt Whitman. His books, with titles like *Homogenic Love and Its Place in a Free Society* (1894), *Iolaus: Anthology of Friendship* (1902), *Prisons, Police, and Punishment* (1905), and *Non-Governmental Society* (1911), explored

Harry Hay (Wikimedia Commons)

radical ideas like anarchism, free love, and the history of homosexuality and its place in civilization. Carpenter's work had a profound effect on the young Hay. In particular, Carpenter's theory that homosexuality had a spiritual component (an idea that we find, too, in some of Walt Whitman's writings), explored in his anthropological and historical studies of homosexuality, encouraged Hay to view homosexuality as more than merely a sexual preference and to emphasize what these early LGBTQ writers understood as the special cultural, psychological, and spiritual aspects of homosexual love.

A second major influence on Hay, first encountered in his youth, was the radical and visionary politics of groups like the International Workers of the World (IWW), also called the "Wobblies." Their vision of brotherhood, personal freedom, and all workers banded together in "one big union" was radical even among other socialists at the time. From his reading of Marxist thinkers, including Joseph Stalin, Hay began to conceive of homosexuals along the lines of a "people" possessing a cultural identity and deserving of political liberation. The notion that homosexuals constituted a political minority was far from obvious before it caught on in the 1960s; that it did can be attributed in large part to the ideas and the early activism of Hay.

Hay graduated from high school in 1929. He attended Stanford University from 1930 to 1932, where he studied international relations. In this period, Hay discovered the underground gay scenes in Los Angeles and San Francisco. In 1931, he came out openly as a homosexual, an unusual thing to do at the time. Hay later described the gay community that he discovered in Los Angeles in the 1930s as frightened, small, and stunted by social stigma and criminalization. He wanted things to change.

Hay supported himself with odd jobs in Hollywood, including as a voice actor, a voice coach, and a screen extra. He met actor Will Geer and the two formed a relationship. Geer was a political activist with strong ties to the leftist movement in Los Angeles. (Geer played Grandpa Walton decades later on the popular 1970s television show, *The Waltons*.) Hay quickly became an active member of the radical left, joining numerous demonstrations for workers' rights. In San Francisco in 1934, the police shot and killed two demonstrators during a general strike in that city. Hay was there, and he witnessed the murders. That shocking event helped to solidify his commitment to revolutionary politics; in the same year, he joined the Communist Party USA.

Hay studied Marxist theory under the auspices of the Party, and he would later become an instructor at the communist People's Educational Center in Los Angeles, teaching classes to working people on Marxism and revolutionary theory. He had a particular interest in folk music and taught courses on the subject at the center, which led to meetings with Woody Guthrie and Pete Seeger. The communists, however much they influenced Hay, were not accepting of his homosexuality. The Party encouraged Hay to marry a woman, as did his Jungian analyst. In 1938, he married Anita Platky, who was also a Communist Party member, and in 1939 the two moved to New York City.

Hay worked in several low-paying jobs in New York, and he was a member of the Communist Party's theater committee there. For the Party, he organized workers' theater groups in the city. Hay and his wife returned to Los Angeles in 1942. After the war, Hay had an increasingly difficult time finding work. The Federal Bureau of Investigation (FBI) was by now targeting him for his subversive ideas and activities. (A common harassment tactic employed by the agency was to visit employers or future employers of a suspected Communist in order to "ask questions." Because this made prospective employers nervous, it effectively guaranteed long-term unemployment or at least under-employment.) Hay and Anita adopted and raised two children before their divorce in 1951.

"*Give yourself permission to enjoy being gay. You do have to give yourself permission. You have been told you may not. Give yourself permission to be free.*"

Alfred Kinsey's groundbreaking book, *Sexual Behavior in the Human Male*, was published in 1948. It had a profound impact on Hay. Kinsey claimed that ten percent of all males in the US population engaged in some homosexual activity. (Later estimates have been lower.) To Hay, this was not only startling news, it was grounds for rethinking the place of homosexuals in society. Hay had thought that there might be as many as several hundred homosexuals in any U.S. city, but Kinsey's report suggested that the number was many thousands. If this group, who had been hidden for so long, actually comprised a significant segment of the population, then there was a good chance that by organizing homosexuals—along the lines of an oppressed minority—social norms and U.S. law might eventually be changed. Hay, familiar with the methods of organizing workers and other groups, began to think seriously about organizing homosexuals.

The single largest problem that Hay faced at this point was not opposition from the state but fear of public exposure on the part of the gay men he wanted to organize. It was extremely uncommon to be "out" in that era. Arrests for indecency, for frequenting gay bars, and for engaging in similar criminalized activities could and did ruin many men's lives. Between 1948 and 1950, Hay considered and rejected several organizational ideas (including "Bachelors' Anonymous") before founding the "Society of Fools" in November 1950. Its initial membership was only Hay and several of his friends. In 1951, they changed their name to the Mattachine Society, an obscure reference to a medieval French secret society of men from the theater who used anonymity (they wore masks) to mock the political order.

In 1952, one of the founding members, Dale Jennings, was arrested for indecent behavior in a park. The Mattachine Society's others founding members decided to take the unusual step of organizing publicly in order to fight the charge. They organized the Citizens Committee to Outlaw Entrapment and began to publicize the case. Hay found a lawyer who would take the case—a labor lawyer who had studied Marxism under Hay at the Southern California Labor School and who normally represented dock workers. At trial, according to Hay's later recollection, the judge dismissed the charges against Jennings when the arresting officer was caught in a lie on the witness stand. The case is thought to be the first legal challenge to police entrapment of a homosexual in Los Angeles history. Largely as a result of this victory, the Mattachine Society's membership began to grow exponentially, estimated at several thousand by 1953. Also in 1953, a Los Angeles newspaper wrote about the society and "outed" Hay as not only a homosexual but a Communist. In order to protect the society, and under pressure from others in the organization, Hay and his fellow radical founding members all stepped down and handed the reins to a less radical leadership.

In 1955, Harry Hay was called to testify before a subcommittee of the House Un-American Activities Committee. After this event, Hay laid low for a number of years. The Mattachine Society, meanwhile, continued its activism on behalf of homosexuals, and instituted a number of rules to maintain a safely benign public profile, believing that this was the best way to win their cause. For example, members were encouraged to dress conservatively during their public demonstrations, and the group distanced itself from both political radicals and bohemians.

Hay, meanwhile, went in the other direction. As the counter culture developed in California in the 1960s, Hay began publicly wearing pearls, dresses, and clothing influenced by Native Americans, declaring that he never wanted to be mistaken for a heterosexual again. He met a manufacturer of kaleidoscopes, John Burnside, in the early 1960s, and the two became romantic partners. They would remain together until Hay's death forty years later in 2002.

When the Stonewall uprising occurred in New York City in 1969, the initial event led to several days of unrest that was covered by the press in New York City. It also led to the first large-scale march for gay rights in United States history—the Gay Pride march that was held in several cities around the country in 1970 to commemorate Stonewall. Also after Stonewall, a number of gay liberation organizations were founded that were more radical than Mattachine subsequent to Hay's departure, including the Gay Liberation Front (GLF). Hay chaired the Los Angeles chapter of the GLF. In later life, Hay would become a founder of the "Radical Faeries," a neo-pagan queer community with an international presence. Their first meeting took place in 1979 at an ashram in Arizona. Hay described the faeries as a "way of life" more than a "movement."

Significance

Throughout his adult life as an activist, Hay was committed to an anti-assimilationist vision for the homosexual community. Hay combined influences from Marxism and the spiritual and political writings of earlier homophiles such as Edward Carpenter. He was both a proud and active member of the United States Communist Party and the key founder of the Mattachine Society, one the nation's first organizations to fight publicly for the rights of gay people. Hay accepted great personal hardships for the sake of his visionary and radical commitments, including intimidation from the FBI and being called to testify before a the House Un-American Activities Committee during the so-called Red Scare.

Although the Mattachine Society, following Hay's departure, continued to perform activist work on behalf of gay rights and to bravely publish and distribute its newsletter, it came to be seen as conservative in the wake of the counter-culture and the Stonewall uprising. By the end of the 1970s the Mattachine Society was essentially defunct. Nevertheless, the society, together with its lesbian counterpart, the Daughters of Bilitis, and a group that splintered from Mattachine called ONE, Inc., were instrumental in paving the way for everything that came after Stonewall. The infrastructure they developed—newsletters, meetings, national coordination—was vital to the later success of the post-Stonewall movement. Above all, their work made public discourse around LGBT people political rather than moral, psychological, or strictly legal.

Hay did all of this out of the limelight. Hay fought for gay freedom when it wasn't fashionable to do so—when it was, in fact, a dangerous underground activity. When the movement for LGBTQ rights made headway towards acceptance in the 1970s and 1980s, he began to decry the tendency to assimilationism within the movement. He criticized the habit of, in his words, "parodying" heterosexuals. Hay remained unafraid to hold unpopular, even wildly controversial, opinions. In the 1990s, he criticized the AIDS activist group ACTUP because he felt that their tenor and tactics smacked of heterosexual machismo, and he supported the National Man-Boy Love Association (NAMBLA), a controversial group that promoted homosexual pederasty.

The world at large might never have known of Harry Hay but for the efforts of some young LGBTQ historians who were working in the 1970s, themselves at liberty to do their work in part as a result of Hay's lifetime of effort. Among them was Jonathan Ned Katz, whose *Gay American History: Lesbians and Gay Men in the U.S.A.* was published in 1976, and John D'Emilio, who wrote *Sexual Politics, Sexual Communities: The Making of a Homosexual Minority in the United States, 1940-1970*, published in 1983. Katz's book publicized the previously obscure history of the founding of Mattachine, and D'Emilio's book placed Hay in a prominent role, as an instrumental figure in originating the idea that homosexuals are a minority community.

Dewayne Dean

FURTHER READING

Cusac, Anne-Marie. "Meet Pioner of Gay Rights, Harry Hay." *The Progressive*. September, 1999. http://progressive.org/mag_cusachay.

D'Emilio, John. *Sexual Politics, Sexual Communities: The Making of a Homosexual Minority in the United States, 1940-1970*. Chicago: U of Chicago Press, 1983.

Hay, Harry and Will Roscoe, ed. *Radically Gay: Gay Liberation in the Words of its Founder*. Boston: Beacon Press, 1996.

Katz, Jonathan Ned. *Gay American History: Lesbians and Gay Men in the U.S.A.*

Levy, Dan. "Ever the Warrior: Gay Rights Icon Harry Hay Has No Patience for Assimilation." *San Francisco Chronicle*, June 23, 2000. http://www.sfgate.com/default/article/Ever-the-Warrior-Gay-rights-icon-Harry-Hay-has-3240144.php

Timmons, Stuart. *The Trouble with Harry Hay: Founder of the Modern Gay Movement*. Boston: Alyson Publications, 1990.

AILEEN CLARKE HERNANDEZ

Civil rights and feminist leader

Born: May 23, 1926; Brooklyn, New York City
Died: February 13, 2017; Tustin, California
Area of Achievement: Social reform, women's rights, labor movement, civil rights

As president of the National Organization for Women, director of the International Ladies' Garment Workers Union, and commissioner of the Equal Employment Opportunity Commission (EEOC), Hernandez represented the interests of women and ethnic minorities in the forefront of social reform. She was the first African American woman to hold a national office as EEOC commissioner, and she became a critic of mainstream, organized feminism for its focus on issues affecting mainly white, upper-middle-class women.

EARLY LIFE

Aileen Clarke Hernandez was born in Brooklyn, New York, to Charles and Ethel Clarke, who had emigrated from Jamaica and eventually became US citizens. Her mother was a costume maker and seamstress in the New York theater district, and her father worked in the art-supply business. Hernandez and her brothers were taught to cook and sew because her parents believed that no gender distinctions should be made in employment. They also emphasized that people should not be treated differently because of race or gender. This family value left an indelible mark on Hernandez, and it would deeply influence her life and career.

Hernandez graduated from Bay Ridge Public School as class valedictorian and, in 1943, from Bay Ridge High School as class salutatorian. She received a scholarship to attend Howard University in Washington, DC; served as editor and writer for the campus paper, *The Hilltop*; and wrote a column for the *Washington Tribune*. In 1946, she received honors in Kappa Mu Society, Howard's counterpart to Phi Beta Kappa.

Hernandez's political philosophy was molded by her college years in Washington, during the postwar period. She joined the student chapter of the National Association for the Advancement of Colored People (NAACP) and demonstrated against the racial discrimination of the National Theatre, Lisner Auditorium, and the Thompson restaurant chain. Moving south for her college years at Howard, she experienced even more discrimination as she traveled by train and waited for the segregated taxis in Washington, which were always the last in line. Believing that a "democratic government requires full participation by all citizens," she supported equal rights for African American World War II veterans returning to an unchanged, segregated America.

After graduating magna cum laude from Howard in 1947 with a degree in sociology and political science, Hernandez traveled to Norway as part of the International Student Exchange Program and studied comparative government. Having recovered at home from an attack of tuberculosis, she attended New York University; the University of California, Los Angeles; and the University of Southern California. In 1959, she was awarded a master's degree in government, summa cum laude, from Los Angeles State College. Southern Vermont College would grant her an honorary doctorate in humane letters in 1979.

> "*I have become increasingly distressed by the growing alienation of minority women who have joined feminist organizations like NOW. They are truly the 'women in the middle,' isolated within their minority communities because of their espousal of the feminist cause and isolated in the feminist movement because they insist on attention to issues which impact heavily on minorities.*"

Life's Work

While attending New York University for graduate school, Hernandez accepted an internship to the International Ladies' Garment Workers Union (ILGWU) Training Institute. She was hired in 1951 and transferred to the ILGWU Pacific Coast region in California as an organizer. Eventually she served for eleven years in the ILGWU's West Coast office in Los Angeles as an education director and public relations director. Her duties ranged from organizing social affairs to mobilizing strikes, pickets, and legislative lobbies. She also was responsible for naturalization classes for foreign-born union employees. In 1957, she married Alfonso Hernandez, a Mexican American garment worker she had met in Los Angeles. They divorced in 1961.

In 1961, Hernandez's career shifted from union work to politics, after managing a victorious campaign for Alan Cranston as California state controller. She was appointed assistant chief of the California Division of the Fair Employment Practice Commission (FEPC) in 1962. In this position she supervised a staff of fifty in four field offices. While serving with the FEPC, she initiated the Technical Advisory Committee (TACT). The TACT report was a comprehensive analysis of industrial testing as it affects the hiring of minorities and the results prompted revisions in tests used by employers as a criterion for hiring.

By this time, Hernandez had acquired recognition for her work in labor relations and fair employment practices. With the recommendation of California governor Edmund G. "Pat" Brown, US president Lyndon B. Johnson appointed her the first woman to the five-member Equal Employment Opportunity Commission (EEOC). Her duties included coordinating the activities of state and local commissions with the national EEOC. During her term on the commission, commercial airlines overturned their traditional policy of firing female flight attendants when they married, and she helped focus the commission on racial discrimination in construction unions and the gender discrimination, implicit or overt, in many labor laws pertaining to women. After eighteen months of service, she resigned from the EEOC because she felt that the commission lacked any power to enforce its own policies. In 1967, she established her own consulting firm in San Francisco, California, called Aileen C. Hernandez Associates, to advise businesses, government agencies, labor organizations, and private groups in urban affairs.

Hernandez was present in 1966 at the Third National Conference of the State Commissions on Women in Washington, DC. Betty Friedan, author of the 1963 best seller *The Feminine Mystique*, also was there, and they spoke of establishing a Civil Rights movement for women. The National Organization for Women (NOW) was created at this conference, and Friedan was chosen as its first president. Initially declining an offer to become a national vice president, Hernandez accepted a 1967 appointment as vice president of the Western region. In 1970 she succeeded Friedan as president of NOW.

Hernandez's leadership and articulation of the women's movement were major assets. Until 1971 many African American women viewed the women's movement as the elitist preserve of white, upper-middle- class women. Hernandez considered NOW an extension of the Civil Rights movement for all women. In one interview, Hernandez addressed the issue head-on when she said,

Until women, black as well as others, gain a sense of their own identity and feel that they have a real choice in society, nothing is going to happen in civil rights. It's not going to happen for Blacks; it's not going to happen for Mexican Americans; it's not going to happen for women.

Hernandez served as NOW president until September 1971. Also in 1971 she helped to organize the National Women's Political Caucus, which encourages women to run for public office and is a forum for women's issues. However, Hernandez's relation with NOW became troubled after her tenure as president. She started the Minority Women's Task Force in 1972, sending out a survey to minority women; the response revealed that only 10 percent of NOW's membership was made up of minorities, and many minority members felt isolated. Hernandez herself criticized NOW for neglecting minority issues during its focus on promoting the Equal Rights Amendment. She was also unhappy with the paucity of minority representation among the organization's leadership. In 1979 she severed her connection with NOW, although she later attended its anniversary celebrations.

In 1973, Hernandez chaired the summer meeting in Boston of the International Feminist Planning Conference, bringing together women from thirty countries. At the invitation of the US State Department and the Konrad Adenauer Foundation, in 1975 she attended the International Conference on Minorities and the Metropolis in Bonn, Germany. She traveled to the People's Republic of China with an American rights group in 1978. That same year, with the National Commission, she made a fact-finding tour of South Africa. The 1981 report of that regional study by the commission *South Africa: Time Running Out* received praise for its analysis of apartheid and US policy in South Africa.

Hernandez continued to build her consulting business, employing four associates and, depending on the project load, as many as thirty staff employees. Specializing in such critical urban issues as transportation, equal opportunity, health, education, economic development, criminal justice, environment, and housing, Aileen C. Hernandez Associates had among its clients United Parcel Service, Standard Oil of California, the National Catholic Conference on Interracial Justice, the Ford Foundation, the Bay Area Rapid Transit District, and the California Department of Health Services.

Hernandez persevered in volunteering her organizational skills. She was vice chair of the National Urban Coalition and of the National Advisory Council of the American Civil Liberties Union, and was chair of Citizen's Trust, a socially conscious investment group. She served on the Secretary's Advisory Committee on the Rights and Responsibilities of Women for the US Department of Health and Human Services and worked with the California Women's Agenda. She was coordinator for Black Women Stirring the Waters and was a board member of the Pesticide Education Center, the National Women's Museum, the Wellesley Center for Research on Women, the Garden Project, the Meilejohn Civil Liberties Union, the Center for Women Policy Studies, the Center for the Common Good, and the Citizen's Commission on Civil Rights. She also became a life trustee of the Urban Institute and a member of the Ms. Foundation for Women.

Hernandez continued to travel frequently to attend conferences and teach. In 1993 she was the Tish Sommers lecturer at the Institute for Health and Aging of the University of California, San Francisco; was a Regents Scholar in Residence in 1996 at the University of California, Santa Barbara; and taught at the University of California, Berkeley. In 2000 she was part of a conference encouraging cooperation between women in the United States and China.

The numerous awards in recognition of her public service are impressive. She was chosen as woman of the year in 1961 by the Community Relations Conference of Southern California. Howard University honored her in 1968 for distinguished postgraduate achievement in the fields of labor and public service, and that same year she received the Charter Day Alumni Post Graduate Achievement in Labor and Public Services Award. The San Francisco Examiner named her one of the ten most distinguished women of the San Francisco Bay Area in 1969. The Trinity Baptist Church of San Mateo County presented her the Bicentennial Award in 1976.

Equal rights advocates commended Hernandez in 1981 for her service to the women's movement, and in 1984 she was honored by the Friends of the San Francisco Commission on the Status of Women. In 1985, the San Francisco League of Women Voters named her among the ten women who make a difference, the National Urban Coalition recognized her service to urban communities, and the San Francisco Black Chamber of Commerce presented her with the Parren J. Mitchell Award for dedicated service to the African American community. The

Memorial United Methodist Church commended her services to humanity in 1986, and Gamma Phi Delta Sorority made her an honorary member.

Hernandez also received awards in appreciation from the National Institute for Women of Color in 1987 and, in the following year, from the Western District Conference on the National Association of Negro Business and Professional Women's Clubs. The Northern California American Civil Liberties Foundation presented her with its Earl Warren Civil Liberties Award in 1989. In 1995 the San Francisco Planning and Urban Research Association gave her its Silver Spur Award. She received the Eleanor Roosevelt Award from the Democratic Women's Forum in California in 1996 and the Ella Hill Hutch Award in 1997. Hernandez was also a founder of the San Francisco-based discussion group Black Women Stirring the Waters. The members of the group published a book in 1997 featuring essays from 44 of the group's members. In 2006, Hernandez was one of the women chosen for the National Women's History Project, a non-profit organization dedicated to creating educational materials that honor and commemorate the achievements of American women.

Hernandez passed away from complications related to dementia on February 13, 2017. The ACLU's deputy director Dorothy Ehrlich, who had known Hernandez from the 1970s, noted that "Aileen Hernandez's entire life embodied the movement forward for women and people of color, and her significant role in that history will never be forgotten. NOW's president Terry O'Neill wrote: "NOW's commitment to intersectional feminism is a direct legacy of Aileen Hernandez's unshakable belief in diversity and racial justice."

Significance

Hernandez's contributions to labor relations, the women's movement, antiracism and equal opportunity efforts, political activism, and community service comprise an extensive list of accomplishments. Her dedication to public service made her both a national and an international figure in the forefront of social reform. She was the first African American woman to hold a national office as EEOC commissioner, and she became one of the first active critics of mainstream feminism for its focus on issues affecting mainly white, upper-middle-class women to the detriment of women of color.

Emily Teipe, updated by Micah L. Issitt

Further Reading

Banner, Lois W. *Women in Modern America: A Brief History.* 2nd ed. San Diego: Harcourt, 1984. Print.

Barakso, Maryann. *Governing NOW: Grassroots Activism in the National Organization for Women.* Ithaca: Cornell UP, 2004. Print.

Baxandall, Rosalyn, and Linda Gordon. "Second-Wave Feminism." *A Companion to American Women's History.* Ed. Nancy A. Hewitt. Malden: Blackwell, 2002. Print.

Dreyfus, Joel. "Civil Rights and the Women's Movement." *Black Enterprise* 8 (1977): 35–37. 45. Hernandez, Aileen Clarke. Interview by Kate Raphael. *Women's Magazine.* KPFA, Berkeley, 29 Apr. 2013. Radio.

Hernandez, Aileen Clarke. Interview by Michael Krasny. Forum with Michael Krasny. *Natl. Public Radio.* KQED, San Francisco, 11 Mar. 2013. Radio.

Lewis, Ida. "Conversation: Ida Lewis and Aileen Hernandez." *Essence* (1971).

Makers: Women Who Make America. Dir. Barak Goodman. PBS, 2013. TV miniseries.

Samuel Gridley Howe

Educator and social reformer

Born: November 10, 1801; Boston Massachusetts
Died: January 9, 1876; Massachusetts
Area of Achievement: Abolitionism, medicine, social reform

Howe was a universal reformer who made his greatest contributions to the education of the blind, the deaf-blind, and the mentally disabled. His monumental efforts significantly enhanced social concern for persons with disabilities in the United States.

Early Life

Samuel Gridley Howe was the son of Joseph Howe and Patty Gridley Howe, both of old New England stock. His father was a cordage manufacturer and steadfast Jeffersonian Republican. A man of principle, as his son was to be, he accepted government bonds in payment for purchases during the War of 1812 and suffered serious financial losses. Samuel attended Boston Latin School and was frequently harassed for his father's politics. The only one of three brothers to attend college, Samuel entered Brown, rather than Federalist-dominated Harvard, in 1817. Young Howe excelled at campus pranks, but his academic performance was mediocre. As a Unitarian among Baptists,

Samuel Gridley Howe (Wikimedia Commons)

Howe once again learned to appreciate the position of the underdog—a useful trait for a future philanthropist.

Being graduated in 1821, Howe enrolled at Harvard Medical School and began to apply himself, enjoying especially anatomy and dissection. After commencement, however, he decided against a traditional practice. Stirred by the Greek War of Independence, a popular cause of the time, Howe left for the Peloponnisos, arriving in early 1827. In Greece he played many roles with distinction. As a physician, he served Greek forces on land and sea. As the agent of American relief committees, he distributed emergency rations, briefly returning to the United States to raise additional funds. Once back in Greece, he developed and ran sizable work relief programs. For his exertions, Howe was knighted by the Greek king as a Chevalier of the Order of the Holy Savior. With the war all but over, Chev, as his friends now called him, returned to Boston in April, 1831. Tall, dark, and handsome, not yet sporting the beard of later years, Howe was a knight-errant seeking a new cause to uplift humanity.

LIFE'S WORK

As luck would have it, the projected New England School for the Blind, incorporated in 1829, needed a director in order to become a reality; the trustees of the school offered Howe the job. Excited by the challenge, he accepted immediately and sailed for Europe to study current techniques for educating the blind. Howe soon became convinced that European efforts were either too intellectual or too mechanical. A more balanced curriculum, he believed, including physical education and greater encouragement of self-reliance, was required. After imprisonment in Prussia for assisting Polish refugees, Howe returned to Boston in July, 1832. During the following August, the first school for the blind in the nation opened its doors with seven students and three staff members.

As director, Howe tried to tailor the curriculum—reading, writing, mathematics, geography, music, physical education, and manual training—to the needs and abilities of the individual student. He fashioned letters of twine and glued them to cards for reading instruction; he invented an improved method of raised printing that significantly lowered costs of manufacture. (Braille was not yet in use.) Howe trooped his students before legislative committees and popular audiences to secure funds, went out into the country to recruit students, and traveled to other states to promote more schools for the blind. As a result of his strenuous activity, the school, renamed Perkins Institution, soon required larger quarters.

In 1837, Howe heard of Laura Bridgman, an eight-year-old who, at the age of two, had lost her sight and hearing through scarlet fever. Howe, who believed in phrenology and innate mental dispositions, was confident that the child could be taught, despite near-universal opinion that the deaf-blind were completely uneducable. He induced her parents to enroll Laura at Perkins.

For several tedious months, Howe tried to get Laura to match raised words with physical objects and make words of letters. Suddenly one day, Laura understood that here was a way to communicate her thoughts to other minds; her face "lighted up with a human expression." This was the greatest single moment in Howe's career. John Greenleaf Whittier proclaimed that Howe was "the Cadmus of the blind." Charles Dickens, who met Laura Bridgman in 1842, lionized Howe's accomplishment in *American Notes* (1842). Howe soon became a world-renowned figure.

Howe's international stature certainly aided his election as a Whig to the Massachusetts House of Representatives in November, 1842. Though only a freshman legislator, he chaired the committee on public charities. Working closely with Dorothea Lynde Dix, Howe personally wrote the bill reforming care of the mentally ill, which passed by overwhelming margins in March, 1843.

In April, 1843, Howe married Julia Ward, who was of a prominent New York family. Their marriage was frequently tempestuous; their personalities did not mesh well. Prideful, demanding, and eighteen years her senior, Howe never approved of Julia's literary aspirations. He normally placed his many reform interests ahead of his wife and his eventual family of six children.

After returning to work in September, 1844, after a European honeymoon, Howe immediately joined his friend Horace Mann, secretary of the state Board of Education, in a battle to reform the Boston grammar schools. In 1845, Howe turned to education of those with mental impairments, undertaking an extensive, two-year training program that he followed up with a comprehensive report to the legislature. Once again, the lawmakers followed his bidding and established in 1848 the Massachusetts School for the Idiotic and Feeble-Minded Youth, another first in American history. Howe served as superintendent of that institution as well as of Perkins until his death in 1876.

Although Howe disapproved of slavery, he remained aloof from agitation until the admission of Texas drew him into the fray. During the Mexican War, Howe became a Conscience Whig, running unsuccessfully for Congress in 1846; in 1851, he helped orchestrate the election of his close friend Charles Sumner to the U.S. Senate. In response to the Kansas-Nebraska Act, Howe moved toward radical abolitionism.

In 1854, Howe was an organizer of both the New England Emigrant Aid Company and the Massachusetts Kansas Aid Committee, the latter formed to obtain guns for antislavery settlers. In January, 1857, John Brown visited Howe and other Boston supporters (the "Secret Six"), obtaining money from the committee and several token guns from Howe personally. In March, 1858, the group gave Brown additional funding to liberate slaves, a plan that culminated in the Harpers Ferry raid of October, 1859. When authorities uncovered Brown's correspondence, Howe fled, panic-stricken, to Canada on the flimsy pretext that he was promoting education of the blind. Involvement of the nation's foremost humanitarian in Brown's scheme further unnerved the South and increased sectional tensions.

During the Civil War, Howe returned to less violent philanthropy. He helped to establish the United States Sanitary Commission in June, 1861, serving on its board for the duration. The commission made important recommendations for "preserving and restoring the health of the troops," which doubtless reduced fatalities. Howe was also a member of the three-man American Freedmen's Inquiry Commission set up in 1863 to investigate the condition of free blacks and make proposals for their future welfare. The commission laid the foundations for the later Freedmen's Bureau.

In 1863, Massachusetts governor John Andrew named Howe chairman of the new Massachusetts Board of State Charities, created to coordinate eleemosynary institutions and programs. After the war, Howe, who strongly disagreed with the sign language system used at the American Asylum in Hartford, sought a charter for a school for the deaf that would teach finger spelling and articulation. The legislature again complied, incorporating Clarke Institution at Northampton in 1867.

> "Nowhere is wisdom more necessary than in the guidance of charitable impulses. Meaning well is only half our duty; Thinking right is the other, and equally important, half."

Although in declining health after the war, Howe embarked in 1871 on his last crusade. President Ulysses S. Grant, manipulated by speculators, favored annexing Santo Domingo. The Senate rejected the treaty, in part because of Charles Sumner's virulent opposition, but Grant named an investigative commission in hopes of recouping support. Despite his long friendship with Sumner, Howe agreed to serve and after a visit to the island became converted to annexation. Howe apparently had hopes of concluding his career as a territorial governor who in philosopher-king fashion would reform Santo Domingo into a tropical paradise. Such dreams were doomed by continuing Senate opposition.

After the disappointing conclusion of the Dominican affair, Howe's health steadily deteriorated. In constant pain and severely depressed, he collapsed on January 4, 1876, and died five days later. Several hours before the end, Laura Bridgman (symbolically on behalf of all those who had or would benefit from his tireless philanthropy) kissed the unconscious Howe farewell.

Significance

Samuel Gridley Howe lived in an optimistic age, in a city and state seething with the ferment of reform; not only was he in harmony with the spirit of his times, he was a symbol of the age as well. In those heady days, true heroism was seen by many as victory over social evil and human suffering. As the foremost philanthropist in the nation, Howe was, in the words of John Greenleaf Whittier, "The Hero."

A Whig in politics and a Unitarian in religion, Howe was a Yankee elitist who accepted the essential goodness of God and humanity and the inevitability of progress. A nineteenth century romantic, Howe rejected John Locke's concept of knowledge drawn solely from the five senses for belief in innate mental dispositions. This thinking as well as Howe's emphasis on self-reliance was clearly in line with that of his friend Theodore Parker and other Transcendentalists. Like many other Americans of the era, Howe was also strongly influenced by phrenology. This pseudoscience (which posited a body-mind unity) maintained that a balanced education, both intellectual and physical, could influence cerebral growth and skull dimensions. Howe's phrenological and vaguely Transcendentalist assumptions frequently guided his reform endeavors. His temporary obsession with the abolitionist movement during the 1850's was typical of most antebellum reformers.

Howe was involved in many causes, but his major impact on American society was in his efforts for the education of people with disabilities. He firmly believed that most people with physical and mental disabilities could become independent and productive citizens. His refusal to accept traditional prejudices concerning the capabilities of the blind, the deaf-blind, the deaf, and the mentally impaired led him to found institutions and develop instructional strategies still important today. Howe's most enduring legacy may be his creation of a continuing public consciousness that disabilities can be surmounted, that, in the words of his life motto, Obstacles Are Things to Be Overcome.

Parker Bradley Nutting

FURTHER READING

Dickens, Charles. *American Notes for General Circulation*. London: Chapman and Hall, 1842. Reprint. London: Oxford University Press, 1966. Though frequently critical of things American, Dickens was extremely impressed by Howe's work. He quotes extensively from Howe's annual *Reports* to the Perkins trustees concerning the education of Laura Bridgman, a source not readily available to the interested reader.

Freeberg, Ernest. *The Education of Laura Bridgman: First Deaf and Blind Person to Learn Language*. Cambridge, Mass.: Harvard University Press, 2001. One of two recent books about Howe's relationship with Bridgman. Although Gitter (see below) provides more biographical information, Freeberg focuses on Howe's specific methods for educating Bridgman, describing how he was influenced by Unitarianism and phrenology. Howe, Freeberg maintains, sought to make Bridgman's education a model of "moral discipline" so he could gain greater insight into human nature.

Gitter, Elisabeth. *The Imprisoned Guest: Samuel Howe and Laura Bridgman, the Original Deaf-Blind Girl*. New York: Farrar, Straus and Giroux, 2001. Describes how and why Howe educated Bridgman, explaining the social, intellectual and cultural context in which Howe and Bridgman transformed public perception of people with multiple disabilities.

Lamson, Mary Swift. *Life and Education of Laura Dewey Bridgman, the Deaf, Dumb, and Blind Girl*. Boston: New England Publishing, 1878. Lamson was one of Laura's teachers. She quotes extensively from her own journal, those of other teachers, and from Howe's *Reports*. A very personal account, it reveals the difficulties of working with Howe.

Richard, Laura E. *Laura Bridgman: The Story of an Opened Door*. New York: D. Appleton, 1928. A full-length biography, written by Howe's daughter, who was Laura Bridgman's namesake. Strong on the relationship between Howe and Bridgman. Includes source materials not readily available.

―――, ed. *Letters and Journals of Samuel Gridley Howe*. 2 vols. Boston: Dana Estes, 1906. Collection contains excerpts from Howe's letters, journals, and annual *Reports*, connected by a running commentary. The period to 1832 is accorded the same weight as the rest of Howe's life. Despite such unevenness, this is the closest thing to a printed collection of Howe's papers.

Sanborn, Franklin Benjamin. *Dr. S. G. Howe: The Philanthropist*. New York: Funk & Wagnalls, 1891. The first scholarly biography, still worth consulting. The author, one of the Secret Six, is laudatory, but the book contains extensive, frequently revealing quotations from original sources. Strong on the antislavery days.

Schwartz, Harold. *Samuel Gridley Howe: Social*

Reformer, 1801-1876. Cambridge, Mass.: Harvard University Press, 1956. Based on extensive research in the Howe manuscripts in Houghton Library at Harvard. Places Howe solidly in his intellectual and social milieu. Notes influence of phrenology. A very balanced work.

DOLORES HUERTA

Labor leader

Born: April 10, 1930; Dawson, New Mexico
Area of Achievement: Labor movement, social reform, women's rights, civil rights

Cofounder of the United Farm Workers Association with César Chávez, Huerta earned renown through contract negotiations with California growers during the Delano grape strike the crowning achievement of one of the greatest victories in the history of American workers. Her role as a Chicana labor leader in the male-dominated culture of farm workers made her a champion of the women's movement as well.

EARLY LIFE

Dolores Huerta (WEHR-tah) was born Dolores Fernández in the mining community of Dawson, New Mexico. Her mother, Alicia Chávez, was a second-generation New Mexican, and her father, Juan Fernández, was of American Indian and Mexican heritage. Her father later became a union activist and served in the state legislature. Huerta's parents were divorced while she was quite young, and she was reared by her mother and grandfather in Stockton, California. Her mother worked in a cannery and saved enough money to buy two small hotels and a restaurant while establishing her household in an integrated working-class community. (Her mother often housed farm worker families for free in the hotels.) Dolores, along with her two brothers, grew up assuming that women and men were equal, drawing on the example of her mother, who never favored her sons above her daughter and who became a business entrepreneur on her own.

Huerta grew up in a racially mixed neighborhood of farm workers and other laborers of Chinese, Latino, American Indian, Filipino, African American, Japanese, or Italian descent. As a result, she learned to appreciate the rich diversity of a range of ethnic cultures at a young age. This absence of cultural or sex discrimination, in combination with her egalitarian family background, contributed to Dolores's leadership style in later life. Because she suffered no sense of inferiority at home and subsequently no acceptance of a secondary role in life or in her later career, Dolores came to maturity convinced that she was not required to accept the traditional feminine role of women as submissive domestic partners. Instead, she rebelled against conventional restraints on women and competed directly with her male colleagues.

Dolores was a dedicated Girl Scout in a multiethnic troop, participating in fundraising campaigns to support the USO and its entertainment programs for the armed forces during World War II; she was one of two winners in a national essay contest held by the Scouts. After graduating from an integrated high school in Stockton in 1947, Dolores married her high school sweetheart, Ralph Head, in 1950. The marriage ended in divorce after the birth of their daughters Celeste and Lori. Dolores's mother took care of the children while Dolores studied for a teaching degree at Stockton College. Although she eventually received a provisional teaching credential, she became dissatisfied with a career as a teacher. A dawning awareness of the pervasiveness of social injustice confronting the

Dolores Huerta (Wikimedia Commons)

Mexican American community and other ethnic minorities led Dolores in a new direction in 1955.

In that year, Dolores met Fred Ross, an organizer for Saul Alinsky's Industrial Areas Foundation who was trying to encourage the growing political consciousness of members of Mexican American communities throughout California. Ross started the Community Service Organization (CSO), a self-help association that led voter registration drives, pushed for more Chicanos on police forces, lobbied for Spanish-speaking staff at hospitals and government offices, and campaigned for sewers and community centers in the barrios. Because of her newfound civic activism and devotion to the work of the CSO, Dolores's marriage to her second husband, Ventura Huerta, also ended in divorce.

LIFE'S WORK

It was through her activities with the CSO that Dolores Huerta eventually became active as a labor organizer among migrant workers in California's San Joaquin Valley. She first came in contact with César Chávez when she was introduced to him by Ross in 1955 while both were working for the CSO. In 1960 she founded the Agricultural Workers Association. By that time, Huerta was a full-time lobbyist for the CSO in Sacramento and sometimes in Washington, D.C., pressuring politicians to support disability insurance, unemployment insurance, and minimum wage bills for farm workers. She was instrumental in securing the passage of bills that extended social insurance and welfare benefits to farm workers and immigrant workers, such as a bill for a Spanish version of the California driver license test in 1960, the repeal of the Bracero program in 1962, and, in 1963, legislation to include California farm workers in Aid to Families with Dependent Children. Nevertheless, she was convinced that these workers could never escape poverty through the CSO strategy of pressure-group politics. What they needed was a union.

At about the same time, Chávez was reaching the same conclusion. By 1962, Chávez had presented the CSO with a program outlining a strategy for the unionization of farm workers. When this program was rejected, he left the organization. While his wife, Helen Chávez, worked in the fields to support their family of eight children, Chávez organized small meetings of workers sympathetic to the idea of a union of agricultural laborers. The Farm Workers Association (FWA), a precursor of the United Farm Workers (UFW) union, was founded in Fresno, California, in September, 1962, at a convention attended by about three hundred delegates practically the entire membership. It was organized primarily by Chávez, but the first person he called upon to work with him organizing the Mexican American farm workers into a union was Huerta, who promptly left her post with the CSO to work with Chávez.

When Huerta began her labor organizing efforts, she was pregnant with the seventh of her eleven children (she had two by her first husband, five by her second, and four by her live-in lover, Richard Chávez, the brother of César). Because of the demands of her work, Huerta was frequently absent from home, and her children spent much of their childhood in the care of her friends or family. Her union work was always her first priority, to the consternation and outrage of the more traditional adherents to Latin culture. Huerta clearly loved her children and was loved by them in return, but she refused to allow motherhood to deter her from her work. Even her colleague Chávez disapproved of her divorces, her decision to live with his brother, and her seemingly chaotic way of raising her children. Nevertheless, he understood that the union was the center of her life just as it was for him.

> "When you have a conflict, that means that there are truths that have to be addressed on each side of the conflict. And when you have a conflict, then it's an educational process to try to resolve the conflict. And to resolve that, you have to get people on both sides of the conflict involved so that they can dialogue."

The foundation of the UFW union was laid during the bitter Delano grape strike of 1965-1970. The farm workers of the 1960's often lived in mind-numbing poverty and toiled under inhumane conditions. The bulk of the workforce spoke little English, was often of illegal residency status, could not vote, and was poorly educated. As a result, the workers were easily exploited by the powerful growers in the agribusiness industry of California. The growers often used deadly pesticides, primarily DDT, in the fields, ignoring the devastating health effects these chemicals had on both the workers and their unborn children. Pickers were paid by the bushel or basket rather than the hour. A field overstaffed with pickers, therefore, could result in a day's labor with little or no pay for the worker. There were no health and welfare benefits, no

Huerta speaking at the Democratic National Convention, 2016. (Wikimedia Commons)

medical insurance, and no low-cost housing for the mainly transient workforce. Workers were forced to live in cars, shacks, and tents; many workers had no other place to sleep than the chemical-laden fields in which they had worked earlier in the day.

The grape-growing industry was perhaps the worst offender in terms of working conditions and pesticide use in all of California. Because of this, it became the logical site of the 1965 labor battle known as the Delano grape strike with Huerta and Chávez at the forefront. The strike began at dawn, when the workers moved out into the fields around Delano. The pickets met them carrying National Farm Workers Association (NFWA) banners with the union's symbol of a black Aztec eagle on a red flag with the single Spanish word "Huelga" (strike). The pickets led the workers off the fields of Delano and the five-year battle began. In 1966, Huerta became the first person to negotiate a farm workers' contract when, as NFWA's representative, she concluded a deal with the Schenley Wine Company. The strike continued on other fronts, and before it ended in 1970, Huerta had been arrested twenty-two times for strike-related efforts.

As quickly as the UFW pickets pulled work crews out, these laborers were replaced by scabs, or strike-breakers, trucked in from Mexico and Texas by the growers. The union's pickets and organizers were harassed and arrested continually by local police, under the influence of the powerful growers. Support for the farm workers was growing, both within the labor movement and on a national level. Senator Robert Kennedy embraced their cause and became their champion. Powerful unions, including the United Auto Workers (UAW), Amalgamated Clothing Workers, and the Packinghouse Workers rallied behind the striking grape pickers and provided relief in the form of fresh pickets, food, and money. It was against this backdrop of national labor and political support that Chávez and Huerta made the decision to escalate the strike to a nationwide struggle by declaring a universal consumer boycott. This boycott initially targeted individual growers and products, but eventually led to the boycott of all California-grown grapes. Hundreds of workers were delegated throughout the country to promote and organize the boycott, while Huerta organized in New York City. She was an eloquent and powerful public speaker, and her speeches expressed the deep desires and struggles of all poor and dispossessed peoples, not just those who worked the fields.

The UFW boycott was successful. Trade unionists across the country joined forces with the farm workers, and a new consciousness of the Chicano in the United States was born as a result of the Huelga. On May 30, 1970, the first table grapes bearing a union label a black eagle on a red flag were shipped to market. The grapes came from seven growers who, unable to withstand the effects of the boycott, had signed contracts with the UFW. On July 29, twenty-six Delano growers filed into the UFW union hall to sign the contracts that ended the bitter five-year battle. As negotiated by Huerta, the workers received an hourly wage of $1.76, a guaranteed yearly increase of fifteen cents per hour, and a twenty-five-cent bonus per box picked. In addition, the growers were required to contribute to a health and welfare plan and to low-cost housing for their workers. Most importantly, the growers agreed not to use certain pesticides, and DDT was banned forever from California vineyards. Huerta's efforts also fostered the California Agricultural Labor Relations Act of 1975.

While championing amnesty for undocumented immigrant farm workers and fighting the federal guest worker programs of the 1980's, Huerta continued to serve in the UFW as negotiator and vice president into the 1990's. She became notorious in the union for her fervor and tenacity; stories are told of growers begging to face anyone at the negotiating table except Huerta. Huerta and Chávez continued their aggressive style of Chicano trade unionism through periodic use of the consumer boycott, most notably against Gallo Wine, the Dole Company, and California table grapes. They worked together to create the Robert Kennedy Medical Plan, Juan De La Cruz Farm Workers Pension Fund, Farm Workers Credit Union, and National Farm Workers Service Center. In the wake of Chávez's death in 1993, Huerta, in her sixties, continued as an eloquent and frequent speaker and organizer on behalf of workers, Mexican Americans, and women. Her fervor elicited both praise and criticism. In 2006, for example, in a graduation address before Tucson High School in Arizona, she denounced programs against illegal immigration, leading to outrage among state and local officials.

In 2002, Huerta received $100,000 as part of the Puffin Foundation/National Institute Award for Creative Citizenship. With this money she founded the Dolores Huerta Foundation, of which she is president. The non-profit foundation offers aid in community organizing, research in private and public policies affecting workers and immigrants, and educational programs.

Huerta became a board member of People for the American Way and for the Feminist Majority Foundation, took an active role in supporting political candidates, and became secretary-treasurer emeritus of the UFW. In 2003

DDT Ban Takes Effect

Dolores Huerta's work on behalf of immigrant farm workers was instrumental in the banning of DDT by the U.S. Environmental Protection Agency, which issued the following press release on December 31, 1972.

The general use of the pesticide DDT will no longer be legal in the United States after today, ending nearly three decades of application during which time the once-popular chemical was used to control insect pests on crop and forest lands, around homes and gardens, and for industrial and commercial purposes.

An end to the continued domestic usage of the pesticide was decreed on June 14, 1972, when William D. Ruckelshaus, Administrator of the Environmental Protection Agency, issued an order finally cancelling nearly all remaining Federal registrations of DDT products. Public health, quarantine, and a few minor crop uses were excepted, as well as export of the material.

The effective date of the EPA June cancellation action was delayed until the end of this year to permit an orderly transition to substitute pesticides, including the joint development with the U.S. Department of Agriculture of a special program to instruct farmers on safe use of substitutes.

The cancellation decision culminated three years of intensive governmental inquiries into the uses of DDT. As a result of this examination, Ruckelshaus said he was convinced that the continued massive use of DDT posed unacceptable risks to the environment and potential harm to human health.

Major legal challenges to the EPA cancellation of DDT are now pending before the U.S. Court of Appeals for the District of Columbia and the Federal District Court for the Northern District of Mississippi. The courts have not ruled as yet in either of these suits brought by pesticide manufacturers.

DDT was developed as the first of the modern insecticides early in World War II. It was initially used with great effect to combat malaria, typhus, and the other insect-borne human diseases among both military and civilian populations.

A persistent, broad-spectrum compound often termed the "miracle" pesticide, DDT came into wide agricultural and commercial usage in this country in the late 1940s. During the past 30 years, approximately 675,000 tons have been applied domestically. The peak year for use in the United States was 1959 when nearly 80 million pounds were applied. From that high point, usage declined steadily to about 13 million pounds in 1971, most of it applied to cotton.

The decline was attributed to a number of factors including increased insect resistance, development of more effective alternative pesticides, growing public and user concern over adverse environmental side effects—and governmental restriction on DDT use since 1969.

she held a short-term appointment as a regent for the University of California.

Huerta's leadership in labor issues and humanitarian causes was widely honored. In 1993 she was inducted into the National Women's Hall of Fame. She has won many awards, including the Outstanding Labor Leader Award from the California State senate, the American Civil Liberties Union's Roger Baldwin Medal of Liberty, the Ellis Island Medal of Freedom, the Eugene V. Debs Foundation Outstanding American Award, the Consumers' Union Trumpeter's Award, the Community of Christ International Peace Award, and the Eleanor Roosevelt Human Rights Award, presented by U.S. president Bill Clinton in 1998. In 1993, *Ms.* magazine named her its Woman of the Year, and *Ladies' Home Journal* placed her on its list of 100 Most Important Women of the Twentieth Century. She received honorary doctorates from six universities, including Princeton (2006), and had five grade schools and one high school named for her.

Significance

Huerta's dedicated and focused work with the Chicano trade union movement was based on four philosophical axioms: to establish a strong sense of identity, to develop a sense of pride, to maintain always the value of services to others, and to be effective and true to oneself. She was convinced of the need to lead through persuasion and personal example, rather than intimidation. She agrees with the vitality of ideas and the necessity of criticism, but for Huerta, action through responsible commitment and moral choice is the key to creating a just society.

More than a liberal, ethnic unionist, Huerta also is proud of her work as a feminist, a Chicano activist, and, above all, a humanist. Her cause transcends the narrow scope of unionism. As Huerta stated at an organizing rally at Santa Clara University in 1990:

> I would like to be remembered as a woman who cares for all fellow humans. We must use our lives to make the world a better and just place to live, not just a world to acquire things. That is what we are put on the earth for.

Also, Huerta's skills as a negotiator are entirely self-taught. In fact, before the Delano grape strike she had never read a union contract. In addition to negotiating the UFW's first contracts, she had organized for the strike in the fields, in boycott offices, and in union election halls as well as served as a picket herself. In retrospect, however, it is her skill, tenacity, combativeness, and cunning as a negotiator that truly separates Huerta from her peers in the labor movement. Her contract negotiations with the California growers marked the crowning achievement of one of the greatest victories ever in the history of American workers.

Huerta has been profiled in two documentary films, the 1979 film *Chicana* and the 2009 film *Crushing Love*, both directed by documentarian Sylvia Morales. Over the course of her career, Huerta has received numerous awards and honorary degrees for public and community service and four elementary schools in California have been named in her honor. In 2012, President Barack Obama presented Huerta with the Presidential Medal of Freedom.

Derrick Harper West, updated by Micah L. Issitt

Further Reading

Acuña, Rodolfo. *Occupied America: A History of Chicanos*. 5th ed. New York: Pearson Longman, 2004. A general history of Chicanos, now a classic. Detailed sections on Chicano agricultural labor organizing, tracing Chicano labor struggles to the turn of the century. Also details labor struggles in other sectors of the economy. Well referenced, with an excellent index.

Coburn, Judith. "Dolores Huerta: La Passionaria of the Farmworkers." *Ms.*, November, 1976. An interview with Huerta during a union election dispute in Sacramento, California, in 1975.

Foner, Philip S. *Women and the American Labor Movement: From World War I to the Present*. New York: Free Press, 1980. A historical overview, though dated, of the American labor movement since World War I with an emphasis on the roles of women, both as labor leaders and as workers.

Garcia, Richard A. "Dolores Huerta: Woman, Organizer, and Symbol." *California History 71* (Spring, 1993): 57-71. This article, appearing in the journal of the California Historical Society, explores the philosophical and ethical underpinnings of Huerta's labor activism.

Hatch, Robert, and William Hatch. *The Hero Project*. New York: McGraw-Hill, 2006. Written for high school readers, this book has an informative biographical sketch of Huerta, followed by a question-and-answer interview about her interests and participation in social reform, especially her activism on behalf of farm workers.

Hayden, Tom. "Prize for Dolores Huerta." *Nation*, December 23, 2002. In an editorial, Hayden, a former

California state senator and supporter of Huerta, explains why she received the Puffin Prize from the Nation Institute for her participation in the Community Service Organization and the United Farm Workers.

Meier, Matt S. *Mexican American Biographies: A Historical Dictionary, 1836-1987.* New York: Greenwood Press, 1988. Meier, an expert on Mexican American history, includes a profile on Huerta in this biographical dictionary. Although brief, the sketch on Huerta does provide a fine summary of her activities on behalf of "la causa."

Schiff, Karenna Gore. *Lighting the Way: Nine Women Who Changed Modern America.* New York: Hyperion Books, 2005. Among Schiff's nine profiles is Huerta, and the long biographical sketch in this book discusses her background and her support of farm workers, Mexican immigrants, the Community Service Organization, César Chávez, various important strikes and boycotts, feminism, and her concern about pesticides. Includes photographs.

LARRY ITLIONG

Filipino American labor organizer

Born: October 25, 1913; San Nicolas, Philippines
Died: February 8, 1977; Delano, California
Also known as: Larry Dulay Itliong; "Seven Fingers"
Area of Achievement: Labor rights

An important figure in the farm labor movement, Larry Itliong organized Filipino farm workers who were toiling alongside Mexican Americans and others in the fields of California. In 1965, he launched the Delano Grape Strike, a key event in twentieth-century American labor history, and he worked with Cesar Chávez and Dolores Huerta to form the United Farm Workers of America (UFW).

EARLY LIFE

Larry Dulay Itliong was born on October 25, 1913 in San Nicolas in the Philippines to Artemio and Francesca Itliong. Itliong's family was poor and he dropped out of school after the sixth grade. In 1929, when he was 14, he decided to travel to America to try for a better life. Itliong found work on farms in Washington state and, later, in a cannery in Alaska. It was at the Alaskan cannery that Itliong lost three fingers in an accident; for the rest of his life his nickname would be "Seven Fingers."

In the 1920 and 1930s, tens of thousands of Filipinos, mostly young men, came to the United States to work as migrant laborers. The Philippines had been a United States territory since the Spanish-American War in 1898. This made it far easier for Filipinos to enter the United States compared to other Asians. By 1930, according the United States Census, there were 45,200 Filipinos living in the United States, Itliong being one of them. Over 30,000 of these were in California, and the vast majority were farm workers.

LIFE'S WORK

Conditions for migrant workers in the West in the 1930s were difficult. Itliong held numerous temporary jobs in several states including Montana, South Dakota, California, Washington, and Alaska. In addition to farm work, he did other kinds of manual labor such as laying railroad track. Typically, migrant workers were housed by the business owners who employed them, but the housing was often temporary, crowded, and ramshackle.

Itliong, who became active in the labor movement almost as soon as he became a laborer, had plenty of opportunity to fraternize with Communists and other radicals in migrant worker camps up and down the coast. Militant left-wing politics and large strikes were more common in the 1930s than they were at any time since. This was the environment in which Itliong cut his teeth as a labor organizer.

During World War II, Itliong served in the United States Army. (He was a cook on a transport ship in the Pacific.) Following the war, he settled in Stockton, California. Now in his thirties, Itliong gradually took on increasingly important roles in labor unions, primarily as a point man for their Filipino membership. In 1959, he became the leader of the Agricultural Workers Organizing Committee (AWOC), a union composed mostly of Filipino workers. Agricultural workers in the 1960s in California typically lived in extreme poverty and worked in inhumane conditions at the mercy of the agribusiness industry. They were exposed to deadly pesticides like DDT as well as to long hours in the harsh sun. They often worked stooped over in the fields from sunrise to sunset, and they had no health benefits or medical insurance.

In May 1965, AWOC held a strike in California's Coachella Valley against grape growers. The grape industry was one of the worst offenders in terms of conditions, pay, and pesticide use. The strikers noted that the owners were paying workers from Mexico better than they paid Filipinos, and they demanded higher wages. The strike was a risk, but it was also carefully calculated; the grapes were ready to be picked, and the picking season in Coachella Valley was known to be unusually brief. The owners agreed to pay the workers a higher wage rather than let the grapes rot in the fields. Because of the success of this strike, Itliong decided to organize workers further north in Delano, California, and strike against the grape growers there. A large group gathered on the evening of September 8, 1965, in the Delano Filipino Community Center. Itliong spoke to them of the success of the strike in Coachella, and the Delano Filipino community voted to strike.

Not infrequently among farm workers, as historically among workers in other sectors, when a union comprised of mostly one ethnicity voted to strike, workers of another ethnicity would not support them or would even become scabs, or strikebreakers. The Delano Grape Strike was successful because, for the first time in California farm worker history, Mexican workers—who far outnumbered Filipinos—agreed to strike with the Filipinos. That decision was spearheaded by labor leader César Chávez, the head of the National Farm Workers Association (NFWA), which was comprised mostly of Mexican workers. Itliong approached Chávez to discuss the matter and to ask for Chávez's support for the strike, and the gambit succeeded. On September 16, the mostly Mexican NFWA joined the mostly Filipino AWOC on the picket lines. The Delano Grape Strike would soon expand across the state and last for five years. Today it is recognized as a key event in the history of the labor movement in the United States.

The alliance between the two labor groups was so strong that they soon merged, forming the United Farm Workers (UFW). Chávez quickly rose to fame as the leader of the UFW, and Itliong served as the union's assistant director. The ever-widening grape strike was the key focus of the UFW. As California grape growers broke strikes by shipping in new workers from Texas and Mexico, new strikes would begin. Support for the farm workers increased significantly as the strike wore on, with figures as prominent as Senator Robert Kennedy championing the workers. The UFW received support from other powerful unions, including the United Auto Workers (UAW) and the Amalgamated Clothing Workers. The strike made national headlines, and the UFW escalated the strike into a nationwide consumer boycott of grapes grown in California. Itliong was the UFW's national boycott coordinator.

After the grape strike ended with a contract negotiated between the strikers and the grape growers, Itliong decided to leave his position at the UFW. In 1972, he was a delegate at the Democratic National Convention. He briefly led a group called the Filipino American Political Association, and he helped plan a strike against Safeway supermarkets in 1974. In 1977, Itliong died after a battle with Lou Gehrig's disease. He was sixty-three years old.

Significance

The Filipino farmworkers who immigrated to the United States in the 1920s and 1930s are sometimes called *manongs,* a word meaning *uncles.* The designation refers to their status as young and unmarried men. Today Itliong is considered one of the most prominent of the *manong* generation of Filipino immigrants and is increasingly well-known as a leader of the farm worker strikes that were led by the United Farm Workers (UFW) in the 1960s. And yet his name was almost lost in time. When the first accounts of the farm worker movement were written in the 1970s, it was common to downplay the role of Filipino workers and to focus almost exclusively on Chávez, a charismatic and media-savvy figure.

> "*If I don't like you, I'll tell you, you know. But if I know you're wrong, I'll tell you you're wrong... But if you don't tell me I'm wrong, how can I correct myself... and how can we progress? Especially in this country... Here in the United States, there's very few of us. The least we can do is to be able to understand and be able to work with each other.*"

Recognition of Itliong's achievements only really took off in the twenty-first century and above all in California. The City of Carson declared October 25, 2010, to be Larry Itliong Day, a gesture that was repeated by Los Angeles County the following year. Itliong's story was told in a documentary film called *The Delano Manongs: Forgotten Heroes of the UFW* in 2013. And in 2018, a children's book was released that tells Itliong's story.

Itliong's life was in many ways defined by United States colonialism, by poverty, and by racism. He was never able to complete more than a sixth grade education, and he worked for years in extraordinarily difficult jobs for little pay and without the legal protections or benefits afforded to most workers. Thanks to the labor movement, however, and the practices and ideas that it espoused—the dignity of labor, the value of equality, the right of workers to strike—Itliong found the means and the strength to oppose injustice. When he launched the Delano grape strike with a roomful of Filipino migrant workers in 1965, he wasn't making a bid for fame or power. He was making a bid for fairness, and for others, on a very local level. When the grape strike was over, Itliong declined to continue in a position at the national level; he was not seeking the spotlight.

We owe our knowledge of Larry Itliong and his work for the Filipino farm workers in California to the Filipino community itself, and to those writers and scholars who have worked to preserve his story.

D. Alan Dean

Further Reading

Bacon, David. "How Filipino Migrants Gave the Grape Strike Its Radical Politics." *Dollars & Sense*, May/June 2018. http://dollarsandsense.org/archives/2018/0518bacon.html.

Bardacke, F. *Trampling Out the Vintage*. Verso: Brooklyn, NY, 2011.

Mabalon, Dawn Bohulano, and Gayle Romasanta. *Journey for Justice: The Life of Larry Itliong*. Bridge & Delta Publishing, 2018.

Rodriguez, Noreen Naseem. "Meet the Manongs: the Untold Stories of Filipino Farmworkers." (PDF) October 19, 2012. http://www.naseemrdz.com/site/assets/files/1034/meetthemanongsfarmworkerbiographies.pdf.

"Larry Itliong: Forgotten Filipino Labor Leader." *New York Times*, Oct. 19, 2012.

Jesse Jackson

Religious leader, activist, and politician

Born: October 18, 1941; Greenville, South Carolina
Also known as: Jesse Louis Jackson; Jesse Louis Burns (birth name)
Areas of Achievement: Civil rights; Government and politics; Religion and theology; Social issues

Jackson, a civil rights leader who began his career with Martin Luther King, Jr., during the 1960's, became the second African American (Shirley Chisholm was the first) to mount a major campaign for president of the United States, an effort that presaged the successful campaign of Barack Obama for the same office a quarter century later.

Early Life

Jesse Louis Jackson was born in 1941 in Greenville, South Carolina, to Helen Burns, a sixteen-year-old single mother. Jackson's father was Burns's next-door neighbor, Noah Louis Robinson, who was married to another woman. A former professional boxer, Robinson was well known in Greenville's black community. When Jackson was two, Burns married Charles Jackson, who adopted the boy.

As a child, Jackson was constantly teased for being a "nobody" with "no daddy," taunting that likely fueled his strong ambitions later in life. His difficult childhood also propelled Jackson to identify with disadvantaged people and to help them realize, as his popular chant would later phrase it, "I am somebody." Jackson's grandmother also helped raise his self-esteem. He ranked tenth in the class of 1959 at Greenville's segregated Sterling High School. By his senior year, Jackson had become a National Junior Honor Society member and a leader on civil rights issues, encouraging other students to fight discrimination with protests and boycotts.

Jackson, who was a quarterback in high school, was awarded a football scholarship at the University of

Jesse Jackson (Library of Congress)

Illinois, Chicago. Jackson thought he would escape racial prejudice by leaving the South but soon discovered that was not the case. He left the University of Illinois after attending school for only parts of 1959 and 1960. Jackson has said that racism prevented him from playing quarterback at Illinois, and that African Americans were allowed to play only running back, lineman, or defensive end. A report by ESPN.com suggests, however, that the university's starting quarterback at the time was African American. Jackson also asserted that a public-speaking instructor discriminated against him. After two semesters at the university, Jackson was put on academic probation. He enrolled in predominantly black North Carolina Agricultural and Technical College (A&T), where he was elected president of the student body and earned a bachelor's degree in sociology.

LIFE'S WORK

Jackson married Jacqueline Lavinia Brown on December 31, 1962, in Greenville. Their first child, Sanita, was born July 16, 1963. The Jacksons had four other children: Jesse Louis, Jr. (1965, later known as Jesse Jackson, Jr.), Jonathan Luther (1966), Yusef DuBois (1970), and Jacqueline Lavinia, Jr. (1975). Jesse Jackson, Jr., has served as Illinois's Second District congressional representative.

Jackson was fully engaged in the Civil Rights movement by the time he graduated from A&T in 1964. While in college, Jackson led marches into segregated restaurants and public buildings. In 1965, he marched with Martin Luther King, Jr., in Selma, Alabama. Jackson enrolled in the Chicago Theological Seminary but withdrew after two and one-half years of study without completing a divinity degree. He was ordained a Baptist minister in 1968, without the degree. Jackson received an honorary doctorate in theology from the Chicago Theological Seminary in 1990; his master of divinity degree was awarded for previous credits (he lacked three courses) and life experience ten years later.

Jackson joined King's Southern Christian Leadership Conference (SCLC) and participated in nonviolent protests against segregation full time. Jackson played an important role in opening the Chicago office of Operation Breadbasket, the economic-opportunity arm of the SCLC, during 1966. Operation Breadbasket used "selective buying" (a form of boycott) to support black companies

Jackson speaks on a radio broadcast from the headquarters of Operation Push, at its annual convention. One of the aims of the organization is to open the world of business to small black owned businesses. Rev. Jackson is credited for helping to make Chicago the black banking capital in the country. He helped persuade white companies to stop taking profits they earned from black consumers to the white suburbs. (National Archives and Records Administration)

and pressure white businesses into hiring African Americans. For four years, beginning in 1967, Jackson was the SCLC's national director. Jackson was in King's party at the Lorraine Motel in Memphis when King was shot to death April 4, 1968. The assassination vaulted Jackson into the national media spotlight. After King's death, however, rifts developed within the SCLC. Jackson clashed with Ralph Abernathy, an assistant to King who also was a leader in the SCLC. In 1971, Abernathy suspended Jackson, saying Jackson had used the group to burnish his own reputation. Jackson resigned from the SCLC that year and formed his own organization, Operation PUSH (People United to Save Humanity).

> "*You must not surrender. You may or may not get there, but just know that you're qualified and hold on and hold out. We must never surrender. America will get better and better. Keep hope alive!*"

In 1979, Jackson was asked by President Jimmy Carter to visit South Africa while it was still under its apartheid regime. Jackson denounced the regime's discriminatory

> **Jackson and Rainbow/PUSH**
>
> Jesse Jackson founded Operation PUSH (People United to Save Humanity) following his suspension from the Southern Christian Leadership Conference in 1971. He announced the founding in front of a portrait of Martin Luther King, Jr. Jackson promised to begin "a rainbow coalition" that would unite people across racial lines to advocate for better economic conditions for the poor. Operation PUSH became Jackson's platform for national and international activism. In 1976 Jackson founded PUSH-Excel to encourage children and teenagers to succeed. Jackson used upbeat public rallies to encourage young people's self-esteem and responsibility, daring his audiences to forsake ghetto-defined notions of prestige.
>
> In the early 1980's, Jackson turned his attention to politics. He used his "rainbow coalition" movement as a platform to help elect Harold Washington as Chicago's first black mayor in 1983. A year later, he ran for president as a Democrat. His platform emphasized increasing employment opportunities for poor people and women. In 1985, he formed the National Rainbow Coalition to advocate for equal rights for African Americans, other minorities, women, and homosexuals. The coalition merged with Operation PUSH in 1996 to form the Rainbow/PUSH Coalition.
>
> Jackson's political platform reflected the priorities of the Rainbow/PUSH organization, including creation of a program to rebuild national infrastructure and provide jobs, reversal of Reagan-era tax cuts (using the money to finance social welfare programs), cuts in military spending, a single-payer national health care system, support for small farmers, support for the Equal Rights Amendment, opposition to South Africa's apartheid (with economic sanctions), support for public education, and support for a Palestinian state.

doctrine. That year, he also toured the Middle East, where he supported the Palestine Liberation Organization and its leader Yasir Arafat, who was widely called a terrorist in United States political circles. In 1983, Jackson negotiated the release of U.S. Navy lieutenant Robert Goodman, who had been shot down and captured in Syria as he was bombing Syrian troops in Lebanon. Jackson made a dramatic appeal to Syrian president Hafez al-Assad. Having initially expressed skepticism about Jackson's unofficial mission, President Ronald Reagan welcomed Jackson and Goodman to the White House on January 4, 1984. Jackson's trips abroad brought him international fame, and his Syrian success helped burnish his political reputation. In June of 1984, while actively campaigning for president, Jackson traveled to Cuba at Fidel Castro's invitation and helped secure the release of twenty-two U.S. citizens who had been imprisoned there.

In the 1984 presidential race, Jackson received more than 3.2 million votes in Democratic primaries, many of them cast by new voters, many of whom were young and non-white. He won primaries and caucuses in the District of Columbia and four states: Louisiana, South Carolina, Virginia, and Mississippi. After the campaign, Jackson launched the National Rainbow Coalition, whose goal was equal rights for all Americans. The coalition later merged with Operation PUSH to form the Rainbow/PUSH Coalition. In 1988, Jackson again campaigned for the Democratic presidential nomination, with wider support than in the 1984 election. He won 6.9 million primary votes and finished first in eleven races: Mississippi, Puerto Rico, Virginia, the District of Columbia, South Carolina, Vermont, Alabama, Georgia, Louisiana, Delaware, and Michigan. Jackson finished second within the party to Massachusetts governor Michael Dukakis, who lost to George H. W. Bush in the general election.

During the 1990's, Jackson supported Bill Clinton's campaigns, rallying African American support to help Clinton win two terms. Jackson also served as a shadow senator (nonvoting representative) for the District of Columbia between 1991 and 1997. In 1997, Clinton appointed Jackson as a U.S. special envoy to Kenyan president Daniel arap Moi, to promote a free election. Two years later, during the war in Kosovo, Jackson went to Belgrade to negotiate the release of three U.S. prisoners of war from the Serbian government. In 2001, shortly after receiving a Medal of Freedom from Clinton, Jackson admitted to having fathered a daughter with staff member Karin Stanford in 1999. CNN reported that the Rainbow/PUSH Coalition had paid Stanford thousands of dollars in moving expenses and contract work.

In 2003, in a speech that drew hundreds of thousands of people in London's Hyde Park, Jackson condemned

U.S. president George W. Bush's advocacy of war in Iraq. He returned to the United Kingdom in November, 2004, to facilitate peace talks in Northern Ireland, and in 2005 to take part in the minority outreach program Operation Black Vote in England. In August, 2005, Jackson met with Venezuelan president Hugo Chavez to ease tensions after American right-wing televangelist Pat Robertson had suggested that Chavez should be assassinated.

Significance

Although Jackson's two presidential campaigns did not succeed, they presaged by almost twenty-five years the successful run of another Chicago community activist and orator, Barack Obama. Obama, a Democrat like Jackson, emphasized inclusion and minority participation at the national political level in the United States. Throughout his prolific career, Jackson has served as an example of political action based on personal convictions. He has championed the rights of the underrepresented and underprivileged, raised the self-esteem of young black men and women, and carried on the message of the Civil Rights movement.

Bruce E. Johansen

Further Reading

Bruns, Roger. *Jesse Jackson: A Biography*. Westport, Conn.: Greenwood Press, 2005. Presents positive and negative aspects of Jackson's life and career. Includes numerous photographs.

Haskins, James. *Jesse Jackson: Civil Rights Activist*. Berkeley Heights, N.J.: Enslow, 2000. This book, aimed at high school readers, provides a sketch of Jackson's work in civil rights—from his youth to the years with Martin Luther King, Jr., to international journeys in more recent years.

Jackson, Jesse L. *Straight from the Heart*. Edited by Roger D. Hatch and Frank E. Watkins. Philadelphia: Fortress Press, 1987. A collection of essays, sermons, and speeches by Jackson, outlining his philosophies and political vision. Jackson mounted his second presidential campaign the year after this book's release.

Landess, Thomas, and Richard Quinn. *Jesse Jackson and the Politics of Race*. Ottawa, Ill.: Jameson Books, 1985. Covers Jackson's work from the 1960's to the early 1980's, when his national political platform was evolving along with his Rainbow Coalition.

Reynolds, Barbara A. *Jesse Jackson: America's David*. Washington, D.C.: JFJ Associates, 1985. Positions Jackson as David to the Goliath of corporate interests and the historical legacy of racism.

Marsha P. Johnson

Gay liberation activist

Born: August 24, 1945; Elizabeth, New Jersey
Died: July 6, 1992; New York City, New York
Also known as: Malcolm Michaels, Jr.
Area of Achievement: LGBTQ rights

Poor, black, queer, and gender-nonconforming, Marsha P. Johnson lived in New York City, where she was active in the gay liberation movement in the 1970s. Although she was a figure very local to New York City, in recent years Marsha P. Johnson has become an icon in the LGBTQ rights movement, especially among transgender activists and queer people of color.

Early Life

Marsha P. Johnson, who as an adult identified herself variously as gay, as a drag queen, and as a transvestite, was born Malcolm Michaels Jr. in Elizabeth, New Jersey, on August 24, 1945. Her father, Malcolm Michaels Sr., worked on an assembly line at a General Motors plant. Her mother, Alberta Claiborne, worked as a housekeeper. Marsha had six brothers and sisters. Altogether they were a conventional working class African American family in Elizabeth. Marsha joined her family in attending an African Methodist Episcopal Church when she was growing up. Later in life, she would become a devout Catholic.

When she was only five years old, Marsha experimented with wearing dresses. Neighborhood boys teased her relentlessly for it, and, as a result, she stopped wearing dresses until she was much older. Her family shared the aversion to homosexuality that was typical of the era. Johnson later recalled that her mother once told her that homosexuals were lower than dogs.

Johnson graduated from high school in 1963. Shortly after, she packed a bag and, with only $15 to her name, moved to New York City.

Life's Work

Johnson initially found work waiting tables. She settled in Greenwich Village, which at that time still had many inexpensive apartments and attracted a young, bohemian, and radical crowd. It was also home to a large population of gay men, and Johnson found she was able to create a life for herself there. She quickly befriended another transgender woman, Sylvia Rivera, who lived on the streets. Sylvia was a young teen when they first met; Johnson an older teen. The two would remain close friends. By 1966, Johnson was also living on the street and supporting herself through prostitution.

Although homosexuality was still criminalized and pathologized, even in New York City, there was a growing sense that open-minded people should be more tolerant. Further, the social and political movements of the 1960s –feminism, civil rights, and the peace movement – had spread an ethos and a language of liberation among many gay men and lesbians. In 1965, the Mattachine Society—a "homophile" organization with a national membership—had organized picket marches in New York, Washington DC, and Philadelphia to demand basic rights for homosexuals. This turned into the "Annual Reminder," a demonstration held every year until 1969, when it was quickly supplanted by the more militant activism of the post-Stonewall era.

A handful of gay bars in New York in the 1960s were important places for homosexuals to meet and socialize, but they were illegal. Disorderly conduct laws were routinely invoked to forbid openly serving homosexual bar patrons. Other laws regulated gender-normative dress. Worse, the police in New York City, as in most cities in the country, routinely entrapped gay men in order to arrest them. The gay bars that existed in New York were mostly owned and operated by the Mafia in cooperation with the corrupt New York City Police Department (NYPD), who received kickbacks from the mob. One of these bars was called the Stonewall Inn, located on Christopher Street in the Village.

The bars were routinely raided by the same police who profited from the arrangement with the Mafia that kept the bars open; in this way, they could make plenty of arrests while still profiting from graft. By the late sixties, the raids had become a scripted non-event for both the Mafia and the police. Records from the era show that every gay bar in the city was raided an average of once a month in the late sixties. The police would tip off the Mafia in advance when a raid was scheduled. The only ones to suffer were the arrested patrons, who could lose their jobs or face prison time as a result.

One of these routine raids occurred at the Stonewall Inn late Friday night, after midnight, on June 27, 1969. As the police lined up the patrons outside the bar to check their identification, some of them began to resist or to mock the police. Tensions mounted, and the resistance grew into a full-fledged riot. Before long, hundreds of gay men, transvestites, and others had set fire to the Inn, overturned police vehicles, lobbed Molotov cocktails, and even uprooted a parking meter to use it as a battering ram to access the Inn after about ten police officers locked themselves inside to hide from the crowd. One of the more famous and memorable responses on the part of some rioters was to form chorus kicklines and face off against the Tactical Patrol Force (TPF), who had been called in to subdue them.

The uprising lasted until the early hours of the morning, and it was followed by five more days and nights of unrest in the streets. The morning after the raid, graffiti outside the bar read, "Support Gay Power!" and "Legalize Gay Bars!" It was an historic turning point, and people knew it. The morning after the second night of rioting, an activist printed five thousand flyers and distributed them in Greenwich Village; the flyers read in part, "The nights of Friday, June 27, 1969 and Saturday, June 28, 1969 will go down in history…" Within months, several gay liberation groups were formed in the city, and in 1970 the first anniversary of the uprising was commemorated with the first Gay Pride march—an event that made the front page of the *New York Times*.

> *"Now they got two little nice statues in Chariot Park to remember the gay movement. How many people have died for these two little statues to be put in the park for them to recognize gay people? How many years has it taken people to realize that we are all brothers and sisters and human beings in the human race? I mean how many years does it take people to see that? We're all in this rat race together!"*

As the myth of Stonewall grew in importance, many of the details about what happened were obscured in lore and hearsay. It was true that the Stonewall Inn was a popular hangout for all types of gay people, including cross dressers and street hustlers as well as middle class white men. Johnson claimed to have been the first drag queen to frequent the Stonewall Inn after it opened. A legend arose that Johnson had thrown the first brick at a cop the night of the riot; another report had her throwing a shot glass at a mirror in the bar and shouting "I got my civil rights"—a so-called "shot glass heard round the world." But Johnson herself has said that she wasn't in the bar that evening. Instead, she arrived at around 2:00 a.m. after the riot had already begun.

Johnson may not have thrown the first brick, but she became an important figure in the militant gay liberation movement that was born immediately after Stonewall. She was an early member of the Gay Liberation Front (GLF), the first gay organization to use the word "gay" in its name. The GLF had a political program that was all over the map and never really settled upon. They cared little, however, for some things that would come to define gay rights in later decades: the right to serve in the military, for example. Like many of the radical movements of the era, they wanted a fundamental restructuring of American society. This included an end to militarized colonialism and and an end to capitalism. They were not in principle non-violent, and they aligned themselves with the Black Power movement. They called for a revolution, and they meant it.

The year after Stonewall, Johnson and her friend Sylvia Rivera founded the Street Transvestite Action Revolutionaries (STAR). They rented a tenement at 213 East Second Street and it became a place where homeless transgender youth could live or crash. The two ran the house less like social workers than like left-wing, revolutionary "drag mothers" (a term from the drag ball culture that was famously documented in the film *Paris is Burning*). At its peak, STAR was active in New York City, Chicago, California, and England.

In the 1970s, Johnson was a fixture in Greenwich Village. She was sometimes called the "mayor of Christopher Street," and she was known for her broad smile, a warm demeanor, and her attention-grabbing costumes: she often wore flowers in her hair and garish, red plastic high heels. She, like Sylvia and like many of the youth that they helped, worked as a prostitute to make ends meet. She was a fixture, too, in the gay nightlife scene in New York in the 1970s, and she performed with a drag performance troupe called Hot Peaches. In 1975, Johnson was photographed by Andy Warhol for a group of screen prints called "Ladies and Gentlemen," a series of portraits of drag queens who frequented the Gilded Grape, a nightclub.

Johnson also suffered from mental illness. She had her first breakdown in 1970, and she was hospitalized in Bellevue numerous times in the following years. Although in 1980 she was invited to ride in the lead car at the Gay Pride Parade, the following decade saw Johnson's mental health decline as she become increasingly subject to volatile mood swings and erratic behavior. From 1980 until her death, she lived in the home of a good friend, Randy Wicker. In 1992, Johnson's body was found floating in the Hudson River. Although there was some evidence of a violent assault, the police initially ruled her death a suicide. However, in November 2012, transgender activist Mariah Lopez succeeded in getting the New York police department to reopen the case as a possible homicide.

Significance

Changing attitudes towards what we today call gender non-conforming behavior has led to a re-evaluation of several figures who were previously considered marginal in LGBTQ history, among them Johnson and her friend Sylvia Rivera. A 2012 documentary called *Pay It No Mind: The Life and Times of Marsha P. Johnson* brought Johnson into vogue for a new generation. The 2017 Netflix documentary, *The Death and Life of Marsha P. Johnson*, follows trans woman and friend of Johnson's Victoria Cruz of the Anti-Violence Project as she investigates Johnson's murder. Like *Pay It No Mind*, it relies on archival footage and interviews

Johnson has become a hero to many in the gay rights community and a hero to many in the transgender community. This is a salutary development, but it would be a shame to thoroughly assimilate Johnson to contemporary concerns or categories. Johnson's politics, for example, were genuinely revolutionary: "We believe in picking up the gun, starting a revolution if necessary," she said. The quote has not been buried by contemporary admirers; in fact, it appeared in a 2018 *New York Times* belated obituary. But it is framed by the writer there as a "reference to the radical politics of the time," as though the statement can simply be bracketed while others—the parts we like—are brought forward. Similarly, the term *transgender* wasn't really in use in the 1960s or 1970s; Johnson, like most in those days, did not make the distinction that we now make between "doing drag" and "being trans." Johnson was, variously, gay, a "queen," or a transvestite in her own eyes—or, at least, in her own words. She sometimes went out in her male persona, Malcolm.

With those caveats in place, the life of Marsha P. Johnson was a remarkable one that should be studied, celebrated, and also mourned. Johnson came from a background that almost guaranteed not just an anonymous life but an extremely hard life, too. She was black, queer, poor, gender nonconforming, and she worked as a street prostitute. She made waves in New York City's gay politics, coming into conflict with the emerging rights movement in the 1970s not only for reasons of gender variance and race, but because of her status as members of an "underclass" of transgender prostitutes and because of her revolutionary beliefs.

D Alan Dean

FURTHER READING

Armstrong, Elizabeth & Suzanna Crage. "Movements and Memory: The Making of the Stonewall Myth." *American Sociological Review*, 2006, Vol. 71 (October 724–751).

Carter, David. *Stonewall: The Riots that Sparked the Gay Revolution*. New York: St. Martins, 2004.

Chan, Sewell. "Marsha P. Johnson: A Transgender Pioneer and Activist Who was a Fixture of Greenwich Village Street Life." *New York Times,* March 8, 2018. https://www.nytimes.com/interactive/2018/obituaries/overlooked-marsha-p-johnson.html

Duberman, Martin. *Stonewall*. New York: Plume, 1993.

The Death and Life of Marsha P. Johnson. (Documentary film.) Directed by David France. Netflix, 2017.

Pay It No Mind: Marsha P. Johnson (Documentary film.) Directed by Michael Kasino. Redux Pictures, 2012.

MOTHER JONES

Irish-born labor organizer

Born: May 1, 1830; Cork City, Ireland
Died: November 30, 1930; Adelphi, Maryland
Area of Achievement: Labor movement, oratory, social reform, women's rights

As a labor organizer and fiery and captivating orator, Jones inspired workers and breathed life into union organizing efforts in the early twentieth century.

EARLY LIFE

The birth date of Mother Jones is in dispute, as are other critical facts about her early life. This uncertainty is not unusual for poor and working-class people whose lives are often not recorded in traditional ways. Even births, deaths, marriages, and work history may not be documented. In her autobiography, Jones herself gave 1830 as her birth year, but she gave other dates in interviews throughout her life. Most historians agree on 1830, although one cites 1839 and another 1843. Jones's father migrated to the United States from Ireland and worked as a laborer building canals and railroads. The family followed and settled initially in Toronto, Canada, where young Jones went to school, graduating in 1858 or 1859.

Little is known of her father and mother or her siblings. Jones taught school in Michigan in 1859, worked as a dressmaker in Chicago in 1860, and again taught school in Memphis, Tennessee. In Memphis, she met George Jones, a member of the Iron Workers' Union, and in 1861 they were married. George Jones and all the couple's children died in the yellow fever epidemic of 1867. In her autobiography, Mother Jones claims to have had four children, but some evidence exists to suggest it may have been one or three. No one disputes the fact that Jones was alone after 1867 with no family and no permanent home.

Jones left Memphis in 1867 to return to Chicago, where she resumed working as a dressmaker for the wealthy. In 1871, she was burned out of her home and lost all of her possessions in the great Chicago Fire. Following the fire, she began attending nightly lectures at the Knights of Labor building, which was located near the

Mother Jones (Library of Congress)

place where many homeless refugees from the fire were camping out. Records of these years of her life are scarce, but it is known that Mother Jones traveled during the 1870's and 1880's from one industrial area to another speaking and organizing, usually in connection with the Knights of Labor. In 1877, she was in Pittsburgh for the first nationwide industrial strike, that of the railroad workers. In 1886, she was in Chicago, active in organizing for the eight-hour work day. In 1890, when the Knights of Labor District 135 and the National Union of Miners and Mine Laborers merged to form the United Mine Workers of America (UMWA), Jones became a paid organizer for the union. She was approximately sixty years old and about to enter the national stage. She was thought of as "the Miners' Angel," the most dangerous woman in the country, or America's most patriotic citizen, depending on the point of view of the different people who encountered her.

> *"If they want to hang me, let them. And on the scaffold I would shout, 'Freedom for the working class!'"*

LIFE'S WORK

Until her health failed in the late 1920's, Jones traveled the nation speaking and organizing not only for coal miners but also for workers in the textile, railway, and steel industries. She figured in most major strikes in the United States in the early 1900's but was repeatedly drawn to the coalfields of Pennsylvania, Colorado, and West Virginia. For a time, she was active in Socialist Party politics, particularly in the campaigns of Eugene V. Debs. She supported Mexican revolutionary Pancho Villa in his fight for better wages and living conditions for Mexican workers, who were often used as strikebreakers, particularly in Western mines. She did not support woman suffrage or other social reform efforts of her era that were not founded solely on working-class rights.

Her speeches reveal that Jones saw herself as an agitator and educator charged with the tasks of teaching the American working class about the nature of capitalism and mobilizing an international working-class movement. In 1909, she told the national convention of the UMWA that she was there to "wake you up." At a UMWA district convention in 1914 she explained, "I hold no office only that of disturbing." In 1920, near the end of her public speaking career, she summarized her mission: "I am busy getting this working man to understand what belongs to him, and his power to take possession of it."

Jones was so effective at "disturbing" workers that corporate and government officials often went to great extremes to keep her from speaking. She was arrested many times, imprisoned, and forcefully escorted out of strike zones where she had been called to help organize. Her success as an educator is less easily documented, but her speeches and audience responses reveal a talented, tireless woman who was able to move people to action while instructing them about the nature of their conflicts and their place in history.

Conditions in mines and mining communities in the early 1900's were stark. Wages were low, mines were unsafe, rates of deaths and disabling injuries were very high, and children were often employed. Miners lived in company-owned housing and were often paid in scrip, a substitute currency that could be redeemed only at company stores. If miners tried to improve their conditions through union organizing, they and their families were evicted from houses, and armed guards (often from the Baldwin-Felts detective agency) were hired by the companies to fight the organizing efforts.

In the face of these conditions Jones devised a wide array of organizing strategies, as the 1897 UMWA strike at Turtle Creek mine, near Pittsburgh illustrates. She spoke to ten thousand miners and sympathizers, urging them to fight. Then she organized farmers in the region to provide food to strikers and escorted the farmers and their wagons to strike headquarters where the food was distributed. She called on neighborhood women to donate a "pound" of something to the cause and urged factory workers to come to miners' meetings and donate.

As in many other strikes, Jones made certain that women and children were actively involved and featured in national news coverage of the conflicts. At Turtle Creek, she organized wives of miners into groups of pickets and demonstrators and positioned the children of miners at the front of parades. In one parade fifty little girls marched with homemade banners, one of which read "Our Papas Aren't Scared."

Jones was often in West Virginia in these early years of the twentieth century. In 1902, she worked in the southern coalfields, but she was successful in organizing only in the Paint Creek and Cabin Creek areas near Charleston, the state capital. While trying to organize the northern part of the state, she was arrested and briefly imprisoned. For several years she traveled across the country to protest child labor, organize miners in the West, and support striking brewery workers, textile workers, copper miners,

"Mother Jones Lives" at the traditional Workers May Day Rally and March in Chicago, May 2018. (Wikimedia Commons)

and smelter workers. Then in 1912 and 1913, once again working as a UMWA organizer, Mother Jones returned to West Virginia's southern coalfields. She faced down armed mine guards to allow union meetings and threatened to encourage West Virginia miners to arm themselves and fight back. She was imprisoned again, tried by a state military militia court, convicted of a charge of conspiracy to commit murder, and sentenced to prison for twenty years. She served eighty-five days, passing her eighty-fourth birthday in jail, before national public outcry and the promise of a congressional investigation prompted that state's newly elected governor to free her.

In her final organizing effort with West Virginia mines, Jones attempted to halt the spontaneous 1921 march of thousands of miners on Logan. It was an unusual role for the aging firebrand, and she was not able to stop the march, later known as the Battle of Blair Mountain (1921). That bloody confrontation left many dead and injured. The determined coal miners proved powerless in the face of armed Baldwin-Felts detectives, the state militia, and the six thousand federal troops and twenty military airplanes sent by President Warren G. Harding to support the coal operators and prevent the union men from marching into nonunion territory. The battle halted organizing efforts in West Virginia until national legislation authorized collective bargaining in 1932.

Organizing miners in Colorado was as difficult as in West Virginia. Jones made her first visits there in 1903 soon after John D. Rockefeller, Sr., bought control of Colorado Fuel and Iron Company and the Victor Fuel Company. These early organizing efforts were not successful and led to a split between Jones and the UMWA leadership over organizing strategy. She did not return to the UMWA payroll until 1911.

In 1913, miners in southern Colorado went on strike for higher wages; an eight-hour day; coal weighing to be monitored by miners; free choice of stores, schools, doctors, and boarding houses; enforcement of Colorado laws; and abolition of the mine guard system. Although most of these provisions were already law in Colorado, the state did not implement them in the southern fields. When the miners went on strike, they were evicted and lived in tent cities through the bitter cold Colorado winter.

Jones joined the striking miners there in the fall of 1913 and returned in December and again in January. Between January and March of 1914, Jones, then in her early eighties, was arrested many times and spent more than a month in basement jail cells in Colorado. Refusing to be silenced, she smuggled out an open letter to the American people that was read and published across the country. She was not in Colorado in April when the state militia attacked the family tent camp, killing thirty-two, including many women and children. Subsequent state and national investigations into this incident, known as the Ludlow Massacre (1914), were extremely critical of the actions of the governor, the state militia, and Colorado Fuel and Iron Company.

When Jones wrote about her life she always identified her cause with the miners. After her death on November 30, 1930, she was buried as she had requested at the Miners Cemetery in Mount Olive, Illinois. A choir of coal miners sang her final tribute.

SIGNIFICANCE

Jones is remembered as a great labor agitator and a tremendously effective public speaker. Stories of her visits to coal camps, leadership at rallies and demonstrations, and confrontations with company and government officials are part of a living oral history of resistance in mining communities. Her memory continues to inspire the labor movement. When women mobilized in a 1989 UMWA strike against the Pittston Coal Group, they identified themselves as the "Daughters of Mother Jones" as they carried out actions in her name, such as occupying company headquarters and holding vigils outside jails where union officials were imprisoned.

The message of Jones's life is that ordinary people, indeed unlikely people, can make important contributions to improving workers' lives. She was homeless and alone; she was poor and sometimes in prison; yet Jones used the resources she had mind, voice, wit, spirit, and energy to influence conditions for workers in America.

Sally Ward Maggard

FURTHER READING

Fetherling, Dale. Mother Jones, the Miners' Angel: Portrait. Carbondale: Southern Illinois University Press, 1974. This first full-scale biography on Jones presents a sympathetic yet balanced portrait.

Gorn, Elliott J. Mother Jones: The Most Dangerous Woman in America. New York: Hill and Wang, 2001. Chronicles Jones's life and work, placing her accomplishments within a wider political and cultural context.

Jones, Mother. The Autobiography of Mother Jones. Edited by Mary Field Parton. Chicago: Charles Kerr, 1974. First published in 1925; later editions (1972, 1974) add useful introductions. Insights into coal strikes, early twentieth century labor leadership, and Jones's spirit and personality. Unfortunately marred by inaccuracies and serious omissions.

---. The Correspondence of Mother Jones. Edited by Edward M. Steel. Pittsburgh: University of Pittsburgh Press, 1985. A collection of all known letters, notes, and telegrams (eight communications are added in Steel's 1988 collection of Jones's speeches and writings). Illustrates development of her political views over the course of her life.

---. Mother Jones Speaks: Collected Writings and Speeches. Edited by Philip S. Foner. New York: Monad Press, 1983. The most comprehensive work and best reference source in conveying the full range of Jones's intellect and activities. Includes speeches, testimony before congressional committees, articles, interviews, letters, an extensive bibliography, and historical background information.

---. The Speeches and Writings of Mother Jones. Edited by Edward M. Steel. Pittsburgh: University of Pittsburgh Press, 1988. Collection of thirty-one speeches believed to have been accurately recorded and transcribed in their entirety. Also includes seventeen articles Jones penned for newspapers and socialist periodicals. A helpful "Biographical Notes" section identifies people in her speeches. A good introduction to her life with historical context for her speeches and activities.

Long, Priscilla. Mother Jones: Woman Organizer And Her Relations with Miners' Wives, Working Women, and the Suffrage Movement. Boston: South End Press, 1976. Examines Jones's position as a female leader in the labor movement and her relationships with working-class women and with women's rights organizations of her era.

Schiff, Karenna Gore. Lighting the Way: Nine Women Who Changed Modern America. New York: Miramax Books/Hyperion, 2005. Mother Jones is one of the nine women profiled in this book about women who were social reformers.

FRANK KAMENY

Gay rights activist

Born: May 21, 1925; New York City, New York
Died: October 11, 2011; Washington, D.C.
Also known as: Franklin Edward Kameny
Area of Achievement: Social Reform; Politics/Law

When Kameny was fired in 1957 from a government job in Washington D.C. because he was a homosexual, he took the unusual step of fighting back. Kameny sued the government, and his case spent years in the court system. Although he eventually lost, Kameny devoted the rest of his life to being a gadfly and a gay rights activist, bravely confronting the government, the police, the psychiatric community, and the media in order to fight homophobia and change laws and opinions.

EARLY LIFE

Frank Kameny was born in New York City on May 21, 1925. As a boy, he was unusually gifted in math and science; he was also unusually ambitious in his school studies. He graduated from high school when he was only sixteen years old and, in the same year, he joined the freshman class at Queens College in Queens, New York.

Before Kameny was able to finish his college degree, World War II intervened. He was drafted into the United States Army and served honorably in Europe until the war ended in 1945. Returning immediately to school, he

Frank Kameny (Wikimedia Commons)

graduated with a bachelor's degree in physics in 1948. He then went to Harvard University for graduate studies. In 1956, he was awarded a doctorate in astronomy.

Life's Work

Kameny, doctoral degree in hand, moved to Washington D.C. where he taught for a year at Georgetown University. In 1957, he found work with the United States Army Map Service. His career was quickly derailed, however, when only a few months into his post, his supervisors learned of a prior arrest on a so-called "vice" charge. Kameny, like thousands of gay men in the 1950s, had been targeted by police for homosexual activity—in this case, for cruising in a restroom. When his supervisor raised the matter, Kameny insisted that his private life was his business and not his employers'. Soon after, he was fired.

During the Cold War, gay people were classified by the United States government as "security risks" and were sought out and fired from their jobs. A 1950 Senate investigation put the matter this way: "It is generally believed that those who engage in overt acts of perversion lack the emotional stability of normal persons." For this reason, they claimed, "sex perverts" constituted a danger to the country. In the McCarthy era, more people lost their jobs for being alleged homosexuals than for being Communists. In the 1950s and 1960s, the United States Federal Bureau of Investigation (FBI) kept files on known homosexuals in cities across the country—not just homosexual government employees, but anyone who was discovered to be a homosexual. The FBI and local police routinely tracked them, noting their favorite bars and restaurants and the names of their friends. The United States Post Office kept lists of addresses where printed material pertaining to homosexuality was mailed, and they shared the information with authorities.

Many thousands of gay people were purged from the military and from government jobs under suspicion of being homosexual. Frank Kameny's plight was a drop in the bucket. But Kameny did something extremely unusual—and risky—in response to his firing. Rather than slink away in shame, he openly contested the firing and the laws that enabled it.

Kameny was young, highly educated, and naturally gifted with both extraordinary persistence and a certain relish for the wonky, bureaucratic institutions and procedures of Washington DC, the city he would call home for the rest of his life. He wrote appeals to the Army Map Service, to the Civil Service Commission, and to congressional committees. He filed complaints with the U.S. District Court for the District of Columbia and the U.S. Court of Appeals. He was rejected again and again. He couldn't even interest a lawyer anymore when he decided to file an appeal with the United States Supreme Court.

> "*The person who really needs the psychotherapy... is not the homosexual youngster who gets dragged to the psychiatrist's office by his mother, but the mother, to relieve her anxieties about his homosexuality.*"

Although Kameny's Supreme Court petition ended in the Court declining to hear his case, the document that he wrote and submitted to the Court—long neglected by historians of the gay rights movement—was the first time anyone confronted the United States judicial system on behalf of gay people using the language of rights and constitutionally guaranteed freedoms. But Kameny went even further. His petition took on the moral opprobrium that was attached to homosexuality and challenged it

Kameny standing in front of signs once used during protests. (Wikimedia Commons)

using stirring language: "Petitioner asserts, flatly, unequivocally, and absolutely uncompromisingly, that homosexuality, whether by mere inclination or by overt act, is not only not immoral, but that for those choosing voluntarily to engage in homosexual acts, such acts are moral in a real and positive sense, and are good, right, and desirable, socially and personally." The petition was the forerunner to and model for many other court filings that Kameny—and soon enough, others—would write on behalf of numerous government employees through the 1960s, until the law that barred homosexuals was finally lifted in 1971.

In 1961, Kameny and his friend Jack Nichols founded the Washington D.C. branch of the Mattachine Society, originally founded by Harry Hay in 1950 in Los Angeles. Kameny was the president of the D.C. chapter. The Mattachine Society of Washington D.C. initiated letter writing campaigns to various government officials and was joined by the National Capital Area Civil Liberties Union in fighting legal battles against discriminatory federal employment policies.

After seeing the success of marches in the civil rights movement, Kameny borrowed the tactic. In 1965, he organized the first march ever held in Washington D.C. on behalf of gay rights. Although only ten brave gay men and women showed up to carry pickets and march in front of the White House, it was the start of something big. Over the next three or four years, more marches were held in cities along the east coast. These may have been small, but knowledge about them traveled throughout the gay community. They undoubtedly contributed to the heightened sense of political possibility that ignited into a wildfire with the Stonewall riots in 1969 in New York City.

Kameny took on not only the government but the body of experts whose knowledge declared homosexuality to be a pathology or a mental disorder. "*We* are the experts on ourselves, and we will tell the experts they have nothing to tell us!" he said. For years, he spoke out against the psychiatric profession's models and classifications regarding homosexuality. Kameny believed that the designation of homosexuality as an illness derived more from prejudice than from reason, and he argued that the psychiatric profession's ideas about homosexuality were muddled and wrong. He attended professional conferences in the field, spoke on panels, and organized his own. In one famous photograph, Kameny is seated somberly at a table heading a panel at the 1972 annual meeting of the American Psychiatric Association (APA); the man next to him, a gay psychiatrist afraid of losing his career, is wearing a mask and wig to protect his identity.

In 1973, Kameny won; the APA removed homosexuality from its manual of mental disorders. Always attuned to the workings of power through social institutions, Kameny wryly noted that the psychiatrists had deigned to "cure" them all, "instantaneously, en masse," on December 15, 1973.

Kameny was active in D.C. politics and with various other gay rights causes in the 1970s, 1980s, and 1990s.

He founded the Gay and Lesbian Activist Alliance, the National Gay and Lesbian Task Force, and the National Gay Rights Lobby, and in 1975 he became the first openly gay city appointee when he became a Commissioner with the D.C. Commission on Human Rights. Building on his work fighting federal employment discrimination in the 1960s, he worked with gay rights groups and gay service members to challenge the ban of homosexuals in the military and to fight dishonorable discharges. Kameny was invited to attend the December 22, 2010, ceremony where President Barack Obama signed the Don't Ask, Don't Tell Repeal Act of 2010.

By the 2000s, Kameny's foundational role in the gay rights movement was becoming increasingly clear to historians. The Smithsonian Institution acquired the pickets that Kameny saved from the 1965 march, and the Library of Congress assembled a vast exhibition of materials demonstrating the central role of Frank Kameny in gay rights history.

In 2015 Kameny was finally recognized as a veteran and received a U.S. Veterans Administration memorial headstone, at Washington, D.C.'s Congressional Cemetery at his memorial site; the headstone was dedicated during a ceremony on the morning of November 11, 2015, Veteran's Day. In front of that headstone lays a marker inscribed with the slogan "Gay is Good". Kameny coined that slogan, and in a 2009 AP interview said about coining it, "If I am remembered for anything I hope it will be that."

Significance

The LGBTQ rights movement is often said to have begun with the Stonewall riots in 1969. Although the riots pumped tremendous new energy into the movement, it is something of a useful myth to say that the movement was "born" in that moment. Prior to Stonewall, there had been much activism and even other riots, like the Compton Cafeteria riot in San Francisco in August 1966. More importantly, there were organizations that were committed to the fight for gay rights and that were active across the country since the 1950s—in particular, there was the Mattachine Society and the Daughters of Bilitis. These groups staged demonstrations, carried pickets, wrote letters to newspapers and officials, petitioned lawmakers, and, through their mailing lists, magazines, and newsletters, organized and informed a community of homosexuals across the country. But if one single *individual* were to be named as the "founder" of the gay rights movement—rather than one single event or an organizational effort—then many historians would agree that that individual should be Frank Kameny.

In the late 1950s and early 1960s, after his firing from a federal job in Washington DC, Kameny pursued the first known civil rights claim based on sexual orientation in any United States court. His petition to the Supreme Court from 1961 has come to be recognized as a foundational document not only of the gay rights movement but of United States history. It was displayed by the Library of Congress in 2011 in an exhibition of major documents that created the United States and formed its legal framework. The curators' decision was a challenge to the way we have come to conceptualize gay rights: rather than seeing the struggle for gay rights as having taken place primarily in the streets, Frank Kameny reminds us that the struggle also took place in purposeful discussions about the meaning of the Constitution and the idea of liberty, and in passionate debate with—and challenges to—our social, political, and professional institutions.

D. Alan Dean

Further Reading

Cuthbert, Mike, and Frank Kameny. "Gay Rights Pioneer Blazed the Trail." *AARP*, 5 June 2009, www.aarp.org/politics-society/rights/info-06-2009/Frank_Kameny_Video.html.

Faderman, Lillian. *The Gay Revolution: The Story of the Struggle*. New York, NY: Simon & Schuster, 2015.

Johnson, David K. *The Lavender Scare: The Cold War Persecution of Gays and Lesbians in the Federal Government*. Chicago: U of Chicago Press, 2004.

Long, Michael G. *Gay Is Good: The Life and Letters of Gay Rights Pioneer Frank Kameny*. Syracuse, NY: Syracuse UP, 2014.

Rainbow History Project. *"Gay is Good": Gay and Lesbian Organizing in D.C., 1961–1975*. Rainbow History Project Digital Collections. http://rainbowhistory.omeka.net/exhibits/show/gayisgood/organizing-nationwide.

Helen Keller

Social reformer and writer

Born: June 27, 1880; Tuscumbia, Alabama
Died: June 1, 1968; Easton, Connecticut
Area of Achievement: Social reform, literature, education

Helen Keller (Library of Congress)

Blind and deaf since early childhood, Keller exemplified by her life of activism the full empowerment potential of disabled persons who receive appropriate adaptive education. She served as a spokesperson and fundraiser for the benefit of those who are unable to see or hear.

EARLY LIFE

Helen Keller was born in a small town in northern Alabama to Kate Adams Keller and Captain Arthur Keller, a Confederate Civil War veteran. At nineteen months, Helen suffered an illness that left her unable to see, hear, or, eventually, speak (in Keller's time, these disabilities were termed "blind," "deaf," and "mute"). She remained locked in this lonely state of sensory deprivation until she reached the age of six, when her family employed Anne Sullivan, the twenty-year-old daughter of working-class Irish immigrants, as her tutor. Sullivan herself was visually impaired.

With Sullivan's devoted, creative, and stubborn help, Keller soon rediscovered the concept that concrete things are associated with linguistic symbols in her case, the letters of the manual alphabet spelled into her hand. Once that breakthrough was made and communication was reestablished, the young girl worked quickly to master manual lip-reading, handwriting, typewriting, Braille, and basic vocal speech. Helen's recovery of communication was aided by the residue of language skills that had developed before she went deaf, by a stimulus-rich home environment, by the early age at which her adaptive education began, and by her own remarkable intelligence and perseverance. Accompanied and assisted by her tutor, Helen attended the Perkins Institution for the Blind (Boston), the Horace Mann School of the Deaf (New York), the Wright-Humason School for the Deaf (New York), and, eventually, Gilman's preparatory Cambridge School for Young Ladies and Radcliffe College (both in Cambridge, Massachusetts), from which she was graduated with honors. While she was still a schoolgirl, Keller began her lifelong career of philanthropic fundraising, collecting contributions for the education of a destitute blind and deaf boy when she was eleven, giving a tea to benefit the kindergarten for the blind when she was twelve, and campaigning for money to start a public library in Tuscumbia when she was thirteen.

She also began her career as a writer early. In her childhood, she published several short pieces, but those early successes were also accompanied by what she later referred to as "the one cloud in my childhood's bright sky." In 1892, she wrote a short story called "The Frost King," which she sent as a birthday present to Michael Anagnos at the Perkins Institution for the Blind, who published it in one of the institution's reports. The story was discovered to be remarkably similar to Margaret T. Canby's "The Frost Fairies." The twelve-year-old child was accused of willful plagiarism and was interrogated for many hours. The experience traumatized her so deeply that, although she loved stories, she never wrote fiction again, remaining anxious and uncertain about which were her own ideas and which were impressions she had gathered from other writers. Helen's literary creativity turned toward autobiography.

When she was a sophomore at Radcliffe, she was asked by the editors of *Ladies' Home Journal* to write her life story in monthly installments. With the help of John Macy, a Harvard English instructor, and Sullivan (who eventually married Macy), Keller completed the project, which was later published in 1902 as *The Story of My Life*.

LIFE'S WORK

After her 1904 graduation from Radcliffe with honors in German and English, Keller continued to write. *The World I Live In* was published in 1908; *The Song of the Stone Wall*, in 1910; and *Out of the Dark: Essays, Letters, and Addresses on Physical and Social Vision*, in 1913.

She also wrote a number of magazine articles, primarily inspirational pieces. Some critics objected to the visual and auditory imagery in her work, criticizing it as mere "hearsay" or even offering it as evidence of outright fraud. As time went by, however, the disbelief with which some people greeted Keller's accomplishments gradually faded. This widening public estimation of what was possible for the deaf and blind significantly enlarged the field of opportunities available to all disabled people after Keller.

Sullivan married Macy soon after Keller's graduation, but the partnership between the two women continued into Keller's adulthood. (Keller never married; her engagement at age thirty-six to Peter Fagan was thwarted by her family.) The two women began to lecture together. Keller would speak her lectures and, because Keller's voice was still very difficult for strangers to understand, Sullivan would interpret. Their lectures served to increase public comprehension of the life of the perceptually impaired.

As Keller gained experience, moving through the world on Sullivan's arm, her scope of interest enlarged from human limitations caused by visual and auditory impairment to include human limitations caused by gender, by class, and by nationalism. She began to see the welfare of all people as being interdependent. She worked for woman suffrage. A pacifist to the core, she spoke against the vast amount of money her country poured into military expenditures. She read Marx and Engels, and in 1909 she joined the Socialist Party, of which John Macy was also a member. At the advent of World War I, she became a member of the Industrial Workers of the World. She wrote and lectured in defense of socialism, supported the union movement, and opposed the United States' entry into World War I. She remained sympathetic toward socialist causes all of her life, but in 1921 she decided to focus her energies on raising money for the American Foundation for the Blind.

Around the time of World War I, the advent of modernism in literature caused Keller's sentimental, rather flowery prose to seem less fashionable. An assertive and political single woman in her middle years, Keller was less comprehensible to the American public than she had been as a child. Her income from her writing diminished, and, after years of refusing it, she finally accepted a yearly stipend from capitalist Andrew Carnegie. Financial issues became more and more important as Sullivan's health deteriorated and Macy descended into alcoholism.

> *"Optimism is the faith that leads to achievement; nothing can be done without hope."*

Financial pressure prompted Keller and Sullivan to venture into vaudeville. Between 1920 and 1924, their lectures were a great success on Harry and Herman Weber's variety circuit. Besides further deepening public understanding of blindness and deafness, their years of vaudeville gave them the opportunity to meet and develop friendships with many of the famous people of the day, including Sophie Tucker, Enrico Caruso, Jascha Heifetz, and Harpo Marx. Throughout her life, Keller's extensive acquaintance with influential people was part of the power she wielded in the world. (She was received in the White House by every U.S. president from Grover Cleveland to John F. Kennedy.)

During the 1920's, Keller and Sullivan also traveled frequently on fundraising tours for the American Foundation for the Blind, an agency that Keller supported until her death. She also continued to write. In 1927,

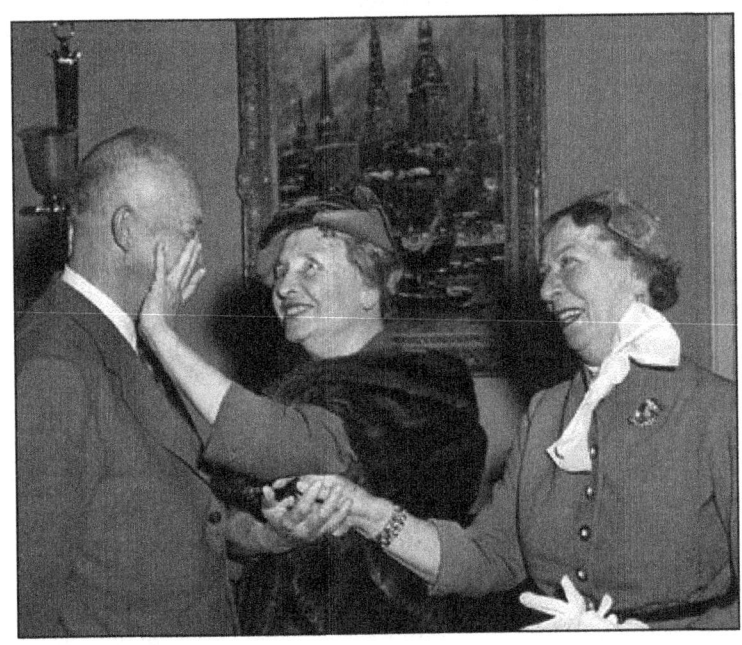

President Eisenhower with Keller and her companion Polly Thompson. (Wikimedia Commons)

she published *My Religion*, an explanation of her understanding of the alternative reality described by the eighteenth century visionary Emanuel Swedenborg. In 1930, *Midstream: My Later Life* appeared as well.

The 1930's saw more of Keller's books produced: *Peace at Eventide* was brought out in 1932, and *Helen Keller's Journal, 1936-1937* was published in 1938. Keller deplored the rise of the Nazis and supported John L. Lewis's union strikes. Sullivan died in 1936. After the death of her primary life-partner, Keller relied mainly on Polly Thompson, a Scots immigrant who had been assisting her since 1915. They remained together until Thompson's death in 1960.

In 1955, Keller published *Teacher, Anne Sullivan Macy: A Tribute by the Foster-Child of Her Mind*, a biography of Sullivan. She continued to be active on behalf of the blind and deaf until around 1962. In 1964, Keller was awarded the Presidential Medal of Freedom, the country's highest civilian honor. She died in her sleep at the age of eighty-seven.

Keller's life was filled with activity: writing, lecturing, studying, and traveling. Her significance was not simply based on her untiring work on behalf of the constituency that a childhood misfortune and her own choice selected for her. By all accounts, she was a woman of great spiritual authority. Religious faith, the self-mastery needed to overcome tragedy, and a powerful and loving teacher produced in Keller one of the spiritually radiant figures of her time, whose power was based not only on what she did or who she knew, but also on who she was and the direct effect of her presence on those whose lives she touched.

SIGNIFICANCE

Keller worked her entire life for the betterment of the disabled. She wrote. She lectured. She exerted her considerable influence over public institutions and powerful people. She raised funds for a number of agencies serving the disabled. She acted as a catalyst for the organization of state commissions for the blind. She helped to educate the American public about the prevention of gonorrheal blindness in newborn babies. The work that she did earned for her numerous humanitarian awards and citations.

The fruits of Keller's work were important, but what is even more important is that she did that work at all. She came into a world that had extremely limiting ideas about what was possible for a deaf and blind woman to accomplish. The disabled were seen as less than fully human; deaf and blind people were still being locked away in mental institutions in the world into which Keller was born. In that world, the mere existence of a powerful, educated, assertive figure such as Keller was profoundly significant. Each lecture she gave, each article she wrote defied stereotypes and served to change the attitudes and expectations of her society. Her public life as an active woman who could not see or hear in the "normal" sense truly altered the intellectual horizons around her. When she died, she left a world that had been radically changed by her life.

Donna Glee Williams

FURTHER READING

Gibson, William. *The Miracle Worker.* New York: Samuel French, 1956. The original play that examined the early years of the relationship between Helen Keller and Anne Sullivan.

Houston, Jean. *Public Like a Frog: Entering the Lives of Three Great Americans.* Wheaton, Ill.: Theosophical Publishing, 1993. Concise biographical sketches of Emily Dickinson, Thomas Jefferson, and Helen Keller, highlighting their spirituality. This work is unique in that the biographies are interspersed with personal growth exercises that invite the reader's imaginative participation in crucial moments of the subjects' lives.

Keller, Helen. *Midstream: My Later Life.* New York: Greenwood, 1968. The story of Keller's life from around 1904 until 1927. Describes her work for the blind, her lecturing and writing career, her experiences in Hollywood, and her relationships with some well-known public figures, including Mark Twain, Alexander Graham Bell, and the Carnegie family.

---. *The Story of My Life.* New York: Collier Macmillan International, 1972. The best-known of Keller's autobiographical works, this book tells the story of her first two decades and includes a selection of letters that illustrate the development of her language skills from the age of seven to adulthood. Contains a useful short introduction by Lou Ann Walker.

---. *Teacher, Anne Sullivan Macy.* Garden City, N.Y.: Doubleday, 1955. Keller's respectful and loving account of Sullivan's life. Seeks to redress what Keller saw as an imbalance between excessive public attention on herself and neglect of Sullivan's accomplishments.

Lash, Joseph P. *Helen and Teacher: The Story of Helen Keller and Anne Sullivan Macy.* New York: Delacorte, 1980. This long dual biography, part of the Radcliffe Biography series, acknowledges the long, fruitful relationship between Keller and Sullivan.

Nielsen, Kim E. *The Radical Lives of Helen Keller.* New

York: New York University Press, 2004. Biography focusing on Keller's political views, describing her radicalism and anti-capitalist activism.

_____, ed. *Helen Keller: Selected Writings*. New York: New York University Press, 2005. Collection of Keller's letters, excerpts of manuscripts, and other writings that provide insight into her life and ideas.

MARTIN LUTHER KING, JR.

Civil Rights activist and religious leader

Born: January 15, 1929; Atlanta, Georgia
Died: April 4, 1968; Memphis, Tennessee
Areas of achievement: Civil rights; Religion and theology; Social issues

Leader of the African American movement for civil rights and legal equality in the United States, King was known for his stirring speeches and his use of nonviolent resistance to racial segregation and discrimination.

Martin Luther King (Library of Congress)

EARLY LIFE

Martin Luther King, Jr., was born January 15, 1929, in Atlanta, Georgia, the son of a prominent minister who soon became pastor of Atlanta's Ebenezer Baptist Church. His family was part of the African American elite that lived and worked along Auburn Avenue in Atlanta, and King's early life was one of comparative privilege and comfort. His father's travel and study in Germany resulted in King's name being changed from Michael to Martin Luther in 1934, in honor of the founder of the Protestant Reformation. King earned a bachelor of arts degree in sociology in 1948 from Atlanta's Morehouse College, a bachelor of divinity degree from Crozier Seminary in 1951, and a Ph.D. from Boston University in 1955. He married Coretta Scott on June 18, 1953, in Heiberger, Alabama. They had four children. While King sang in a choral event that accompanied the opening of *Gone with the Wind*—a film criticized for its depictions of African Americans—in Atlanta in 1939, he also refused to yield his seat on a bus in rural Georgia in 1944, until a teacher persuaded him to do so. His early life seemed to have prepared him for a comfortable pastorate or a university teaching position, but he concluded that he should pursue a vocation where he was most needed.

LIFE'S WORK

In 1954, King assumed the pastorate at the Dexter Avenue Baptist Church in Montgomery, Alabama. The church had historically catered to the African American elite in Jim Crow Alabama. Almost immediately, King urged his congregants to register to vote and to join the National Association for the Advancement of Colored People (NAACP). In December, 1955, he became president of the Montgomery Improvement Association, which spearheaded a yearlong boycott of that city's buses to compel an end to segregated seating. After their success in December, 1956, King and other leading southern African American ministers established the Southern Christian Leadership Conference (SCLC) in 1957. The Atlanta-based ministerial alliance helped orchestrate and support civil rights activism across the South. In 1958, King published his first book, *Stride Toward Freedom: The Montgomery Story*, a memoir of the bus boycott. In 1960, he became the associate pastor of Ebenezer Baptist Church.

King believed that nonviolent protest would incite violent reaction by the South's politicians and police, winning the moral high ground for African Americans while highlighting the pervasive racism of the region. Such moral drama, he believed, might bring about important external pressure on the South to grant full civil rights to African Americans. King grounded his activism in his personal faith, but he also drew heavily on philosopher Reinhold Niebuhr's ideas concerning the reality of evil and the irony of racism in United States history, Mahatma Gandhi's belief in the power of passive resistance, and Henry David Thoreau's notion of civil disobedience.

King's evolving strategies to achieve political and social ends met with successes and failures. Attempting to assist the Student Nonviolent Coordinating Committee (SNCC) in registering African American voters in Albany, Georgia, in 1961 and 1962, King went to jail rather than pay a fine following his arrest. The Albany police chief, Laurie Pritchett, released King after three days, responding to King's nonviolent tactics with moderation and denying King public martyrdom. In addition, the SCLC, NAACP, and SNCC became mired in jurisdictional disputes that undermined the movement's unity.

More successful was the SCLC-directed campaign in Birmingham, Alabama, in 1963. There, Eugene "Bull" *Martin Luther King, Jr., and Coretta Scott King in 1964.* (Library of Congress) Connor, the public safety commissioner, had protesters doused by high pressure fire hoses and attacked by police dogs, then arrested. Television stations filmed these demonstrations, recording images that were seared into the national consciousness. King was jailed again and wrote his *Letter from Birmingham City Jail* (1963), which justified his involvement as a minister, a Christian, and a citizen in protesting the race discrimination in jobs and by law enforcement in Birmingham. The city's leaders, facing the loss of business and a deluge of negative publicity, agreed to endmost of their overt discrimination.

March on Washington for Jobs and Freedom (Wikimedia Commons)

> "*Life's most persistent and urgent question is: 'What are you doing for others?'*"

From August of 1963 through March of 1965, King's appeal to Christian morality and a color-blind application of the Constitution reached its zenith, attracting support from whites in addition to African Americans. King's stirring "I Have a Dream" speech, delivered from the steps of the Lincoln Memorial on August 28, 1963, as part of the massive March on Washington for Jobs and Freedom, became the rhetorical high point of the entire Civil Rights movement. King called for a democracy based on character, rather than skin pigmentation. In 1965, after the initial march from Selma to Montgomery, Alabama, was violently halted by white law-enforcement officials at the Edmund Pettus Bridge, King participated in a second, successful march that inspired President Lyndon B. Johnson to push for and sign the Voting Rights Act of 1965, which outlawed discriminatory voting practices in the South and gave the national government the task of ensuring voting rights in states where minorities had been historically excluded from the democratic process. In 1964, King was awarded the Nobel Peace Prize.

Three major events eroded the broad national support for the Civil Rights movement. First, race riots in the Watts section of Los Angeles in 1965 caused many white observers to see African Americans as figures of lawless violence, rather than long-suffering, nonviolent protesters. The emergence of the Black Power movement augmented this shift in perception. Second, the escalation of the Vietnam War diverted national attention from problems at home to the Cold War abroad. Finally, in 1966,

> **Montgomery Bus Boycott**
>
> Having endured discriminatory treatment on city buses in Montgomery, Alabama, for decades, African American citizens conducted a daylong bus boycott on December 5, 1955, the day Rosa Parks was tried for failing to yield her seat in accordance with the city's segregation ordinance. At a mass meeting that evening, Martin Luther King, Jr., was selected to head the organization that would extend the boycott. At the time, King was selected because he had not been a resident of Montgomery long enough to have made enemies in a city whose African American leadership was divided against itself. As head of the Montgomery Improvement Association, King came to national attention for his charismatic speaking. He was arrested and his home firebombed by white supremacists, but his organizational skills and belief that biblical teachings supported African American claims to equal citizenship under the Constitution steeled the 385-day boycott. The protest led to the Supreme Court affirming a lower court decision that struck down the municipal bus segregation ordinance. It also made King a national leader in the emerging Civil Rights movement.

King took his nonviolent resistance movement to Chicago to crusade for economic justice, which he increasingly portrayed as a root cause of African American disempowerment, hopelessness, and anger among the young. His movement, however, did not find unjust laws that could be challenged morally in the streets and constitutionally in the courts, and northern whites responded to his marches with violence and vitriol eerily similar to the violence in the South.

Increasingly, King came to see a connection between the violence associated with the Vietnam War and the attempts to maintain white supremacy at home. On April 4, 1967, he delivered a stirring address at New York's Riverside Church, making an explicit the connection between domestic and imperialist violence and materialism, which reduced people to things. His criticism of U.S. foreign policy drew a backlash from many of his former supporters, including President Johnson, and sharply divided the white liberal community. The following year, King continued his crusade for economic justice, which included a march on Washington and a demand for a bill of rights for America's poor. His ongoing focus on economic injustice led him to intervene in a strike by sanitation workers in Memphis, who protested their systematic dehumanization by municipal managers. On April 4, 1968, he was assassinated by James Earl Ray at the Lorraine Motel in Memphis, Tennessee, after delivering his "Been to the Mountaintop" address. In the wake of the assassination, riots erupted in many U.S. cities. Ray was captured by agents of the Federal Bureau of Investigation after a large manhunt.

Significance

King was the foremost leader of the Civil Rights movement, an eloquent and influential challenger of the national acquiescence to racism and inequality. His protest campaigns led to major federal laws affecting voting rights and housing. He became a symbol for diversity and tolerance, and his emphasis on nonviolent civil disobedience provided an example for generations of activists. Although he is best remembered for challenging racial discrimination, King's concern went beyond civil rights to include attacks on poverty at home and imperialism abroad. The creation of a national holiday in his honor, the first such holiday for an African American, illustrated his status as a national icon, rather than solely an African American one.

Edward R. Crowther

Further Reading

Burns, Stewart. *To the Mountaintop: Martin Luther King, Jr.'s Sacred Mission to Save America, 1955-1968*. San Francisco: HarperCollins, 2004. Especially rich in oral history, Burns's work emphasizes King's humanity and internal struggles.

Fairclough, Adam. *Better Day Coming: Blacks and Equality, 1890-2000*. New York: Penguin Books, 2001. An accessible overview of the Civil Rights movement in the twentieth century and King's role in it.

Garrow, David J. *Bearing the Cross: Martin Luther King, Jr., and the Southern Christian Leadership Conference*. New York: William Morrow, 1986. A Pulitzer Prizewinner, this biography is extensively researched.

King, Martin Luther, Jr. *A Call to Conscience: The Landmark Speeches of Dr. Martin Luther King, Jr.* Edited by Clayborne Carson and Kris Shepard. New York: Warner Books, 2001. A stirring collection of twelve of

King's greatest speeches; an audio edition also is available.

Lewis, David L. *King: A Biography*. New York: Praeger, 1970. Despite appearing before many of King's papers were made public, Lewis's study is especially insightful. Sitkoff, Harvard. *King: Pilgrimage to the Mountaintop*. New York: Hill & Wang, 2008. An outstanding short, interpretive biography that portrays King as a radical and polarizing figure whose prophetic voice impeached widely held assumptions about race, religion, and national destiny.

Thornton, J. Mills, III. *Dividing Lines: Municipal Politics and the Struggle for Civil Rights in Montgomery, Birmingham, and Selma*. Tuscaloosa: University of Alabama Press, 2002. Without peer in its explanation of the contours of the Civil Rights movement and King's role in three key cities.

JOHN L. LEWIS

Labor leader

Born: February 12, 1880; Cleveland, Iowa
Died: June 11, 1969; Alexandria, Virginia
Areas of Achievement: Labor movement, social reform

As president of the United Mine Workers union and founder of the Congress of Industrial Organizations, Lewis dominated the progress of organized labor in the United States from the 1920's through the 1960's.

EARLY LIFE

John Llewellyn Lewis was the son of Thomas Lewis and Louisa (née Watkins) Lewis, who had been born in Wales and had migrated to the United States in the 1870's. John was the eldest of six sons and two daughters. Thomas worked as a coal miner whenever he could find work, but, having been placed on an employer blacklist for leading a miners' strike in 1882, he often had to fill in with other jobs, such as working as a night watchman.

Young Lewis only went as far as the eighth grade before leaving school to supplement his father's meager and irregular income. He sold newspapers in Des Moines, Iowa, for a few years until the abolition of the blacklist in 1897 allowed his father to return to Lucas, where Lewis, then age seventeen, joined him in the coal mines. Lewis worked there until 1901 and then set off on a working tour of Western mining communities, toiling in copper, silver, gold, and coal mines in Montana, Utah, Arizona, and Colorado. Soon after returning to Lucas in 1906, he married Myrta Edith Bell, the daughter of a local doctor. They would have three children: Margaret Mary (who died in childhood), Florence Kathryn, and John Llewellyn II.

Shortly before Lewis's marriage, the Lucas miners elected him as a delegate to the national convention of the United Mine Workers of America (UMWA), the largest union affiliated with the American Federation of Labor (AFL). A few years later, in 1909, he moved his family to Panama, Illinois, and continued his union activity. He was selected president of the Panama miners' local union and soon thereafter was appointed state legislative agent for District 12 of the UMWA. It was in this capacity that he convinced the Illinois legislature to pass a comprehensive package of mine safety and workmen's compensation laws by exploiting the Cherry, Illinois, mine disaster of 1911 that killed 160 men.

Samuel Gompers (founder and president of the AFL), impressed by Lewis's obvious leadership talents, took the young labor activist under his wing and made him a national legislative representative for the AFL in late 1911. This job took Lewis to Washington, D.C., where he was able to learn valuable lessons regarding the politics and

John L. Lewis (Library of Congress)

management of labor organization. He also continued his rise through the ranks of the UMWA. In 1916, he served as temporary chair of the UMWA's national convention and, in 1917, he was elected vice president of the union.

Lewis had his first taste of national-level labor confrontation when, in 1919, he became acting president of the union for Frank J. Hayes, who had become too debilitated by alcoholism to carry out his duties. Several months after assuming this position, Lewis called for a strike when mine operators rejected the union's demand for a 60 percent wage hike, a six-hour workday, and a five-day workweek. A federal court issued an injunction against the strike, but, in November, 1919, Lewis defied the injunction, ordering 425,000 men out of the mines.

The strike lasted two months and, after a face-to-face meeting with President Woodrow Wilson, Lewis was forced to call the miners back to work. They did gain a wage increase of approximately 30 percent, but their other demands went unsatisfied. The rough, bulky, bushy-eyebrowed Lewis did gain a reputation for toughness during the strike, however, and he parlayed this into an official UMWA presidency in 1920. He would hold this position until he retired in 1960.

LIFE'S WORK

Lewis assumed the presidency of the UMWA at a time when the coal industry had begun to experience serious difficulties. Coal output had skyrocketed between 1916 and 1919 to meet wartime needs but, once World War I was over, demand dropped back to more normal levels, causing a glut of coal on the market. In addition, mine owners with union workers faced rising competition from nonunion mines in the South and from "captive" mines owned by steel companies and railroads. In an effort to meet these threats, unionized producers began to lower both prices and miners' wages. Lewis refused to agree to this wage-reduction strategy and, in 1922, he called a strike. Miners did win a wage increase to $7.50 a day as a result of this strike, but many only worked irregularly as the crisis persisted.

> "Let the workers organize. Let the toilers assemble. Let their crystallized voice proclaim their injustices and demand their privileges. Let all thoughtful citizens sustain them, for the future of Labor is the future of America."

In the years that followed, the situation in the coal industry continued to deteriorate. More than three thousand mines shut down during the 1920's and UMWA membership dropped from a high of 500,000 in 1922 to 150,000 by 1930. Lewis responded by urging coal operators to increase their productivity and thereby halt the precipitous decline in regular miner employment. He opposed pay cuts that were made to keep unprofitable operations in business and instead favored the closing of these marginal mines and the introduction of increased mechanization in remaining ones to make them more efficient and competitive and thus a stable source of employment for his members. Factions within the UMWA opposed Lewis's proposals and organized a series of wildcat strikes to protest his emphasis on mechanization (which they believed would cost even more jobs). This struggle within the UMWA, which also contributed to the decline in membership, culminated at the national convention of 1930, where his opponents made a concerted effort to unseat him. Lewis still had enough support within the UMWA, however, to resist these attempts and to purge the leaders of this opposition from the union.

As the Depression tightened its grip on the United States after 1930, it also aggravated the problems within the coal industry. Coal sales continued to slump, and thousands of miners lost their jobs. The UMWA, in an increasingly weakened position, could do little to resist employer attempts to reduce the wages of miners who managed to keep their jobs. It was at this point that Lewis turned to the national government for help. Although he had been a Republican throughout the 1920's and had even supported Herbert Hoover in 1932, Lewis recognized that the Democrat who defeated his man in that election, Franklin D. Roosevelt, was sympathetic to labor's plight and might come to its aid. Accordingly, Lewis swung to Roosevelt and the Democratic Party and participated actively in the New Deal. He became a labor adviser to the president, a member of the Labor Advisory Board, and a member of the National Labor Board. This close relationship between the UMWA and the Roosevelt administration benefited both parties. Because of the passage of the Guffey Act of 1935, National Labor Relations Act (or Wagner Act) of 1935, and section 7A of the National Industrial Recovery Act of 1933, miners received a substantial daily pay raise, a shortened workday, and the right to bargain collectively through their own representatives. The UMWA recovered as a result, and, by 1935, its membership was approaching one-half million again. Roosevelt, on the other hand, received the grateful votes of coal miners, relative labor peace in the mines, and large contributions from the UMWA to his campaign treasury.

Meanwhile, trouble was brewing in the AFL, and Lewis, as usual, was at the center of it. Lewis had decided that "industrial unionism" (where all workers in a given industry, regardless of their particular trade, would be part of a single union that represented them all) was the best way for workers to fight for their rights, and he tried to convince the AFL, which represented workers by their trade, to adopt this policy. At the AFL national convention of 1935, however, his proposal was soundly rejected. In response, Lewis resigned as vice president of the AFL in November, 1935, and formed a new omnibus labor organization based on industrial unionism, one that eventually became the Congress of Industrial Organizations (CIO). Lewis's UMWA led the way in affiliating with this new organization, and it was soon joined by many others. By 1938, the CIO included forty-four unions and more than four million members.

As president of the CIO, Lewis also began the hard struggle to organize automobile and steelworkers and affiliate them with his organization. Employing such tactics as the sit-down strike, he did force the automobile industry to recognize the CIO in 1937. He then convinced the nation's largest steel manufacturer, United States Steel, to accept the CIO (also in 1937). The smaller steel companies, however, such as Bethlehem and Republic Steel, put up strong resistance to Lewis's organizing efforts, forcing him to call a strike against them in May, 1937.

Marred by violence, the strike dragged on until late summer of that year, and Lewis ultimately accepted a compromise settlement that fell short of his initial goals.

The strike also provoked a break between Lewis and Roosevelt. Lewis became disappointed and frustrated at the president's lack of support for the so-called Little Steel strike and tried to rally labor behind his Republican opponent, Wendell Willkie, in the election of 1940. Roosevelt nevertheless won easily, but he never forgave Lewis for his defection. Temporarily defeated, Lewis resigned as president of the CIO and devoted his full attention to his UMWA.

Lewis (right) confers with Thomas Kennedy (left), Secretary-Treasurer of the UMW, and Pery Tetlow (center), president of UMW District 17, at the War Labor Board conference January 15, 1943, about the anthracite coal miners' strike. (Library of Congress)

Lewis opposed American involvement in World War II and stuck to this position right up to the Japanese attack on Pearl Harbor on December 7, 1941. Although he declared his support for the American war effort after this attack, his "noninvolvement" stand up to Pearl Harbor had alienated many of his former allies among the leadership of the CIO. In 1942, therefore, he pulled the UMWA out of the CIO and purged CIO sympathizers from his union.

Lewis did not allow the war to stop him from fighting for the coal miners. In 1943, he declared that the wage increase authorized by the War Labor Board was inadequate and called a strike. The conflict lasted nearly a year, and, during its course, the government temporarily took over the nation's mines and Roosevelt even appealed directly to the miners to return to work. In the end, though, Lewis won a two-dollars-per-day pay increase for his men. He called another strike in 1945 and won again, gaining an increase in overtime pay, the establishment of one-hour travel pay to and from work, and paid vacations for miners. Lewis authorized still another strike in March, 1946, which resulted in a small pay increase and, more important, the establishment of a pension and welfare fund for miners, financed by a five cents per ton royalty on all coal produced.

In October, 1946, Lewis called his third strike in fourteen months in an attempt to reduce the miners' workweek to less than fifty-four hours. A federal court judge issued a restraining order against this work stoppage. When Lewis ignored the order, the judge found him to be in criminal and civil contempt and fined him ten thousand dollars and the UMWA $3.5 million. The Supreme Court upheld the judge's order, and Lewis had no choice but to call off the strike.

In between the two strikes in 1946, Lewis had reaffiliated the UMWA with the AFL. This reconciliation lasted only a year before Lewis, after a disagreement with other AFL leaders over the organization's position regarding the new Taft-Hartley Act, withdrew the UMWA again. It would remain unaffiliated with both the AFL and CIO during the rest of his presidency.

Lewis authorized more coal strikes in 1948 and 1949 and, despite court injunctions, fines, and the strict provisions of the Taft-Hartley law, he won further wage increases, a seven-hour workday, and increases in employer contributions to the pension and welfare fund. At the time of Lewis's retirement from the UMWA presidency, a post he had held for forty years, miners earned $24.24 a day and possessed a pension fund of $1.3 billion. Lewis also devoted much of his efforts during the 1950's to improving safety in coal mines and played a major role in obtaining the passage of the Federal Mine Safety Law of 1952.

Following his retirement, Lewis served as a trustee for the union's pension and welfare fund; in 1964, he received the Presidential Medal of Freedom from President Lyndon B. Johnson. Lewis died in Washington, D.C., on June 11, 1969, at the age of eighty-nine.

Significance

Lewis transformed the coal industry and the American labor movement. When he became president of the UMWA in 1920, miners were paid seven dollars a day; they had no travel-time pay, no paid vacations, no welfare and pension fund; they had to supply their own tools; and they received no state compensation for mine accidents. In 1960, after forty years of Lewis's leadership, they made more than twenty-four dollars a day, had one hour's paid travel-time per day, a week's paid vacation, a huge pension and welfare fund, and used tools supplied by their employers. All states paid compensation for miners killed or injured in work-related accidents, and, moreover, Lewis had persuaded the federal government to enact rules regarding mine safety that were enforced by a joint operator-miner committee. Lewis not only had greatly improved the material condition of coal miners in the United States but also had made them partners with their employers in determining conditions inside the mines.

Lewis's influence spread far beyond the coalfields. His partnership with Franklin D. Roosevelt from 1932 to 1940 played a large role in determining the prolabor stance of the early New Deal and helped forge the alliance with organized labor that served the Democratic Party so well in future decades. Through his founding of the CIO in 1935 and his organizing efforts on its behalf, Lewis not only established industrial unionism on a solid and permanent foundation in the United States but also helped create the powerful United Automobile Workers and United Steel Workers unions. In addition, Lewis shaped the nature of modern collective bargaining between unions and management. By employing such tactics as the sit-down strike and through his willingness to call strikes whenever the interests of his men were threatened, regardless of the powers lined up against him, Lewis made organized labor a force to be reckoned with in the United States, one that insisted that it share in the decisions that affected it.

Lewis could be stubborn, vain, autocratic, and even abusive, given to labeling his opponents as "communists." Yet the organized labor movement in the United States made gigantic gains under his uncompromising leadership, and the American worker, not only the coal miner, is much better off because of him.

Christopher E. Guthrie

Further Reading

Alinsky, Saul. *John L. Lewis: An Unauthorized Biography.* New York: G. P. Putnam's Sons, 1949. The author was a formidable organizer himself and he appreciates Lewis's talents in this regard. Yet he is also at pains to point out what he sees as weaknesses in Lewis's character, abilities, and tactics. This book is a good, balanced portrait of Lewis the man and Lewis the organizer.

Carnes, Cecil. *John L. Lewis.* New York: Robert Speller, 1936. Published shortly after Lewis founded the CIO in 1935, this book provides a rather colorless account of his career up to that point.

Dubofsky, Melvyn, and Warren Van Tine. *John L. Lewis: A Biography.* Urbana: University of Illinois Press, 1977. This book is not only the most comprehensive and well-written study of Lewis; it is also an often brilliant analytical survey of the American labor movement from 1920 to 1960.

Kurland, Gerald. *John L. Lewis: Labor's Strong-Willed Organizer*. Charlotteville, N.Y.: SamHar Press, 1973. A short (one-hundred-page) general examination of Lewis's life and work. It will provide the interested reader with the highlights of Lewis's career but little else.

McFarland, C. K. *Roosevelt, Lewis, and the New Deal, 1933-1940*. Fort Worth: Texas Christian University Press, 1970. A good and concise investigation of the relationship between Lewis and Roosevelt up until their official split during the presidential election in 1940, this book falls a little short in explaining the long-range repercussions of this seven-year partnership.

Preis, Art. *Labor's Giant Step: Twenty Years of the CIO*. New York: Pathfinder Press, 1972. In the course of tracing the first two decades of the CIO, the author also presents a fairly objective portrait of Lewis's role in creating and then almost destroying the organization.

Wechsler, James A. *Labor Baron: A Portrait of John L. Lewis*. New York: William Morrow, 1944. Reprint. Westport, Conn.: Greenwood Press, 1972. Emphasizes Lewis's negative side and downplays his positive achievements.

Zieger, Robert H., and Gilbert J. Gall. *American Workers, American Unions: The Twentieth Century*. 3d ed. Baltimore: Johns Hopkins University Press, 2002. This history of the American labor movement includes information about Lewis.

Malcolm X

Black nationalist leader

Born: May 19, 1925; Omaha, Nebraska
Died: February 21, 1965; New York City, New York
Also known as: Malcolm Little (birth name); El-Hajj Malik el-Shabazz
Areas of Achievement: Religion and theology; Social issues

One of the most charismatic and dynamic personalities of the Civil Rights era, Malcolm X was the public face of the Nation of Islam and a strong defender of the rights and interests of African Americans.

Early Life

Malcolm X was the son of Earl Little, a Baptist preacher who actively participated in Marcus Garvey's Universal Negro Improvement Association. Malcolm inherited his light complexion from his mother, Louise Little, whose father was of Scottish ancestry, and he was given the nickname "Red" because of the tinge of his hair. Initially he took pride in his skin color, but in later life he said that he "hated every drop of that white rapist's blood that is in me." While Malcolm was a baby, the family moved to Lansing, Michigan, after reportedly being forced to leave Omaha by the Ku Klux Klan. When he was six years old, his father died under mysterious circumstances, leaving the family in poverty. Eight years later, his mother was declared legally insane and committed to a mental asylum, where she lived for twenty-six years. The siblings were split up, and Malcolm was sent to live with a series of white foster parents.

Although Malcolm succeeded academically in junior high school, he increasingly became embittered toward white authority figures. In his autobiography, he wrote that he dropped out of school after his eighth-grade teacher told him that his ambition to become a lawyer was not a "realistic goal for a nigger." Like many young men in such circumstances, he became involved in petty

Malcolm X (Library of Congress)

crimes and was sent to reform schools. In 1941, at the age of sixteen, he moved to Boston to live with his half sister, Ella Collins, and two years later he moved to New York City. While holding a number of low-paying jobs, he increasingly participated in the night life of the zoot suiters and was attracted to the money that could be acquired from the sale of drugs, robbery, racketeering, and prostitution. According to biographer Bruce Perry, some of Malcolm's former associates reported that he sometimes worked as a gay hustler. When ordered to register for the draft in 1943, he later claimed to have escaped military service by telling the examining officer that he hoped to steal guns and kill white people.

After returning to Boston in 1945, Malcolm participated in several burglaries of wealthy white residences. In early 1946, he was arrested, convicted, and sentenced to eight to ten years in the Massachusetts State Prison, where he developed an appetite for reading. His brother Reginald introduced him to the teachings of Elijah Muhammad, the founder of the Nation of Islam (NOI), whose heterodox version of the Islamic religion included the notion that whites were inherently wicked. Despite his earlier antireligious perspective, Malcolm became an enthusiastic convert and began a personal correspondence with Muhammad.

LIFE'S WORK

After he was paroled in 1952, Malcolm X began to work as a full-time minister and recruiter for the Nation of Islam. Reflecting his new identity, he replaced his "white slave-master" surname of Little with "X," which represented the unknown name of his African ancestors. A talented orator and charismatic leader, Malcolm also was a tireless worker and completely dedicated to the Nation's mission. Within two years, he was promoted to minister of New York Temple No. 7, and he helped to establish temples in several northern cities. In 1957, he became the Nation's national representative, the second most powerful position in the organization. His leadership was an important factor in the growth of the Nation's membership from five hundred in 1952 to twenty-five thousand in 1963. In 1958, he married Betty X (later called Betty Shabazz); the couple eventually had six daughters.

Malcolm's electrifying speeches attracted a great deal of support among discontented African Americans, and he became something of an icon for the Nation in the national media. He was a staunch follower of its strict moral code and gender conventions. In private, he reportedly expressed skepticism about whether all of the organization's religious doctrines were literally true. Gradually he developed his own ideology of Black Nationalism, which he defined as economic autonomy, organized self-defense, racial and cultural pride, and eventually a separate nation for African Americans. Many white Americans saw Malcolm as a racist who preached a dangerous and vindictive message, especially after the broadcast of the 1959 television documentary on the Nation of Islam titled *The Hate That Hate Produced*.

Malcolm was particularly critical of the nonviolent strategy utilized by Martin Luther King, Jr., whom he called a "chump" for the white establishment. Malcolm called for African Americans to defend their interests "by any means necessary." An example of his disciplined form of militancy occurred in 1957, when a black Muslim, Hinton Johnson, was refused medical attention while in police custody. Malcolm assembled Temple 7's menacing paramilitary force, the Fruit of Islam, in front of the police station, where officials quickly agreed to provide Johnson with appropriate treatment. Malcolm referred to the 1963 March on Washington as "the farce on Washington." He admired and frequently praised left-wing revolutionary leaders in other countries, such as Fidel Castro and Patrice Lumumba. After President John F. Kennedy's

Malcolm X being interviewed by reporters. (Library of Congress)

that Muhammad was not practicing the code of sexual morality required of members. In addition, he strongly disagreed with the prophet's refusal to engage in political activities. On March 8, 1964, Malcolm publicly announced his separation from the organization, explaining that he was going to organize a Black Nationalist organization that would strive to "heighten the political consciousness" of African Americans. On March 26, 1964, after a Senate hearing on the Civil Rights Act, he had a one-minute meeting with King, the only time the two men met.

In Cleveland on April 3, 1964, Malcolm delivered perhaps his most famous speech, titled "The Ballot or the Bullet," which called for racial unity and militancy in the pursuit of freedom. Emphasizing the need for Black Nationalism, he stated: "No, I'm not an American. I'm one of the twenty-two million black people who are the victims of Americanism." While advising members of his race to exercise their right to vote judiciously, he warned that if white society continued to deny them full racial equality, it would be necessary to take up arms in a revolution that would require "bloodshed."

> "We declare our right on this earth to be a human being, to be respected as a human being, to be given the rights of a human being in this society, on this earth, in this day, which we intend to bring into existence by any means necessary."

Having left the Nation of Islam, Malcolm moved in the direction of a more orthodox form of Sunni Islam, and he studied Sunni doctrines under Dr. Mahmoud Shuwarbi. On April 13, he left the United States for Saudi Arabia to participate in the Hajj (pilgrimage), where he was treated as a visiting dignitary. Returning home on May 21, he took a Sunni name, El-Hajj Malik El-Shabazz, and announced that he had learned from the pilgrimage that not all white men were devils. That summer, he established a religious organization, Muslim Mosque, Inc., as well as a secular group, the Organization of Afro-American Unity. The media's attention on Malcolm's activities intensified the anger of Black Muslims at his defection, and there were indications that his life might be in danger. On December 4, an article written by Boston minister Louis Farrakhan declared that "such a man as Malcolm is worthy of death." On February 14, 1965, Malcolm's home in Queens burned to the ground.

Malcolm's Pilgrimage to Mecca

After undertaking the Hajj—the pilgrimage to Mecca required of orthodox Muslims with financial means, Malcolm X wrote his followers "A Letter from Mecca," asserting that the experience had caused him to modify some of his previous "thought-patterns" about race relations. Never before had he "witnessed such sincere hospitality and overwhelming spirit of true brotherhood as is practiced by people of all colors and races." Declaring that Islam "is the one religion that erases from its society the race problem," he concluded that if white Americans could only learn to acknowledge "the Oneness of God," then perhaps they might accept "the Oneness of man—and cease to measure, and hinder, and harm others in terms of their 'differences' in color."

Scholars disagree about the extent to which "A Letter from Mecca" accurately expressed Malcolm's perceptions in 1964. He must have known that not all Muslims of the world eschewed racial discrimination and exploitation. Some commentators argue that the main goal of the letter was to promote Islam by presenting an idealized description of race relations under the religion. Shawna Maglangbayan suggests that Malcolm possibly "mistook the momentary, euphoric fervor" of a religious pilgrimage for "a permanent state of amity among peoples of all colors." Bruce Perry has suggested that the letter was the attempt of a "gifted politician" to justify his "shift in political position without undermining his credibility." Most commentators, nevertheless, accept Malcolm's claim that the Hajj caused him to modify his earlier assumptions about the inherent racism and selfishness of whites.

---

assassination in 1963, he characterized the event as the "chickens coming home to roost," adding that seeing chickens return home "always made me glad." The remarks provoked a widespread outcry by the public, and Muhammad responded by prohibiting Malcolm from speaking for ninety days.

By the time of his silencing, Malcolm had already begun to split from the NOI. He had obtained information

On February 21, 1965, in Manhattan's Audubon Ballroom, Malcolm was speaking at a meeting of the Organization of Afro-American Unity when three armed men rushed the stage. Malcolm was shot once in the chest with a shotgun, followed by fourteen rounds from handguns. He was pronounced dead shortly after reaching the hospital. Angry onlookers subdued one of the attackers, Thomas Hayer, and several eyewitnesses claimed to recognize the two men who escaped. All three were NOI members. At trial, Hayer confessed, but the other two insisted on their innocence. The three men were found guilty of first-degree murder, sentenced to life imprisonment, and eventually paroled. Several conspiracy theorists have alleged that law-enforcement officials knew about the assassination before it occurred, especially after it was learned that at least one Federal Bureau of Investigation (FBI) agent had infiltrated the Nation. Although Farrakhan denied any direct involvement, he later admitted that he had "created the atmosphere" that led to Malcolm's murder.

SIGNIFICANCE

Malcolm X was one the most influential black leaders of the twentieth century. Numerous African Americans, especially in northern and Western urban areas, looked to him as the most effective spokesman for their frustrations and anger about continuing inequality. In addition to promoting the development of black pride, his teachings provided part of the foundation of the Black Power movement. He was responsible for much of the spread of Islam in the United States, but his influence was much more important in the realm of racial issues than in religion. Although he did not directly support the Civil Rights movement, many historians have concluded that his militant rhetoric encouraged African Americans to push aggressively for equal rights, while convincing some moderate whites that social change was necessary to maintain peace.

Thomas Tandy Lewis

FURTHER READING

Carson, Clayborne. *Malcolm X: The FBI File*. New York: Carroll & Graf, 1991. Compilation of FBI reports from 1953 to 1965, revealing much about Malcolm's activities and the Federal Bureau of Investigation's agenda.

Cone, James H. *Martin and Malcolm and America: A Dream or a Nightmare*. Maryknoll: Orbis Books, 1991. Cone argues that a creative interplay between Malcolm and King had an impact on both of them and on the movements they led.

Dyson, Michael E. *Making Malcolm: The Myth and Meaning of Malcolm X*. New York: Oxford University Press, 1995. The first half evaluates the different "Malcolms" in popular culture and academic studies; the second half examines Malcolm's relationship to contemporary social movements.

Jenkins, Robert L. *The Malcolm X Encyclopedia*. Westport, Conn.: Greenwood Press, 2002. Useful reference for obtaining quick information about people, events, ideas, and organizations related to Malcolm.

Malcolm X and Alex Haley. *The Autobiography of Malcolm X*. 1965. Reprint. New York: Random House, 1987. A classic work that frankly discusses Malcolm's youthful mistakes. Essential reading for anyone interested in African American history or race relations.

Marable, Manning. *Malcolm X: A Life of Reinvention*. New York: Viking, 2011. This well-researched biography reexamines widely accepted beliefs about Malcolm X's life and death.

Perry, Bruce. *Malcolm: The Life of the Man Who Changed Black America*. Barrytown, N.Y.: Station Hill Press, 1991. A scholarly biography that challenges the accuracy of parts of Malcolm's autobiography and argues that his hard exterior concealed a sensitive and vulnerable man.

Terrill, Robert F. *Malcolm X: Inventing Radical Judgment*. East Lansing: Michigan State University Press, 2007. Analysis of Malcolm's rhetoric, emphasizing that he worked within a speech tradition that he modified.

CHERRÍE MORAGA

Playwright, scholar, and feminist

Born: September 25, 1952; Los Angeles, California
Area of Achievement: Scholarship, theater, social issues, gay and lesbian issues

Known for her autobiographical works that explore the multifaceted aspects of her Chicana lesbian identity and multigenerational familial relationships, Moraga is also a prolific playwright and community activist. Her works explore the complex connections of sexuality, race, gender, and class and the inequities and challenges experienced by women of color.

Cherríe Moraga (Wikimedia Commons)

Early Life

Cherríe Moraga (cheh-REE moh-RAH-gah) was born Cher'rie Cecilia Lawrence in the Los Angeles area, California, to parents Elvira and Joseph. Moraga is the youngest of three children born to a Chicana mother and an Anglo father, and Moraga's work is influenced by the relationship between her parents and by her struggles to integrate the different aspects of her racial identity. When she was nine, Moraga and her family relocated to San Gabriel, California, where she was daily exposed to her mother's extended family and Chicano familial connections. The influence of family, the style of her family's oral storytelling, and the significance of female familial bonds are apparent in Moraga's works.

Moraga and her siblings were the first generation in her family to pursue college degrees, and Moraga completed her teaching degree in English at Immaculate Heart College in 1974. Moraga began to write creatively and grappled with her lesbian consciousness while attending college. In 1975, Moraga came out as a lesbian and began to write openly about her sexuality. In 1977, she relocated to the San Francisco area. Influenced by the racism and heterocentrism in the largely white feminist movement and the sexism and heterocentrism within the Black Power and Chicano movements, her writing became focused on the matters affecting women of color because of societal oppressions based on class, race, and sexuality. She received her M.A. from San Francisco State University in 1980.

Life's Work

Moraga's experiences with her identities and her desire to pursue a career as a writer and playwright led her to New York City after she received her M.A. degree. In 1981, Moraga co-founded Kitchen Table: Women of Color Press, whose primary goal was to publish works by women of color. Moraga also coedited, along with Gloria Anzaldúa, the foundational feminist text, *This Bridge Called My Back: Writings by Radical Women of Color* (1983). This anthology contains essays, poems, and narratives by a multitude of writers, including Moraga, on various subjects that impact the lives of women of color.

Moraga's autobiographical text, *Loving in the War Years: Lo que nunca pasó por sus labios*, was published in 1983 and considered groundbreaking for its exploration of lesbian identity, the potential violence that impacts the lives of lesbians of color, the critique of Chicana familial relationships and histories, and Moraga's use of Spanish in her prose and poetry throughout the text.

> "*Remember you live in a community. You have a responsibility to be accountable to your family and your community as well as yourself.*"

Giving up the Ghost (1986) became the first of many plays written by Moraga and confronts issues of sexual violence, the oppression felt by women of color because of societal injustices, and lesbian sexuality and love. This work was followed by *Shadow of a Man* (1992), *Heroes and Saints, and Other Plays* (1994), *Heart of the Earth: A Popol Vuh Story* (2000), *The Hungry Woman: A Mexican Medea* (2000), *Watsonville: Some Place Not Here* (2000), *Circle in the Dirt: El Pueblo de East Palo Alto* (2002), *Waiting for Da God* (2004), *Digging up the Dirt* (2010), and *New Fire: To Put Things Right Again* (2012). Her most recent play, *The Mathematics of Love* debuted in 2017 in San Francisco. Her plays have considered issues of oppressive mythologies, community activism, and the lived experiences of women of color.

In 1993, Moraga published *The Last Generation*, a collection of poems and essays that analyze the loss of culture in Chicano communities and the inclusion of homosexual-identified individuals in a Chicano future. She later published *Waiting in the Wings: Portrait of a Queer*

Motherhood (1997), an autobiographical text sharing her experiences in becoming a mother. Moraga's most recent poetry collection was published in 2011, entitled *A Xicana Codex of Changing Consciousness: Writings, 2000-2010*.

Moraga has spent much of her career as an educator, serving as the artist-in-residence in the Department of Drama at Stanford University and teaching courses such as Creative Writing and Latino/Queer Performance. She has received numerous awards for her works and community activism.

Significance

In Loving in the War Years, Moraga articulated her experiences in coming to consciousness as a Chicana lesbian struggling to find her identity in the liminal spaces between white and Chicano cultures, between her sexuality and a homophobic society, and between her generation and those of Chicanas before her. These personal revelations about sexuality and racial identity, as well as commentary on the oppressions experienced by women of color everywhere, have impacted the evolution of homosexual, Chicana, and feminist studies. Her consistent efforts to address these issues as a playwright, essayist, poet, activist, and educator are Moraga's legacy.

Erin Ranft, updated by Micah L. Issitt

Further Reading

Kevane, Bridget A., and Juanita Heredia. *Latina Self-Portraits: Interviews with Contemporary Women Writers*. Albuquerque: University of New Mexico Press, 2000. Contains an interview with Moraga in which she shares her insights and opinions about connections between the Chicano community and academia, about writing, and about the utility and importance of language.

Moraga, Cherríe, and Gloria Anzaldúa. *This Bridge Called My Back: Writings by Radical Women of Color*. Berkeley, Calif.: Third Woman Press, 2002. This third edition of the text includes the original introductions and preface, an introduction by Moraga in which she reflects on the publication of *This Bridge*, and commentary on the political, economic, and social issues that continue to impact women of color.

Sternback, Nancy Saporta. "'A Deep Racial Memory of Love:' The Chicana Feminism of Cherríe Moraga." In *Breaking Boundaries: Latina Writing and Critical Readings*, edited by Asunción Horno-Delgado, Eliana Ortega, Nina M. Scott, and Nancy Saporta Sternbach. Amherst: University of Massachusetts Press, 1989. An examination of Moraga's Loving in the War Years and its influential and groundbreaking Chicana lesbian feminist content.

Yarbro-Bejarano, Yvonne. *The Wounded Heart: Writing on Cherríe Moraga*. Austin: University of Texas Press, 2001. A close reading of Moraga's work on the body, sexuality, and desire.

Bree Newsome

Civil Rights activist and artist

Born: c. 1984; Charlotte, North Carolina
Also known as: Brittany Ann Newsome
Area of achievement: Activism

In 2015, following the murder of nine African Americans in a church in South Carolina, activist Bree Newsome shimmied up a flagpole at the South Carolina State House and removed the Confederate flag that had flown there—

Bree Newsome. (Alberto E. Rodriguez/Getty Images)

amid strong controversy—ever since 1962.

Early Life

Bree Newsome was born Brittany Ann Newsome in Charlotte, North Carolina. She moved with her family to the Maryland suburbs of Washington DC in 1986 when her father, Dr. Clarence G. Newsome, a professor of religious studies at Duke University, took a job as the dean of the Howard University School of Divinity. Bree had an early interest in the arts, and her parents encouraged her talents. When she was only seven years old, she wrote her first song on the piano; she would later found a funk band. Every summer, Bree traveled from Maryland to Charlotte, North Carolina, to be with her grandmother and extended family.

Newsome attended Oakland Mills High School in Columbia, Maryland. While she was there, she made an animated short film that won her a $40,000 scholarship from the National Academy of Television Arts and Sciences. She then studied film at the Tisch School of the Arts at New York University. Her senior project, a short horror film called *Wake*, won several awards and screened at several film festivals, including the Cannes Film Festival in 2010.

Life's Work

Newsome's first national attention came with the success of a music video that she made with her funk band, Powerhouse. The video, called "Shake It Like an Etch-A-Sketch" mocked Republican politician Mitt Romney and circulated widely on social media in 2012. Newsome first experience with political activism came in 2013, when she was inspired by the Reverend William Barber II. Beginning in April 2013, Barber led regular civil-rights protests in North Carolina's state capital, Raleigh. These events, called "Moral Mondays," drew press from around the nation and earned Barber recognition as one of the most important progressive leader the South. They also galvanized many young people, including Bree Newsome. She became involved in other protests and demonstrations, and over the next year or two traveled to various places in the country to participate in protests, including Florida to protest the killing of Trayvon Martin and Ohio to protest the killing of John Crawford. (Crawford was an African-American man who was shot and killed by police inside a Wal-Mart while talking on his cell phone and holding a piece of store merchandise that he was going to buy—a BB gun. No charges were filed against the officers.)

The events that led to Bree's most famous moment as an activist began on June 17, 2015, in Charleston, South Carolina, when Dylann Roof walked into a prayer service at Emanuel African Methodist Episcopal Church. Roof, who was nineteen years old and a self-declared white supremacist, shot and killed nine people in the church, all of them African Americans, including the pastor and state senator Clementa Pinckney. One other person was injured. Roof later confessed that he committed the shooting with the hope of starting a race war. The incident led to a national discussion about lingering ideologies of white racial superiority in America and about the legacy of slavery and the Confederacy in the South. In particular, a debate was reignited regarding the meaning of the Confederate flag, a controversial symbol in popular culture since its resurgence around the time of the Civil War centennial.

"I removed the flag not only in defiance of those who enslaved my ancestors in the southern United States, but also in defiance of the oppression that continues against black people globally in 2015, including the ongoing ethnic cleansing in the Dominican Republic. I did it in solidarity with the South African students who toppled a statue of the white supremacist, colonialist Cecil Rhodes. I did it for all the fierce black women on the front lines of the movement and for all the little black girls who are watching us. I did it because I am free."

South Carolina's State House had been implicated in the flag controversy like no other government institution. In 1961, ostensibly to mark the anniversary of the Civil War, the Confederate flag was flown over the State House dome. Then, in 1962, South Carolina's lawmakers decreed that the Confederate flag would henceforth be flown atop the dome on a permanent basis. This was understood, nearly universally, to be a gesture of thumbing the nose at the civil rights movement. In 1980, South Carolina's lawmakers passed a resolution rescinding that 1962 order. From 1980 onward, the Confederate flag was flown instead from a pole in the courtyard in front of the building and not atop the dome. In the days after the killings, the Republican governor of South Carolina, Nikki Haley, gave an impassioned speech calling on lawmakers to permanently remove the flag from the State House. President Barack Obama, likewise, asked that it be moved to a museum. Newsome and other activists, meanwhile, were discussing removing the flag in a direct action. Newsome was, in fact, already on a train riding to Columbia, South Carolina's capitol, when she heard President Obama's eulogy and remarks about the flag.

Ten days after the killings, on June 27, 2015, Newsome shimmied up the thirty-foot flagpole wearing climbing gear and a protective helmet. By the time she reached the top, police were already waiting at the base of the pole. She informed them that she was prepared to be arrested and go to jail. Newsome was charged with a misdemeanor: defacing a monument on capitol grounds. Her act of civil disobedience quickly made headlines around the world. Within a few hours, more than $60,000 dollars was raised for legal costs, although the fine was only $3,000. Since that memorable moment, Newsome has given many interviews and spoken at colleges and other venues around the country.

Significance

Although the flag was raised again a mere forty-five minutes after Newsome's action, the symbolism of the gesture was powerful, and the action itself was visually compelling. On July 10, 2015, the flag was officially taken down by order of governor Nikki Haley. It was given to the South Carolina Confederate Relic Room and Military Museum. In 2016 Newsome was given the NAACP Image Award. Newsome has settled into work as a community activist in her home in Charlotte, where she focuses on access to affordable housing; she continues to work as an artist as well.

Dewayne Dean

Further Reading

Contrera, Jessica. "Who Is Bree Newsome? Why the Woman Who Took Down the Confederate Flag Became an Activist." Washington Post. June 28, 2015. https://www.washingtonpost.com/news/arts-and-entertainment/wp/2015/06/28/who-is-bree-newsome-why-the-woman-who-took-down-the-confederate-flag-became-an-activist/

Evans, Kelley D. "Bree Newsome's Social Justice Fight Continues Two Years After Taking Down the Confederate Flag in South Carolina." The Undefeated. September 11, 2017. https://theundefeated.com/features/bree-newsome-social-justice-fight-two-years-after-taking-down-the-confederate-flag-in-south-carolina/

Queen Noor

Queen Dowager of Jordan, activist, architect

Born: August 23, 1951; Washington, D.C.
Full name: Queen Noor al-Hussein
Birth name: Lisa Najeeb Halaby
Also known as: Noor al-Hussein
Area of Achievement: Government and politics, architecture and design, social issues

As queen of Jordan from 1978 to 1999, Noor al-Hussein implemented numerous projects to improve the life of the people of her adopted country. Queen Noor has continued to work for peace, cross-cultural understanding, and other important social concerns worldwide.

Early Life

Lisa Najeeb Halaby was born August 23, 1951, in Washington, D.C., the eldest of three children. Her father, Najeeb Elias Halaby, a Syrian American, worked as a test pilot and airline executive and in the United States

Queen Noor (Wikimedia Commons)

government. Her mother, Doris Carlquist Halaby, a Swedish American, was a homemaker.

During the early 1960s, Halaby attended Cathedral School in Washington, D.C., where she was became interested in politics and civil rights. In 1965, her family moved to New York, where Halaby finished high school at Concord Academy. Although she was accepted to Stanford University in California, Halaby decided to become part of the first co-ed class at Princeton University in New Jersey in 1969. She graduated in 1974 with a bachelor's degree in architecture and urban planning.

Halaby first met King Hussein bin Talal, the king of Jordan, in 1977, when he and his wife visited the airport where Halaby worked for her father. She met him again in April 1978, months after the death of his wife. They married on June 15, 1978. Prior to the marriage, Halaby quit her job, learned Arabic, converted to Islam, and gave up her American citizenship. After she converted to Islam, King Hussein named her Noor, which means "spiritual light of saintliness" in Arabic. At the time of their marriage, Noor was twenty-six years old and King Hussein was forty-three. Queen Noor became the first American-born queen of an Arab country. King Hussein had eight children from three previous marriages, whom Queen Noor helped raise as her own. Queen Noor also had four children of her own: Prince Hamzah, born on March 29, 1980, Prince Hashim, born on June 10, 1981, Princess Iman, born on April 24, 1983, and Princess Raiyah, born on February 9, 1986.

> "*Today, there is no excuse for any one of us to sit back and go, 'Ugh! There's nothing I can do about it.' Because there is always something that can be done.*"

Life's Work

Following her marriage, Queen Noor was plunged into the political, economic, and religious dynamics of the Middle East, including the long-running Arab-Israeli conflict. She supported King Hussein's ongoing efforts to promote peace in the region and was dedicated to taking care of her children and stepchildren. She worked on improving Jordan's health care system and on the issue of poverty in the country. She also worked to improve

Noor Al Hussein Foundation and King Hussein Foundation

Queen Noor al-Hussein chairs both the Noor Al-Hussein Foundation (NHF) and the King Hussein Foundation (KHF). The profits from her autobiography, Leap of Faith (2003), benefit the KHF. The NHF programs were started in 1979 to support community development, education, microfinance, family health, women's empowerment, sustainable development, and environmental conservation. In 1985, by royal decree, all of the programs were gathered together into the nonprofit, nongovernmental organization NHF, which also acts to implement the community development initiatives of the King Hussein Foundation. The NHF promotes best practice programs through the Jubilee Institute (Center for Excellence in Education), Institute for Family Health, Community Development Program, Tamweelcom–the Jordan Micro Credit Company, Information and Research Center, National Center for Culture and Performing Arts, and National Music Conservatory.

The King Hussein Foundation (KHF) and King Hussein Foundation International (KHFI) were founded in 1999 to promote peace, health services, education, leadership, economic empowerment, sustainable community development, tolerance, and cross-cultural dialogue, and to conduct research and make policy recommendations through national, regional, and international programs. In 2000, the KHFI began annually awarding the King Hussein Leadership Prize, which recognizes the leadership of individuals, groups, or organizations that promote sustainable development, human rights, tolerance, social equity, or peace. In 2007, Queen Noor launched the annual Media and Humanity Program during New York City's Tribeca Film Festival. The program promotes film and media projects that focus on the similarities across cultures, especially in the Middle East and Muslim world.

opportunities for women and to preserve the nation's history and culture.

In 1979, Queen Noor established the Royal Endowment for Culture and Education, a program designed to promote higher education, culture, and the arts. In 1981, she began the Jerash Festival of Culture and Arts in the city of Jerash, which has two well-preserved Roman theaters. The annual event attracts hundreds of artists, musicians, and performers, and tens of thousands of visitors. It also serves as a showcase for Jordanian culture and architecture. Queen Noor also worked to build Jordan's tourism industry and created the National Handicrafts Development Project to encourage Jordanians to take pride in their native craftwork and clothing, as well as help teach them how to make a living selling handicrafts.

In 1984, Noor created the Jubilee School, an independent co-educational school for gifted children from various backgrounds. Underprivileged children attended on scholarships, and its graduates attended well-respected colleges throughout the world. In addition, Queen Noor established the National Music Conservatory to teach Arabic and Western music and train music teachers. Queen Noor developed the Arab Children's Congress to promote unity among Arab nations by allowing children from different Arab countries to gather for two weeks to learn about each other through drama and art.

In 1998, King Hussein was diagnosed with lymphoma, a type of cancer, and he died on February 7, 1999. Queen Noor broke Muslim tradition by attending her husband's funeral. She continued her humanitarian work after her husband's death and published her memoir, Leap of Faith: Memoirs of an Unexpected Life, in 2003, which became a New York Times best-seller and was reprinted in seventeen languages.

Significance

Queen Noor maintains a busy schedule of speeches and international work promoting world peace, conflict prevention, development, and improved understanding of Arab and Muslim culture and politics. She has been a longtime advocate for Arab-Israeli peace, and the list of organizations that she supports and has founded is extensive, ranging in focus from cancer research to conservation and environmentalism, to women's and children's issues.

She founded the Noor Al-Hussein Foundation in 1985 and the King Hussein Foundation in 1999. Queen Noor also co-founded the Alliance of Civilizations Media Fund, a nonprofit organization composed of private media entities, the United Nations, and global philanthropists that uses media technology to foster cross-cultural understanding.

Queen Noor has served as a commissioner on the International Commission on Missing Persons, which searches for missing people from armed conflicts in the Balkans and whose groundbreaking forensic DNA system is used by governments worldwide. Since 1998, she has been an advisor to and global advocate for the International Campaign to Ban Landmines. She works with the Landmine Survivors Network and has worked to promote and implement the Ottawa Mine Ban Treaty. Queen Noor is a founding leader of Global Zero, an international movement working for the world-wide elimination of nuclear weapons and represented the organization at the 2009 United Nations Security Council meeting. In 2015, Noor received the Woodrow Wilson Award for public service from the Smithsonian Institution.

Virginia L. Salmon, updated by Micah L. Issitt

Further Reading

Lafferty, Elaine. "Queen Noor: The Next Chapter." *Ms.* 13 (Fall 2003): 32–39. Print. Interview with the queen briefly discussing her early life and then focusing on her work since 1999, including with women in Arab nations.

Noor, Queen. *Leap of Faith: Memoirs of an Unexpected Life*. New York: Miramax/Hyperion, 2003. Print. Noor's autobiography, discussing living in two different cultures and providing an account of the politics and history of Jordan and the surrounding countries during a very turbulent time.

Raatma, Lucia. *Queen Noor: American-Born Queen of Jordan*. Minneapolis: Compass Point, 2006. Print. Includes a timeline, bibliography, glossary, illustrations, and sidebars.

Rosa Parks

Civil Rights activist

Born: February 4, 1913; Tuskegee, Alabama
Died: October 24, 2005; Detroit, Michigan
Area of achievement: Civil rights

On December 1, 1955, Parks refused to give up her seat

Rosa Parks (Wikimedia Commons)

on a city bus to a white passenger. She was arrested and convicted for violating a local ordinance. This was the beginning of the Montgomery bus boycott, which had a profound effect on the Civil Rights movement.

Early Life

Rosa Louise Lee McCauley Parks was born on February 4, 1913, in Tuskegee, Alabama. Her father, James McCauley, was a carpenter, and her mother, Leona McCauley, was a schoolteacher. Parks had one brother, Sylvester. The family later moved to Pine Level, Alabama, with Parks's grandmother, Rose Edwards. Parks was homeschooled by her mother until the age of eleven, and later Parks attended the Montgomery Industrial School for girls. This private institution focused on self-worth and was influential in Parks's development. She attended Alabama State Teachers College High School but did not graduate because her grandmother became ill. Parks valued her family, and later she took on the responsibility of caring for her mother and brother. Years later, in 1934, Parks earned her high school diploma. When she prepared to attend college, her mother became ill, and again Parks had to abandon her educational plans.

> "People always said that I didn't give up my seat because I was tired, but that isn't true. I was not tired physically, or no more tired than I usually was at the end of a working day. I was not old, although some people have an image of me as being old then. I was forty-two. No, the only tired I was, was tired of giving in."

Parks married Raymond Parks on December 18, 1932. Because of segregation, her husband did not receive a formal education; instead, he was educated by his mother and taught himself as much as possible. He was a barber who was involved in the Montgomery chapter of the National Association for the Advancement of Colored People (NAACP). Parks later joined her husband in the organization and helped mobilize a voter-registration drive in Montgomery. Parks was the youth adviser for the NAACP, and she also worked as a seamstress.

Although Parks had devoted hundreds of hours of time working on cases of murders and rapes of African Americans that had come to the attention of the NAACP, her efforts had come to naught. It was not until Parks refused to give up her seat on a bus to a white man on December 1, 1955, that she made history. Her act sparked similar actions all over the South and throughout the rest of the country. The Montgomery bus boycott was organized, and African Americans refused to ride the Montgomery city buses until the law of segregation was abolished. Around the United States, sit-ins and marches were organized to support the cause of integration and racial equality.

Life's Work

All of the attention surrounding Parks made it difficult for her to secure a job in Montgomery. She and her husband relocated to Detroit, Michigan, where they experienced years of financial struggle. Parks later worked as an administrative assistant for U.S. congressman John F. Conyers.

In 1987, Parks founded the Rosa and Raymond Parks Institute for Self-Development, in memory of her husband. She consistently believed that each person could make a difference, and that children are the key to future success. The institute offers a Pathway to Freedom

Parks being fingerprinted by Deputy Sheriff D.H. Lackey after being arrested for boycotting public transportation, Montgomery, Alabama, February, 1956. (Wikimedia Commons)

Program, which affords youngsters ages eleven and twelve a chance to meet with national leaders and to participate in Freedom Rides.

On April 21, 1998, a groundbreaking ceremony was held at the arrest site of Parks for the Rosa Parks Library and Museum. Troy State University hosts the Rosa Parks Museum and Library, which opened on December 1, 2000, the forty-fifth anniversary year of her arrest. Parks attended the state of the union address in January, 1999, and received a standing ovation when President Bill Clinton acknowledged her. In 2000, Parks met with Pope John Paul II in St. Louis and read a statement, asking for racial healing.

In an effort to share her story, Parks wrote four books, which detailed her life and her arrest. The books are *Rosa Parks: My Story* (1992), *Quiet Strength* (1994), *Dear Mrs. Parks: A Dialogue with Today's Youth* (1996), and *I Am Rosa Parks* (1997). Parks received the NAACP Image Award for Outstanding Literary Work for the book *Dear Mrs. Parks*.

Parks appeared in the television series *Touched by an Angel*; she received the NAACP Image Award for Best Supporting Actress for her performance. Another historical moment was the filming of *The Rosa Parks Story*, which took place in Montgomery, Alabama, in 2001 and aired February 24, 2002, on the Columbia Broadcasting System (CBS).

On February 4, 2005, when Parks turned ninety-two years old, students from Detroit Public Schools reenacted Parks's arrest. She enjoyed the performance and marveled at the excellent work of the youngsters. This was another example of how her role in history impacts future generations.

Parks died of natural causes on October 24, 2005. For two days her casket was placed in the Rotunda of the U.S. Capitol. This honor is given to presidents when they die. People came from all over the country to pay respects to the mother of the Civil Rights movement.

Significance

When Parks refused, quietly and calmly, to give up her seat on a city bus in deference to a white man, she gave impetus to the Civil Rights movement. Parks was the first living person to be honored with a state holiday. In Michigan, the first Monday following February 4 is designated Mrs. Rosa Parks Day. Michigan also honored her with the Rosa L. Parks Learning Center, which opened in 1998. The center, located at Botsford Commons, a senior community in Michigan, encourages young people to provide computer instruction to senior citizens. This successful program has built strong relationships across generations. Parks participated, and she was part of the first graduating class on November 24, 1998. Parks received the Congressional Gold Medal in 1999, a prestigious honor that prominent leaders, such as George Washington and Nelson Mandela, have received. Parks touched many with her quiet nature, her humble personality, and her dignified carriage.

Tammy K. Baggett

Further Reading

Ashby, Ruth. *Rosa Parks: Freedom Rider*. New York: Sterling, 2008. This is the courageous story of Parks and how she refused to give up her seat to a white man on a city bus.

Bjornlund, Lydia D. *Rosa Parks and the Montgomery Bus Boycott*. Detroit: Lucent Books, 2007. A detailed account of the Montgomery bus boycott, from the beginning challenges to victory. A chronological chart is included.

DeGezelle, Terri. *Rosa Parks and the Civil Rights Movement*. Chicago: Heinemann Library, 2000. A book for young readers summarizes the life of Parks and her involvement in civil rights.

Kohl, Herbert R. *She Would Not Be Moved: How We Tell the Story of Rosa Parks and the Montgomery Bus Boycott*. New York: New Press, 2005. An account of Rosa Parks and her role in the Civil Rights movement.

Parks, Rosa. *Quiet Strength*. Grand Rapids, Mich.: Zondervan, 1994. Parks gives her version of the day that launched the Montgomery bus boycott. She said she had no intention of being arrested; she just spoke up for herself.

Schraff, Anne E. *Rosa Parks: Tired of Giving In*. Berkeley Heights, N.J.: Enslow, 2005. The book presents a look at Parks, the Montgomery bus boycott, and the moment that changed history.

ALICE PAUL

Suffragist

Born: January 11, 1885; Mount Laurel, New Jersey
Died: July 9, 1977; Moorestown, New Jersey
Area of Achievement: Women's rights, government and politics

The leader of the radical wing of the women's suffrage movement that helped ensure the passage of the Nineteenth Amendment, Paul also introduced the Equal Rights Amendment.

EARLY LIFE

Born to a wealthy Quaker (Society of Friends) family, Alice Paul entered the women's movement at a very early age. Her father, William Paul, served as president of the Burlington County Trust Company, and her mother, Tacie Parry Paul, was clerk of the Moorestown Friends' Meeting. Both strongly encouraged young Alice's interest in equal rights.

Paul's early life focused almost entirely on her Quaker heritage. The Friends created a humane, optimistic religion during the seventeenth century, and they were one of the few sects that preached equality between the sexes. The fact that the Quakers allowed women to become missionaries and ministers created a unique religious environment. Although not much is known about Paul's childhood, many scholars agree that it was the egalitarian,

Alice Paul (Library of Congress)

flexible, and tolerant nature of Quaker society that allowed her to develop as perhaps America's greatest radical feminist.

Although both of Paul's parents encouraged her independent attitudes, her mother served as her chief mentor. Her father died before she reached adulthood. Tacie Paul was one of many Quaker women (such as Lucretia Mott) who were involved in the nineteenthcentury American woman suffrage movement.

Paul followed in her mother's footsteps, enrolling in the Moorestown Quaker school and later graduating from another Friends' institution, Swarthmore College. During these formative years, She also used Lucretia Mott as her role model. Mott, one of the founders of the American woman suffrage movement, helped organize the first women's rights convention in 1848 at Seneca Falls, New York, where she and Elizabeth Cady Stanton wrote the Declaration of Sentiments. Paul began her great crusade for equal rights as a graduate student at England's Woodbridge Quaker College and the London School of Economics, where she joined Emmeline, Christabel, and Sylvia Pankhurst, the radical British feminists who taught her the aggressive tactics that later produced American congressional support for the Nineteenth Amendment.

During Paul's years in Britain, she formed a close, lifelong friendship with another American suffragist, Lucy Burns, who also belonged to the Pankhursts' Women's

Social and Political Union. Nearing the end of this political apprenticeship, Paul resolved to bring confrontational feminism to the United States.

LIFE'S WORK

When Paul returned to the United States in 1910, she found Susan B. Anthony's bill granting women the right to vote still stalled in a congressional committee. Even though Anthony had submitted her bill in 1896, American women still lacked "The Franchise." Paul concluded that the situation in America called for drastic measures.

Paul persuaded the National-American Woman Suffrage Association (NAWSA) to allow her to coordinate its lobbying effects in Congress and promptly organized a huge march on the White House backed by a suffrage army estimated at a half-million people. Her dramatic entrance into Washington politics duly impressed the new president, Woodrow Wilson, whose inauguration occurred the next day. Immediately after the opening of the new Congress, Paul employed her aggressive tactics on the returning politicians to secure the Anthony Bill's release from committee to the floor of the House of Representatives. It would have been an overwhelming task for any lobbyist. Given Paul's extreme shyness, introverted Quaker personality, and lack of rhetorical skills, the bill that Congress passed, the president signed, and the states ratified became a signal triumph for her organizational genius.

During World War I, Paul quickly became the radical leader of the feminist movement. First, she changed NAWSA's lobbying focus from the states to the national legislature. She became a public relations expert at a time in history when such experts were rare. Paul's training in British circles enabled her to overcome opposition from the Washington, D.C., police, who wanted her marchers to parade on Sixteenth Street in front of the foreign embassies (instead of picketing the White House). She stood her ground, insisting that the ladies must be seen by the president and First Lady. She won the debate the first of many such victories resulting in the ratification of the Nineteenth Amendment to the Constitution.

Paul conferring with English members of the newly formed International Advisory Committee of National Woman's Party at the American Woman's Club in London. Left to right, seated - Alice Paul, Elizabeth Robins, Viscountess Rhondda, Dr. Louisa Martindale, Mrs. Virginia Crawford, Dorothy Evans. Left to right, standing - Mrs. Pethick-Lawrence, Alison Neilans, Florence Underwood, Miss Barry. (Library of Congress)

> "The Woman's Party is made up of women of all races, creeds and nationalities who are united on the one program of working to raise the status of women."

In 1917, when the United States declared war on Germany and President Wilson declared that the "world must be made safe for democracy," Paul decided that the time was right for another parade and picketing of the White House. "Why should American women support the war to make the world safe for democracy," her pickets emphatically asked, "when they have no democracy since they cannot vote?" When the White House called the police, Paul and her loyal "soldiers," facing arrest and imprisonment, followed tactics learned in England and refused to eat. Force-fed by law enforcement officials afraid of the possible public outcry produced by the hospitalization or death of a suffragist, Paul turned that tactic as well to the advantage of her cause.

Not everyone in the suffrage movement approved of Paul's tactics. More radical than the mainstream

NAWSA's moderate leadership, she organized the National Woman's Party in 1913. The Quaker activist incorporated the party on September 20, 1918, but kept it largely inactive until the passage of the Nineteenth Amendment became a certainty.

After the Congress and the states approved woman suffrage, Paul reactivated the National Woman's Party in 1921. Although most women perhaps believed that equal rights would result automatically from the ratification of the Nineteenth Amendment, Paul and her colleagues remained unconvinced.

The principal philosophical ideas Paul wrote into the National Woman's Party platform reflected her skepticism that voting rights would lead to equal rights. Women, she argued, would no longer constitute the "governed half" of the American people. In the future, they would participate equally in all aspects of life. The National Woman's Party organized most of the serious agitation such as jail-ins, marches, fasts, and picketing that occurred before the ratification of the Nineteenth Amendment. When ratification occurred, the more moderate NAWSA transformed itself into the League of Women VotersLeague of Women Voters. Paul, however, believed that the battle would not be over until equal rights had been achieved for all Americans, regardless of sex.

For Paul, true freedom extended far beyond the simple attainment of suffrage. She single-mindedly pursued the goal of removing all legal obstacles for women throughout the United States. After careful consideration and examination of the tactics and strategies that won the battle for woman suffrage, she concluded that the only means to legal equality was the passage of a federal Equal Rights Amendment (ERA). This was an extremely radical idea when Paul introduced it in 1923 at Seneca Falls, New York, where the first women's rights convention had been held in 1848. The central point she expressed focused on the philosophy that women would never be subjugated again "in law or in custom, but shall in every way be on an equal plane in rights." In this way, her Woman's Party gave birth to the Equal Rights Amendment.

Paul's proposed amendment split the women's movement. Some women believed that voting rights naturally would produce equality, making a second amendment unnecessary. Since the ERA radically redefined power relationships between men and women, even stronger opposition than originally existed to the Nineteenth Amendment developed within the male establishment.

Critics dismissed Paul as either a harmless but misguided "bleeding heart liberal" or a dangerously deranged radical. Democrats and Republicans alike warned the public against being receptive to her ideas. As the nation turned more conservative during the 1920s, with the election of President Warren Harding and the widespread repudiation of progressivism, the popularity of Paul and her party declined, and she did not resurface as a significant force until the reintroduction of the ERA in 1972.

Following Paul's creation of the National Woman's Party and the introduction of the Equal Rights Amendment, the popularity of women's rights declined in the United States during the Depression of the 1930s. As the fight for jobs excluded more and more American women, Paul took her campaign to Europe, where she founded the World's Woman's Party. Since Paul always expressed strong opposition to the League of Nations' failure to allow female political participation, she continued her lobbying efforts on behalf of women until the organization collapsed during World War II. When the League gave way to the United Nations, Paul played a key role in introducing an equal rights provision in the preamble to the U.N. charter.

Following Paul's European experiment, she returned to the United States, where she resumed her efforts to pass the new, revamped Equal Rights Amendment. During the late 1960s, Paul campaigned against the Vietnam War while working for the ERA. Still marching and fighting for equal rights at the age of eightyfive, she finally surrendered to old age and moved to a Quaker nursing home in her native Moorestown, New Jersey, where America's great radical feminist died on July 9, 1977, at the age of ninety-two. She never lived to see the passage of the amendment to which she had devoted her entire life.

SIGNIFICANCE

Few leaders in the politics of women's liberation were more significant than Alice Paul. Her longevity and radical proclivities outdistanced others who garnered more press and historical notice. For sixty-five years, from 1912 until her death in 1977, Paul stood ready to give her best to the cause of equal rights.

Despite her reputation for radical measures, Paul was not an abrasive personality. Although some thought her insensitive, perhaps what they perceived was the absent-mindedness of an intellectual who received her Ph.D. in sociology in 1912, before she launched her suffrage career. She understood both the politics and the economics of equal rights. The real struggle, she once argued, would not be won in state or even national legislatures. Women would have to win economically before they could win politically. Political forms would crystallize, she hypothesized, only when women had gained economic power. More important, she emphasized that having money was not enough. Knowing how to use money to attain political ends was the key.

Paul was not as well known as other feminists Susan B. Anthony, Lucretia Mott, and Elizabeth Cady Stanton. Her strategies and tactics, however, have since been considered to have been paramount in obtaining the Nineteenth Amendment to the Constitution. Although she died without realizing victory in her struggle to institute the Equal Rights Amendment, many of the goals she sought came to pass nevertheless, partly because of the half-century of supreme effort she exerted to realize her great dream.

J. Christopher Schnell

FURTHER READING

Barker-Benfield, G. J., and Catherine Clinton, eds. *Portraits of American Women: From Settlement to the Present*. New York: St. Martin's Press, 1991. A collection of scholarly articles on significant American women from Pocahontas to Betty Friedan. The article on Alice Paul by Christine A. Lunardini presents a particularly effective analysis.

Becker, Susan D. *The Origins of the Equal Rights Amendment: American Feminism Between the Wars*. Westport, Conn.: Greenwood Press, 1981. An analysis of Paul's postsuffrage role in reorganizing the women's movement along the international lines of the World's Woman's Party.

Butler, Amy E. *Two Paths to Equality: Alice Paul and Ethel M. Smith in the ERA Debate, 1921-1929*. Albany: State University of New York Press, 2002. Paul and Smith were proponents of equal rights for women but they had different views about the best way to attain those rights. This book explains their differences and its impact on the cause of women's rights.

Flexner, Eleanor. *Century of Struggle: The Woman's Rights Movement in the United States*. Rev. ed. Cambridge, Mass.: The Belknap Press of Harvard University Press, 1975. A classic history of the women's movement (highlighting Alice Paul's role) by one of the great feminist historians.

Gallagher, Robert S. "I Was Arrested, of Course . . ." *American Heritage* 25, no. 2 (February, 1974): 16-24, 92-94. A fascinating and penetrating interview conducted with Paul three years before her death.

Irwin, Inez Haynes. *The Story of Alice Paul and the National Woman's Party*. Fairfax, Va.: Denlinger's, 1977. This is the primary history of the National Woman's Party.

Morgan, David. *Suffragists and Democrats: The Politics of Woman Suffrage in America*. East Lansing: Michigan State University Press, 1972. This is a narrow British interpretation of the politics of the American woman suffrage movement.

Stevens, Doris. *Jailed for Freedom*. New York: Boni & Liveright, 1920. Reprint. Freeport, N.Y.: Books for Libraries Press, 1971. This primary source focuses on the radical feminists who campaigned for the vote between 1913 and 1919. The work includes a valuable chapter on "General Alice Paul."

ELIZABETH PERATROVICH

Native Alaskan civil rights activist

Born: July 4, 1911; Petersburg, Alaska
Died: December 1, 1958; Seattle, Washington
Also known as: Kaaxgal.aat (Tlingit language), Elizabeth Wanamaker (maiden name)
Area of achievement: Native Leaders; Social Reform

In the 1940s, Elizabeth Peratrovich campaigned tirelessly for equal rights for Alaskan Natives. The powerful personal testimony that she gave to the Alaskan legislature prior to the passage of Alaska's Anti-Discrimination Act of 1945 has become legendary. In 1998, her work on behalf of equal rights was officially recognized with the establishment of Elizabeth Peratrovich Day by the Alaskan legislature.

EARLY LIFE

Kaaxgal.aat, later known as Elizabeth Peratrovich, was born on July 4, 1911. She was by birth a member of the Tlingit nation of Native Alaskans. The Tlingit historically reside along the southeastern coast of Alaska. When she was still a young child, Kaaxgal.aat was orphaned and adopted by a Tlingit couple named Andrew and Mary Wanamaker who lived in the Tlingit village of Klawock. Her adopted father, Andrew, worked as a fisherman and was also a Presbyterian lay minister called to mission to the Tlingit people.

Elizabeth graduated from Ketchikan High School in Ketchikan, Alaska, then attended Sheldon Jackson College in Sitka and the Western College of Education in Bellingham, Washington. When she was twenty years old, Elizabeth married Roy Peratrovich, who was also a Tlingit. Between 1936 and 1941, Roy worked variously as a policeman, as Klawock's chief clerk, as a judge, and as Klawock's postmaster. He eventually became the mayor of Klawock.

Life's Work

In 1941, Roy and Elizabeth moved to the capital city of Alaska, Juneau. There they encountered a degree of anti-Native prejudice that they hadn't known previously. Wanting to buy a home, they encountered entrenched obstacles and extensive discrimination. Certain neighborhoods were forbidden to them as homeowners, and many businesses in Juneau had window signs that said, "No Dogs or Indians Allowed." Native Alaskan children were banned from Juneau's public school system. Some restaurants who allowed entry to indigenous people enforced segregated seating, and all movie theaters in Juneau were segregated.

Elizabeth had a strong sense of right and wrong, and the injustice of the discrimination troubled her greatly. She was a college graduate, something rare for a Native Alaskan woman, and she had a self-confident demeanor and a natural gift for public relations. She could speak her mind directly and naturally, yet without causing offense. Elizabeth put these strengths to use in her battle against discrimination. Over the next several years, Elizabeth organized groups, attended meetings, and sat through many hearings of the Alaska legislature. She often went with her young children, sitting through the proceedings with her knitting while the children ran among the seats and the aisles. She also took many Native Alaskan women under her wing, and would advise them on things like how to speak up in social settings—asking sales people for help, for example.

Within a few years, thanks to the extensive campaigning and organizing conducted by the Peratroviches and others, there was a growing sense that the discrimination needed to be addressed through legislation. In 1943, an anti-discrimination bill was defeated in the Alaska legislature. In 1945, a nearly identical bill was introduced, and this time it had support from a number of influential territorial senators, although others opposed it. One of the bill's opponents was territorial senator Allen Shattuck. Who is reported to have asked dismissively from the senate floor, "Who are these people, barely out of savagery, who want to associate with us whites with 5,000 years of recorded civilization behind us?" Elizabeth was seated in the gallery listening to the proceedings. As the formal debate concluded, she set her knitting to the side, rose, and asked for permission to speak. Contemporary accounts noted that she was well-dressed and had a "regal" bearing. According to the memory of witnesses, she began by saying: "I would not have expected that I, who am barely out of savagery, would have to remind gentlemen with 5,000 years of recorded history behind them of our Bill of Rights." The wry remark has become legendary. She went on to describe her personal experiences with discrimination, as well as the experiences of her friends. Unfortunately, there is no surviving document of the testimony given by Peratrovich that day. She did not leave a copy of her speech, and the Alaskan legislature in that period did not make transcripts of legislative hearings. We do have, however, a report that appeared the following day in the *Daily Alaska Empire* newspaper: "It was the neatest performance of any witness yet to appear before this session, and there were a few red senatorial ears as she regally left the chambers."

> "I would not have expected that I, who am barely out of 'savagery,' would have to remind gentlemen with five thousand years of recorded civilization behind them, of our Bill of Rights."

The bill passed by an 11-5 margin. When it was signed into law by Governor Gruening on February 16, 1945, it was the first legislation to address discrimination to be passed in any state (or territory) since the Civil War era. On the evening of the day the bill became law, Elizabeth and Roy celebrated with dinner and dancing in the lounge at one of Juneau's most expensive hotels, the Baranof. The venue was not chosen casually: until that very day, the business had refused admittance to Native Alaskan patrons.

For the next ten years, Elizabeth focused her advocacy on health care for Native Alaskans. In 1955, when Roy took a job with the Bureau of Indian Affairs, Elizabeth moved with him to Oklahoma, and the following year, she traveled to Tennessee to attend a conference on adult Indian education. The conference organizers had invited a young African American minister to speak to them about desegregation. Peratrovich heard him talk and was favorably impressed; his name was Martin Luther King, Jr. Two years later, in 1958, Peratrovich died following an extended battle with cancer. She was forty-seven years old.

Significance

Elizabeth Peratrovich's name is associated with the first anti-discrimination legislation to be passed in any U.S. state or territory in the twentieth century: Alaska's Anti-Discrimination Act of 1945. Alaska's civil rights movement, while not widely known, was an important precursor to the civil rights movement of the 1960s. In 1989, Alaska recognized Peratrovich's contribution to history by declaring February 16 to be "Elizabeth Peratrovich Day."

Dewayne Dean

Further Reading

A Recollection of Civil Rights Leader Elizabeth Peratrovich, 1911-1958. Juneau, Alaska: The Tlingit and Haida Central Council, 1991.

Boochever, Annie and Roy Peratrovich, Jr. *Fighter in Velvet Gloves: Alaska Civil Rights Hero Elizabeth Peratrovich.* Fairbanks, Alaska: University of Alaska Press, 2019.

Imel, Susan and Gretchen Bersch. *No Small Lives: Handbook of North American Early Women Adult Educators, 1925-1950.* Charlotte, NC: Information Age Publishing, 2015.

Kiffer, Dave. "Alaska Celebrates Civil Rights Pioneer: Peratrovich's Efforts Pre-Dated Martin Luther King." *Stories In the News.* Feb. 18, 2008. http://www.sitnews.us/Kiffer/Peratrovich/021808_e_peratrovich.html

Metcalfe, Peter. *A Dangerous Idea: The Alaska Native Brotherhood and the Struggle for Indigenous Rights.* Fairbanks, Alaska: University of Alaska Press, 2014.

Ai-jen Poo

Labor activist

Born: ca. 1974; Pittsburgh, Pennsylvania
Area(s) of significance: Activism

At the age of 26, Poo founded Domestic Workers United, a grass-roots organization of maids and other domestic workers, often immigrants, that achieved extraordinary success in passing laws to protect a vulnerable and often exploited workforce.

Ai-jen Poo (Wikimedia Commons)

Early Life

Ai-jen Poo was born in Pittsburgh, Pennsylvania. Her parents had emigrated from Taiwan as graduate students; her father, Mu-ming Poo, is a molecular neurobiologist, and her mother, an oncologist. She has one sister, Ting Poo, a film editor. In his native country, then led by Chiang Kai-shek, Mu-ming had been a pro-democracy activist, and Poo was deeply influenced by his activities. (He now teaches and conducts research at the University of California, Berkeley.) She was even more deeply influenced by her mother, who ran the household despite studying for a PhD in chemistry, working initially as a lab technician, and learning English.

Poo attended the academically rigorous Phillips Academy in Andover, Massachusetts. Her propensity for activism was evident early on, and she once skipped an address by President George H. W. Bush (himself a Phillips alum) in order to take part in a pro-choice rally. Upon graduating from the school in 1992, Poo, who was considering becoming a professional potter, entered Washington University in St. Louis, Missouri. After a year

The U.S. Department of Labor's Policy Office Forum on "The Gig Economy and Developing Positive Platforms". Featuring Poo, Sheila Marcelo (Care.com), Marina Gorbis (Institute for the Future), Devin Fidler (Institute for the Future), Natalie Foster (Institute for the Future), and Mary Beth Maxwell (U.S. Department of Labor). (Wikimedia Commons)

there, she transferred to Columbia University in New York City, excited to be in one of the cultural capitals of the world.

She soon switched her focus from pottery and art to women's studies. Columbia, on the Upper West Side of Manhattan, had long been known for its tradition of student activism and volunteerism, and Poo fit right into that environment. She was arrested in 1995 for blocking one of the city's major bridges during a protest against police brutality, and the following year she took part in campuswide protests demanding more culturally diverse classes.

While in college Poo also began volunteering at the New York Asian Women's Center, which ran a shelter for victims of domestic abuse, and she was involved with the Committee Against Anti-Asian Violence (CAAAV), which hired her as a paid staff member upon her graduation from Columbia in 1996.

Life's Work

While working at the CAAAV, Poo spearheaded a project to organize Asian immigrant women working in low-paying service jobs. It was an era in which several of New York City's garment factories were closing their doors and firing the predominantly female laborers; many of those whose immigration paperwork was in order became home health-care aides, while the undocumented among them flocked to restaurant kitchens, beauty parlors, and casual maid services. None of those situations was enviable: the women typically worked at least twelve hours per day and still remained below the poverty line.

Although the project began with Asian women—mainly Filipina workers—Poo quickly saw the need to branch out into a citywide, multiethnic effort. She was particularly moved by one Jamaican woman who approached her after hearing of her work. The woman had been lured to the United States as a teen, believing she could work as a live-in nanny and maid while attending school. Instead, her employers kept her busy from sunrise until late into the night, with no time to attend high school. Even worse, she never saw a dime of her promised wages: the couple employing her claimed they were sending the checks straight to her parents, but because they restricted her access to mail, she could never be certain that they were actually doing so. After almost two decades, she finally escaped with the help of one of the couple's children. In 2000, with the help of coworkers from CAAAV, Poo created and was lead organizer of Domestic Workers United, which in 2007 became an affiliate of a larger umbrella group, the National Domestic Workers Alliance (NDWA). Soon after its formation, Poo became the director of the NDWA.

Poo and her staffers made dozens of trips to Albany to lobby New York State lawmakers to enact legislation protecting the rights of low-wage domestic workers. They were generally accompanied by large groups of the workers, who donned matching shirts and gathered on the steps of the New York State Capitol building to make their voices heard. After Assemblyman Keith Wright (D-Manhattan) and Senator Diane Savino (D-Brooklyn/Staten Island) introduced such a bill into the state legislature in 2004, some of the workers were invited to share their life stories. Among the most moving, Poo has recalled, was that of an elderly Colombian woman who worked for more than one hundred hours per week, cooking, cleaning, and providing child care for a family of six. For that, she was paid about three dollars per hour—money she used in part to buy insulin for her own child. Living in a sewage-filled basement, she was fired suddenly with no severance pay and no other job lined up.

Other workers told harrowing stories of withheld pay, sexual harassment, and similar such indignities.

On November 29, 2010, the state's Domestic Workers' Bill of Rights took effect, three months after Governor David Paterson signed it. The law, which was the first of its kind in the nation, entitles domestic workers in New York State to overtime pay, one day off per week, three paid days off a year after one year with the same employer, and inclusion in the state's Human Rights Law, which protects against sexual harassment and discrimination. The law applies even to undocumented workers. Since passage of the New York law, Hawaii, California, and Massachusetts have followed suit, and other states have organized taskforces or taken other steps toward enacting similar legislation.

In recent years Poo has turned her attention to the issues surrounding elder care and the estimated three million home-care providers in the United States. To that end, in 2011 Poo spearheaded a new organization called Caring Across Generations, for which she is a codirector. The organization is devoted to encouraging a cultural shift in the way Americans feel about aging, multigenerational relationships, and caregiving; advocating for effective government policies; and building a platform for multigenerational civic engagement. She has also written a book on the topic, *The Age of Dignity: Preparing for the Elder Boom in a Changing America* (2015).

> "It's precisely the people who are considered the least 'likely' leaders who end up inspiring others the most. Everyday people and everyday acts of courage eventually change everything."

SIGNIFICANCE

In 2014, Ai-jen Poo, as director of the National Domestic Workers Alliance, was awarded a John D. and Catherine T. MacArthur Foundation fellowship. She was also recognized by Time magazine as one of the world's most influential people. Despite such accolades, Poo is widely recognized as a humble person who prefers the spotlight to be on the National Domestic Workers Alliance, rather than on herself.

Mari Rich

FURTHER READING

Alonso, Nathalie. "The Home Front." Columbia College Today. Columbia College Today, Fall 2012. Web.

Ehrenreich, Barbara. "The Nannies' Norma Rae." T Magazine. New York Times, 1 May 2011. Web.

Poo, Ai-jen. "America's Most Invisible Workforce Is the One We Need the Most." Guardian. Guardian News and Media, 29 Sept. 2014. Web.

Shah, Angilee. "Ai-jen Poo: The Rock Star of Community Organizing." Dame Magazine. Dame Media, 24 May 2012. Web.

Swarns, Rachel. "A Capstone in a Career Spent Fighting for the Rights of Domestic Workers." New York Times. New York Times, 21 Sept. 2014. Web.

Weiner, Joann. "MacArthur Fellow Ai-jen Poo on Why She Fights for the Rights of Domestic Workers." Washington Post. Washington Post, 18 Sept. 2014. Web.

A. PHILIP RANDOLPH

Civil rights activist and labor leader

Born: April 15, 1889; Crescent City, Florida
Died: May 16, 1979; New York City, New York
Also known as: Asa Philip Randolph; Phil Randolph
Areas of Achievement: Civil rights; Journalism and publishing; Labor

A. Philip Randolph (Library of Congress)

Civil rights leaders meet with President John F. Kennedy in the Oval Office of the White House after the March on Washington, D.C. Photograph shows (left to right): Willard Wirtz (Secretary of Labor); Floyd McKissick (CORE); Mathew Ahmann (National Catholic Conference for Interracial Justice); Whitney Young (National Urban League); Martin Luther King, Jr. (SCLC); John Lewis (SNCC); Rabbi Joachim Prinz (American Jewish Congress); Randolph, with Reverend Eugene Carson Blake partially visible behind him; President John F. Kennedy; Walter Reuther (labor leader), with Vice President Lyndona Johnson partially visible behind him; and Roy Wilkins (NAACP). (Library of Congress)

Randolph was the founder and leader of the first effective African American labor union, and he was largely responsible for some of the earliest gains of the Civil Rights movement.

EARLY LIFE

Asa Philip Randolph was the second son of the Reverend James Randolph, a minister in the African Methodist Episcopal Church, and Elizabeth Robinson Randolph, a skilled seamstress. In 1891, the family moved to Jacksonville, Florida, where James accepted the call to serve as pastor of a small church with poor parishioners. From his father's example, Randolph learned eloquence, integrity, and a strong determination to resist racial discrimination. He disappointed his father, however, when at an early age he expressed disinterest in the ministry. He and his brother, James, Jr., were outstanding students at the Cookman Institute, one of the few high schools for African Americans in Florida. Randolph sang in the school choir, was a star on the baseball team, and was valedictorian of the 1907 graduating class.

In 1911, hoping to pursue a career as an actor, Randolph moved to New York City, which became his permanent home. For the next few years, he held a series of odd jobs and participated in productions of Harlem's Shakespearean Society. From 1912 to 1917, he took courses at the City College of New York and Columbia University. Through his studies, he became acquainted with left-wing socialists and the writings of Karl Marx. Persuaded that socialism would bring about social justice and put an end to racial discrimination, he became an active member of the Socialist Party. In 1914, he married a beauty-shop operator, Lucille Campbell Greene, who shared his socialist convictions and supported him financially for the next several years.

LIFE'S WORK

About 1914, Randolph made the acquaintance of Chandler Owen, a fellow socialist who had considerable knowledge in the field of economics. The two men formed a partnership to promote progressive causes, particularly civil rights for African Americans and improved conditions for workers. In 1916, they organized a labor union for elevator and switchboard operators, which they controlled for almost a year. In 1917, with the financial support of Randolph's wife, they created and became joint editors of the monthly magazine *The Messenger*, which they called "the only radical Negro magazine in America." A landmark during the early stage of the "New Negro" movement, the magazine became the most influential black publication in the country for several years. Like many intellectuals of the left, Randolph and Owen firmly opposed involvement in World War I, advising African Americans to resist the draft and refuse to fight for a country that treated them so badly. In 1918, they were arrested and indicted for violating the Espionage Act, but the judge dismissed the charges, saying he doubted that the two young African Americans understood the significance of their words.

In 1919, when the Socialist Party split over whether to support the Soviet Union, Randolph remained loyal to the noncommunist faction of the party. He was chosen to be the party's candidate for New York state controller in 1920 and secretary of state in 1922—without much success. Initially, he presented a favorable view of the Communist Party in *The Messenger*, but by the middle of the

Randolph and the Fair Employment Practices Commission

In the summer of 1940, jobs in defense industries were growing rapidly, but discrimination limited most African Americans' access to the new prosperity. That September, A. Philip Randolph and Walter Francis White, head of the National Association for the Advancement of Colored People (NAACP), discussed the matter with President Franklin D. Roosevelt. The meeting failed to produce any concrete results. Influenced by Mahatma Gandhi's mass protests in India, Randolph decided to organize the March on Washington Movement, which he hoped would bring at least ten thousand African American protestors to the nation's capital. By the summer of 1941, the response had become so great that Randolph increased his goal to 100,000 marchers. Roosevelt and members of the administration were alarmed by the possibility that such a demonstration might lead to violence and harm America's democratic image.

On June 18, 1941, Roosevelt and other political leaders held a meeting with Randolph and White at the White House. When Roosevelt requested that the demonstration be called off, Randolph replied that it would be impossible unless the president issued an executive order banning discrimination in the defense industries and the military. On June 25, Roosevelt signed Executive Order 8802, creating the Fair Employment Practices Commission (FEPC), which had the task of preventing "discrimination in the employment of workers in defense industries or government because of race, creed, color, or national origin." When Randolph found the FEPC lacking in effectiveness, he again threatened to bring a mass demonstration to Washington unless things improved. In 1943, yielding for a second time, Roosevelt issued Executive Order 9346, which strengthened the commission's powers. Although enforcement was uneven, the FEPC was the nation's first federal agency designed to promote equal opportunity, which established a crucially important precedent for the Civil Rights movement.

---

decade he had assumed a strong anticommunist stance. He was even more hostile toward Marcus Garvey's Universal Negro Improvement Association, joining in the "Garvey Must Go" campaign for two reasons: a belief that Garvey ignored the issue of class conflict and opposition to the notion that African Americans should return to Africa. Escalating conflicts among left-wing African Americans exacerbated the financial difficulties of *The Messenger*, which went out of business in 1928.

As subscriptions to the magazine declined, Randolph increasingly focused his efforts on more direct ways to improve conditions for African American workers. In 1925, he helped organize employees of the Pullman Company into the Brotherhood of Sleeping Car Porters (BSCP), and the members elected him as president. Three years later, the BSCP became the first African American union to be affiliated with the American Federation of Labor (AFL). In negotiations, Randolph was patient and pragmatic but determined to get the best terms possible for his union. Amendments to the Railway Labor Act of 1934 strengthened his bargaining power, and three years later, despite the Great Depression, he signed a contract that provided significant gains in pay and improvements in working conditions. In 1935, when African American communists, liberals, and democratic socialists joined in a popular-front organization, the National Negro Congress (NNC), the diverse group chose Randolph as the first president. In August, 1939, however, the pact between Nazi Germany and Stalinist Russia made it impossible for communists and non-communists to cooperate. Randolph resigned from the presidency of the NNC with the remark that it was "hard enough being black without also being red."

In 1941, Randolph was the main organizer of the March on Washington movement. He used the threat of a mass demonstration to persuade President Franklin D. Roosevelt to issue Executive Order 8802, which outlawed discrimination in defense industries and established the Fair Employment Practices Committee (which later became the Fair Employment Practices Commission). In 1948, after a new draft law failed to desegregate the armed forces, Randolph and his colleague Bayard Rustin organized the League for Nonviolence Civil Disobedience Against Military Segregation. In a meeting with President Harry S. Truman on March 22, Randolph predicted that African Americans would no longer be willing to participate in a segregated Army, and he even advised young black men to refuse induction into such an Army. Randolph's pressure was one of the factors that led to Truman's Executive Order 9981, issues on July 24, which required an end to military discrimination and implicitly disallowed segregation. Although disappointed that the order was not worded more clearly, Randolph agreed to call off the campaign.

> *"Patriotism has no appeal to us; justice has. Party has no weight with us; principle has. Loyalty is meaningless; it depends on what one is loyal to."*

In 1950, Randolph was one of the major founders of the Leadership Conference on Civil Rights, which coordinated campaigns for civil rights legislation. However, during the 1950's, most of his efforts were devoted to union activities. In 1955, he was elected vice president of the executive council of the newly merged American Federation of Labor and Congress of Industrial Organizations (AFL-CIO). In this position, he tried to promote equal opportunity within unions. At the 1959 convention of the AFL-CIO, he introduced a resolution calling for the expulsion of segregated unions, but the leadership firmly vetoed the resolution. Dissatisfied with organized labor's unwillingness to push harder for racial equality, Randolph was the leading force behind the creation of the Negro American Labor Council, and he served as its president from 1960 to 1966.

In 1962, the seventy-two-year-old Randolph was persuaded that the time was ripe for a mass demonstration in support of civil rights legislation, and he joined with other black leaders to plan the project, naming it the March on Washington for Jobs and Freedom. Randolph insisted that Rustin be put in charge of organizing the event, although some of the leaders feared that Rustin's homosexuality would tarnish the movement's image. On August 28, 1963, Randolph was the first speaker to address the assembly of 200,000 people, although his words were overshadowed historically by Martin Luther King, Jr.'s iconic "I Have a Dream" speech. The event was a huge success and helped persuade Congress to pass the Civil Rights Act of 1964.

In 1964, Randolph presided over the establishment of the A. Philip Randolph Institute, and he led the organization's efforts to provide a minimum income to all citizens. Because of his anticommunist views, he never took a firm stand against the U.S. policy in the Vietnam War, although he defended King's opposition to the war as morally consistent with the Civil Rights movement. He was highly critical of Stokely Carmichael and other leaders of the Black Power movement, and he declared in 1966 that "black power has tones of black racism." However, he remained a man of the political left. In 1969, he rejoined the Socialist Party, confessing that he as always considered himself to be "part of the democratic socialist movement." Randolph died on May 16, 1979, in New York City.

Significance

Randolph's espousal of massive, nonviolent protests in support of civil rights had major consequences for future generations of African Americans. Rustin said of Randolph, "With the exception of W. E. B. Du Bois, he was probably the greatest civil rights leader of the twentieth century until Martin Luther King." Randolph's tenure as president of the Brotherhood of Sleeping Car Porters from 1928 until his retirement in 1968 was crucial in improving the conditions of an important segment of the black community. His vision and pragmatic strategies helped bring about three major reforms: the creation of the Fair Employment Practices Committee, the desegregation of the armed forces, and passage of the 1964 Civil Rights Act.

Thomas Tandy Lewis

Further Reading

Anderson, Jervis. *A. Philip Randolph: A Biographical Portrait*. New York: Harcourt Brace Jovanovich, 1973. An excellent source that is readable and full of interesting information and anecdotes.

Garfinkel, Herbert. *When Negroes March: The March on Washington Movement in the Organizational Politics for FEPC*. New York: Athenaeum, 1969. Valuable account of how Randolph's threat of a large demonstration resulted in the creation of the Fair Employment Practices Committee.

Kersten, Andrew E. *A. Philip Randolph: A Life in the Vanguard*. New York: Rowman & Littlefield, 2006. A relatively concise account of Randolph's accomplishments as a labor and civil rights leader.

Miller, Calvin C. *A. Philip Randolph and the African American Labor Movement*. Greensboro, N.C.: Morgan Reynolds, 2005. Emphasizes Randolph's work with the Brotherhood of Sleeping Car Porters while also summarizing other aspects of his long career. Written primarily for young readers.

Pfeffer, Paula. *A. Philip Randolph: Pioneer of the Civil Rights Movement*. Baton Rouge: Louisiana State University Press, 1990. Argues that Randolph's ideologies and strategies provided the blueprint for the civil rights achievements of the 1950's and 1960's.

Taylor, Cynthia. *A. Philip Randolph: The Religious Journey of An African American Labor Leader*. New York: New York University Press, 2006. Emphasizes Randolph's appreciation for the moral influences of black churches and greatly minimizes his support for the Humanist Manifesto of 1973.

Wright, Sarah E. *A. Philip Randolph: Integration in the Workplace*. Englewood Cliffs, N.J.: Silver Burdett Press, 1990. A useful summary of Randolph's life and career for young readers.

SYLVIA RIVERA

Gay liberation and transgender activist

Born: July 2, 1951; New York City, New York
Died: February 19, 2002; New York City, New York
Also known as: Ray Rivera
Area of achievement: Social Reform

Co-founder with Marsha P. Johnson of a collective to support homeless youth, transgender, and gender-queer people of color in New York City in the 1970s, Sylvia Rivera was a prominent activist in the gay liberation movement until she was shut out by its more mainstream leadership. In the 1990s and 2000s, when transgender issues took on greater urgency, Rivera was re-discovered and hailed as a pioneer of transgender activism.

EARLY LIFE

Ray "Sylvia" Rivera was born on July 2, 1951 in New York City to Puerto Rican and Venezuelan parents. Not long after her birth, her father, Jose Rivera, abandoned his wife and child. When Ray was three years old, her mother committed suicide. An orphan, Rivera was raised by her Venezuelan grandmother. Ray's effeminate behavior met with strong disapproval from her grandmother and from other boys in the neighborhood who bullied Ray. When Rivera was only ten years old, she ran away from home for the first time. By age eleven, Rivera was living on the streets in New York and working as a prostitute in the gritty Times Square area. She was taken in by older prostitutes, in particular by a group of drag queens and other homosexual outcasts who formed a rough, contingent community and supported themselves primarily through sex work. She was named Sylvia by the drag queens who adopted her.

LIFE'S WORK

Sylvia began frequenting the gay bars of pre-Stonewall New York when she was young, finding community with other sexual minorities. The gay bars that existed in New York City at that time were mostly owned and operated by the Mafia who worked in cooperation with a corrupt New York City Police Department. The bars were routinely raided but not closed down; in this way, the police were able to make arrests while also profiting from graft. By the late sixties, the raids had become a scripted non-event for both the Mafia and the police. Records from the era show that every gay bar in the city was raided an average of once a month in the late sixties. These raids could be devastating for the patrons who were arrested, leading to job loss and conflict with family and friends.

One of these raids occurred at the Stonewall Inn late Friday night, after midnight, on June 27, 1969. As the police lined up the patrons outside the bar to check their identification, some of them began to resist or to mock the police. Tensions mounted, and the resistance grew into a full-fledged riot. Before long, hundreds of gay men, transvestites, and others threw bottles, overturned police vehicles, and lobbed Molotov cocktails. When police officers, not anticipating resistance, locked themselves inside the bar for self-protection, the crowd uprooted a parking meter to use it as a battering ram while others tried to set the Inn on fire.

The uprising lasted until the early hours of the morning. It was followed by five more days and nights of similar unrest in the streets. It was an historic turning point, and people knew it. The morning after the second night of rioting, an activist printed five thousand flyers and distributed them in Greenwich Village. The flyers read in part, "The nights of Friday, June 27, 1969 and Saturday, June 28, 1969 will go down in history…" Many accounts of what happened acknowledge the pivotal role of some of society's most disenfranchised groups in the Stonewall Uprising—young people who were living on the streets, poor gay people of color, drag queens, and prostitutes. Sylvia Rivera spoke for all of them when she later recalled, "We were the frontliners…. We had nothing to lose."

> "*I was a radical, a revolutionist. I am still a revolutionist...I am glad I was in the Stonewall riot. I remember when someone threw a Molotov cocktail, I thought, 'My god, the revolution is here. The revolution is finally here!'*"

The events of Stonewall profoundly affected Sylvia Rivera and her close friend Marsha P. Johnson. The pair were among the most colorful and outspoken of their tribe, a group of transvestite prostitutes, sometimes homeless, who were not yet outside the pale of the gay liberation movement at a time when the movement itself was nascent and all of it on the fringes of society. Left-wing revolutionary rhetoric spoke of uprisings of the dispossessed, and Rivera and Johnson, galvanized by Stonewall, became firmly revolutionary in their outlook. Over the next several years, the gay liberation movement became divided between a more mainstream core, often white and middle-class, who sought to obtain legal rights within the American economic and political system, and a more radical wing that wanted revolutionary change to that system. Rivera and Johnson were among the latter; they forged ties with the Black Panthers and with the Young Lords, a socialist Puerto Rican group that had arisen from a street gang. Rivera was by most mainstream measures an eccentric in her appearance and behavior, and she was part of an under-class that was rarely acknowledged, even in left-wing theory. She was proud that Huey Newton, one of the founders of the Black Panthers, had personally welcomed her as a comrade, and that the macho Young Lords in New York City had categorically done the same.

In 1970, the year after Stonewall, Rivera and Johnson founded the Street Transvestite Action Revolutionaries (STAR). They rented a tenement at 213 East Second Street and it became a place where homeless transgender youth could access shelter, food, health and other services, and even live together communally. They were inspired by social programs that were being operated by the Black Panthers and other revolutionary organizations on behalf of their communities. She later recalled, "STAR was for the street gay people, the street homeless people, and anybody that needed help at that time." Housing was often a problem for street youth who were gender nonconforming; at most of the shelters in the city, they faced discrimination and harassment. "Marsha and I had always sneaked people into our hotel rooms. And you can sneak 50 people into two hotel rooms." At its peak, STAR was active in New York City, Chicago, California, and England.

The first gay liberation rally (later "pride") was organized in the same year. By 1973, the rally's more mainstream organizers were marginalizing transvestites, drag queens, and what today would be called gender-queer people in order to win better press for the rest of the gay community. At the rally in Washington Square Park in Manhattan in 1973, Rivera wanted to address the crowd to tell them about the work that STAR was doing to help poor gays and lesbians and members of the gender-queer and drag community. Organizers withheld the microphone from her for hours before relenting. When she finally took the stage to speak, the crowd began to jeer. Speaking over them, she began, "Y'all better quiet down." Then, in an impassioned speech she excoriated the crowd: "I've been trying to get up here all day for your gay brothers and your gay sisters in jail, that write me every motherfucking week and ask for *your* help, and you all don't do a goddamn thing for them." She continued, "I have been beaten; I have had my nose broken; I have been thrown in jail; I have lost my job; I have lost my apartment—all for gay liberation. And you all treat me this way?" The experience was a turning point for Rivera. Profoundly disillusioned and hurt, she suffered a breakdown. Eventually STAR disbanded, and Rivera spent many of the following years living homeless in an encampment on one of the West Village piers.

Rivera's friend Marsha P. Johnson was found dead in the Hudson River in 1992. In 1995, Rivera tried to commit suicide. Through these difficult years, Rivera maintained several prominent friends, including the gay journalist Randy Wicker. Not long after her suicide attempt, she was interviewed for a PBS series, *The Question of Equality*. Around this time, her life began to change for the better. She found a place to live, and she found a lover and a job. Even when she herself had been homeless, Rivera remained active helping other homeless gay and transgender people, especially those suffering from AIDS in the 1980s and 1990s. She became increasingly recognized as a special person with a compelling story, and she was invited to give talks at events and venues around the city. She was even invited to Italy's Millennium March in 2000, where she was called the "mother of all gay people."

In 2001, she resurrected STAR, changing the name slightly to incorporate the new term *transgender* in place of the older *transvestite*. The term *transgender* emerged in the 1990s to describe all kinds of gender-nonconforming people, including drag queens. Sylvia spoke of herself variously as a gay man, a gay woman, and a drag queen. She also rejected any form of gender reassignment surgery for herself. Writing about her gender, she said, "I'm tired of being labeled. I don't even like the label 'transgender....' I just want to be who I am."

Rivera lived for most of the last five years of her life at Transy House, a transgender collective that was formed in 1995. She became an active member of the Metropolitan Community Church of New York, where she attended services regularly, volunteered at the food pantry, and advocated tirelessly for the poor and the homeless. She eventually became the food pantry's director. Her compassion for people living in poverty and the efforts she took to aid them—not just gay or queer people, but everybody—have been widely recognized. After her death, the church re-named its food pantry the Sylvia Rivera Food Pantry, and its shelter for homeless youth was named Sylvia's Place. Rivera, who struggled with alcoholism for many years, died of liver cancer in 2002.

SIGNIFICANCE

Rivera, like her friend Marsha P. Johnson, worked from the margins of society and the fringes of the gay right movement to help not only transgender and gender-queer people, but the poor and homeless as well. Inspired by the social movements, programs, and living arrangements of revolutionary groups like the Black Panthers and other left-wing communities, Rivera organized STAR, the Street Transvestite Action Revolutionaries, to provide a home for those who needed one, to create community, and to advocate for revolutionary change. In the twenty-first century, as issues of gender identity became prominent, figures like Sylvia Rivera and Marsha P. Johnson were reclaimed as founders of the movement for transgender rights.

Dewayne Dean

FURTHER READING

Armstrong, Elizabeth & Suzanna Crage. "Movements and Memory: The Making of the Stonewall Myth." *American Sociological Review*, 2006, Vol. 71 (October 724–751).

Carter, David. *Stonewall: The Riots that Sparked the Gay Revolution*. New York: St. Martins, 2004.

Duberman, Martin. *Stonewall*. New York: Plume, 1993.

Feinberg, Leslie. "Street Transvestite Action Revolutionaries." *Workers' World*. September 24, 2006. https://www.workers.org/2006/us/lavender-red-73/

Rivera Sylvia. "Queens In Exile, The Forgotten Ones." *Street Transvestite Action Revolutionaries: Survival, Revolt, and Queer Antagonist Struggle*. Untorelli Press, 2013.

Stryker, Susan. *Transgender History: The Roots of Today's Revolution*. Berkeley, CA: Seal Press, 2017.

BAYARD RUSTIN

LGBTQ activist

Born: March 17, 1910; West Chester, Pennsylvania
Died: August 24, 1987; New York City, New York
Areas of Achievement: Gay and lesbian issues; Government and politics; Labor; Social issues

Rustin worked for civil rights, social justice, and world peace for more than fifty years. His major achievement was organizing the 1963 March on Washington, the pinnacle of the African American Civil Rights movement. Rustin also was a prominent figure in the early stages of the gay and lesbian rights struggle.

EARLY LIFE

Bayard Taylor Rustin was born in West Chester, Pennsylvania, in 1910 to Florence Davis, who was in her teens. He never knew his father. Rustin grew up believing that his grandparents, who raised him, were his parents; he did

Bayard Rustin (Library of Congress)

not learn the truth until he was eleven. He also realized that he was gay during his youth and confided in his grandmother, Julia Davis Rustin, who responded with understanding. Julia, a Quaker, positively influenced Rustin's moral and social perspectives.

West Chester also shaped Rustin's character. The community had been part of the Underground Railroad that harbored escaped slaves in the nineteenth century. However, West Chester was racially segregated in the 1920's and the Ku Klux Klan was active in the town. While still a teenager, Rustin challenged segregation as an individual and by leading groups of African American peers. Confident, persuasive, and undaunted by arrests, Rustin proved adept at organizing people for social change.

In high school, Rustin excelled in athletics, singing, debating, and public speaking, and graduated near the top of his class. However, financial hardship and the Great Depression of the 1930's prevented Rustin from earning a college degree.

LIFE'S WORK

Rustin moved to New York City in the 1930's. He found work singing until political activism took over. The American Communist Party's opposition to racism led Rustin to join the party and work as a recruiter, but he quit in objection to its compromises on integration at the start of World War II. Rustin's disillusionment with communism mirrored the experiences of Langston Hughes, Richard Wright, and other prominent African Americans. The brief affiliation would haunt him in the future.

Rustin's activism for organized labor, racial integration, and pacifism accelerated in the 1940's. African American labor leader A. Philip Randolph and Rustin began their long working relationship during that time. Rustin joined the Fellowship of Reconciliation, an international peace organization, and the Congress of Racial Equality (CORE). Both groups benefited from Rustin's speaking and organizing tours. He endured arrests and beatings, but won over people with his convictions and charisma.

Rustin's opposition to the military draft brought his activism and sexual relationships under scrutiny by the Federal Bureau of Investigation (FBI). His refusal to serve in World War II led to a prison term of more than two years. In 1947, Rustin joined an integrated group of activists for the first Freedom Rides aimed at desegregating interstate bus travel in the South. These actions landed Rustin in a North Carolina jail, for which he worked on a chain gang. His published accounts of the experience helped abolish North Carolina's chain gangs.

> *"When an individual is protesting society's refusal to acknowledge his dignity as a human being, his very act of protest confers dignity on him."*

Rustin's agenda became increasingly international in the 1950's. He campaigned against nuclear weapons and went abroad to support Africans and Asians in their struggles against Western domination. At home, friends as well as foes disapproved of Rustin's sexuality. He served another jail term, this time for "perverted" behavior (1953). Controversy over his sex life complicated Rustin's work as an architect of the Civil Rights movement in the 1950's and 1960's. The movement needed his experience as an activist, organizer, and tactician. He mentored the much younger Martin Luther King, Jr., during the 1955 Montgomery bus boycott, shaping King's message and methods. However, Rustin's radical roots and stigmatized sexuality made him a target for critics seeking to discredit the movement, and civil rights allies feared a scandal.

The King-Rustin partnership put both men on the defensive. Rustin kept a low profile even while coordinating the March on Washington. The demonstration gave King a global audience and led to major civil rights legislation. Rustin took a new role directing the A. Philip Randolph Institute, a liberal think tank (1965-1979). An insider with access to President Lyndon B. Johnson, Rustin modified his beliefs and strategies, provoking controversy by supporting the Vietnam War. Discord within the Civil Rights movement took a toll on Rustin, whom some Black Nationalists labeled a traitor. His organization of a memorial march after King's 1968 assassination was one of Rustin's last major public acts of the 1960's. In his later years, Rustin worked against South Africa's apartheid and committed himself to the struggle for gay and lesbian rights. He died of heart failure at the age of seventy-five in New York City.

SIGNIFICANCE

Although Rustin was one of the most important black leaders of the twentieth century, his contributions to the Civil Rights movement—including a key role in the legendary March on Washington—were long overlooked. His refusal to be ashamed of his race and sexuality drove a lifetime of activism to combat discrimination and prejudice in all forms.

Ray Pence

FURTHER READING

Anderson, Jervis. *Bayard Rustin: Troubles I've Seen—A Biography*. Berkeley: University of California Press, 1998. The first major Rustin biography, aimed at general readers, covers the civil rights leader's life and work.

D'Emilio, John. *Lost Prophet: The Life and Times of Bayard Rustin*. New York: Free Press, 2003. A lengthy, well-researched scholarly portrait of Rustin as a gay and lesbian rights pioneer.

Podair, Jerald E. *Bayard Rustin: American Dreamer*. Lanham, Md.: Rowman & Littlefield, 2009. A comprehensive account of Rustin's achievements, suited to academic and general audiences.

EDWARD SNOWDEN

Activist

Born: June 21, 1983; Elizabeth City, North Carolina
Area(s) of significance: Activism; dissidence; government and politics

A skilled computer programmer, Edward Snowden spent years working in computer network security as an employee and contractor for the Central Intelligence Agency (CIA) and the National Security Agency (NSA), which gave him access to top-secret government information. In 2013 Snowden leaked a number of secret documents, publicly revealing an elaborate domestic spying program run by the NSA.

Edward Snowden (Wikimedia Commons)

EARLY LIFE

Edward Joseph Snowden was born in Elizabeth City, North Carolina, on June 21, 1983, the second of two children. His father, Lon, was in the Coast Guard. His mother, Elizabeth "Wendy" Snowden, worked as a chief deputy clerk for administration and information technology for the US District Court in Baltimore, Maryland. When Snowden was nine, the family moved to Crofton, Maryland, outside of Annapolis. He attended Arundel High School, but dropped out during his sophomore year in 1998 after coming down with mononucleosis. Snowden took community college courses at Anne Arundel Community College in computer science and later earned his GED. His parents divorced in 2001 and he moved with his mother to Ellicot City, Maryland, and worked for a friend's small technology company.

In May 2004, inspired by the terrorist attacks on the World Trade Center three years earlier, he joined the Army Special Forces. Snowden reported to Fort Benning in Georgia for basic training, but grew disillusioned with the attitudes of his fellow recruits. He broke both of his legs in a training accident and was discharged in September. Snowden moved back to Maryland where he found a job as a security guard for the University of Maryland's Center for Advanced Study of Language, an NSA facility.

LIFE'S WORK

Shortly after taking the security job, the CIA hired Snowden as a computer engineer working on information technology (IT) security. He later spent six months in training in the CIA's technology specialist school. In 2007 he was transferred to Geneva, Switzerland, and worked for the CIA at the United States Mission to the United Nations maintaining computer network security. Just like with the army, Snowden was disappointed in the work practices of CIA agents he observed and the government's war activities that he read about in internal documents. He resigned from the organization in 2009.

"There have been times throughout American history where what is right

Snowden speaking with Chris Anderson and Tim Berners Lee at TED on a telepresence robot, beaming in from a secret location in Russia. (Wikimedia Commons)

is not the same as what is legal. Sometimes to do the right thing you have to break the law."

In 2010 he took a job in Tokyo, Japan, working for Dell, a computer technology company that did contract work for the NSA. Through Dell, he worked with NSA officials to safeguard networks against Chinese hackers. In 2011 Dell transferred him back to Maryland where served as lead technologist for the CIA. At this point, Snowden had had worked with the NSA long enough to know about the organization's mass surveillance program—an extensive operation that included monitoring the e-mails and cell phone calls of ordinary citizens. In 2012 Dell sent him to Hawaii to do more contract work for the NSA at their Central Security Service on Oahu, where he could view and download all but the highest level security information. In early 2013 he took a job with the consulting and contracting firm Booz Allen Hamilton and, through the company, took another position in cyber security for the NSA. He worked as a system administrator, a role that provided him with wide-ranging access to NSA computers and allowed him to access documents without being traced. He downloaded top-secret documents onto thumb drives. By this time, Snowden had already reached out to two journalists, filmmaker Laura Poitras and writer Glenn Greenwald, who would later leak the documents.

In May 2013 Snowden flew to Hong Kong. His correspondence with Poitras and Greenwald had been conducted using complicated security mechanisms to ensure the secrecy of their project. The three finally met in person in Hong Kong in June. The London *Guardian* published the first document—one of the hundreds of thousands Snowden had downloaded—a few days later on June 6, 2013. Over the next few weeks, additional documents were published by the *Guardian* and the *Washington Post* revealing the extent of the NSA's warrantless domestic surveillance and the United States' international espionage practices. Among the most significant of the revelations was that of the PRISM program, which allowed the NSA access to the systems of large tech companies, such as Google and Apple, and how those companies may have collaborated with the NSA on their surveillance efforts. (Both newspapers continued to publish additional leaked documents for months afterwards.)

In an interview with the *Guardian* published on June 9, 2013, Snowden revealed himself as the whistleblower. The United States Department of Justice filed a criminal complaint against Snowden on June 14, charging him with three felonies: stealing government property, revealing classified information, and transferring classified documents to unauthorized parties. The government sought to extradite Snowden from Hong Kong, but the autonomous region did not fulfill the request. On June 23, he flew to Moscow, and was forced to stay in the airport for five weeks until given temporary asylum by the Russian government in August. He made a formal request for clemency from the United States, but it was denied in November 2013.

When Snowden's temporary asylum expired on August 1, 2014, he was authorized to stay in Russia for another three years. Further extensions have granted him the right to stay in Russia at least until 2020. Snowden is in high demand as a speaker; he has given talks in many countries via satellite and remains a vocal advocate against unauthorized government surveillance. Edward Snowden's longtime girlfriend, Lindsay Mills, joined him in Moscow where they live together.

In 2016, Snowden became the president of the Freedom of the Press Foundation, an organization that attempts to protect journalists from hacking and government surveillance.

SIGNIFICANCE

Edward Snowden is a polarizing figure who has had a

major cultural impact on American culture and policy. He is lauded by some as the most significant whistle-blower of the recent past; he was named *Time* magazine's Person of the Year in 2013. Many books have been written about him and he was the subject of Poitras's documentary about their meeting, *Citizenfour*, which won an Academy Award in 2015. He is also a wanted criminal and, according to some government officials, a traitor, who reportedly inflicted so much damage on US military security that it could take billions of dollars to fix.

Snowden and the information he brought to light have remained big news since June 2013, but by 2015 policies began to reflect real change. Congress voted in June 2015 to rein in the NSA program that collects phone records with the USA Freedom Act, which stated that the section of the USA Patriot Act that the NSA had previously used to justify bulk collection could not be used after six months. Apple and Google improved encryption on their devices to protect customers' data from government surveillance. A federal appeals court ruled on May 7, 2015 that collecting Americans' phone records without a warrant is illegal.

In 2016, Oliver Stone directed the film Snowden, a biographical thriller about Snowden's life as a whistleblower. It was based on the books The Snowden Files by Luke Harding and Time of the Octopus by Anatoly Kucherena. It starred Joseph Gordon-Levitt as Snowden and included an all-star supporting cast: Shailene Woodley, Melissa Leo, Zachary Quinto, Timothy Olyphant, Tom Wilkinson, and Nicolas Cage. The movie had to be financed through France and Germany and filmed in Germany as no US companies or studios were willing to support it. Stone and Gordon-Levitt met with Snowden in Moscow during production and Snowden even makes a cameo appearance as himself at the end of the film, saying: "I think the greatest freedom that I've gained is the fact that I no longer have to worry about what happens tomorrow, because I'm happy with what I've done today."

Molly Hagan

Further Reading

Bamford, James. "The Most Wanted Man in the World." Wired. Condé Nast, 22 Aug. 2014. Web.

Burrough, Bryan, Sarah Ellison, and Suzanna Andrews. "The Snowden Saga: A Shadowland of Secrets and Light." Vanity Fair. Condé Nast, May 2014. Web.

Marbella, Jean, Shashank Bengali, and David S. Cloud. "Details about Edward Snowden's Life in Maryland Emerge." Baltimore Sun. Baltimore Sun, 10 June 2013. Web.

Savage, Charlie, and Jonathan Weisman. "N.S.A. Collection of Bulk Call Data Is Ruled Illegal." New York Times. New York Times, 7 May 2015. Web.

Shane, Scott. "Snowden Sees Some Victories, From a Distance." New York Times. New York Times, 19 May 2015. Web.

Elizabeth Cady Stanton

Social reformer

Born: November 12, 1815; Johnstown, New York
Died: October 26, 1902; New York City, New York
Area of Achievement: Women's rights

Stanton was one of the founders of the organized women's rights movement in the United States and served as one of its chief leaders during the second half of the nineteenth century.

Elizabeth Cady Stanton (Library of Congress)

EARLY LIFE

Elizabeth Cady Stanton was born Elizabeth Cady, the fourth of the six children of Daniel and Margaret Cady who survived childhood. Through her mother she was descended from a wealthy family, the Livingstons, who were part of the political elite of New York. Her mother's father, James Livingston, was an officer in George Washington's army during the American Revolution and a member of the New York state legislature. Elizabeth's father, Daniel Cady, was a successful lawyer who served in the New York state legislature and the U.S. House of Representatives, and, after 1847, he was a member of the New York State Supreme Court. Daniel Cady was a conservative in his political views and became an active member of the Federalist Party. Elizabeth's parents were

---

Early Exposure to the Law

In her autobiography, Elizabeth Cady Stanton recalls how she became aware of the gross unfairness to women of statutory laws, about which she read in her father's law office when she was young.

"As my father's office joined the house, I spent there much of my time, when out of school, listening to the clients stating their cases, talking with the students, and reading the laws in regard to woman. In our Scotch neighborhood many men still retained the old feudal ideas of women and property. Fathers, at their death, would will the bulk of their property to the eldest son, with the proviso that the mother was to have a home with him. Hence it was not unusual for the mother, who had brought all the property into the family, to be made an unhappy dependent on the bounty of an uncongenial daughter-in-law and a dissipated son. The tears and complaints of the women who came to my father for legal advice touched my heart and early drew my attention to the injustice and cruelty of the laws. As the practice of the law was my father's business, I could not exactly understand why he could not alleviate the sufferings of these women. So, in order to enlighten me, he would take down his books and show me the inexorable statutes. The students, observing my interest, would amuse themselves by reading to me all the worst laws they could find, over which I would laugh and cry by turns. One Christmas morning I went into the office to show them, among other of my presents, a new coral necklace and bracelets. They all admired the jewelry and then began to tease me with hypothetical cases of future ownership. 'Now,' said Henry Bayard, 'if in due time you should be my wife, those ornaments would be mine; I could take them and lock them up, and you could never wear them except with my permission. I could even exchange them for a box of cigars, and you could watch them evaporate in smoke.'

"With this constant bantering from students and the sad complaints of the women, my mind was sorely perplexed. So when, from time to time, my attention was called to these odious laws, I would mark them with a pencil, and becoming more and more convinced of the necessity of taking some active measures against these unjust provisions, I resolved to seize the first opportunity, when alone in the office, to cut every one of them out of the books; supposing my father and his library were the beginning and the end of the law. However, this mutilation of his volumes was never accomplished, for dear old Flora Campbell, to whom I confided my plan for the amelioration of the wrongs of my unhappy sex, warned my father of what I proposed to do. Without letting me know that he had discovered my secret, he explained to me one evening how laws were made, the large number of lawyers and libraries there were all over the State, and that if his library should burn up it would make no difference in woman's condition. 'When you are grown up, and able to prepare a speech,' said he, 'you must go down to Albany and talk to the legislators; tell them all you have seen in this office—the sufferings of these Scotch women, robbed of their inheritance and left dependent on their unworthy sons, and, if you can persuade them to pass new laws, the old ones will be a dead letter.' Thus was the future object of my life foreshadowed and my duty plainly outlined by him who was most opposed to my public career when, in due time, I entered upon it."

Source: Elizabeth Cady Stanton, *Eighty Years and More: Reminiscences, 1815-1897* (New York, 1898), chapter 2.

strict Presbyterians who held firmly to traditional Calvinist doctrines of predestination and the depravity of human nature. As a child, Elizabeth found this version of religion frightening, even to the point of having nightmares that the Devil was attempting to possess her.

Several events in Elizabeth's childhood helped awaken her to the realization that women held a subordinate position in American society. Her father wanted very much to have a son, but each of Elizabeth's three brothers died young. At the death of his third son, Daniel Cady openly lamented to Elizabeth that she was not a boy. Part of the impetus for Elizabeth's refusal to accept a traditional female sex role may have stemmed from her attempt to be the son her father so fervently desired. A second instance that brought a new awareness of the disadvantage of being female occurred in her father's law office. Hearing of a case in which a female friend sought unsuccessfully to reclaim property she had purchased with her own money, but of which she had been deprived because of a state law transferring a woman's property to her husband when she married, Elizabeth became so upset that she attempted to cut the relevant pages out of her father's law books.

Even as a child, Elizabeth displayed intellectual ability considerably beyond that of the average youth. Believing that becoming a learned person was essential if she were to be equal to boys, she began the study of Greek at the age of eleven, later winning a prize at the Johnstown Academy for her achievements in this area. In spite of her outstanding academic record, she was not allowed to enroll at Union College, which admitted only boys, and had to be content with a girls' boarding school, Troy Female Seminary, which she attended from 1830 to 1833. Although most girls' boarding schools at this time were primarily finishing schools, concentrating on developing their students' social skills, Troy was unusual in that it attempted to provide academic training comparable to that which colleges provided men. The seminary encouraged its students to be self-reliant and provided careful training in writing skills, which Elizabeth later believed to have contributed to her success as an author.

After graduation from Troy Female Seminary, Elizabeth did not seek a career and at this point displayed little evidence that she would become a reformer. Even in this period, however, she occasionally displayed those qualities of independence and a militant opposition to efforts to place women in a subordinate position that marked her later life. She became the head of a young women's association that raised funds to enable an aspiring minister to attend seminary. When the recipient of their funds was invited to deliver a special sermon and chose to speak on women's inferiority, Elizabeth rose from her seat in the front pew and led the other young women out of the church in a gesture of protest.

During the 1830s, Elizabeth was increasingly drawn into the abolitionist movement; reform effort by her cousin Gerrit Smith. Her cousin's home was a station on the Underground Railroad, and the accounts of their experiences by fugitive slaves made a lasting impression on Elizabeth. It was while attending an anti-slavery meeting that Elizabeth met the man who eventually became her husband. Henry Stanton was a member of the executive committee that directed the activities of the American Anti-Slavery. He was a gifted public speaker who had risked his life on several occasions by speaking against slavery to hostile crowds. When he proposed marriage to Elizabeth, her parents were totally opposed, because they considered abolitionists to be fanatics.

Marriage to Henry was an important turning point in Elizabeth's life, for he was not wealthy, and she knew that the social elite of New York would never accept them as long as he remained an abolitionist. Nevertheless—and even though her parents remained opposed and did not attend her wedding—Elizabeth married Henry in May, 1840. In two important respects, the marriage ceremony reflected her emerging feminist consciousness: At her request, the traditional bride's promise to obey her husband was deleted from the wedding vows, and, while adding her husband's name, she retained her own name.

> "*To deny political equality is to rob the ostracised of all self-respect; of credit in the market place; of recompense in the world of work; of a voice among those who make and administer the law; a choice in the jury before whom they are tried, and in the judge who decides their punishment.*"

LIFE'S WORK

Almost immediately after their marriage, Elizabeth and Henry left for London to attend an international anti-slavery convention. This proved to be a traumatic experience for her. Many male delegates feared that association with feminism would harm the abolitionist cause and opposed allowing women to be delegates. The first major issue discussed at the conference was whether women delegates should be allowed to participate on an equal basis with men. It was eventually decided that women should not be allowed to sit on the convention floor with men and should not be permitted to speak at the conference. Stanton was deeply angered by the treatment accorded women and resolved to organize a women's rights convention when she returned to the United States. Although eight years passed before that conference was held, her treatment at the London convention was directly responsible for convincing her that women must join together in an organized effort if they were to progress toward equality.

After their return to New York, Stanton became immersed in domestic activities. She had seven children between 1842 and 1859, and her husband considered it her responsibility to rear them. Partly because Henry was often away from home, sometimes for as long as eight months, Stanton was frequently depressed and resented the burdens of housework and child rearing. In her speeches and writings in later years, she often stressed birth control as of central importance in improving the position of married women; it is likely that her remarks at least partially reflected her own experiences.

After discovering that other women shared her sense of discontent, Stanton organized a women's rights convention at Seneca Falls, New York, at which women's grievances could be expressed. The Woman's Rights Convention (1848) was intended to be a local event, and she did not expect a large turnout. Nevertheless, more than three hundred persons came for the convention, including a number of prominent reformers from nearby Rochester. Stanton wrote the key document discussed by the convention, a list of women's grievances that she called the Declaration of Sentiments.

The declaration was modeled after the Declaration of Independence and drew upon the same natural-rights arguments to justify an end to discrimination based on sex. The list of grievances was lengthy and covered a wide spectrum: the admission of women to institutions of higher education, the right to enter professions such as law and medicine, the right of employed married women to retain their earnings, and an end to the double standard of sexual morality. Resolutions on these points received the unanimous support of those at the convention. A resolution proposing woman suffrage, however, proved far more controversial and passed by only a bare majority. Even Stanton's husband, Henry, opposed the suffrage resolution. After the convention, Stanton's father attempted to persuade her to remove her name from the list of those who had signed the Declaration of Sentiments, but she refused to do so. Her decision to persevere was an important turning point in her emergence as a nationally prominent feminist reformer.

During the years after the Seneca Falls convention, Stanton continued her activities on behalf of women's rights but was also active in other reform movements. In 1852, angry because the New York State temperance organization discriminated against women, she helped found the Women's State Temperance Society of New York. Her advocacy of the temperance movement reflected a belief that excessive drinking by men often had serious consequences for women.

Because of the brutality often exhibited by drunken men toward their wives, Stanton urged that the grounds for divorce be expanded to include consistent heavy drinking. The majority of the women members were too conservative to consider Stanton's suggestion that the grounds for divorce be liberalized, and when they refused to reelect her as president, she withdrew from the organization. She also remained active in the abolitionist movement, urging the immediate emancipation of slaves, and opposed Abraham Lincoln's candidacy for the presidency in 1860 on the grounds that he was too moderate on the

Address of Stanton before the Senate Committee on Privileges and Elections, 1878. (Library of Congress)

slavery issue and might compromise with the South. When, after the war, constitutional amendments were proposed extending the suffrage and civil rights to blacks, Stanton campaigned to have the amendments extended to women. Opposition to this step by her abolitionist friends contributed to its failure and drove a wedge between them; this was widened when she, in turn, argued against the Fourteenth and Fifteenth amendments because she feared the newly enfranchised black men would be hostile to woman suffrage.

In 1851, Stanton met Susan B. Anthony and initiated a friendship that had an important influence on the American feminist movement in the second half of the nineteenth century. Stanton persuaded Anthony to become involved in the campaign for women's rights, and the two worked closely on behalf of that cause for the next forty years. Stanton was a talented writer and public speaker but disliked the administrative work necessary to conduct a major campaign. Anthony excelled at such work, however, and thus the two formed an effective team. Although Anthony later received more public recognition for her role in bringing about woman suffrage, she was the junior partner in the relationship and acknowledged that Stanton was the true founder of the organized women's rights movement in the United States.

With the assistance of Anthony, Stanton promoted the cause of woman suffrage in a variety of ways. In 1866, she ran for Congress as an independent in order to test the constitutional right of a woman to hold public office. In the following year, she conducted an extensive campaign in Kansas, speaking throughout the state on behalf of a state constitutional amendment on woman suffrage.

In 1871, Stanton and Anthony made a speaking tour around the West, seeking to stimulate support for woman suffrage. In 1878, Stanton was responsible for the introduction of a woman suffrage amendment to the Constitution in Congress, a measure that was reintroduced in each subsequent Congress until it was passed in 1920. She appeared in Congress almost every year until late in her life to speak on behalf of the woman suffrage amendment. Perhaps her most important contribution to that movement was the major part she played in establishing and directing the National Woman Suffrage Association. Stanton and Anthony formed the NWSA in 1869, and Stanton served as its president until 1890, when it merged with the rival American Woman Suffrage Association. A prolific writer, Stanton joined with Anthony in coediting three volumes of *History of Woman Suffrage* (Stanton et al.) (1881-1886), an invaluable source on the American woman suffrage movement.

Although woman suffrage was her major concern, Stanton never restricted her reforming efforts to one issue. She frequently shocked female audiences by her ideas on marriage and divorce. This caused friction between her and Anthony, who maintained that the cause of woman suffrage was being harmed by associating it with radical proposals for easier divorce. Stanton also alarmed Anthony with her criticisms of the Church. She believed that the Church was a major force maintaining the subordinate position of women, and from 1878, Stanton endeavored to persuade the NWSA to take a public stand against this.

Unsuccessful in that effort, Stanton then attempted to establish a committee of women to prepare a revised version of the Bible that would eliminate its sexist language. Eventually she proceeded on her own to write an extensive commentary on the biblical passages that directly discussed the status of women. Published in 1895 as *The Woman's Bible*, (Stanton and Gage), it defended women against the claim that they were responsible for Original Sin because of Eve's behavior in the Garden of Eden. Stanton was deeply hurt when the work was repudiated by other woman suffrage leaders, who feared that it would lead the public to dismiss the suffrage movement as irreligious.

Although her eyes began to fail during the last years of her life (she was completely blind by the time of her death), Stanton continued to write on women's issues until her death, on October 26, 1902, in New York City. She continued to enjoy life during old age, but her last years were marred by the breakdown of her friendship with Anthony and the efforts of woman suffrage leaders to distance themselves from her because of their belief that *The Woman's Bible* would prove harmful to their cause.

SIGNIFICANCE

The position of women in American society has changed considerably since the mid-nineteenth century, and Stanton was one of the central figures helping to bring about that change. As the founder of the organized women's rights movement in the United States and its recognized leader during the second half of the nineteenth century, she was a vital figure in an important and continuing reform movement. Although often remembered primarily in connection with the woman suffrage issue, she viewed suffrage as a means by which reforms could be instituted in other areas affecting women rather than an end in itself.

Although she held important offices in women's organizations, Stanton was equally important as a publicist whose writings articulated the reasons that feminists wished to alter relationships between the sexes. Her writings on these issues were so extensive that it would be appropriate to consider her the chief theorist or intellectual of the late nineteenth-century women's rights movement.

Since her death, Stanton's contribution to the American women's suffrage movement has been overshadowed by that of Anthony. This is in part because many of the women's suffrage activists in the generation immediately after Stanton's death did not share her views on issues other than suffrage. The revival of feminism in the United States since 1960, however, has brought a renewed interest in her life and work, partly because she did emphasize that the nonpolitical forces that kept women in a subordinate position were as important as those that were political.

Harold L. Smith

FURTHER READING

Banner, Lois. Elizabeth Cady Stanton: A Radical for Women's Rights. Boston: Little, Brown, 1980. The best single volume on Stanton's life and thought. It presents her as the philosopher of the feminist movement and is especially helpful on her theories.

DuBois, Ellen Carol, ed. Elizabeth Cady Stanton, Susan B. Anthony: Correspondence, Writings, Speeches. New York: Schocken Books, 1981. This is an excellent collection of the correspondence between Stanton and Anthony, which also includes many of Stanton's more important speeches and articles. The critical commentary by DuBois is helpful in placing the documents in context.

Flexner, Eleanor. Century of Struggle: The Woman's Rights Movement in the United States. Cambridge, Mass.: Harvard University Press, 1959. Widely regarded as the best history of the campaign for woman suffrage. It includes some references to Stanton but focuses on the movement itself rather than on its leaders.

Forster, Margaret. "Elizabeth Cady Stanton, 1815-1902." In Significant Sisters. New York: Oxford University Press, 1984. A well-written chapter in a book about prominent feminists. It makes extensive use of Stanton's letters and other original sources in conveying a vivid sense of her personality.

Griffith, Elisabeth. In Her Own Right: The Life of Elizabeth Cady Stanton. New York: Oxford University Press, 1984. A detailed account of Stanton's life based upon extensive research in primary sources. It is a psychological study that excels in discussing Stanton's private life.

Kern, Kathi. Mrs. Stanton's Bible. Ithaca, N.Y.: Cornell University Press, 2001. Examines Stanton's non-sexist Bible, published in 1895. Kern argues Stanton's biblical commentary alienated her from less radical feminists and may have delayed passage of the woman suffrage amendment.

Lutz, Alma. Created Equal: A Biography of Elizabeth Cady Stanton. New York: John Day, 1940. This was the first scholarly biography of Stanton. It is a clear, objective, narrative account that concentrates more on her political activities than on her thought.

Stanton, Elizabeth Cady. Eighty Years and More: Reminiscences, 1815-1897. London: T. Fisher Unwin, 1898. Reprint. New York: Schocken Books, 1971. Written near the end of her life, Stanton's autobiography provides the fullest account of her life from her own point of view. Although invaluable for its firsthand information, it is brief on some events in her life and omits others entirely, and thus must be supplemented by other sources.

Wellman, Judith. The Road to Seneca Falls: Elizabeth Cady Stanton and the First Women's Rights Convention. Urbana: University of Illinois Press, 2004. Chronicles the events that took place during the historic women's rights meeting, describing how abolitionism, radical Quakerism, and the campaign for legal reform shaped the convention's proceedings—and Stanton's life.

MARY TAPE

Chinese-born activist and photographer

Born: 1857; China
Died: October 9, 1934; Berkeley, California
Also known as: Mary McGladery
Area of Achievement: Activism, art

Tape is best known for her role in the 1885 California Supreme Court case Tape v. Hurley, in which her eight-year-old daughter Mamie sued a San Francisco school that denied her admission due to her Chinese heritage. She also received local acclaim for her talent as an amateur photographer.

Mary Tape (far right) (Wikimedia Commons)

EARLY LIFE

Mary Tape was born in China in 1857 and immigrated to the United States by 1868, settling in San Francisco. She lived in Chinatown for a time before becoming a resident of the children's home run by the Ladies' Protection and Relief Society. While at the home, Tape met the institution's matron, Mary McGladery, who taught her to speak and read English. Tape was so strongly influenced by McGladery that she adopted her teacher's name as her own; her original name is not known.

In the spring of 1875, Mary met Joseph Tape (originally Jeu Dip), a deliveryman who had emigrated from China in 1869. They married on November 16, 1875, and later had four children. Joseph established a successful business that allowed the family to purchase a home as well as vacation and rental properties.

LIFE'S WORK

The Tapes valued education, and as established residents of San Francisco, they wanted their children to be educated in the local public school system that they supported through taxes. Although California state law provided for segregated public education for nonwhite students, children of Chinese ancestry were denied even this between 1871 and 1885, reflecting the significant anti-Chinese sentiment of the period. Many Chinese-American children received no education, while others had tutors, were homeschooled, or attended religious schools. In 1878, the Chinese community in California petitioned the state legislature for public education opportunities, but the petition was rejected.

When their eldest daughter, Mamie, was refused admittance to the local public school because of her Chinese heritage, the Tapes first enlisted the Chinese consulate to argue on their behalf. In response, the superintendent of San Francisco schools cited the California Constitution, which referred to the Chinese as "dangerous to the well-being of the state," as justification for barring Mamie and other Chinese-American children from enrolling. The Tapes then sued the principal of the Spring Valley School, Jennie Hurley, and the San Francisco Board of Education. In March of 1885, the Supreme Court of California ruled in *Tape v. Hurley* that Chinese-American children born in the United States and residing within a public school district were guaranteed the right to a public school education by both the U.S. Constitution and California law.

Following this decision, the California legislature passed a law that allowed the establishment of segregated schools for Chinese children and prohibited students from attending any other public school when a Chinese school was available. Tape wrote a strongly worded letter to the board of education protesting this injustice and pledging that her own children would never attend a segregated school. Despite her pledge, Tape eventually sent her eldest children to the newly established Chinese school. Early in the 1890s, Tape moved with her family to Berkeley, California, where her children were able to attend non-segregated schools.

While living in Berkeley, Tape, a skilled amateur photographer, became known for developing her own photographs and creating slides for use with a magic lantern, an early image-projecting device. She received a great deal of attention for her artistic talent and knowledge of chemicals and darkroom principles, though many of the reports on her work focused on the fact that she was a Chinese woman participating in an activity dominated by Caucasian men. Tape also created paintings and decorative dishes, some of which appeared in exhibits decades after her death.

"What right have you to bar my children out of the school because she is a Chinese Decend. They is no other worldly reason that you could keep her out, except that. I suppose, you all goes to churches on Sundays! Do you call that a Christian act to compel my little children to go so far to a

school that is made in purpose for them."

Significance

Tape played a significant role in the movement against school segregation, establishing in *Tape v. Hurley* a precedent that continued to be referenced in cases of discrimination. Though Chinese-American children remained segregated in some California communities into the 1930s, the process of school segregation ultimately came to an end nationwide following the 1954 Supreme Court case *Brown v. Board of Education*.

Judy A. Johnson

Further Reading

Kuo, Joyce. "Excluded, Segregated, and Forgotten: A Historical View of the Discrimination against Chinese Americans in Public Schools." *Chinese America: History and Perspectives* (2000): 32–48. Print. Provides an overview of anti-Chinese discrimination in public schools and includes several references to the Tape case.

Ngai, Mae. *The Lucky Ones: One Family and the Extraordinary Invention of Chinese America*. Boston: Houghton, 2010. Print. Details the history of the Tape family, including the lives of Mary and Joseph's children.

Thompson, Daniella. *The Tapes of Russell Street: An Accomplished Family of School Desegregating Pioneers*. Berkeley Architectural Heritage Association, 30 Apr. 2004. Web. 7 Mar. 2012. Discusses Tape's early life, experience with segregation, and artistic talents and includes several of her photographs.

Reies López Tijerina

Activist

Born: September 21, 1926; Falls City, Texas
Died: January 19, 2015; El Paso, Texas
Areas of achievement: Activism; social issues

During the 1960's and 1970's, Tijerina led a militant struggle to restore Spanish colonial land grants in New Mexico to the grantees' descendants.

Early Life

Reies López Tijerina (RAY-ehz LOH-pehz TEE-heh-REE-nah) was born on September 21, 1926, near Falls City, Texas. His father, Antonio, was a cotton sharecropper; his mother, Herlinda, was a strong-willed woman accustomed to carrying heavy cotton sacks on her back. Tijerina had three brothers and three sisters.

The Great Depression was particularly hard on cotton producers, forcing the Tijerina family to join the massive stream of migrant farmworkers who moved almost constantly in search of employment. During summers, the family usually worked in Michigan, then scraped out a living in San Antonio during the winter months. Like other Mexican Americans, Tijerina experienced a great deal of prejudice and discrimination. By the age of fifteen, he had begun talking back to white employers, and he resented his father's subservient behavior. As he matured, Tijerina became increasingly convinced that most Anglos were fundamentally unjust and hypocritical.

Like many children of migrant workers, Tijerina had limited opportunities for formal schooling and never graduated from high school. Influenced by his pious mother, however, he took a keen interest in religion, often reading the Bible during breaks in the field. Particularly attracted to the practical ethics of Jesus Christ, he had little concern for "otherworldly" doctrines such as the Trinity and the afterlife. Deciding to become a Protestant minister, Tijerina enrolled in 1944 at the Assembly of God Bible Institute in El Paso, Texas. His theological ideas were considered unorthodox at the school, and he withdrew in 1947 without graduating. Shortly thereafter, he married a fellow student, Mary Escobar, and for most of the next ten years, he traveled around the country as an itinerant minister. During this period, he developed close ties to many Mexican American communities and perfected his skills in public speaking and persuasion.

Life's Work

Tijerina became convinced that Christian churches were either unwilling or unable to promote social justice, and he decided to leave the ministry. In 1956, he led a group of seventeen families to southern Arizona with the goal of establishing a utopian commune. After a flood destroyed most of the commune, Tijerina experienced a vision in which three "interplanetary messengers or angels" informed him that he had been chosen for a special mission. He wrote in his autobiography: "I believed in what I saw and planned on obeying, fulfilling the mission."

In early 1957, Tijerina was accused of theft, and that July, he was formally charged with participating in a failed jailbreak scheme to free one of his brothers. Hearing rumors of an Anglo conspiracy to have him killed, he fled Arizona and was a fugitive for the next four years. By moving frequently, he successfully evaded law enforcement officers until the statute of limitations expired. The resulting stress, however, was particularly difficult on his wife, and the couple formally divorced in 1963.

While in northern New Mexico, Tijerina learned about the century-old grievance of poor Mexican American farmers in the region. In the Treaty of Guadalupe Hidalgo (1848), which ended the Mexican-American War, the U.S. government had agreed to respect property ownership based on Spanish and Mexican grants but refused to recognize communal lands (*ejido*) assigned to groups of farmers. Some of the land had been annexed as national forests, and thousands of acres were purchased by speculators. Infuriated by these accounts of Anglo greed and theft, Tijerina promised to try to help the farmers to regain possession of their ancestral lands. In order to learn more about the grants, he spent several months in Mexico examining archives and discussing the matter with legal scholars.

> "*There is a powerful expression of our yearning. But now that we have the revolutionary spirit, we must not lose sight of the brotherhood awareness. Temper the revolutionary spirit. Culture identification is needed, but we must not let it lead us to hatred*"

In 1963, Tijerina founded the Federal Alliance of Land Grants (La Alianza Federal de Mercedes), which grew to about fourteen thousand members in two years. He explained that its purpose "was to give the Indo-Hispanic people of the Southwest pride in their heritage, and to force the Anglo to respect him, just like we respect them." For a number of months in 1965, Tijerina publicized the land issue with a daily radio program, *The Voice of Justice*. On July 2, 1966, he mobilized a nonviolent march from Albuquerque to Santa Fe with the goal of drawing attention to the issue of land grants. Although the governor and media expressed sympathy for the farmers, the march failed to prompt any change.

Tijerina decided that a more militant strategy was necessary. On October 15, 1966, three hundred alliance members occupied the Echo Amphitheater portion of the Kit Carson National Park, arguing that a section of the park had been included in the San Joaquín land grant. The occupiers made citizens' arrests of two park rangers for trespassing. After five days, the occupation ended when government authorities moved in and arrested Tijerina and four others. The five men were charged with assault but released on bond. When the alliance held a meeting in Coyote on June 3, 1967, district attorney Alfonso Sánchez alleged communist influence and ordered that the meeting be disbanded. Although Tijerina escaped, eleven members were arrested and then jailed in Tierra Amarilla.

On June 5, 1967, Tijerina led three carloads of armed supporters to the courthouse in Tierra Amarilla. Their intent was to free their comrades and to make a citizens' arrest of Sánchez, who was not in the courthouse at the time. During the raid, a prison guard, Eulogio Salazar, and a sheriff's deputy were wounded. Tijerina and several followers escaped into the mountains. The National Guard, state police, and local officers conducted the largest manhunt in New Mexico's history. Five days after the raid, Tijerina was taken into custody when he was recognized by a gas station attendant. Salazar, who swore in a hearing that Tijerina was the one who shot him, was brutally murdered on January 2, 1968, but the crime was never solved. While awaiting trial, Tijerina was elected to lead the Chicano delegation of the Poor People's Campaign, and he helped plan many of the demonstrations. In May and June, he marched with major civil rights leaders in Albuquerque, Denver, Kansas City, Louisville, and Washington, D.C

Tijerina's first trial for the Tierra Amarilla shootout was held in Albuquerque in late 1968. He was allowed to defend himself with the help of two court-appointed lawyers. The judge was sympathetic, instructing the jury that a citizens' arrest included the right to use reasonable force. Acquitted of all charges relating to the raid, Tijerina was at the height of his popularity and held several large rallies.

Tijerina's problems with the law, however, continued. In March, 1969, his second wife, Patsy, with his encouragement, protested by burning a large federal sign at the Santa Fe National Forest. When armed forest rangers suddenly appeared, Tijerina threatened a ranger with his M-1 rifle, claiming the right of self defense. He was arrested and released on bail. A few months later, he traveled to Washington with the intention of placing Warren Burger, nominee for chief justice of the Supreme Court, under citizens' arrest; however, as Tijerina waited outside the Senate chamber, Burger dodged the arrest by exiting through a back door. Tried in federal court in September, 1969, for the Tierra Amarilla courthouse raid, Tijerina was found guilty and sentenced to nine years in prison. In October, New Mexico prosecuted him a second time for various charges relating to the Tierra Amarilla shootout, and this time the jury found him guilty of assaulting Salazar.

Tijerina's prison sentences added up to a combined twenty-six years. On July 26, 1971, however, the federal government released him on the condition that he not hold any leadership position in the Federal Alliance of Land Grants. Although he still faced prison time from his New Mexico convictions, the state kept him imprisoned for only six months in 1974. After his final release, Tijerina retained symbolic importance but no longer was a major activist leader with a large following. In 1994, he moved to Mexico, only to return to the United States in 2006. As he aged, Tijerina became less confrontational and emphasized the need for Anglo-Latino reconciliation.

Tijerina died in El Paso, aged 88, on January 19, 2015.

Significance

During the 1960's, Tijerina was a militant spokesman and skillful organizer in the struggle for Latino pride and civil rights. Although he did not achieve his goal of winning legal recognition for preconquest communal land grants, his crusade promoted awareness of a historical injustice that affected thousands of poor farmers and ranchers. His extremist and violent tactics, however, detracted from his effectiveness, causing most of mainstream society to disregard the idealist ends that he espoused.

Thomas Tandy Lewis

Further Reading

Acuña, Rodolfo. *Occupied America: A History of Chicanos.* New York: Pearson Longman, 2004. A standard work in the Chicano studies field that emphasizes anti-Latino discrimination in the Southwestern U.S.

Blawis, Patricia Bell. *Tijerina and the Land Grants: Mexican Americans in Struggle for Their Heritage.* New York: International Publishers, 1971. Clearly written and well organized, this history casts Tijerina and his actions in a positive light.

Ebright, Malcolm. *Land Grants and Lawsuits in Northern New Mexico.* 3d ed. Santa Fe, N. Mex.: Center for Land Grant Studies, 2008. Scholarly historical study of Spanish and Mexican land grants in New Mexico.

Nabokov, Peter. *Tijerina and the Courthouse Raid.* Berkeley: Ramparts Press, 1970. Interesting and balanced account by a journalist who interviewed Tijerina, but its organization is rather confusing.

Rosales, F. Arturo. *Chicano: The History of the Mexican American Civil Rights Movement.* Houston, Tex.: Arte Público Press, 1997. Provides a historical context for Tijerina's life and career.

Tijerina, Reies. *They Called Me "King Tiger."* Translated by José Angel Gutiérrez. Houston, Tex.: Arte Público Press, 2000. Fascinating memoir in which Tijerina clearly and frankly describes his ideology and version of events.

Sojourner Truth

Activist

Born: c. 1797; Swartekill, New York
Died: November 26, 1883; Battle Creek, Michigan
Area of Achievement: Abolitionism, social issues, women's rights

Truth, born a slave, walked to freedom to become an example of courage and survival. Although she was an illiterate woman, she was able to reach white and black audi-

Sojourner Truth (National Portrait Gallery)

ences through her speeches and her biography. She challenged white supremacy, claiming her rights through legal action and civil disobedience, and proposed ideas to alleviate the suffering of her people.

EARLY LIFE

Sojourner (soh-JUHRN-uhr) Truth was born a slave around 1797 in Hurley, Ulster County, New York, near the Hudson River. She was the second youngest of ten or twelve children of James and Elizabeth, but as a child she knew only one sibling. Her birth name was Isabella Baumfree.

Truth and her family were the property of Colonel Johannes Hardenbergh, who owned nearly two million acres between the Hudson and Delaware rivers in Ulster County. Hardenbergh died when Truth was an infant, and she and her family became the property of his son, Charles.

In 1807, after the death of Charles Hardenbergh, Truth was sold to John Neely, a merchant from Twaalfskill, New York (near present-day Kingston). She was about nine years old. After one or two years, the Neelys sold her to Martinus Shryver, a fisherman and tavern keeper. Shryver, in turn, sold Truth in 1810 to John J. Dumont of New Paltz Landing, where she remained until 1826.

With the Dumont family, Truth did farm work and household chores. In 1814, she married another slave named Thomas, whom Dumont seems to have selected for her, and they lived together for about ten years. They had five children, four of whom—Diana, Peter, Elizabeth, and Sophia—lived past infancy. The fifth may have died in infancy or early childhood.

In 1817, the New York state legislature passed a law decreeing that all New York slaves born before July 4, 1799, would be freed on July 4, 1827. Dumont promised Truth and Thomas that he would free them on July 4, 1826, a year earlier than the law required. However, Truth subsequently injured her hand and lost her ability to work quickly; Dumont, arguing that she owed him additional work because of her inefficiency, broke his promise. In the fall of 1826, Truth walked off the Dumonts' property carrying her infant daughter, Sophia.

She went to the home of Levi Rowe, a Quaker whom she expected to help her. However, she found him on his deathbed. Rowe sent her to the home of Isaac and Maria Van Wagenen in Wagondale, New York (presentday Bloomington).

The Van Wagenens took in Truth and gave her work as a free person. However, when Dumont learned that she was at the Van Wagenen house, he went to claim her as his property. To prevent Truth's reenslavement, the Van Wagenens paid him twenty-five dollars for Truth and Sophia. Truth remained with them for about a year and adopted their last name, becoming Isabella Van Wagenen. While working for the family, Truth learned that her five-year-old son, Peter, had been sold illegally and taken to Alabama. Determined to rescue her son, she confronted the Dumonts, who did not recognize her claim. With support from Quaker friends, she hired a lawyer who, in 1828, succeeded in having Peter returned to his mother.

Truth and Peter moved to New York City in late 1828, leaving Sophia with the Van Wagenens. She joined the Zion African Church and worked as a housekeeper for various families. In 1835, Truth was accused of poisoning her employer but was able to prove that she did not commit the crime. During her fourteen years in New York City, Truth came into contact with employers and other African Americans who were very religious. Several went on to become prominent abolitionists. In this context, Truth had a spiritual experience in which she felt called to become a traveling evangelist. To pursue this calling, she adopted the name "Sojourner Truth." "Sojourner" reflected that she would travel the land, and "Truth" her determination to speak the truth. Thus, in 1843, she set out from New York on her mission.

> "That man over there says that women need to be helped into carriages, and lifted over ditches, and to have the best place everywhere. Nobody ever helps me into carriages, or over mud-puddles, or gives me any best place! And ain't I a woman? Look at me! Look at my arm! I have ploughed and planted, and gathered into barns, and no man could head me! And ain't I a woman? I could work as much and eat as much as a man — when I could get it — and bear the lash as well! And ain't I a woman? I have borne thirteen children, and seen most all sold off to slavery, and when I cried out with my mother's grief, none but Jesus heard me! And ain't I a woman?"

LIFE'S WORK

Truth began preaching in Connecticut and Northampton, Massachusetts; there, she found many supporters associated with the Northampton Association, which had been founded by abolitionists, idealists, and workers to pursue equal rights for all. Truth remained with the association until 1846, working as a laundress. During her stay with the Northampton Association, she met prominent abolitionists such as William Lloyd Garrison, editor of *The Boston Liberator* and president of the American Anti-Slavery Society, and Frederick Douglass. In 1846, Truth began dictating her autobiography to Olive Gilbert; in 1850, it was published as *Narrative of Sojourner Truth* and marked her emergence as an abolitionist and women's suffrage advocate.

In 1851, Garrison invited Truth to accompany him and his friend, George Thompson, a radical member of the British parliament, on a trip into western New York. Truth made the trip with Thompson, making speeches and selling her book. In Ohio, Truth assisted the Ohio Woman's Rights Convention and delivered a famous speech on equal rights for African-American women, which was later published as "Ain't I a Woman?" In 1853, Truth journeyed to Andover, Massachusetts, and asked Harriet Beecher Stowe, the author of *Uncle Tom's Cabin* (1852), to help promote her autobiography. Stowe wrote a short article about the book. Ten years later, based on this brief encounter, Stowe wrote "Sojourner Truth, the Libyan Sibyl" for the *Atlantic Monthly*.

In 1857, Truth joined the community of Harmonia, a racially mixed settlement of progressive abolitionists and spiritualists, located six miles west of Battle Creek, Michigan. She was joined there by her daughters, Diana, Elizabeth, and Sophia, who had been legally freed. Her grandsons, James Caldwell and Samuel Banks, became her traveling companions. In 1860, Truth moved to the town of Battle Creek.

With the outbreak of the Civil War in 1861, Truth became deeply involved in politics. She openly challenged slavery and championed the Union cause. In 1862, Truth accompanied Josephine Griffing, a radical feminist, to Indiana, violating a state law prohibiting the entry of black people. She was chased by a mob and arrested. In 1863, when President Abraham Lincoln signed the Emancipation Proclamation and gave orders to recruit African-American troops to fight for the Union, Truth went door to door to collect Thanksgiving food for the soldiers of the First Michigan Colored Regiment, stationed at Camp Ward in Detroit. In 1864, Truth collected more food and clothing from the people of Battle Creek for the Camp Ward troops. Around this time, she addressed the troops and sang a song that she had composed in honor of the regiment.

The Civil War and social struggles of the 1860s moved Truth to make her first trip to Washington, D.C., in 1864, accompanied by her grandson, Banks. She carried a new edition of her autobiography and her portrait printed on postcards. Under her picture was printed the message "The Shadow Supports the Substance." In Washington, Truth and her white companion Lucy Colman met Lincoln; he signed her autograph book, "For Auntie Sojourner Truth, October 29, 1864." In later years, Truth would also visit President Andrew Johnson and Ulysses S. Grant.

Truth stayed in Washington from 1864 to 1867. During her stay, she saw and experienced the racial discrimination that pervaded everyday life. Although streetcars had been desegregated by federal law in 1865, conductors did not want to stop for black passengers. Truth insisted on riding in the streetcars, even when she was humiliated and assaulted, forcing conductors to respect the law.

In Washington, D.C., Truth worked for the National Freedmen's Relief Association and the Freedmen's Bureau, aiding black refugees from the southern states. The poor conditions in which freed African Americans lived—characterized by cramped housing, crime, and joblessness—led her to argue that her people needed work, not government money. Truth proposed that the government provide land for free African Americans. Massachusetts senator, Charles Sumner advised her to collect signatures to pressure Congress to authorize land grants. From 1870 to 1871, Truth and Banks toured New England and the mid-Atlantic region collecting signatures. Her tour was cut short when Banks fell ill, and they returned to Battle Creek, where he died in 1875. Subsequently, the exodus of many freed African Americans to Kansas in 1879 upstaged Truth's plan, but she supported it enthusiastically.

In Battle Creek, at the urging of her friend Frances Titus, Truth updated her *Narrative of Sojourner Truth*, adding her speeches and scrapbook. During the fall of 1883, Truth fell gravely ill. She died before dawn on November 26.

SIGNIFICANCE

Truth was born a slave and became a nationally known advocate for the abolition of slavery and equal rights for women. Truth viewed her advocacy as a religious calling to put her faith into practice. Her escape from slavery and her adherence to her principles in the face of personal hardship and tragedy made her a powerful symbol of the abolitionist and women's rights causes.

F. Sonia Arellano-Lopez

Further Reading

Bordewich, Fergus M. *Bound for Canaan: The Underground Railroad and the War for the Soul of America.* New York: HarperCollins, 2005. Offers historical background on the activities of the abolitionists who befriended and assisted Truth.

Claflin, Edward Beecher. *Sojourner Truth and the Struggle for Freedom.* New York: Barron's Educational Series, 1987. Provides a brief and straightforward account of Truth's life.

Gilbert, Olive. *Narrative of Sojourner Truth, a Bondswoman of Olden Time.* 1878. Reprint. New York: Oxford University Press, 1994. This reprint is the version updated with support from Frances Titus, which includes Stowe's article on Truth, excerpts of letters, speeches, and scrapbook material.

Mabee, Carleton. "Sojourner Truth and President Lincoln." *The New England Quarterly* 61, no. 4 (December, 1988): 519-529. A compelling article demystifying the diverse versions of the meeting between Truth and Lincoln.

Painter, Nell Irvin. *Sojourner Truth: A Life, a Symbol.* New York: W. W. Norton, 1996. Scholarly biography of Truth that includes information on the social, economic, and political conditions under which she lived.

Harriet Tubman

Abolitionist

Born: c. 1820; Dorchester County, Maryland
Died: March 10, 1913; Auburn, New York
Area of Achievement: Abolitionism, social issues, women's rights

Tubman escaped slavery and then dedicated her life to helping others do the same. Her commitment to freedom fueled an intense passion for the abolitionist movement and led her to serve as a Union Army nurse and spy during the Civil War. She also forged ties with the women's suffrage movement and spoke eloquently in support of women's and African-Americans' rights.

Early Life

Harriet Ross Tubman was born Araminta Ross around 1820 to Harriet and Benjamin Ross in Bucktown, Dorchester County, Maryland. She decided to take her mother's name when she was older. Tubman and her eight siblings were born on the plantation of Edward Brodess. She began work as a domestic servant at the age of about six years and also was rented out to other households for the same purpose. She often was severely beaten and poorly treated. As a teenager, she preferred to work in the field, where it was easier to escape the brutality of overbearing mistresses and the unwanted sexual advances of her masters.

Ultimately, field work did not provide Tubman with enough protection from the cruelty of slavery. Between the years of 1834 and 1836, she suffered trauma to her head as a result of being struck by a metal weight. The weight was thrown at an escaping slave by the overseer, and Tubman jumped in the way, attempting to prevent the escapee's capture. The impact of the two-pound metal weight against her head nearly killed her. Her skull was badly crushed, resulting in sleeping spells, headaches, and dizziness that she endured for the rest of her life. However, Tubman claimed that the injury also left her with heightened dreams and prophecies. She said that these visions showed her the future and led her on journeys in which she liberated slaves from the South. Her visions were nurtured by her exposure to evangelical teachings and African-influenced cultural traditions.

Harriet Tubman (Wikimedia Commons)

After Tubman's injury, no buyer was interested in purchasing or renting her services because she was considered damaged property. Tubman's fear that she might one day be sold to a more abusive master because of her injury fueled her desire to escape. Her first flight took place in 1849. At the time, she was being rented from her master by a man called Doctor Thompson. She had lived on his property for two years with her husband, John Tubman, whom she married in 1844. Although John was a free man, he lived with Tubman in the slave quarters. Even though Tubman did her best to convince her husband to accompany her on the journey, he refused.

Tubman, far left, with family and neighbors, circa 1887, at her home in Auburn, NY. Left to right: Harriet Tubman; Gertie Davis (adopted daughter) behind Tubman; Nelson Davis (husband and 8th USCT veteran); Lee Chaney (neighbor's child); "Pop" John Alexander (elderly boarder in Tubman's home); Walter Green (neighbor's child); Blind "Aunty" Sarah Parker (elderly boarder); and Dora Stewart (great-niece). (Wikimedia Commons)

LIFE'S WORK

In 1849, Tubman escaped to freedom. She traveled by night, guided only by the North Star, until she reached Philadelphia, a free state. She was aided by abolitionists on the Underground Railroad, who helped her evade capture and identify who would help along the journey. Upon arriving in Philadelphia, however, Tubman found herself confused and saddened. The success of reaching the so-called Promised Land was complicated by a painful realization. She was alone in a strange land without family, friends, or community. While she understood that most of the people she knew did not possess the courage to attempt what she had done, her loneliness prompted her to return and secure the freedom of her family members. She constructed a plan that led her to being called the Moses of her people.

> *"I had crossed de line of which I had so long been dreaming. I was free; but dere was no one to welcome me to de land of freedom, I was a stranger in a strange land, and my home after all was down in de old cabin quarter, wid de ole folks, and my brudders and sisters. But to dis solemn resolution I came; I was free, and dey should be free also; I would make a home for dem in de North, and de Lord helping me, I would bring dem all dere."*

First, Tubman secured employment as a domestic laborer, cooking and cleaning house for northern white women. The money she earned cleaning houses was equally divided between her living expenses and a return trip to Baltimore, Maryland, where she rescued her enslaved sister and her two children. In December of 1850, Tubman, her sister Mary Ann Bowley, and Mary Ann's husband and two children arrived in Philadelphia. Tubman's success in her first venture set the stage for a return a few months later in which she safely delivered her brother and two other men to safety. It was not until the fall of 1851 that she returned to free her husband, John. However, John had remarried and still refused to travel with her. Eager to continue her mission, Tubman abandoned thoughts of helping him and quickly identified a group of slaves who were willing to flee. She also brought this group safely to Philadelphia. Almost from the beginning, Tubman's mission to free slaves reached beyond her own family. From 1851 to 1857, she made at least eleven trips into slave country, and she eventually freed all of her brothers and sisters and her parents during the ten years that she conducted the Underground Railroad.

Tubman viewed the problems facing African Americans, women, and humanity as indelibly intertwined, and her life's work began to reflect this belief. Tubman set about developing relationships with women involved in the suffrage movement, such as, Susan B. Anthony, and intensified her relationships with staunch abolitionists such as William Grant Still and John Brown. She believed that the nation could take its greatest strides toward liberation and equality when people—no matter their creed, color, or gender—worked in concert.

It was this belief that led to Tubman's decision to assist the Union Army in the Civil War. She worked for the Army for four years as a nurse and spy, without any recognition or financial compensation. She was deployed by the governor of Massachusetts to the South at the beginning of the Civil War in the position of spy and scout and under the direction of Colonel James Montgomery. Tubman organized a group of black men to scout the inland waterways of South Carolina for Union raids. She also nursed wounded soldiers back to health and taught newly freed African-Americans strategies for survival and sustenance. Although efforts were made by Secretary of State William H. Seward to secure a pension for her years of service, she was unsuccessful.

After a period of about four years, Tubman left the Army to continue her work, giving speeches on slavery, abolition, and suffrage. Through her powerful oratory, Tubman urged many slaves to find their way to freedom by educating them about the abolition movement. In December of 1860, Tubman was invited to Boston by Gerrit Smith to speak at a large antislavery meeting. Although Tubman was illiterate, people in attendance were startled by her eloquence at the podium. However, her oratory was merely an outgrowth of the shrewd critical thinking faculties upon which she had to rely greatly as the most successful conductor of the Underground Railroad.

Near the end of her life, Tubman transformed her New York home into a boardinghouse to providing care for old and disabled African Americans. Tubman died of pneumonia on March 10, 1913, after a two-year residence in the Harriet Tubman Home for Aged and Indigent Colored People. Booker T. Washington was a featured speaker at her funeral service.

SIGNIFICANCE

During her lifetime Tubman was internationally renowned as a conductor on the Underground Railroad, abolitionist, Civil War spy, nurse, suffragist, and humanitarian. Tubman accomplished a great deal during a time of intense racial, social, political, and economic upheaval. Her primary goal was to secure the freedom of enslaved people and to end the institution of slavery. Her deep commitment to this goal led her to associate with all types of people regardless of race, gender, or class. As the debate over slavery intensified, Tubman was a respected spokesperson for the abolitionist movement.

Kidogo A. Kennedy

FURTHER READING

Bordewich, Fergus M. *Bound for Canaan: The Epic Story of the Underground Railroad, America's First Civil Rights Movement*. Boston: HarperCollins, 2006. Details the history of the Underground Railroad, emphasizing the real lives and stories of participants.

Bradford, Sarah E. H. *Harriet Tubman: The Moses of Her People*. Introduction by Butler A. Jones. New York: G. R. Lockwood and Son, 1886. Reprint. New York: Corinth Books, 1961. A republication of the 1886 expanded version of the 1869 original book, this is an important source for information on Tubman's life. Bradford interviewed Tubman and also included comments about her by a number of leading nineteenth-century Americans.

Clinton, Catherine. *Harriet Tubman: The Road to Freedom*. Boston: Back Bay Books, 2005. Thorough and well-researched biography of Tubman that fleshes out many of her contemporaries, famous and obscure, and examines Tubman's remarkable lifetime accomplishments.

Humez, Jean M. *Harriet Tubman: The Life and the Life Stories*. Madison: University of Wisconsin Press, 2003. Collection of primary source materials, including letters, diaries, memorials, and speeches, that provide a description of Tubman's life and personality. The materials document Tubman's relationships with abolitionist John Brown, Abraham Lincoln, Frederick Douglass, Sojourner Truth, and others.

Larson, Kate Clifford. *Bound for the Promised Land: Harriet Tubman, Portrait of an American Hero*. New York: Ballantine, 2004. Comprehensive account of Tubman's life, based in part on sources such as court records, contemporary newspapers, wills, and letters.

Petry, Ann. *Harriet Tubman: Conductor on the Underground Railroad.* New York: Amistad, 1996. Children's book whose narrative provides a compelling biography of Tubman and history of the Underground Railroad.

Nat Turner

Leader of a slave rebellion

Born: October 2, 1800; Southampton County, Virginia
Died: November 11, 1831; Jerusalem (now Courtland), Virginia
Also known as: Nathaniel Turner; Nat (birth name); General Turner; Captain Nat
Area of Achievement: Social issues

Enraged by a system that enslaved him and guided by religious visions, Turner led a bloody slave rebellion through the Virginia countryside, killing dozens of white plantation owners and their families. Turner's Rebellion was one of the most significant slave revolts in United States history.

Early Life

Nathaniel Turner, whose birth name was recorded simply as "Nat," was born on Benjamin Turner's Southampton County, Virginia, plantation to Nancy, a slave and domestic servant. Turner's father, whose name is unknown, ran away when Turner was eight or nine years old and left the young boy to be raised by his mother and paternal grandmother, Bridget. Turner learned to read and was raised a Christian. When he was twelve years old, Turner became a field hand, working from sunrise to sunset plowing, hoeing, and tending animals.

As a teenager, Turner began preaching at secret slave meetings and came to believe that he had been appointed to save fellow slaves from oppression. In 1821, he escaped from his master and spent a month in the woods, but he experienced a vision that prompted him to return voluntarily to the plantation. Turner married a fellow slave named Cherry the next year. On May 12, 1828, another vision persuaded Turner that he had been chosen to fight a battle against a serpent. His revelations and role as a lay preacher led Turner to be dubbed "The Prophet" by some of his followers.

Turner's ownership passed from Benjamin Turner to his son Samuel Turner. When Samuel Turner died, Turner was sold to Thomas Moore for four hundred dollars and Cherry was sold to a nearby plantation owned by Giles Reese for forty dollars. Upon Moore's death, Turner became the property of nine-year-old Putnam Moore. When Moore's mother remarried, Turner fell under the control of her new husband, Joseph Travis.

Nat Turner (Wikimedia Commons)

Life's Work

In February, 1831, a solar eclipse provided Turner with a sign that God wanted him to direct a rebellion against slave owners. Initially planned for the Fourth of July but suspended when Turner became sick, the revolt was rescheduled after yet another astronomical event. The sun appeared to be a bluish-green color on August 13; Turner accepted this as an indication that he should pursue his earlier plans. On August 21, Turner, Hark Travis, Nelson Williams, Henry Porter, Sam Francis, Will Francis, and Jack Reese met at Giles Reese's nearby Cabin Pond. In the early hours of the next day, Turner and his followers murdered Joseph Travis, his wife, and their family; they then traveled to other plantations and repeated their actions. They killed many of the white men, women, and children they encountered. As they proceeded under the guidance of Turner, the slaves moved toward Jerusalem, Virginia, the county seat, and other slaves joined them. After nearly two days had passed, they had slain between fifty-five and sixty-five white people. The band of slaves was weary, and some among them were under the influence of alcoholic beverages that they had found along their way. Some of the group disbanded, but Turner continued to seek fresh recruits.

In the meantime, the Virginia state militia and other armed citizens began to unite. A frenzy resulted; church bells rang, and people in the South were filled with panic. Two groups of militia were near the James W. Parker farm when Turner's men arrived there. The Battle of Parker's Farm ensued, taking the lives of some of the rebels while some others dispersed. Afterward, Turner turned south with his remaining followers to seek more recruits at the large plantation of Thomas Ridley. The militia awaited them there and at the Harris Farm, their final stop, as well.

These counterattacks were brutal and equally heinous. The militiamen managed to capture or kill the majority of Turner's group, as well as many others who were innocent of wrongdoing. The remainder of Turner's band retreated; Turner escaped initial capture and survived in the woods for six weeks. On September 17, 1831, Virginia governor John Floyd delivered a proclamation that described Turner and offered a five-hundred-dollar reward. A slave named Nelson reported seeing Turner on October 15. Fifteen days later, Turner was caught by Benjamin Phipps. On November 1, 1831, Turner's lawyer, slave owner Thomas Gray, recorded the *Confessions of Nat Turner*. Four days later, Tuner was tried, convicted, and sentenced to hang for his role in the rebellion. After his execution on November 11, Turner's body was dismembered. Joseph Travis's heirs were paid $375 for the loss of his "property."

> *"I heard a loud noise in the heavens, and the Spirit instantly appeared to me and said the Serpent was loosened, and Christ had laid down the yoke he had borne for the sins of men, and that I should take it on and fight against the Serpent, for the time was fast approaching when the first should be last and the last should be first."*

SIGNIFICANCE

Tuner's rebellion sent shock waves through the South. The hysteria that ensued resulted in the murder of many innocent people. The event led several southern states to pass tougher slave laws and more strictly enforce existing statutes. Abolitionists faced increased hostility. Over time, the details of the rebellion have become more difficult to verify. Literary and fictional treatments of the rebellion have created stereotypes and misconceptions that have further compounded the mysteries that surround Turner.

Cynthia J. W. Svoboda

FURTHER READING

Bisson, Terry. *Nat Turner*. New York: Chelsea House, 1988. Part of the Black Americans of Achievement Series. Describes NatTurner as a slave revolt leader.

French, Scott. *The Rebellious Slave: Nat Turner in American Memory*. Boston: Houghton Mifflin, 2004. Examines the various depictions of Turner's legacy in American culture, including his *Confessions* and the controversial novel by William Styron, *The Confessions of Nat Turner* (1967).

Greenberg, Kenneth S., ed. *Nat Turner: A Slave Rebellion in History and Memory*. New York: Oxford University Press, 2003. A series of essays that includes an examination of who Turner was, a review of his confessions, stories of the rebellion, and observations of how he is remembered.

IDA B. WELLS-BARNETT

Activist and journalist

Born: July 16, 1862; Holly Springs, Mississippi
Died: March 25, 1931; Chicago, Illinois
Area of Achievement: Civil rights, journalism and publishing, women's rights

Wells-Barnett applied investigative journalism to the pervasive crime of lynching, publishing statistical and anecdotal evidence that showed the brutality and injustice of racial violence. She was a vocal proponent of African-American civil rights and women's rights throughout her career.

EARLY LIFE

Ida B. Wells-Barnett was born in Holly Springs, Mississippi, on July 16, 1862, to slaves James Wells and Elizabeth Warrenton. Her father, the only son of his former master, received training and became a skilled carpenter long before his freedom. Well respected as a free

Ida B. Wells-Barnett (Wikimedia Commons)

wage-earner after the Civil War, he also achieved the rank of Freemasonry Master Mason in the Freemasons.

As a young girl, Wells-Barnett received basic education from the Freedmen's Aid Society of the Episcopal Church. At age sixteen, after both her parents' deaths, she earned a teaching certificate in order to support her five siblings. Because of her father's Masonic rank, the local Masons helped her obtain a teaching position. Wells-Barnett first became aware of the injustice of Jim Crow segregation when she was forcibly removed from a first-class rail car despite having a valid ticket. Wells-Barnett's teaching career took her to Memphis, where she discovered new opportunities in journalism. She found writing more fulfilling than teaching and soon dedicated herself to an anti-lynching campaign.

Life's Work

Writing for *The American Baptist* and other newspapers under the pen name Iola, Wells-Barnett attracted a national audience. She became known as "The Princess of the Press." By 1889, she had acquired one-third ownership in a Memphis newspaper, *Free Speech*. After a local school refused to renew her teaching contract because of an article she had written, she turned to journalism and newspaper ownership full time.

Wells-Barnett increased *Free Speech's* subscriber base by nearly 40 percent. Her involvement as owner, editor, and writer turned the paper into a force in the fight for racial justice. In 1891, three Memphis businessmen— one of whom was a close friend of Wells-Barnett—were targeted by a white mob because their grocery store was competing with a nearby white-owned store. After the businessmen fought back, injuring some of the attackers, they were lynched. The murders deeply affected Wells-Barnett and drove her to shift her focus from civil rights in general to lynching specifically.

Wells-Barnett's militant articles about lynching stirred controversy in Memphis. After her newspaper's offices were destroyed by a mob, she left the city for New York. She took a job with *The New York Age*, an African-American weekly publication that also had broad white readership. She launched a public-speaking career in October, 1892, as well. That year, Wells-Barnett wrote an article for *The New York Age* in which she attacked the myth that lynching was a form of vigilante justice for black men who raped white women; she used data to expose the attitudes toward race and sexuality that underlay the southern culture of racial violence. The article became the pamphlet "Southern Horrors: Lynch Law in All Its Phases," published by the end of 1892. The speaking tour that followed took her across the United States and to the United Kingdom. She became an international figure in the campaign against lynching.

> "The way to right wrongs is to turn the light of truth upon them."

In 1893, Wells-Barnett helped to organize a boycott of the World's Columbian Exhibition in Chicago and contributed to a pamphlet titled "The Reason Why the Colored American Is Not in the World's Columbian Exhibition," which was distributed at the event. The trip culminated in her decision to move to Chicago, where she spent the remainder of her life. In Chicago, she began writing for newspaper owner and attorney Ferdinand Barnett's *The Chicago Conservator*. In 1895, she and Barnett were married. They had four children. Although she remained active in the national anti-lynching campaign, of which she was a founding member, she scaled back her activism to focus on her family.

Over the subsequent decades, Wells-Barnett balanced

activism with motherhood. She provided the means and the leadership for the creation of the National Association of Colored Women (NACW). She also canvassed the state to promote suffrage for women and establish the first suffrage association for African-American women in Chicago. Her political interests eventually led her to run for a state senate seat in the 1930s. An active champion of social justice, she developed strategies for the antilynching campaign that would be used by activists generations later.

Wells-Barnett died in Chicago, still actively pursuing the cause of justice for all. Her bid for political office, a campaign to prevent the appointment of a North Carolina judge to the U.S. Supreme Court, and work on her autobiography filled the last days of her life.

Significance

Wells-Barnett's investigative reporting and forceful editorials forced her readers—black and white—to confront the cruelty and injustice of lynching. She devoted her career to disproving the myths about race and gender that contributed to the prevalence of lynching in the South. She also worked more generally for African-American civil rights and women's rights and suffrage.

Kay J. Blalock

Further Reading

Bay, Mia. *To Tell the Truth Freely: The Life of Ida B. Wells*. New York: Hill and Wang, 2009. This thorough biography offers insight into the life and times of Wells-Barnett and analysis of her impact.

Giddings, Paula J. *Ida, a Sword Among Lions: Ida B. Wells and the Campaign Against Lynching*. New York: Amistad, 2008. Drawing on Wells-Barnett's words and several published and unpublished works, this biography presents a well-researched look at her role in the African-American reform movements.

Schechter, Patricia A. *Ida B. Wells-Barnett and American Reform, 1880-1930*. Chapel Hill: University of North Carolina Press, 2001. Examines and analyzes Wells-Barnett's ideas and activism in terms of gender and race.

Schraff, Anne. Ida B. *Wells-Barnett: "Strike a Blow Against a Glaring Evil."* Berkeley Heights, N.J.: Enslow, 2008. Biography for younger readers, offering an accessible overview of Wells-Barnett's life's work.

Wells-Barnett, Ida B. *Crusade for Justice: The Autobiography of Ida B. Wells*. Edited by Alfreda M. Duster. Chicago: University of Chicago Press, 1970. This posthumously published autobiography was edited by Wells-Barnett's daughter.

---. *The Memphis Diary of Ida B. Wells*. Edited by Miriam Decosta-Willis. Boston: Beacon Press, 1995. Wells-Barnett's diary offers an intimate look at the anti-lynching crusader as a young woman.

Elie Wiesel

German-born writer and activist

Born: September 30, 1928; Sighet, Romania
Died: July 2, 2016; Manhattan, New York City
Areas of Achievement: Literature; activism

Since emerging from the Nazi concentration camps as a teenager in 1945, Wiesel has dedicated his life to writing, to teaching, and to humanitarian outreach. He is committed to raising global awareness of social injustice and of genocide.

Early Life

Elie Wiesel (Wikimedia Commons)

President George W. Bush, joined by The Dalai Lama, welcomes Wiesel, Wednesday, October 17, 2007, to the ceremony at the U.S. Capitol in Washington, D.C., for the presentation of the Congressional Gold Medal to The Dalai Lama. (Wikimedia Commons)

Elie Wiesel (EH-lee vee-ZEHL) was born in 1928 in Sighet, a town in Transylvania (now Romania). His father, Shlomo, and his mother, Sarah, raised their four children in the teachings of the Orthodox Jewish faith. Wiesel, the third child and only son, had a comfortable childhood, and he had a passionate interest in Jewish spirituality and knowledge.

Beginning in 1933, the Nazis gained power in Germany and began a ruthless expansionist campaign across Europe, with an ultimate goal to murder all the Jews. The turning point in Wiesel's youth was when the Nazis entered Sighet. Over a short span of time, the Nazis forced the Jews of Sighet into a ghetto, then into a smaller ghetto, and ultimately into Nazi concentration camps. Wiesel conveyed the horror the Jews experienced at the hands of the Nazis in his first publication, *Un di Velt hot geshvign* (1956; *Night*, 1960), wherein he described the circumstances of the ghettoes, the train transport to Auschwitz, and the entrance into the infamous Nazi concentration camp. Wiesel was fifteen years old when he was deported to Auschwitz, where his mother and sister Tziporah were murdered immediately upon arrival. In January, 1945, as the Russians approached Auschwitz, the Nazis forced the prisoners to go on a death march through the snow, pushing them deeper into Germany. Wiesel's father died in the Buchenwald concentration camp shortly after their arrival; in April, 1945, Wiesel was among the prisoners liberated at Buchenwald.

At the war's end, Wiesel, still a teenager, was taken to an orphanage in France, where he later discovered that his two older sisters had survived. As a young adult, he was a journalist for a Tel Aviv newspaper; in the mid-1950's, he moved to the United States, becoming a citizen in 1963. In 1969, he married Marion, who has translated many of his books that he wrote in French into English; their only child, a son, was born in 1972. Wiesel taught at several colleges prior to becoming a professor at Boston University in 1976, where he became a member of both the philosophy and the religion departments. Over time, his publications on the Holocaust and on Jewish themes have gained him an international audience.

"What hurts the victim most is not the cruelty of the oppressor but the silence of the bystander."

Life's Work

Wiesel re-created his life from the Holocaust's ruins, building on his strengths in writing and in fluency in languages. He used his literary skills as a journalist and, later, as an author; because he traveled widely, his ability to speak multiple languages helped him gain an understanding of the world. He vowed to write an account of his wartime experience but decided to wait ten years before doing so. After the decade was over, Wiesel wrote a lengthy book (more than eight hundred pages) in Yiddish, *Un di velt hot geshvign* (and the world kept silent), published in Argentina. The title is significant because Wiesel has been consistently preoccupied with silence, particularly in the face of atrocity: the silence of the world that could possibly have prevented the Holocaust and the silence of God. Wiesel later pared down his Yiddish text into a much leaner version, written in French, titled *La Nuit* (1958). Although it took several decades for *La Nuit*, and its 1960 English version, *Night*, to achieve significant status, the book ultimately became a seminal text of Holocaust memoirs.

Wiesel's literary reputation could have been built on *Night* alone, which has been published in more than thirty

> **A Passionate Defense of All Persecuted People**
>
> Elie Wiesel has maintained an abiding commitment to alleviate social injustice. If the autobiographical *Night* (1956) were Wiesel's only accomplishment, he would have given readers a great gift, but he has continued to use his talents to help others who suffer. His numerous public speaking engagements, his many publications, and his leadership on national and international committees have, at various times, propelled onto a global stage people and situations that might otherwise have been neglected. Wiesel has raised awareness on such diverse plights as the suffering of indigenous peoples in Nicaragua and Argentina, the circumstances facing war refugees, and the ongoing genocide in Africa. He has spoken up for those whose voices the world could not, or would not, hear, such as the Jews who lived in then-Soviet Russia and the Africans dying from famine. Moreover, Wiesel is not afraid to confront or to challenge the powerful. He urged then-U.S. president Ronald Reagan not to visit a German cemetery in which many Nazis were buried; he also encouraged German leaders to go to Israel and apologize for what Nazi Germany had done. Believing in the power of education, Wiesel and his wife established the Elie Wiesel Foundation for Humanity, which promotes human rights.

languages, but he is a prolific author. He has written more than fifty well-received books in a variety of genres, including fiction, autobiography, essays, and drama. His literary work ranges widely in scope, but two central patterns emerge: Jewish history and the Holocaust. Some people credit him for creating the term Holocaust, although that is arguable. His writing is not limited solely to the subject of the Holocaust, but his experiences during that event shaped his literary vision and his religious thought. His writing draws upon events in his life and upon Jewish history and rabbinic wisdom. Wiesel is particularly intrigued by questions; as in the case of the Holocaust, sometimes the answers do not satisfy, but the questions must be asked.

Wiesel is an educator in addition to being an author and a humanitarian. He uses the classroom, his writings, and speaking engagements to work to alleviate the suffering caused by racial, religious, or social bigotry. His commitment to raising awareness about oppression and genocide caused U.S. president Jimmy Carter to appoint Wiesel as the chairman of the President's Commission on the Holocaust (1978). Wiesel was a founding chairman of the United States Holocaust Memorial Museum. His tireless efforts in confronting social injustice around the world resulted in him receiving the Nobel Peace Prize in 1986.

In *Night*, Wiesel describes a spiritual break with God. This break, however, was not a divorce; Wiesel's life and writings reveal a man with a passionate love of, and reverence for, Jewish culture and wisdom. His writings indicate a deep engagement with Jewish history and a dynamic, but not simple, relationship with God. Many consider Wiesel the elder statesman of the Holocaust and a key figure in the creation of a world where genocide can no longer occur.

Wiesel died on the morning of July 2, 2016 at his home in Manhattan, aged 87. Utah senator Orrin Hatch paid tribute to Wiesel in a speech on the Senate floor the following week, where he said that, "With Elie's passing, we have lost a beacon of humanity and hope. We have lost a hero of human rights and a luminary of Holocaust literature."

SIGNIFICANCE

Wiesel is, for many, the public face and the human voice of the Holocaust survivor. With *Night*, subsequent memoirs, and an extensive bibliography, Wiesel compels the world to look with horror at violence, neglect, and genocide. Thanks to his prolific writing and speaking engagements, Wiesel reminds the world of the Holocaust victims and what they experienced. Because of his suffering under the Nazis, which includes the murder of his parents and his sister, Wiesel maintains an abiding commitment to alleviate social injustice and to raise awareness of the disenfranchised. Wiesel's writings on the Holocaust and on Jewish thought have sold widely and well. He has received many honors from organizations, colleges, and countries; among the most prestigious are the U.S. Presidential Medal of Freedom, the U.S. Congressional Gold Medal, the rank of Grand-Cross from the French Legion of Honor, honorary knighthood from the British government, and the Nobel Peace Prize.

Deborah Lee Prescott

FURTHER READING

Bayer, Linda N. *Elie Wiesel: Spokesman for Remembrance.* New York: Rosen, 2000. A review of Wiesel's life, describing his struggle to survive in the concentration camps and his Life's Work in reminding the world about the horrors of genocide. Suitable for juvenile audience.

Wiesel, Elie. *All Rivers Run to the Sea.* New York: Knopf, 1995. Wiesel covers such significant events as his Sighet childhood, the Holocaust, the French orphanage, and his adult career as a journalist, educator, and author.

---. *From the Kingdom of Memory.* New York: Summit, 1990. In this collection of essays and speeches, Wiesel remembers his hometown of Sighet; also included are his Nobel Peace Prize speech and lecture.

---. *Night.* Rev. ed. New York: Hill and Wang, 2006. Many readers consider this the premier memoir of the Holocaust. Terse, with ellipses indicating passages that defy human speech, Wiesel conveys Nazi cruelty.

---. *The Trial of God.* New York: Schocken, 1995. Based on an event he witnessed at Auschwitz, Wiesel's drama places God on trial in the seventeenth century after a pogrom against the Jews.

STEM

The United States has historically been a world leader in STEM fields—Science, Technology, Engineering, and Mathematics. (The acronym was born in a meeting at the National Science Foundation in the 1980s). Scientific and technological innovation are essential to the success of the economy and vital to the strength of the nation. The interest in STEM as a national issue with international ramifications began long before the term was coined. The National Academy of Sciences was founded by President Abraham Lincoln in 1863 and tasked with advising Congress and the executive branch on new developments in science and technology. A sense of urgency emerged in the era of Sputnik and the Cold War between the Soviet Union and the United States. In the middle of the arms race, presidents Dwight D. Eisenhower and John F. Kennedy both encouraged American competitiveness in science, technology, engineering, and mathematics. NASA was founded by Eisenhower in 1958, and Kennedy announced the goal of putting an American on the moon.

Scientists rank high in public perceptions. When asked to rank various occupations by their prestige, one survey showed that the only occupation Americans hold in higher regard is that of firefighter. However, despite the importance of scientists both in real terms and as figures in public perception, there remains a lack of interest among American students in STEM majors and in STEM careers. The United States Department of Education, for example, has found that only 16% of high school students were interested in a STEM career and were proficient in mathematics. STEM education remains a critical topic. Without adequate STEM educational opportunities leading to the emergence of robust science and technology leaders, our country's economic well-being will be at risk. The good news for students and young people today is that there is tremendous opportunity for those with an interest in STEM.

An optical communications system using hollow optical fibres. (Wikimedia Commons)

Benjamin Banneker

Astronomer, inventor, and civil rights activist

Born: November 9, 1731 ; Baltimore County, Colony of Maryland
Died: October 9, 1806 ; Oella, Maryland
Also known as: Benjamin Bannaky (birth name)
Areas of Achievement: Invention; Science and Technology

Banneker was part of a team of surveyors entrusted to survey the federal territory that became Washington, D.C. A self-taught astronomer who compiled successful almanacs, he also constructed a clock from memory that ran for some fifty years.

Early Life

Benjamin Banneker was the grandson of a white woman named Molly Welsh, an English immigrant who indentured herself for seven years in exchange for safe passage to America. Once Molly gained her freedom, she purchased a modest farm and two African male slaves to help work the land. One of them— rumored to be a chieftain or an African king—was called Banneky and, later, Banneker. Molly set him free, married him, and had four daughters. One daughter, Mary, married a native African and had four daughters and a son. That son was Benjamin Banneker.

Molly taught her grandson to read from the Bible, but he was a fast learner and soon knew more about it than she did. Hungry to learn, he also studied biography, history and travel, and eventually surpassed his entire family in his studies.

At age twenty-two, Banneker decided to make a clock out of hand-carved wood. This would not have been remarkable under normal circumstances, but Banneker had never even seen a clock. Clocks did exist in North America at that time, but they were not abundant. Banneker had seen a watch once or twice, and he knew what a sundial was, but that was the extent of his experience. Nevertheless, with no formal clock making skills, he used his memory to convert complicated diagrams of wheels and gears into three-dimensional wooden clock parts. Word of his accomplishment spread, and Banneker's home soon became a point of interest for the area. People came from miles around to see the homemade clock he

Benjamin Banneker (Wikimedia Commons)

hung in a corner of his cabin. It ran for more than fifty years.

Banneker fascinated almost everyone he encountered; whereas most African Americans of the eighteenth century were uneducated slaves, he was knowledgeable and well rounded. He developed a reputation as a man "acquainted with everything of importance that was passing through this country."

Life's Work

For all his intelligence, Banneker lived a mostly isolated life as a tobacco planter and beekeeper. This was probably because he only knew one or two other free black men; the rest were slaves and had no interaction with him.

At the age of fifty-seven, Banneker became interested in astronomy. A friend opened his personal library to Banneker and loaned him equipment and astronomy books, including one written in French. Without any assistance, Banneker soon mastered all the complex mathematical formulas necessary to calculate when the sun or moon would eclipse, and the exact time every star would rise. He was so dedicated to astronomy that each night he wrapped himself in a heavy cloak and lay out under the stars to study the heavens. He slept in the mornings, woke

> ### Banneker's Correspondence with Thomas Jefferson
>
> While Benjamin Banneker searched for a publisher for his almanacs, he found the most unlikely opportunity to speak out for his race. Secretary of State Thomas Jefferson's book *Notes on the State of Virginia* (1784) made sweeping claims about African Americans requiring less sleep, lacking forethought, and even "secreting less by the kidneys [*sic*] and more by the glands of the skin, which gives them a very strong and disagreeable odour." Banneker took the opportunity to address Jefferson's narrow-minded conclusions, offering his almanac as proof that black men were not intellectually inferior.
>
> Banneker's August 19, 1791, letter asked Jefferson and others in authority to "wean yourselves from those narrow prejudices which you have imbibed with respect to them [African Americans], and as Job proposed to his friends, 'Put your Souls in their Souls' stead.'"
>
> Such shocking advice from an "inferior" to a white man could have had deadly consequences. However, on August 30, 1791, Jefferson replied. "Nobody wishes more than I," he wrote, "to see such proofs as you exhibit, that nature has given to our black brethren talents equal to those of the other colors of men, and that the appearance of a want of them is owing merely to the degraded condition of their existence...."
>
> Jefferson ended his letter with an eloquence typically reserved for men of high social standing: "I am with great esteem, Sir your most [obedient] servant." Jefferson also sent copies of Banneker's almanac to experts in the field, including members of the Philanthropic Society.

in the afternoons, chided himself for his laziness, and rushed to complete his neglected chores. Scholars heard of Banneker's intelligence and took turns mailing difficult math equations for him to solve. Not only did Banneker solve the equations; he composed equations of his own—in verse—and mailed them off for others to solve.

When Banneker was fifty-nine years old, the Federal Territory (Washington, D.C.) was being surveyed, and a surveyor assigned by President George Washington hired Banneker to be his assistant. After this important job was completed, Banneker returned home to his astronomy. He compiled his calculations and predictions into a farmer's almanac, which was eventually published and brought him much fame. Banneker used his celebrity to fight racism and war and to produce social change. He even sent a letter and a handwritten copy of his almanac to the secretary of state, Thomas Jefferson, in an attempt to prove that African Americans were just as intelligent as other races. Impressed, Jefferson replied to Banneker's letter and sent copies of the almanac to the secretary of the Academy of Sciences at Paris and members of the Philanthropic Society.

After a time, Banneker sold his land and bought an annuity to live on. This amount, along with the money earned from his almanacs (which sold well for more than ten years), allowed him to live comfortably and continue his studies in peace.

Banneker was a solitary man. He never married, but lived with his mother in the same little log cabin in which he had been born until her death. Afterward, he lived alone with his books and his astronomy equipment until the day of his own death on October 9, 1806, at the age of seventy-four.

> "*The colour of the skin is in no way connected with strength of the mind or intellectual powers.*"

Significance

Banneker was the first African American man of science. He was not the first to build a clock, but clocks were scarce, and he was the first in his region to build one completely from memory. He was a self-taught mathematician and astronomer and one of the earliest spokespersons for his race, petitioning the powerful Thomas Jefferson to reconsider the racist stereotypes of the times. At one time, Banneker was considered the most intelligent and distinguished black person in America.

Rita Lorraine Hubbard

Further Reading

Bedini, Silvio A. *The Life of Benjamin Banneker: The First African-American Man of Science*. 2d rev. ed. Baltimore: Maryland Historical Society, 1999. An excellent study of Banneker, based on careful review of secondary materials, previously unused material from private archives, and Banneker's journal. This edition includes photographs and information on Banneker's African roots.

Cerami, Charles. *Benjamin Banneker: Surveyor, Astronomer, Publisher, Patriot*. New York: J. Wiley, 2002. A clearly and simply written biography that examines Banneker's life and the breadth of his career.

Litwin, Laura Baskes. *Benjamin Banneker: Astronomer and Mathematician*. Berkeley Heights, N.J.: Enslow, 1999. A biography of Banneker for young-adult readers, covering his life and achievements.

Miller, John Chester. *The Wolf by the Ears: Thomas Jefferson and Slavery*. New York: Free Press, 1977. Miller examines the correspondence between Banneker and Jefferson in the context of Jefferson's life and slavery in the United States.

STEVEN CHU

Scientist, educator, and government official

Born: February 28, 1948 ; St. Louis, Missouri
Area of Achievement: Science, education, government and politics

Steven Chu was appointed by President Barack Obama as the twelfth sssssss. He had earlier won a Nobel Prize in Physics for discovering a technique that uses lasers to trap and study atoms.

EARLY LIFE

Steven Chu was born on February 28, 1948, in St. Louis, Missouri. His father, Ju Chin Chu, was a chemical engineer who immigrated to the United States in 1943 from Taicang, a town near Shanghai, China. Steven's mother, Ching Chen Li, came to the United States to study economics in 1945. Unable to return to China because of political unrest there, the couple decided to raise their family in the United States. Chu has one older brother and one younger brother. Chu was born after his father had accepted a position at Washington University in St. Louis.

The son of academics, Chu was an excellent student. He had a particular fondness for physics and mathematics. He also loved constructing mechanical things, which nurtured the spatial intuition that later proved valuable to him as a scientist. After graduating from high school, Chu enrolled at University of Rochester, where he pursued his passion for physics and mathematics. He later attributed his career as a physicist to the introductory textbook *Lectures on Physics* by Richard P. Feynman. Feynman's use of new ideas to solve complex problems inspired Chu to want to become a theoretical physicist.

After his graduation in 1970, Chu began his graduate work at the University of California, Berkeley. His work at Berkeley convinced him that experimental re-search was his field of interest, and he soon began work on a doctoral thesis. During this period, a revolutionary new theory proposed a unification of two fundamental forces in the universe, electromagnetism and the weak nuclear force. Many physicists were eagerly seeking verification of this theory. Chu built a laser to study atomic transitions and the absorption of right and left polarized light. After receiving his doctorate in 1976, he remained at Berkeley to complete this project. A few months before Chu and his collaborators gathered their evidence for neutral weak interactions into print, scientists working with the Stanford Linear Accelerator uncovered the confirmatory evidence and published their results.

LIFE'S WORK

Although Chu was part of the faculty at Berkeley, he was encouraged to take a position elsewhere in order to

Steven Chu (Wikimedia Commons)

Ed Moses, Principal Associate Director of the National Ignition Facility at Lawrence Livermore National Laboratory (left), shows a model of an ignition target to Chu. (Wikimedia Commons)

expand and deepen his expertise. In the fall of 1978, Chu joined Bell Telephone Laboratories in New Jersey, where he worked as an independent researcher. Chu undertook a spectroscopic study of positronium, an atom composed of a negative and positive electron. Previous attempts to study the properties of positronium had failed because of its extremely brief existence. By developing improved laser techniques, Chu and his colleagues were able to study a few of these atoms, and, later, even larger quantities, culminating in one of the most precise measurements of a quantum electro dynamic atomic system. Chu's success in this study led to him being named as head of Bell's Quantum Electronic Research Department in 1983.

In 1984, Chu developed the technique of laser cooling and trapping atoms. His 1985 paper reporting his results, "Three-dimensional Viscous Confinement and Cooling of Atoms by Resonance Radiation Pressure," was published in the academic journal *Physical Review Letters*. The central feature of Chu's method was confining the atom under study in a space, or "box," created by three pairs of laser beams. This technique proved to be extraordinarily valuable in studying other "optically trapped atoms." In 1987, Chu accepted a professorship at Stanford University, where he extended his laser technique to new applications, investigating different parts of molecules and using laser beams as "optical tweezers." He also used this method to study DNA molecules. In 1997, Chu won the Nobel Prize in Physics, which he shared with two other scientists who had helped create the method of cooling and trapping atoms with lasers.

Chu is also involved in energy issues. He encourages students to become involved in combating global climate change, which he sees as potentially devastating to American agriculture if it continues unabated. He pursued these concerns as director of the Lawrence Berkeley National Laboratory, a position he assumed in 2004. Chu succeeded in making the laboratory a center of research on energy problems. The lab worked closely with US Department of Energy.

> "As the saying goes, the Stone Age did not end because we ran out of stones; we transitioned to better solutions. The same opportunity lies before us with energy efficiency and clean energy."

In 2009, Chu was named the twelfth US secretary of energy by President Barack Obama. Chu is the first Nobel Prize winner appointed to the position. As energy secretary, Chu has worked to carry out President Obama's plans to develop wind, solar, geothermal, and other renewable energy sources, while also emphasizing efforts to increase the energy efficiencies of motor vehicles, buildings, and industries.

In August 2011 Chu praised an advisory panel report on curbing the environmental risks of natural-gas development. Chu responded to the panel's report on hydraulic fracturing, the controversial drilling method that is enabling a U.S. gas boom while bringing fears of groundwater contamination. The report called for better data collection of air and water data, as well as "rigorous" air pollution standards and mandatory disclosure of the chemicals used in the hydraulic fracturing process. Chu said that he would "be working closely with my colleagues in the Administration to review the recommendations and to chart a path for continued development of this vital energy resource in a safe manner".

Chu resigned as energy secretary on April 22, 2013. He returned to Stanford as Professor of Physics and Professor of Molecular & Cellular Physiology.

Significance

Chu's discovery of atom cooling and trapping has led to many applications, such as highly sensitive gyroscopes and an instrument that can measure gravity more precisely than any previous technique. Over the course of his career, Chu has helped develop new ways to manipulate DNA molecules, and his method has proved valuable in the study of many other molecules important in the structure and functioning of living things. Environmentalists and others concerned about the United States' overreliance on fossil fuels believe that Chu's advocacy of alternative energy and nuclear power has proven significant.

Washington University in St. Louis and Harvard University awarded him honorary doctorates during their 2010 and 2009 commencement exercises, respectively. He was awarded an honorary degree from Yale University during its 2010 commencement. He was also awarded an honorary degree from the Polytechnic Institute of New York University, the same institution at which his father taught for several years, during its 2011 commencement. Penn State University awarded him an honorary doctorate during their 2012 commencement exercises. In 2014, Chu was awarded an honorary doctorate from Williams College, during which he gave a talk moderated by Williams College Professor Protik Majumder. Chu was also awarded an honorary doctorate from Amherst College in 2017, where he later gave a lecture titled "Climate Change and Needed Technical Solutions for a Sustainable Future" in March 2018.

Robert J. Paradowski

FURTHER READING

Chang, Laura. *Scientists at Work: Profiles of Today's Groundbreaking Scientists from Science Times*. New York: McGraw, 2000. Print. Profiles fifty scientists, including Steven Chu. Originally published in a weekly supplement of the *New York Times*.

Ekspong, Gösta, ed. *Nobel Lectures in Physics, 1996–2000*. Hackensack: World Scientific, 2003. Print. Contains the Nobel lecture delivered by Chu along with a biography and analysis of the significance of his work.

May, Mike. "Interview: Steven Chu." *American Scientist* 86.1 (Jan.–Feb. 1998): 1. Print. Discusses Chu's work with atom cooling and its applications in accessible terms.

ALBERT EINSTEIN

German-born scientist

Born: March 14, 1879 ; Ulm, Germany
Died: April 18, 1955 ; Princeton, New Jersey
Areas of Achievement: Science and technology; social issues

One of the greatest scientific minds in history, Einstein revised classical notions of matter, energy, light, gravity, time, and space. His equations gave rise to the two most important advances of modern physics, the theory of relativity and quantum mechanics.

EARLY LIFE

Albert Einstein (IN-stin) was born into a Jewish family in Germany in 1879. His father, Hermann, was a businessman; his mother, Paulina Koch, came from a wealthy family that provided financial assistance to the Einsteins as needed. Einstein showed interest in geometry and in mechanical and magnetic objects. Undoubtedly these

Albert Einstein (Wikimedia Commons)

early preoccupations, similar to those of Sir Isaac Newton at a young age two hundred years earlier, were important factors in preparing the minds of Newton and Einstein for the great conceptual breakthroughs they would make as adults. Einstein also studied the violin, which would become his lifelong hobby.

His family was not observant, and Einstein, skeptical of the tenets of traditional Judaism, decided against a Bar Mitzvah when he was thirteen. He also found the authoritarian German gymnasium system of education stifling. In 1895, he finished high school in Aarau, Switzerland and then graduated from the Zurich Polytechnic Institute. Although he had been fascinated by the paradoxes of modern physics since his teenage years, he did not excel as a student. In 1900, he graduated with the lowest examination scores of any of the Polytechnic graduates.

In 1903, he married Mileva Marić, who had also been a student at the Polytechnic Institute; they would have three children. Unable to obtain an academic position, Einstein became a clerk in the Swiss patent office, which allowed him time to contemplate scientific questions. In 1905, he was awarded his Ph.D. in physics.

LIFE'S WORK

In a burst of scientific brilliance that is paralleled in the history of physics only by Newton's discoveries in the year 1666, Einstein published five papers in 1905 that transformed modern science. His March paper solved the riddle of the photoelectric effect by proposing the quantum photon theory of light. His April and May papers advanced the theory of the atom, solving the mystery of Brownian motion. His June paper proposed the special theory of relativity, postulating that while motion is relative to an observer's frame of reference, that is, the observer's position and velocity, the speed of light is the same, regardless of the direction or velocity of either its source or its observers. To reconcile this paradox, Einstein reevaluated traditional notions of space and time. His fifth paper, in September, proposed the equivalence of matter and energy according to the famous formula $E = mc^2$, paving the way for the later development of atomic energy and weapons.

It took the world several years to realize that in these papers, an obscure clerk from the Swiss patent office had revised Newtonian physics. Einstein was rewarded with prestigious professorships in Germany and the Nobel Prize in Physics. In 1916, Einstein published his greatest achievement, the general theory of relativity, incorporating gravity into a four-dimensional model of space-time. When observations during a 1919 solar eclipse confirmed his theories, he became world famous.

In Germany, however, Einstein was exposed to increasing anti-Semitism. Paul Weyland, a German nationalist, organized the Study Group of German Scientists for the Preservation of Pure Science, which held a vitriolic meeting in Berlin's Philharmonic Hall on August 24, 1920. The Nobel Laureate Philipp Lenard advocated for a Germanic science untainted by Jewish influence. Even a little-known rabble-rouser picked up on the controversy,

---

The Theory of Relativity

The summit of Albert Einstein's scientific achievements was his theory of relativity. It is one of the pivotal intellectual conceptions of humankind, revising fundamental principles of space, time, and gravity. Einstein had a great appreciation for the physicists who preceded him, and his theory can be seen as systematizing Galileo Galilei's relativity of motion, Isaac Newton's gravitational theories, Ernst Mach's inertial principle, the tensor analysis of Carl Gauss and Bernhard Riemann, and the electromagnetic field equations of Hendrik Lorentz and James Maxwell. Einstein formulated the theory in two parts: special and general relativity. His special theory of relativity described uniform motion in an inertial system without reference to a gravitational field. His general theory of relativity accounted for gravity not as a force, as conceived by Newton, but as the geometrical curvature of space-time by the presence of matter. As Newton's breakthrough on gravity is traditionally attributed to his observation of a falling apple, Einstein attributed his insights to imagining an object seeming to fall in a nongravitational field due to mechanical acceleration. Einstein called this concept—the principle of equivalence of gravity and acceleration—the happiest thought of his life. The theory of relativity was confirmed by calculations of the Perihelion precession of Mercury and the curvature of light due to the sun's gravitational field. Einstein's theory of relativity is a bedrock of modern physics, essential to understanding gravity and the effects of mass on the space-time continuum.

complaining in a January 3, 1921, article in the *Volkischer Beobachter* newspaper that "[s]cience, once our greatest pride, is today being taught by Hebrews." The author of that article: Adolf Hitler.

In 1919, Einstein and his wife divorced, and Einstein later married his cousin Elsa. In the spring of 1921, Einstein took a two-month tour of the United States, where he was celebrated as a great physicist and a hero of modern Judaism. However, his visit aggravated a tension in the Jewish establishment. On the one side were European Zionists, such as Chaim Weizmann, who accompanied Einstein to raise funds for the planned Hebrew University of Jerusalem; on the other side were leaders of American Jewry, such as Louis Brandeis, Felix Frankfurter, Bernard Baruch, and the Guggenheim family, who emphasized success and even assimilation in the United States. Amid the rancor, Einstein tried to stay aloof. He came away from the trip more deeply committed to a Jewish homeland and also impressed with the enthusiasm of Americans.

Where Einstein had once been the scientific revolutionary, he became ambivalent about making startling discoveries in quantum physics. Einstein was alarmed by the challenges that quantum mechanics posed to notions of causality and the determinate nature of the universe. A spiritual man, Einstein found repugnant any theory of physics that seemed to deny a rational, orderly conception of the universe.

With the ominous rise of Nazi power, Einstein and his second wife immigrated to the United States in October, 1933, where Einstein accepted a position at the Institute for Advanced Study in Princeton, New Jersey. The newly installed Nazi regime reacted angrily. Einstein's works were included in a book burning, and his bank accounts were confiscated. Nazi aggression caused Einstein to rethink his commitment to absolute pacifism.

Einstein and Leó Szilárd, along with other refugees such as Edward Teller and Eugene Wigner, "regarded it as their responsibility to alert Americans to the possibility that German scientists might win the race to build an atomic bomb, and to warn that Hitler would be more than willing to resort to such a weapon." To make certain the US was aware of the danger, in July 1939, a few months before the beginning of World War II in Europe, Szilárd and Wigner visited Einstein to explain the possibility of atomic bombs, which Einstein, a pacifist, said he had never considered. He was asked to lend his support by writing a letter, with Szilárd, to President Roosevelt, recommending the US pay attention and engage in its own nuclear weapons research. In addition to the letter, Einstein used his connections with the Belgian Royal Family and the Belgian queen mother to get access with a personal envoy to the White House's Oval Office. Some say that as a result of Einstein's letter and his meetings with Roosevelt, the US entered the "race" to develop the bomb, drawing on its "immense material, financial, and scientific resources" to initiate the Manhattan Project.

> "*Everybody is a genius. But if you judge a fish by its ability to climb a tree, it will live its whole life believing that it is stupid.*"

For Einstein, "war was a disease ... [and] he called for resistance to war." By signing the letter to Roosevelt, some argue he went against his pacifist principles. In 1954, a year before his death, Einstein said to his old friend, Linus Pauling, "I made one great mistake in my life—when I signed the letter to President Roosevelt recommending that atom bombs be made; but there was

International Committee on Intellectual Cooperation (League of Nations). Plenary session in the Palais Wilson, between 1924 and 1927. (Wikimedia Commons)

some justification—the danger that the Germans would make them ..."

Einstein became an American citizen in 1940. Not long after settling into his career at the Institute for Advanced Study (in Princeton, New Jersey), he expressed his appreciation of the meritocracy in American culture when compared to Europe. He recognized the "right of individuals to say and think what they pleased", without social barriers, and as a result, individuals were encouraged, he said, to be more creative, a trait he valued from his own early education.

In the postwar period, Einstein strove to formulate a unified theory of relativity, electromagnetism, and particle physics. Although he never achieved this objective, he pioneered efforts to find a unified field theory. He became outspoken in favor of internationalism, pacifism, and his bond with the Jewish people. He spoke in favor of equal rights for African Americans, and he advocated nuclear disarmament. He favored a Jewish homeland in Palestine and insisted that Jews and Arabs be treated equally; he cosigned a December 4, 1948, letter to *The New York Times*, denouncing the U.S. speaking tour of Israeli militia leader Menachem Begin for his violent and ultranationalist methods. Einstein retained his bond to the Hebrew University of Jerusalem, serving on its board and donating his collected papers to the university. In 1952, he declined the presidency of Israel. He died of heart failure in 1955.

SIGNIFICANCE

One of the greatest scientific minds in history, Einstein revised classical notions of matter, energy, light, gravity, time, and space. His equations gave rise to the two most important advances of modern physics, the theory of relativity and quantum mechanics, foreshadowing modern discoveries of an expanding universe, gravitational lensing, displacement of spectral lines, and black holes. Einstein has become an iconic figure throughout the world representing scientific progress and genius. In addition, Einstein promoted peace, internationalism, and civil rights. A theoretical scientist on the level of Newton, and a humane and advanced social thinker, Einstein is one of the most significant figures of modern history.

Howard Bromberg

FURTHER READING

Cropper, William. "Adventure in Thought: Albert Einstein." In *Great Physicists: The Life and Times of Leading Physicists from Galileo to Hawking*. New York: Oxford University Press, 2004. Insightful chapter puts Einstein's science in the context of physicists who preceded and followed him.

Isaacson, Walter. *Albert Einstein: His Life and Universe*. New York: Simon and Schuster, 2007. Full-length biography based on Einstein papers released in 2006.

---. "How Einstein Divided America's Jews." *The Atlantic* 304, no. 5 (December, 2009): 70-74. In-depth account of Einstein's 1921 trip to the United States, which the author asserts strengthened his support of Zionism.

Jerome, Fred. *Einstein on Israel and Zionism: His Provocative Ideas About the Middle East*. New York: St. Martin's Press, 2009. Controversially argues that Einstein's support for Israel as a home for the Jewish people is a myth.

Speregen, Devra. *Albert Einstein: The Jewish Man Behind the Theory*. Philadelphia: Jewish Publication Society of America, 2006. A young-adult book emphasizing Einstein's Jewish roots and his commitment to Israel.

GRACE MURRAY HOPPER

Mathematician and computer scientist

Born: December 9, 1906 ; New York City, New York
Died: January 1, 1992 ; Arlington, Virginia
Area of Achievement: Invention, science and technology

Hopper was a U.S. naval officer who eventually rose to the rank of rear admiral. She is best known for her work on the development of COBOL as a computer programming language. She also created a large variety of computer software that was innovative in terms of the problems addressed.

EARLY LIFE

Grace Brewster Murray was the eldest of three children born to Walter Fletcher Murray, an insurance broker, and Mary Campbell Van Horne Murray of New York City. Her family was fairly well off, and she spent her childhood summers at the family cottage on Lake Wentworth in Wolfeboro, New Hampshire. Her father encouraged her not to follow the traditional roles that women typically followed at that time. From her surveyor grandfather, John Van Horne, she learned about angles and curves, which may have led to her interest in a

Grace Murray Hopper (Wikimedia Commons)

mathematics career, although she credited her mother's interest in the subject as being the main influence. Murray received her bachelor's degree in mathematics and physics from Vassar College in 1928, graduating Phi Beta Kappa, and earned a master's degree in mathematics from Yale University in 1930. In 1934, she became the first woman to receive a doctorate in mathematics from Yale. Her dissertation was titled "New Types of Irreducibility Criteria" and was written under the tutelage of famed algebraist Øystein Ore.

Murray married Vincent Foster Hopper in 1930, when she was twenty-three years old. Hopper was an honors graduate of Princeton University and later earned a doctorate in literature at Columbia University. The couple separated in the early 1940's and were divorced in 1945. He died shortly afterward in the final days of World War II. They had no children.

Grace Hopper served as a faculty member at Vassar College from 1931 to 1943, at which time she joined the U.S. Navy's Bureau of Ordnance at Harvard University as a mathematical officer, working under Howard Aiken. Her great-grandfather Alexander Russell had been a rear admiral, and she had always been interested in the Navy. At the age of thirty-seven, she was initially considered too old for the Navy, but her specialty in mathematics was crucial, and the Navy relented and accepted her. There was also a problem with her weight: At 105 pounds, she was sixteen pounds underweight for her height of five feet, six inches. However, she was granted a waiver. Because of her educational background, she was sent to Midshipman's School and graduated at the top of her class in 1944, becoming a lieutenant (junior grade).

Her first job was as one of the initial programmers on the Navy's Mark I—the first large-scale digital computer. The Mark I was fifty-one feet long, eight feet tall, and eight feet wide and was considered a marvel of modern science. It contained five hundred miles of electrical wire and over 750,000 parts. The computer was used to calculate aiming angles for guns in various types of weather to determine the flight path of artillery shells. Hopper and her assistants had to keep the computer running twenty-four hours a day during the war. In 1946, much of her wartime knowledge was incorporated into a book that she coauthored with James Conant—A Manual of Operation for the Automatic Sequence Controlled Calculator.

"*Humans are allergic to change. They love to say, "We've always done it this way." I try to fight that. That's why I have a clock on my wall that runs counter-clockwise.*"

Life's Work

Following the war, Hopper was released from active duty, but she remained in the Naval Reserve. She joined the Harvard faculty at the Computation Laboratory, where she continued her work on the Mark II and Mark III. From 1949 to 1967, she worked as a mathematician for Eckert-Mauchly Computer Corporation, which was later acquired by Sperry Rand Corporation. From 1967 through September of 1986, she was on active duty with the Navy. She was promoted to commodore in 1983 at the age of seventy-six. When she retired from the Navy as a rear admiral in 1986, Hopper was the oldest-serving officer at that time and the first female admiral in the history of the Navy. Late in her career, at the age of eighty, she joined Digital Equipment Corporation, where she worked from 1986 to 1988.

At Sperry Rand, Hopper had the opportunity to work on the Universal Automatic Computer, better known as UNIVAC, which operated one thousand times faster than the Navy's old Mark I. The UNIVAC was the first commercial electronic computer. It used vacuum tubes instead of the electromechanical relay switches of the Mark calculating machines. In 1952, she invented the compiler, an intermediate program that translated English-language instructions into computer language. She also was the first to use now standard computer tools such as subroutines, formula translation, code optimization, and symbolic manipulation.

Hopper is best known for creating the computer programming language known as Common Business Oriented Language (COBOL). COBOL was the first language that allowed a programmer to talk to a computer with words rather than with numbers. Before COBOL, computer programs were written either in assembly code or some type of machine code. Hopper felt that programmers should be able to communicate with computers in English.

Hopper is also known for popularizing the term "bug" to describe a computer glitch. Today, correcting problems in computer software is known as "debugging." Hopper used the term "bug" when she traced an error in the Mark II to a real bug—a moth trapped in a relay switch. The moth was removed and taped to a computer log book. Initially, "bug" referred to problems with hardware, but in the 1950's Hopper extended the meaning of "debug" to include fixing software programming errors.

Most of Hopper's inventions dealt with software. Her innovative ideas included computer programs to track the life cycle of crop-eating locusts, a weather computer, software to manage water reserves, and programs to track wave motions at the bottom of the ocean. In 1966, she was promoted to commander in the Naval Reserve, but she had reached the legal limit of twenty years' service and was forced to retire. However, within six months, the Navy decided that it needed her back to work on COBOL. In 1967, at the age of sixty, she returned to active duty. Her new job was to combine versions of COBOL into a USA Standard COBOL.

In her later years, Hopper was a venerable figure, nicknamed "Amazing Grace" for her accomplishments and her ability to motivate audiences. During her career, she was granted more than thirty-seven honorary degrees, including ones from the University of Pennsylvania, Long Island University, and the Newark College of Engineering. Other honors included her selection for the 1969 "man of the year" award (she was the initial recipient of this award) from the Data Processing Management Association. In 1991, she was awarded the nation's first National Medal of Technology by President George H. W. Bush. In 1994, more than two years after her death, she was inducted into the National Women's Hall of Fame. The Navy later launched an Aegis-guided missile destroyer named for her, the USS Hopper. Hopper died in 1992 and was buried in Arlington National Cemetery with full military honors.

Hopper at the UNIVAC keyboard, circa 1960. (Wikimedia Commons)

Significance

Hopper's scientific achievements made her a legend in computer circles internationally. She began as one of the first programmers on the Navy's Mark I computer and progressed to become the first programmer on the first commercial computer, the UNIVAC. Her work with language compilers made computer programming easier. Following her introduction of COBOL, she published more than fifty articles on software and programming languages. Her innovative ideas for the use of computers inspired others to use computers creatively.

> **COBOL: A Computer Programming Language**
>
> Grace Murray Hopper is best known for creating the Common Business Oriented Language (COBOL), a programming language that permitted programmers to communicate with computers by means of the English language rather than through numbers. Hopper attributed the idea for COBOL to her difficulty in balancing her checkbook. Early computers were programmed using a machine code that used numbers. Hopper had learned to add, subtract, multiply, and divide using a numbering system to the base eight, known as the octal system, which used digits 0 through 7. Unfortunately, Hopper became so adept at using the base-eight system that she inadvertently used it when she added and subtracted in her checkbook. Thus, her checkbook did not balance because she was not using the decimal system.
>
> To alleviate the problem of programmers having to use the octal system, she suggested that the Universal Automatic Computer (UNIVAC), the first commercial electronic computer, be programmed to understand English commands. Initially ridiculed by other programmers, Hopper developed the B-0 compiler, later known as FLOW-MATIC, which by 1956 had enabled the UNIVAC to understand twenty English-like phrases. By 1959, this compiler had led to the first standardized universal computer language—COBOL. COBOL was used to retrieve accounting, billing, and payroll data, and the program was easy to use. Hopper then created the manuals to enable others to learn COBOL and to program their own computers. Nicknamed the "Grandmother of COBOL" and "Amazing Grace," Hopper was recalled to active duty in the Navy in 1967 to continue her work on COBOL.

As a naval officer, and later at Digital Equipment Corporation, she traveled throughout the world speaking to thousands about the future of computers. She was honored on television shows such as 60 Minutes and was the subject of documentaries. Hopper's work essentially allowed non-computer specialists to work directly with computers. Computers were made accessible to the average businessperson; in turn, businesses were more successful because of the wide availability of computer technology, which led to economic growth throughout the world.

Dale L. Flesher

FURTHER READING

Billings, Charlene W. *Grace Hopper: Navy Admiral and Computer Pioneer.* Hillside, N.J.: Enslow Elementary, 1989. One of many children's books about Hopper.

Hopper, Grace Murray, and James Bryant Conant. *A Manual of Operation for the Automatic Sequence Controlled Calculator.* Cambridge, Mass.: Harvard University Press, 1946. Much of Hopper's wartime knowledge can be found in this work.

Hopper, Grace Murray, and Steven L. Mandell. *Understanding Computers.* St. Paul, Minn.: West, 1984. This textbook was quite successful when it was first published, and it was accompanied by a student study guide and a videotape.

Mitchell, Carmen L. *The Contributions of Grace Murray Hopper to Computer Science and Computer Education.* Ann Arbor, Mich.: University Microfilms, 1995. A doctoral dissertation written at the University of North Texas that includes analysis of many of Hopper's published writings on computers and programming.

Whitelaw, Nancy, and Janet Hamlin. *Grace Hopper: Programming Pioneer.* New York: W. H. Freeman, 1995. This straightforward biography, written for children in grades 4-8, includes several humanizing anecdotes, including the fact that she had a clock that ran backward.

Williams, Kathleen Broome. *Grace Hopper: Admiral of the Cyber Sea.* Annapolis, Md.: Naval Institute Press, 2004. A well-written biography that analyzes Hopper's contributions to computer science. Focuses on her indefatigable character that carried her through social barriers.

Edwin Powell Hubble

Astronomer

Born: November 20, 1889 ; Marshfield, Missouri
Died: September 28, 1953 ; San Marino, California
Area of Achievement: Astronomy

Twentieth-century American astronomer Edwin Hubble is credited with the discovery that countless galaxies exist beyond the Milky Way, previously believed to be the only galaxy in the universe. He also identified the outward expansion of those galaxies, disproving the centuries-old belief that the universe was static. He produced the first outline of the observable universe, revolutionizing conceptions of its size, structure, processes, and history.

Edwin Powell Hubble (Wikimedia Commons)

Early Life

Edwin Powell Hubble was born in Marshfield, Missouri, the third of eight children born to Virginia Lee James, a homemaker, and John Powell Hubble, a businessman. He moved with his family when he was twelve years old to Wheaton, Illinois, and in 1906 won a scholarship to the University of Chicago, where he studied physics, chemistry, astronomy, and mathematics, as well as Latin, Greek, and French. He graduated in 1910 and was selected as a Rhodes Scholar, spending the next three years in England at Queens College, Oxford University. There, perhaps in compliance with his father's wishes, Hubble studied Roman and English law, although he retained his love of astronomy. John Hubble died in 1913, and that year Edwin completed his studies at Queens and returned to the United States, where he taught Spanish, physics, and mathematics at New Albany High School in Indiana.

At the end of the school year in 1914, Hubble wrote to his former astronomy professor Forest Ray Moulton to tell him that he wanted to enter a graduate program in astronomy, but lacked the necessary funds. With Moulton's help, Hubble obtained a position as an assistant at the Yerkes Observatory of the University of Chicago, and Hubble began work on a doctoral degree in astronomy, completing his degree in 1917.

Following graduation, Hubble was offered an astronomer position by George Ellery Hale, director of the Mount Wilson Observatory in Southern California; but instead, he applied for an officer's commission in the US Army during World War I, serving in France and attaining the rank of major. Honorably discharged in 1919, Hubble then joined the staff of the Wilson Observatory, a position he held for more than three decades until his death. Hubble married Grace Burke in 1924; they had no children.

Life's Work

In 1923, Hubble used the 100-inch Hooker Telescope, then the largest telescope in the world, to view Cepheid variables in what was then known as the Andromeda nebula. Cepheids are stars that cycle from brighter to dimmer and back over a fixed period of time. They had been used to measure the distance between objects in the galaxy since the early 1900s, when American astronomer Henrietta Swan Leavitt's observations of Cepheid brightness made it possible for scientists to use mathematical calculations to determine galactic distances. Using Cepheid stars, Hubble was able to prove that the Andromeda nebula was an independent galaxy and not a cluster of gasses and stars in the Milky Way as was previously believed.

In 1924, Hubble gained international recognition and was acknowledged for launching a new era in celestial inquiry when the *New York Times* reported his findings that spiral nebulae, which appeared as whirling clouds, are in fact galaxies—stellar systems that are immense, of varying size, and at great distances from the Milky Way galaxy. This revolutionized mainstream conceptions of the size and expanse of the universe.

In 1925, Hubble developed the Hubble sequence, or the Hubble tuning-fork diagram, a classification scheme for galaxies based on their shape or appearance. He categorized galaxies into three broad types: spiral, elliptical, and lenticular, with variations within each type. The small percentage of galaxies that did not fit into this three-tiered scheme were classified as irregulars. This classification system of galaxies remains in use today.

By 1929, Hubble, with his assistant Milton Humason, produced evidence that the outer galaxies were receding from each other at thousands or even hundreds of thousands of miles per second. He proposed that groups of galaxies were bound by gravity and would travel together in space, showing a relationship between the speed of recession of the galaxies and their distance from each other: The farther a galaxy is, the faster it appears to be receding. This distance-velocity relation is called Hubble's law.

In 1936, Hubble published his major findings in the book *The Realm of the Nebulae* (1936), which contained his views on the structure of the universe and its expanding nature. Hubble's findings revealed innumerable galaxies throughout the universe, comparable in size to the Milky Way and separated by unimaginably large voids. He also determined that, if considered on a large-enough scale, the universe is isotropic (it has neither a centernor an edge) and homogenous (it is generally the same in composition throughout).

> "We do not know why we are born into the world, but we can try to find out what sort of a world it is — at least in its physical aspects."

In 1931, Einstein publicly thanked Hubble for his evidence of a dynamic universe, which supported cosmological considerations in the general theory of relativity more concisely than had Einstein's own rationale. Using Hubble's findings, scientists could determine the rate at which galaxies move and the distance that separates them. Furthermore, by retracing galaxies' paths, astronomers could infer the amount of time that has passed since all matter and energy in the universe existed in a state of utmost density. The number they reached using this technique, called the "Hubble time," gave a close estimate of the age of the universe, believed to be about 13.7 billion years. Thus, Hubble and other astronomers provided the observational reasons, and Einstein and other physicists provided theoretical reasons, for assuming an explosive origin to the universe and its subsequent expansion, popularly called the big bang theory.

In 1942, the United States was involved in World War II, and Hubble was asked by the government to lead the US Army's Ballistics Research Laboratory at the Aberdeen Proving Ground in Maryland. He remained there until December of 1945, when he returned to Mount Wilson Observatory. He was awarded the Medal of Merit for his services at Aberdeen. Back at Wilson, Hubble continued his work on cosmology, seeking to learn whether the expansion of the universe would cease or continue forever. In 1949, Hubble was the first to use the newly

The 100 inch Hooker telescope at Mount Wilson Observatory near Los Angeles, California. This is the telescope that Hubble used to measure galaxy redshifts and discover the general expansion of the universe. (Wikimedia Commons)

Hubble Confirms That the Universe Is Expanding

In 1929, Edwin Powell Hubble announced that the greater the distance to a given galaxy, the faster it is traveling away from the Milky Way galaxy. This discovery was of major importance, because it implied that the universe was expanding, lending support to what became known as the big bang theory of the creation of the universe.

Hubble's revolutionary conclusions were based on the discoveries of at least two preceding astronomers. In 1911 and 1912, Harvard astronomer Henrietta Swan Leavitt analyzed Cepheid variables, a type of star whose brightness fluctuates at regular intervals. She determined the relationship between a Cepheid's brightness (or luminosity) and its rate of fluctuation (or period), which became an important measure in determining the star's distance from the Earth. Around the same time, astronomer Vesto Melvin Slipher at Lowell Observatory in Arizona was studying the light emitted from distant stars and noted that some of them exhibited "redshift," meaning their light had a slightly longer wavelength and was therefore skewed slightly toward the red end of the visible spectrum.

Redshift is a manifestation of the Doppler effect, which says that waves coming from a moving source are shorter as the source approaches an observer and longer as the source moves away. Thus, redshift indicated that the observed stars must be moving away from the Earth. Slipher had no reliable way of measuring distances, however; it was left to Hubble to put together Slipher's redshift observations with distance measurements based on Leavitt's observations.

Hubble began work in 1919 with the 60-inch telescope on Mount Wilson, near Pasadena, California, when he returned from service in World War I; he then moved to the 100-inch Hooker Telescope at the same location. He studied objects within the Milky Way, such as novas (exploding stars), stars associated with gaseous nebulae, and variable stars. By 1922, he had published a paper noting the differences between the gaseous nebulae and those that were suspected of being more remote. Along the way, he determined that the Milky Way is just one out of a huge number of galaxies in the universe. He was eventually able to conclude that the farther a celestial object is from Earth, the faster it is receding—a conclusion now called Hubble's law.

Hubble's observations comported with Albert Einstein's general theory of relativity and lent powerful credence to the theory of an expanding universe postulated in 1927 by Belgian astronomer Georges Lemaître. Further extrapolations by Lemaître and others led to the big bang theory, the most commonly accepted scientific theory of the origin of the universe.

completed 200-inch Hale Telescope at Mount Palomar in California.

Hubble died in 1953 from heart failure.

Significance

Hubble's natural inclinations, curiosity, and talents prompted him to decipher and analyze the riddles of the universe. By the time of his death, he had become the world's foremost astronomer. The Hubble crater on the moon and Asteroid 2069 Hubble are named in his honor. The Hubble Space Telescope, put into orbit in 1990, has supplied valuable research data and images that have lead to many discoveries in the field of astrophysics. In fact, the telescope was used to observe supernovae of a special type in order to continue research on the expansion of the universe, whose leaders were honored with the 2011 Nobel Prize in Physics.

Hubble's discoveries that the universe is made up of countless and ever-changing and moving galaxies formed the basis of modern cosmology. He equipped cosmology with a new vocabulary and a new set of concepts for further study. His work initiated a fundamental shift in the pattern of cosmological thought comparable to the work of Nicolas Copernicus and Galileo Galilei.

Timothy C. Miller

Further Reading

Christianson, Gale E. *Edwin Hubble: Mariner of the Nebulae*. New York: Farrar, 1995. Print. A comprehensive and detailed biography of Hubble.

Hetherington, Norriss S. *Hubble's Cosmology: A Guided Study of Selected Texts.* Tucson: Pachart, 1996. Print. An interpretative, evaluative framework for understanding some original Hubble papers.

Hubble, Edwin. *The Realm of the Nebulae.* 1936. New Haven: Yale UP, 1982. Print. Hubble's own story of his research.

Kanipe, Jeff. *Chasing Hubble's Shadows: The Search for Galaxies at the Edge of Time.* New York: Hill and Wang, 2006. Print. Interprets findings of the Hubble Space Telescope on the expansion of the universe.

Sharov, Alexander S., and Igor D. Novikov. *Edwin Hubble, the Discoverer of the Big Bang Universe.* Trans. Vitaly Kisin. Cambridge: Cambridge UP, 2005. Print. Recounts the growth of Hubble's scientific thought and consequential discoveries.

MAE C. JEMISON

Scientist and astronaut

Born: October 17, 1956 ; Decatur, Alabama
Area(s) of significance: Business, medicine, science and technology

Jemison opened the field of space exploration to African American women but also dedicated her substantial later career to education and to using her experience as a business leader to find solutions to medical and environmental problems.

EARLY LIFE

Mae Carol Jemison was born to Charlie and Dorothy Jemison in Decatur, Alabama, less than thirty miles from Huntsville, home of the Marshall Space Center. Jemison, her mother, and her siblings Ada Sue and Ricky moved to Chicago, Illinois, when Jemison was three years old, leaving her father in his native Alabama before he joined them two months later. Jemison spent most of her childhood in Chicago and considered the city her hometown. In kindergarten, she declared her intention to become a scientist to a disbelieving teacher. Her innate intelligence, ambition, and the example of her mother's return to college to become a teacher fueled Jemison's determination to achieve her own goals.

As a young girl, Jemison grew up amid gangs in the primarily African American neighborhood of Woodlawn and witnessed the Chicago riots of 1968. When she was ten years old, her family moved to an all-white neighborhood that slowly integrated over the next few years. In spite of the obstacles, Jemison pursued science and began studying sickle cell anemia while still in high school. She finished high school at age fifteen and graduated from Stanford University with degrees in chemical engineering and African and African American studies at age nineteen. Jemison received her medical degree from Cornell University in 1981.

LIFE'S WORK

Jemison's professional life allowed her to contribute to the advancement of science in both the medical field and the national space program, which led to her role as the first female African American astronaut in 1992.

While Jemison was a high school student, she researched sickle cell anemia for a science fair project. She studied samples in a laboratory and worked with other scientists to form a working hypothesis. As an undergraduate, she intended to work in the biomedical field but instead opted to forgo a prestigious and lucrative medical career to join the Peace Corps. Jemison served for more than two years as the Peace Corps area medical officer for the African countries of Liberia and Sierra Leone and later returned to the United States to work in medicine.

Mae C. Jemison (Wikimedia Commons)

During Jemison's service in the Peace Corps, a volunteer became seriously ill and was diagnosed with malaria. As the volunteer's condition worsened, Jemison became convinced that the disease was actually meningitis with life-threatening complications that could not be dealt with in Sierra Leone. Jemison called for an Air Force hospital plane based in Germany for a military medical evaluation. The embassy questioned Jemison's authority, but she told them she did not need permission to make a medical decision. Jemison took the trip with the sick volunteer, staying up with them for over 56 hours. The volunteer survived the experience.

After undergoing a rigorous selection process, Jemison participated in the prestigious National Aeronautics and Space Administration (NASA) astronaut program from June, 1987, through March, 1993. While in the space program, she also worked in launch support at the Kennedy Space Center and dealt with computer software in the Shuttle Avionics Integration Laboratory.

Beginning September 12, 1992, Jemison was part of the crew of the space shuttle Endeavour. Her flight was the fiftieth space shuttle flight in the space program's history. During that eight-day flight, Jemison served as the science mission specialist on STS-47 Spacelab J, the first joint mission between the United States and Japan. The mission also was noted for including the first Japanese astronaut.

While on Endeavour, Jemison and her colleagues conducted forty-four experiments—twenty-four in materials science and twenty in life science, which meshed well with her medical and engineering background. Overall, Jemison spent about 190 hours in space on her only shuttle flight.

> "Never be limited by other people's limited imaginations. If you adopt their attitudes, then the possibility won't exist because you'll have already shut it out... You can hear other people's wisdom, but you've got to re-evaluate the world for yourself."

After leaving the space program in 1993, Jemison made a special cameo on the popular science fiction television show *Star Trek: The Next Generation* as Lieutenant Palmer. In 1994, she formed a science camp for teenagers, the Earth We Share, which focuses on global problem solving. Jemison was a professor of environmental studies at Dartmouth College from 1995 to 2002 and later joined the staff at Cornell University as a professor-at-large.

Using her extensive engineering and medical knowledge, Jemison became the chief executive officer of Bio-Sentient Corporation, a biomedical technology firm, and president of the Jemison Group, a technologically oriented company with projects such as improving health care in developing nations. Jemison was one of a number of scientists and researchers who made bids for the 100 Year Starship plan, a long term study towards the creation of a plan for human exploration of space and interstellar travel. Jemison's organization had the winning bid in 2012, and Jemison served as principal of the organization. The organization held symposia in 2013, 2014, and 2015, offering scientists and artists interested in the subject of interstellar travel.

In 2018, she collaborated with Bayer and National 4-H Council for the initiative called "Science Matters" which was aimed at encouraging young children to understand and pursue agricultural sciences.

Significance

Jemison made history as the first female African American astronaut and has remained a role model for her innovative work in medical research, computer science, and engineering, all of which were historically male professions. Jemison also has shown versatility and ambition with her achievements in space exploration, education, and business leadership. Jemison is the recipient of nine honorary doctorate degrees, an inductee of the Women's Hall of Fame and has been considered one of the most influential African American women in science.

Bonnye Busbice Good, updated by Mwah L. Issitt

Further Reading

Alagna, Magdelena. *Mae C. Jemison: The First African American Woman in Space.* New York: Rosen, 2003. This biography describes Jemison's obstacles, career, and achievements as she pursued her efforts in science.

Black, Sonia. *Mae Jemison.* New York: Mondo, 2000. Brief biography written for children.

Gates, Henry Louis, Jr. "Mae Jemison." In *In Search of Our Roots: How Nineteen Extraordinary African Americans Reclaimed Their Past.* New York: Crown, 2009. In this intriguing source, Gates traces the ancestry of notable African Americans. In the chapter on Jemison, she shares memories of her youth, and Gates helps her construct her family tree, locating records of enslaved ancestors and seeking out their African tribal origins.

Haskins, Jim. *Black Stars: African American Women Scientists and Inventors.* New York: Scholastic, 1997. This collection of biographies written for students includes a chapter on Jemison.

Jemison, Mae. *Find Where the Wind Goes: Moments From My Life.* New York: Scholastic, 2001. Written to encourage young readers, this series of vignettes describes how Jemison persevered in her youth to become a doctor and astronaut.

KATHERINE G. JOHNSON

Scientist and mathematician

Born: August 26, 1918 ; White Sulfur Springs, West Virginia
Also known as: Katherine Coleman Goble Johnson; Katherine Coleman (birth name)
Area of Achievement: Science and technology

A pioneering space scientist who broke racial and gender barriers, Johnson specialized in mathematics and physics during a career spanning more than thirty years with the National Aeronautics and Space Administration (NASA). She was an indispensable member of teams that launched some of America's most successful exploratory programs, including the Mercury, Apollo, and space shuttle missions.

EARLY LIFE

Katherine Coleman Goble Johnson was the youngest of four children born to farmer and part-time janitor Joshua Coleman and former teacher Joylette Coleman. Fascinated with numbers from an early age, she entered school early and quickly advanced because of her mathematical genius. Her hometown of White Sulphur Springs, West Virginia, offered education for African American schoolchildren only through eighth grade, so her father moved the family 125 miles to Institute, West Virginia, to provide Katherine and her older siblings—Charles, Margaret, and Horace—additional opportunities.

At the age of ten, Johnson entered West Virginia State High School, affiliated with West Virginia Collegiate Institute (later renamed West Virginia State University). The high school principal took particular interest in the precocious youngster and engendered in her a lifelong interest in astronomy. Johnson graduated at age fourteen after taking special courses in advanced math and analytic geometry, and then enrolled at West Virginia Collegiate Institute on a full scholarship. In 1937, she graduated summa cum laude with a bachelor of science degree, majoring in math and French. Johnson afterward began graduate studies in mathematics and physics. In 1939, she married fellow graduate student James Francis Goble; the couple would eventually become parents to three daughters: Constance, Joylette, and Kathy. In 1940, Johnson was forced to withdraw from the graduate program because her husband became ill with an inoperable brain tumor. She subsequently went to work as a teacher in rural schools in Virginia and West Virginia.

LIFE'S WORK

In the early 1950's, Johnson learned of openings for research mathematicians at the Langley Research Center of the National Advisory Committee for Aeronautics, the precursor of the National Aeronautics and Space Administration (NASA). She applied and, in 1953, was hired as a human computer, necessitating her family's move to Langley, Virginia. Part of a pool of women assigned to complete complicated mathematical calculations related to aeronautics, she quickly demonstrated her analytic and computing abilities. Despite the racial and gender

Katherine G. Johnson (Wikimedia Commons)

discrimination that prevailed within the organization, Johnson was accepted and treated as an equal because of the accuracy of her work.

In 1956, Johnson's husband succumbed to cancer. Three years later, she married Korean War veteran Lieutenant Colonel James A. Johnson. By then, Johnson was an integral part of NASA's previously all-male Flight Mechanics Branch. As an aeronautics technologist and research mathematician, she was instrumental in figuring launch windows, spacecraft trajectories, and orbits and made contributions to avionics, backup plans, and navigational charts for some of NASA's most important early missions, which helped propel the United States to the forefront of space exploration. In 1959, Johnson was part of the team that successfully launched Alan Shepard, the first American in space, and it was her work that provided a precise splashdown for his 1961 Mercury capsule. In 1962, when electronic computers first were introduced to calculate the flight of John Glenn, the first American to orbit the Earth, Johnson was the person called upon to check the computer's accuracy and verify its figures. In 1969, as a member of NASA's Space Controls Branch, she was primarily responsible for calculating the outward- and inward-bound trajectories for the trailblazing Apollo 11 mission, in which Neil Armstrong became the first person to set foot on the moon. During a career that spanned thirty-three years—in which she co-rote more than twenty-five scientific and technical papers—Johnson also worked on such projects as the Earth Resources Satellite, the space shuttle, and plans for a mission to Mars. She retired from NASA in 1986. Inspired by their mother's achievements, Johnson's daughters followed in her footsteps: Kathy and Constance became teachers, and Joylette spent many years as a computer analyst at Lockheed Martin.

"I was excited at something new, always liked something new, but give credit to everybody who helped. I didn't do anything alone but try to go to the root of the question and succeeded there."

President Barack Obama presented Johnson with the Presidential Medal of Freedom, one of 17 Americans so honored on November 24, 2015. She was cited as a pioneering example of African-American women in STEM.

On May 5, 2016, a new 40,000-square-foot (3,700 m^2) building was named "Katherine G. Johnson Computational Research Facility" and formally dedicated at the agency's Langley Research Center in Hampton, Virginia. The facility officially opened its doors on September 22, 2017. Johnson attended this event, which also marked the 55th anniversary of astronaut Alan Shepard's historic rocket launch and splashdown, a success Johnson helped achieve.

The highly acclaimed film *Hidden Figures*, released in December 2016, was based on the non-fiction book of the same title by Margot Lee Shetterly, which was published earlier that year. It follows Johnson and other female African-American mathematicians (Mary Jackson and Dorothy Vaughan) who worked at NASA. Taraji P. Henson plays Johnson in the film. Appearing alongside Henson at the 89th Academy Awards, Johnson received a standing ovation from the audience. In an earlier interview, Johnson offered the following comment about the movie: "It was well-done. The three leading ladies did an excellent job portraying us." In a 2016 episode of the NBC series *Timeless*, titled "Space Race", the mathematician is portrayed by Nadine Ellis.

Johnson at NASA Langley Research Center in 1980. (Wikimedia Commons)

Significance
Throughout her career at NASA, Johnson garnered numerous accolades for her work. In 1967, she received the Lunar Orbiter Spacecraft and Operations Team Award and the Apollo Group

Achievement Award; the latter honor included a souvenir flag that had flown to the moon. She also received Langley Research Center Special Achievement Awards in 1971, 1980, 1984, 1985, and 1986. After retiring, she was granted an honorary doctorate of laws in 1998 from the State University of New York, Farmingdale. The next year, she was named West Virginia State University outstanding alumna of the year. In 2006, she was commencement speaker at Capitol College in Maryland, where she was awarded an honorary doctorate of science.

Jack Ewing

FURTHER READING

Carey, Charles W., Jr. *African Americans in Science: An Encyclopedia of People and Progress*. 2 vols. Santa Barbara, Calif.: ABC-CLIO, 2008. This reference examines the work, contributions, and achievements of African Americans such as Johnson in more than thirty different fields of scientific endeavor.

Godwin, Robert, ed. *Apollo 11: The NASA Mission Reports*. Burlington, Ont.: Collector's Guide, 2002. Part of a three-volume set containing both written text and DVDs of lunar footage, this is a complete postmission report of the historic Apollo 11 project, incorporating technical data, diagrams, medical information, and crew observations.

Lang, Mozell P. "Katherine G. Johnson." In *Contributions of African American Scientists and Mathematicians*. Orlando, Fla.: Harcourt, 2007. Accessible biography of Johnson aimed at younger students.

MARY GOLDA ROSS

Cherokee aerospace engineer

Born: August 9, 1908 ; Park Hill, Oklahoma
Died: April 29, 2008 ; Los Altos, California
Area of achievement: Aeronautics; STEM; Native Leaders

The first female engineer at Lockheed, Ross worked on design concepts for interplanetary space travel and earth-orbiting missions.

EARLY LIFE

Mary Golda Ross was born in 1908 in Park Hill, Oklahoma, to William Wallace Ross and his wife Mary Henrietta Moore Ross. Park Hill, located in Cherokee County, Oklahoma, became an important center for Cherokee resettlement following the Cherokees' forced removal from the southeastern United States, an event known as the "Trail of Tears." Ross attended school in nearby Tahlequah, Oklahoma, also an important Cherokee city. It was declared the capital of the Cherokee Nation in 1839. Today, in addition to being the county seat of Cherokee County, it is the capital of the two federally recognized Cherokee tribes based in Oklahoma: the United Keetoowah Band of Cherokee Indians and the modern Cherokee Nation. Today in Tahlequah, Oklahoma, street signs and business signs are printed both in English and in Cherokee. Here, Mary Golda Ross finished high school at the age of sixteen. She then attended Northeastern State Teachers' College, also in Tahlequah. When Ross went to register for classes, she was asked to declare a major. Unfamiliar with that term, she expressed puzzlement. The registrar asked her what her favorite subject was in high school. Responding "math," she thus entered college as a mathematics major. She earned her bachelor's degree in mathematics in 1928 when she was twenty years old. When Ross graduated from college, only about seven percent of young people between the ages eighteen and twenty-four in the United States were enrolled in higher education; about forty percent of all bachelor's degrees in 1928 were awarded to women.

LIFE'S WORK

Ross spent nine years after her graduation working in schools in Oklahoma teaching math and science. In 1937, now age twenty-eight, she decided that she wanted to see more of the world than Oklahoma. She took the civil service exam that year relocated to Washington DC, where she worked as a statistical clerk at the Bureau of Indian Affairs (BIA). The BIA, recognizing that she would be more valuable to the Native American community working in education, reassigned her to the Santa Fe Indian School in Santa Fe, New Mexico, where she worked as a student advisor. Taking classes in the summer at Colorado State College of Education, she obtained a master's degree in 1938.

In late 1941, the United States entered World War Two. In 1942, while visiting friends in California, Ross learned that the Lockheed Corporation was experiencing a shortage of workers with strong mathematics and technical backgrounds because of the war. She applied for a job and was hired. Ross was assigned to a team of engineers who were working to correct a design problem with the corporation's P-38 Lightning aircraft. The P-38 was a military plane, one of the fastest in use at the time. After the war, Lockheed kept Ross and even paid for her to attend UCLA for a degree in engineering. She also studied aeronautics and missile and celestial mechanics.

In 1952, she was transferred to Lockheed's "Skunk Works," a top-secret think tank, where she began working on a classified program to develop technology for space travel. Other than the secretary, she was the only woman at Skunk Works. She is credited with having contributed design concepts for interplanetary space travel as well as for earth-orbiting space missions. She worked on the design of the Agena rocket, a type of rocket used in hundreds of space flight missions from 1959 to 1987. She was a co-author of numerous technical reports, too, including the NASA Planetary Flight Handbook, for which she wrote about the design of "flyby" missions to Venus and Mars. Reflecting years later on the work that she did for Lockheed and NASA, she said, "We were taking the theoretical and making it real." Much of her work remains classified, even today.

Ross retired in 1973. She began focusing her energy on promoting STEM education for Native American youth and for women. She was a member of the Society of Women Engineers. When she was ninety-six years old, Ross participated in the opening ceremonies of the National Museum of the American Indian at the Smithsonian in Washington DC, wearing a traditional Cherokee dress. She died in 2008; in her will, she bequeathed an endowment of $400,000 to the museum.

> "To function efficiently in today's world, you need math. The world is so technical, if you plan to work in it, a math background will let you go farther and faster."

SIGNIFICANCE

Ross is an inspiration not only to Native Americans or to American women, but to all of us. In 2018, she was honored by the United States Mint, who stamped her image on the 2019 Native American dollar. Rising from humble origins in her Cherokee community in Oklahoma, Ross earned a bachelor's degree in mathematics when she was twenty years old, and her lifetime work for Lockheed and for NASA was foundational to the development of the United States space program.

D. Alan Dean

FURTHER READING

Agnew, Brad. "Golda Ross Left Teaching to Support War Effort. *Tahlequah Daily Press*, March 20, 2016. https://www.tahlequahdailypress.com/news/golda-ross-left-teaching-to-support-war-effort/article_c500cbc4-eeba-11e5-9b57-2b127651fcb5.html.

Howard, Jenny. "Meet Mary Golda Ross, One of the First Native Americans in Engineering." *Massive Science*, May 17, 2018. https://massivesci.com/articles/mary-golda-ross-cherokee/

Blakemore, Erin. "Google Doodle Honors Little-Known Math Genius Who Helped America Reach the Stars." *Smithsonian Magazine*, March 29, 2017. https://www.smithsonianmag.com/smithsonian-institution/little-known-math-genius-helped-america-reach-stars-180962700/

Synar, Edwina. " Remember the Ladies: Mary Golda Ross — Aerospace Pioneer." *Tahlequah Daily Press*, February 15, 2019. https://www.tahlequahdailypress.com/cnhi_network/remember-the-ladies-mary-golda-ross-aerospace-pioneer/article_eeeeafdf-38c1-5afd-bd21-0a888dcd5216.html.

STEVE WOZNIAK

Technologist and entrepreneur

Born: August 11, 1950 ; San Jose, California
Area(s) of significance: Business; computers and technology

As a young man, Wozniak was adept at building computers and using them to entertain and to solve problems. Together with his friend Steve Jobs, he created the revolutionary Apple computer. In the twenty-first century, the company Wozniak helped create has remained at the forefront of technological innovations that have revolutionized the way we live.

EARLY LIFE

Stephan Gary Wozniak, also known as "Woz," was born on August 11, 1950, in San Jose, California. As an electrical engineer, his father, Jerry, encouraged his son's love of electronics from an early age. His mother, Margaret, was a homemaker, devoting her time to raising her children, who also included Leslie and Mark. Wozniak was shy and loved to read. In the fourth grade, he discovered

Steve Wozniak (Wikimedia Commons)

that he loved mathematics. The following year, he discovered ham radios and learned Morse code. By the time he was eleven, Wozniak was writing computer games. At the age of thirteen, he won an award at the Bay Area Science Fair for his 10-bit parallel digital computer.

Wozniak began taking electronics classes in high school and was hired by an electronics company to program its computers using Fortran. With a grant from the National Science Foundation, he also took mathematics classes at local colleges. Despite a love of practical jokes that caused him to be suspended for a short time, Wozniak graduated from Homestead High with honors in 1968. During a year attending the University of Colorado, he spent much of his time on computers. Returning to California, he attended a local college in Sunnyvale and got a job programming and running diagnostics on computers at Tenet, Inc. He and his friend Bill Fernandez spent their spare time designing a computer that they dubbed Cream Soda. His junior year found Wozniak attending the University of California, Berkeley.

Life's Work

By 1973, Wozniak was working at Hewlett-Packard in Palo Alto, California, which placed him in an ideal position for the upcoming computer revolution. He renewed his friendship with Steve Jobs, a high school computer geek serving an internship at Hewlett-Packard. In March 1975, the two friends attended the first meeting of the Homebrew Computer Club in Menlo Park, California. Although Jobs was five years younger, he and Wozniak found that their interest in computers outweighed the age difference. Homebrew was one of many such clubs that had sprung up in response to the release of the Altair computer kit, which allowed computer hobbyists to build their own computers. The club gave members a venue for sharing their developing knowledge. An electronics whiz, Wozniak was convinced that he could build his own computer now that the price of parts had begun to drop. After saving his money, he managed to complete his computer by January 1976.

Wozniak's computer, which became the Apple I, would be considered primitive by today's standards, but it was revolutionary for its time. Jobs encouraged him to sell his creation. It was sold without a case, a power supply, a monitor, or a keyboard. By that time, Bill Gates and Paul Allen were already selling their operating system, MS-DOS. At the National Computer Conference, an enterprising but less than honest member of Homebrew stole discarded Microsoft tapes from the garbage and carried them back to Homebrew, where they were freely distributed and used. On February 3, 1976, an open letter from Gates decrying the piracy appeared in the club's newsletter and in other publications regularly perused by hobbyists. Together, Wozniak and Jobs designed the Blue Box, a device that allowed them to bypass telephone charges. It made them a small profit but could have resulted in jail time.

> "*If you love what you do and are willing to do what it takes, it's within your reach. And it'll be worth every minute you spend alone at night, thinking and thinking about what it is you want to design or build. It'll be worth it, I promise.*"

While Wozniak worked at Hewlett-Packard, Jobs continued to live at home, earning money by writing computer games for Atari. In their spare time, the friends played with game development. Atari subsequently asked them to design Breakout, a spin-off of Atari's popular Pong game. Wozniak was responsible for circuitry, problem-solving, and diagram writing. They designed the game to use only 43 chips, at a time when most games were using more than 120 chips.

Despite the drawbacks of the Apple I, Jobs was astute enough to understand its potential to make money. He convinced Wozniak that they should start their own company in order to sell it, but Wozniak was initially hesitant to leave the financial safety of his job at Hewlett-Packard. He agreed to go into business with Jobs, however, and Apple was founded on April 1, 1976. Wozniak steadily improved his computer design, working mostly in the garage at the home of Jobs's parents. Within a year, the Apple II was introduced. Wozniak said later that both Apple I and Apple II were created for fun rather than profit.

In October 1976, Wozniak finally yielded to persuasion and left Hewlett-Packard to devote his efforts to Apple. In January 1977, after Mike Markkula, the marketing guru whom Jobs and Wozniak had hired to guide them through the early days, invested $250,000 in the company, it was incorporated as Apple Computer, Inc., and was relocated to Cupertino. As Apple continued to expand, it eventually needed an entire campus in Silicon Valley to house its operations.

Selling for $1,298, the Apple II was the first computer that did not need to be assembled after purchase. Using the BASIC programming language and a printed circuit board, it also contained its own keyboard, power supply, speakers, graphics, and game paddles and had 4K of memory, a user's manual, and a demonstration cassette. However, it was still dependent on a television monitor and on a cassette recorder and tapes. By 1979, however, Apple computers contained floppy disk drives for storing data. As Apple grew, Wozniak had less time to spend on computer design. Since most development work was done by teams of developers, Wozniak took on a public relations role.

The Apple III was introduced in 1980 as a rival to IBM personal computers. It was expensive at $2,995, and sales were disappointing. It was discontinued at the end of the following year. After time off to complete his education, Wozniak returned to work at Apple in 1982, but he chose to work as an engineer rather than as an executive. Although bitter infighting seemed to be tearing the company apart, Wozniak attempted to remain above the fray. Released in 1983, the Lisa (the Mac XL) was the most user-friendly computer released to that time, containing folders, pull-down menus, and an entire megabyte of random access memory (RAM). At $9,995, however, it was beyond the means of the average home user.

Wozniak at Kansasfest, 2013. Kansasfest is the only annual convention dedicated to the Apple II computer. (Wikimedia Commons)

On February 7, 1981, with Wozniak at the controls, a plane carrying him, his fiancée (Clark), Clark's brother, and his girlfriend crashed, causing Wozniak to suffer a short-term memory loss and leading to a reevaluation of his life. Wozniak decided to return to Berkeley to resume work on a degree. After a year of taking classes, Berkeley officials allowed him to use his continuing work at Apple for course credit. He finally graduated in 1986 and delivered the commencement speech at his graduation.

Wozniak gave up his active role in Apple in 1987. Along with a fellow Apple engineer, he founded CL-9 (Cloud 9), concentrating on creating a universal infrared remote control, which became the first programmable remote control in history. Wozniak continued to serve as a consultant for Apple, but his friendship with Jobs steadily unraveled. They remained in contact until Jobs's death in 2011 but were never again close friends. Wozniak remained a nominal employee of Apple, however, and continued to receive an annual salary. Wozniak founded the company Wheels of Zeus (WOZ) in 2001 to develop wireless global positioning system (GPS) technology. That venture lasted until 2006, the same year Wozniak published his autobiography. He was portrayed in the films *Jobs* (2013) and *Steve Jobs* (2015), consulting on the latter for historical accuracy.

Wozniak devoted his post-Apple years to philanthropic causes in San Jose, establishing the Technology Museum of Innovation and the Children's Discovery Museum and contributing to the Cleveland Ballet. He also remained active in the electronics industry, helping to develop such diverse items as the first programmable universal television remote control and wireless GPS equipment. He worked to get computers into schools and remains active in the battle against the infringement of electronic freedom and in providing legal counsel for computer hackers. In 2009, he became chief scientist for the Salt Lake City–based company Fusion-io.

In 2018 Woz won the "Human of the Year Award" at The Human Project Summit. Woz nominated Ryan Wolfington from The Inspiring Children Foundation program to receive the award with him. Foundation Executive Director Trent Alenik and mentor program founder and youth leader Cherrial Odell accepted the award on behalf of Ryan Wolfington and the Foundation.

SIGNIFICANCE

In contrast to Jobs, Wozniak always preferred to be an engineer rather than a manager or the head of a large company. He has always said that he created both Apple I and Apple II for fun and not for profit. Other insights into his personality and his values are perhaps revealed in his decision to go back to college at a point in his life when he had already found success as the creator of the Apple computer, or in his decision to become a teacher. Although Wozniak wasn't involved with Apple to become rich or powerful, he nevertheless had an incalculable impact on today's world.

Elizabeth Rholetter Purdy

FURTHER READING

Carlton, Jim. *Apple: The Inside Story of Intrigue, Egomania, and Business Blunders*. New York: Random House, 1997. Print.

Deutschman, Alan. "Thanks for the Future." *Time* 7 Nov. 2011: 8–13. Print.

Kendall, Martha E. *Steve Wozniak ... Inventor of the Apple Computer*. New York: Walker, 1994. Print.

Levy, Steven. *The Perfect Thing: How the iPod Shuffles Commerce, Culture, and Coolness*. New York: Simon, 2006. Print.

Linzmayer, Owen W. *Apple Confidential: The Real Story of Apple Computer*. San Francisco: No Starch, 1999. Print.

Wozniak, Steve, with Gina Smith. *iWoz: From Computer Geek to Cult Icon; How I Invented the Personal Computer, coFounded Apple, and Had Fun Doing It*. New York: Norton, 2006. Print.

CHIEN-SHIUNG WU

Chinese-born scientist

Born: May 31, 1912 ; Liuhe, China
Died: February 16, 1997 ; New York City, New York
Also known as: C. S. Wu
Areas of achievement: Science and technology

Chien-Shiung Wu is best known for conducting the 1956 experiment that proved that "weak" interactions among decaying particles are not always symmetrical. The results disproved the principle of conservation of parity, the basic law of physics that postulated complete symmetry between left and right. Wu was also involved in experiments with uranium and the development of more sensitive radiation detectors for the Manhattan Project.

EARLY LIFE

Chien-Shiung Wu was born near Shanghai, China, to Fuhua Fan and Zhongyi Wu, a former engineer and a principal at an elementary school for girls. Wu's father founded the school in order to educate women, and he

Chien-Shiung Wu (Wikimedia Commons)

advised his daughter to ignore obstacles and keep moving forward. To promote the education and freedom of women, her mother encouraged parents to send their daughters to school, and she also spoke out against the practice of binding the feet of young girls.

> *"There is only one thing worse than coming home from the lab to a sink full of dirty dishes, and that is not going to the lab at all!"*

Growing up in a family environment that was conducive to learning, Wu was constantly exposed to books about science and mathematics. With the support and encouragement of her father, she developed self-confidence and curiosity. In 1922, after attending her father's school, Wu transferred to a boarding school, the Soochow School for Girls, and enrolled in its normal school program. Because Wu was very interested in mathematics, physics, and chemistry, she studied these subjects by herself from borrowed books. Graduating with high honors in 1930, Wu entered the National Central University in Nanjing. After obtaining a bachelor of science degree in physics in 1934, she taught and did research in X-ray crystallography with Shanghai's National Academy of Sciences. An uncle's financial assistance allowed Wu to travel to the United States in 1936, where, instead of attending the University of Michigan as planned, Wu entered the University of California Berkeley. She received graduate and research training under the guidance of prominent physicists Ernest Lawrence, Emilio Segre, and J. Robert Oppenheimer, and eventually became an expert in nuclear fission.

After obtaining a PhD in physics from UC Berkeley in 1940, Wu married fellow student and physicist Luke Yuan in 1942. They would have one child, Vincent, who is also a physicist. Wu went on to teach at Smith College in Northampton, Massachusetts, and briefly at Princeton University, before joining the Manhattan Project at Columbia University in 1944. Wu worked with a team of Columbia scientists in using diffusion techniques to separate common uranium from its fissionable isotopes.

After World War II, Wu was retained by Columbia as a research scientist. In 1954, she became a US citizen.

Life's Work

Wu devoted four decades to research and teaching. Her work on beta decay–later discussed in her book *Beta Decay* (1966), a respected publication among physicists–helped to support Enrico Fermi's theory of weak interactions.

In 1956, Wu began an experiment that would come to be known as the "Wu experiment," seeking to prove a theory developed by Tsung-Dao Lee, a colleague at Columbia, and Chen-Ning Yang, a physicist at the State University of New York in Stony Brook. The fundamental laws of physics had shown complete symmetry between left and right. Approached by Lee and Yang to test a new

---

The Manhattan Project

In September 1942, the Manhattan Project acquired 59,000 acres of land along the Clinch River in eastern Tennessee with the goal of creating an atomic bomb. The greatest challenge facing the project was the accumulation of sufficient quantities of fissionable material. Physicists had identified a likely candidate in uranium-235 (U-235). Natural uranium is only seven-tenths of 1 percent U-235. The remainder is overwhelmingly uranium-238 (U-238), which could not be made to fission with any process available during the 1940s. U-235 cannot be chemically separated from U-238; it must be physically separated using processes that rely on the 1.2 percent difference in mass between the two isotopes.

The Manhattan Project settled on two methods to separate U-235 from U-238. In electromagnetic separation, the uranium was rendered into a gas (uranium hexafluoride); the gas ionized and was then electrically propelled through a magnetic field. The lighter U-235 followed a more sharply curved path than the U-238, and the isotopes ended their journeys at two different places. In gaseous diffusion, the uranium hexafluoride was pumped through a series of porous barriers with millions of submicroscopic openings per square inch. The gas molecules containing U-235 trickled through the barriers at a slightly higher rate than those with U-238. After the gas passed through several thousand such barriers, the concentration of U-235 was significantly enhanced. In three years, the Y-12 electromagnetic separation team and K-25 gaseous diffusion team together separated enough U-235 for a single atomic bomb.

The experiments of Columbia University physicists (left to right) Wu, Y.K. Lee, and L.W. Mo confirmed the theory of conservation of vector current. In the experiments, which took several months to complete, proton beams from Columbia's Van de Graaff accelerator were transmitted through pipes to strike a 2mm Boron target at the entrance to a spectrometer chamber. (Wikimedia Commons)

theory, Wu and her collaborators designed and executed an experiment to show that the weak interactions among decaying particles were not always symmetrical with respect to left and right. The evidence of their research undermined the principle of conservation of parity, earning Lee and Yang the Nobel Prize in physics in 1957. Although Wu did not share the Nobel Prize with Lee and Yang, she was recognized as a top experimental physicist. As a result, her ideas and work were highly regarded by Nobel laureates and leaders in physics.

Wu was promoted to full professor at Columbia University in 1958, and was appointed Michael I. Pupin Professor of Physics in 1973. After conducting extensive research on beta decay, Wu moved on to study sickle-cell anemia. Throughout her forty-year career at Columbia, she trained numerous graduate students and postdoctoral fellows. She retired from teaching in 1981, as Pupin Professor Emerita of Physics. She then traveled as an advisor and lecturer in China and Taiwan. In 1995, a group that included four Nobel laureates established the Wu Chien-Shiung Foundation in Taiwan. One of the foundation's objectives is to cultivate outstanding talent in the sciences.

Wu identified three ingredients vital to her scientific achievements: a supportive husband, a home close to work, and good child care. These arrangements allowed her to work long hours in the laboratory. She observed that the only obstacle that blocks women from making progress in the field of science is "unimpeachable tradition."

Significance

Chien-Shiung Wu was a pioneer in physics and the only Chinese American woman to play an active role in the Manhattan Project. The results of her famous 1956 experiment held vast ramifications for physicists everywhere, and her subsequent work on beta decay continues to be a standard reference. The significance of her contributions has been recognized by numerous awards and honors, including the National Medal of Science (1975) and the Wolf Prize in Physics (1978), as well as honorary doctoral degrees from colleges and universities such as Princeton, Harvard, and Dickinson. Wu was the first woman to be the president of the American Physical Society (1975). Wu inspired young scientists to pursue scientific careers. Her life experience underscores the significance of growing up in an intellectually stimulating home environment and a willingness to take risks. She managed to make important contributions in a male-dominated, prestigious field.

Joyce Tang

Further Reading

Byers, Nina, and Gary Williams, eds. *Out of the Shadows: Contributions of Twentieth-Century Women to Physics.* New York: Cambridge UP, 2006. Print. An introductory examination of Wu's career and significant accomplishments, highlighting many aspects of her biography.

McGrayne, Sharon Bertsch. *Nobel Prize Women in Science: Their Lives, Struggles, and Momentous Discoveries.* 2nd ed. Secaucus: Carol, 1998. Print. Author considers the gender disparities among Nobel laureates, citing Wu as an example of a woman who succeeded in her field.

Reynolds, Moira Davison. *American Women Scientists: 23 Inspiring Biographies, 1900–2000.* Jefferson: McFarland, 1999. Print. Includes an extensive and well-detailed biographical sketch of Wu, describing her education and professional research; also provides background on her family.

Appendixes

APPENDIX

Chronological List of Entries

First Name	Last Name	Birth year
Benjamin	Franklin	1706
Benjamin	Banneker	1731
George	Washington	1732
daniel	Boone	1734
John	Adams	1735
	Kamehameha I	1736
Patrick	Henry	1736
Thomas	Paine	1737
	Nanyehi	1738
Thomas	Jefferson	1743
Abigail	Adams	1744
James	Madison	1751
Alexander	Hamilton	1755
John	Marshall	1755
Andrew	Jackson	1767
Dolley	Madison	1768
William	Clark	1770
Meriwether	Lewis	1774
Stephen	Decatur	1779
	Sacagawea	1788
John	Ross	1790
Thomas L.	Jennings	1791
Sojourner	Truth	1797
John	Brown	1800
Nat	Turner	1800
Samuel Gridley	Howe	1801
Dorothea	Dix	1802
John	Deere	1804
William Lloyd	Garrison	1805
Robert E.	Lee	1807
Abraham	Lincoln	1809
Margaret	Fuller	1810
Harriett Beecher	Stowe	1811

First Name	Last Name	Birth year
Elizabeth Cady	Stanton	1815
Henry David	Thoreau	1817
Frederick	Douglass	1817
Walt	Whitman	1819
Susan B.	Anthony	1820
Harriet	Tubman	1820
Clara	Barton	1821
Elizabeth	Blackwell	1821
Mary Baker	Eddy	1821
Elizabeth Cabot	Agassiz	1822
	Red Cloud	1822
Mary Ann Shadd	Cary	1823
Stonewall	Jackson	1824
	Geronimo	1829
Emily	Dickinson	1830
Belva A.	Lockwood	1830
Mother	Jones	1830
	Sitting Bull	1831
Andrew	Carnagie	1835
Olympia	Brown	1835
John	Muir	1838
	Lili'uokalani	1838
John D.	Rockefeller	1839
Chief	Joseph	1840
Loreta Janeta	Velasquez	1842
	Crazy Horse	1842
Lola	Rodriguez de Tio	1843
Cathay	Williams	1844
Sarah	Winnemucca	1844
Edmonia	Lewis	1845
Alexander Graham	Bell	1847
Thomas Alva	Edison	1847
George	Eastman	1854

First Name	Last Name	Birth year
Robert M.	La Follette	1855
Eugene V.	Debs	1855
Booker T.	Washington	1856
Louis D.	Brandeis	1856
Ida	Tarbell	1857
Clarence	Darrow	1857
Mary	Tape	1857
Theodore	Roosevelt	1858
Juliette Gordon	Low	1860
John J.	Pershing	1860
Jane	Addams	1860
George Washington	Carver	1861
Charles Evans	Hughes	1862
Ida B.	Wells-Barnett	1862
Susan La Flesche	Picotte	1865
John R.	Mott	1865
Anne	Sullivan	1866
Wilbur	Wright	1867
Madame C. J.	Walker	1867
W. E. B.	Du Bois	1868
Emma	Goldman	1869
Orville	Wright	1871
Learned	Hand	1872
Lee	de Forest	1873
Mary McLeod	Bethune	1875
Garrett	Morgan	1877
Margaret	Sanger	1879
Luisa	Capetillo	1879
Albert	Einstein	1879
Jeanette	Rankin	1880
Helen	Keller	1880
John L.	Lewis	1880
Franklin D.	Roosevelt	1882
Norman	Thomas	1884
Eleanor	Roosevelt	1884
Chester W.	Nimitz	1885
Alice	Paul	1885
Georgia	O'Keefe	1887
Marcus	Garvey	1887
Richard	Byrd	1888
Margaret	Chung	1889
A. Philip	Randolph	1889
Edwin	Hubble	1889
Dwight D.	Eisenhower	1890
Zora Neale	Hurston	1891
Earl	Warren	1891
Bessie	Coleman	1892
Mercedes de	Acosta	1893
Omar Nelson	Bradley	1893
Huey	Long	1893
Fabiola Cabeza de Baca	Gilbert	1894
Jack	Dempsey	1895
Babe	Ruth	1895
Jimmy	Doolittle	1896
Amelia	Earhart	1897
Felisa	Rincon de Gautier	1897
Margaret Chase	Smith	1897
Dorothy	Day	1897
William O.	Douglas	1898
Duke	Ellington	1899
Helen G.	Douglas	1900
Adlai E.	Stevenson II	1900
Margaret	Murie	1902
Lou	Gehrig	1903
Pura	Belpré	1903
Ralph	Bunche	1903
Ella	Baker	1903
Charles Richard	Drew	1904
Anna May	Wong	1905

First Name	Last Name	Birth year	First Name	Last Name	Birth year
Oveta Culp	Hobby	1905	Sue Kunitomi	Embrey	1923
William J.	Brennan	1906	James	Baldwin	1924
Grace Murray	Hopper	1906	Shirley	Chisholm	1924
Katharine	Hepburn	1907	Daniel	Inouye	1924
Rachel	Carson	1907	Maria	Tallchief	1925
Mary A.	Hallaren	1907	Robert F.	Kennedy	1925
James	Stewart	1908	Frank	Kameny	1925
Edward R.	Murrow	1908		Malcolm X	1925
Thurgood	Marshall	1908	Ruth	Asawa	1926
Mary Golda	Ross	1908	Ralph	Abernathy	1926
Bayard	Rustin	1910	Aileen Clarke	Hernandez	1926
Babe Didrikson	Zaharias	1911	Reies Lopez	Tijerina	1926
Elizabeth	Peratovich	1911	Althea	Gibson	1927
Hazel Ying	Lee	1912	Patsy Takemoto	Mink	1927
harry	hay	1912	Cesar	Chavez	1927
Chien-Shiung	Wu	1912	Fred	Rogers	1928
Jesse	Owens	1913	Maya	Angelou	1928
Hedy	Lamarr	1913	Mari-Luci	Jaramillo	1928
Larry Dulay	Itliong	1913	Helen Fabela	Chavez	1928
Rosa	Parks	1913	Elie	Wiesel	1928
Jonas	Salk	1914	Martin Luther	King, Jr.	1929
Billie	Holiday	1915	Neil	Armstrong	1930
Thomas	Merton	1915	George	Soros	1930
Walter	Cronkite	1916	Harvey	Milk	1930
Katharine	Graham	1917	Sandra Day	O'Connor	1930
John F.	Kennedy	1917	Barbara	Harris	1930
Fannie Lou	Hamer	1917	Dolores	Huerta	1930
Gertrude	Elion	1918	Toni	Morrison	1931
Betty	Ford	1918	Martha E.	Bernal	1931
Katharine	Johnson	1918	Dave	Thomas	1932
Jackie	Robinson	1919	Nina	Simone	1933
John	Glenn	1921	Susan	Sontag	1933
Betty	Friedan	1921	Ruth Bader	Ginsberg	1933
Stan	Lee	1922	Bill	Russell	1934
Alan	Shepard	1923	Ralph	Nader	1934
Chuck	Yeager	1923	Geraldine	Ferraro	1935

First Name	Last Name	Birth year	First Name	Last Name	Birth year
Barbara	Jordan	1936	Steve	Wozniak	1950
Madeleine	Albright	1937	Sally	Ride	1951
Colin	Powell	1937	Lynda	Carter	1951
Sister Thea	Bowman	1937	Queen	Noor	1951
Judy	Blume	1938	Sylvia	Rivera	1951
Martha P.	Cotera	1938	bell	hooks	1952
Lourdes	Casal	1938	David	Ho	1952
Nancy	Kwan	1939	Cherrie	Moraga	1952
Marian Wright	Edelman	1939	Giannina	Braschi	1953
Jack	Nicklaus	1940	Jane	Delgado	1953
Bruce	Lee	1940	Elaine	Chao	1953
Joan	Baez	1941	Judy	Chu	1953
Jesse	Jackson	1941	Oprah	Winfrey	1954
Muhammed	Ali	1942	Sandra	Cisneros	1954
Aretha	Franklin	1942	Norma V.	Cantu	1954
Robert D.	Ballard	1942	Condoleezza	Rice	1954
Patricia	Bath	1942	Sonia	Sotomayor	1954
Gloria	Anzaldúa	1942	Barbara	Carrasco	1955
Shannon W.	Lucid	1943	Bill	Gates	1955
Vilma Socorro	Martinez	1943	Indra	Nooyi	1955
Antonia	Novello	1944	Martina	Navritilova	1956
Avi	Weiss	1944	Huping	Ling	1956
August	Wilson	1945	Ann	Curry	1956
Wilma	Mankiller	1945	Nora	Volkow	1956
Marsha P.	Johnson	1945	Heather	Fong	1956
Judy	Baca	1946	Zaid	Shakir	1956
Martin	Wong	1946	Mae	Jemison	1956
Dolly	Parton	1946	Ellen	Ochoa	1958
Deepak	Chopra	1946	Keith	Haring	1958
Sally	Priesand	1946	Andrea	Jung	1958
Mazie	Hirono	1947	Ellen	Degeneres	1958
Christa	McAuliffe	1948		Prince	1958
Al	Gore	1948	Maya	Lin	1959
Steven	Chu	1948	Winona	LaDuke	1959
Joseph	LeDoux	1949	Kimberle Williams	Crensahw	1959
Henry Louis	Gates, Jr.	1950	Jean Michel	Basquiat	1960

First Name	Last Name	Birth year	First Name	Last Name	Birth year
Maria	Hinojosa	1961	Nikki	Haley	1972
Barack	Obama	1961	Rachel	Paulose	1973
Michael	Jordan	1963	Ai-Jen	Poo	1974
Sunita	Williams	1965	Ta-Nehisi	Coates	1975
Jhumpa	Lahiri	1967	Michelle	Kwan	1980
Van	Jones	1968	Serena	Williams	1981
Tammy	Duckworth	1968	Edward	Snowden	1983
Sheryl	Sandberg	1969	bree	newsome	1984
Sanjay	Gupta	1969	M. Hasna	Maznavi	1986
	Selena	1971	Emma	Gonzalez	1999

Alphabetical List of Entries

Last Name	First Name	Last Name	First Name
Abernathy	Ralph	Brown	John
Acosta	Mercedes de	Brown	Olympia
Adams	Abigail	Bunche	Ralph
Adams	John	Byrd	Richard
Addams	Jane	Cantu	Norma V.
Agassiz	Elizabeth Cabot	Capetillo	Luisa
Albright	Madeleine	Carnagie	Andrew
Ali	Muhammed	Carrasco	Barbara
Angelou	Maya	Carson	Rachel
Anthony	Susan B.	Carter	Lynda
Anzaldúa	Gloria	Carver	George Washington
Armstrong	Neil	Cary	Mary Ann Shadd
Asawa	Ruth	Casal	Lourdes
Baca	Judy	Chao	Elaine
Baez	Joan	Chavez	Cesar
Baker	Ella	Chavez	Helen Fabela
Baldwin	James	Chisholm	Shirley
Ballard	Robert D.	Chopra	Deepak
Banneker	Benjamin	Chu	Judy
Barton	Clara	Chu	Steven
Basquiat	Jean Michel	Chung	Margaret
Bath	Patricia	Cisneros	Sandra
Bell	Alexander Graham	Coates	Ta-Nehisi
Belpré	Pura	Coleman	Bessie
Bernal	Martha E.	Cotera	Martha P.
Bethune	Mary McLeod	Crazy Horse	
Blackwell	Elizabeth	Crensahw	Kimberle Williams
Blume	Judy	Cronkite	Walter
Boone	daniel	Curry	Ann
Bowman	Sister Thea	Darrow	Clarence
Bradley	Omar Nelson	Day	Dorothy
Brandeis	Louis D.	de Forest	Lee
Braschi	Giannina	Debs	Eugene V.
Brennan	William J.	Decatur	Stephen

Last Name	First Name	Last Name	First Name
Deere	John	Gilbert	Fabiola Cabeza de Baca
Degeneres	Ellen	Ginsberg	Ruth Bader
Delgado	Jane	Glenn	John
Dempsey	Jack	Goldman	Emma
Dickinson	Emily	Gonzalez	Emma
Dix	Dorothea	Gore	Al
Doolittle	Jimmy	Graham	Katharine
Douglas	Helen G.	Gupta	Sanjay
Douglas	William O.	Haley	Nikki
Douglass	Frederick	Hallaren	Mary A.
Drew	Charles Richard	Hamer	Fannie Lou
Du Bois	W. E. B.	Hamilton	Alexander
Duckworth	Tammy	Hand	Learned
Earhart	Amelia	Haring	Keith
Eastman	George	Harris	Barbara
Eddy	Mary Baker	hay	harry
Edelman	Marian Wright	Henry	Patrick
Edison	Thomas Alva	Hepburn	Katharine
Einstein	Albert	Hernandez	Aileen Clarke
Eisenhower	Dwight D.	Hinojosa	Maria
Elion	Gertrude	Hirono	Mazie
Ellington	Duke	Ho	David
Embrey	Sue Kunitomi	Hobby	Oveta Culp
Ferraro	Geraldine	Holiday	Billie
Fong	Heather	hooks	bell
Ford	Betty	Hopper	Grace Murray
Franklin	Aretha	Howe	Samuel Gridley
Franklin	Benjamin	Hubble	Edwin
Friedan	Betty	Huerta	Dolores
Fuller	Margaret	Hughes	Charles Evans
Garrison	William Lloyd	Hurston	Zora Neale
Garvey	Marcus	Inouye	Daniel
Gates	Bill	Itliong	Larry Dulay
Gates, Jr.	Henry Louis	Jackson	Stonewall
Gehrig	Lou	Jackson	Andrew
Geronimo		Jackson	Jesse
Gibson	Althea	Jaramillo	Mari-Luci

Last Name	First Name	Last Name	First Name
Jefferson	Thomas	Low	Juliette Gordon
Jemison	Mae	Lucid	Shannon W.
Jennings	Thomas L.	Madison	Dolley
Johnson	Marsha P.	Madison	James
Johnson	Katharine	Malcolm X	
Jones	Van	Mankiller	Wilma
Jones	Mother	Marshall	John
Jordan	Michael	Marshall	Thurgood
Jordan	Barbara	Martinez	Vilma Socorro
Joseph	Chief	Maznavi	M. Hasna
Jung	Andrea	McAuliffe	Christa
Kamehameha I		Merton	Thomas
Kameny	Frank	Milk	Harvey
Keller	Helen	Mink	Patsy Takemoto
Kennedy	Robert F.	Moraga	Cherrie
Kennedy	John F.	Morgan	Garrett
King, Jr.	Martin Luther	Morrison	Toni
Kwan	Michelle	Mott	John R.
Kwan	Nancy	Muir	John
La Follette	Robert M.	Murie	Margaret
LaDuke	Winona	Murrow	Edward R.
Lahiri	Jhumpa	Nader	Ralph
Lamarr	Hedy	Nanyehi	
LeDoux	Joseph	Navritilova	Martina
Lee	Hazel Ying	newsome	bree
Lee	Bruce	Nicklaus	Jack
Lee	Stan	Nimitz	Chester W.
Lee	Robert E.	Noor	Queen
Lewis	Edmonia	Nooyi	Indra
Lewis	John L.	Novello	Antonia
Lewis and Clark		Obama	Barack
Lili'uokalani		Ochoa	Ellen
Lin	Maya	O'Connor	Sandra Day
Lincoln	Abraham	O'Keefe	Georgia
Ling	Huping	Owens	Jesse
Lockwood	Belva A.	Paine	Thomas
Long	Huey	Parks	Rosa

Last Name	First Name	Last Name	First Name
Parton	Dolly	Sitting Bull	
Paul	Alice	Smith	Margaret Chase
Paulose	Rachel	Snowden	Edward
Peratovich	Elizabeth	Sontag	Susan
Pershing	John J.	Soros	George
Picotte	Susan La Flesche	Sotomayor	Sonia
Poo	Ai-Jen	Stanton	Elizabeth Cady
Powell	Colin	Stevenson II	Adlai E.
Priesand	Sally	Stewart	James
Prince		Stowe	Harriett Beecher
Randolph	A. Philip	Sullivan	Anne
Rankin	Jeanette	Tallchief	Maria
Red Cloud		Tape	Mary
Rice	Condoleezza	Tarbell	Ida
Ride	Sally	Thomas	Dave
Rincon de Gautier	Felisa	Thomas	Norman
Rivera	Sylvia	Thoreau	Henry David
Robinson	Jackie	Tijerina	Reies Lopez
Rockefeller	John D.	Truth	Sojourner
Rodriguez de Tio	Lola	Tubman	Harriet
Rogers	Fred	Turner	Nat
Roosevelt	Eleanor	Velasquez	Loreta Janeta
Roosevelt	Franklin D.	Volkow	Nora
Roosevelt	Theodore	Walker	Madame C. J.
Ross	John	Warren	Earl
Ross	Mary Golda	Washington	Booker T.
Russell	Bill	Washington	George
Rustin	Bayard	Weiss	Avi
Ruth	Babe	Wells-Barnett	Ida B.
Sacagawea		Whitman	Walt
Salk	Jonas	Wiesel	Elie
Sandberg	Sheryl	Williams	Sunita
Sanger	Margaret	Williams	Serena
Selena		Williams	Cathay
Shakir	Zaid	Wilson	August
Shepard	Alan	Winfrey	Oprah
Simone	Nina	Winnemucca	Sarah

Last Name	First Name	Last Name	First Name
Wong	Martin	Wu	Chien-Shiung
Wong	Anna May	Yeager	Chuck
Wozniak	Steve	Zaharias	Babe Didrikson
Wright	Orville and Wilbur		

Subject Index

#

442nd Regimental Combat Team 578, 579

A

abolition 292, 293, 301, 311, 315, 393, 552, 686, 741, 753, 758, 762, 767, 769, 782, 783, 839, 850, 894, 897
Abu Noor University 737
Academy of Motion Picture Arts and Sciences 275
Accords, Oslo 739
acquired immunodeficiency syndrome 96, 405, 415
Action Comics 196
addiction 186, 204, 322, 427, 428, 429, 431, 432
Advisory Committee on the Rights and Responsibilities of Women 819
Affirmative Action 777
Affordable Care Act 554, 697
Agassiz School for Girls 149
Agricultural Labor Relations Act 773, 826
Agricultural Workers Organizing Committee 829
Agriculture Adjustment Act 704, 705
AIDS 56, 58, 71, 96, 97, 127, 192, 307, 374, 405, 408, 409, 415, 416, 417, 422, 427, 431, 817, 878
Air Corps 11, 213, 215, 372, 442
Air Force 4, 5, 12, 17, 20, 31, 43, 44, 45, 213, 433, 434, 457, 547, 640, 684, 737, 738, 922
Albany Congress 551
Alcatraz 488
alcoholism 13, 175, 364, 418, 663, 672, 699, 702, 750, 845, 851, 879
Allied forces 44, 295, 399, 460, 461
All-Star Game 89, 90, 104, 105
"Aloha 'Oe." 484
al-Qaeda 628, 635
Altair 8800 126
Alvarado School Arts Workshop 49
American academy of Arts and Letters 367, 368
American Anti-Slavery Society 314, 315, 751, 768, 894
American Colonization Society 313, 314, 604, 768, 805
American Expeditionary Force 458, 460, 461, 462
American Federation of Labor 592, 781, 782, 850, 875, 876
American Folklore Society 365
American Foundation for the Blind 164, 845
American Indian 8, 58, 60, 69, 165, 249, 250, 473, 477, 480, 487, 488, 490, 493, 508, 623, 681, 745, 824, 926
American Institute for the Prevention of Blindness 264
American Inter-Seminary Missionary Alliance 732
American Journal of Psychiatry 413, 430
American League 83, 104, 109
American Library Association (ALA) 340, 341, 342, 343
American Medical Association (AMA) 396, 397, 406, 446
American Missionary Association 768
American Peace Society 314
American Psychological Association (APA) 391, 392, 415
American Red Cross 281, 282, 385, 387, 388, 389, 390
American Revolution 249, 438, 540, 551, 559, 562, 567, 569, 570, 623, 624, 665, 668, 710, 713, 741, 748, 884
Ames Research Center 28
Amherst College 279, 281, 354, 911
Amnesty International 172, 173
Annapolis Convention 560, 693
Antarctica 224, 253, 254, 255, 307
Antares (lunar module) 35, 36
antebellum 292, 769, 823
Anthony Comstock 424, 425
anti-Chinese 889, 890
anti-gay 96
anti-Japanese 798
anti-lesbian 96
anti-Semitism 332, 912
antislavery 311, 312, 313, 314, 315, 316, 375, 376, 552, 688, 751, 761, 768, 789, 822, 823, 897
antiwar 172, 173, 318, 539, 589, 592, 631, 632, 633, 650, 808
Apache 467, 474, 475, 476, 477
Apollo 11 3, 5, 6, 7, 35, 304, 924, 925
Apple I 927, 928, 929
Apple II 928, 929
Appomattox 452, 453, 454, 689
Arctic 15, 237, 238, 252, 253
Are You There God? It's Me, Margaret 343, 344
Arlington National Cemetery 19, 443, 461, 916
Armed Services Committee 18, 443, 639
Army Commendation Medal 443

Arthur Ashe Stadium 88
Articles of Confederation 560, 680, 693
Art Spiegelman 197
Asian American 20, 22, 37, 50, 128, 129, 157, 158, 190, 191, 192, 218, 219, 367, 368, 399, 526, 529, 530, 541, 547, 548, 571, 614, 615, 625
Asian American Voters Coalition 192
assassination 173, 206, 304, 338, 373, 428, 497, 522, 590, 600, 656, 682, 685, 688, 832, 849, 856, 857, 880
Associated Press 88, 91, 116, 117, 640
Association on American Indian Affairs 69
Atlanta Compromise 166
Atlantic Monthly 128, 134, 150, 223, 351, 362, 376, 894
Atlantic Records 181
Auschwitz 739, 902
Australian Open 95, 113, 114, 115
Avon 128, 129, 130, 143, 173
Avon Foundation for Women 129
ayurveda 397

B

Back to Africa 803, 804, 805
Baker v. Carr 519, 655
Balanchine 68, 69, 70
ballet 67, 68, 69, 70, 174, 633
banned books 343
Barnard College 319, 363, 365, 366, 535
Barrymore, John 185
Baseball Hall of Fame 105
Battle of Bull Run 452, 463
Battle of Shiloh 286, 463
Battle of the Little bighorn 472, 474, 504
Bay Area Police Watch 227
Bay of Pigs 647, 652, 684
Beginners All-purpose Symbolic Instruction Code (BASIC) 126
Bell Telephone Company 267
Beloved Woman 488, 493
Berkeley School for Girls 535
Best Actor 186, 213, 383
Best Actress 185, 186
Best Picture 197, 212, 217, 383
Best Supporting Actress 216, 217, 383, 865
Bethune-Cookman College 152, 153
Betty Ford Center 672, 674
Beverly Hills 67, 118, 211
Bill, Buffalo 504, 505
Bill, Jones 636
Bill, Lockwood Bill 595

Bill & Melinda Gates Foundation 125, 127
Bill of Rights 301, 566, 569, 574, 576, 579, 690, 694, 713, 870, 873
birth control 184, 185, 423, 424, 425, 426, 427, 555, 778, 808, 886
Black Elk 470, 473, 496
Black Hills 469, 470, 471, 472, 495, 496, 504
Black Nationalism 855, 856
Black Panther (comic) 197, 349, 351
Black Power 382, 836, 848, 857, 858, 876
Black Star Line 804, 805
Bluecoats 470, 471, 472
Board of Naval Commissioners 441
Bob dylan 171, 173
Booth, John Wilkes 689
Boston Celtics 89, 106, 107
Boston Marathon 38, 39
Boston Red Sox 104, 109
Boston Tea Party 551, 568, 601, 622, 665
Boy Scouts of America 4, 159
braille 821, 844
breast cancer 129, 175, 211, 307, 373, 619, 663, 672, 673, 674, 813
British Royal Air Force 43
Broadway 6, 81, 86, 97, 185, 186, 212, 214, 219, 308, 334, 335, 338, 378, 380, 382, 383, 535, 636
Bronze Star 443, 579
Brooklyn Bridge 122
Brooklyn Dodgers 103, 104, 111
Brotherhood of Locomotive Firemen 781
Brotherhood of Sleeping Car Porters 875, 876
Brown vs. Board of Education 147, 509
Bryn Mawr College 186, 565
Buddhist 362, 571, 715
Budget Committee 614
Buffalo soldiers 465
Bureau of Indian Affairs 419, 489, 490, 870, 925
Burr, Aaron 439, 561, 563, 603, 675, 680
Burwell v. Hobby Lobby 555, 644

C

Cable News Network (CNN) 304, 405, 545
California Arts Council 50
California gold rush 59
California Institute of the Arts 55
calypso 334
Camelot 685
camera 5, 18, 206, 227, 261, 282, 283, 284, 285, 286, 289, 306, 323, 324, 373, 611

Campfire Girls 161
Cape Canaveral 17, 25, 26, 35
Cape Cod 223, 241, 245
capitalism 119, 124, 346, 518, 592, 650, 651, 708, 765, 779, 806, 807, 836, 838
capital punishment 353, 519, 533, 607, 608, 620, 666, 696
Captain America 196
Captain James Cook 481
Caring Across Generations 873
Carnegie Corporation 124, 522
Carnegie Council on Children 796
Carnegie Foundation for the Advancement of Teaching 124
Carnegie Hall 124, 189
Carnegie Institution 124
Carnegie-Mellon University 124
Carnegie Steel 122, 123, 124, 807
Cary Grant 185, 186, 213
Castro, Fidel 323, 371, 684, 770, 833, 855
Castro Street 611, 612, 613
Castro Village Association 612
cataract 264
Catholic Worker 777, 779, 780
CBS Evening News 303, 304
Cedars-Sinai Medical Center 408
censorship 342, 343, 344, 346, 592, 770, 778, 798
Censorship Bureau 331
Central Intelligence Agency (CIA) 881
Central Park 565
Challenger 6, 25, 26, 27, 30, 31, 32, 33, 45
Chamberlain, Wilt 107, 108
Chan, Jackie 195
Charlestown 761
Cherokee Nation 487, 488, 489, 490, 499, 925
Cherokee Nation Community Development Department 489
Chicago Bulls 88, 89, 91
Chicago Haymarket bombings 807
Chicago riots 921
Chicana 55, 56, 209, 349, 352, 353, 609, 610, 753, 754, 755, 775, 824, 828, 857, 858, 859
Chicano 55, 347, 349, 351, 352, 353, 391, 753, 754, 755, 771, 772, 826, 827, 828, 858, 859, 891, 892
Chinese American 130, 157, 158, 159, 192, 219, 399, 529, 530, 931
Chinese nationalism 20
Choctaw 69, 467
Chris Evert 95, 97

Christian Science 616, 720, 721, 722, 723
Chrysler Corporation 6
Churchill, Winston 323, 460, 705
Church of Christ, Scientist 718, 720, 721
Church of England 549, 693
Church of the Advocate 724, 725
City College 30, 103, 362, 402, 420, 529, 627, 874
Civil disobedience 171, 847, 848, 861, 892, 893
Civil Rights Act 614, 641, 744, 856, 876
Civil Rights Memorial 62
civil rights movement 329, 465, 678, 842, 860, 871
Civil Service 223, 708, 841
Civil Works Administration 704
Clay, Henry 122, 498, 653, 676, 687, 807
Clean Energy Corps 229
Clean Energy Jobs Bill 229
Clean Water Protection Act 530
Cold War 1, 17, 19, 27, 171, 301, 435, 437, 446, 514, 515, 634, 635, 646, 648, 669, 671, 684, 685, 779, 841, 843, 848, 905
Collins, Harper 100, 105, 108, 201, 202, 231, 365, 401, 515, 629, 849, 895, 897
Colonel Nelson Miles 472, 479
Columbia Accident Investigation Board 32
Columbia Records 181, 189, 200
comic books 195, 196, 197, 349
Commission on the Status of Women 701, 819
Committee Against Anti-Asian Violence 872
Committee for National Defense 153
Committee on Canonical Affairs and Church Governance 718
Committee on Education and the Workforce 571
Committee on Foreign Relations 697
Committee on Un-American Activities 323, 324
Commodore Records 189
Common Business Oriented Language 916, 917
Common Sense 622, 624, 625, 665, 667
communism 139, 374, 539, 647, 651, 657, 808, 880
Community Service Organization 772, 773, 774, 824, 825, 829
Confederacy 448, 450, 451, 452, 453, 454, 462, 463, 464, 490, 498, 860
Confiscation Act of 1861 464
Congressional Black Caucus 528
Congressional Medal of Honor 12, 253
Congressional Space Medal of Honor 7, 24
Congress of Industrial Organizations 783, 850, 852, 876
Congress of Racial Equality 338, 880
conservation 221, 223, 234, 236, 237, 238, 239, 592, 614, 707, 862, 863, 929, 931

Constitutional Convention 563, 569, 602, 666, 693, 694, 710, 712
Continental Army 433
Continental Congress 551, 559, 560, 561, 568, 623, 664, 665, 679, 693
contraception 424, 425, 426
Convention on the Elimination of All Forms of Discrimination Against Women 513
Cornell University 316, 368, 411, 553, 732, 802, 888, 921, 922
Corpus Christi 16, 17, 208, 209, 466
Corpus Christi Naval Air Training Center 16
Cotton Club 179
Council of American-Islamic Relations 726
country music 198, 199, 200, 202
Country Music Association 201
Crazy Horse 469, 470, 471, 472, 473, 474
crop rotation 270
Cuban Missile Crisis 304, 588, 647, 685
Cultural Revolution 157

D

Daily Eagle 378, 381
Dartmouth College 205, 383, 922
Dateline NBC 307
Daughters of the American Revolution 748
Dave Thomas Foundation for Adoption 141
DC Comics 196
D day 304
DDT 224, 225, 616, 825, 826, 827, 829
death penalty 532, 533, 607, 741
Declaration of Conscience 639, 640, 641, 642
Declaration of Independence 315, 551, 665, 667, 679, 681, 682, 741, 759, 886
Deep South 271
Deere and Company 277, 278, 279
Defense of Marriage Act (DOMA) 698
Democracy Now! 233, 234
Democratic National Committee 318, 637, 700
Democratic National Convention 18, 182, 528, 536, 541, 544, 578, 584, 585, 647, 696, 697, 703, 757, 813, 826, 830
Democratic Women's Caucus 615
Department of Health, Education, and Welfare 446, 447, 585
Department of Homeland Security 548
Department of Labor 229, 526, 616, 872
desegregation 85, 323, 338, 364, 519, 576, 607, 608, 646, 656, 657, 794, 795, 871, 876

Dexter Avenue Baptist Church 744, 847
Distinguished Service Cross 579
DNA 403, 404, 863, 910, 911
Dollywood 200, 201
Domestic Workers' Bill of Rights 873
Don't Ask, Don't Tell Repeal Act 530, 843
draft dodging 77
"Dream Team" 90
Dr. Susan Picotte Memorial Hospital 419
dry cleaning 291
dry scouring 291, 292

E

Early Childhood Education Act 614
Earth Day 221
EarthKam 32
Eastman Kodak Company 285
Education and Labor Committee 528
Edwards Air Force Base 4, 5, 31, 44
Eleanor Roosevelt Humanitarian Award 343
Emancipation Proclamation 59, 315, 464, 689, 789, 791, 894
Emanuel African Methodist Episcopal Church 860
Emergency Banking Act 704
Emmy Awards 176, 177, 216, 304, 306
Empire State Building 196, 197
Energy Independence and Security Act 229
England Anti-Slavery Society 313
Enter the Dragon 193, 194, 195
environmentalism 60, 62, 223, 226, 228, 234, 863
Environmental Protection Agency (EPA) 225
Episcopal Church 210, 227, 596, 724, 725, 726, 834, 860, 874, 900
Equal Access to Quality Education Act 530
Equal Employment Opportunity Commission (EEOC) 817, 818
Equal Rights Amendment (ERA) 673, 868
Esquire magazine 397
Every Man a King 599, 600, 601
Expanded and Improved Medicare for All Act 530

F

Facebook 136, 137, 138, 173
Face the Nation 528, 641
Fair Employment Practice Commission 818
Fantastic Four 196
farmer's almanac 908
fast food 140, 141
Faulkner, William 367, 369, 717

Federal Aid Highway Act 670
Federal Alliance of Land Grants 891, 892
Federal Bureau of Investigation (FBI) 215, 216, 815, 841, 857, 880
Federal Court of Appeals 553
Federalist Party 312, 562, 563, 666, 884
Federal Reserve System 592
Federal Trade Commission (FTC) 301, 592, 616
Feinstein, Diane 612
Fellowship of Reconciliation 650, 880
feminism 138, 353, 490, 596, 610, 753, 755, 799, 801, 802, 808, 809, 817, 820, 829, 835, 867, 885, 888
Ferry, Harpers 240, 449, 452, 760, 761, 762, 792, 822
First Amendment 301, 517, 518, 519, 520, 539, 566, 600, 607, 608, 693, 715, 776, 777, 783
First Baptist Church 744
Fist of Fury 194
Flight Mechanics Branch 924
Food and Drug Administration (FDA) 401
Forbes 115, 131, 132, 139, 140, 217, 248, 629
Ford, Henry 119, 270
Ford Motor Company 405
Fortas, Abe 553, 607, 656
Fort Laramie 494
Fourteenth Amendment 517, 557, 576, 751, 752
Fox News 230
Framingham State College 25
Franco-Prussian War 159, 388
Freedmen's Bureau 822, 894
Freedom of Speech 532, 538, 539, 540, 572, 576, 607, 639, 783, 807
Freedom's Journal 292
Free Federation of Workers 766
French and Indian War 491, 711
French Open 86, 95, 113, 114
Frida Kahlo 55, 427
Friedan, Betty 377, 799, 801, 803, 818, 869
Fruit of Islam 855
Fugitive Slave Act 315, 759, 768
Fundamentalist 234
fur trade 257

G

Galapagos 246, 701
Garden Grove mosque 726
Gay and Lesbian Activist Alliance 843
Gay Liberation Front 816, 836
Gay Pride march 816, 835
gay rights 96, 97, 530, 610, 611, 612, 814, 816, 836, 840, 841, 842, 843

Gender Equity Act 615
genealogy 360
General Custer 471, 504
General Douglas MacArthur 437, 456, 669
General Electric (GE) 88, 125, 129, 131, 287, 297, 298, 327
General Motors (GM) 3, 616, 834
Geneva Medical College 393, 394
geography 258, 346, 479, 544, 566, 821
geology 245, 247, 248, 627
George III, King 568, 625
Gethsemani 729, 730
Gettysburg Address 689
Ghigau 491, 492
G.I. Bill 437, 743
Gibbons v. Ogden 603
Girl Guides 160, 161
Girl Scouts of America 25, 162
Golden Gloves 75
golf 6, 36, 85, 87, 88, 95, 97, 98, 99, 100, 117, 135, 141, 184, 670
google 629
Gore, Bush 554, 557, 620
gospel 180, 181, 182, 236, 717, 724, 734, 780
graffiti 53, 54, 55, 57, 71, 835
Grammy Awards 180, 182, 183, 201, 203
Grammy Hall of Fame 180, 189
Grand Canyon 221, 236, 709
Grand Ole Opry 198, 201
Great Depression 3, 85, 106, 155, 156, 195, 210, 336, 405, 410, 600, 651, 704, 724, 771, 797, 875, 880, 890
Great Plains 276
Green Job Corps 228, 229
Green Jobs Act 229
Green Party 233, 617
Green v. School Board 519
Guantanamo Bay 698
Gulf War 38, 528, 626, 628, 629
gun control 217, 698, 809, 810, 811

H

hair care products 142, 143, 144
Hampton Institute 165, 166
Harlem 85, 86, 87, 178, 179, 188, 190, 263, 334, 336, 337, 338, 339, 340, 342, 363, 364, 365, 650, 757, 779, 792, 874
Harlem Renaissance 178, 342, 363, 364, 365, 792
Harlem Writers Guild 334
Harvard Business School 136, 526

Harvard Law Review 317, 564, 696
Harvard Law School 516, 519, 524, 553, 555, 564, 615, 645, 696, 776
Hebrew Union College 735, 736
Hemingway, Ernest 367
Heritage Foundation 401, 526
Hindu 38, 130, 331, 559, 715
Hiroshima 653
His Horse Looking 469, 470
Hispanic American 582
Hispanic Health and Nutrition Examination Survey 400, 401
Historic Cookery 156
Hitchcock, Alfred 214
Hitler, Adolf 100, 101, 294, 323, 442, 461, 514, 651, 705, 913
HIV 71, 408, 409, 417, 431
HIV/AIDS 71, 408, 409, 431
Hoffa, Jimmy 587
Hogg, David 810, 811
Hole, Woods 223, 245, 246, 247, 421
Hollywood Walk of Fame 77, 219
holocaust 779
homeland security 530, 548
Hong Kong 20, 91, 128, 190, 191, 192, 193, 194, 195, 409, 882
Horace Mann School for the Deaf and Hard of Hearing 265
House Foreign Affairs Committee 536, 537
House Naval Affairs Committee 639
House of Burgesses 568, 679, 711
House Un-American Activities Committee 816
Houston Post 303, 445, 446
Houston, Texas 27, 28, 30, 36, 38, 303, 444, 582
Howard University 154, 178, 263, 280, 281, 338, 350, 363, 368, 521, 522, 606, 767, 769, 813, 817, 819, 860
hubble telescope 154, 178, 263, 280, 281, 338, 350, 363, 368, 521, 522, 606, 767, 769, 813, 817, 819, 860
Hulk 196, 197
Hull House 746, 747, 748, 749
human immunodeficiency virus (HIV) 417
Humanitarian Award 343, 406
Human Rights Campaign 97, 542
Humphrey Bogart 186
Hunkpapa Lakota 503
Hyde Park 13, 700, 702, 703, 704, 833
hydropathy 719

I

I Know Why the Caged Bird Sings 216, 334, 335
Imagination Library 201
Indian American 39, 366, 367, 559
Indianapolis 23, 143, 144, 234, 441, 633, 695, 710, 749, 753, 781
Indian Council of Fire Achievement Award 69
Indian Removal Bill of 1830 497
Indian Wars 459, 461, 465, 477, 480
Industrial Workers of the World (IWW) 845
Institute for Exploration 247
Institute for the Study of Nonviolence 172
Institute of International Education 321
Interior and Insular Affairs Committee 614
internal combustion engine 40
International Business Machines (IBM) 126
International Group for Historic Aircraft Recovery 14
International Karate Tournament 194
International Labor Organization 639
International Ladies' Garment Workers Union 817, 818
International Missionary Council 733
International Peace Congress 596
International Space Station (ISS) 28, 29, 37, 38, 39
International Tennis Hall of Fame 88, 96
Internet Explorer 126
internment camps 49, 50, 798
Iraq War 406, 542, 626, 697
Iroquois 467, 489, 490
ISIS 698
It's a Wonderful Life 211, 213, 214

J

Japanese American 49, 577, 578, 579, 613, 797, 798, 799
Japanese American National Museum 579
Japanese internment 50, 798, 799
jeet kune do 192, 194, 195
Jet Li 195
Jim Crow 10, 167, 582, 717, 744, 799, 847, 900
Johnson Space Center 1, 7, 23, 24, 25, 27, 28, 29, 30, 33, 38
Joint Chiefs of Staff 307, 437, 438, 458, 628, 669
Judaism and the New Woman 736
Judiciary Committee 572, 582, 584, 585, 618
Justice Department 588, 589, 625, 793

K

Kansas-Nebraska Act 688, 759, 822
Katharine Hepburn Medal 186

Katharine Houghton Hepburn Center 186
Katie couric 406
Kennedy Center Honors 69, 182
Kennedy, Jacqueline 209, 683, 684
Kennedy Space Center 2, 5, 23, 24, 31, 36, 922
Kentucky Fried Chicken 141
Khrushchev, Nikita S. 670, 684
kinetoscope 261
Kingfish 80, 599, 600, 601
Kirby, Jack 196, 197
Kitty Hawk, North Carolina 4, 40
Klan, Ku Klux 153, 633, 854, 880
Kodak 261, 282, 283, 284, 285
Korean War 4, 17, 45, 141, 304, 437, 444, 606, 792, 924
kung fu 192, 193, 194, 195

L

Ladies' Home Journal 800, 828, 844
Lafayette, Marquis de 560, 680
Lakota 469, 470, 471, 472, 473, 474, 493, 494, 495, 496, 503, 504, 505, 506
Lama, Dalai 432, 730, 902
Langley Research Center of the National Advisory Committee for Aeronautics 923
Late Show with David Letterman 182
Latina 27, 29, 175, 209, 319, 320, 342, 371, 400, 401, 525, 582, 643, 767, 775, 859
Latin America 55, 172, 208, 346, 370, 572, 574, 575, 577, 581, 709, 766, 770, 776
Latino USA 320
Leadership Conference on Civil Rights 876
League for Nonviolence Civil Disobedience Against Military Segregation 875
League of Nations 701, 747, 764, 868, 913
League of United Latin American Citizens (LULAC) 155
League of Women Voters 445, 527, 700, 764, 819
Lean In 136, 137, 138
Leaves of Grass 329, 378, 379, 380
Legion of Honor 14, 268, 443, 734, 903
Legion of Merit 416, 443
Lewis and Clark 255, 257, 258, 259, 499, 500, 501, 502, 503, 681
LGBT 698, 749, 817
Lifetime Achievement Award 50, 107, 175, 180, 183, 192, 206, 217
light bulb 273, 286, 287, 288, 289

Lincoln Memorial 62, 848
Lindbergh, Charles A. 6, 14, 214, 253
Lindy Lady 14
Lockheed Martin 51, 924
Los Angeles Riots 227
Los Angeles Times 177, 532, 626, 642
Lost Battalion 578
Louis Armstrong 179, 188, 189
Loving v. Virginia 606
lupus 49
Lyndon B. Johnson Space Center 25, 27, 28

M

MacArthur Foundation 348, 796, 873
Madison Square Garden 76, 739, 805
Major League Baseball (MLB) 104
Manhattan Project 913, 929, 930, 931
Manzanar Committee 797, 798, 799
Manzanar War Relocation Authority 797
Marbury v. Madison 603
March for Our Lives 217, 811
March of Dimes 216, 401, 796
March on Washington for Jobs and Freedom 172, 338, 848, 876
Marine Corps 16, 18, 39, 433, 457, 683
Marjorie Stoneman Douglas High School 809, 811
Marshall, George C. 436, 438, 445, 461, 669
Marshall Islands 16
Marshall Plan 683
martial arts 192, 193, 194, 195
Marvel Comics 195, 197
Marxism 793, 815, 816
Massachusetts Institute of Technology (MIT) 35, 128, 366
mass production 760
Mattachine Society 611, 814, 816, 835, 842, 843
Mauro, Fra 35, 36
McCain, John 697
McClure's 301, 326, 327
McKinley Tariff Act 485
McLean Psychiatric Hospital 785
Medicare 400, 401, 530
meditation 397, 429, 737
Mellon Foundation 421
Ménière's syndrome 35
Metro-Goldwyn-Mayer (MGM) 212, 294, 535
Metropolitan Museum 66, 69, 71, 72, 549

Mexican American 52, 55, 341, 347, 348, 349, 391, 392, 524, 525, 582, 608, 609, 610, 818, 825, 829, 890, 891, 892
Mexican American Legal Defense and Educational Fund 524, 608, 609
Mexican-American War 462, 891
Microsoft 125, 126, 127, 128, 927
Mid-Atlantic Ridge 246
Milky Way 918, 919, 920
Minority Women's Task Force 819
Minute Men 599
Miranda v. Arizona 540, 656
Mission Control 23, 24
Miss World USA 174
Mister Rogers' Neighborhood 205, 206, 207
Modernism 66
Mondale, Walter 18, 512, 543, 545
Monmouth Reform Temple 736
Monroe Doctrine 575, 577, 709
Monticello 679
moon 1, 2, 5, 7, 19, 26, 35, 36, 38, 688, 729, 905, 907, 920, 924, 925
Morse code 927
most valuable player (MVP) 89, 105, 106
motion pictures 211, 261, 271, 274, 289, 535, 612
muckraking 301, 326, 327
Muller v. Oregon 516
mural 10, 51, 52, 53, 55, 57, 58
Museum of American Graffiti 71
Museum of Modern Art 72
Muslim 76, 77, 140, 339, 373, 715, 726, 727, 728, 737, 738, 855, 856, 862, 863
Muslim Public Affairs Council 727
Mussolini, Benito 327, 651, 705

N

Nagasaki 653
Naismith Memorial Basketball Hall of Fame. 90
NASA Manned Spacecraft Center 5
Nashville Songwriters Hall of Fame 201
National Academy of Television Arts 207, 860
National Aeronautics and Space Administration (NASA) 4, 28, 34, 45, 670, 922, 923
National Aeronautics Association's Collier Trophy 7
National Alliance for Hispanic Health 399, 400
National and International Blindness Prevention Program 263

National Association for the Advancement of Colored People (NAACP) 105, 144, 166, 210, 217, 281, 296, 527, 585, 605, 606, 607, 609, 701, 744, 757, 790, 792, 794, 818, 847, 864, 875
National Association for the Repeal of Abortion Laws 801
National Association of Colored Women 153, 901
National Association of Hispanic Journalists 320
National Association of Wage Earners 153
National Association of Women Business Owners 558
National Basketball Association (NBA) 88, 89, 106, 108
National Book Award 225, 335, 367, 368, 373
National Book Critics Circle Award 373
National Christian Scientist Association 721
National Coalition Against Censorship 343
National Collegiate Athletic Association (NCAA) 89, 106
National Consumers' League 632
National Defense Education Act 670
National Domestic Workers Alliance 872, 873
National Endowment for the arts 345
National Equal Rights Party 596
National Farm Workers Association 772, 773, 774, 775, 830
National Freedmen's Relief Association 894
National Gay and Lesbian Task Force 843
National Gay Rights Lobby 843
National Geographic Society 14, 236, 237, 247, 248, 444, 737
National Guard 461, 891
National Honor Society 205
National Humanities Medal 367, 369
National Industrial Recovery Act 704, 705, 851
National Institute of Mental Health (NIMH) 391, 411
National Institute on Drug Abuse (NIDA) 430
National Institutes of Health (NIH) 411, 430
National Inventors Hall of Fame 264, 271, 404
National Labor Board 851
National Labor Relations Act 704, 851
National League 84, 105, 111
National Mall 69
National Medal of Arts 63, 201, 348
National Medal of Technology 63, 201, 348
National Music Conservatory 862, 863
National Negro Business League 166, 296
National Negro Congress 875
National Organization for Women (NOW) 528, 544, 800, 818
national park 221, 238

National Park Service 238, 762
National Political Congress of Black Women 528
National Public Radio (NPR) 304, 319
National Recovery Act 575
National Research Council 281
National Research Science Award 391
National School Walkout 811
National Science Foundation 263, 411, 905, 927
National Security Agency (NSA) 881
National Security Council 512, 513, 635, 647
National Student Federation of America 321
National Traffic and Motor Vehicle Safety Act 616
National Woman Suffrage Association 595, 751, 764, 887
National Women's Hall of Fame 32, 69, 154, 443, 490, 528, 749, 769, 828, 916
National Women's Political Caucus 544, 796, 801, 819
National Women's Studies Association 756
Nation of Islam 77, 339, 854, 855, 856
Native Son 337, 338, 339, 359
Naval Academy 34, 37, 252, 455
Naval War College 34, 455
Naval Women's Reserve 399
navigation 1, 31
NBC Nightly News 307
Negro American Labor Council 876
Negro Welfare League 9
Never Again MSD 811
New Age 232, 397
New Brunswick Islamic Center 737
New Deal 445, 523, 536, 565, 600, 646, 651, 670, 701, 702, 704, 705, 706, 851, 853, 854
New Left 808
Newsweek 33, 130, 317, 432, 546, 559, 590, 641
New York City Ballet 67, 68
New York Giants 83, 110
New York Public Library. 340, 341
New York Yankees 82, 83, 85, 110, 111
Nez Perce 477, 478, 479, 480
Nez Perce War 477, 479, 480
Niagra Falls 477, 479, 480
Nikumaroro 15
Nineteenth Amendment 636, 764, 866, 867, 868, 869
Nobel Peace Prize 521, 522, 524, 555, 557, 596, 695, 697, 701, 731, 733, 734, 748, 848, 903, 904
Nobel Prize 368, 369, 403, 404, 405, 409, 909, 910, 912, 920, 931
North American Free Trade Agreement 617
North Atlantic Treaty Organization 513, 669

Northern Pacific Railroad 470, 504
Northern Paiute 506
North Pole 252, 253, 255

O

Oahu 481, 482, 483, 578, 614, 882
Obamacare 554, 697, 698
Obergefell v. Hodges 554
Oberlin College 59, 361, 369, 734
Occupational Safety and Health Administration 616
Occupy Wall Street 173
oceanography 32, 245, 247
Office of Advanced Research and Technology 6
Office of Exploration 30, 32
Office of Strategic Services 522
Ohio State University 19, 98, 101
Ojibwe 59, 232, 233
Oklahoma Indian Territory 478, 480
Olympics 73, 75, 76, 88, 90, 92, 93, 99, 100, 101, 102, 103, 105, 106, 113, 114, 115
Open Orthodox 738
Operation Cobra 437
Operation Desert Shield 38, 629
Operation Iraqi Freedom 541, 542
Operation Overlord 437
ophthalmology 263, 264
orbital flight 5, 17, 18, 19
Oregon Trail 470, 494
origami 49
Osage Nation 68
Osama Bin Laden 628
Oscars 628
Oval Office 322, 542, 874, 913

P

Pacific Asian American Women Bay Area Coalition 548
Pacific theater 16, 705
Palestinian Liberation Organization 739
Pancho Villa 460, 462, 838
Parkinson's disease 77, 327
Park Slope 53
Patton, George S. 436, 461
Pawnee 493, 494
Paxon Field 9
Peabody Award 304, 360
Peace Corps 156, 526, 581, 684, 921, 922
Pearl Harbor 11, 20, 213, 224, 295, 399, 455, 578, 632, 705, 797, 798, 852

Pele 481
PEN 346, 348, 367, 370, 373
Pennsylvania Assembly 550, 551, 623
Pennsylvania Railroad 121, 124, 133
Pennsylvania Rock Oil Company 133
Pentagon Papers 318
People for the American Way 827
People magazine 175, 209
People's Republic of China (PRC) 670, 819
People United to Save Humanity (PUSH) 832, 833
PepsiCo 130, 131, 132
Perkins Institution for the Blind 844
Persian Gulf War 528, 628, 629
personal computer 126, 629
Pete Seeger 171, 815
PGA Tour 98, 99
Phi Beta Kappa 136, 564, 732, 818, 915
Philadelphia Convention 552, 559, 561
phonograph 261, 268, 286, 288, 289
photography 18, 53, 58, 95, 247, 254, 282, 283, 284, 285, 373, 374
Pittsburgh Courier 724
Planned Parenthood 426, 427, 619, 736
plantation 165, 255, 256, 257, 269, 331, 375, 453, 464, 569, 578, 598, 613, 675, 690, 691, 692, 812, 895, 898, 899
police brutality 227, 228, 872
polio 420, 421, 422, 423, 446, 700, 703, 704, 812, 813
Pond, Walden 240, 241, 242
Poor People's March 335
Poor Richard's Almanack 550
Populist 592, 593
positron emission tomography (PET) 428
Potomac 325, 452, 453, 582, 680
President Benjamin Harrison 236
President Bill Clinton 69, 141, 216, 335, 336, 409, 446, 490, 524, 528, 545, 553, 581, 610, 621, 643, 674, 775, 865
President Calvin Coolidge 565, 804
President George Bush 565, 804
President George H. W. Bush 416, 525, 526, 546, 628, 871, 916
President George W. Bush 139, 183, 201, 206, 229, 230, 526, 527, 614, 625, 626, 633, 634, 636, 739, 902
President Gerald Ford 102
President Grover Cleveland 236, 596
President Harry S. Truman 153, 399, 437, 457, 640, 646, 669, 701, 875

President Herbert Hoover 289, 445
Presidential Citizen's Medal 409
Presidential Medal of Freedom 32, 63, 91, 97, 107, 177, 183, 206, 217, 226, 238, 304, 323, 336, 369, 370, 490, 514, 615, 621, 641, 674, 828, 846, 853, 903, 924
President Jimmy Carter 102, 238, 553, 580, 610, 613, 614, 832
President Lyndon B. Johnson 5, 304, 588, 848, 853, 880
President Richard Nixon 618, 684
President Ronald Reagan 6, 12, 305, 526, 618, 634, 739, 833
President Rutherford B. Hayes 789, 791
President's Commission on the Holocaust 903
President Ulysses S. Grant 221, 478, 595, 822
President Warren G. Harding 461, 839
President William Howard Taft 565, 592
President William McKinley 708, 807
President Woodrow Wilson 460, 631, 638, 700, 734, 764, 851
Princeton University 128, 212, 248, 365, 368, 374, 520, 577, 604, 615, 642, 644, 645, 649, 653, 734, 862, 915, 930
Professional Golf Association (PGA) 97
Prohibition 111, 533, 646
Project Mercury 5, 17, 18, 19, 33, 34
Proposition 8 698
Provincial Freeman 768
Public Broadcasting System (PBS) 206
Public Interest Research Group 416, 616
Public Service Commission 598
Public Works Administration 704
Pulitzer Prize 180, 197, 212, 317, 318, 319, 335, 365, 366, 367, 368, 369, 382, 383, 683, 774, 793
Pullman Strike 782, 784
Pura Belpré Awards 341, 342
Purchase, Louisiana 251, 258, 464, 499
Purdue University 4, 14, 31
Pure Food and Drug Act 709
Puritan 381, 393, 552, 661, 758, 762
Purple Heart 541, 579
Purple Rain 203

Q

Quaker 131, 173, 248, 311, 312, 313, 380, 402, 418, 420, 622, 690, 691, 732, 750, 751, 753, 866, 867, 868, 880, 893
Queen Elizabeth II 38

Queen Victoria 160, 484

R

race relations 282, 342, 360, 635, 791, 856, 857
Radcliffe College 149, 150, 163, 765, 844
Radio Corporation of America (RCA) 274
Radio-Keith-Orpheum (RKO) 213
ragtime 177, 178
Rainbow/PUSH Coalition 833
Reader's Digest 202, 225, 364, 461, 524
rebellion 313, 366, 427, 449, 452, 463, 482, 486, 758, 898, 899
Reconstruction 152, 165, 582, 689, 741, 769, 785, 792
Red Clay 489
Red Cloud Agency 471, 472
Red Cloud's War 470
Red Cross 13, 281, 282, 331, 385, 387, 388, 389, 390, 700
Redding, Otis 182
Reform Judaism 736
Richmond Mural Project 52
Rico, Puerto 53, 339, 340, 342, 344, 345, 370, 371, 415, 416, 636, 765, 766, 767, 833
Robert H. Goddard Memorial Trophy 7
Rock and Roll Hall of Fame 173, 183, 190, 204
Rockefeller Foundation 56, 135, 228
Rockefeller Institute for Medical Research 135
Rocky Mountains 135, 257, 502
Rodney King 227
Roe v. Wade 539, 553, 673
roll film 282, 283, 284, 285
Rough Riders 389, 708, 709
Royal Flying Corps 13
Rules Committee 528

S

Safety Device Company 297
San Diego State University 28
Sandpiper pipeline 233
Sandwich Islands 481, 482
San Francisco School of the Arts 49, 50
Sarah Palin 558, 559, 697
Schwab, Charles 123
Science and Health 720, 721, 723
Scott, Dred 688
Scout, Eagle 4, 7
sculpture 49, 50, 59, 60, 62, 510, 760
Second Lieutenant J. L. Gratton 469

Secretary of State 93, 127, 292, 460, 511, 513, 514, 515, 562, 603, 633, 897, 908
Securities Exchange Act 704
Sedition Act 667
segregation 77, 101, 102, 147, 152, 166, 167, 296, 338, 582, 592, 606, 633, 647, 654, 655, 702, 726, 757, 794, 832, 847, 849, 864, 876, 880, 890, 900
self-made 138, 144, 167, 552, 569
self-taught 150, 299, 828, 907, 908
Senator Joseph McCarthy 519, 587, 639, 640, 652, 670, 683
Seneca Falls 309, 751, 866, 868, 886, 888
separate but equal 166, 606, 607, 655
September 11, 2001 230, 406, 580, 615, 628, 635
sexism 8, 10, 88, 307, 334, 352, 754, 776, 806, 858
Shakespeare, William 185, 308, 333, 597
Shawnee 69, 249, 250
Shenandoah Valley 252, 449, 450, 454, 465
Sherman Antitrust Act 134, 135, 327, 708
Shoshone 499, 500, 501, 502, 507
Shoshone, Lemhi 499
Shuttle Avionics Integration Laboratory 23, 922
Sierra Club 97, 236, 238
Sierra Nevada 235
Silent Spring 223, 224, 225, 226
Sinatra, Frank 190
Sioux 418, 467, 469, 470, 471, 473, 474, 493, 495, 496, 503, 504, 506
Sioux War 495, 496
Sister Thea Bowman Black Catholic Educational Foundation 718
Six Nations Reserve 265
skin care products 142
smallpox 310, 385, 418, 465
Smithsonian Institution 1, 10, 42, 53, 69, 77, 512, 843, 863
Socialism 650, 652, 653
Socialist Party 649, 650, 651, 652, 653, 780, 782, 783, 784, 838, 845, 874, 876
Social Security Administration 704
soHo 54
SONY 113, 114
sound barrier 1, 43, 44, 45, 641
South Carolina State House 859
Southern Christian Leadership Conference (SCLC) 744, 757, 832, 847
South Pole 253, 254, 255
Southwest Pacific Area 456
space race 924

space shuttle 2, 6, 16, 18, 23, 24, 27, 28, 29, 30, 31, 32, 33, 36, 38, 45, 320, 922, 923, 924
SpaceX 39
Spanish-American War 159, 160, 389, 707, 829
Spanish Civil War 427, 808
Spencer Tracy 185
Spider-Man 196, 197
Spotted Tail 469, 470, 472
Springfield Republican 355
Sputnik 4, 17, 670, 905
Square Deal League 599
Stamp Act 568, 569, 622, 664, 665
Standard Oil Company 132, 133, 134, 135, 301, 325, 326, 328, 598
State of the Union 558
steel plow 276
Steffi Graf 95, 114
Stephen Wise Free Synagogue 736
Steve McQueen 194
Steven Spielberg 216
Stonewall Inn 835, 877
Stonewall riot 878
Street Transvestite Action Revolutionaries (STAR) 836, 878
Student Nonviolent Coordinating Committee (SNCC) 757, 812, 848
Student Struggle for Soviet Jewry 739
submarine 245, 246, 248, 271, 611
Sun Oil Company 724
Superman 196
Supreme Council of the United Orders of Railroad Employees 782
Susan G. Komen Foundation 175
Swarthmore College 30, 796, 866
swimming 37, 39, 115, 186, 503, 654, 795
synaptic self 413, 414, 415

T

Tape v. Hurley 888, 889, 890
Teamsters Union 587
TEDtalk 137
Tejano 208, 209
telegraph 121, 266, 267, 268, 273, 286, 287, 288, 476, 479, 494, 782
telemedicine 264
telephone 31, 125, 265, 266, 267, 268, 288, 337, 442, 638, 673, 782, 927
telescope 3, 918, 919, 920

temperance 59, 212, 278, 312, 314, 315, 393, 418, 596, 720, 741, 753, 767, 769, 886
Temple Beth El 736
Temple University 164, 405, 780, 801
Tennessee Valley Authority 670
tennis 30, 85, 86, 87, 88, 94, 95, 96, 97, 103, 105, 112, 113, 114, 115, 184, 252, 345
terrorism 514
The Age of Reason 623
The American Magazine 327
The Carol Burnett Show 200
The Christian Science Monitor 616, 723
The Dial 240
The Dukes of Hazzard 175
The economist 346
The Ed Sullivan Show 68, 87
The Federalist 559, 561, 562, 563, 694, 695
The Feminine Mystique 377, 799, 800, 801, 803, 818
the Free Press 312
The Gospel of Wealth 119, 123, 124
The Green Hornet 194
the *Guardian* 882
Their Eyes Were Watching God 216, 364
The Liberator 241, 313, 314, 315, 316, 788
The Messenger 874, 875
The Miracle Worker 163, 846
The New England Courant 549
The New Yorker 7, 72, 136, 138, 227, 231, 339, 366, 367, 546, 811
The New York Times 229, 350, 351, 380, 397, 507, 554, 769, 810, 835, 911, 918
The New York Tribune 309
The North Star 768, 788, 789
The Oprah Winfrey Show 215, 216, 335, 360, 407
theory of relativity 911, 912, 914, 919, 920
The Pennsylvania Gazette 550
The Philadelphia Story 185, 186, 213
The Porter Wagoner Show 199
The Rights of Man 623
The Seven Storey Mountain 728, 729, 730
The Spirit of Liberty 565, 566, 567
The Today Show 306, 307
The Tonight Show with Johnny Carson 200, 214
The View 230, 307, 397
The Wall Street Journal 643
The Woman Rebel 424, 425
ticker-tape parade 6, 86
Time magazine 182, 190, 231, 320, 350, 407, 409, 544, 873, 883

Times Square 54, 55, 877
Titanic 245, 246, 247, 248
Title IX 509, 613, 614, 615
Torah 736, 740
track-and-field 115, 116
Trail of Tears 487, 488, 489, 498, 499, 678, 925
transcendental 309, 377, 737
transgender 834, 835, 836, 837, 877, 878, 879
Trappist 728, 730
Treaty of Paris 667
Truman Doctrine 683
Truth-in-Securities Act 704
tuberculosis 162, 240, 265, 327, 373, 385, 398, 418, 419, 476, 521, 701, 746, 766, 785, 818
Tuskegee Institute 122, 166, 167, 271, 792, 804
Twain, Mark 122, 723, 846
Twentieth Century Fox Studios 194
Twenty Hours Forty Minutes (1928) 14
typhoid fever 41, 355, 418, 663

U

Uncle Tom's Cabin 337, 374, 375, 376, 377, 894
Underground Railroad 764, 768, 880, 885, 895, 896, 897, 898
Unitarian 309, 313, 357, 765, 820, 823
United Airlines 6
United Auto Workers 826, 830
United Farm Workers UFW) 55, 745, 771, 772, 773, 774, 775, 798, 824, 825, 829, 830
United Mine Workers of America (UMWA) 838, 850
United Nations Children's Fund (UNICEF) 416
United Nations Commission on Human Rights 545
United Nations Educational, Scientific, and Cultural Organization (UNESCO) 156
United Press 303
United Service Organization (USO) 295
United States Astronaut Hall of Fame 24, 29
United States Biological Survey 238, 243
United States Civil Service Commission 708
United States Conference of Catholic Bishops 718
United States Constitution 305, 584, 741
United States Department of Transportation 526
United States Holocaust Memorial Museum 903
United States Naval Academy 34, 37, 455
United States Naval Test Pilot School 38
United States Post Office 677, 841
United States Strategic Bombing Survey 646

United Way of America 526
Universal Automatic Computer (UNIVAC) 917
Universal Franchise Association 595
Universal Negro Improvement Association 803, 804, 805, 806, 854, 875
Universal Peace Union 596
Up from Slavery 166, 167, 168, 804
USA Freedom Act 883
U.S. Ambassador to the United Nations 512, 558
USA Patriot Act 883
US Army's Ballistics Research Laboratory 919
US Attorney General 625
U.S. Department of Health and Human Services 400
U.S. Department of Labor 229, 872
US Figure Skating Championships 91, 92
US Fish and Wildlife Service 223
U.S. Olympic Hall of Fame 102
U.S. Open 85, 86, 95, 96, 113
U.S. Patent Office 267, 290, 291, 292
US secretary of energy 909, 910
USS enterprise 11
USS Hornet 6, 11

V

vaccine 385, 408, 420, 421, 422, 423, 446
Valley Forge 602, 711
Vanderbilt 119, 428, 432, 556
Vanity Fair 200, 883
Vassar College 317, 915
veterans 13, 61, 388, 412, 437, 541, 542, 579, 800, 818
Veterans Administration (VA) 437, 438, 843
Veterans' Affairs Committee 528
Vietnam Veterans Memorial 60, 61, 62, 63
Vietnam Veterans Memorial Fund 61, 62
Vietnam War 45, 61, 62, 76, 77, 171, 172, 197, 304, 305, 318, 349, 374, 539, 571, 627, 641, 730, 779, 798, 811, 848, 849, 868, 876, 880
Violence Against Women Act 620
Virginia State College 281
Vostok 1 1, 4, 34
Voting Rights Act 609, 744, 745, 848

W

Walden 240, 241, 242, 254
Wall Street 138, 173, 192, 287, 643, 704
War Department 445, 458, 471, 688
Warner Bros. 177, 193, 194, 195, 203, 204

War of 1812 251, 258, 290, 438, 440, 676, 691, 692, 695, 707, 820
Warren Commission 656, 685
Washington Post 16, 27, 301, 316, 317, 318, 319, 351, 397, 432, 515, 626, 674, 738, 861, 873, 882
Watergate 301, 304, 316, 318, 319, 578, 584, 585, 616, 671, 674
Wayne, John 87, 186
Way of the Dragon 194
Wendy's 119, 141, 142
Western Electric 272
Western Union 267, 287, 288
West Los Angeles College 55
West Point 435, 436, 448, 449, 451, 452, 455, 459, 668, 669, 711
westward expansion 221, 473, 508
West Wing 673
Whiskey Rebellion 256, 562, 681, 712
White House press secretary 230
White Night riots 612
Whitney Museum 49, 55, 58, 72
Wilderness Act of 1964 237, 238
Wilderness Road 249
Wilderness Society 238
Wild West 477, 504
Wimbledon 85, 86, 87, 88, 95, 97, 113, 114
Windows 95 126
Woman's Rights Convention 751, 886, 894
Women Airforce Service Pilots (WASP) 20
Women in Community Service 443, 444
Women in Military Service for America 443
Women's Armed Services Integration Act 443, 640
Women's Army Auxiliary Corps (WAAC) 442, 445
Women's Army Corps (WAC) 21, 443
Women's Educational Equity Act 614, 615
Women's International League for Peace and Freedom 632, 748
Women's Mosque 726, 727, 728
Women's National Indian Association 418
Women's Peace Party 631
Women's Political Council 744
Women's Sports Hall of Fame 88
Women's Tennis Association 113
Wonder Woman 174, 175, 176
Wong, Suzie 190, 191, 192
Woodstock 782
Works Progress Administration (WPA) 704
World Camp of the Girl Scouts 161
World Figure Skating Championships 92
World Jewish Congress 739
World Population Conference 426
World Series 84, 85, 105, 109, 110, 111
World's Fair 272
World's Student Christian Federation 733, 735
World Trade Center 62, 346, 628, 881
Wounded Knee 473, 480, 496, 505, 506, 745
Wright Company 41, 42
Wright field 11, 44
Wright-Patterson Air Force Base 4

X

X-15 4
X-Men 196, 197
XYZ affair 602

Y

Yellowstone 221, 251, 479, 501
Yeshivat Chovevej Torah 740
Yeshivat Maharat 740
Yosemite National Park 221, 235, 236
Young Lords 878
Young Men's Christian Association (YMCA) 732
Young Women's Christian Association (YWCA) 153
Yo-Yo Boing! 344, 345, 346

Z

Zaytuna College 737, 738
Zionism 517, 518, 807, 914
Zuckerberg, Mark 137